My Family Tree

The Mason and Carey Bloodline

By

Stephanie Mason

My Family Tree

My Family Tree

The tree represents the family, and they are praying to their ancestors for guidance. Seasons come and go. The tree, which represents family, is planted by the rivers of water. I shall not be moved, over the course of time, what was is no more. What is shall be, the past reaching to the present, creating a bridge which is my family tree.

My Family Tree

Editorial Review

Stephanie M. Mason's "My Family Tree: The Mason & Carey Bloodline" is a heartfelt journey into her family lineage's rich history and resilient spirit. Through meticulous research and personal anecdotes, Mason beautifully weaves together the story of her ancestors, honoring their struggles and triumphs. Her narrative style invites readers to connect deeply with each generation, portraying a vivid tapestry of African-American heritage that spans centuries.

In conclusion, "My Family Tree: The Mason & Carey Bloodline" is a poignant tribute to resilience and family legacy. This book has the potential to resonate even more deeply with readers, preserving and celebrating the enduring spirit of the Mason and Carey bloodline for generations to come.

All rights reserved; No portion of this book may be reproduced without the express written permission of the author.

All photos are from the archives of the Mason/Carey families. All rights reserved.

© 2025 SMM Media Ltd.

My Family Tree

Dedication

I'M DEDICATING OUR FAMILY TREE TO:

My Heavenly Father The Great **"I AM"**

My loving parents: Norma J. Mason and (in loving memory of Eugene N. Mason)

My sister, Iris A. Nicholas

My cousins, my aunt, and uncle helped me with the start of my journey with this book:

(In loving memory of Cousin Frances R. Strickland)

(In loving memory of Cousin Mildred E. Peppers)

Cousin, Maria J. Strickland

(In loving memory of Aunt Litha R. Mason)

(In loving memory of Uncle William A. Mason (Tony)

Mrs. Tess Haney

(My Mentor, Best Friend, and Co- Researcher)

(In loving memory of Bishop, Rev. Gary M. Simpson – Spiritual Leader)

(In loving memory of Minister William C. Roberson – My Mentor, Best Friend, and Consultant)

This book is a personal memoir for my family members whose voices have been lost to time.

I love you, and thank you so much for walking with me on this long journey!

My Family Tree

Table of Contents

Dedication	iv
Introduction	9
Surviving Slavery	10
Traveling Into History	12
The Slave Codes	14
The Black Codes and Pig Laws	16
Sharecropping	17
The Boarding House	18
Reading Notes	19
The Generation Break Down	21
The Mason Bloodline	24
Education In The Shadow	26
The Saponi	269
Bishop, {Rev.} Gary Marcus Simpson	304
Introduction	305
Virginia	305
West Virginia	305
The Underground Railroad	305
Editor's Note	307
The Carey Bloodline	309
The Civil War – Slaves, Soldiers, Spies	309
The Storm	458
Living Testimonies	460
When God Calls	506
The Journey	507
A Word of Inspiration	508
Will The Circle Be Unbroken	509

My Family Tree

In Loving Memory	511
A Poem For Black Hearts	565
From our Family Albums	567
Postscript	619
DNA Results	620
Carey and Mason Bloodline – Index	621
References	646

My Family Tree

Dear Family, Friends, and My Readers,

The purpose of me writing this book was not only to learn about my family history on both sides but also to show us as a family coming out of darkness and into the light. Each of us has experienced life in different ways. Some of us have struggled and had victories along the way, always putting our best foot forward with the talents we were given to achieve our goals. Most of us have just started or are close to being finished with the goals that we have laid out for ourselves to achieve. Life for us as a family has stayed strong because we always try to keep God at the center of our table. We are that family that prays together, and we will always stay together with God on our side. I want to share and show connections within the family of what I have learned with you.

Thank you, "Happy Reading."

– Stephanie M. Mason – Author

My Family Tree

The first and only house *Hazel L. and Napoleon J.* owned when they moved from North Carolina. They were the 5th generation of the Mason family line. The house would be passed down to their great-grandson, *Trever Anthony Jackson,* who was too young to inherit their house. His mother, *Euphonia Tracy Jackson,* took over until he was of age. This house was built in March 1952 on the west-side of Detroit.

My Family Tree

Introduction

The following compilation represents over 20 years of effort. It has been a labor of love, passion for family, a thirst for knowledge, and a desire that the memories of family not fade into obscurity.

I am thankful for the members of the families of both lines who have contributed to compiling the information that exists. Without their assistance, so much might have been lost to the ages.

It is asked that family members reading this who have information please come forward to help make the records just that much more complete to maintain the memories for future generations.

Because our lines continue, the story has by no means ended. Let other members come forth, adding new records, completing existing records, and filling in the gaps so that a richer, more detailed picture emerges.

Let the love of family ever grow stronger.

Stephanie M. Mason

Author

My Family Tree

Surviving Slavery

"...and gather together the dispersed of Judah from the four corners of the earth."

- **Isaiah 11:12**

When one thinks of slavery in America, the general thought focuses on the Atlantic Slave Trade that brought millions of Africans to these foreign shores. Many think that the slave trade had its beginnings in concert with the colony in Jamestown, Virginia (1619) and continued through the turmoil of the Civil War.

Those who have done their homework know that the African Diaspora goes back even further to the extraction of African natives by Portugal, Spain, and then the rest of Europe (Palmer, 1999). Others will know that Congress abolished slavery as an active business venture in 1807 and that the Black Market for slaves endured (Schomburg, n.d.). England passed a similar law in the same year, banning the slave trade to America but leaving intact trade in Cuba and Brazil (Black Presence, n.d.).

The rich bounty of resources in Africa, stable societies, and positive social interactions among indigenous peoples were a source of jealousy, and European countries became bound and determined to undermine African life and customs through slavery, missionary assignments, colonization, and outright war (Falconbridge, 1792). As few know that age old societies, such as Kongo/N'Dongo (Angola), resisted slave activity until they, too, were overrun (Rogers, J. A., 1947).

The archives of the University of South Florida, among others, reveal that the first slaves brought to the American shore landed in the Spanish colonies of Florida in the latter part of the 1500s. It would not be long before there was a free black community near St. Augustine. As part of Spain's effort to weaken British control and influence, the position was that any slave escaping the British-held colonies would be granted asylum and welcomed. The free community near St. Augustine was developed into a military defense position known as *Fort Moses,* the first free black settlement. For a time, the area provided a distinct difference from life experienced on America's slave plantations.

Estimates by various historians place the numbers brought to these shores as low as nine million slaves and, by others, upward of twenty-five million slaves. The bottom line is that even in a strange land, separated from family, customs, worship, and language, these dark-skinned people survived, grew strong, established new families, and endured, longing for (and sometimes fighting for) the day when they and their children would be free.

While many celebrate the passage of the Thirteenth Amendment, abolishing slavery, and generations today still remember **Juneteenth** as a day of celebration, the last bastions of slavery would cling to American society, especially in the South, through the Civil War, Reconstruction, Jim Crow and more than one era of Civil Rights.

The men and women whose names appear on these pages, whose statements speak to succeeding generations, and whose family lines trace back to a time of infamy are a testament to the resilience,

My Family Tree

endurance, and hope that embraces each of us. May the memory of their sacrifices ever be with us as a guide into our tomorrow.

My Family Tree

Traveling Into History

As may be readily seen, many of the records listed here are incomplete; some by reason of sparse availability of documents, some by reason of personal reticence, and some by reason of memories growing dim with time. Yet, the effort has been enlightening, broadening scope, and a better understanding of the history that our bloodline has helped shape. For instance:

Cedar Grove Baptist Church Cemetery has a rich history to tell. It is believed to be the second oldest African–American church and cemetery in Mocksville, North Carolina – Davie County, within the Fork Community. The church was started in 1863 by *Rev. Thornton Hairston* in the surrounding woods within the Fork Community. The children of slaves orchestrated the gathering of the Fork Community during slavery days for church and meetings among slaves (Find a grave.com, 2018). The *Masons* built the foundation of the church after slavery ended for their families and future generations to come. At one time, the *Masons* owned the church and land that encompasses *Cedar Grove Baptist Church Cemetery,* which is a Historical Landmark. There are 180 graves, not including seven unmarked graves. This is a private cemetery for African-Americans – *our Mason bloodline*. It serves as the final resting place for one-half of the *Mason* line. There are some families that were buried there, and I could not draw a connection within the family, but the journey was enlightening.

Foy Cemetery was located on *James Foy's* private property (an eminent African-American Farmer) in Winston Township, North Carolina – Forsyth County (was also known as *Old Evergreen Cemetery)*, which turned into *Evergreen Cemetery,* which had a 10-acre site, serves as one of the oldest and largest memorial centers in Forsyth County (Find a grave.com, 2018). *Old Evergreen Cemetery* was built Sunday, July 1, 1928, for the region, a private cemetery for African-Americans. *Smith-Reynolds Airport* brought the property to expand the airport but kept the name of the cemetery and attached *Smith-Reynolds Airport* to the cemetery. The city has ownership over *Evergreen Cemetery,* which is now called *New Evergreen Cemetery.* All three cemeteries are Historical Landmarks and serve as resting places for African-Americans. The *Old Evergreen* was relocated in the early 1940s. There are 1,332 marked graves remaining in the wooded complex area of *Smith Reynolds Airport* but around about 700 graves were relocated to the new cemetery. The Works Progress Administrative helped orchestrate the movement of *Old Evergreen Cemetery* to its new location. The *New Evergreen Cemetery* opened in 1944 to replace *Old Evergreen.* People who were buried at *Old Evergreen Cemetery* and re-interred at *New Evergreen* may not be in their database system at the new location yet. Some of the graves may be unknown to this day. These three cemeteries serve as the final resting place for one-fourth of the *Mason* line.

Odd Fellows Cemetery was established in 1911 in Winston Township by the *Twin City Lodge* and the *Winston Star Lodge*, both are African-American fraternal organizations, which is one of the oldest and largest African-American Cemetery in Winston-Salem, North Carolina – Forsyth County. *Odd Fellows Cemetery* dates back to the Civil War and is a Historical Landmark. It was said that African-Americans decorated the graves themselves to remember their loved ones instead of headstones. They marked the graves in varieties of ways by using plants, shells, white quartz, colored glass, and "offerings" on top of the graves, such as pottery, saucers, bowls, pots, and marbles (Find a grave.com, 2018). It serves as the final resting place for one-fourth of the *Mason* line.

My Family Tree

- ❖ (Two different families with the same last name have an asterisk in front of the name)
- ❖ The Mason side consists of 16 main branches of the family tree: Conard, Cunningham, Dubose, *Elliott, Green, Hege, Jefferson, Little, Malone, Mason, Orr, Roberson, Snow, Workman, and Younger.
- ❖ Many established Boarding Houses as a means of economic survival
- ❖ The jobs they held after slavery included Railroad Workers, Tobacco Factory Workers, Domestic Workers, Ministers, Homemakers, Farmers or Farm Laborers (known as Sharecroppers), Laundress, Black Smiths, some voluntary or involuntary in the military or held military Draft Registration Cards
- ❖ Tuesday, May 13, 1913, Winston Township merged into Winston-Salem in North Carolina

My Family Tree

The Slave Codes

In 1715, North Carolina enacted a set of slave codes to control the movement of slaves while away from the plantation and restrict gatherings. As fewer indentured servants were available, greater control of labor was desired to maintain the economy. Later laws even restricted the manner and conditions by which a slave could be freed, requiring the approval of the local courts.

During the colonial era, slavery was not as prevalent in North Carolina as in other parts of the South. In the period from 1729 to 1767, the slave population of North Carolina grew from a mere 6,000 slaves to around 40,000. In 1774, the Provincial Congress banned the import of slaves to keep down the number of runaways, especially those enticed by the British.

Before the revolution, there were several free black families in North Carolina that included the descendants of mixed unions. During the 18th century, there was a migration of free blacks from Virginia, with the number of free blacks in the area increasing for almost twenty years after the war.

The 1831 slave rebellion fomented by *Nat Turner* created widespread unrest and discomfort among slave owners. What had been unimaginable had taken place – armed revolt and purposeful resistance. Scores of whites' lives had been lost in mere days. Where a sentiment of disregard had been the standard, a new attitude of egregious cruelty took hold. The old rules of how to treat and control dark-skinned property had to be enhanced, reinforced, and studiously enforced.

Where some rules had theretofore only been implied by word of mouth, new rules were set in place, often put in writing, and set as law. Prohibitions against slaves being educated – especially learning to read and write, were seemingly etched in stone. All pretense of a slave being a human was cast aside – with ever-increasing rules against marriage, property rights, assembly, and rights to speech being created and enforced. Never again would white society allow the possibility of slaves to conspire to revolt.

Punishment for the violation of various slave codes varied from public whipping, public humiliation, and/or special auctions. Whites who encouraged or had knowledge of the violations and did not step forward were fined $100 or had to serve jail time, and the slave would receive 39 lashes. It was not uncommon for a slave found in violation of the codes to be sentenced to death by hanging. Private lynching was a means by which slave masters would provide examples to other slaves and people of color of the consequences of any act of rebellion or even minor resistance to their authority.

The slave experience was that of dehumanizing brutality. Runaway slaves who were caught could only expect tremendous cruelty in response to their actions. There was every likelihood that other slaves – including family members and other slaves – would be forced to witness their punishment.

Slaves and their offspring were put to work at a young age. Their slave life began at the age of 5 or 6 years old, carrying water out into the fields for the overseers and the field slaves. Sometimes, they were used as human fans on extremely hot days to cool the master, his wife, and their guests down or to bring drinks and snacks.

My Family Tree

The laws put in place in the old colonies transferred into the laws of the new states, and even after the Civil War, the traditions of these laws would be maintained under the guise of Jim Crow. Even the advances of Civil Rights would not erase the emotional fervor that was maintained in the hearts and minds of many of the ensuing generations of white citizens.

As a people, we are grateful to historic figures such as *Frederick Douglass*, who would show the world that the intellectual abilities and humanity of people of color were a reality against which there could be no argument. In the same vein, some of the experiences revealed herein stand in testament to the spirit and strength of various men and women whose journeys are equally a part of history.

My Family Tree

The Black Codes and Pig Laws

In the first two years after the Civil War, a few laws were passed, forcing blacks to work for low wages. Some Northern States had already had the Black Codes in place before the Civil War ended. Their main purpose of using the Black Codes was to control the conduct and hold restrictions against people of color. The South systematized the Black Codes by upholding their laws that allowed people of color certain rights, which were legalized marriages, possession of property (and what kind of property they could own), and limited their access to the courts. People of color were prohibited from testifying against whites in a court of law, reporting any crimes against whites, and even serving on a jury.

In 1877, Southern States enforced a series of laws intended to undermine the lives of people of color with strict contracts that penalized any of them for leaving a job without their debts being paid off. Blacks had to get written consent from their previous employers before starting a new job. The Pig Laws targeted people of color to penalize them for crimes, which were not having proper paperwork for farm animals, farm equipment, or products for farming. Without proper paperwork, they were accused of stealing. People of color were prohibited and found violations of being homeless, unemployed, making or selling liquor, schools (black churches) had to be segregated, possession of most firearms, and having a post bond to travel within and out of states. These codes were set in stone, and a lot of misdemeanors were treated as felonies with strict sentences and fines against people of color. County Sheriffs could hire out blacks who were homeless or unemployed to white employers to work off their fines most of the time. The Pig Laws restricted people of color from having equal political rights, rights to attend public schools, rights to vote, freedom of speech, and equal treatment under their laws until the 14th and 15th Amendment was passed and put into motion. People of color are still fighting for these rights today.

The Federal Government conducted over 2,000 interviews with former slaves in the United States during the 1930s to see what their lives were like during and after slavery. This assignment was named Writers' Project, and later, it was renamed to Works Progress Administration. The book was called *Born in Slavery:* Slave Narratives from the Federal Writer's Project.

My Family Tree

Sharecropping

The post-Civil War era was a time of economic upheaval. The old plantation system was, by and large, a relic to be dismantled and discarded. The need for crops – food – was felt on both sides of the racial divide, but labor was still a critical issue.

While General William Tecumseh Sherman's field order provided parcels of land to an estimated 30,000 former slaves along the Georgia coast, there were yet millions of former slaves who had to make their way in a time of uncertainty. Through the efforts of the Freedmen's Bureau, white landowners were directed to develop contracts with former slaves for their services. Often, instead of wages, an agreement was made that the former slave would keep a portion of the harvest. Many landowners found ways to abuse the system, and new codes were developed that corrupted the system. A yearlong contract was designed to force the indebtedness of former slaves. Often, disputes resulted in former slaves being arrested, thus transferring contract labor into forced labor – sometimes referred to as chain gangs.

In other cases, short-term contracts were developed with much the same result. Former slaves were charged rent for what was once slave housing; in addition, there were additional costs for supplies, clothing, tools, and seeds. By the time of the harvest, the bills presented far exceeded the ability of the former slave to pay – again resulting in forced labor. Yet, many former slaves were able to eke out a living and indeed, were able to save money to buy their own tracts of land. For all the trials and tribulations former slaves had to endure, the continuity of time prevailed, leading to growth, maturity, and the dawn of a new era for people of color.

My Family Tree

The Boarding House

The Boarding House was an integral part of life for many communities (black and white). For the proprietor, it was an economic fail-safe, a source of income, and a way to keep one's head above water in troubled financial situations. For the boarders, it was a respite from expensive hotels or life on the street. The Boarding House provided benefits for both – a means of income on the one hand, a warm bed, and a meal on the other.

As urban centers began to grow because of developing industry, workers sought shelter in these areas as they sought employment. In the North and the South, the Boarding House provided a means to get and hold jobs for railroad workers, coal miners, tradesmen, construction workers, teachers, seamstresses, and more. It has been speculated that by the latter part of the 19th century, virtually one-third of the urban populations in America were boarders.

A Boarding House most often was a family home, with rooms converted for temporary use by lodgers. Rooms could be rented for a night, a week, or even longer (not unlike today's Bed and Breakfast). Sometimes the Boarding House could occupy up to least six or more tenants depending on the size of the house. It was uncommon not to have a boarder or boarders living with your family. Sometimes, boarders became friends and were treated like family members.

The Boarding House provided services, such as specified mealtimes, handyman, laundry, and cleaning services. Sometimes, the services were included in the lodging cost. Sometimes, there was an extra charge. The house had rules and regulations concerning common areas, visitors, pets, weapons, smoking, and drinking. Visitors, if allowed, usually could not stay overnight. Some Boarding Houses catered to women or men only. Women and men could have children with them, but it was their responsibility to look after them. Many Boarding Houses had strictly enforced curfews and quiet time.

The operation of a Boarding House was very much a part of our family history; it was a foundation, a source of sustenance, and a focus of life from which members could begin to experience life and make their way into a larger world.

My Family Tree

Reading Notes

Birth (b.)
Death (d.)
Senior I
Junior II, III, IV
Unknown: No information was found, documentation remains incomplete, or no record has been located for review and inclusion.
Not Available (N/A): Family members who are still alive or those who did not want to participate at this current time.
Place of Birth (POB.)
Place of Death (POD.)
Doctor of Philosophy (PhD)
Registered Pharmacist (D.Ph.)

For each family line, the children are listed first.

There are three different family lines of *Mason*. The other two *Mason* families were married on my dad's father's side.

The United States Federal Census Mortality Schedule is documented every ten years, just like the Census. The Census Mortality Schedule collects information which included demographic information – name, sex, race, length of residence, marital status, person's parents, trade or occupation, disease or cause of death, the number of days being ill, place of birth, and place of death, in which state, county or territory the individual died in; and the name of the attending physician.

The main purpose of the Census Mortality Schedule was use for discover and document chromosomal signs and illnesses or diseases that caused death among Chinese descent, Native-American descent, and Africans or African-American descent were often included, especially if they were slaves (Ancestry.com, 1997-2022).

The first United States Federal Census began on Monday, August 2, 1790. The data that was collected was in three categories: whites, free blacks, other free races, and slaves. Slaves made up three-fifths of the count that went toward a state's demographic statistics used to control the apportionment of congressional seats. The United States Census had a separate form when it came to slaves in the 1790's through 1860, and they were counted under the name of their owners. Native-Americans were first counted in the 1900s Census, both on and off the reservations. In collecting demographic information relating to people of color, there were a lot of errors made within the documentation, such as misspelled names, birth, marriage, and death records were incomplete, wrong or unsure information that was given out by other family members, friends, or neighbors about a person in their absence.

My Family Tree

The bottom line was a lot of people back then, blacks and whites were illiterate, and history has shown that documenting information for people of color was not as prevalent as for whites. In the 1500s, education was not free until the 1920s. Students who could afford to go to school and who lived far away from home made dealt with owners of Boarding Houses to live with them in exchange for tutoring them or their children when they could not pay for a room but only school. People would pay for a tutor to teach them the basics until the Smith – Towner 557 bill was passed Thursday, April 1, 1920, in the United States, which started the movement for compulsory public education.

My Family Tree

The Generation Break Down

	Father's side			Mother's side		
First Generation	Name	Birth (b)	Death (d)	Name	Birth (b)	Death (d)
	Lethia Elliott	Unknown	Unknown	Flora Carrington	Unknown	Unknown
	Rachael Hege Conard	1806	1923	Abe Carrington	Unknown	Unknown
	Matt Conrad	Unknown	Unknown	Louise Constans Carey	1840	Unknown
	Isabela Elliott	1808	Unknown	Miles Carey [1]	1831	Unknown
	Benjamin Orr	1782	1885	Jane White Palmer	Unknown	Unknown
				Joshua Palmer	Unknown	Unknown
				Jim Anderson	Unknown	Unknown
				Jane E. Alison White	1805	Unknown
				George White	1800	Unknown
				Adaline Summers McCrary	Unknown	Unknown
				Newton McCrary	Unknown	Unknown
Second Generation	Caroline Elliott Orr	1833	1920	Elizabeth Witherspoon Cowan	1836	1897
	Washington A. Orr [1]	1834	Unknown	Charles Cowan [1]	1824	1900
	Diana Malone Hege	1839	1931	Mary C. Summers White	1849	1915
	Lewis E. Hege [1]	1840	1918	George R. White	1828	1913
	Isie Elliott Roberson	1849	1921	Lucia Cunningham	1838	Unknown
	E. C. Gan Cunningham	Unknown	Unknown	Rubin Cunningham	1820	Unknown
	Loveless Roberson	1837	Unknown	Susan Beverly Carrington	1831	Unknown
	Ann Green	Unknown	Unknown	Abraham Carrington	1830	1920
	Edwin Green	Unknown	Unknown	Laura Palmer Carey	1853	1933
	Eliza Little Workman	1830	1912	Charles Carey	1855	Unknown
	Franklin Workman	1822	Unknown	Elvira Anderson Bass	1845	1929
	Charlotte Hodge Younger	Unknown	Unknown	James Bass	1850	1910
	Jeff Younger	Unknown	Unknown			
	Emily Gwynn Snow	Unknown	Unknown			
	Sam Snow	Unknown	Unknown			

My Family Tree

Generation	Name	Birth	Death	Name	Birth	Death
Third Generation	Henrietta Hatchett Cunningham Jefferson	(1858) 1860	1948	Susan Jane (Sookey) Cowan Cornelius	1860	1914
	James Henderson Jefferson	1842	1923	Augustus (Gus) Cornelius	Unknown	Unknown
	Henderson Younger	1865	Unknown	Lillie Belle Carrington Carey	1884	1941
	William Snow	1865	1910	James A. Carey	1873	1948
	Isabelle Dubose Mason	Unknown	Unknown	Martha Cunningham Bass	1871	Unknown
	Robert (Bud) Mason	Unknown	Unknown	Joseph Bass	1867	1928
	Annie Cornelius Hege Orr	1865	1945	Grace E. White	1890	Unknown
	Isaac Orr	1884	1946	Jay Hugh White	1882	1960
	Carrie Green Workman	1869	Unknown	Maggie McCall White	Unknown	Unknown
	Henry Workman	1865	1924	Annie Lee Cornelius White	1889	1965
Fourth Generation	Euphonia Bernice Orr Workman	1902	1987	Ana Barber Cowan	Unknown	Unknown
	William Essix Workman	1899	1960	John Cowan	Unknown	Unknown
	Elizabeth Mason	Unknown	Unknown	Helen Bass Carey	1893	1920
	Mary Mason	1873	1900	George Beamon Faulkner	1891	1954
	Ellen Jefferson Mason	1880	1928	Charles Alexander Carey	1895	1944
	Samuel M. Mason	1864	1937	Lucy Nancy Moore	Unknown	Unknown
				Archie Moore [1]	Unknown	Unknown
Fifth Generation	Hazel Lorraine Workman Mason	1918	1995	Levonia Margaret Carey Cowan	1919	1999
	Napoleon Jefferson Mason	1911	1996	Walter White	1915	1983
				Lucille Bruce-Wilson White	1923	1994
				Newell Virgil Moore	1921	1973
				James Avery Cowan	1916	1997
Sixth Generation	Eugene Napoleon Mason	1936	1989	Norma Jean Carey Mason	1939	N/A
Seventh Generation	Rodney Allen Mason	1974	1974			
	Stephanie Michele Mason	1975	N/A			
	Iris Althea Mason Nicholas	1976	N/A			

My Family Tree

	James Russell Nicholas III	1977	N/A			
Eighth Generation	James Rusell Nicholas IV	2014	N/A			

My Family Tree

The Mason Bloodline

The bloodlines (on the *Carey's*) with the same last names are italicized, but only a few families have had convergence.

Ables	Abney	Adams	Aikens	Alexander	*Allen*	Alston
Anthony	Askew	Atkinson	Audrey	Austin	Bailey	*Baker*
Ball	*Barber*	Bares	Barker	Barksdale	Barnett	Barron
Bassett	Benson	Berry	Black	*Bolden*	Booe	Bostic
Bowman	Boyce	Boyd	Brandon	Britton	Brock	*Brown*
Browning	*Bruce*	Bryant	Bryson	Burke	Burrs	Burton
Butler	Byrd	Cain	*Carey*	Carson	Carter	Cason
Chambers	Chaplin	Cherry	Chubbs	Clabona	Clark	Clayton
Clement	Click	Clingman	Clinkscales	Clodfelter	Cochran	Cofield
Coleman	Collie	Conrad	Cooper	*Copeland*	*Cowan*	*Crawford*
Cross	Croston	Crump	*Cunningham*	Cuthrell	*Dalton*	Darr
Davis	Denison	Dennis	Dillard	Dobson	Doulin	Douthit
Downs	Dubose	Eason	Edwards	Elliott	Ellis	Ellis-Young
Ervin	Farris	Fenwick	Few	Fields	Fisher	Floyd
Foster	Foster-Revel	Foster-Williams	Fowler	*Freeman*	Friday	Frohop
Furlow	Gaither	Gay	Gilbert	Gill	Gilliam	Gillon
Gist	*Glenn*	Gooden	Goodwin	Goolsby	Gordon	*Grant*
Gray	Green	Grier	*Griffith*	Gwynn	Hairston	Haith
Haizlip	*Hall*	Hamilton	Hampton	Hargraves	*Harris*	*Hawkins*
Haynes	Heath	Hege	Henley	Herrin	Herron	Holloway
Holman	*Holmes*	Holton	Hooper	*Howard*	Hudson	Hunter
Hyatt	Ijames	Ingram	Ivory	*Jackson*	James	Jefferson
Johnson	*Jones*	Jordan	*Knox*	Lash	Lassiter	Latner
Latten	Law	Lay	Leak	*Lee*	Lewin	*Lewis*
Lindsay	*Lipscomb*	Little	*Lockhart*	Long	Lord	*Lyons*
Mack	Malone	Martin	*Mason*	Mason-Mote	Mathes	McCain
McCall	McCombs	*McDaniel*	McGuire	McLaughlin	McLeod	McMillan
McMiller	McQueen	McVey	Means	Meroney	Michael	*Miller*
Mills	Minton	Mock	*Moore*	*Morrison*	Morrow	Myers

My Family Tree

Myricle	Neely	Nelson	Nicholas	Norman	Oden	Orr
Parker	*Parks*	Pate	*Patterson*	Pauling	Payne	*Pearson*
Peebles	Peppers	Perrell	Pittman	Pledger	Price	Quick
Redmon	Reynolds	Rice	Rivers	*Roberson*	Roberts	Rorie
Rush	Ryder	Sales	Samuels	Sawyer	Scales	*Scott*
Shields	Shoaf	Sieber	Simms	Simpson	Small	Smith
Snow	Solter	Speas	Springs	Stanton	Staples	Steel
Steele	Steelman	*Stiff*	Stokes	Stover	Stickland	Sturdevant
Suggs	Sullivan	Tate	Tatum	*Taylor*	Thomas	Thompson
Thornton	Thues	*Tillman*	Tomlin	Travis	Troy	*Turner*
Vance	Van Easton	Vaughters	*Walker*	Wall	Wallace	Ware
Warren	Watkins	Watson	Watt	Watts	Weaver	Webber
Webster	West	*White*	Whitfield	Whitworth	*Williams*	Williamson
Willis	*Wilson*	Winford	Winfred	Winton	*Witherspoon*	Wright
Wooden	Woodward	Woody	Workman	*Young*	Younger	Zeglen

My Family Tree

Education In The Shadow

Few living today, particularly those counted as millennials, can begin to imagine or understand the struggles faced by our ancestors living through slavery. Even more foreign to common thought patterns may be the concept that, for slaves – and indeed for many people of color – learning to read and write was often undertaken under the threat of death.

For instance, South Carolina law in 1740 "…made teaching a slave to write a crime" (Webb, L. D., 2006). Georgia soon followed, and other southern states established laws prohibiting the education of slaves.

The reasoning was that "…education contributed to slave unrest" (2. Ibid.). In spite of such laws, it has been established that by the start of the Civil War, as much as "…5% of the slave population was literate" (3. Ibid.).

Various slaves learned to read and write, quietly teaching others to support the ultimate goal of liberty. Often, the learning took the form of listening, repeating, mimicry, and other surreptitious activities, even though discovery could mean "…beatings, amputations, even death" (5. Ibid.).

There was a concept among the white community and among various slave owners that some Christian teaching would help keep slaves under control. Much of the religious teaching among slaves "…insisted upon fidelity and obedience as Christian values in servants and upon the authority of Paul" (Gundaker, G., 2007). The attitude of control persisted even beyond Reconstruction and may even be seen in today's education. Some things change ever so slowly as to seem unchanging.

The standard in American society was that education was essential for growth and progress – for whites. Black education was generally relegated to trades training so that successive generations of workers would continually be available. However, the seed of liberty had been sown, and various members of the black community were determined that they, too, would benefit from educational pursuits. No sacrifice was too great if future generations might grow up free, with dignity and the understanding of their value as humans and citizens.

America slowly accepted the education of blacks, and after the turn of the 20th century, recognized segregated education as the standard. It would not be until the mid-50s that *Brown v BOE Topeka* would bring to an end the abominable doctrine of separate but equal. This ruling would come after a series of legal victories spearheaded by noted attorney and Civil Rights advocate *Thurgood Marshall* (who would later become the first black Justice on the United States Supreme Court). In 1936, his efforts paved the way for blacks to attend law school at the University of Maryland. In 1938, equally successful efforts opened the doors for blacks at the law school of the University of Missouri.

My Family Tree

According to the United States Freedmen's Bureau for Miscellaneous Records for 1865 – 1872 ... John R. Brie was listed as Isabela slave master in Carver Creeks Township, North Carolina – Bladen County.

Great – Great – Great Grandmother Line of Eugene Napoleon Mason – Maternal (His Mother's Side)

The Family Line of Isabela Elliott

The First Generation

Name	Isabela Elliott
Date Of Birth	1808
Place Of Birth	North Carolina – Mecklenburg County
Date Of Death	Unknown
Age At Death	Unknown
Place Of Death	Unknown
Occupation	Keeping House
Married	Unknown
Notes	She was a slave. According to the 1880 Census, she was illiterate. Her children were Caroline Elliott Orr and Samuel Springs. At the age of 72, she was a boarder living between both of her children's homes.

Her (2) Children

According to the United States Freedmen's Bureau Records for 1865 – 1872 ... the prominent Orr family of North Carolina – Mecklenburg County were John H. Orr and then his son, Dr. M. M. Orr, the slave masters of Benjamin Orr and his son, Washington A. Orr [1].

The Second Generation

Name	Caroline Elliott Orr
Date Of Birth	Thursday, April 25, 1833
Place Of Birth	Charlotte Township, North Carolina – Mecklenburg County
Date Of Death	Tuesday, August 3, 1920
Age At Death	87

My Family Tree

Place Of Death	Henderson, North Carolina – Vance County
Occupation	Farm Hand/Domestic Worker/Homemaker
Married	Washington A. Orr [1]
Notes	She had one set of twins. According to the 1880 Census, their home was a boarding house with boarders, including her mother (Isabela Elliott), William May, and Amanda Elizabeth Orr Biggers (not a family member). Amanda Elizabeth Orr Biggers was born Thursday, November 11, 1858, in Pineville Township, North Carolina – Mecklenburg County, and died Friday, February 8, 1935 (age 76). According to the 1910 Census, Caroline, Washington, [1], Amanda, and Amanda's husband, Wallace Amzi Biggers, were slaves and illiterate. Amanda worked as a Domestic Worker at the Orr's home after slavery ended. Wallace Amzi Biggers was born on Sunday, August 13, 1854, and died on Monday, June 1, 1925 (age 70). Amanda and Wallace were both buried side-by-side at Philadelphia Presbyterian Church Cemetery in Mint Hill, North Carolina – Mecklenburg County.

Name	**Washington A. Orr I**
Date Of Birth	1834
Place Of Birth	Sharon Township, North Carolina – Mecklenburg County
Date Of Death	Unknown
Age At Death	Unknown
Place Of Death	North Carolina – Mecklenburg County
Occupation	Section Hand – Railroad Worker
Married	Caroline Elliott Orr
Notes	He was known by his nickname, "Wash." At various times, Wash would use the name Isaac when it suited him. His father was Benjamin Orr, born Tuesday, January 1, 1782, and died March 1885 (age 103) in North Carolina – Mecklenburg County.

Name	**Samuel Springs**
Date Of Birth	1840

My Family Tree

Place Of Birth	Pineville Township, North Carolina – Mecklenburg County
Date Of Death	Unknown
Age At Death	Unknown
Place Of Death	North Carolina – Mecklenburg County
Occupation	Farmer
Married	Esther Lee Springs (born 1850), North Carolina – Mecklenburg County
Notes	He was born a slave. According to the 1880 Census, Esther and Samuel were illiterate. His nephew and two nieces were James A. Orr, Malinda Orr Steel, and Venus Orr Barnett, and his sister Caroline Elliott Orr were boarders at their home in the 1880s. His nickname was "Sam." Their children were Amos Springs and James Springs.

Great – Great Grandparent Line of Eugene Napoleon Mason– Maternal (His Mother's Side)

The Family Line of Caroline Elliott Orr and Washington A. "Wash" Orr [1]

The connection to the family line was Caroline, the daughter of Isabela Elliott.

The Second Generation

Caroline Elliott Orr	-	See Entry Page 27-28
Washington A. "Wash" Orr [1]	-	See Entry Pages 28

Their (12) Children

Name	Robert Orr
Date Of Birth	1857
Place Of Birth	Pineville Township, North Carolina – Mecklenburg County
Date Of Death	Unknown
Age At Death	Unknown
Place Of Death	North Carolina – Mecklenburg County
Occupation	Farm Hand-Laborer
Married	Single

My Family Tree

Notes	He was born a slave. According to the 1870 Census, he was illiterate.

Name	**Isaac Orr**
Date Of Birth	March 1884
Place Of Birth	Charlotte Township, North Carolina – Mecklenburg County
Date Of Death	Friday, April 5, 1946
Age At Death	62
Place Of Death	Winston-Salem, North Carolina – Forsyth County
Occupation	Section Hand on Railroad – Laborer
Married	Annie Cornelius Hege Orr
Notes	Isaac and his father worked for the same company. He was buried on Tuesday, April 9, 1946, a widower.

Name	**Annie Cornelius Hege Orr**
Date Of Birth	1865
Place Of Birth	Winston Township, North Carolina – Forsyth County
Date Of Death	Saturday, November 3, 1945
Age At Death	79 – 80
Place Of Death	Winston-Salem, North Carolina – Forsyth County
Occupation	Retired – Domestic Worker/Housewife
Married	(1) William E. Brown (2) Isaac Orr
Notes	She was born into slavery. Her nickname was "Ann." Her parents were Diana Malone Hege and Lewis E. Hege [I]. Married Monday, September 17, 1880, in Winston Township, North Carolina – Forsyth County, at the age of 15. William E. Brown was born in 1866 and died in 1900 (age 33-34) in North Carolina. They were married for 20 years. His parents were Isabella Brown and James I. Brown,

My Family Tree

	from Wilkesboro, North Carolina – Wilkes County. According to the 1900 Census, Annie was a widow. (2) Married Tuesday, December 13, 1904, in North Carolina – Forsyth County. According to the 1910 Census, Annie and Isaac were both literate. They were married for 40 years. She did not have any children by either of her husbands but adopted their daughter, Euphonia Bernice Orr Workman. In the 1920 Census, their home was noted as a Boarding House with two residents. Annie was buried on Thursday, November 8, 1945. Annie and Isaac were both buried at Evergreen Cemetery.

Name	Mary Orr
Date Of Birth	1861
Place Of Birth	Pineville Township, North Carolina – Mecklenburg County
Date Of Death	October 1870
Age At Death	8 – 9
Place Of Death	North Carolina
Occupation	None
Married	Single
Notes	She was born into slavery. Mary was burned to death in a fire, and her name was listed on the United States Federal Census Mortality Schedule in North Carolina from 1855 to 1880.

Name	Lee Orr
Date Of Birth	1867
Place Of Birth	Pineville Township, North Carolina – Mecklenburg County
Date Of Death	Unknown
Age Of Death	Unknown
Place At Death	Manhattan, New York – New York County
Occupation	Day Laborer

My Family Tree

Married	Francis James Orr
Notes	He could not read or write, according to the 1910 Census.

Name	**Francis James Orr**
Date Of Birth	Wednesday, May 16, 1866
Place Of Birth	South Carolina – Fairfield County
Date Of Death	Thursday, October 31, 1946
Age At Death	80
Place Of Death	Manhattan, New York – New York County
Occupation	Domestic Worker/Housewife
Married	Lee Orr
Notes	Married on Wednesday, August 21, 1895, in Charlotte Township, North Carolina – Mecklenburg County. Her parents were Mariah Holmes James and Benjamin James, both from South Carolina. Francis lived at 67 Macomb Pl. in Manhattan at the time of her death, a widow. She was buried on Tuesday, November 5, 1946, in Charlotte, North Carolina – Mecklenburg County.

Name	**Washington A. Orr II**
Date Of Birth	January 1863
Place Of Birth	Pineville Township, North Carolina – Mecklenburg County
Date Of Death	Saturday, September 15, 1923
Age At Death	60
Place Of Death	Charlotte Township, North Carolina – Mecklenburg County
Occupation	General Farmer
Married	Ella Audrey Orr
Notes	He was born into slavery. His nickname was "Wash II." In the 1920 Census noted that Wash II owned his own home and land and was mortgage-free.

My Family Tree

	He lived at 1309 Irwin in Charlotte at the time of his death. He was buried on Sunday, September 16, 1923.

Name	Ella Audrey Orr
Date Of Birth	Monday, September 10, 1877
Place Of Birth	Charlotte Township Ward 11, North Carolina – Mecklenburg County
Date Of Death	Sunday, February 21, 1965
Age Of Death	87
Place Of Death	Charlotte Township, North Carolina – Mecklenburg County
Occupation	Domestic Worker/Housewife
Married	Washington A. Orr [II]
Notes	Her parents were Emily Robinson Audrey and Joe Audrey. Married on Sunday, March 23, 1890, in Pineville Township, North Carolina – Mecklenburg County, and they were married for 33 years. According to the 1910 Census, Ella and Wash [II] were both literate, and her maiden name was spelled Ardrey. Their children: Lillian Orr Burton, James B. Orr, Emma Orr McCombs, Enzelia Orr, Jessie B. Orr McCain, Ella Mae Orr Watts, Eunice Orr Oden, Jane Orr, Lolo Orr, and George A. Hyatt. Ella lived at 15131 Pharr Street in Charlotte at the time of her death, a widow. Ella was buried on Thursday, February 25, 1965. Ella and Washington [II] were both buried at China Grove Church Cemetery in City China Grove, North Carolina – Rowan County.

Name	Charley Orr
Date Of Birth	1864
Place Of Birth	Pineville Township, North Carolina – Mecklenburg County
Date Of Death	Unknown
Age At Death	Unknown
Place Of Death	Unknown
Occupation	General Farmer

My Family Tree

Married	Millie Barber Orr (b. February 1871)
Notes	He was born into slavery. Married Thursday, January 5, 1885, in Charlotte Township, North Carolina – Mecklenburg County. Census records noted that his name was spelled Chas., short for Charles, Charlie, or Charley. An earlier 1900 Census indicates that Millie had six children, but only three survived. Their children Cora Orr McLaughlin, Walter Orr, Lillie Orr, Infant Orr, Ione Orr, and Joe Orr. According to the 1910 Census, Millie and Charley were both literate. In the 1920 Census, it was noted that their home was turned into a Boarding House with one resident. Millie and her mother, Charlotte Barber, were born in South Carolina.

Name	Thomas Orr
Date Of Birth	Saturday, March 13, 1875
Place Of Birth	Charlotte Township, North Carolina – Mecklenburg County
Date Of Death	Friday, April 5, 1946
Age At Death	71
Place Of Death	Charlotte Township, North Carolina – Mecklenburg County
Occupation	Farm Laborer
Married	Stella Orr (b. 1876)
Notes	According to the 1880 Census, he was illiterate.

Name	Venus Orr Barnett
Date Of Birth	Saturday, March 17, 1877
Place Of Birth	Pineville Township, North Carolina – Mecklenburg County
Date Of Death	Unknown
Age At Death	Unknown
Place Of Death	Philadelphia, Pennsylvania – Philadelphia County
Occupation	Farm Laborer/Housewife

My Family Tree

Married	Charles Barnett
Notes	The 1880 Census noted that the couple were both illiterate, and her first name was spelled as Veney or Venia.

Name	**Charles Barnett**
Date Of Birth	March 1876
Place Of Birth	Charlotte Township, North Carolina – Mecklenburg County
Date Of Death	Sunday, April 29, 1945
Age At Death	69
Place Of Death	Philadelphia, Pennsylvania – Philadelphia County
Occupation	Farm Laborer
Married	Venus Orr Barnett
Notes	Their marriage was recorded as Thursday, December 16, 1897, in Charlotte Township, North Carolina – Mecklenburg County. His parents were Sue Morrow Barnett and Doc Barnett.

Name	**James A. Orr**
Date Of Birth	1868
Place Of Birth	South Carolina
Date Of Death	Unknown
Age At Death	Unknown
Place Of Death	North Carolina
Occupation	Day Laborer
Married	(1) Mary E. Whitworth Orr (b. 1877) (2) Maggie Tate Orr
Notes	At the age of 2, he was sent to live with his father's family. Caroline adopted him after his mother, Violet Orr, had passed. According to the 1890 Census, he was noted as illiterate.

My Family Tree

	(1) Marriage on Thursday, September 15, 1898. (2) Marriage on Wednesday, January 30, 1889. Both marriages took place in Gaston, North Carolina – Northampton County. Mary's father was Titus Whitworth.

Name	**Malinda Orr Steel**
Date Of Birth	Thursday, June 10, 1869
Place Of Birth	Pineville Township, North Carolina – Mecklenburg County
Date Of Death	Monday, November 3, 1952
Age At Death	83
Place Of Death	Greensboro, North Carolina – Guilford County
Occupation	Retired – Domestic Worker – Wash Woman/Housewife
Married	John Steel
Notes	According to the 1920 Census, Malinda and John were both literate. They lived at 610 E. Market Street in Greensboro at the time of their deaths and were homeowners. She was buried on Wednesday, November 5, 1952, at Maplewood Cemetery in Greensboro, North Carolina – Guilford County, a widow.

Name	**John Steel**
Date Of Birth	1871
Place Of Birth	South Carolina – York County
Date Of Death	Thursday, March 20, 1941
Age At Death	69 – 70
Place Of Death	Charlotte Township, North Carolina – Mecklenburg County
Occupation	Plumbing Director
Married	Malinda Orr Steel
Notes	Married Tuesday, October 17, 1916, in Rowan, North Carolina – Rowan County – married for 25 years. His parents were Lydia Steel and Clark

My Family Tree

	Steel. He was buried in March 1941 at Pinewood Cemetery in Charlotte Township, North Carolina – Mecklenburg County.

Name	**Louisa Sadler Orr Alexander**
Date Of Birth	1869
Place Of Birth	Pineville Township, North Carolina – Mecklenburg County
Date Of Death	Thursday, January 17, 1924
Age At Death	54 – 55
Place Of Death	Charlotte Township, North Carolina – Mecklenburg County
Occupation	Domestic Worker/Housewife
Married	Jefferson Alexander
Notes	Her twin brother was Alexander Orr. According to the 1880 Census, she was noted as illiterate. Her nickname was "Lou." Their children were Mary Elizabeth Alexander (b. 1900 – d. 1915, age 14–15), Cornelius Vanderbilt Alexander (b. 1895 – d. 1971, age 75–76), Sarah Alexander McVey, and Dorothy L. Alexander Webber. Louisa lived on Mannse Road in Charlotte Township. She was buried on Saturday, January 19, 1924.

Name	**Jefferson Alexander**
Date Of Birth	1861
Place Of Birth	North Carolina – Mecklenburg County
Date Of Death	Monday, March 8, 1926
Age At Death	64 – 65
Place Of Death	Charlotte Township, North Carolina – Mecklenburg County
Occupation	Farm Laborer
Married	Louisa Sadler Orr Alexander
Notes	He was born into slavery. Known by his nickname, "Jeff." Married on Thursday, April 28, 1887, in Charlotte Township, North Carolina – Mecklenburg County – married for 37 years. He was a widower when he died. His parents were Amanda Alexander and Jackson Alexander. His

My Family Tree

	dad's nickname was "Jack." Louisa, Mary, and Jefferson were all buried side-by-side at Cherokee Street Baptist Church Cemetery in Kings Mountain, North Carolina – Cleveland County.

Name	**Alexander Orr**
Date Of Birth	1869
Place Of Birth	Pineville Township, North Carolina – Mecklenburg County
Date Of Death	Unknown
Age Of Death	Unknown
Place At Death	Unknown
Occupation	Farm Laborer
Married	Alice Wallace Orr
Notes	He went by three different nicknames: "Elick," "Aleck," or "Alex." According to the 1880 Census, he was listed as illiterate, even though he attended school. Their children were Annie Orr Walker, Lawrence Orr, and Thomas Orr.

Great – Great – Great Grandmother Line of Eugene Napoleon Mason – Maternal (His Mother's Side)

The Family Line of Rachael Hege Conrad and Matt Conrad

The First Generation

Name	**Rachael Hege Conrad**
Date Of Birth	1806
Place Of Birth	North Carolina – Davidson County
Date Of Death	Friday, June 1, 1923
Age At Death	116 – 117
Place Of Death	Lexington, North Carolina – Davidson County
Occupation	Farm Laborer

My Family Tree

Married	Matt Conrad
Notes	She was a slave. Their child was Lewis E. Hege [I]. They had him out of wedlock, and his last name was not changed. In the 1880 Census, her first name was spelled as Rachel, and the couple had a boarder named George Fries (b. 1795, North Carolina), who worked as a field laborer and stayed with them until his death. Rachael was buried on Sunday, June 3, 1923, at Midway Cemetery in Lexington, North Carolina – Davidson County, a widow.

Great – Great Grandparents of Eugene Napoleon Mason – Maternal (His Mother's Side)

The Family Line of Diana Malone Hege and Lewis E. Hege [I]

The Second Generation

Name	Lewis E. Hege I
Date Of Birth	1840
Place Of Birth	Winston Township, North Carolina – Forsyth County
Date Of Death	Saturday, June 15, 1918
Age At Death	77 – 78
Place Of Death	Winston-Salem, North Carolina – Forsyth County
Occupation	Laborer Yardman
Married	(1) Diana Malone Hege (2) Eliza Wilson Hege (b. 1865)
Notes	He was born a slave. According to the 1880 Census, he could read but could not write. Lewis [I] was 68, and Eliza was 43 when they married on Wednesday, December 16, 1908, in Broadbay Township, North Carolina – Forsyth County. They did not have any children together. Lewis [I] was buried on Monday, June 17, 1918, at Saint Philips African Moravian Graveyard Section II Cemetery in Winston-Salem, North Carolina – Forsyth County.

Name	Diana Malone Hege
Date Of Birth	1839
Place Of Birth	Montgomery, Alabama – Montgomery County

My Family Tree

Date Of Death	1931
Age At Death	91 – 92
Place Of Death	Winston-Salem, North Carolina – Forsyth County
Occupation	Domestic Worker/Homemaker
Married	Lewis E. Hege [1]
Notes	She was born a slave. According to the 1880 Census, she was illiterate, with four different spellings of her first name: Diana, Dinah, Deana, or Dena. Diana and Lewis married on Tuesday, March 20, 1866, in Winston Township, North Carolina – Forsyth County, in (Judgement in Civil Action, the Superior Court) a marriage of 41 years. She was divorced when she died.

Their (6) Children

Name	Lewis E. Hege II
Date Of Birth	September 1879
Place Of Birth	Winston Township, North Carolina – Forsyth County
Date Of Death	Friday, March 22, 1918
Age At Death	38
Place Of Death	Winston-Salem, North Carolina – Forsyth County
Occupation	R. J. Reynolds – Tobacco Industry – Copper Worker
Married	Gertrude Carter Hege
Notes	Listed as literate in the 1880 Census. He was buried on Sunday, March 24, 1918, at Bellevue Cemetery in Winston-Salem, a widower. His body was removed from Bellevue Cemetery and re-interred in 1968 at Nat Watkins Cemetery in Walkertown, North Carolina – Forsyth County.

Name	Gertrude Carter Hege
Date Of Birth	1879
Place Of Birth	Winston Township, North Carolina – Forsyth County
Date Of Death	Wednesday, March 20, 1918

My Family Tree

Age At Death	38 – 39
Place Of Death	Winston-Salem, North Carolina – Forsyth County
Occupation	Domestic Worker/Homemaker
Married	Lewis E. Hege II
Notes	Married on Friday, September 2, 1898, in Winston Township, North Carolina – Forsyth County, and they had been married for 20 years. Gertrude and Lewis II lived at 922 Fuller Street in Winston-Salem at the time of their deaths and were homeowners. Their children were Deborah Hege (b. 1902 – d. Monday, October 31, 1921, POD. Columbus, Ohio – Franklin County, age 18–19) and Roscoe Hege (b. 1903). Roscoe married Louise Hairston Hege (b. 1905) on Tuesday, January 16, 1923, in Winston-Salem, North Carolina – Forsyth County. Louise's mother was Mollie Ellis Hairston. Gertrude's parents were Mary Leak Carter and Nash Carter.

Name	**Lula Hege Boyd**
Date Of Birth	Saturday, January 5, 1878
Place Of Birth	Winston Township, North Carolina – Forsyth County
Date Of Death	Wednesday, July 30, 1947
Age At Death	69
Place Of Death	Greenville, North Carolina – Pitt County
Occupation	Domestic Worker/Homemaker
Married	Preston Boyd (b. 1873), POB. Simpsonville, North Carolina – Rockingham County
Notes	Listed as literate in the 1880 Census. Married on Sunday, July 22, 1894, in Winston Township, North Carolina – Forsyth County. Preston's parents were Fannie Boyd (b. 1851) and Washington Boyd (b. 1830). Washington's nickname was "Wash." Fannie and Wash were slaves.

Name	**Arabelle Hege**
Date Of Birth	1862
Place Of Birth	Winston Township, North Carolina – Forsyth County

My Family Tree

Date Of Death	Unknown
Age At Death	Unknown
Place Of Death	North Carolina – Forsyth County
Occupation	Domestic Worker
Married	Single
Notes	Born into slavery. According to the 1880 Census, she was illiterate. Her nickname was "Bell."

Name	John W. Hege
Date Of Birth	Friday, January 14, 1870
Place Of Birth	Winston Township, North Carolina – Forsyth County
Date Of Death	Wednesday, September 21, 1887
Age At Death	17
Place Of Death	Winston Township, North Carolina – Forsyth County
Occupation	R. J. Reynolds – Tobacco Industry – Worker
Married	Single
Notes	According to the 1880 Census, he could read but could not write, even though he attended school. He was buried in September 1887 at Saint Philips African Moravian Graveyard Section II Cemetery in Winston Township, North Carolina – Forsyth County.

Name	Thomas Hege
Date Of Birth	1873
Place Of Birth	Winston Township, North Carolina – Forsyth County
Date Of Death	Unknown
Age At Death	Unknown
Place Of Death	Unknown

My Family Tree

Occupation	Unknown
Married	Julia White Hege
Notes	According to the 1880 Census, he was able to read and write. His first name was listed as Thos., the short form of Thomas. His father was Anderson Hege. He married Julia White Hege on Saturday, July 20, 1895, in Winston Township, North Carolina – Forsyth County. Julia's parents were Zepha White and Bill White.

The connection to the family line was Annie, the daughter of Diana Malone Hege and Lewis E. Hege [1].

Annie Cornelius Hege Orr - See Entry Page 30-31
Isaac Orr - See Entry Page 30

Great – Great Grandparents of Eugene Napoleon Mason – Paternal (His Father's Side)

The Family Line of Isie Elliott Roberson, E. C. Gan Cunningham, and Loveless Roberson

The Second Generation

Name	**Isie Elliott Roberson**
Date Of Birth	1836
Place Of Birth	Milton Township, North Carolina – Caswell County
Date Of Death	Tuesday, June 14, 1921
Age At Death	84 – 85
Place Of Death	Winston-Salem, North Carolina – Forsyth County
Occupation	General Domestic Worker
Married	(1) E. C. Gan Cunningham (2) Loveless Roberson
Notes	Isie and her mother (Lethia Elliott) were slaves. The 1880 Census noted various spellings of her first name: Isie, Icey, Isa, or Isey. Lethia Elliott was a boarder at their home until her death. Loveless Roberson was born in January 1837 and was also a slave. In the early 1880 Census, the couple lived in a boarding house. The 1910 Census recorded Loveless's first name as Lovelace or Loveless, and his last name was traced as Robinson, Robenson, Robertson, or Roberson; he was illiterate. His occupation changed from Farm Laborer to Domestic Servant. Neither Isie nor her mother was literate, according to the 1910 Census. Isie and Loveless were

My Family Tree

	married in 1865 in Milton Township, North Carolina – Caswell County, lasting 35 years. The 1920 Census recorded her birth as 1836, but her death certificate listed her birth as (May 1849), matching her headstone. Isie's father was listed as unknown on her death certificate. She was buried on Friday, June 16, 1921, at Oddfellows Cemetery. At the time of her death, she lived at 1507 Cromartie Street in Winston-Salem, a widow and homeowner. Her children were Henrietta Hatchett Cunningham Jefferson, and James Roberson.

Isie (2) Children

Name	**Henrietta Hatchett Cunningham Jefferson**
Date Of Birth	June 1860 (or 1858)
Place Of Birth	Milton Township, North Carolina – Caswell County
Date Of Death	Sunday, December 26, 1948
Age At Death	88
Place Of Death	Milton Township, North Carolina – Caswell County
Occupation	Laundries/Homemaker
Married	(1) James Henderson Jefferson (b. Monday, October 10, 1842 – d. Friday, September 7, 1923, age 81) (2) Henderson Younger (3) William Snow
Notes	Henrietta was born a slave. The 1880 Census listed her as Mulatto with two different birth years. Her parents were Isie Elliott Cunningham Roberson and E. C. Gan Cunningham. She had 12 children, but only seven survived. At age 23, she was a widow. Her children included Walter Jefferson [1], Glenn Jefferson, Ellen Jefferson Mason, Brownie Younger Bassett, Priscilla Younger, and Dorotha Younger. She was illiterate according to the 1910 Census, and her first name was spelled as Harriet in some documents, but the correct spelling was Henrietta. She lived at 1507 Cromartie Street in Winston-Salem at the time of her death and was a homeowner. Her first husband was James Henderson Jefferson, also a slave. According to the 1910 Census, James's name was documented as Tim or Taz, with the last name listed as Jeffrey, but the correct spelling was Jefferson. Henrietta adopted Icy A. Snow Holton and Eliza Younger Pearson as her daughters when she married their father.

Name	**Henderson Younger**

My Family Tree

Date Of Birth	1834
Place Of Birth	Halifax, Virginia – Halifax County
Date Of Death	Unknown
Age At Death	Unknown
Place Of Death	North Carolina – Forsyth County
Occupation	Farmer
Married	(1) Nelly J. Carey Younger (b. 1847) (2) Martha Younger (3) Henrietta Hatchett Cunningham Younger
Notes	Henderson was born a slave. The 1880 Census noted he was illiterate and listed as Mulatto. He was a widower when he married Nelly. (1) Marriage on Monday, May 21, 1866, in Charlotte Township, Virginia – Charlotte County. Nelly's mother was Nancy Carey. Nelly and Henderson had a child named Jeff Younger (b. 1869). (3) Marriage on Wednesday, October 26, 1881, in Milton Township, North Carolina – Caswell County. His parents were Charlotte Hodge Younger and Jeff Younger.

Name	**William Snow**
Date Of Birth	December 1865
Place Of Birth	Mount Airy, North Carolina – Surry County
Date Of Death	Thursday, March 3, 1910
Age At Death	44
Place Of Death	Winston-Salem, North Carolina – Forsyth County
Occupation	Farmer
Married	Henrietta Hatchett Cunningham Snow
Notes	He was born at the end of slavery. The 1880 Census noted he was illiterate. Married Tuesday, February 11, 1902, in Winston Township, North Carolina – Forsyth County. They had been married for eight years with no children from their marriage. His parents were Emily Gwynn Snow and Sam Snow. He was buried in March 1910 at Mountain View Cemetery in Mount Airy, North Carolina – Surry County.

My Family Tree

Name	James Roberson
Date Of Birth	September 1864
Place Of Birth	Milton Township, North Carolina – Caswell County
Date Of Death	Unknown
Age At Death	Unknown
Place Of Death	North Carolina
Occupation	United States – Army/Worker at Bryce Hospital
Married	Susan Johnson Roberson (b. 1863), occupation – Farm Hand
Notes	He was born into slavery. According to the 1880 Census, he was able to read and write. In the 1910 Census, he was listed Mulatto, and his last name was spelled in different ways Robinson, Robenson, Robertson, or Roberson. His father was Loveless Roberson. Married Thursday, October 9, 1884, in Milton Township, North Carolina – Caswell County. He served during WWI and was honorably discharged from the Army. Susan's parents were Laura Johnson (b. 1815), POB. Virginia, a Domestic Worker, and Haywood Johnson (b. 1815), POB. North Carolina, a Farmer. In the 1910 Census Susan's family last name was spelled Johnston.

Henrietta (3) Children with James Henderson Jefferson

Name	Walter Jefferson I
Date Of Birth	Tuesday, May 12, 1874
Place Of Birth	Milton Township, North Carolina – Caswell County
Date Of Death	Unknown
Age At Death	Unknown
Place Of Death	Columbus, Ohio – Franklin County
Occupation	Farm Laborer
Married	Roxie Martin Jefferson (b. 1881), POB. Virginia
Notes	Roxie's father was Sid Martin. According to the 1880 Census, noted he was listed Mulatto and that he was literate. Married Saturday, March 31,

My Family Tree

	1900 in Winston Township, North Carolina – Forsyth County. Their children: Sadie Jefferson (b. September 1900), Mary Bell Jefferson (b. Thursday, February 19, 1903), POB. Columbus, Ohio – Franklin County and Walter Jefferson [II] (b. Tuesday, June 11, 1901 – d. Monday, February 17, 1908) POD. Columbus, Ohio – Franklin County, age 6), Walter [II] was buried Wednesday, February 19, 1908, at Green Lawn Cemetery in Columbus, Ohio – Franklin County. Walter [II] lived at 791 Hamlet Street in Columbus at the time of his death. Sadie and Walter [II] POB. Winston Township, City Ward 2, North Carolina – Forsyth County.

Name	**Glenn Jefferson**
Date Of Birth	1875
Place Of Birth	Milton Township, North Carolina – Caswell County
Date Of Death	Unknown
Age At Death	Unknown
Place Of Death	Mocksville, North Carolina – Davie County
Occupation	Farm Laborer
Married	Unknown
Notes	According to the 1880 Census noted that he was listed Mulatto and that he was literate.

The connection to the family line was Ellen Jefferson Mason, the daughter of Henrietta Hatchet Cunningham Jefferson and James Henderson Jefferson, and Ellen's husband – Samuel M. Mason, was the son of Isabelle Dubose Mason and Robert Mason.

Name	**Ellen Jefferson Mason**
Date Of Birth	Saturday, February 28, 1880
Place Of Birth	Milton Township, North Carolina – Caswell County
Date Of Death	Thursday, January 26, 1928
Age At Death	47
Place Of Death	Mocksville, North Carolina – Davie County
Occupation	Domestic Worker/Homemaker

My Family Tree

Married	Samuel M. Mason
Notes	She joined an organization named the Eastern Star. According to the 1880 Census records, she was listed Mulatto. Ellen and Samuel were both literate, according to the 1910 Census. Their children Raymond D. Mason [I], Mildred Ann Mason Hege, Cornelius Mason, Cleophus Mason, Margaret Mason McCall, Veada Mason Pittman, Napoleon Jefferson Mason, Suphonia M. Mason Johnson, and Brownie Mae Mason Ryder. Ellen was buried on Sunday, January 29, 1928. It was reported to (find-a-grave.com) that she was the daughter of Henrietta Hatchett Jefferson and James Henderson Jefferson.

Name	**Samuel M. Mason**
Date Of Birth	Tuesday, January 5, 1864
Place Of Birth	Mocksville, North Carolina – Davie County
Date Of Death	Monday, March 29, 1937
Age At Death	73
Place Of Death	Winston-Salem, North Carolina – Forsyth County
Occupation	Farmer/Janitor
Married	(1) Elizabeth Mason (2) Mary Mason (3) Ellen Jefferson Mason
Notes	He was born into slavery, and when slavery ended, he was still an infant. He eventually joined an organization named the Freemasons. His nickname was "Sam." His parents were Isabelle Dubose Mason and Robert Mason. He was buried Sunday, April 4, 1937, as a widower. Ellen and Samuel were both buried side-by-side at Cedar Grove Baptist Church Cemetery. There was a discrepancy about his birth year being 1864, but it was recorded on his death certificate that his birth year was 1874. The elders of the family and one of his younger sons, Napoleon, stated that his dad's birth year was 1864, and his headstone was correct. Later it was found that Sam wrote in his big daily journal that he was born in 1864. (1) Marriage in 1883. Elizabeth's child with Samuel: Addie Mason Haizlip. (2) Married in 1896, lasting for 4 years. Mary was a Domestic Worker. Mary joined an organization named the Eastern Star and their children – Etta Mason Webster, Green Mason, Ella M. Mason Neely, Nebraska Mason, and Nevada Mason. According to the 1900 Census, Mary was literate. Mary Mason (b. Wednesday, November 5, 1873 POB.

My Family Tree

	Mocksville, North Carolina – Davie County – d. Thursday, July 26, 1900, age 26, POD. Winston Township, North Carolina – Forsyth County. (3) Marriage Saturday, October 13, 1901, lasting 27 years. All of his marriages took place in Mocksville, North Carolina – Davie County. Census records noted that Sam owned his home, farm, and land and was mortgage-free. Census noted that he turned his home into a Boarding House with a few residents. Sam and his wives all lived at 1112 East 12th Street, Winston-Salem, at the time of their deaths.

Henrietta (5) Children with Henderson Younger

Name	**Brownie Younger Bassett**
Date Of Birth	Wednesday, January 8, 1890
Place Of Birth	Milton Township, North Carolina – Caswell County
Date Of Death	Sunday, October 20, 1968
Age At Death	78
Place Of Death	Winston-Salem, North Carolina – Forsyth County
Occupation	Retired – R. J. Reynolds – Tobacco Industry – Tobacco Roller/Homemaker
Married	(1) Lemuel Arthur Adams (2) Daniel Benjamin Bassett [I]
Notes	(1) Married Wednesday, October 28, 1908 in Winston Township, North Carolina – Forsyth County. (1) b. 1885 – d. 1918, POB. Winston Township and POD. Winston-Salem, North Carolina – Forsyth County (age 35). (1) His parents were Isabel Adams and Jack Adams. She did not have any children from her first marriage. According to the 1920 Census, Brownie and Daniel were both literate. The Census noted that Brownie bore 5 children, but only 4 survived. Their children were Helen W. Bassett, Walter A. Bassett, Dr. Golden F. Bassett Wall, Daniel Benjamin Bassett [II], and Jethro Benjamin Bassett. Brownie was buried on Monday, October 24, 1968. Brownie lived at 1507 Cromartie Street in Winston-Salem at the time of her death, a widow and homeowner. This house was passed down through 3 generations within the family.

Name	**Daniel Benjamin Bassett I**
Date Of Birth	Thursday, September 28, 1893

My Family Tree

Place Of Birth	Martinsville, Virginia – Henry County
Date Of Death	Sunday, April 14, 1935
Age At Death	41
Place Of Death	Greensboro, North Carolina – Guilford County
Occupation	Farmer/Pastor – Disciple Church
Married	Brownie Younger Bassett
Notes	Married Monday, December 27, 1920 in Winston-Salem, North Carolina – Forsyth County and they had been married for 15 years. His parents were Martha Jane Price Bassett and William Henry Bassett. He held a Draft Registration Card Tuesday, June 5, 1917, in Winston-Salem from the United States Army during WWI (1917-1918). His nickname was "Dannie or Dan." He lived at 606 Eric in Greensboro at the time of his death as a homeowner. Daniel was buried on Monday, April 15, 1935.

Name	**Icy A. Snow Holton**
Date Of Birth	Thursday, July 29, 1886
Place Of Birth	Winston Township, North Carolina – Forsyth County
Date Of Death	November 1962
Age At Death	76
Place Of Death	Winston-Salem, North Carolina – Forsyth County
Occupation	Domestic Worker/Homemaker
Married	James Holton [I]
Notes	Icy's parents were Emma Snow and William Snow. She was listed Mulatto and was literate in the 1910 Census. Their children: Thelma Holton (b. 1908), Bruce E. Holton (b. 1919), Harry Holton (b. 1923), John Holton (b. 1927), James Holton [II] (b. 1914), Icy Holton and Priscilla E. Holton Gilliam (b. 1916), Priscilla's husband – George Gilliam [II] (b. 1913), married Friday, March 23, 1934, in Winston-Salem, North Carolina – Forsyth County. George's parents were Callie Gilliam and George Gilliam [I]. Icy A. and James [I], children POB. Winston Township and Winston-Salem, North Carolina – Forsyth County.

My Family Tree

Name	James Holton I
Date Of Birth	1880
Place Of Birth	Winston Township, North Carolina – Forsyth County
Date Of Death	Tuesday, March 19, 1935
Age At Death	54 – 55
Place Of Death	Winston-Salem, North Carolina – Forsyth County
Occupation	Day Laborer
Married	Icy A. Snow Holton
Notes	His parents were Ona Holton and Paul Holton. Married Saturday, September 24, 1904 in Winston Township, North Carolina – Forsyth County. The 1910 reports also noted that their last name was spelled two different ways: Halton or Holton.

Name	Eliza Younger Pearson
Date Of Birth	December 1887
Place Of Birth	Winston Township, North Carolina – Forsyth County
Date Of Death	Unknown
Age At Death	Unknown
Place Of Death	Winston-Salem, North Carolina – Forsyth County
Occupation	Domestic Worker/Housewife
Married	Richard Pearson (b. 1879), POB. and POD. Winston Township, North Carolina – Forsyth County
Notes	In the 1910 Census, it was noted that she was literate. Married Sunday, February 14, 1904, in Winston Township, North Carolina – Forsyth County. Her mother was Martha Younger. His parents were Bell Pearson and Miles Pearson.

My Family Tree

Name	Priscilla Younger
Date Of Birth	September 1889
Place Of Birth	Winston Township, North Carolina – Forsyth County
Date Of Death	Unknown
Age At Death	Unknown
Place Of Death	Winston-Salem, North Carolina – Forsyth County
Occupation	R. J. Reynolds – Tobacco Industry – Worker
Married	Unknown
Notes	According to the 1910 Census, she was literate.

Name	Dorotha Younger
Date Of Birth	May 1897
Place Of Birth	Winston Township, North Carolina – Forsyth County
Date Of Death	Friday, July 19, 1912
Age At Death	15
Place Of Death	Winston Township, North Carolina – Forsyth County
Occupation	Domestic Worker
Married	Single
Notes	According to the 1910 Census, she was illiterate. She lived at 1046 Oak Street in Winston Township at the time of her death. She was buried Saturday, July 20, 1912, at Happy Hill Cemetery in Winston Township, North Carolina – Forsyth County.

The Great Grandparents of Eugene Napoleon Mason – Paternal (His Father's Side)

According to the United States Freedmen's Bureau Records for 1865 – 1872 ... the prominent Mason family of North Carolina – Fairfax County was George Mason, the slave master of Robert Mason.

My Family Tree

The Family Line of Isabelle Dubose Mason and Robert Mason

The Third Generation

Name	Robert Mason
Date Of Birth	Unknown
Place Of Birth	North Carolina – Fairfax County
Date Of Death	Unknown
Age At Death	Unknown
Place Of Death	North Carolina
Occupation	Farmer
Married	Isabelle Dubose Mason
Notes	He was a slave. His nickname was "Bud" or "Bob."

Name	Isabelle Dubose Mason
Date Of Birth	Unknown
Place Of Birth	North Carolina – Fairfax County
Date Of Death	Unknown
Age At Death	Unknown
Place Of Death	Fulton Township, North Carolina – Davie County
Occupation	Domestic Worker/Housewife
Married	Robert Mason
Notes	She was a slave. Her nickname was "Lizzie" or "Eliza." The 1910 Census noted that Eliza and Bud had a servant named Henrietta Ford (age 12) living with them, and they were literate.

Their (2) Children

Samuel M. Mason	-	See Entry Page 47-49
Elizabeth Mason	-	See Entry Page 48
Mary Mason	-	See Entry Page 48-49

My Family Tree

Ellen Jefferson Mason - See Entry Page 47-48

Name	**Ennis Mason**
Date Of Birth	Sunday, July 18, 1847
Place Of Birth	Mocksville, North Carolina – Davie County
Date Of Death	Sunday, March 6, 1938
Age At Death	90
Place Of Death	North Carolina – Davidson County
Occupation	Retired – General Farmer
Married	Bettie Hairston Mason
Notes	He was born a slave. The 1900 Census and his death record had his wife's maiden name as his last name. He was buried under his wife's maiden name, too. The 1930 Census noted that he was literate and could pass for a white man. The bank tried to repossess his land and house when it was discovered that he was a black man, but he initiated legal remedies and won, remaining a homeowner. He was buried on Monday, March 7, 1938. Both he and his wife were buried at Cedar Grove Baptist Church Cemetery, and he was a widower until he died.

Name	**Bettie Hairston Mason**
Date Of Birth	1850
Place Of Birth	North Carolina – Davie County
Date Of Death	1914
Age At Death	63 – 64
Place Of Death	Fulton Township, North Carolina – Davie County
Occupation	Domestic Worker/Homemaker
Married	Ennis Mason
Notes	She was born a slave. Her father was Tom Hairston. She was buried in 1914 in North Carolina. Their daughters: Jettie Ann Hairston Mason Brown and Ida Mary Mason Carter.

My Family Tree

The Great Grandparents of Eugene Napoleon Mason – Maternal (His Mother's Side)

The Family Line of Annie Cornelius Hege Orr and Isaac Orr

The Third Generation

Annie Cornelius Hege Orr	-	See Entry Page 30-31
Isaac Orr	-	See Entry Page 30

Their Child

Name	**Euphonia Bernice Orr Workman**
Date Of Birth	Tuesday, October 1, 1902
Place Of Birth	Columbus, Ohio – Franklin County
Date Of Death	Saturday, January 17, 1987
Age At Death	84
Place Of Death	Winston-Salem, North Carolina – Forsyth County
Occupation	Retired – R. J. Reynolds – Tobacco Industry – Stemmer Worker/Homemaker
Married	William Essix Workman
Notes	She was a full-blooded Native American – Cherokee. Adopted by the Orr family as an infant. Her first name was listed as Effanna in the Census. She stated on her marriage license that she did not know her biological parents' names but her adoptive parents and was listed as black. She joined the Eastern Star. Took over her (adopted) parents' house after her mother passed; her father lived with them as a boarder. The house is a Historical Landmark. She was buried Saturday, January 24, 1987, a widow until she died. They lived at 808 Marcenia in Winston-Salem, homeowners. Both were buried side-by-side at Evergreen Cemetery; middle names were spelled wrong on their headstones. She had eight children, but only five survived: Hazel Lorraine Workman Mason, Grace Louise Workman Browning, William Robert Workman [1], Eugene N. Workman, Edward Ray Workman, Treva Mae Workman, James Leonard Workman, and Richard LeRoy Workman [1].

Name	**William Essix Workman**
Date Of Birth	Tuesday, July 11, 1899

My Family Tree

Place Of Birth	Greenville, South Carolina – Greenville County
Date Of Death	Wednesday, May 25, 1960
Age At Death	60
Place Of Death	Winston-Salem, North Carolina – Forsyth County
Occupation	Retired – R. J. Reynolds – Tobacco Industry – Stemmer Worker/United States Army
Married	Euphonia Bernice Orr Workman
Notes	According to the 1910 Census, the couple was literate and attended school. He used his middle name as his first name, recorded with the spelling "Essex." He joined the Freemason organization and served in the United States Army during WWI from (1917 to 1918). Married Friday, June 20, 1919, in Lexington, North Carolina – Davidson County, a marriage of 41 years. Buried Sunday, May 29, 1960. His parents were Carrie Green Workman and Henry Workman.

The Great Grandparents of Eugene Napoleon Mason – Maternal (His Mother's Side)

The Family Line of Carrie Green Workman and Henry Workman

The Third Generation

Name	Henry Workman
Date Of Birth	May 1874
Place Of Birth	Paris Mountain, South Carolina – Greenville County
Date Of Death	Saturday, March 22, 1924
Age At Death	49
Place Of Death	Winston-Salem, North Carolina – Forsyth County
Occupation	General Farmer
Married	Carrie Green Workman
Notes	Married in 1892 in South Carolina. His parents were Eliza Little Workman and Franklin Workman, both of whom were slaves. He was buried Sunday,

My Family Tree

	March 23, 1924, at Bellevue Cemetery and re-interred at Nat Watkins Cemetery in Walkertown, North Carolina – Forsyth County in 1968.

Name	**Carrie Green Workman**
Date Of Birth	August 1869
Place Of Birth	Paris Mountain, South Carolina – Greenville County
Date Of Death	Unknown
Age At Death	Unknown
Place Of Death	Unknown
Occupation	Homemaker/R. J. Reynolds Tobacco Industry – Stemmer Worker
Married	(1) Henry Workman (2) MG Griffith
Notes	Her parents were Ann Green and Edwin Green. The 1900 Census noted that Carrie and Henry were married for 8 years and had a boarder living with them. In the 1930s, Carrie was a boarder at their son's home. Carrie and Henry could both read, but it was documented in the 1910 Census records that Henry could not write.

Their Child

The connection to the family line was William, the son of Carrie Green Workman and Henry Workman, William's wife – Euphonia was the daughter of Annie Cornelius Hege Orr and Isaac Orr.

William Essix Workman	-	See Entry Page 55-56
Euphonia Bernice Orr Workman	-	See Entry Page 55

The Grandparents of Eugene Napoleon Mason – Paternal (His Father's Side)

The Family Line of Elizabeth Mason, Mary Mason, Ellen Jefferson Mason, and Samuel M. Mason

The Fourth Generation

Elizabeth Mason	-	See Entry Page 48
Mary Mason	-	See Entry Page 48-49
Ellen Jefferson Mason	-	See Entry Page 47-48
Samuel M. Mason	-	See Entry Page 47-49

My Family Tree

Elizabeth Child with Samuel

Name	Addie Mason Haizlip
Date Of Birth	Friday, March 7, 1890
Place Of Birth	Mocksville, North Carolina – Davie County
Date Of Death	Tuesday, January 4, 1966
Age At Death	75
Place Of Death	Winston-Salem, North Carolina – Forsyth County
Occupation	Boarding House – Keeper
Married	(1) U Grant Haizlip (2) James A. Herrin
Notes	According to the 1900 Census, she was literate and attended school. Her child: Lillie Mae Haizlip Warren, was listed as Mulatto. The 1920 Census records noted that James was a lodger at Addie's home. (2) Marriage on Saturday, September 11, 1920, in Winston-Salem, North Carolina – Forsyth County. She kept her first husband's last name for legal purposes. (2) His parents were Susie Herrin and Rufus Herrin. Federal records spelled her first married name as Haislip, but her death certificate spelled it Haizlip. Her mother was Elizabeth Mason. Addie lived at 1118 East 12th Street in Winston-Salem at the time of her death; she was a widow and homeowner, living on her dad's street. She was buried on Saturday, January 8, 1966, at Evergreen Cemetery.

Name	U Grant Haizlip
Date Of Birth	October 1876
Place Of Birth	North Carolina
Date Of Death	Sunday, December 2, 1917
Age At Death	41
Place Of Death	Winston-Salem, North Carolina – Forsyth County
Occupation	Day Laborer
Married	Addie Mason Haizlip

My Family Tree

Notes	Married Monday, September 22, 1902, in Winston Township, North Carolina; a marriage of 15 years. His parents were Mary Ann Lash Haizlip and George Fountain Haizlip (b. 1842 – d. 1927, age 84–85). U Grant had a living Will in Probate Court on Tuesday, January 22, 1918, in Winston-Salem, North Carolina – Forsyth County. He was buried in December 1917 at Odd Fellows Cemetery. His parents were slaves.

Mary (5) Children with Samuel M. Mason

Name	Etta Mason Webster
Date Of Birth	Thursday, June 2, 1887
Place Of Birth	Winston Township City Ward 2, North Carolina – Forsyth County
Date Of Death	Unknown
Age At Death	Unknown
Place Of Death	Unknown
Occupation	Retired – R. J. Reynolds – Tobacco Industry – Worker/Homemaker
Married	(1) Unknown (2) G. O. Webster
Notes	According to the 1900 Census, she was literate and attended school. She did not have any children from her first marriage but had children from her second husband. Their children are Lillie Mae Webster Jones and Otis Webster.

Name	Ella M. Mason Neely
Date Of Birth	Friday, July 7, 1894
Place Of Birth	Winston Township City Ward 2, North Carolina – Forsyth County
Date Of Death	Wednesday, June 15, 1966
Age At Death	71
Place Of Death	Columbus, Ohio – Franklin County
Occupation	Retired – R. J. Reynolds – Tobacco Industry – Worker/Housewife
Married	Cicero Clarence Neely [1]
Notes	According to the 1900 Census, she was literate and attended school. She was buried in June 1966 at Green Lawn Cemetery in Columbus, Ohio –

My Family Tree

	Franklin County, a widow. Their children were Cicero Clarence Neely II and William H. Neely.

Name	**Cicero Clarence Neely I**
Date Of Birth	Sunday, August 5, 1888
Place Of Birth	Winston Township City Ward 2, North Carolina – Forsyth County
Date Of Death	Friday, November 18, 1932
Age At Death	44
Place Of Death	Loveland, Ohio – Hamilton County
Occupation	Day Laborer
Married	Ella M. Mason Neely
Notes	According to the 1900 Census, he was literate. Married Sunday, March 15, 1914, in Davie, North Carolina – Davidson County, a marriage of 18 years. He was buried Tuesday, November 22, 1932, at Evergreen Cemetery. They both lived at 538 Elliott Street in Loveland at the time of their deaths and were homeowners. His parents were Elsie Hawkins Neely and Henry Neely.

Name	**Nebraska Mason**
Date Of Birth	Winston Township City Ward 2, North Carolina – Forsyth County
Place Of Birth	Unknown
Date Of Death	Unknown
Age At Death	Unknown
Place Of Death	Unknown
Occupation	Unknown
Married	Unknown
Notes	

My Family Tree

Name	Nevada Mason
Date Of Birth	Winston Township City Ward 2, North Carolina – Forsyth County
Place Of Birth	Unknown
Date Of Death	Unknown
Age At Death	Unknown
Place Of Death	Unknown
Occupation	Unknown
Married	Unknown
Notes	

Name	Green Mason
Date Of Birth	Thursday, December 26, 1896
Place Of Birth	Winston Township City Ward 2, North Carolina – Forsyth County
Date Of Death	Tuesday, June 3, 1930
Age At Death	33
Place Of Death	Winston-Salem, North Carolina – Forsyth County
Occupation	R. J. Reynolds – Tobacco Industry – Worker / United States – Army
Married	Alice Roberson Mason
Notes	- Listed as literate, Mulatto, and attended school in the 1900 Census. - At age 16, he lived with his sister Etta. - Served in the U.S. Army during WWI, registered Monday, July 15, 1918, and was honorably discharged. - Child: Dorothy Williams (b. 1902 – d. Friday, March 18, 1921, age 18 – 19). She was buried Sunday, March 20, 1921, at Oddfellows Cemetery.

Ellen (9) Children with Samuel M. Mason

Name	Raymond D. Mason [1]

My Family Tree

Date Of Birth	Sunday, February 4, 1900
Place Of Birth	Manteo, North Carolina – Dare County
Date Of Death	Monday, February 13, 1984
Age At Death	84
Place Of Death	Columbus, Ohio – Franklin County
Occupation	Retired – Tankage Plant Worker
Married	Roxanna S. Smith Mason
Notes	- Illiterate according to the 1910 Census, but literate by 1930. - Buried in February 1984. - Both he and Roxanna were buried at Union Cemetery in Columbus, Ohio – Franklin County.

Name	**Roxanna S. Smith Mason**
Date Of Birth	Thursday, August 16, 1906
Place Of Birth	Moncure, North Carolina – Chatham County
Date Of Death	Tuesday, September 29, 1964
Age At Death	58
Place Of Death	Columbus, Ohio – Franklin County
Occupation	Domestic Worker/Homemaker
Married	Raymond D. Mason [I]
Notes	- First name was spelled as Roxella in the 1920 Census. - Married on Monday, July 20, 1925, in North Carolina – Chatham County, they had been married for 39 years. - Buried on Friday, October 2, 1964. - Her parents were Henrietta Smith and Jordan Smith. - Their children: Alberta R. Mason Samuels, Dorthea M. Mason White, Lois Mason Croston, Raymond A. Mason [II], Melvin Mason, and Ella M. Mason.

Name	**Mildred Ann Mason Hege**

My Family Tree

Date Of Birth	Wednesday, December 2, 1903
Place Of Birth	Fork Township, North Carolina – Wayne County
Date Of Death	Wednesday, December 7, 1988
Age At Death	85
Place Of Death	Winston-Salem, North Carolina – Forsyth County
Occupation	Homemaker
Married	Jesse Lee Hege
Notes	- The 1910 Census noted that she was literate. - Buried in December 1988, a widow and homeowner. - Mildred and Jesse were both buried at Evergreen Cemetery. - The 1930 records reported that she had four children, but only three survived. - Their children: Charlie Lee Hege, James Hege, John Thomas Hege [I], and Frances Rebecca Hege Strickland.

Name	**Jesse Lee Hege**
Date Of Birth	Thursday, September 5, 1907
Place Of Birth	Fulton Township, North Carolina – Davie County
Date Of Death	Monday, May 19, 1969
Age At Death	61
Place Of Death	Winston-Salem, North Carolina – Forsyth County
Occupation	Retired – United States Army / Retired – Cook
Married	(1) Mildred Ann Mason Hege (2) Mary Wilma Dobson Hege (3) Sallie Hege
Notes	- Served in the United States Army during WWI from (1917–1918) and was honorably discharged. - (1) Marriage Wednesday, December 14, 1921, in Fulton Township, North Carolina – Davie County, a marriage of 48 years. - The 1920 Census noted that his first name was spelled Jessie. - Jesse was not legally divorced from his first wife when he married his second or his third wife. - When he died, Mildred received his life benefits because they were still

My Family Tree

	married. - Buried Saturday, May 24, 1969, at Cedar Grove Baptist Church Cemetery. - Lived at 710 Glenn Avenue in Winston-Salem at the time of his death. - His parents were Cora Young Hege (b. 1879) and Paten Richard Hege (b. Wednesday, December 18, 1878 – d. Wednesday, December 2, 1959, age 80), both born in Fulton Township, North Carolina – Davie County.

Name	Cornelius Mason
Date Of Birth	Sunday, April 16, 1905
Place Of Birth	Mocksville, North Carolina – Davie County
Date Of Death	Sunday, October 10, 1971
Age At Death	66
Place Of Death	New Brunswick, New Jersey – Middlesex County
Occupation	Retired – Crane Operator
Married	Eva Parker Mason
Notes	The 1910 Census noted that he was illiterate, but by 1930 he was literate.

Name	Eva Parker Mason
Date Of Birth	Wednesday, August 6, 1905
Place Of Birth	Kentucky
Date Of Death	Monday, January 5, 1981
Age At Death	75
Place Of Death	New Brunswick, New Jersey – Middlesex County
Occupation	Housewife
Married	Cornelius Mason
Notes	- Married Thursday, May 3, 1928, in New York – Chautauqua County, a marriage of 43 years. - Her parents were Elizabeth Gay Parker and George Parker.

My Family Tree

	- Their children: Mary Ellen Mason, Richard Mason, Bobby Mason, Robert Mason [1], George Mason, and Elizabeth Mason Smith.

Name	**Cleophus Mason**
Date Of Birth	Monday, March 30, 1908
Place Of Birth	Mocksville, North Carolina – Davie County
Date Of Death	Unknown
Age At Death	Unknown
Place Of Death	Columbus, Ohio – Franklin County
Occupation	Retired – General Contractor/United States – Army – Retired
Married	(1) Unknown (2) Clarabelle Berry Mason
Notes	- In the 1930 Census noted that he was literate. - Served in the United States Army during WWII – registered Tuesday, December 14, 1943, in Fulton Township, North Carolina – Forsyth County and was honorably discharged. - Married twice with no children from either marriage.

Name	**Clarabelle Berry Mason**
Date Of Birth	Friday, July 12, 1912
Place Of Birth	Columbus, Ohio – Franklin County
Date Of Death	Monday, June 22, 1986
Age At Death	73
Place Of Death	Columbus, Ohio – Franklin County
Occupation	Retired – Private Maid
Married	Cleophus Mason
Notes	- Married Saturday, May 16, 1950, in Columbus, Ohio – Delaware County. - Her parents were Anna Whitfield Berry and Albert Berry. - Her nickname was "Carol" or "Carol Bell." - She was a widow when she died.

My Family Tree

Name	**Margaret Mason McCall**
Date Of Birth	Friday, August 26, 1910
Place Of Birth	Mocksville, North Carolina – Davie County
Date Of Death	Unknown
Age At Death	Unknown
Place Of Death	Columbus, Ohio – Franklin County
Occupation	Domestic Worker/Housewife
Married	Robert Raymond McCall [I]
Notes	- The 1920 Census listed her as illiterate, but by 1930, she was literate. - Their child: Robert Raymond McCall [II].

Name	**Robert Raymond McCall I**
Date Of Birth	Saturday, April 14, 1906
Place Of Birth	White Hall, Alabama – Lowndes County
Date Of Death	Sunday, October 3, 1982
Age At Death	76
Place Of Death	Columbus, Ohio – Franklin County
Occupation	Day Laborer
Married	Margaret Mason McCall
Notes	- His parents were Hattie Ivory McCall and Duncan McCall. - Married Thursday, July 14, 1927, in Columbus, Ohio – Franklin County.

Name	**Veada Mason Pittman**
Date Of Birth	Sunday, April 27, 1913
Place Of Birth	Mocksville, North Carolina – Davie County

My Family Tree

Date Of Death	Sunday, April 14, 1991
Age At Death	77
Place Of Death	Ward 2, New Brunswick City, New Jersey – Middlesex County
Occupation	Retired – R. J. Reynolds – Tobacco Industry – Stemmer Worker/Housewife
Married	William Pittman [I] (b. 1904), North Carolina
Notes	- According to the 1930 Census, she was a boarder at her sister Mildred's home at the age of 16. - Her brother-in-law, Clifton Pittman, was also a boarder at their home. - Their children: Ralph Pittman, William Pittman [II], Judy Pittman, Carolyn Pittman, and Alfreda Pittman. Their children were born in New Brunswick City, New Jersey – Middlesex County.

Name	Napoleon Jefferson Mason
Date Of Birth	Thursday, July 6, 1911
Place Of Birth	Mocksville, North Carolina – Davie County
Date Of Death	Saturday, May 11, 1996
Age At Death	84
Place Of Death	Detroit, Michigan – Wayne County
Occupation	Retired – R. J. Reynolds – Tobacco Industry – Worker/Auto Assembly Line Worker – Chrysler Corp/Packard Motor Plant/Tiger Stadium – Concession Stand Worker
Married	Hazel Lorraine Workman Mason
Notes	He joined an organization named the Freemason. He was buried on Friday, May 17, 1996. He was a widower until he died. Hazel and Napoleon both lived at 15799 Alden Street in Detroit at the time of their deaths, homeowners. Hazel and Napoleon were both buried side-by-side at Woodlawn Cemetery in Detroit, Michigan – Wayne County. Mr. Mason has a live testimony that talks about his life and an obituary.

Name	Hazel Lorraine Workman Mason
Date Of Birth	Sunday, October 27, 1918

My Family Tree

Place Of Birth	Winston-Salem, North Carolina – Forsyth County
Date Of Death	Wednesday, September 13, 1995
Age At Death	76
Place Of Death	Southfield, Michigan – Oakland County
Occupation	Retired – R. J. Reynolds – Tobacco Industry – Worker/Auto Assembly Line Worker – Desoto Chrysler / Homemaker
Married	Napoleon Jefferson Mason
Notes	Her parents were Euphonia Bernice Orr Workman and William Essix Workman. Married Friday, June 12, 1936, in Winston-Salem, North Carolina – Forsyth County, a marriage of 59 years. She joined an organization named the Eastern Star. She was buried on Monday, September 18, 1995. Mrs. Mason has a live testimony that talks about her life and an obituary. Their children were Eugene Napoleon Mason (Gene), William Anthony Mason (Tony), Robert Stanley Mason (Bobby), and Euphonia C. Mason Jackson (Phonia).

Name	**Suphonia M. Mason Johnson**
Date Of Birth	Wednesday, September 20, 1916
Place Of Birth	Mocksville, North Carolina – Davie County
Date Of Death	Thursday, September 2, 1993
Age At Death	77
Place Of Death	Philadelphia, Pennsylvania – Philadelphia County
Occupation	Housewife
Married	(1) George Lewis (2) Houston Johnson
Notes	She did not have any children from either of her marriages. She changed her first name as an adult to Peggy M. Mason.

Name	**Brownie Mae Mason Ryder**
Date Of Birth	Monday, July 5, 1920
Place Of Birth	Mocksville, North Carolina – Davie County

My Family Tree

Date Of Death	Saturday, July 12, 1975
Age At Death	55
Place Of Death	Columbus, Ohio – Franklin County
Occupation	Retired – R. J. Reynolds – Tobacco Industry – Worker/Housewife
Married	Widow
Notes	She never remarried before she died.

The Grandparents of Eugene Napoleon Mason – Maternal (His Mother's Side)

The Family Line of Euphonia Bernice Orr Workman and William Essix Workman

The Fourth Generation

Euphonia Bernice Orr Workman	-	See Entry Page 55
William Essix Workman	-	See Entry Page 55- 56

Their (8) Children

Hazel Lorraine Workman Mason	-	See Entry Page 67-68
Napoleon Jefferson Mason	-	See Entry Page 67

Name	**Grace Louise Workman Browning**
Date Of Birth	Saturday, January 28, 1922
Place Of Birth	Winston-Salem, North Carolina – Forsyth County
Date Of Death	Tuesday, July 7, 1981
Age At Death	59
Place Of Death	Detroit, Michigan – Wayne County
Occupation	Detroit City Worker – Wayne County Auditor
Married	Elwood B. Browning
Notes	She joined an organization named the Eastern Star. She was buried on Tuesday, July 11, 1981. Mrs. Browning has an obituary that talks about her life. Their children: Marva L. Browning Grant and Mona L. Browning Cooper.

My Family Tree

Name	**Elwood B. Browning**
Date Of Birth	Tuesday, November 22, 1910
Place Of Birth	Bowling Green, Kentucky – Warren County
Date Of Death	Monday, January 18, 1993
Age At Death	82
Place Of Death	Detroit, Michigan – Wayne County
Occupation	Retired – United States – Armed Forces/UAW Union Member
Married	Grace Louise Workman Browning
Notes	He served in the United States Armed Forces during WWII from Friday, September 1, 1939 – Sunday, September 2, 1945, and was honorably discharged. Married Saturday, September 13, 1947, in Lucas, Ohio – Richland County, a marriage of 34 years. He joined an organization named the Freemasons. He was buried on Friday, January 22, 1993. He died a widower and homeowner. Grace and Elwood were both buried side-by-side at Glen Eden Lutheran Cemetery in Livonia, Michigan – Wayne County. Mr. Browning has an obituary that talks about his life. His parents were Alma Davis Browning (b. 1893) and Charles Browning (b. 1889). Alma and Charles were married Saturday, July 17, 1909, in Bowling Green, Kentucky – Warren County.

Name	**William Robert Workman I**
Date Of Birth	Monday, January 20, 1919
Place Of Birth	Winston-Salem, North Carolina – Forsyth County
Date Of Death	Thursday, March 10, 2005
Age At Death	86
Place Of Death	Winston-Salem, North Carolina – Forsyth County
Occupation	Retired – Sherwood Treating Worker
Married	Melba Elizabeth Thompson Workman
Notes	He had three years of high school education. He was enlisted in the United States Army during WWII and was honorably discharged Monday, March

	11, 1946. He was buried Saturday, March 12, 2005, in North Carolina, and he was a widower when he died and a homeowner. Mr. Workman has an obituary that talks about his life.

Name	Melba Elizabeth Thompson Workman
Date Of Birth	Tuesday, November 9, 1920
Place Of Birth	Martin, Tennessee – Weakley County
Date Of Death	Monday, May 13, 2002
Age At Death	81
Place Of Death	Winston-Salem, North Carolina – Forsyth County
Occupation	Homemaker
Married	William Robert Workman [I]
Notes	Their children: William R. Workman [II], Melba Louise Lindsay Workman Bostic, and Lenora W. Workman Cochran.

Name	Eugene N. Workman
Date Of Birth	Thursday, August 8, 1935
Place Of Birth	Winston-Salem, North Carolina – Forsyth County
Date Of Death	Sunday, July 5, 1936
Age At Death	11 Months Old
Place Of Death	Winston-Salem, North Carolina – Forsyth County
Occupation	None
Married	Single
Notes	He lived at 603 Oriole in Winston-Salem at the time of his death. He was buried Tuesday, July 7, 1936, at Bellevue Cemetery and re-interred at Nat Watkins Cemetery in Walkertown, North Carolina – Forsyth County in 1968.

My Family Tree

Name	Edward Ray Workman
Date Of Birth	Tuesday, February 3, 1925
Place Of Birth	Winston-Salem, North Carolina – Forsyth County
Date Of Death	Unknown
Age At Death	Unknown
Place Of Death	In the Army during WWII
Occupation	None
Married	Single
Notes	He held a Draft Registration Card from the United States Army during WWII in 1943, and he joined the United States Army with his brother William. Edward never made it back home from the war.

Name	Treva Mae Workman
Date Of Birth	Unknown
Place Of Birth	Winston-Salem, North Carolina – Forsyth County
Date Of Death	Died in infancy after five days
Age At Death	Five days old
Place Of Death	Winston-Salem, North Carolina – Forsyth County
Occupation	None
Married	Single
Notes	She lived at 603 Oriole in Winston-Salem at the time of her death. Treva was buried on the property, according to the elders of the family, but no death record was found.

Name	James Leonard Workman
Date Of Birth	Sunday, October 8, 1933
Place Of Birth	Winston-Salem, North Carolina – Forsyth County

My Family Tree

Date Of Death	Saturday, April 25, 2009
Age At Death	75
Place Of Death	Charleston, South Carolina – Berkeley County
Occupation	Retired – United States Armed Forces/Day Laborer
Married	Evelyn T. Workman
Notes	He served in the United States Armed Forces during WWII from Friday, September 1, 1939 – Sunday, September 2, 1945, and was honorably discharged. He was buried in April 2009 in Charleston, South Carolina – Berkeley County, a homeowner.

Name	**Richard LeRoy Workman I**
Date Of Birth	Saturday, December 11, 1926
Place Of Birth	Winston-Salem, North Carolina – Forsyth County
Date Of Death	Thursday, January 1, 2009
Age At Death	83
Place Of Death	Winston-Salem, North Carolina – Forsyth County
Occupation	Barber – Shop Owner
Married	Mildred Delores Cherry Workman
Notes	Mildred and Richard were homeowners.

Name	**Mildred Delores Cherry Workman**
Date Of Birth	Friday, September 2, 1932
Place Of Birth	Winston-Salem, North Carolina – Forsyth County
Date Of Death	Sunday, February 13, 2000
Age At Death	67
Place Of Death	Winston-Salem, North Carolina – Forsyth County

My Family Tree

Occupation	Housewife
Married	Richard LeRoy Workman [I]
Notes	Their child: Richard LeRoy Workman [II] (b. Wednesday, August 10, 1960, POB. and POD. Winston-Salem, North Carolina – Forsyth County – d. Monday, August 15, 1960, age 5 Days Old). He was buried Monday, August 15, 1960, at Evergreen Cemetery.

The Parents of Eugene Napoleon Mason

The Family Line of Hazel Lorraine Workman Mason and Napoleon Jefferson Mason

The connection to the family line was Hazel, the daughter of Euphonia Bernice Orr Workman and William Essix Workman, and Hazel's husband – Napoleon, was the son of Ellen Jefferson Mason and Samuel M. Mason.

The Fifth Generation

Hazel Lorraine Workman Mason - See Entry Page 67-68
Napoleon Jefferson Mason - See Entry Page 67

Their (4) Children

Name	**Eugene Napoleon Mason**
Date Of Birth	Monday, November 23, 1936
Place Of Birth	Winston-Salem, North Carolina – Forsyth County
Date Of Death	Wednesday, October 11, 1989
Age At Death	52
Place Of Death	Detroit, Michigan – Wayne County
Occupation	Retired – Auto Assembly Line Worker – Ford Motor Company
Married	Norma Jean Carey Mason
Notes	His nickname was "Gene." He was buried Saturday, October 14, 1989, at Westlawn Cemetery in Wayne, Michigan – Wayne County. Mr. Mason has a live testimony that talks about his life and an obituary.

My Family Tree

Name	**Norma Jean Carey Mason**
Date Of Birth	Wednesday, October 18, 1939
Place Of Birth	Holden, West Virginia – Logan County
Date Of Death	N/A
Age At Death	N/A
Place Of Death	N/A
Occupation	Retired – Nurse/Homemaker/Janitor/Cook – Private School
Married	Eugene Napoleon Mason
Notes	Her nickname is "Jean or Jeanne." Married Saturday, July 1, 1967, in Detroit, Michigan – Wayne County, a marriage of 23 years. Theirs was the first matrimonial ceremony performed by Bishop, Rev. Gary M. Simpson at the **Temple of I AM** and in the name of **I AM**. She is a widow and homeowner. Mrs. Mason has a living testimony about her life. Norma is the "Mother of the Church" at the **Temple of I AM**. Norma had 3 children, but only 2 survived: Rodney A. Mason, Stephanie M. Mason, and Iris A. Mason Nicholas. Her parents were Levonia Margaret Carey Cowan and Walter White.

Name	**William Anthony Mason**
Date Of Birth	Saturday, January 22, 1938
Place Of Birth	Winston-Salem, North Carolina – Forsyth County
Date Of Death	Monday, August 3, 2020
Age At Death	82
Place Of Death	Detroit, Michigan – Wayne County
Occupation	Retired – Daimler Chrysler Worker – Floor Supervisor/Board Member – Bake College/PhD
Married	Litha Ruth Walker Mason
Notes	His nickname was "Tony or T-Bird." He was buried on Friday, August 7, 2020. Litha and William were both buried side-by-side in an immurement at Woodlawn Cemetery in Detroit, Michigan – Wayne County. He was a widower until he died. Litha and William were homeowners. Mr. Mason has a living testimony that talks about his life and an obituary. The promise

My Family Tree

| | that Tony made with his older brother (Eugene) was kept for over 30 years, all the way until he died. He was a Father Figure to his younger nieces (Stephanie M. Mason and Iris A. Mason Nicholas). Litha and Tony were a support team for their sister-in-law (Norma J. Mason). |

Name	**Litha Ruth Walker Mason**
Date Of Birth	Saturday, March 20, 1937
Place Of Birth	Locust Grove, Georgia – Henry County
Date Of Death	Monday, April 22, 2019
Age At Death	82
Place Of Death	Detroit, Michigan – Wayne County
Occupation	Retired – Secretary – Seamstress – Winkelman's Warehouse/Homemaker
Married	William Anthony Mason
Notes	Married Saturday, March 19, 1960, in Detroit, Michigan – Wayne County, a marriage of 59 years. She was buried on Wednesday, May 1, 2019. Mrs. Mason has a living testimony that talks about her life and an obituary. Their children: Jenean E. Mason, Theodore C. Mason, and Anthony T. Mason. Her parents were Estella Lewis Walker (b. Tuesday, May 16, 1916, POB. Butler, Georgia – Henry County – d. Tuesday, January 28, 1992, POD. Detroit, Michigan – Wayne County, age 75) and Theortic Calvin (T. C.) Walker. Estella was buried Saturday, February 1, 1992, at Westlawn Cemetery in Wayne, Michigan – Wayne County, a widow and homeowner. Her grandparents were Alice Patricia Parker Lewis and Leonard Radney Lewis. Her adopted daughters are Venus R. Mason Thues, Iris A. Mason Nicholas, and Stephanie M. Mason.

Name	**Robert Stanley Mason**
Date Of Birth	Friday, February 2, 1940
Place Of Birth	Winston-Salem, North Carolina – Forsyth County
Date Of Death	Sunday, August 10, 2014
Age At Death	74

My Family Tree

Place Of Death	Garfield Heights, Ohio – Cuyahoga County
Occupation	Retired – Auto Worker – Supervisor – Daimler Chrysler
Married	(1) Peggy Mason (2) Louise Lockhart Mason (3) Annette Mason (4) Ann Mason (5) JoAnn McGuire Mason
Notes	His nickname was "Bobby." He was cremated Wednesday, August 13, 2014, in Garfield Heights, Ohio – Cuyahoga County, a homeowner. (1) Peggy Mason (b. 1944 – d. 1987, age 42 – 43), POD. Ohio, (2) Louise Lockhart Mason (b. 1951), married Wednesday, June 1, 1988, and divorced Wednesday, April 25, 2001), (5) JoAnn McGuire Mason (b. 1958), married Tuesday, March 6, 2007. His children: Tyrone Mason, Linda Mason Gill (b. December 1952), Terrence Mason (b. Friday, July 4, 1958), and Rashad Amin Mason (b. Thursday, May 15, 1986), POB. Ohio, his mother is Louise. Mr. Mason has an obituary that talks about his life.

Name	**Euphonia C. Mason Jackson**
Date Of Birth	Saturday, June 13, 1943
Place Of Birth	Winston-Salem, North Carolina – Forsyth County
Date Of Death	Thursday, January 16, 1986
Age At Death	42
Place Of Death	Detroit, Michigan – Wayne County
Occupation	Homemaker/Auto Assembly Line Worker – Daimler Chrysler
Married	Horace Ronald Jackson
Notes	Her nickname was "Phonia." She was buried Monday, January 20, 1986, at Westland Cemetery in Wayne, Michigan – Wayne County. Mrs. Jackson has an obituary that talks about her life. Their children: Euphonia T. Jackson, Horace R. Jackson, and Eric C. Jackson.

Name	**Horace Ronald Jackson**
Date Of Birth	Thursday, November 7, 1940

My Family Tree

Place Of Birth	Riverdale, Georgia – Clayton County
Date Of Death	Tuesday, March 8, 2016
Age At Death	75
Place Of Death	Detroit, Michigan – Wayne County
Occupation	Retired – United States Army/Auto Assembly Line Worker – Ford Motor Company
Married	Euphonia C. Mason Jackson
Notes	Married Saturday, September 16, 1961, in Detroit, Michigan – Wayne County, a marriage of 25 years, a widower, and they were homeowners.

The Family Line of Norma Jean Carey Mason and Eugene Napoleon Mason

The connection to the family line is Norma, the daughter of Levonia Margaret Carey Cowan and Walter White and Norma's husband – Eugene, was the son of Hazel Lorraine Workman Mason and Napoleon Jefferson Mason.

The Sixth Generation

Norma Jean Carey Mason - See Entry Page 75
Eugene Napoleon Mason - See Entry Page 74

Their (3) Children

Name	**Rodney Allen Mason**
Date Of Birth	Saturday, January 12, 1974
Place Of Birth	Detroit, Michigan – Wayne County
Date Of Death	Wednesday, January 16, 1974
Age At Death	4 Days Old
Place Of Death	Detroit, Michigan – Wayne County
Occupation	None
Married	Single
Notes	His body was donated to science on Wednesday, January 16, 1974.

My Family Tree

Name	**Stephanie Michele Mason**
Date Of Birth	Friday, June 20, 1975
Place Of Birth	Detroit, Michigan – Wayne County
Date Of Death	N/A
Age At Death	N/A
Place Of Death	N/A
Occupation	Certified Dental Assistant/Full-Time Caregiver/Business Manager
Married	Single
Notes	Author/Poet. Ms. Mason has a living testimony about her life. Iris and Stephanie manage all their mother's affairs, and Stephanie is in charge of their mother's medical team services, as their mother is in her golden years.

Name	**Iris Althea Mason Nicholas**
Date Of Birth	Monday, November 1, 1976
Place Of Birth	Detroit, Michigan – Wayne County
Date Of Death	N/A
Age At Death	N/A
Place Of Death	N/A
Occupation	Retail Store Manager/Homemaker/Caregiver
Married	James Russell Nicholas III
Notes	Married on Saturday, June 23, 2012. Marriage performed by Bishop, Rev. Gary M. Simpson at the **Temple of I AM** in Detroit, Michigan – Wayne County. Mrs. Nicholas has a living testimony about her life.

Name	**James Russell Nicholas III**
Date Of Birth	Wednesday, March 16, 1977

My Family Tree

Place Of Birth	Detroit, Michigan – Wayne County
Date Of Death	N/A
Age At Death	N/A
Place Of Death	N/A
Occupation	Chef/Chauffeur/Caretaker
Married	Iris Althea Mason Nicholas
Notes	His parents are AlFreda E. Williams Nicholas (b. Friday, July 26, 1957), POB. Montgomery, Alabama – Montgomery County. AlFreda was married twice. AlFreda's first husband was James Russell Nicholas [II] (b. Sunday, August 13, 1950, POB. Layland, West Virginia – Fayette County – d. Saturday, May 15, 1993, POD. Detroit, Michigan – Wayne County, age 42). James [II]'s parents were Kathryn L. Freeman Tonye, and James Russell Nicholas [I]. James [II] was buried in May 1993 at Westlawn Cemetery in Wayne, Michigan – Wayne County. AlFreda's second husband is Willie James Parker (b. Thursday, March 27, 1969), POB. Sylacauga, Alabama – Talladega County, nickname "Will or Daddy Will." Mr. Nicholas has a living testimony about his life. Iris and James are homeowners.

Their Child

Name	**James Russell Nicholas IV**
Date Of Birth	Thursday, June 19, 2014
Place Of Birth	Royal Oak, Michigan – Oakland County
Date Of Death	N/A
Age At Death	N/A
Place Of Death	N/A
Occupation	N/A
Married	N/A
Notes	At birth: 3 lbs and 11 oz – 17 ½ inches. Our miracle baby "Mr. Yam or JJ."

My Family Tree

The Family Line of Audrey F. Holloway Mason and Theodore Cornelius Mason

The connection to the family line is Theodore, the son of Litha Ruth Walker Mason and William Anthony Mason.

The Seventh Generation

Name	**Theodore Cornelius Mason**
Date Of Birth	Tuesday, April 4, 1967
Place Of Birth	Detroit, Michigan – Wayne County
Date Of Death	N/A
Age At Death	N/A
Place Of Death	N/A
Occupation	Auto Assembly Line Worker – Chrysler
Married	(1) Audrey F. Holloway Mason (2) Suzanne Maria Zeglen Mason
Notes	(1) Marriage Friday, October 14, 1994, in Redford, Michigan – Wayne County. (2) Marriage Friday, September 1, 2017, in Novi, Michigan – Oakland County. Theodore and Audrey were divorced in Michigan. His nickname is "Ted." Mr. Mason has a living testimony about his life. Suzanne and Ted are homeowners.

Theodore Cornelius Mason (2) Children with Audrey F. Holloway Mason

Name	**Amber Rose Mason**
Date Of Birth	Friday, June 19, 1998
Place Of Birth	Redford Township, Michigan – Wayne County
Date Of Death	N/A
Age At Death	N/A
Place Of Death	N/A
Occupation	Student at College/Bank Teller
Married	N/A

My Family Tree

Notes	

Name	**Anthony Jefferson Mason**
Date Of Birth	Thursday, January 18, 2007
Place Of Birth	Redford Township, Michigan – Wayne County
Date Of Death	N/A
Age At Death	N/A
Place Of Death	N/A
Occupation	Student
Married	N/A
Notes	

The Family Line of Grace Louise Workman Browning and Elwood B. Browning

The connection to the family line was Grace, the daughter of Euphonia Bernice Orr Workman and William Essix Workman.

The Fifth Generation

Grace Louise Workman Browning - See Entry Page 69
Elwood B. Browning - See Entry Page 70

Their (2) Children

Name	**Marva Lorraine Browning Grant**
Date Of Birth	Wednesday, June 25, 1947
Place Of Birth	Detroit, Michigan – Wayne County
Date Of Death	N/A
Age At Death	N/A
Place Of Death	N/A
Occupation	Retired – Florida City Worker

My Family Tree

Married	Thomas Dale Grant
Notes	Married Thursday, September 11, 1997, and divorced Wednesday, December 13, 2000, in Miami, Florida – Dade County. Currently living in Plantation, Florida – Broward County. His nickname is "Tommy."

Name	**Mona Louise Browning Cooper**
Date Of Birth	Sunday, January 27, 1952
Place Of Birth	Detroit, Michigan – Wayne County
Date Of Death	N/A
Age At Death	N/A
Place Of Death	N/A
Occupation	Retired – Senior Personnel Manager – Florida Dept. Corrections
Married	(1) McMiller (2) Willie James Cooper
Notes	(2) Marriage Thursday, February 27, 1992, in Florida. Currently living in Plantation, Florida – Broward County.

Mona Louise Browning Cooper (2) Children

Name	**LaShawn Maria McMiller**
Date Of Birth	February 1969
Place Of Birth	Detroit, Michigan – Wayne County
Date Of Death	N/A
Age At Death	N/A
Place Of Death	N/A
Occupation	Associate Broker – Real Estate in Florida
Married	N/A
Notes	Her mother is Mona Louise Browning McMiller. Currently living in Plantation, Florida – Broward County.

My Family Tree

Name	Justin Merrick Malone
Date Of Birth	Friday, November 23, 1984
Place Of Birth	Detroit, Michigan – Wayne County
Date Of Death	Sunday, September 22, 2024
Age At Death	39
Place Of Death	Pompano Beach, Florida – Broward County
Occupation	Self-Employed
Married	Single
Notes	He has two beautiful children.

The Family Line of Euphonia C. Mason and Horace Ronald Jackson

The connection to the family line was Euphonia C., the daughter of Hazel Lorraine Workman Mason and Napoleon Jefferson Mason.

The Sixth Generation

Euphonia C. Mason Jackson - See Entry Page 77
Horace Ronald Jackson - See Entry Page 77-78

Their (3) Children

Name	Euphonia Tracy Jackson
Date Of Birth	Monday, February 26, 1962
Place Of Birth	Detroit, Michigan – Wayne County
Date Of Death	Sunday, July 18, 1999
Age At Death	37
Place Of Death	Detroit, Michigan – Wayne County
Occupation	Hairdresser /Daimler Chrysler – Assembly Line Worker
Married	Single
Notes	She always went by her middle name, "Tracy." She passed two months before her marriage to David Thomas. She was buried Saturday, July 24, 1999, at Detroit Memorial Park Cemetery in West Redford Township,

My Family Tree

	Michigan – Wayne County. Her grandparents (Hazel and Napoleon) gave her son a gift for life. Her children: Trevor A. Jackson and Trina Thomas. Ms. Jackson has an obituary that talks about her life.

Name	Horace Reginale Jackson
Date Of Birth	Friday, March 17, 1967
Place Of Birth	Detroit, Michigan – Wayne County
Date Of Death	N/A
Age At Death	N/A
Place Of Death	N/A
Occupation	N/A
Married	N/A
Notes	

Name	Eric Creighton Jackson
Date Of Birth	Monday, August 15, 1966
Place Of Birth	Detroit, Michigan – Wayne County
Date Of Death	N/A
Age At Death	N/A
Place Of Death	N/A
Occupation	N/A
Married	N/A
Notes	

My Family Tree

Euphonia Tracy Jackson (2) Children

Name	**Trever Anthony Jackson**
Date Of Birth	Thursday, November 11, 1982
Place Of Birth	Detroit, Michigan – Wayne County
Date Of Death	N/A
Age At Death	N/A
Place Of Death	N/A
Occupation	CEO/Founder "Good Food LLC" – Chief
Married	Single
Notes	His children – Z'Riah Jackson and Zaiden Jackson – twins. Hazel and Napoleon passed their house down to their great-grandson Trever, a home of good memories, love, support, safety, and lessons. He was 13 years old when they passed. His great-grandparents told him he would always have a home there and a car when he was old enough to take it over. He was always Grandma's helper in the kitchen.

Name	**Trina Thomas**
Date Of Birth	Saturday, October 15, 1994
Place Of Birth	Detroit, Michigan – Wayne County
Date Of Death	N/A
Age At Death	N/A
Place Of Death	N/A
Occupation	Hotel Management
Married	Single
Notes	Her parents were Euphonia Tracy Jackson and David Thomas.

My Family Tree

The Family of Mary Frances Clinkscales Harris and William Anthony Mason

The connection to the family line was William, the son of Hazel Lorraine Workman Mason and Napoleon Jefferson Mason.

The Sixth Generation

Mary Frances Clinkscales Harris - See Entry Below
William Anthony Mason - See Entry Page 75-76

Their Child

Name	**Venus Renee Mason Thues**
Date Of Birth	Saturday, September 29, 1956
Place Of Birth	Detroit, Michigan – Wayne County
Date Of Death	N/A
Age At Death	N/A
Place Of Death	N/A
Occupation	Homemaker/Book Author/Full-Time Caretaker
Married	(1) Barry Allen Floyd (2) Jerome Anthony Thues
Notes	Her mother was Mary Frances Clinkscales Harris (b. Sunday, November 23, 1930, POB. West Point, Georgia – Troup County – d. Sunday, November 3, 2019, POD. Detroit, Michigan – Wayne County, age 88). Mary was buried Tuesday, November 12, 2019, at Mount Hope Memorial Gardens in Livonia, Michigan. Their children: Lakeisha R. Thues Stiff and Jessica M. Thues. Mrs. Mason Thues has a living testimony about her life.

Name	**Jerome Anthony Thues**
Date Of Birth	Thursday, August 7, 1952
Place Of Birth	Detroit, Michigan – Wayne County
Date Of Death	N/A
Age At Death	N/A
Place Of Death	N/A
Occupation	College Advisor/Life Counselor

My Family Tree

Married	Venus Renee Mason Thues
Notes	Married Wednesday, April 3, 1985, in Detroit, Michigan – Wayne County. His parents were Jessie Mae Thues and Willie Thues. The Thues family adopted him as a child, but his last name was Smith before he was adopted. His nickname is "Rick." Jerome's sons are James Thues and Royale Thues. Mr. Thues has a living testimony about his life. Venus and Rick are homeowners.

Litha Ruth Walker Mason (3) Children with William Anthony Mason

Name	Jenean Evette Mason
Date Of Birth	Wednesday, December 30, 1964
Place Of Birth	Detroit, Michigan – Wayne County
Date Of Death	N/A
Age At Death	N/A
Place Of Death	N/A
Occupation	Health Services Administrator – Baker College/Caretaker
Married	Single
Notes	Ms. Mason has a living testimony about her life. Her parents passed their house down to her before they died.

Theodore Cornelius Mason - See Entry Page 81
Audrey F. Holloway Mason - See Entry Page 81

Name	Anthony Troy Mason
Date Of Birth	Friday, January 6, 1961
Place Of Birth	Detroit, Michigan – Wayne County
Date Of Death	N/A
Age At Death	N/A
Place Of Death	N/A
Occupation	N/A

My Family Tree

Married	Sandar Lewin Mason (b. Thursday, May 4, 1967)
Notes	Their children: Austin S. Mason and Ashley S. Mason.

Barbara Ware Child with William Anthony Mason

Name	Gregory Ware
Date Of Birth	Monday, October 17, 1955
Place Of Birth	Detroit, Michigan – Wayne County
Date Of Death	N/A
Age At Death	N/A
Place Of Death	N/A
Occupation	N/A
Married	N/A
Notes	

The Family Line of Sandar Lewin Mason and Anthony Troy Mason

The connection to the family line is Anthony, the son of Litha Ruth Walker Mason and William Anthony Mason.

The Seventh Generation

Sandar Lewin Mason - See Entry Page 89
Anthony Troy Mason - See Entry Page 88-89

Their (2) Children

Name	Austin Shane Mason
Date Of Birth	Friday, February 26, 1999
Place Of Birth	Falls, Virginia – Fairfax County
Date Of Death	N/A
Age At Death	N/A

My Family Tree

Place Of Death	N/A
Occupation	College Student
Married	N/A
Notes	

Name	Ashley Sherrin Mason
Date Of Birth	Sunday, September 24, 2000
Place Of Birth	Falls, Virginia – Fairfax County
Date Of Death	N/A
Age At Death	N/A
Place Of Death	N/A
Occupation	College Student
Married	N/A
Notes	

The Family Line of Venus Renee Mason Thues and Jerome Anthony Thues

The connection to the family line is Venus, the daughter of Mary Frances Clinkscales Harris and William Anthony Mason.

The Seventh Generation

Venus Renee Mason Thues - See Entry Page 87
Jerome Anthony Thues - See Entry Page 87-88

Their (2) Children

Name	Lakeisha Renee Thues Stiff
Date Of Birth	Saturday, March 25, 1978
Place Of Birth	Detroit, Michigan – Wayne County
Date Of Death	N/A

My Family Tree

Age At Death	N/A
Place Of Death	N/A
Occupation	Entertainment Executive/Magazine Editor
Married	William Stiff
Notes	Married Monday, December 5, 2005, in Detroit, Michigan – Wayne County. Their children: Madison R. Stiff and Jordan J. Stiff. Mrs. Stiff has a living testimony about her life.

Name	**Jessica Marie Thues**
Date Of Birth	Monday, October 27, 1986
Place Of Birth	Detroit, Michigan – Wayne County
Date Of Death	N/A
Age At Death	N/A
Place Of Death	N/A
Occupation	Medical Assistant
Married	N/A
Notes	Ms. Thues has a living testimony about her life.

Jessica Marie Thues Child

Name	**Ramiyah Kimberly White**
Date Of Birth	Friday, May 28, 2004
Place Of Birth	Detroit, Michigan – Wayne County
Date Of Death	N/A
Age At Death	N/A
Place Of Death	N/A
Occupation	Student

My Family Tree

Married	N/A
Notes	Ramiyah's father was Vernon Edward White, born Thursday, December 18, 1986, and died Thursday, May 20, 2004, in Detroit, Michigan – Wayne County (age 17), Single.

The Family Line of Eva Parker Mason and Cornelius Mason

The connection to the family line was Cornelius, the son of Ellen Jefferson Mason and Samuel M. Mason.

The Fifth Generation

Eva Parker Mason - See Entry Page 64-65
Cornelius Mason - See Entry Page 64

Their (6) Children

Name	Mary Ellen Mason
Date Of Birth	1936
Place Of Birth	Ward 4, New Brunswick, New Jersey – Middlesex County
Date Of Death	N/A
Age At Death	N/A
Place Of Death	N/A
Occupation	N/A
Married	N/A
Notes	

Name	Richard Mason
Date Of Birth	Wednesday, April 16, 1930
Place Of Birth	Pennsylvania – Erie County
Date Of Death	Wednesday, October 15, 1980
Age At Death	50
Place Of Death	New Jersey – Monmouth County

My Family Tree

Occupation	Day Laborer
Married	Single
Notes	

Name	**Robert Mason I**
Date Of Birth	Friday, April 17, 1931
Place Of Birth	Pennsylvania – Erie County
Date Of Death	Saturday, January 19, 2002
Age At Death	70
Place Of Death	New Brunswick, New Jersey – Middlesex County
Occupation	Day Laborer
Married	Marguerite Mason
Notes	His twin brother was Bobby. Their son: Robert Mason [II].

Name	**Bobby Mason**
Date Of Birth	Friday, April 17, 1931
Place Of Birth	Pennsylvania – Erie County
Date Of Death	N/A
Age At Death	N/A
Place Of Death	N/A
Occupation	N/A
Married	N/A
Notes	His twin brother was Robert [I].

My Family Tree

Name	George Mason
Date Of Birth	1933
Place Of Birth	New Brunswick, New Jersey – Middlesex County
Date Of Death	N/A
Age At Death	N/A
Place Of Death	N/A
Occupation	N/A
Married	N/A
Notes	

Name	Elizabeth Mason Smith
Date Of Birth	Monday, June 1, 1925
Place Of Birth	Pennsylvania – Erie County
Date Of Death	Wednesday, December 9, 1992
Age At Death	67
Place Of Death	New Jersey
Occupation	Housewife
Married	(1) Oberian Lee (2) Earnest Wooden (3) Myron Smith
Notes	(1) Married on Friday, January 8, 1954; divorced on Thursday, March 18, 1982, in Texas; (28 years). (2) Born on Tuesday, August 1, 1922, in Georgia; died on Monday, November 17, 1997 (age 75) in New Brunswick, New Jersey – Middlesex County; father was Ben Fields.

The Family Line of Mildred Ann Mason Hege and Jesse Lee Hege

The connection to the family line was Mildred, the daughter of Ellen Jefferson Mason and Samuel M. Mason.

My Family Tree

The Fifth Generation

Mildred Ann Mason Hege - See Entry Page 62-63
Jesse Lee Hege - See Entry Page 63-64

Their (4) Children

Name	Charlie Lee Hege
Date Of Birth	Friday, September 29, 1922
Place Of Birth	Fork Township, North Carolina – Wayne County
Date Of Death	Sunday, May 9, 1973
Age At Death	50
Place Of Death	Fulton, North Carolina – Davie County
Occupation	R. J. Reynolds – Tobacco Industry – Worker
Married	Margaret Hege
Notes	Buried May 1973 at Evergreen Cemetery. Their child: Leah Hege, was born in Fork Township, North Carolina – Wayne County.

Name	James Hege
Date Of Birth	Tuesday, October 2, 1923
Place Of Birth	Fork Township, North Carolina – Wayne County
Date Of Death	Wednesday, November 21, 1923
Age At Death	1 Month and 19 Days
Place Of Death	Fulton Township, North Carolina – Davie County
Occupation	None
Married	Single
Notes	Buried November 1923 at Evergreen Cemetery.

Name	John Thomas Hege I

My Family Tree

Date Of Birth	Tuesday, April 7, 1925
Place Of Birth	Fork Township, North Carolina – Wayne County
Date Of Death	Friday, June 16, 1961
Age At Death	36
Place Of Death	Durham, North Carolina – Durham County
Occupation	R. J. Reynolds – Tobacco Industry – Worker
Married	Lucille Boozer Woody Hege
Notes	Buried Friday, June 22, 1962.

Name	**Lucille Boozer Woody Hege**
Date Of Birth	Tuesday, June 12, 1928
Place Of Birth	Winston-Salem, North Carolina – Forsyth County
Date Of Death	Tuesday, February 12, 1963
Age At Death	34
Place Of Death	Winston-Salem, North Carolina – Forsyth County
Occupation	Domestic Worker/Housewife
Married	John Thomas Hege [I]
Notes	Buried on Saturday, February 16, 1963; widow at death; both were buried at Evergreen Cemetery; lived at 4220 Carven Road in Winston-Salem at the time of their death, homeowners. Married on Sunday, February 25, 1945, for 17 years; parents: Eliza Herron Woody and Roosevelt Woody; children: Equila Francena Hege Miller, Carolyn Collen Hege Anthony, Vendetta Hege Simpson, John Thomas Hege [II].

Name	**Frances Rebecca Hege Strickland**
Date Of Birth	Tuesday, May 25, 1926
Place Of Birth	Fork Township, North Carolina – Wayne County

My Family Tree

Date Of Death	Thursday, September 19, 2013
Age At Death	87
Place Of Death	Winston-Salem, North Carolina – Forsyth County
Occupation	Retired – Medical Assistant/Homemaker/Sunday School Teacher
Married	Samuel L. Strickland III
Notes	Frances and Samuel took over her mother's house to ensure smooth operation and caretaking; the house is a Historical Landmark in Winston-Salem; buried on Thursday, September 26, 2013, known as "Mama Frances." Their daughters: Mildred E. Strickland Peppers, Maria J. Strickland, Suzette D. Strickland Willis; both buried at Evergreen Cemetery; widow at death. She has an obituary about her life.

Name	**Samuel L. Strickland III**
Date Of Birth	Friday, July 6, 1923
Place Of Birth	Jackson, Georgia – Gaston County
Date Of Death	Thursday, December 26, 1985
Age At Death	62
Place Of Death	Winston-Salem, North Carolina – Forsyth County
Occupation	United States Army/Retired R. J. Reynolds Tobacco Industry – Machine Operator
Married	Frances Rebecca Hege Strickland
Notes	Served during WWII as CPL; brother Cam L. was PFC; both honorably discharged from the Army; married Saturday, November 2, 1946, in Winston-Salem, North Carolina; the marriage lasted 39 years; buried Sunday, December 29, 1985. His parents were Frona "Fronie" Lay Strickland (b. Saturday, August 1, 1896 – d. Friday, November 19, 1954, age 58) and Samuel F. Strickland II (b. Wednesday, December 19, 1894 – d. Sunday, December 6, 1959, age 64). Samuel III's parents and *Cam* POB. Jackson, Georgia – Gaston County and POD. Winston-Salem, North Carolina – Forsyth County. His parents, *Cam* and *Samuel*, all worked at R. J. Reynolds – as tobacco industry workers.

My Family Tree

> Samuel F [II]'s parents were Vallie Few Strickland and Samuel Strickland [I].
> Cam L. Strickland (b. Wednesday, April 6, 1921 – d. Wednesday, December 5, 1973, age 52).
> Cam's wife – Thelma W. Strickland (b. Friday, December 30, 1921), POB. North Carolina – d. Saturday, November 17, 1984, age 62). Thelma and Cam, both POD. Winston-Salem, North Carolina – Forsyth County. Fronie's parents were Lula Shields Lay and John Lay. Samuel [III]'s parents, Thelma and Cam, were buried side-by-side at Evergreen Cemetery. All three of Samuel's nicknames were "Sam."

The Family Line of Ella M. Mason Neely and Cicero Clarence Neely [I]

The connection to the family line was Ella, the daughter of Mary Mason and Samuel M. Mason.

The Fifth Generation

Ella M. Mason Neely - See Entry Page 59-60
Cicero Clarence Neely [I] - See Entry Page 60

Their (2) Children

Name	**Cicero Clarence Neely II**
Date Of Birth	Wednesday, August 23, 1922
Place Of Birth	Winston-Salem, North Carolina – Forsyth County
Date Of Death	Wednesday, November 21, 2001
Age At Death	79
Place Of Death	Columbus, Ohio – Franklin County
Occupation	Retired – R. J. Reynolds – Tobacco Industry – Worker
Married	Betty J. Burrs Neely
Notes	

Name	**Betty J. Burrs Neely**
Date Of Birth	Monday, February 14, 1921
Place Of Birth	Winston-Salem, North Carolina – Forsyth County
Date Of Death	Tuesday, October 14, 2008

My Family Tree

Age At Death	87
Place Of Death	Columbus, Ohio – Franklin County
Occupation	Retired – R. J. Reynolds – Tobacco Industry – Worker/Homemaker
Married	Cicero Clarence Neely II
Notes	Her parents were Emerline Butler Burrs and Clarence Burrs. Married Friday, December 6, 1940, in Columbus, Ohio – Franklin County. They both lived at 1076 Parkview Blvd in Columbus until they died, homeowners. She died a widow. Betty and Cicero were both buried side-by-side at Glen Rest Memorial Estate in Reynoldsburg, Ohio – Franklin County.

Name	**William H. Neely**
Date Of Birth	Thursday, September 17, 1931
Place Of Birth	Winston-Salem, North Carolina – Forsyth County
Date Of Death	Friday, May 5, 1978
Age At Death	46
Place Of Death	Gastonia, North Carolina – Gaston County
Occupation	Day Laborer
Married	Leah M. Chubbs Neely
Notes	

Name	**Leah M. Chubbs Neely**
Date Of Birth	Wednesday, August 19, 1931
Place Of Birth	Columbus, Ohio – Franklin County
Date Of Death	N/A
Age At Death	N/A
Place Of Death	Gastonia, North Carolina – Gaston County

My Family Tree

Occupation	Housewife
Married	William H. Neely
Notes	Her parents were Dixie Ware Chubbs and Raymond Chubbs. They married on Tuesday, August 23, 1949, in Columbus, Ohio – Franklin County.

The Family Line of Frances Rebecca Hege Strickland and Samuel L. Strickland III

The connection to the family line was Frances, the daughter of Mildred Ann Mason Hege and Jesse Lee Hege.

The Sixth Generation

Frances Rebecca Hege Strickland - See Entry Page 96-97
Samuel L. Strickland III - See Entry Page 97-98

Their (3) Children

Name	**Suzette De-Carroll Strickland Willis**
Date Of Birth	Wednesday, November 2, 1966
Place Of Birth	Winston-Salem, North Carolina – Forsyth County
Date Of Death	N/A
Age At Death	N/A
Place Of Death	N/A
Occupation	Business Planning Analyst/Caretaker
Married	Joel Stephen Willis
Notes	Mrs. Willis has a living testimony about her life.

Name	**Joel Stephen Willis**
Date Of Birth	Saturday, February 8, 1964
Place Of Birth	High Point, North Carolina – Davidson County
Date Of Death	N/A
Age At Death	N/A

My Family Tree

Place Of Death	N/A
Occupation	Category Manager/America Tire Distributors
Married	Suzette De-Carroll Strickland Willis
Notes	Married on Saturday, February 25, 2003, in Winston-Salem, North Carolina – Forsyth County. His parents are Mary Willis and Joe V. Willis. Mr. Willis has a living testimony about his life. Joel's daughter – Raven Willis.

Name	**Maria Jeanette Strickland**
Date Of Birth	Thursday, January 12, 1950
Place Of Birth	Winston-Salem, North Carolina – Forsyth County
Date Of Death	N/A
Age At Death	N/A
Place Of Death	N/A
Occupation	Caretaker/Hair Stylist – Salon Owner
Married	N/A
Notes	Maria and the rest of the family (down south) were – Mama Frances's caregivers. Mama Frances passed her house down to her daughters before she passed, but it was Maria who took over the house. This house has been passed down through three generations within the family and will always stay in the family. Ms. Strickland has a living testimony about her life.

Name	**Mildred Elizabeth Strickland Peppers**
Date Of Birth	Saturday, June 12, 1948
Place Of Birth	Winston-Salem, North Carolina – Forsyth County
Date Of Death	Tuesday, November 7, 2016
Age At Death	68
Place Of Death	Winston-Salem, North Carolina – Forsyth County

My Family Tree

Occupation	Retired – Teacher/PhD – Treasurer – Winston-Salem State University/Homemaker – Caretaker/Sunday School Teacher – Deaconess
Married	Ronald Carl Peppers
Notes	Her nickname was "Skinner." She was buried on Saturday, November 12, 2016; she was a widow when she died. They were homeowners. Mildred and Ronnie were both buried side-by-side at Evergreen Cemetery. Mrs. Peppers had an interview with The Winston-Salem Journal – News Article in North Carolina, a live testimony that talks about her life and an obituary. Their children; Frances V. Peppers, Blanche Y. Peppers Sawyer, and Joneice C. Peppers Pledger.

Name	**Ronald Carl Peppers**
Date Of Birth	Thursday, January 12, 1950
Place Of Birth	Dillon, South Carolina – Dillon County
Date Of Death	Saturday, April 12, 2008
Age At Death	58
Place Of Death	Winston-Salem, North Carolina – Forsyth County
Occupation	United States – Marine Corp – Retired/R. J. Reynolds – Tobacco Industry – Worker/Postal Worker
Married	Mildred Elizabeth Strickland Peppers
Notes	Married Thursday, November 22, 1973, in Winston-Salem, North Carolina – Forsyth County, a marriage of 35 years. He served in the United States Marine Corps and was honorably discharged. His nickname was "Ronnie or Pepp." He was buried on Sunday, April 13, 2008. His siblings are Rugina Peppers, James A. Peppers (Belinda), and sister-in-law Linda Peppers. His parents were Sarah Lee Peppers and Jonnie Peppers. Mr. Peppers has an obituary about his life.

Their (3) Children

Name	**Frances Vencelia Peppers**
Date Of Birth	Friday, August 9, 1963
Place Of Birth	Winston-Salem, North Carolina – Forsyth County
Date Of Death	N/A

My Family Tree

Age At Death	N/A
Place Of Death	N/A
Occupation	Electrical Engineer – NAVFAC
Married	Single
Notes	She is a homeowner. Ms. Peppers has a living testimony about her life.

Name	**Blanche Yvonne Peppers Sawyer**
Date Of Birth	Thursday, October 15, 1964
Place Of Birth	Winston-Salem, North Carolina – Forsyth County
Date Of Death	N/A
Age At Death	N/A
Place Of Death	N/A
Occupation	Chief Executive Officer – Sawyer's Design
Married	Darren Antwon Sawyer
Notes	Their children: Xavier J. Sawyer and Alexander J. Sawyer. Mrs. Sawyer has a living testimony about her life. Blanche and Darren are homeowners.

Name	**Darren Antwon Sawyer**
Date Of Birth	Friday, August 9, 1963
Place Of Birth	Virginia Beach, Virginia – Virginia Beach County
Date Of Death	N/A
Age At Death	N/A
Place Of Death	N/A
Occupation	Captain – United States – Navy – Retired
Married	Blanche Yvonne Peppers Sawyer

My Family Tree

Notes	His parents were Alva Jean Davis Sawyer (b. Thursday, January 2, 1947 – d. Tuesday, September 30, 1969, buried October 1969, age 22) and Donald R. Sawyer (b.1941 – d. 2018, age 76 –77). Both parents' POD. Winston-Salem, North Carolina – Forsyth County and were buried at Evergreen Cemetery. Alva's parents were Grace Davis and John Davis. Darren served and retired from the United States Navy with an honorable discharge. Married on Saturday, April 27, 1991, in Winston-Salem, North Carolina – Forsyth County. Mr. Sawyer has a living testimony about his life.

Name	**Joneice Conchetta Peppers Pledger**
Date Of Birth	Wednesday, September 3, 1975
Place Of Birth	Winston-Salem, North Carolina – Forsyth County
Date Of Death	N/A
Age At Death	N/A
Place Of Death	N/A
Occupation	Senior Lab Technician – Ingredion
Married	Willie Lee Pledger II
Notes	Her nickname is "Jo." Mrs. Pledger has a living testimony about her life. Joneice and Will are homeowners.

Name	**Willie Lee Pledger II**
Date Of Birth	Sunday, December 31, 1972
Place Of Birth	Winston-Salem, North Carolina – Forsyth County
Date Of Death	N/A
Age At Death	N/A
Place Of Death	N/A
Occupation	Retired – United States – Navy / Retired North Carolina State Correctional Officer
Married	Joneice Conchetta Peppers Pledger

My Family Tree

Notes	Married on Saturday, May 22, 1999, in Winston-Salem, North Carolina – Forsyth County. Willie II served in the United States Navy, retired from naval service, and was honorably discharged. His nickname is "Will or Pledger." Mr. Pledger has a living testimony about his life. His parents were Whilhelmenia Levonia Jackson Pledger (b. Friday, November 18, 1949, POB. North Carolina – Forsyth County – d. Monday, September 9, 2019, age 69), POD. Elizabeth City, North Carolina – Pasquotank County and Willie Lee Pledger I (b. Friday, October 24, 1947), POB. North Carolina – Washington County. Whilhelmenia and Willie I were married Saturday, February 26, 1972, in Winston-Salem, North Carolina, a marriage of 47 years and homeowners. Whilhelmenia's parents were Louise Johnson Jackson and Willie Gladden Jackson. Willie I's parents were Rodena Pledger and Willie Lee Britton. Rodena and Willie I both lived at 902 Anderson Street in Elizabeth City at the time of their death; they were homeowners.

The Family Line of Joneice Conchetta Peppers Pledger and Willie Lee Pledger II

The connection to the family line is Joneice, the daughter of Mildred Elizabeth Strickland Peppers and Ronald Carl Peppers.

The Seventh Generation

Joneice Conchetta Peppers Pledger - See Entry Page Above
Willie Lee Pledger II - See Entry Page Above

Their (2) Children

Name	Jadon Carl Pledger
Date Of Birth	Thursday, September 13, 2001
Place Of Birth	Winston-Salem, North Carolina – Forsyth County
Date Of Death	N/A
Age At Death	N/A
Place Of Death	N/A
Occupation	College Student
Married	N/A
Notes	

My Family Tree

Name	Carrington Sabory Pledger
Date Of Birth	Friday, November 17, 2006
Place Of Birth	Winston-Salem, North Carolina – Forsyth County
Date Of Death	N/A
Age At Death	N/A
Place Of Death	N/A
Occupation	High School Student
Married	N/A
Notes	

The Family Line of Blanche Yvonne Peppers Sawyer and Darren Antwon Sawyer

The connection to the family line is Blanche, the daughter of Mildred Elizabeth Strickland Peppers and Ronald Carl Peppers.

The Seventh Generation

Blanche Yvonne Peppers Sawyer - See Entry Page 103
Darren Antwon Sawyer - See Entry Page 103-104

Their (2) Children

Name	Xavier J. Sawyer
Date Of Birth	Wednesday, October 5, 1994
Place Of Birth	Portsmouth, Virginia – Norfolk County
Date Of Death	N/A
Age At Death	N/A
Place Of Death	N/A
Occupation	Business Accountant
Married	N/A
Notes	

My Family Tree

Name	Alexander J. Sawyer
Date Of Birth	Wednesday, October 15, 1997
Place Of Birth	Portsmouth, Virginia – Norfolk County
Date Of Death	N/A
Age At Death	N/A
Place Of Death	N/A
Occupation	Engineer
Married	N/A
Notes	

The Family Line of Lucille Boozer Woody Hege and John Thomas Hege [I]

The connection to the family line was John [I], the son of Mildred Ann Mason Hege and Jesse Lee Hege.

The Sixth Generation

Lucille Boozer Woody Hege - See Entry Page 96
John Thomas Hege [I] - See Entry Page 95-96

Their (4) Children

Name	Equila Francena Hege Miller
Date Of Birth	1944
Place Of Birth	Winston-Salem, North Carolina – Forsyth County
Date Of Death	N/A
Age At Death	N/A
Place Of Death	N/A
Occupation	N/A
Married	Errie Johnson Miller [II] (b. Saturday, May 20, 1939 – d. Wednesday, April 11, 2012, age 72)
Notes	Married on Friday, October 14, 1960, at the age of 16 in Winston-Salem, North Carolina – Forsyth County. Their marriage lasted for 51 years. He was buried on Monday, April 16, 2012. He retired from R. J. Reynolds –

My Family Tree

	as a Tobacco Worker. His parents were Alice M. Johnson Miller and Errie Johnson Miller[1]. Census records spelled her first name two different ways: Equila or Aquila. Their children: Cassandra Miller Sales and Richard Leon Miller.

Name	Carolyn Collen Hege Anthony
Date Of Birth	Sunday, October 20, 1946
Place Of Birth	Winston-Salem, North Carolina – Forsyth County
Date Of Death	Friday, April 1, 1988
Age At Death	41
Place Of Death	Winston-Salem, North Carolina – Forsyth County
Occupation	R. J. Reynolds – Tobacco Industry – Presser Worker
Married	Edward Alvis Anthony
Notes	She was buried Wednesday, April 6, 1988, at Evergreen Cemetery. They planned to be buried together. She was buried under her maiden name, and he was not buried next to her.

Name	Edward Alvis Anthony
Date Of Birth	Tuesday, August 7, 1945
Place Of Birth	North Carolina – Forsyth County
Date Of Death	Saturday, March 27, 2010
Age At Death	64
Place Of Death	Winston-Salem, North Carolina – Forsyth County
Occupation	R. J. Reynolds – Tobacco Industry – Worker
Married	Carolyn Collen Hege Anthony
Notes	Married on Wednesday, October 20, 1965, and divorced in North Carolina – Forsyth County. His parents were Pearl Brandon Anthony (b. 1913) and Henry Alvis Anthony (b. Saturday, October 28, 1899 – d. Tuesday, January 13, 1981, age 81). Henry was buried Saturday, January 17, 1981, at Bethlehem Meth Church Cemetery in Pfafftown, North Carolina –

My Family Tree

	Forsyth County, a widower. Henry was a retired worker from the R. J. Reynolds – Tobacco Industry. Pearl and Henry both lived at 9606 Glenn Road in Winston-Salem at the time of their death, homeowners. Henry held a United States Army Draft Registration Card from (1917-1918) in North Carolina – Yadkin County. Pearl and Henry were married on Thursday, July 4, 1940, in Winston-Salem, North Carolina – Forsyth County, and married for 41 years. Pearl's parents were Augusta Brandon and Walter Brandon. Henry's parents were Martha Douthit Anthony and Edward Anthony.

Name	Vendetta Hege Simpson
Date Of Birth	Saturday, May 15, 1948
Place Of Birth	Winston-Salem, North Carolina – Forsyth County
Date Of Death	N/A
Age At Death	N/A
Place Of Death	N/A
Occupation	Housewife
Married	Gayberns Lamard Simpson (b. Wednesday, November 9, 1949)
Notes	Her children: Harold Hege and Tameka Hege. Married on Saturday, October 12, 1968, in Winston-Salem, North Carolina – Forsyth County. His parents were Dorothy Speas Simpson and Arthur Simpson. Gayberns was born in North Carolina.

Name	John Thomas Hege II
Date Of Birth	Saturday, October 21, 1950
Place Of Birth	North Carolina – Forsyth County
Date Of Death	N/A
Age At Death	N/A
Place Of Death	N/A
Occupation	N/A

My Family Tree

Married	Sandra Kay Simpson Hege (b. Saturday, May 16, 1953), POB. North Carolina – Forsyth County
Notes	Married on Monday, March 8, 1971, in Winston-Salem, North Carolina – Forsyth County. Her parents were Rosena Gist Simpson and Earl Simpson.

The Family Line of Equila Francena Hege Miller and Errie Johnson Miller II

The connection to the family line is Equila, the daughter of Lucille Boozer Woody Hege and John Thomas Hege [1].

The Seventh Generation

Equila Francena Hege Miller - See Entry Page 107-108
Errie Johnson Miller II - See Entry Page 107-108

Their (2) Children

Name	**Cassandra Miller Sales**
Date Of Birth	Friday, September 20, 1968
Place Of Birth	Winston-Salem, North Carolina – Forsyth County
Date Of Death	N/A
Age At Death	N/A
Place Of Death	N/A
Occupation	N/A
Married	Unknown
Notes	Her child: Cavicka S. Miller Williamson. The Census shows that her first name was spelled Careka.

Name	**Richard Leon Miller**
Date Of Birth	1963
Place Of Birth	Winston-Salem, North Carolina – Forsyth County
Date Of Death	N/A
Age At Death	N/A
Place Of Death	N/A

My Family Tree

Occupation	Minister
Married	Doris Faya Quick Miller (b. 1953)
Notes	Her parents were Leatha Adams Quick and Earnest Quick. Married Tuesday, March 31, 1987, in Winston-Salem, North Carolina – Forsyth County.

The Family Line of Emerline Lord Fowler and Alex Fowler [1]

The Third Generation

Name	**Emerline Lord Fowler**
Date Of Birth	1850
Place Of Birth	Virginia
Date Of Death	Unknown
Age At Death	Unknown
Place Of Death	Jerusalem, North Carolina – Davie County
Occupation	Keeping House/Housewife
Married	Alex Fowler [1] (b. 1834), POB. Virginia POD. Jerusalem, North Carolina – Davie County, occupation – Farmer
Notes	It was reported to the Census that they were brought from Virginia to North Carolina as slaves. According to the 1920 Census, the couple were literate.

Their (7) Children

Name	**Alex Fowler II**
Date Of Birth	1873
Place Of Birth	Jerusalem, North Carolina – Davie County
Date Of Death	Unknown
Age At Death	Unknown
Place Of Death	Jerusalem, North Carolina – Davie County
Occupation	Farmer Laborer

My Family Tree

Married	Unknown
Notes	According to the 1920 Census, he was literate.

Name	**Mary Fowler**
Date Of Birth	1864
Place Of Birth	Jerusalem, North Carolina – Davie County
Date Of Death	Unknown
Age At Death	Unknown
Place Of Death	Jerusalem, North Carolina – Davie County
Occupation	Farmer Laborer
Married	Unknown
Notes	She was born into slavery. According to the 1920 Census, she was literate.

Name	**Willie Mae Fowler**
Date Of Birth	1868
Place Of Birth	Jerusalem, North Carolina – Davie County
Date Of Death	Unknown
Age At Death	Unknown
Place Of Death	Jerusalem, North Carolina – Davie County
Occupation	Farmer Laborer
Married	Unknown
Notes	According to the 1920 Census, she was literate.

Name	**Margaret Fowler**

My Family Tree

Date Of Birth	1875
Place Of Birth	Jerusalem, North Carolina – Davie County
Date Of Death	Unknown
Age At Death	Unknown
Place Of Death	Jerusalem, North Carolina – Davie County
Occupation	Domestic Worker
Married	Unknown
Notes	According to the 1920 Census, she was literate.

Name	Isaac Fowler
Date Of Birth	1878
Place Of Birth	Jerusalem, North Carolina – Davie County
Date Of Death	Unknown
Age At Death	Unknown
Place Of Death	Jerusalem, North Carolina – Davie County
Occupation	Farmer Laborer
Married	Connie Hairston Fowler (b. 1882)
Notes	According to the 1920 Census, he was literate. Married on Monday, April 14, 1902, in Winston Township, North Carolina – Forsyth County. Her parents were Fannie Hairston and Salem Hairston.

Name	Maggie Fowler Mason
Date Of Birth	Monday, October 11, 1880
Place Of Birth	Jerusalem, North Carolina – Davie County
Date Of Death	Friday, September 16, 1948

My Family Tree

Age At Death	67
Place Of Death	Salisbury, North Carolina – Rowan County
Occupation	Farm Laborer
Married	Robert M. Mason [II]
Notes	According to the 1930 Census, Maggie was literate, while Robert was able to read but could not write. Her death certificate documented her birth year as 1884, but her headstone has the year as 1880. The elders of the family stated that her headstone was correct. She was buried in September 1948. Maggie and Robert [II] were both buried at Cedar Grove Baptist Church Cemetery, and she was a widow when she died. They lived at Route 3 in Mocksville until their deaths, homeowners. Their children include Annie E. Mason, Beatrice Mason, Susan Mason Fowler, Edwin Mason, Odell Buck Mason, Lizzie Mason, Esther Mason Aikens, Alexander Mason, Ernest I. Mason, Bessie Mae Mason Davis, Johnsie J. Mason Brown, Robert Mason [I], Jessie Mae Mason Parks, Earl Mason, Infant Mason, Charlie Mason, Catherine Mason Chaplin, and James Mason.

Name	**Robert M. Mason II**
Date Of Birth	September 1868
Place Of Birth	Mocksville, North Carolina – Davie County
Date Of Death	Friday, November 23, 1945
Age At Death	77
Place Of Death	Salisbury, North Carolina – Rowan County
Occupation	General Farmer
Married	Maggie Fowler Mason
Notes	His parents were Eliza "Lizzie" Smith Mason (b. May 1845, Virginia – d. Thursday, August 26, 1915, Fulton Township, North Carolina – Davie County, age 70). Eliza was buried on Friday, August 27, 1915. She was a widow when she died, and Robert M. Mason [I]. Eliza and Robert [I] were slaves. Eliza's parents were Tame Smith and Simon Smith. His father's second wife was Emma Mason, also from North Carolina – Davie County. Robert [II] was buried on Sunday, November 25, 1945. His sibling was Charlie Mason (b. 1872, North Carolina – Davie County – d. Saturday, July 26, 1924, POD. Winston-Salem, North Carolina – Forsyth County,

	age 51–52). Charlie's wife was Priscilla Hargraves Mason (b. 1875), married Friday, July 25, 1890, in North Carolina – Rowan County. Their child was Aaron Mason (b. 1900), POB. North Carolina. Charlie was buried on Sunday, August 3, 1924. Eliza and Charlie were both buried at Cedar Grove Baptist Church Cemetery. Charlie lived at 336 East 8th in Winston-Salem at the time of his death, was a homeowner, and worked as a Tobacco Worker at American Tobacco Company. Priscilla's parents were Louisa Hargraves and Osborn Hargraves.

Name	Robert Flood Fowler
Date Of Birth	Tuesday, September 6, 1887
Place Of Birth	Fulton Township, North Carolina – Davie County
Date Of Death	Friday, November 28, 1930
Age At Death	43
Place Of Death	Winston-Salem, North Carolina – Forsyth County
Occupation	General Farmer
Married	Bessie Mason Fowler
Notes	According to the 1910 Census, he was literate. He was buried in December 1930.

Name	Bessie Mason Fowler
Date Of Birth	Monday, March 25, 1889
Place Of Birth	North Carolina – Davie County
Date Of Death	Monday, December 25, 1944
Age At Death	55
Place Of Death	Winston-Salem, North Carolina – Forsyth County
Occupation	Domestic Worker/Homemaker
Married	Robert Flood Fowler
Notes	According to the 1920 Census, she was literate. Buried Thursday, December 28, 1944. Parents: Emma Mason and Robert M. Mason I. Bessie

My Family Tree

	and Robert were both buried at Evergreen Cemetery – Smith Reynolds Airport. They lived at 704 E – 3rd Street in Winston-Salem at the time of their deaths, homeowners. Their children: Willie Fowler, Minnie M. Fowler Black, Rosella Flood Fowler James, and Lester LeRoy Fowler.

The Family Line of Maggie Fowler Mason and Robert M. Mason II

The connection to the family line was Robert M. II, the son of Eliza Smith Mason and Robert M. Mason I.

The Fourth Generation

Maggie Fowler Mason - See Entry Page 113-114
Robert M. Mason II - See Entry Page 114-115

Their (18) Children

Name	Annie E. Mason
Date Of Birth	Tuesday, October 26, 1909
Place Of Birth	Fulton Township, North Carolina – Davie County
Date Of Death	Sunday, November 20, 1920
Age At Death	11
Place Of Death	Fulton Township, North Carolina – Davie County
Occupation	None
Married	Single
Notes	According to the 1920 Census, she was literate. Buried on Monday, November 21, 1920, at Cedar Grove Baptist Church Cemetery.

Name	Beatrice Mason
Date Of Birth	Tuesday, October 2, 1906
Place Of Birth	Fulton Township, North Carolina – Davie County
Date Of Death	Tuesday, November 18, 1958
Age At Death	52
Place Of Death	Charlotte, North Carolina – Mecklenburg County

My Family Tree

Occupation	Domestic Worker
Married	Single
Notes	According to the 1920 Census, she was literate. Buried in November 1958 at Cedar Grove Baptist Church Cemetery.

Name	**Susan Mason Fowler**
Date Of Birth	Tuesday, November 20, 1888
Place Of Birth	Fulton Township, North Carolina – Davie County
Date Of Death	Wednesday, July 2, 1930
Age At Death	41
Place Of Death	Lexington, North Carolina – Davidson County
Occupation	Housewife
Married	Widow
Notes	According to the 1920 Census, she was literate. Buried in July 1930 at Raleigh Road African American Cemetery in Lexington, North Carolina – Davidson County.

Name	**Edwin Mason**
Date Of Birth	Wednesday, February 28, 1894
Place Of Birth	Fulton Township, North Carolina – Davie County
Date Of Death	July 1971
Age At Death	77
Place Of Death	Fulton Township, North Carolina – Davie County
Occupation	General Farmer
Married	Bettie Click Mason (b. 1893)
Notes	According to the 1920 Census, he was literate. The Census indicated that his first name was spelled Edd. Married Thursday, April 29, 1915, in North Carolina – Davie County. His nickname was "Ed."

My Family Tree

Name	Odell Buck Mason
Date Of Birth	Saturday, October 6, 1906
Place Of Birth	Fulton Township, North Carolina – Davie County
Date Of Death	Thursday, December 1, 1966
Age At Death	60
Place Of Death	Winston-Salem, North Carolina – Forsyth County
Occupation	Domestic Servant
Married	(1) Alice Mack Mason (2) Louise Harris Mason
Notes	According to the 1920 Census, he was literate. He was buried on Sunday, December 4, 1966. Louise and Odell were both buried at Evergreen Cemetery. Louise, Alice, and Odell all lived at 1010 Peachtree Street Alley in Winston-Salem at the time of their death; they were homeowners.

Name	Alice Mack Mason
Date Of Birth	Wednesday, September 23, 1908
Place Of Birth	Winnsboro, South Carolina – Fairfield County
Date Of Death	Wednesday, January 27, 1965
Age At Death	56
Place Of Death	Winston-Salem, North Carolina – Forsyth County
Occupation	Private Cook
Married	Odell Buck Mason
Notes	Her parents were Aurelia Pearson Mack and John Mack. Married on Friday, July 13, 1928, in Winston-Salem, North Carolina – Forsyth County. She was buried on Thursday, February 1, 1965, at Piedmont Memorial Gardens Cemetery in Winston-Salem, North Carolina – Forsyth County.

Name	Louise Harris Mason

My Family Tree

Date Of Birth	Monday, April 9, 1934
Place Of Birth	North Carolina – Davie County
Date Of Death	Sunday, February 4, 1968
Age At Death	33
Place Of Death	Winston-Salem, North Carolina – Forsyth County
Occupation	Housewife
Married	Odell Buck Mason
Notes	Her parents were Pansy Harris Ervin and Alex Ervin. Louise was buried on Thursday, February 8, 1968. She was a widow. Their child, Benjamin Franklin Mason, was born on Friday, June 18, 1954, in Winston-Salem, North Carolina – Forsyth County, died on Wednesday, March 9, 1955 (age 9 Months Old), and was buried the same day at Evergreen Cemetery.

Name	Lizzie Mason
Date Of Birth	1915
Place Of Birth	Fulton Township, North Carolina – Davie County
Date Of Death	Unknown
Age At Death	Unknown
Place Of Death	Unknown
Occupation	Unknown
Married	Unknown
Notes	According to the 1920 Census, she was literate.

Name	Esther Mason Aikens
Date Of Birth	Saturday, October 12, 1901
Place Of Birth	Fulton Township, North Carolina – Davie County

My Family Tree

Date Of Death	Sunday, February 17, 1946
Age At Death	44
Place Of Death	Winston-Salem, North Carolina – Forsyth County
Occupation	Domestic Worker/Housewife
Married	(1) Baxter Tomlin (b. 1883) (2) Joseph Aikens
Notes	According to the 1920 Census, she was literate. (1) Marriage on Tuesday, November 11, 1919, in Winston-Salem, North Carolina – Forsyth County. She was buried Thursday, February 21, 1946, at Cedar Grove Baptist Church Cemetery. (1) His parents were Caroline Tomlin Denison and George Denison; he was born out of wedlock, and they did not change his last name after they got married.

Name	Alexander Mason
Date Of Birth	Tuesday, July 1, 1913
Place Of Birth	Advance, North Carolina – Davie County
Date Of Death	Monday, February 3, 1936
Age At Death	22
Place Of Death	Winston-Salem, North Carolina – Forsyth County
Occupation	Private Cook
Married	Single
Notes	According to the 1910 Census, he was literate. He was buried Wednesday, February 5, 1936, at Cedar Grove Baptist Church Cemetery. He lived at 1021 Cleveland Street in Winston-Salem at the time of his death, a homeowner.

Name	Ernest I. Mason
Date Of Birth	Friday, September 8, 1899
Place Of Birth	Fulton Township, North Carolina – Davie County
Date Of Death	Wednesday, August 17, 1966

My Family Tree

Age At Death	66
Place Of Death	Mocksville, North Carolina – Davie County
Occupation	General Farmer
Married	Mary Hairston Mason
Notes	The 1910 Census noted that his first name was spelled Earnest. He was buried on Saturday, August 20, 1966.

Name	**Mary Hairston Mason**
Date Of Birth	Tuesday, June 24, 1902
Place Of Birth	Fulton Township, North Carolina – Davie County
Date Of Death	Thursday, February 28, 2002
Age At Death	99
Place Of Death	Mocksville, North Carolina – Davie County
Occupation	Homemaker/Domestic Worker – Laundress
Married	Ernest I. Mason
Notes	Married on Wednesday, March 4, 1925, in North Carolina – Davie County. Both were literate in the 1940 Census. Parents: Molly A. Hairston and Samuel H. Hairston. She was buried on Thursday, February 28, 2002. Three children, two survived: Infant Mason, Marie Mason, and Herbert Gilmer Mason. Considered "Mother of the Church" at Cedar Grove Baptist Church in her obituary. Mary and Ernest were buried side-by-side at Cedar Grove Baptist Church Cemetery, and she was a widow at death.

Name	**Bessie Mae Mason Davis**
Date Of Birth	Sunday, July 22, 1906
Place Of Birth	North Carolina – Davie County
Date Of Death	Wednesday, June 16, 1993
Age At Death	86

My Family Tree

Place Of Death	Hickory, North Carolina – Catawba County
Occupation	Retired – Domestic Worker/Homemaker
Married	Clinton Davis
Notes	Highest education level was 8th grade. Buried in June 1993. They both were buried at Cedar Grove Baptist Church Cemetery. A widow at death. Bessie and Clinton lived at 741 W. 25 ½ Street in Winston-Salem, homeowners. Nicknamed "Big Mama." Children: Maggie M. Davis Cain, Mary Elizabeth Davis, and Mattie Ruth Davis Nelson.

Name	**Clinton Davis**
Date Of Birth	Monday, March 14, 1910
Place Of Birth	Gaffney, South Carolina – Cherokee County
Date Of Death	Saturday, January 30, 1960
Age At Death	49
Place Of Death	Winston-Salem, North Carolina – Forsyth County
Occupation	Day Laborer
Married	Bessie Mae Mason Davis
Notes	Parents were Mary Smith Davis and Cleveland Davis. Married on July 3, 1926, in North Carolina – Davidson County; married for 34 years. Buried in February 1960 at Evergreen Cemetery. According to the 1930 Census, Bessie and Clinton were boarders living with Lula M. Mason Goolsby and John Hairston Goolsby [1].

Name	**Johnsie J. Mason Brown**
Date Of Birth	Friday, December 25, 1914
Place Of Birth	Fulton Township, North Carolina – Davie County
Date Of Death	Monday, August 25, 1952
Age At Death	37
Place Of Death	Lexington, North Carolina – Davidson County

My Family Tree

Occupation	Domestic Worker/Housewife
Married	Clarence Odell Brown [I]
Notes	According to the 1920 Census, she was literate. Her first name had various spellings – Jonice, Johnsie, Johnsy, or Jonsie in the Census records. Johnsie and her child (Infant Brown) were buried on Wednesday, August 27, 1952. Her death certificate documented her birth year as 1915; Clarence stated it was a clerical error. Johnsie had 10 children, but only 9 survived. Their children include Clarence Odell Brown [II], Jessie Brown, Robert Mason Brown, Jane Brown, Wayne Brown, Daniel Brown, Onelle Brown, Frank James Brown [I], Infant (Girl) Brown, and Lou Etta Brown.

The connection to the family line was Clarence, the son of Jettie Ann Hairston Mason Brown and Jesse James Brown [I].

Name	**Clarence Odell Brown I**
Date Of Birth	Monday, March 31, 1913
Place Of Birth	Fulton Township, North Carolina – Davie County
Date Of Death	Tuesday, September 5, 1994
Age At Death	81
Place Of Death	Winston-Salem, North Carolina – Forsyth County
Occupation	Retired – Furniture Finisher
Married	(1) Johnsie J. Mason Brown (2) Juanita Cuthrell Brown (b. Monday, July 6, 1925 – d. Tuesday, November 29, 2016, age 91)
Notes	According to the 1920 Census, he was literate. (1) Married on Wednesday, June 14, 1933, in Mocksville, North Carolina – Davie County; a marriage of 19 years. He was a Freemason. His parents were Jettie Ann Hairston Mason Brown, and Jesse James Brown [I]. Clarence lost his wife and child during childbirth. He was buried on Tuesday, September 5, 1994. Johnsie and their infant daughter were buried at Cedar Grove Baptist Church Cemetery. Clarence and Juanita were both buried side-by-side where his first wife and child. All three lived at 204 Cedar Grove Church Road in Mocksville at the time of their death as homeowners.

Name	**Robert Mason I**

My Family Tree

Date Of Birth	Monday, March 14, 1898
Place Of Birth	Fulton Township, North Carolina – Davie County
Date Of Death	Wednesday, October 6, 1954
Age At Death	56
Place Of Death	Salisbury Township, North Carolina – Rowan County
Occupation	Farmer/United States Air Force – Korea – Retired
Married	Janet Secreca Britton Mason (b. 1908), POB. North Carolina
Notes	They lived together as a common-law marriage that was reported to the 1910 Census in North Carolina. The 1920 Census noted that they were both literate. They officially put their marriage on paper on Thursday, April 12, 1928, in Mocksville, North Carolina – Davie County. He served during WWI as PVT (344 Service BN OMC). He was buried on Sunday, October 10, 1954, at Shiloh Baptist Church Cemetery in Mocksville, North Carolina – Davie County. Their children: Helen Faith Mason, Elizabeth Victoria Mason Johnson, and Robert Mason [II]. According to the 1930 and 1940 Census notes, the spelling of her first name was Ceneca Alcrese Britton Mason. Janet preferred to use her middle name.

Name	**Jessie Mae Mason Parks**
Date Of Birth	Thursday, February 13, 1913
Place Of Birth	Fulton Township, North Carolina – Davie County
Date Of Death	Friday, July 11, 1980
Age At Death	67
Place Of Death	Winston-Salem, North Carolina – Forsyth County
Occupation	Caterer – Paul Meyers Catering
Married	William Garlin Parks
Notes	According to the 1920 Census, she was literate. She was buried on Wednesday, July 16, 1980, at Piney Grove Church Cemetery in Winston-Salem, North Carolina – Forsyth County. Jessie Mae lived at 4656 Indiana Avenue in Winston-Salem at the time of her death, a widow, and homeowner.

My Family Tree

Name	**William Garlin Parks**
Date Of Birth	Saturday, July 9, 1910
Place Of Birth	North Carolina
Date Of Death	Tuesday, February 22, 1972
Age At Death	61
Place Of Death	Winston-Salem, North Carolina – Forsyth County
Occupation	Shipping Department
Married	Jessie Mae Mason Parks
Notes	He was buried on Saturday, February 26, 1972, at Evergreen Cemetery. His parents were Ophelia Gray Parks and Allen Parks. William lived at 4656 Walcott Street in Winston-Salem until he died as a homeowner.

Name	**Earl Mason**
Date Of Birth	December 1897
Place Of Birth	Fulton Township, North Carolina – Davie County
Date Of Death	Friday, November 8, 1935
Age At Death	37
Place Of Death	Gastonia, North Carolina – Gaston County
Occupation	Day Laborer
Married	Ola Mason (b. 1901)
Notes	According to the 1920 Census, he was literate, and his first name was spelled as Early. Ola and Earl owned their farm. Married in 1923 in North Carolina – Davie County.

Name	**Infant Mason**
Date Of Birth	November 1900
Place Of Birth	Fulton Township, North Carolina – Forsyth County

My Family Tree

Date Of Death	November 1900
Age At Death	0
Place Of Death	Fulton Township, North Carolina – Forsyth County
Occupation	None
Married	Single
Notes	

Name	**Charlie Mason**
Date Of Birth	1908
Place Of Birth	Fulton Township, North Carolina – Davie County
Date Of Death	Thursday, July 27, 1978
Age At Death	69 – 70
Place Of Death	Midway, North Carolina – Davidson County
Occupation	Farmer
Married	Catherine Bailey Mason
Notes	According to the 1920 Census, he was literate. He was buried on Monday, July 31, 1978, at Evergreen Cemetery as a widower. He lived on Shoaf Road in Midway, North Carolina.

Name	**Catherine Bailey Mason**
Date Of Birth	Tuesday, May 7, 1907
Place Of Birth	North Carolina – Davie County
Date Of Death	Sunday, September 24, 1967
Age At Death	60
Place Of Death	Mocksville, North Carolina – Davie County

My Family Tree

Occupation	Housewife
Married	Charlie Mason
Notes	Her parents were Lillie Bailey and Griffin Bailey. Married on Saturday, July 28, 1928, in Winston-Salem, North Carolina – Forsyth County, a marriage of 39 years. She was buried on Thursday, September 28, 1967, at Piney Grove United Methodist Church Cemetery in Advance, North Carolina – Davie County. Their child: Joseph Bailey Mason.

Name	Catherine Mason Chaplin
Date Of Birth	Sunday, January 7, 1917
Place Of Birth	Fulton Township, North Carolina – Davie County
Date Of Death	Winston-Salem, North Carolina – Forsyth County
Age At Death	78
Place Of Death	Winston-Salem, North Carolina – Forsyth County
Occupation	Domestic Worker/Housewife
Married	Robert Bob Chaplin [I]
Notes	According to the 1920 Census, she was literate. In the 1920 and 1930 Census, her name was spelled Kathleen. Catherine was buried in December 1995, at Cedar Grove Baptist Church Cemetery, a widow. Their children: Robert Bob Chaplin [II], Willie Chaplin, Minnie Chaplin, Margaret Chaplin, Alfonzo Chaplin, Infant (Male) Chaplin (b. and d. Thursday, March 13, 1941), age 0, POB. and POD. Erlanger, North Carolina – Davidson County, buried at home, Margie Ann Chaplin Rice (b. 1943), and Melvin Chaplin [I] (b. Saturday, April 23, 1935 – d. Wednesday, June 29, 2011, age 76). Margie married Alvin on Thursday, January 8, 1959, in Greensboro, North Carolina – Guilford County. Alvin Homer Rice (b. 1941) is the son of Mamie Minton Rice and Paul Rice. Melvin married Dorothy Mae Grier Chaplin (b. 1935, POB. and POD. Winston-Salem, North Carolina – Forsyth County – d. 2016, age 80-81), and her parents were Ilar Grier and John Grier.

Name	Robert Bob Chaplin I
Date Of Birth	Friday, November 7, 1913

My Family Tree

Place Of Birth	North Carolina – Davie County
Date Of Death	Saturday, March 26, 1983
Age At Death	69
Place Of Death	Winston-Salem, North Carolina – Forsyth County
Occupation	Retired – Mason Brick Layer
Married	Catherine Mason Chaplin
Notes	His parents were Louisiana Hairston Chaplin and Thomas Jonas Chaplin. Robert was buried on Thursday, March 31, 1983, at Piedmont Memorial Gardens Cemetery in Winston-Salem, North Carolina – Forsyth County. He took ownership of his brother-in-law William Garlin Parks' home after he passed and lived at 4656 Walcott Street in Winston-Salem at the time of his death. According to the 1920 Census, his parents' first names were spelled Lozianna and Jon.

Name	James Mason
Date Of Birth	Tuesday, December 2, 1901
Place Of Birth	Winston Township, North Carolina – Davie County
Date Of Death	Sunday, December 29, 1985
Age At Death	84
Place Of Death	Winston Township, North Carolina – Davie County
Occupation	Retired – General Farmer/Variety – Department Store Attendant
Married	Thelma Miller Mason
Notes	According to the 1920 Census, he was literate. He was buried on Saturday, January 4, 1986, at Evergreen Cemetery. He lived at 4640 Indiana Ave in Winston-Salem until he died, a widower and homeowner.

Name	Thelma Miller Mason
Date Of Birth	Friday, November 12, 1911
Place Of Birth	North Carolina – Union County

My Family Tree

Date Of Death	Thursday, November 25, 1971
Age At Death	60
Place Of Death	Winston-Salem, North Carolina – Forsyth County
Occupation	Domestic Worker/Homemaker
Married	(1) Eugene Mason (2) James Mason
Notes	(1) Married on Sunday, January 15, 1933, in Fulton Township, North Carolina – Davie County, a marriage of 38 years. Her parents were Almeta Robinson Miller and Isiah Miller. Her child with James was Walter Wade Mason (b. Tuesday, November 8, 1927, POB. Mocksville, North Carolina – Davie County – d. Friday, June 18, 1954, age 26), POD. Winston-Salem, North Carolina – Forsyth County, occupation – Day Laborer and single. Walter was buried in June 1954. She did not have any more children after the death of her son, – Walter. Thelma was buried on Saturday, November 27, 1971. Thelma and her son Walter were both buried at Capernaum Church of Christ Cemetery in Clemmons, North Carolina – Forsyth County.

The Family Line of Bessie Mason Fowler and Robert Flood Fowler

The connection to the family line was Bessie, the daughter of Emma Mason and Robert M. Mason[1], and Bessie's husband – Robert was the son of Emerline Lord Fowler and Alex Fowler[1] – sister of Maggie Fowler Mason.

The Fourth Generation

Bessie Mason Fowler - See Entry Page 115-116
Robert Flood Fowler - See Entry Page 115

Their (4) Children

Name	Willie Fowler
Date Of Birth	Tuesday, February 3, 1903
Place Of Birth	Winston Township, North Carolina – Forsyth County
Date Of Death	Tuesday, June 19, 1990
Age At Death	87
Place Of Death	Winston Township, North Carolina – Forsyth County
Occupation	Retired – United States Army

My Family Tree

Married	Rebecca Solter Fowler
Notes	According to the 1920 Census, he was literate. He served in the United States Army in WWII as a PVT and was honorably discharged. He was buried in June 1990.

Name	**Rebecca Solter Fowler**
Date Of Birth	Sunday, January 17, 1897
Place Of Birth	South Carolina
Date Of Death	Saturday, July 14, 1973
Age At Death	76
Place Of Death	Winston-Salem, North Carolina – Forsyth County
Occupation	Housewife/Domestic Worker
Married	Willie Fowler
Notes	She was buried on Wednesday, July 18, 1973. Rebecca and Willie were both buried at Evergreen Cemetery. They lived at 401 N. E. 27th Street in Winston-Salem at the time of their deaths; they were homeowners. Her parents were Mary P. Smith Solter and John Solter.

Name	**Minnie M. Fowler Black**
Date Of Birth	Monday, January 25, 1915
Place Of Birth	Fulton Township, North Carolina – Davie County
Date Of Death	Thursday, January 29, 1998
Age At Death	82
Place Of Death	Winston-Salem, North Carolina – Forsyth County
Occupation	Retired – Servant – Private Home/Housewife
Married	Robert Bruce Black
Notes	According to the 1920 Census, she was literate. She was buried in February 1998 at Evergreen Cemetery. Minnie and Robert lived at 702 East 3rd Street in Winston-Salem at the time of their death, homeowners.

My Family Tree

	Rosella and Levonz [1] lived at their house as boarders, according to the 1930 Census.

Name	**Robert Bruce Black**
Date Of Birth	Monday, July 5, 1915
Place Of Birth	Winston-Salem, North Carolina – Forsyth County
Date Of Death	March 1984
Age At Death	68
Place Of Death	Winston-Salem, North Carolina – Forsyth County
Occupation	R. J. Reynolds – Tobacco Industry – Worker
Married	Minnie M. Fowler Black
Notes	Married Friday, April 29, 1932, in Virginia – Henry County. They were married for 51 years.

Name	**Rosella Flood Fowler James**
Date Of Birth	Friday, April 27, 1917
Place Of Birth	Winston-Salem, North Carolina – Forsyth County
Date Of Death	Friday, December 11, 1953
Age At Death	36
Place Of Death	Winston-Salem, North Carolina – Forsyth County
Occupation	Domestic Worker/Housewife
Married	Levonz Wallace James
Notes	Her nickname was "Rosa." She was buried on Sunday, December 13, 1953.

Name	**Levonz Wallace James**

My Family Tree

Date Of Birth	Wednesday, April 20, 1904
Place Of Birth	Mount Olive, North Carolina – Stokes County
Date Of Death	Sunday, September 2, 1956
Age At Death	52
Place Of Death	Winston-Salem, North Carolina – Forsyth County
Occupation	R. J. Reynolds – Tobacco Industry – Worker
Married	Rosella Flood Fowler James
Notes	Married on Saturday, June 30, 1934, in Winston-Salem, North Carolina – Forsyth County, a marriage of 22 years. After Rosella died, Levonz moved out of Minnie's and Robert's home. He was buried on Thursday, September 6, 1956. Rosella and Levonz were both buried at Evergreen Cemetery. Levonz lived at 711 Linden Street in Winston-Salem when he died, a widower and homeowner. His parents were Dora Wallace James and Anthony James.

Name	**Lester LeRoy Fowler**
Date Of Birth	Monday, May 16, 1904
Place Of Birth	North Carolina – Davie County
Date Of Death	Tuesday, July 29, 1980
Age At Death	76
Place Of Death	Winston-Salem, North Carolina – Forsyth County
Occupation	Retired – Private Cook
Married	Sue Pearl Barksdale Fowler
Notes	According to the 1920 Census, he was literate. He was buried on Saturday, July 5, 1980. Sue Pearl and Lester were divorced when he died.

Name	**Sue Pearl Barksdale Fowler**
Date Of Birth	Friday, February 25, 1910

My Family Tree

Place Of Birth	Winston-Salem, North Carolina – Forsyth County
Date Of Death	Wednesday, August 27, 1997
Age At Death	87
Place Of Death	Winston-Salem, North Carolina – Forsyth County
Occupation	Retired – Domestic Worker/Housewife
Married	Lester LeRoy Fowler
Notes	Married on Sunday, September 15, 1929, in Winston-Salem, North Carolina – Forsyth County. Sue Pearl was buried in August 1997. They were both buried side-by-side at Evergreen Cemetery, even though they never remarried. Her parents were Sallie Luanna Martin Barksdale (b. Saturday, June 27, 1885 – d. Monday, January 1, 1945, age 59) and Walter Barksdale (b. Monday, August 14, 1882 – d. Saturday, October 20, 1934, age 52). Sue's parents' POB. Laurens, South Carolina – Laurens County and POD. Winston-Salem, North Carolina – Forsyth County. Sallie was buried in January 1945, a widow, and Walter was buried in October 1934. Sallie and Walter were both buried side-by-side at Evergreen Cemetery. They both lived at 1416 Derry Street in Winston-Salem at the time of their deaths; they were homeowners. Sallie's parents were Carolina Austin Martin and Allen Martin. Walter's parents were Eliza Downs Barksdale and Tobe Barksdale.

The Family Line of Bessie Mae Mason Davis and Clinton Davis

The connection to the family line was Bessie Mae (sister of Johnsie) and the daughter of Maggie Fowler Mason and Robert M. Mason [II].

The Fifth Generation

Bessie Mae Mason Davis - See Entry Page 121-122
Clinton Davis - See Entry Page 122

Their (3) Children

Name	**Maggie M. Davis Cain**
Date Of Birth	1928
Place Of Birth	Winston-Salem, North Carolina – Forsyth County
Date Of Death	Unknown
Age At Death	Unknown

My Family Tree

Place Of Death	Unknown
Occupation	Domestic Worker/Housewife
Married	Julius Cain (b. 1929)
Notes	Married on Saturday, March 27, 1948, in Winston-Salem, North Carolina – Forsyth County. His parents were Hattie Cain and William Cain.

Name	**Mary Elizabeth Davis**
Date Of Birth	Monday, August 11, 1930
Place Of Birth	Fulton Township, North Carolina – Forsyth County
Date Of Death	N/A
Age At Death	N/A
Place Of Death	N/A
Occupation	N/A
Married	N/A
Notes	

Name	**Mattie Ruth Davis Nelson**
Date Of Birth	Saturday, August 12, 1933
Place Of Birth	Winston-Salem, North Carolina – Forsyth County
Date Of Death	Saturday, Wednesday 6, 2003
Age At Death	69
Place Of Death	Winston-Salem, North Carolina – Forsyth County
Occupation	Housewife
Married	Harold Nelson (b. 1932)

My Family Tree

Notes	Married on Friday, October 11, 1957, in Winston-Salem, North Carolina – Forsyth County. She was buried on Saturday, August 9, 2003, at Evergreen Cemetery. His parents were Annie Nelson and Eddie Nelson.

The Family Line of Janet Secreca Britton Mason and Robert Mason [I]

The connection to the family line was Robert [II] (brother of Johnsie) and the son of Maggie Fowler Mason and Robert M. Mason [II].

The Fifth Generation

Janet Secreca Britton Mason - See Entry Page 124
Robert Mason [I] - See Entry Page 123-124

Their (3) Children

Name	Helen Faith Mason
Date Of Birth	Wednesday, January 3, 1934
Place Of Birth	Mocksville, North Carolina – Davie County
Date Of Death	Wednesday, July 4, 1934
Age At Death	7 Months 1 Day Old
Place Of Death	Mocksville, North Carolina – Davie County
Occupation	None
Married	Single
Notes	She was buried on Wednesday, July 4, 1934, at Shiloh Baptist Church Cemetery in Mocksville, North Carolina – Davie County.

Name	Robert Mason II
Date Of Birth	Thursday, December 31, 1931
Place Of Birth	Mocksville, North Carolina – Davie County
Date Of Death	Thursday, June 17, 1971
Age At Death	39
Place Of Death	Mocksville, North Carolina – Davie County
Occupation	United States Air Force – Retired/Salesman – Inger Scoll Rand

My Family Tree

Married	Sylvia Ijames Mason
Notes	He served in WWII – as an (AIC) Air Force Fighter in the Korean War. He was buried on Sunday, June 20, 1971, at Shiloh Baptist Church Cemetery in Mocksville, North Carolina – Davie County. He lived on Mill Street in Mocksville at the time of his death.

Name	**Elizabeth Victoria Mason Johnson**
Date Of Birth	Sunday, July 22, 1928
Place Of Birth	Mocksville, North Carolina – Davie County
Date Of Death	Sunday, April 26, 1992
Age At Death	63
Place Of Death	Mocksville, North Carolina – Davie County
Occupation	Licensed Practical Nurse/Housewife
Married	Widow
Notes	She lived at 268 Milling Road in Mocksville when she died, a widow, and homeowner. She was buried in April 1992 at Shiloh Baptist Church Cemetery in Mocksville, North Carolina – Davie County.

The Family Line of Roxanna S. Smith Mason and Raymond D. Mason [I]

The connection to the family line was Raymond D.[I], the son of Ellen Jefferson Mason and Samuel M. Mason.

The Fifth Generation

Roxanna S. Smith Mason - See Entry Page 62
Raymond D. Mason [I] - See Entry Page 61-62

Their (7) Children

Name	**Alberta R. Mason Samuels**
Date Of Birth	Sunday, May 16, 1926
Place Of Birth	Pittsboro, North Carolina – Chatham County
Date Of Death	Tuesday, February 3, 2009
Age At Death	82

My Family Tree

Place Of Death	Columbus, Ohio – Franklin County
Occupation	Retired – Domestic Worker/Housewife
Married	William Samuels II
Notes	She was buried in February 2009; she was a widow when she died. Alberta and (her sister) Dorthea were buried in mausoleums side-by-side at Green Lawn Cemetery in Columbus, Ohio – Franklin County.

Name	**William Samuels II**
Date Of Birth	Monday, December 13, 1920
Place Of Birth	Columbus, Ohio – Franklin County
Date Of Death	Saturday, February 17, 1990
Age At Death	69
Place Of Death	Columbus, Ohio – Franklin County
Occupation	Retired – Farm Laborer
Married	Alberta R. Mason Samuels
Notes	His parents were Della M. Howard Samuels and William Samuels I. Married on Wednesday, September 10, 1947, in Columbus, Ohio – Franklin County, a marriage of 43 years.

Name	**Dorthea M. Mason White**
Date Of Birth	Thursday, August 4, 1927
Place Of Birth	North Carolina – Chatham County
Date Of Death	Thursday, November 15, 1990
Age At Death	63
Place Of Death	Columbus, Ohio – Franklin County
Occupation	Domestic Worker/Housewife
Married	Abney White

My Family Tree

Notes	Her nickname was "Doty." Dorthea was buried in November 1990, a widow.

Name	**Abney White**
Date Of Birth	Sunday, March 9, 1919
Place Of Birth	Columbus, Ohio – Franklin County
Date Of Death	Saturday, October 5, 1985
Age At Death	66
Place Of Death	Columbus, Ohio – Franklin County
Occupation	Day Laborer
Married	Dorthea M. Mason White
Notes	Married on Saturday, January 11, 1947, in North Carolina, a marriage of 43 years. Abney was buried in October 1985 at Green Lawn Cemetery in Columbus, Ohio – Franklin County. His parents were Florence Abney White (b. 1882 – d. 1930, age 47- 48) and Loren White (b. 1877 – d. 1952, age 74 – 75). His grandparents were Mary Ellen Eason Abney (b. 1859 – d. 1930, age 70 – 71) and Augustine B. Abney "Gus" (b. Sunday, March 17, 1857, Ohio – Brown County – d. Tuesday, September 12, 1939, age 82). His parents and grandparents were all buried at Wesley Chapel Cemetery in Hilliard, Ohio – Franklin County, with his grandparents buried side-by-side.

Name	**Lois Mason Croston**
Date Of Birth	Thursday, June 24, 1923
Place Of Birth	Columbus, Ohio – Franklin County
Date Of Death	Friday, September 17, 1999
Age At Death	76
Place Of Death	Clinton Township, Ohio – Franklin County
Occupation	Restaurant Business
Married	Kennard Croston (b. 1925), POB. Ohio, Occupation – Sewer Worker

My Family Tree

Notes	

Name	Robert Raymond McCall II
Date Of Birth	Tuesday, February 28, 1928
Place Of Birth	Columbus, Ohio – Franklin County
Date Of Death	Sunday, May 14, 1944
Age At Death	16
Place Of Death	Marion Township, Ohio – Franklin County
Occupation	None
Married	Single
Notes	While he was living with his Aunt Roxanna and Uncle Raymond [1], they adopted their nephew as their son. His parents were Margaret Mason McCall and Robert Raymond McCall [1]. He was buried on Friday, May 19, 1944, at Green Lawn Cemetery in Columbus, Ohio – Franklin County. He lived at 2208 Alum Creek Drive in Marion Township at the time of his death.

Name	Raymond A. Mason II
Date Of Birth	Friday, January 2, 1931
Place Of Birth	Columbus, Ohio – Franklin County
Date Of Death	Friday, July 13, 2012
Age At Death	81
Place Of Death	Columbus, Ohio – Franklin County
Occupation	Retired – Plant man Worker
Married	Mary Jones Mason
Notes	Married on Monday, November 27, 1947, in Columbus, Ohio – Franklin County. His nickname was "Ray." He was buried in July 2012 at Green Lawn Cemetery in Columbus, Ohio – Franklin County. Her parents were Mary A. Simms Jones and Merriel Jones. Their children: Raymond A.

My Family Tree

	Mason III (Barbara), Evelyn Mason (John Boyce), Gwendolyn Mason (Sam McMillan), Gayle Mason (Eric Troy), Pamela Mason Lewis, Lessee Mason, and Ramonia L. Mason Morrison (John Thomas).

Name	**Melvin Mason**
Date Of Birth	Sunday, April 1, 1934
Place Of Birth	Columbus, Ohio – Franklin County
Date Of Death	Saturday, February 21, 1998
Age At Death	63
Place Of Death	Columbus, Ohio – Franklin County
Occupation	United States Army – Retired/Retired – Sanitary Services
Married	Sally Mae Jones Mason
Notes	Married on Monday, January 19, 1953, and divorced in Columbus, Ohio – Franklin County. He served in the United States Army during WWII in Korea and was honorably discharged. He was buried in February 1998 at Green Lawn Cemetery in Columbus, Ohio – Franklin County.

Name	**Ella M. Mason**
Date Of Birth	Wednesday, October 25, 1939
Place Of Birth	Columbus, Ohio – Franklin County
Date Of Death	Sunday, February 21, 1988
Age At Death	48
Place Of Death	Columbus, Ohio – Franklin County
Occupation	Day Laborer
Married	Single
Notes	

My Family Tree

The Family Line of Johnsie J. Mason Brown and Clarence Odell Brown [1]

The connection to the family line was Clarence [1], the son of Jettie Ann Hairston Mason Brown and Jesse James Brown [1].

The Fifth Generation

Johnsie J. Mason Brown - See Entry Page 122-123
Clarence Odell Brown [1] - See Entry Page 123

Their (10) Children

Name	Clarence Odell Brown II
Date Of Birth	Tuesday, January 1, 1935
Place Of Birth	Fulton Township, North Carolina – Davie County
Date Of Death	Wednesday, September 24, 2003
Age At Death	68
Place Of Death	Fulton Township, North Carolina – Davie County
Occupation	Day Laborer
Married	Single
Notes	

Name	Jessie Brown
Date Of Birth	1936
Place Of Birth	Fulton Township, North Carolina – Davie County
Date Of Death	N/A
Age At Death	N/A
Place Of Death	N/A
Occupation	N/A
Married	N/A
Notes	

My Family Tree

Name	**Robert Mason Brown**
Date Of Birth	Friday, February 25, 1938
Place Of Birth	Fulton Township, North Carolina – Davie County
Date Of Death	N/A
Age At Death	N/A
Place Of Death	N/A
Occupation	N/A
Married	N/A
Notes	

Name	**Jane Brown**
Date Of Birth	Monday, May 14, 1945
Place Of Birth	Mocksville, North Carolina – Davie County
Date Of Death	N/A
Age At Death	N/A
Place Of Death	N/A
Occupation	N/A
Married	N/A
Notes	Her twin brother is Wayne.

Name	**Wayne Brown**
Date Of Birth	Monday, May 14, 1945
Place Of Birth	Mocksville, North Carolina – Davie County
Date Of Death	N/A

My Family Tree

Age At Death	N/A
Place Of Death	N/A
Occupation	N/A
Married	N/A
Notes	His twin sister is Jane.

Name	**Daniel Brown**
Date Of Birth	Friday, April 7, 1944
Place Of Birth	Mocksville, North Carolina – Davie County
Date Of Death	Monday, July 27, 1959
Age At Death	15
Place Of Death	Mocksville, North Carolina – Davie County
Occupation	None
Married	Single
Notes	He was buried on Saturday, August 1, 1959, at Cedar Grove Baptist Church Cemetery.

Name	**Onelle Brown**
Date Of Birth	Wednesday, July 11, 1951
Place Of Birth	Mocksville, North Carolina – Davie County
Date Of Death	N/A
Age At Death	N/A
Place Of Death	N/A
Occupation	N/A
Married	N/A

My Family Tree

Notes	

Name	**Frank James Brown I**
Date Of Birth	Thursday, January 9, 1941
Place Of Birth	Mocksville, North Carolina – Davie County
Date Of Death	Monday, July 17, 2006
Age At Death	65
Place Of Death	Fork, North Carolina – Davie County
Occupation	Minister
Married	Single
Notes	His children: Angela Brown Small, Frank James Brown [II], Keith Brown, and Tony Norman. He was buried on Friday, July 21, 2006, in North Carolina. He lived at 4640 Indiana Ave. in Winston-Salem at the time of his death, a homeowner. The house was passed down for the second time within the family.

Name	**Lou Etta Brown**
Date Of Birth	Saturday, December 23, 1939
Place Of Birth	Mocksville, North Carolina – Davie County
Date Of Death	N/A
Age At Death	N/A
Place Of Death	N/A
Occupation	N/A
Married	N/A
Notes	

My Family Tree

Name	**Infant (Girl) Brown**
Date Of Birth	Monday, August 25, 1952
Place Of Birth	Lexington, North Carolina, Davidson County
Date Of Death	Monday, August 25, 1952
Age At Death	0
Place Of Death	Lexington, North Carolina, Davidson County
Occupation	None
Married	Single
Notes	She was buried on Wednesday, August 27, 1952, at Cedar Grove Baptist Church Cemetery.

The Family Line of Mary Hairston Mason and Ernest I. Mason

The connection to the family line was Ernest I., the son of Maggie Fowler Mason and Robert M. Mason[II].

The Fifth Generation

Mary Hairston Mason - See Entry Page 121
Ernest I. Mason - See Entry Page 120-121

Their (3) Children

Name	**Infant Mason**
Date Of Birth	Thursday, February 8, 1917
Place Of Birth	Fulton Township, North Carolina – Forsyth County
Date Of Death	Thursday, February 8, 1917
Age At Death	0
Place Of Death	Fulton Township, North Carolina – Forsyth County
Occupation	None
Married	Single
Notes	

My Family Tree

Name	Marie Mason
Date Of Birth	Wednesday, May 6, 1925
Place Of Birth	Mocksville, North Carolina – Forsyth County
Date Of Death	Unknown
Age At Death	Unknown
Place Of Death	Unknown
Occupation	Unknown
Married	Unknown
Notes	

Name	Herbert Gilmer Mason
Date Of Birth	Saturday, May 19, 1934
Place Of Birth	Mocksville, North Carolina – Forsyth County
Date Of Death	Tuesday, September 7, 1971
Age At Death	37
Place Of Death	Winston-Salem, North Carolina – Forsyth County
Occupation	Owner – Furniture Company
Married	Blanche Lucille Vaughters Mason
Notes	Herbert was buried on Friday, September 10, 1971. Their children: Perry Lee Mason (b. Thursday, October 8, 1964 – d. Saturday, January 16, 1965 (age 3 Months Old), Perry was buried Monday, January 18, 1965. Herbert and Perry were both buried at Cedar Grove Baptist Church Cemetery and Jimmy Ray Mason (b. Sunday, September 16, 1962). Both children's POB. is Fulton Township, North Carolina – Davie County.

The Family Line of Edna Bell Winford Mason and John Bunyon Mason

The connection to the family line was John Bunyon, the grandson of Lucinda Mason Mason and Spencer Mason.

My Family Tree

The Fourth Generation

Name	**John Bunyon Mason**
Date Of Birth	Friday, September 9, 1895
Place Of Birth	High Point, North Carolina – Guilford County
Date Of Death	Sunday, February 19, 1967
Age At Death	71
Place Of Death	High Point, North Carolina – Guilford County
Occupation	United States – Army Air Corps – Retired/General Farmer/Minister
Married	Edna Bell Winford Mason
Notes	His parents were Nancy Jane Crump Mason and John Henry Mason. He served in the United States Armed Forces during WWI and was honorably discharged. Edna stated an error was made on his headstone for his birth year as 1898. Both his death certificate and military records have his birth year as 1895. He was buried on Thursday, February 23, 1967.

Name	**Edna Bell Winford Mason**
Date Of Birth	Tuesday, January 14, 1902
Place Of Birth	North Carolina – Davie County
Date Of Death	Thursday, September 29, 1987
Age At Death	85
Place Of Death	Mocksville, North Carolina – Davie County
Occupation	Domestic Worker/Housewife
Married	John Bunyon Mason
Notes	Her mother was of Indian descent. According to the 1930 Census, Edna and John were both literate. She was buried in October 1987 as a widow. Edna and John were both buried side-by-side at Cedar Grove Baptist Church Cemetery. Edna and John lived at 803 Mangue Ave in High Point at the time of their death; they were homeowners. Her parents were Mary Belle Doulin Winford and Alexander Winford. Edna's siblings were Dorsey Winford, Fallie Winford Foster, Mary Winford Hairston, Ella

My Family Tree

| | Winford Furlow, Laura Winford, Charlie Robert Winford, Celesta Winford, Emma Winford, Elizabeth O. Winford Mason, Maggie Winford, and Tallie Winford. |

Their (13) Children

Name	William John Bunyon Mason
Date Of Birth	Thursday, October 17, 1918
Place Of Birth	Fulton Township, North Carolina – Davie County
Date Of Death	Monday, April 21, 2008
Age At Death	89
Place Of Death	Jamaica, New York – Queens
Occupation	Retired – General Farm Laborer
Married	Leona Brown Mason
Notes	According to the 1920 Census, he was literate. William preferred to use his middle name. He was a widower when he died.

Name	Leona Brown Mason
Date Of Birth	Sunday, January 20, 1924
Place Of Birth	Fulton Township, North Carolina – Davie County
Date Of Death	Monday, September 23, 1996
Age At Death	72
Place Of Death	Jamaica, New York – Queens
Occupation	Retired – Domestic Worker/Homemaker
Married	William John Bunyon Mason
Notes	Her parents were Jettie Ann Hairston Mason Brown and Jesse James Brown I. Their children: John Louis Mason and William Lewis Mason.

My Family Tree

Name	Fannie P. Mason
Date Of Birth	1921
Place Of Birth	Fulton Township, North Carolina – Davie County
Date Of Death	Unknown
Age At Death	Unknown
Place Of Death	Unknown
Occupation	Unknown
Married	Unknown
Notes	According to the 1930 Census, she was literate. She was a boarder at the home of Willie Mayo, Irene Mayo, and Susie Williams in the 1940s in Ward 3 Winston-Salem, North Carolina – Forsyth County.

Name	Beana Mae Mason Watkins
Date Of Birth	Monday, February 27, 1922
Place Of Birth	Fulton Township, North Carolina – Davie County
Date Of Death	Saturday, February 17, 2018
Age At Death	95
Place Of Death	North Carolina – Davie County
Occupation	Domestic Worker/Housewife
Married	Roscoe Watkins
Notes	According to the 1930 Census, she was literate. The Census notes indicated that her first name was spelled Buna Mae. She was buried in February 2018. Beana and Roscoe were both buried side-by-side at Cedar Grove Baptist Church Cemetery. Their child: Edna Elizabeth Watkins Ball Scott (b. Sunday, September 28, 1941), POB. Fulton Township, North Carolina – Davie County. Edna's first husband – Sherman Preston Ball [II] (b. Friday, August 4, 1950) in Virginia – Arlington County – married Saturday, May 5, 1973. Edna's second husband – LeRoy Franklin Scott [II] (b. 1944), POB. Fulton Township, North Carolina – Davie County. Edna and LeRoy got married Saturday, November 24, 1979, in Mocksville, North Carolina – Davie

My Family Tree

	County. LeRoy's parents were Ruby Brown Scott and LeRoy Franklin Scott [1].

Name	**Roscoe Watkins**
Date Of Birth	Wednesday, January 11, 1911
Place Of Birth	North Carolina – Davie County
Date Of Death	Monday, June 21, 1971
Age At Death	60
Place Of Death	Lexington, North Carolina – Davidson County
Occupation	Truck Driver
Married	Beana Mae Mason Watkins
Notes	He was buried Thursday, June 24, 1971, at Cedar Grove Baptist Church Cemetery. His mother was Catherine Watkins. They lived at 122 Smith Avenue in Lexington at the time of their death; they were homeowners.

Name	**Thomas Fisher Mason**
Date Of Birth	Monday, April 21, 1924
Place Of Birth	Fulton Township, North Carolina – Davie County
Date Of Death	Sunday, May 5, 1991
Age At Death	67
Place Of Death	Far Rockaway Queens, New York
Occupation	Day Laborer
Married	Single
Notes	

My Family Tree

Name	**Nannie B. Mason Mock**
Date Of Birth	Monday, September 24, 1928
Place Of Birth	Fulton Township, North Carolina – Davie County
Date Of Death	Unknown
Age At Death	Unknown
Place Of Death	Washington, DC
Occupation	Domestic Worker/Housewife
Married	Rudolph Mock (b. Thursday, March 29, 1928), POB. Davidson, North Carolina – Davidson County
Notes	His parents were Pearl Mock and Odell Mock. Married on Thursday, December 25, 1947, in Davidson, North Carolina – Davidson County.

Name	**Creolla Ann Mason Holmes**
Date Of Birth	Saturday, January 5, 1929
Place Of Birth	Fulton Township, North Carolina – Davie County
Date Of Death	Unknown
Age At Death	Unknown
Place Of Death	Unknown
Occupation	Housewife
Married	Manuel Odell Holmes
Notes	

Name	**Manuel Odell Holmes**
Date Of Birth	Saturday, February 18, 1922
Place Of Birth	Cotton Grove Township, North Carolina – Davidson County
Date Of Death	Sunday, July 26, 1992

My Family Tree

Age At Death	70
Place Of Death	Winston-Salem, North Carolina – Forsyth County
Occupation	United States – Army/Construction – Pipe Fitter – Ground Worker
Married	Creolla Ann Mason Holmes
Notes	Married on Wednesday, September 15, 1948, in Lexington, North Carolina – Davidson County. His parents were Ophelia Tillman Holmes and Lee Thomas Holmes. His level of education was Grammar School. He served in the United States Army during WWII from Thursday, December 31, 1942 – Wednesday, May 22, 1946, and was honorably discharged. He was buried in July 1992 at the National Cemetery in Salisbury, North Carolina – Rowan County. He lived at 316 Mandala Ave in Lexington and was divorced at the time of his death. His sister was Mary Elizabeth Holmes Brown.

Name	**Pansy Annette Mason Gooden**
Date Of Birth	Wednesday, November 16, 1930
Place Of Birth	Fulton Township, North Carolina – Davie County
Date Of Death	Tuesday, February 13, 1973
Age At Death	42
Place Of Death	Mocksville, North Carolina – Davie County
Occupation	Housewife
Married	(1) Clarence Friday (b. 1924) (2) Widow
Notes	(1) Married on Thursday, July 15, 1948, in Davidson, North Carolina – Davidson County. (1) His parents were Zulla Friday and C. F. Friday. She was buried in February 1973 at Cedar Grove Baptist Church Cemetery.

Name	**Eveline Mason**
Date Of Birth	Friday, March 10, 1933
Place Of Birth	Fulton Township, North Carolina – Davie County
Date Of Death	Saturday, February 10, 1934

My Family Tree

Age At Death	11 Months Old
Place Of Death	Fulton Township, North Carolina – Davie County
Occupation	None
Married	Single
Notes	She was buried Sunday, February 11, 1934, at Cedar Grove Baptist Church Cemetery.

Name	Alex Mason
Date Of Birth	1934
Place Of Birth	Fulton Township, North Carolina – Davie County
Date Of Death	N/A
Age At Death	N/A
Place Of Death	N/A
Occupation	N/A
Married	N/A
Notes	

Name	Leander Mason
Date Of Birth	Thursday, February 28, 1935
Place Of Birth	Fulton Township, North Carolina – Davie County
Date Of Death	N/A
Age At Death	N/A
Place Of Death	N/A
Occupation	N/A
Married	N/A

My Family Tree

Notes	

Name	Charline Mason Gillon
Date Of Birth	Thursday, March 31, 1938
Place Of Birth	Fulton Township, North Carolina – Davie County
Date Of Death	September 1980
Age At Death	42
Place Of Death	Washington, DC
Occupation	Housewife
Married	Charles Lewis Gillon (POB. Virginia – Arlington County)
Notes	Married on Tuesday, February 23, 1960, in Virginia – Arlington County. His parents were Essre Myricle Gillon and George Gillon.

Name	Kenneth Mason
Date Of Birth	Monday, April 15, 1940
Place Of Birth	Fulton Township, North Carolina – Davie County
Date Of Death	N/A
Age At Death	N/A
Place Of Death	N/A
Occupation	N/A
Married	N/A
Notes	

Name	Alfred K. Mason
Date Of Birth	Tuesday, March 17, 1942

My Family Tree

Place Of Birth	Fulton Township, North Carolina – Davie County
Date Of Death	N/A
Age At Death	N/A
Place Of Death	N/A
Occupation	Laborer Worker
Married	Barbara Jean Carson Mason
Notes	

Name	**Barbara Jean Carson Mason**
Date Of Birth	Sunday, June 18, 1944
Place Of Birth	Fulton Township, North Carolina – Davie County
Date Of Death	Friday, July 31, 2009
Age At Death	65
Place Of Death	Fulton Township, North Carolina – Davie County
Occupation	Housewife
Married	Alfred K. Mason
Notes	She was buried on Saturday, August 8, 2009, at Cedar Grove Baptist Church Cemetery. Barbara and Alfred planned to be buried side-by-side.

The Family Line of Nancy Jane Crump Mason and John Henry Mason

The connection to the family line was John Henry Mason, the grandson of Phyllis Ann Brown Hairston Mason and Burrell Mason.

The Third Generation

Name	**Nancy Jane Crump Mason**
Date Of Birth	Thursday, January 15, 1874
Place Of Birth	Mocksville, North Carolina – Davie County

My Family Tree

Date Of Death	Monday, February 21, 1938
Age At Death	64
Place Of Death	Mocksville, North Carolina – Davie County
Occupation	Domestic Worker/Housewife
Married	John Henry Mason
Notes	Married on Sunday, May 4, 1890, in Mocksville, North Carolina – Davie County, a marriage of 45 years. Nancy and John, according to the 1910 Census, noted that both were literate. She was buried in February 1938. Nancy and John were both buried side-by-side at Cedar Grove Baptist Church Cemetery, and she was a widow when she died. Her parents were Mary Crump and Stimson Crump, and they both were slaves.

Name	**John Henry Mason**
Date Of Birth	Wednesday, March 11, 1868
Place Of Birth	Fulton Township, North Carolina – Davie County
Date Of Death	Monday, December 23, 1935
Age At Death	67
Place Of Death	Fulton Township, North Carolina – Davie County
Occupation	General Farmer/Barber – Owner
Married	Nancy Jane Crump Mason
Notes	His parents were Lucinda Mason Mason and Spencer Mason. He was buried on Friday, December 27, 1935. Nancy and John both lived at Route #3 – Box 37 in Fulton Township when they died, homeowners.

Their (7) Children

Name	**Baxter Mason**
Date Of Birth	Wednesday, March 11, 1896
Place Of Birth	Fulton Township, North Carolina – Davie County

My Family Tree

Date Of Death	October 1983
Age At Death	87
Place Of Death	Pennsylvania, Allegheny County
Occupation	Minister of Saint Luke's Baptist Church
Married	Nanna Mason (b. 1898), POB. Kentucky
Notes	According to the 1910 Census, he was literate. The 1940 Census noted that they had a family of four (boarders) living with them. Nanna and Baxter did not have any children.

Name	**Nathaniel A. Mason**
Date Of Birth	Sunday, March 6, 1898
Place Of Birth	Fulton Township, North Carolina – Davie County
Date Of Death	Sunday, September 16, 1962
Age At Death	64
Place Of Death	High Point, North Carolina – Guilford County
Occupation	Farm Laborer/Minister
Married	Mary Taylor Mason (b. 1904)
Notes	According to the 1910 Census, he was literate. He was buried Saturday, September 22, 1962, at Forest Lawn Cemetery in Buffalo, New York – Erie County. He lived at 115 Florida Street in Buffalo at the time of his death, a homeowner. Her mother was Lucy Taylor.

The connection to the family line was Dennis^I and John Bunyon; they were the sons of Nancy Jane Crump Mason and John Henry Mason. Dennis^I's wife – Elizabeth O. Winford Mason, and John Bunyon's wife – Edna Bell Winford Mason (were sisters).

Name	**Dennis De Quincy Mason I**
Date Of Birth	Wednesday, February 8, 1899
Place Of Birth	Fulton Township, North Carolina – Davie County
Date Of Death	Friday, October 22, 1976

My Family Tree

Age At Death	77
Place Of Death	High Point, North Carolina – Guilford County
Occupation	Farmer/Minister
Married	Elizabeth O. Winford Mason
Notes	According to the 1910 Census, he was literate. He was buried on Monday, October 25, 1976, at Carolina Biblical Gardens Cemetery in Jamestown, North Carolina – Guilford County.

Name	Elizabeth O. Winford Mason
Date Of Birth	Wednesday, September 12, 1900
Place Of Birth	North Carolina – Davie County
Date Of Death	Friday, July 10, 1987
Age At Death	86
Place Of Death	High Point, North Carolina – Guilford County
Occupation	Retired – Domestic Worker/Homemaker
Married	Dennis De Quincy Mason [I]
Notes	Her nickname was "Lizzie." Married on Wednesday, January 2, 1918, in Fork, North Carolina – Davie County, a marriage of 58 years. Her parents were Mary Belle Doulin Winford and Alexander Winford (her mother was of Indian descent). They lived at 1311 Cedrow Drive in High Point at the time of their death, homeowners. Their children: Lula Senie Mae Mason Clement, Baxter Sherman Mason, Dennis DeQuincy Mason [II], Mary Elizabeth Mason Booe, Marie Mason Jones, Clydie Mae Mason McQueen, James Mason, John Mason, Virginia Mae Mason Watson, Gennellia Mason Hunter, and Rebecca Mason.

Name	Clydie Mae Mason Redmon
Date Of Birth	Saturday, November 8, 1913
Place Of Birth	Fulton Township, North Carolina – Davie County
Date Of Death	Saturday, March 6, 1965

My Family Tree

Age At Death	51
Place Of Death	Pittsburgh, Pennsylvania – Allegheny County
Occupation	Housewife
Married	Eugene J. Redmon
Notes	The 1940 Census noted that she was a boarder at her brother's (Baxter) home in Pennsylvania. Married on Saturday, August 24, 1946, in Pennsylvania – Allegheny County. Clydie was buried in March 1965.

Name	**Eugene J. Redmon**
Date Of Birth	Wednesday, May 7, 1913
Place Of Birth	Pennsylvania – Allegheny County
Date Of Death	1979
Age At Death	65 – 66
Place Of Death	Pittsburgh, Pennsylvania – Allegheny County
Occupation	Day Laborer
Married	(1) Clydie Mae Mason Redmon (2) Lena E. Redmon (b. 1925 – d. Unknown)
Notes	He was buried in 1979; Clydie, Lena, and Eugene were all buried at Mount Lebanon Cemetery in Mount Lebanon, Pennsylvania – Allegheny County. Lena and Eugene were supposed to be buried side-by-side, but her body was not there. His parents were Ouida Jackson Redmon and Cedric Redmon.

Edna Bell Winford Mason - See Entry Page 147-148
John Bunyon Mason - See Entry Page 147

Name	**Annie Geneva Mason Hairston**
Date Of Birth	Friday, April 3, 1908
Place Of Birth	Lexington, North Carolina – Davidson County
Date Of Death	Saturday, April 25, 1959
Age At Death	51

My Family Tree

Place Of Death	Lexington, North Carolina – Davidson County
Occupation	Farm Laborer/Housewife
Married	Winston Ervin Hairston
Notes	She was buried in April 1959 at Cedar Grove Baptist Church Cemetery.

Name	**Winston Ervin Hairston**
Date Of Birth	Wednesday, February 24, 1909
Place Of Birth	North Carolina – Davie County
Date Of Death	Thursday, August 31, 1967
Age At Death	58
Place Of Death	Lexington, North Carolina – Davidson County
Occupation	Cook Restaurant
Married	Annie Geneva Mason Hairston
Notes	Married on Thursday, November 29, 1928, in Fulton Township, North Carolina – Davie County, and they got divorced after 31 years. He was buried on Monday, September 4, 1967. He lived at 414 Raleigh Road in Lexington at the time of his death as a homeowner. His parents were Ruth W. Hairston Hairston (b. Saturday, October 20, 1883 – d. Saturday, September 28, 1974, age 90) and William Thomas Hairston (b. Thursday, June 28, 1877– d. Tuesday, July 10, 1973, age 96). His parents were born in North Carolina – Stokes County. Winston and his parents were all buried at Buncombe Church Cemetery in Lexington, North Carolina – Davidson County, but his parents were buried side-by-side.

Name	**Zula M. Mason Barker**
Date Of Birth	Wednesday, June 8, 1910
Place Of Birth	Fulton Township, North Carolina – Davie County
Date Of Death	Monday, October 20, 2003
Age At Death	93

My Family Tree

Place Of Death	Fulton Township, North Carolina – Davie County
Occupation	Retired – Farm Laborer/Homemaker
Married	William E. Barker
Notes	She graduated from high school. She was supposed to be buried at Rockfish Memorial Cemetery, but instead, she was buried on Thursday, October 23, 2003, at Cedar Grove Baptist Church Cemetery. She was a widow when she died. Their children: Alberta M. Barker and William N. Barker.

Name	**William E. Barker**
Date Of Birth	Friday, July 6, 1906
Place Of Birth	North Carolina
Date Of Death	Thursday, March 4, 1971
Age At Death	64
Place Of Death	Fayetteville, North Carolina – Cumberland County
Occupation	Painter
Married	Zula M. Mason Barker
Notes	Married on Friday, February 7, 1930, in Mocksville, North Carolina – Davie County, a marriage of 41 years. He was buried on Sunday, March 7, 1971, at Rockfish Memorial Cemetery in Fayetteville, North Carolina – Cumberland County. His parents were Effie Fisher Barker and Llie Barker. Zula and William both lived at 1008 Ellis Street in Fayetteville at the time of their death; they were homeowners.

The Family Line of Jettie Ann Hairston Mason Brown and Jesse James Brown [1]

The connection to the family line was Jettie, the daughter of Bettie Hairston Mason and Ennis Mason.

The Fifth Generation

Name	**Jettie Ann Hairston Mason Brown**
Date Of Birth	Saturday, March 3, 1888
Place Of Birth	Fulton Township, North Carolina – Davie County

My Family Tree

Date Of Death	Thursday, September 27, 1928
Age At Death	40
Place Of Death	Fulton Township, North Carolina – Davie County
Occupation	Domestic Worker/Homemaker
Married	Jesse James Brown [I]
Notes	According to the 1920 Census, she was literate, and Jesse was illiterate. Her parents were Bettie Hairston Mason and Ennis Mason. Her father Ennis was a boarder at their house until he died. Her headstone had a design of the triple links, a recurring symbol among Oddfellows internationally connoting the motto of "Amicitia Amoret Veritas" (a part of the Eastern Star) English: "Friendship, Love, and Truth" with an R in the middle. She was buried on Saturday, September 29, 1928.

Name	**Jesse James Brown I**
Date Of Birth	Wednesday, June 15, 1887
Place Of Birth	Thursday, September 17, 1959
Date Of Death	Fulton Township, North Carolina – Davie County
Age At Death	72
Place Of Death	Mocksville, North Carolina – Davie County
Occupation	General Farmer
Married	Jettie Ann Hairston Mason Brown
Notes	His mother was Hanna Brown Michael (b. Wednesday, November 27, 1878 – d. Thursday, April 19, 1956, age 77). He joined an organization named the Freemason and his headstone had a design of the Freemason symbol. He was buried in September 1959. Jettie and Jesse were both buried side-by-side at Cedar Grove Baptist Church Cemetery, and he was a widower when he died.

Their (10) Children

Name	**Eva Brown Hairston**
Date Of Birth	Friday, June 26, 1908

My Family Tree

Place Of Birth	Fulton Township, North Carolina – Davie County
Date Of Death	Monday, June 9, 1930
Age At Death	21
Place Of Death	Lexington, North Carolina – Davidson County
Occupation	Housewife
Married	Early B. Hairston
Notes	According to the 1920 Census, she was literate. She was buried in June 1930.

Name	**Early B. Hairston**
Date Of Birth	Wednesday, February 15, 1905
Place Of Birth	Fulton Township, North Carolina – Davie County
Date Of Death	Monday, March 30, 1970
Age At Death	65
Place Of Death	Lexington, North Carolina – Davidson County
Occupation	Day Laborer
Married	Eva Brown Hairston
Notes	Married on Saturday, May 9, 1925, in Mocksville, North Carolina – Davie County. In the Census, his name was spelled Erley. He was buried on Thursday, April 2, 1970. Early was divorced from Eva when he died. His parents were Carrie Hairston Hairston (b. Monday, June 25, 1883, POB. North Carolina – Davidson County – d. Sunday, September 20, 1959, age 76), buried on Tuesday, September 22, 1959, and William H. Hairston. Eva, Early, and his mother were all buried at Buncombe Baptist Church Cemetery in Lexington, North Carolina – Davidson County.

Name	**Alberta Mae Brown Hairston**
Date Of Birth	Sunday, December 18, 1910
Place Of Birth	Fulton Township, North Carolina – Davie County

My Family Tree

Date Of Death	Monday, September 5, 1983
Age At Death	72
Place Of Death	Lexington, North Carolina – Davidson County
Occupation	Retired – Domestic Worker/Homemaker
Married	Roy Righteous Hairston
Notes	According to the 1910 Census, she was literate and attended school. She was buried on Saturday, September 10, 1983. She had a daughter with Selman Clabona: Infant Brown (b. and d., age 0) and was buried on Thursday, September 8, 1927, at Cedar Grove Baptist Church Cemetery.

Name	**Roy Righteous Hairston**
Date Of Birth	Sunday, July 12, 1903
Place Of Birth	Davidson City, North Carolina – Davie County
Date Of Death	Friday, November 20, 1992
Age At Death	89
Place Of Death	Lexington, North Carolina – Davidson County
Occupation	Retired – Cement Mixer – Foltz Pipe Company
Married	Alberta Mae Brown Hairston
Notes	Married Wednesday, April 9, 1930, in North Carolina – Davie County, a marriage of 53 years. His level of education was the 6th grade because his father (Righteous) needed his help in the field to grow crops so the family could survive through the winter months. He was buried in November 1992 as a widower. They were both buried side-by-side at Yadkin Star Baptist Church Graveyard Cemetery in Lexington, North Carolina – Davidson County. The only thing written on his headstone was his born year. His parents were Mary Clodfelter Hairston and Righteous Hairston.

Clarence Odell Brown [1] - See Entry Page 123
Johnsie J. Mason Brown - See Entry Page 122-123

Name	**Jesse James Brown II**
Date Of Birth	Monday, October 25, 1915

My Family Tree

Place Of Birth	Fulton Township, North Carolina – Davie County
Date Of Death	Sunday, August 29, 1993
Age At Death	77
Place Of Death	Mocksville, North Carolina – Davie County
Occupation	Retired – Farm Laborer
Married	Lettie F. Goolsby Brown
Notes	According to the 1920 Census, he was literate. His death certificate stated that he was supposed to be buried in September 1993, his final resting place at Cedar Creek Church Cemetery in Mocksville, North Carolina – Davie County, but his body was not there. Instead, he was buried at Cedar Grove Baptist Church Cemetery.

Name	**Lettie F. Goolsby Brown**
Date Of Birth	Thursday, May 8, 1919
Place Of Birth	North Carolina – Davie County
Date Of Death	Tuesday, November 12, 2002
Age At Death	83
Place Of Death	Mocksville, North Carolina – Davie County
Occupation	Retired – Domestic Worker/Homemaker
Married	Jesse James Brown [II]
Notes	Lettie was buried in November 2002. They were both laid side-by-side at Cedar Grove Baptist Church Cemetery, and she was a widow when she died. Her parents were Lula M. Mason Goolsby and John Hairston Goolsby [I]. Their children: John Thomas Brown, Jesse James Brown [III], Kenneth O. Brown, Betty B. Brown Goodwin, Barbara B. Brown Williams, and Jettie Elizabeth Brown Lindsay.

Name	**Hannah Elizabeth Brown Hamilton**
Date Of Birth	Friday, June 28, 1918

My Family Tree

Place Of Birth	Fulton Township, North Carolina – Davie County
Date Of Death	Thursday, November 14, 1991
Age At Death	73
Place Of Death	Winston-Salem, North Carolina – Forsyth County
Occupation	Retired – Domestic Worker/Housewife
Married	Dorce Frank Hamilton [I]
Notes	According to the 1920 Census, she was literate. She was buried in November 1991. Hannah, Dorce, Julia, and George were all buried side-by-side at Goodwill Baptist Church Cemetery in Arcadia, North Carolina – Davidson County, and she was a widow when she died. Their child: Dorce Frank Hamilton [II] (b. Thursday, April 4, 1940), POB. Fulton Township, North Carolina – Davie County.

Name	**Dorce Frank Hamilton I**
Date Of Birth	Friday, June 30, 1911
Place Of Birth	Cleveland, North Carolina – Rowan County
Date Of Death	Monday, October 11, 1982
Age At Death	71
Place Of Death	Clemmons, North Carolina – Forsyth County
Occupation	Retired – Construction Worker
Married	Hannah Elizabeth Brown Hamilton
Notes	Married on Wednesday, July 30, 1930, in North Carolina – Davie County, a marriage of 52 years. He was buried on Saturday, October 16, 1982. Hannah and Dorce both lived at 2824 Inca Lane in Arcadia at the time of their death; they were homeowners. His parents were Julia Friday Hamilton (b. 1888 – d. 1979, age 90–91) and George Henry Hamilton (b. 1890 – d. 1962, age 71–72).

Name	**Ida Doreatha Brown Goolsby**
Date Of Birth	Wednesday, August 22, 1920

My Family Tree

Place Of Birth	Fulton Township, North Carolina – Davie County
Date Of Death	Tuesday, November 19, 2013
Age At Death	93
Place Of Death	Mocksville, North Carolina – Davie County
Occupation	Domestic Worker/Housewife
Married	John Hairston Goolsby II
Notes	According to the 1910 Census, she was literate. She was cremated on Thursday, November 21, 2013, in North Carolina, and she was a widow when she died. Their children: Lula Goolsby Williams, Gwendolyn Goolsby Reynolds, Linda Goolsby Johnson, and John Hairston Goolsby III (Betty).

Lettie F. Goolsby Brown and John Hairston Goolsby II were siblings, and they married into the Brown family.

Name	**John Hairston Goolsby II**
Date Of Birth	Monday, October 30, 1916
Place Of Birth	Fulton Township, North Carolina – Davie County
Date Of Death	Thursday, July 4, 1974
Age At Death	57
Place Of Death	Mocksville, North Carolina – Davie County
Occupation	Hexman Factory Worker
Married	Ida Doreatha Brown Goolsby
Notes	He was buried on Saturday, July 6, 1974, at Cedar Grove Baptist Church Cemetery. Ida stated that John's headstone had the wrong day that he died. His parents were Lula M. Mason Goolsby and John Hairston Goolsby I.

Leona Brown Mason - See Entry Page 148
William John Bunyon Mason - See Entry Page 148

Name	**Addie B. Mae Brown**
Date Of Birth	1925

My Family Tree

Place Of Birth	Fulton Township, North Carolina – Davie County
Date Of Death	1942
Age At Death	16-17
Place Of Death	Fulton Township, North Carolina – Davie County
Occupation	Domestic Worker
Married	Single
Notes	She was buried in 1942, right beside her parents, at Cedar Grove Baptist Church Cemetery.

Name	**Thomas Frank Brown**
Date Of Birth	Monday, May 28, 1928
Place Of Birth	Fulton Township, North Carolina – Davie County
Date Of Death	Monday, October 15, 2001
Age At Death	73
Place Of Death	Lexington, North Carolina – Davidson County
Occupation	Retired – United States Army – Lieutenant
Married	Mary Elizabeth Holmes Brown
Notes	The Census noted that his name was spelled Tom F. Brown. He served in the United States Army during WWII and was honorably discharged. He was buried on Thursday, October 18, 2001.

Name	**Mary Elizabeth Holmes Brown**
Date Of Birth	Friday, December 21, 1928
Place Of Birth	Cotton Grove Township, North Carolina – Davidson County
Date Of Death	Wednesday, July 9, 2003
Age At Death	74

My Family Tree

Place Of Death	Winston-Salem, North Carolina – Forsyth County
Occupation	Housewife/Teacher
Married	Thomas Frank Brown
Notes	Married on Saturday, July 2, 1949, in Davidson, North Carolina – Davidson County, and was married for 52 years. She was buried on Saturday, July 12, 2003, a widow. Mary and Thomas were both buried at Forest Hill Memorial Park Cemetery in Lexington, North Carolina – Davidson County. Her first name was Mary, but she preferred to use her middle name. Her parents were Ophelia Tillman Holmes and Lee Thomas Holmes. Her brother was Manuel Odell Holmes.

Name	**Odell Brown**
Date Of Birth	Unknown
Place Of Birth	Fulton Township, North Carolina – Davie County
Date Of Death	Monday, March 16, 1981
Age At Death	Unknown
Place Of Death	Mocksville, North Carolina – Davie County
Occupation	Day Laborer
Married	Unknown
Notes	He was buried in March 1981 at Cedar Grove Baptist Church Cemetery.

The Family Line of Leona Brown Mason and William John Bunyon Mason

The connection to the family line was Leona, the daughter of Jettie Ann Hairston Mason Brown and Jesse James Brown[1].

The Sixth Generation

Leona Brown Mason - See Entry Page 148
William John Bunyon Mason - See Entry Page 148

<u>**Their (2) Children**</u>

Name	**John Louis Mason**
Date Of Birth	Saturday, March 8, 1941

My Family Tree

Place Of Birth	Fulton Township, North Carolina – Davie County
Date Of Death	Saturday, March 8, 1941
Age At Death	0
Place Of Death	Fulton Township, North Carolina – Davie County
Occupation	None
Married	Single
Notes	He was buried on Sunday, March 9, 1941, at Cedar Grove Baptist Church Cemetery.

Name	William Lewis Mason
Date Of Birth	Sunday, February 7, 1943
Place Of Birth	Fulton Township, North Carolina – Davie County
Date Of Death	N/A
Age At Death	N/A
Place Of Death	N/A
Occupation	N/A
Married	N/A
Notes	

The Family Line of Lettie F. Goolsby Brown and Jesse James Brown [II]

The connection to the family line was Jesse [II], the son of Jettie Ann Hairston Mason Brown and Jesse James Brown [I], Jeese's [II], his wife – Lettie, was the daughter of Lula M. Masin Goolsby and John Hairston [I].

The Sixth Generation

Lettie F. Goolsby Brown - See Entry Page 165
Jesse James Brown [II] - See Entry Page 164-165

Their (6) Children

Name	John Thomas Brown

My Family Tree

Date Of Birth	Thursday, April 24, 1941
Place Of Birth	Fulton Township, North Carolina – Davie County
Date Of Death	N/A
Age At Death	N/A
Place Of Death	N/A
Occupation	N/A
Married	N/A
Notes	

Name	Jesse James Brown III
Date Of Birth	Sunday, March 15, 1936
Place Of Birth	Fulton Township, North Carolina – Davie County
Date Of Death	N/A
Age At Death	N/A
Place Of Death	N/A
Occupation	N/A
Married	Geraldine Tatum Brown
Notes	Their children: Jessica Darlene Brown, Michael Arnelle Brown [I], Derrick Brown, Lucy Michelle Brown Jones, Lawrence Clayton, Cynthia Brown West, and Christopher Brown.

Name	Kenneth O. Brown
Date Of Birth	N/A
Place Of Birth	Fulton Township, North Carolina – Davie County
Date Of Death	N/A

My Family Tree

Age At Death	N/A
Place Of Death	Fulton Township, North Carolina – Davie County
Occupation	N/A
Married	N/A
Notes	

Name	**Betty B. Brown Goodwin**
Date Of Birth	Sunday, January 9, 1944
Place Of Birth	Fulton Township, North Carolina – Davie County
Date Of Death	N/A
Age At Death	N/A
Place Of Death	N/A
Occupation	N/A
Married	(1) Melvin Gaither (2) Widow
Notes	(1) Married on Saturday, June 3, 1961, in Fulton Township, North Carolina – Davie County. (1) His parents were Alice Gaither and Thomas A. Gaither.

Name	**Barbara B. Brown Williams**
Date Of Birth	Wednesday, September 1, 1943
Place Of Birth	Fulton Township, North Carolina – Davie County
Date Of Death	N/A
Age At Death	N/A
Place Of Death	N/A
Occupation	N/A

My Family Tree

Married	Widow
Notes	

Name	**Jettie Elizabeth Brown Williams Lindsay**
Date Of Birth	Monday, October 31, 1938
Place Of Birth	Fulton Township, North Carolina – Davie County
Date Of Death	Wednesday, June 18, 2008
Age At Death	69
Place Of Death	Fulton Township, North Carolina – Davie County
Occupation	Housewife
Married	(1) Widow (2) Harvey Boyd Lindsay
Notes	She was divorced in North Carolina and remarried on Saturday, September 21, 1974, in Winston-Salem, North Carolina – Forsyth County.

Name	**Harvey Boyd Lindsay**
Date Of Birth	Thursday, November 13, 1947
Place Of Birth	North Carolina – Guilford County
Date Of Death	N/A
Age At Death	N/A
Place Of Death	N/A
Occupation	N/A
Married	Jettie Elizabeth Brown Williams Lindsay
Notes	His parents were Levenia Moore Lindsay and Abram Lindsay.

Franklin L. Neely's name was listed in the United States Census Slave Schedule in the 1850s with 7 male slaves (ages ranging from 45 to 4) in North Carolina – Rowan County with George Neely and Henry Neely names listed as his slaves.

My Family Tree

The Family Line of Alsey Lyons Neely and George Neely

The Second Generation

Alsey Lyons Neely
George Neely

Their Child

Name	Henry Neely
Date Of Birth	October 1845
Place Of Birth	Winston Township City Ward 2, North Carolina – Forsyth County
Date Of Death	Thursday, February 9, 1922
Age At Death	76
Place Of Death	North Carolina – Davie County
Occupation	Farmer
Married	Elsie Hawkins Neely
Notes	He was born a slave. Elsie and Henry were illiterate in the 1910 Census. The Census indicated their marriage in 1869 in North Carolina – Forsyth County, a marriage of 31 years. He was buried on Saturday, February 11, 1922, at Piney Grove United Methodist Church Cemetery in Advance, North Carolina – Davie County. In the 1900 Census, they had four of their grandchildren living with them: Clarence Ellis, Zaddie Ellis, Henry Ellis, and Lunlu Hairston. The 1910 Census noted that their grandson Clarence was their servant.

Name	Elsie Hawkins Neely
Date Of Birth	March 1844
Place Of Birth	Virginia
Date Of Death	Friday, February 6, 1925
Age At Death	80
Place Of Death	Winston-Salem, North Carolina – Forsyth County
Occupation	Retired – Domestic Worker/Homemaker

My Family Tree

Married	Henry Neely
Notes	She was born a slave. She traveled from Virginia on a slave ship; her final destination was North Carolina. The 1910 Census noted that her first name was spelled Alicy or Alsey. She had 11 children, but only 7 survived, and she had a chance to see 3 of her children grow up after slavery ended. Her parents were Effie Lyons Hawkins and Richmond Hawkins. She was buried at Cedar Grove Baptist Church Cemetery, and her headstone has the wrong birth year.

Their (5) Children

The connection to the family line was Ella, the daughter of Ellen Jefferson Mason and Samuel M. Mason.

Cicero Clarence Neely [1] - See Entry Page 60
Ella M. Mason Neely - See Entry Page 59

Name	Effie Neely Mason
Date Of Birth	September 1893
Place Of Birth	North Carolina – Davie County
Date Of Death	Monday, April 5, 1937
Age At Death	43
Place Of Death	Winston-Salem, North Carolina – Forsyth County
Occupation	Domestic Worker/Homemaker
Married	Walter Mason
Notes	According to the 1910 Census, she was literate. She lived at 931 ½ Claremont Ave in Winston-Salem at the time of her death as a widow. She was buried on Sunday, April 11, 1937. Their daughters: Katie Mason (b. Saturday, February 24, 1906, – d. Thursday, December 14, 1933, age 27), buried Sunday, December 17, 1933, and Effie Mason (b. Friday, January 21, 1916 – d. Monday, July 2, 1917, age 1), buried Wednesday, July 4, 1917. Effie (mother), Katie, and Effie (daughter) were all buried at Piney Grove United Methodist Church Cemetery in Advance, North Carolina – Davie County. Their children were born and died in North Carolina – Davie County.

The connection to the family line was Walter, the son of Mary Jane Brown Mason and John Henry Mason. John Henry Mason and Lucinda Mason Mason were siblings.

My Family Tree

Name	Walter Mason
Date Of Birth	1875
Place Of Birth	North Carolina – Davie County
Date Of Death	Saturday, April 5, 1924
Age At Death	48 – 49
Place Of Death	Winston-Salem, North Carolina – Forsyth County
Occupation	R. J. Reynolds – Tobacco Industry – Shipping Department
Married	Effie Neely Mason
Notes	According to the 1900 Census, he was literate. His parents were Mary Jane Brown Mason and John Henry Mason. They lived at 1232 E. 11th Street in Winston-Salem, North Carolina – Forsyth County, until they died as homeowners. He was buried on Wednesday, April 9, 1924, at Cedar Grove Baptist Church Cemetery.

Name	George R. Neely
Date Of Birth	Thursday, October 27, 1881
Place Of Birth	Mocksville, North Carolina – Davie County
Date Of Death	Sunday, January 1, 1933
Age At Death	51
Place Of Death	Loveland, Ohio – Hamilton County
Occupation	Day Laborer
Married	Sallie May Farris Neely (b. Friday, November 18, 1892), POB. Kentucky
Notes	Married Thursday, June 22, 1922, in Warren, Ohio – Trumbull County. He was buried in January 1933 at Kerr Cemetery in Symmes Township, Ohio – Hamilton County. He was literate according to the 1910 Census.

Name	George Washington Neely
Date Of Birth	Friday, August 18, 1876

My Family Tree

Place Of Birth	Mocksville, North Carolina – Davie County
Date Of Death	Sunday, February 2, 1964
Age At Death	87
Place Of Death	Goldsboro, North Carolina – Wayne County
Occupation	Farmer
Married	Mary Ann Ijames Neely
Notes	In the 1930 Census, noted that Mary and George were able to read and write. He was buried on Tuesday, February 4, 1964, at Friendship Baptist Church Cemetery in Saluda, North Carolina – Polk County. Mary and George both lived at 1128 Oak Street in Mocksville at the time of their death; they were homeowners.

Name	**Mary Ann Ijames Neely**
Date Of Birth	Friday, September 28, 1877
Place Of Birth	Mocksville, North Carolina – Davie County
Date Of Death	Friday, September 7, 1984
Age At Death	106
Place Of Death	Mocksville, North Carolina – Davie County
Occupation	Housewife/Domestic Worker
Married	George Washington Neely
Notes	Married Thursday, January 28, 1897, in Mocksville, North Carolina – Davie County, and they were married for 67 years. The Census noted that Mary had 6 children, but only 5 survived. Their children: Joshua S. Neely, James K. Neely, Joseph Frank Neely, Beulah Irene Neely, Norman Eugene Neely, and William Odell Neely.

Name	**David L. Neely**
Date Of Birth	Thursday, March 15, 1883
Place Of Birth	Mocksville, North Carolina – Davie County

My Family Tree

Date Of Death	Saturday, January 7, 1967
Age At Death	83
Place Of Death	Fulton Township, North Carolina – Davie County
Occupation	Retired – R. J. Reynolds – Tobacco Industry – Worker
Married	Susan McIver Brown Neely
Notes	Susan and David were able to read and write and reported to the United States Federal Census on Thursday, April 10, 1930, in Winston-Salem, North Carolina – Forsyth County. He was buried on Sunday, January 15, 1967. Susan and David were both buried side-by-side at Cedar Grove Baptist Church Cemetery, and he was a widower when he died, a homeowner.

Name	**Susan McIver Brown Neely**
Date Of Birth	Saturday, May 20, 1882
Place Of Birth	Mocksville, North Carolina – Davie County
Date Of Death	Wednesday, February 10, 1954
Age At Death	71
Place Of Death	Mocksville, North Carolina – Davie County
Occupation	Housewife/Retired – R. J. Reynolds – Tobacco Industry – Worker
Married	David L. Neely
Notes	Married on Sunday, January 3, 1915, in Fulton, North Carolina – Forsyth County – a marriage of 39 years. Her parents were Priscilla Mason Brown (b. 1848) and Wyatt Brown (b. 1842). She was buried in February 1954.

The Family Line of Lucinda Mason Mason, Spencer Mason, Burrell T. Mason, Clayborn Mason, and Colwell Mason

The Second Generation

Name	**Lucinda Mason Mason**
Date Of Birth	Tuesday, January 16, 1855
Place Of Birth	Virginia

My Family Tree

Date Of Death	Wednesday, February 3, 1915
Age At Death	60
Place Of Death	Fulton Township, North Carolina – Davie County
Occupation	Farmer Laborer/Homemaker
Married	Colwell Mason
Notes	She was born a slave. She and her parents were forced to board a slave ship from Virginia going to North Carolina. According to the 1910 Census, she was illiterate. Lucinda had relations with four different Mason men who were Farmers and had children with them: Colwell Mason, Burrell T. Mason, Spencer Mason, and Clayborn Mason. Colwell Mason's father was G. G. Mason. The Census noted that Colwell and Burrell's first names were spelled differently – Colwell or Caldwell, Burrell or Burleson. She was a boarder at her son's (Sherlie) house until she died. She was buried on Thursday, February 4, 1915, at Cedar Grove Baptist Church Cemetery, and she was a widow when she died. Her parents were Sukie Turner Mason (Suckey) (b. 1820), occupation – housewife, and Burrell Mason (Burleson or Burwell) (b. 1812), occupation – Farmer Laborer. Her parents POD., Fulton Township, North Carolina – Davie County. Lucinda's father's second wife was Phyllis Ann Brown Hairston Mason, occupation – housewife. Her father's parents were Silla Bruce Mason and Robert Mason. Lucinda's son, Brachelor Kelly Mason, stated that his mother's mother was Phyllis Ann Brown Hairston Mason, but Lucinda's death record has Sukie Turner Mason (Suckey) as her mother.

Lucinda Mason Mason (8) Children

There is a large headstone at Cedar Grove Baptist Church Cemetery in Mocksville, North Carolina – Davie County, with a listing of all Lucinda's children.

John Henry Mason - See Entry Page 156
Nancy Jane Crump Mason - See Entry Page 155-156

Name	William B. Mason I
Date Of Birth	1881
Place Of Birth	Mocksville, North Carolina – Davie County
Date Of Death	Wednesday, December 13, 1939

My Family Tree

Age At Death	57 – 58
Place Of Death	Concord, North Carolina – Cabarrus County
Occupation	Janitor
Married	(1) Emerline Hairston Mason (2) Fannie Hargraves Mason
Notes	His father was Burrell T. Mason. He was buried on Sunday, December 17, 1939. Emerline and William were both buried side-by-side at Cedar Grove Baptist Church Cemetery.

Name	**Emerline Hairston Mason**
Date Of Birth	1863
Place Of Birth	Mocksville, North Carolina – Davie County
Date Of Death	Saturday, August 8, 1914
Age At Death	50-51
Place Of Death	Salisbury Township, North Carolina – Rowan County
Occupation	Domestic Worker/Homemaker
Married	William B. Mason [I]
Notes	She was born into slavery. Her nickname was "Emma." She was buried on Monday, August 10, 1914. Her headstone has the wrong day she died. Her parents were Nancy Hairston and Frank Hairston, who were slaves. Their children: Emerline Wachovia Mason Hawkins and William B. Mason [II].

Name	**Fannie Hargraves Mason**
Date Of Birth	Sunday, December 14, 1873
Place Of Birth	Lexington, North Carolina – Davidson County
Date Of Death	Wednesday, January 6, 1965
Age At Death	91
Place Of Death	Greensboro, North Carolina – Guilford County

My Family Tree

Occupation	Retired – Domestic Worker/Homemaker
Married	William B. Mason [1]
Notes	She was buried Saturday, January 9, 1965, at Piedmont Memorial Park Cemetery in Greensboro, North Carolina – Guilford County, a widow, but her body was not there. Her parents were Laura J. Hargraves and Henry M. Hargraves.

Name	**Sherlie H. Mason**
Date Of Birth	1886
Place Of Birth	Mocksville, North Carolina – Davie County
Date Of Death	Saturday, November 24, 1945
Age At Death	58-59
Place Of Death	Winston-Salem, North Carolina – Forsyth County
Occupation	Farmer/Pastor/Storekeeper/Colonel
Married	Cora Perrell Mason
Notes	According to the 1910 Census, his name was spelled Sherly, but in later Census records, his name was spelled in various ways: Sherlie, Sherley, Sherly, or Shirley. He served in the United States Army during WWI from (1917 –1918) as a Colonel and was honorably discharged. His death certificate listed his father as unknown, but the elders of the family stated that Spencer Mason was his father. He was buried on Tuesday, November 27, 1945. Cora and Sherlie were both buried at Cedar Grove Baptist Church Cemetery. Cora and Sherlie lived at 1523 1/2 Garfield Street in Winston-Salem when they died; they were homeowners, and he was a widower when he died.

Name	**Cora Perrell Mason**
Date Of Birth	1884
Place Of Birth	North Carolina
Date Of Death	Wednesday, January 6, 1932
Age At Death	47-48

My Family Tree

Place Of Death	Fulton Township, North Carolina – Davie County
Occupation	Housekeeper/Homemaker
Married	Sherlie H. Mason
Notes	Married on Saturday, December 10, 1904, in Winston Township, North Carolina – Forsyth County – married for 28 years. Her parents were Ellen Thompson Perrell and Jacob Perrie Perrell. Cora and Sherlie, according to the 1900 Census, noted that they both were literate. She was buried on Saturday, January 9, 1932. Their children: Buxton F. Mason, Lucille Mason Hamilton, and Thelma Mason.

Name	**Fisher Robert Mason**
Date Of Birth	Tuesday, September 9, 1878
Place Of Birth	Fork, North Carolina – Davie County
Date Of Death	Tuesday, November 23, 1965
Age At Death	87
Place Of Death	High Point, North Carolina – Guilford County
Occupation	Minister/Retired – Principal
Married	Fannie M. Bryant Mason
Notes	He held a Draft Registration Card from the United States Army during WWI (1917-1918). He began preaching in 1898 in North Carolina. He served as principal of the city's grade school from 1908 until 1912. Editor A. B. Caldwell wrote about him in his book, "History of the American Negro and his Institutes," Volume IV, in 1921. It was documented on his death certificate that his father's name was Colwell Mason, but in the interview by A. B. Caldwell, it was stated that his father was Spencer Mason. He was buried on Friday, November 26, 1965, as a widower. Fannie and Fisher's death records had their final resting place at Cedar Grove Baptist Church Cemetery. Fannie, Everett, Lillie, and Fisher were all buried at Oakdale Union Hill Cemetery in Salisbury, North Carolina – Rowan County. Mr. Mason has an obituary that talks about his life.

Name	**Fannie M. Bryant Mason**
Date Of Birth	Saturday, September 27, 1884

My Family Tree

Place Of Birth	Salisbury, North Carolina – Rowan County
Date Of Death	Saturday, June 20, 1959
Age At Death	74
Place Of Death	Trinity, North Carolina – Randolph County
Occupation	Retired – Domestic Worker/Housewife
Married	Fisher Robert Mason
Notes	Married on Wednesday, May 18, 1904, in North Carolina – Davie County, and they had been married for 55 years. She was buried on Wednesday, June 24, 1959. Fannie and Fisher both lived at 531 Radford in High Point at the time of their death; they were homeowners. Her parents were Elizabeth "Bettye" Meroney Bryant and Rev. William H. Bryant. Their children: Everett H. Mason, Lillie Mae Mason Davis, and Frank Edward Bryant Mason II (b. Thursday, March 4, 1920 – d. Wednesday, April 10, 1996, age 76), occupation – Barber. Frank's wife – Gladys Beatrice Haith Mason – (b. 1922 – d. 1997, age 74–75), occupation – Housewife. The 1930 Census indicated that they had 5 boarders living with them.

Name	**Mary Mason Doulin**
Date Of Birth	March 1876
Place Of Birth	Fulton Township, North Carolina – Davie County
Date Of Death	Unknown
Age At Death	Unknown
Place Of Death	Fulton Township, North Carolina – Davie County
Occupation	Housewife/Domestic Worker
Married	Robert Doulin
Notes	According to the 1880 Census, she was illiterate. They got married on Sunday, August 13, 1893, in North Carolina – Davie County, and they had been married for 7 years. The Census noted that she had five children, with three surviving. Mary could read but could not write, and Robert was able to read and write. According to the 1900 Census, their last name was spelled Dulin. Mary's death certificate listed her father as unknown. Their children: Martha Doulin Wallace, John Thomas Doulin I, Fisher S. Doulin, and Mosella Doulin Neely Grant.

My Family Tree

Name	Robert Doulin
Date Of Birth	June 1870
Place Of Birth	Fulton Township, North Carolina – Davie County
Date Of Death	Friday, November 8, 1940
Age At Death	70
Place Of Death	Fulton Township, North Carolina – Davie County
Occupation	Day Laborer
Married	(1) Mary Mason Doulin (2) Lucy B. Steele Doulin
Notes	(1) Married on Sunday, August 13, 1893. (2) Married on Thursday, July 10, 1919, both marriages took place in North Carolina. Lucy B. Steele Doulin was born on Wednesday, June 15, 1870, in North Carolina and died on Wednesday, June 20, 1951, in Fulton Township, North Carolina – Davie County (age 81). Robert was buried in November 1940 at Second Presbyterian Church Cemetery in Mocksville, North Carolina – Davie County. His parents were Laura Law Doulin, born April 1845 in Virginia, who died Monday, February 5, 1934, in Mocksville, North Carolina – Davie County (age 88) and was buried in February 1934, at Smith Grove AME Zion Church Cemetery in Smith Grove, North Carolina – Davie County, and Frederick Doulin. Census records indicated that Laura and Frederick were married for over 35 years. Laura's father was Robert Law.

Name	Penix M. Mason
Date Of Birth	1869
Place Of Birth	Fulton Township, North Carolina – Davie County
Date Of Death	Unknown
Age At Death	Unknown
Place Of Death	Gideon Grove, North Carolina – Davie County
Occupation	Day Laborer
Married	Cora Patterson Mason (born 1873)

My Family Tree

Notes	According to the 1920 Census, he was illiterate, with the spelling of his name as Pinnix. Married on Thursday, December 18, 1890, in Gideon Grove, North Carolina – Davie County. Their sons, James H. Mason, was born on Friday, November 20, 1908, and died on Saturday, November 20, 1909 (age 1). James was buried on Monday, November 22, 1909; he lived at 773 Wash Street in Cincinnati until he died. Jasper Mason was born on Monday, February 10, 1902, and died on Friday, May 8, 1925 (age 22). Jasper was buried on Tuesday, May 12, 1925. James and Jasper were both buried, at Union Baptist Cemetery in Cincinnati, Ohio – Hamilton County, occupation – Day Laborer. Jasper lived at 1025 Mount in Cincinnati until he died. Both of their sons were born and died in Cincinnati, Ohio – Hamilton County.

Name	**Brachelor Kelly Mason**
Date Of Birth	Friday, September 2, 1881
Place Of Birth	Fulton Township, North Carolina – Davie County
Date Of Death	Saturday, March 16, 1968
Age At Death	86
Place Of Death	Charlotte, North Carolina – Mecklenburg County
Occupation	Minister
Married	Marie Antoinette Alston Mason
Notes	His father's name was Colwell Mason. His parents were born slaves. In the Census, his middle name was documented as his first name. He graduated in Theology in 1911 and 1914, holding two degrees – Bachelor of Theology and Bachelor of Arts from Shaw University. Editor A. B. Caldwell wrote about him in his book titled "History of the American Negro and his Institutes," Volume IV, in 1921. He was buried on Wednesday, March 20, 1968. Marie and Brachelor were both supposed to be buried at Cedar Grove Baptist Church Cemetery, but they were both buried at York Memorial Park Cemetery in Charlotte, North Carolina – Mecklenburg County. He was a widower when he died. Mr. Mason has an obituary that talks about his life.

Name	**Marie Antoinette Alston Mason**
Date Of Birth	Wednesday, August 15, 1888

My Family Tree

Place Of Birth	Weldon, North Carolina – Halifax County
Date Of Death	Saturday, July 16, 1949
Age At Death	60
Place Of Death	Charlotte, North Carolina – Mecklenburg County
Occupation	School Teacher/Housewife
Married	Brachelor Kelly Mason
Notes	Married on Thursday, October 9, 1913, in Charlotte, North Carolina – Mecklenburg County – a marriage of 36 years. She was educated at Hartshorn College in Richmond, Virginia. She was buried on Tuesday, July 19, 1949. Her parents were Olivia Mills Alston and Jake Jacob Alston. Their child: William T. Mason.

Name	Estella Novella Mason Williams
Date Of Birth	Thursday, February 28, 1884
Place Of Birth	Mocksville, North Carolina – Davie County
Date Of Death	Monday, June 8, 1931
Age At Death	47
Place Of Death	Jerusalem, North Carolina – Davie County
Occupation	Domestic Worker/Housewife
Married	George Rufus Williams
Notes	According to the 1890 Census, she was illiterate. Her father was Clayborn Mason. She was supposed to be buried on Tuesday, June 9, 1931, at Cedar Grove Baptist Church Cemetery, but her body was not there. Their children: Celestia Williams (b. Saturday, June 26, 1915, and – d. Sunday, June 10, 1917, age 1), buried June 1917, at Cedar Grove Baptist Church Cemetery, Otis Livingston Williams (b. Saturday, April 26, 1913, and – d. Wednesday, March 27, 2002, age 88), Lawrence O'Neal Williams (b. Thursday, May 18, 1911, and – d. Monday, February 4, 2002, age 90), buried February 2002. Lawrence, his parents – Estella and George – were all buried at Bethel Baptist Church Cemetery in Mocksville, North Carolina – Davie County. Estella and George were both buried side-by-side there. Lawrence's wife – Maria Price Williams (b. 1918, and – d. 1940, age 21–22). Maria and Lawrence were married on Tuesday,

My Family Tree

	November 27, 1934, in North Carolina. Jasper Mason Williams (b. Tuesday, June 12, 1917, and – d. Monday, July 10, 1989, age 72) and Pennix Marshall Williams (b. Thursday, September 7, 1905, and – d. Wednesday, October 29, 1975, age 70), POD. Asheboro, North Carolina – Randolph County. Pennix was buried in November 1975. Pennix's wife – Mamie Suggs Williams (b. 1909, and – d. 1992, age 82–83). Mamie and Pennix were both buried side-by-side at Mount Calvary Cemetery in Asheboro, North Carolina – Randolph County. Estella and George's children were born and died in Mocksville, North Carolina – Davie County.

Name	George Rufus Williams
Date Of Birth	Wednesday, February 9, 1881
Place Of Birth	Mocksville, North Carolina – Davie County
Date Of Death	Tuesday, October 27, 1953
Age At Death	72
Place Of Death	Mocksville, North Carolina – Davie County
Occupation	Day Laborer
Married	Estella Novella Mason Williams
Notes	

The Family Line of Elizabeth O. Winford Mason and Dennis De Quincy Mason [1]

The connection to the family line was Dennis [1], the son of Nancy Jane Crump Mason and John Henry Mason.

The Fourth Generation

Elizabeth O. Winford Mason - See Entry Page 158
Dennis De Quincy Mason [1] - See Entry Page 157-158

Their (12) Children

Name	Lula Senie Mae Mason Clement
Date Of Birth	Saturday, April 21, 1923
Place Of Birth	Fulton Township, North Carolina – Davie County

My Family Tree

Date Of Death	Wednesday, November 5, 1986
Age At Death	63
Place Of Death	Mocksville, North Carolina – Davie County
Occupation	Machine Operator/Housewife
Married	George Washington Clement [I]
Notes	Their child: George Washington Clement [II]. She was buried on Sunday, November 9, 1986.

Name	**George Washington Clement I**
Date Of Birth	Tuesday, February 22, 1921
Place Of Birth	Calahaln Township, North Carolina – Davie County
Date Of Death	Friday, August 24, 2012
Age At Death	91
Place Of Death	Mocksville, North Carolina – Davie County
Occupation	Machine Operator
Married	Lula Senie Mae Mason Clement
Notes	Married Saturday, August 16, 1941, in North Carolina – Davie County, married for 45 years. His parents were Ada C. Pate Clement and John Wesley Clement born Friday, January 15, 1847, died Monday, January 1, 1940 (age 92). John was buried in January 1940 at Clement Family Cemetery in Mocksville, North Carolina – Davie County. His parents were married on Sunday, February 11, 1917, in North Carolina – Davie County, married for 23 years. George's brother, William Edward Clement, born Sunday, March 24, 1918, died Sunday, November 6, 1994 (age 76), and William's wife – Beathric C. Clement, born in 1923 and died in 2006 (age 82 – 83). William was buried in November 1994, and George was buried in August 2012. Lula, George, Beathric, and William were all buried side-by-side at Cedar Grove Baptist Church Cemetery.

Name	**Baxter Sherman Mason**
Date Of Birth	Tuesday, July 27, 1920

My Family Tree

Place Of Birth	Mocksville, North Carolina – Davie County
Date Of Death	Sunday, August 15, 1971
Age At Death	51
Place Of Death	North Carolina – Davie County
Occupation	Minister
Married	Edna Elizabeth Ijames Mason Allen
Notes	He was buried on Wednesday, August 18, 1971.

Name	**Edna Elizabeth Ijames Mason Allen**
Date Of Birth	Thursday, June 6, 1918
Place Of Birth	Mocksville, North Carolina – Davie County
Date Of Death	Tuesday, April 21, 2020
Age At Death	101
Place Of Death	Greensboro, North Carolina – Guilford County
Occupation	Housewife/Member of the Eagle Network and Local NAACP
Married	(1) Baxter Sherman Mason (2) Ralph Q. Allen
Notes	(1) Married on Thursday, July 13, 1939, in North Carolina – Davie County, married for 32 years. (2) Married in 1981 in North Carolina – Davie County. She was buried on Sunday, April 26, 2020. Edna and Baxter were both buried at Cedar Grove Baptist Church Cemetery. Her parents were Columbia Veatrice Sturdevant Ijames, born Tuesday, November 20, 1883, in North Carolina – Davie County, died Sunday, April 20, 1958, in Mocksville, North Carolina – Davie County (age 74), and John Alexander Ijames, born Saturday, February 2, 1884, died Thursday, September 22, 1955 (age 71). Edna's parents were married in 1910 in North Carolina and married for 45 years. John was buried Sunday, September 25, 1955, at Clement Grove Church in Mocksville, North Carolina – Davie County. Her grandparents were Angeline Gaither Sturdevant, Asberry Sturdevant, Alice Holman Ijames (born 1860), and Rev. John Wesley Ijames, born in 1862 and died in 1916 (age 53–54). Her children with Baxter: William Sherman Mason,

My Family Tree

	Sylvester Mason (who died at birth), and Columbia DeAnn Mason Stanton (William Ernest Stanton). She has an obituary that talks about her life.

Name	**Dennis De Quincy Mason II**
Date Of Birth	Thursday, June 4, 1925
Place Of Birth	Fulton Township, North Carolina – Davie County
Date Of Death	Sunday, April 25, 2004
Age At Death	78
Place Of Death	Greensboro, North Carolina – Guilford County
Occupation	Retired – Private Cook
Married	Nannie E. Sullivan Mason
Notes	

Name	**Nannie E. Sullivan Mason**
Date Of Birth	Tuesday, April 27, 1926
Place Of Birth	Greenville, South Carolina – Greenville County
Date Of Death	Saturday, March 19, 2011
Age At Death	84
Place Of Death	Greensboro, North Carolina – Guilford County
Occupation	Retired – Domestic Worker/Housewife
Married	Dennis De Quincy Mason II
Notes	Married on Thursday, October 12, 1950, in North Carolina, a marriage of 54 years. She was buried Thursday, March 24, 2011, in Greensboro, North Carolina – Guilford County, a widow. Her parents were Nannie Sullivan and Edward Sullivan. Their children: Dequenay R. Mason, Lucille V. Mason, Dene R. Mason, Valerie Mason Cunningham (Eric Cunningham), Lori Mason Norman (Daniel Norman), and Gail Mason Robinson. Their children were born in Fulton Township, North Carolina – Davie County.

My Family Tree

Name	**Mary Elizabeth Mason Booe**
Date Of Birth	Friday, November 8, 1918
Place Of Birth	Fulton Township, North Carolina – Davie County
Date Of Death	Thursday, December 30, 1993
Age At Death	75
Place Of Death	Inwood, Long Island, New York – Nassau County
Occupation	Beautician
Married	Widowed
Notes	She always went by her middle name. Her level of education was the 11th grade. She was buried in January 1994 at Carolina Biblical Gardens Cemetery in Jamestown, North Carolina – Guilford County, and she was a widow when she died.

Name	**Marie Mason Jones**
Date Of Birth	1927
Place Of Birth	Fulton Township, North Carolina – Davie County
Date Of Death	Unknown
Age At Death	Unknown
Place Of Death	Unknown
Occupation	Unknown
Married	Widow
Notes	

Name	**Clydie Mae Mason McQueen**
Date Of Birth	Friday, March 7, 1930
Place Of Birth	Fulton Township, North Carolina – Davie County

My Family Tree

Date Of Death	Wednesday, February 21, 2007
Age At Death	76
Place Of Death	High Point, North Carolina – Guilford County
Occupation	Housewife
Married	Kinney M. McQueen [II] (b. 1931)
Notes	Married on Saturday, August 11, 1956, in Guilford, North Carolina – Davie County, married for 7 years. They got divorced on Monday, September 16, 1963, in North Carolina – Guilford County. His parents were Estee McQueen and Kinney M. McQueen [I]. Their child: Sylvia Mae McQueen (b. Friday, March 29, 1957), POB. High Point, North Carolina – Guilford County.

Name	**James Mason**
Date Of Birth	Friday, April 15, 1932
Place Of Birth	Fulton Township, North Carolina – Davie County
Date Of Death	N/A
Age At Death	N/A
Place Of Death	N/A
Occupation	N/A
Married	N/A
Notes	His twin brother is John.

Name	**John Mason**
Date Of Birth	Friday, April 15, 1932
Place Of Birth	Fulton Township, North Carolina – Davie County
Date Of Death	N/A
Age At Death	N/A

My Family Tree

Place Of Death	N/A
Occupation	N/A
Married	N/A
Notes	His twin brother is James.

Name	**Virginia Mae Mason Watson**
Date Of Birth	Sunday, December 24, 1933
Place Of Birth	Fulton Township, North Carolina – Davie County
Date Of Death	Saturday, July 27, 1996
Age At Death	62
Place Of Death	Winston-Salem, North Carolina – Forsyth County
Occupation	Housewife
Married	John Thomas Watson
Notes	She was buried in July 1996 as a widow. Virginia and John were both buried side-by-side at Guilford Memorial Park in Greensboro, North Carolina – Guilford County.

Name	**John Thomas Watson**
Date Of Birth	Thursday, January 22, 1925
Place Of Birth	South Carolina – Laurens County
Date Of Death	Sunday, March 17, 1996
Age At Death	71
Place Of Death	High Point, North Carolina – Guilford County
Occupation	Retired – United States Army SSG
Married	Virginia Mae Mason Watson

My Family Tree

Notes	He served in the United States Army during the Korean War and was honorably discharged. He was buried in March 1996.

Name	**Gennellia Mason Hunter**
Date Of Birth	Tuesday, September 1, 1936
Place Of Birth	Fulton Township, North Carolina – Davie County
Date Of Death	Thursday, April 6, 2006
Age At Death	69
Place Of Death	Guilford, North Carolina – Guilford County
Occupation	Housewife
Married	Robert L. Hunter (b. Monday, July 22, 1935)
Notes	Married on Friday, October 26, 1956, in Guilford, North Carolina – Guilford County. His parents were Zeffie Crawford Hunter (b. Saturday, January 23, 1904, and – d. Friday, September 15, 2000, age 96) and Frank William Hunter (b. Monday, May 5, 1902, and – d. Friday, August 26, 1988, age 86). Zeffie was a widow when she died.

Name	**Rebecca Mason**
Date Of Birth	Saturday, April 8, 1939
Place Of Birth	Fulton Township, North Carolina – Davie County
Date Of Death	N/A
Age At Death	N/A
Place Of Death	N/A
Occupation	N/A
Married	N/A
Notes	Her twin was Wyvonnia.

My Family Tree

Name	**Wyvonnia M. Mason Ables**
Date Of Birth	Saturday, April 8, 1939
Place Of Birth	Fulton Township, North Carolina – Davie County
Date Of Death	Sunday, April 27, 2008
Age At Death	69
Place Of Death	High Point, North Carolina – Davie County
Occupation	Director of City Hall of High Point
Married	Eddie Lee Ables [I]
Notes	Her twin was Rebecca. She was buried Wednesday, April 30, 2008, as a widow. Wyvonnia and Eddie [I] were both buried at Carolina Biblical Gardens Cemetery in Jamestown, North Carolina – Guilford County; both of their bodies were not buried there. Their children: Demetrius L. Ables, Edith E. Ables McLeod, and Eddie L. Ables [II].

Name	**Eddie Lee Ables I**
Date Of Birth	Tuesday, January 25, 1938
Place Of Birth	Wagener, South Carolina – Aiken County
Date Of Death	Saturday, September 5, 2009
Age At Death	71
Place Of Death	High Point, North Carolina – Guilford County
Occupation	General Manager/Chief Director/City Councilman
Married	Wyvonnia M. Mason Ables
Notes	Married on Friday, February 9, 1962, in North Carolina, a marriage of 46 years. He was buried on Thursday, September 10, 2009. His parents were Rilla Ables and McQueene Ables.

The Family Line of Edna Elizabeth Ijames Mason Allen and Baxter Sherman Mason

The connection to the family line was Baxter, the son of Elizabeth O. Winford Mason and Dennis De Quincy Mason [I].

My Family Tree

The Fifth Generation

Edna Elizabeth Ijames Mason Allen - See Entry Page 189-190
Baxter Sherman Mason - See Entry Page 188-189

Their (3) Children

Name	**William Sherman Mason**
Date Of Birth	Friday, July 24, 1942
Place Of Birth	Fulton, North Carolina – Davie County
Date Of Death	N/A
Age At Death	N/A
Place Of Death	N/A
Occupation	N/A
Married	N/A
Notes	

Name	**Columbia DeAnn Mason Stanton**
Date Of Birth	Sunday, October 22, 1944
Place Of Birth	Lexington, North Carolina – Davidson County
Date Of Death	N/A
Age At Death	N/A
Place Of Death	N/A
Occupation	N/A
Married	William Ernest Stanton (b. 1947)
Notes	Married Sunday, June 30, 1968 in North Carolina – Davie County.

Name	**Sylvester Mason**

My Family Tree

Date Of Birth	Monday, May 20, 1940
Place Of Birth	Calahaln, North Carolina – Davie County
Date Of Death	Monday, May 20, 1940
Age At Death	0
Place Of Death	Calahaln, North Carolina – Davie County
Occupation	None
Married	Single
Notes	

The Family Line of Bettie Hairston Mason and Ennis Mason

The connection to the family line was Ennis, the son of Isabelle Dubose Mason and Robert Mason.

The Fourth Generation

Bettie Hairston Mason - See Entry Page 54
Ennis Mason - See Entry Page 54

Their (2) Children

Name	**Ida Mary Mason Carter**
Date Of Birth	Friday, August 26, 1881
Place Of Birth	Fulton Township, North Carolina – Davie County
Date Of Death	Monday, July 20, 1914
Age At Death	32
Place Of Death	Fulton Township, North Carolina – Davie County
Occupation	Domestic Worker
Married	Lueco G. Carter
Notes	According to the 1900 Census, she was literate. She was buried on Monday, July 13, 1914; her headstone has her mother's maiden name instead of Mason as her maiden name.

My Family Tree

Name	Lueco G. Carter
Date Of Birth	Friday, December 25, 1874
Place Of Birth	North Carolina
Date Of Death	Friday, July 4, 1930
Age At Death	55
Place Of Death	Fulton Township, North Carolina – Davie County
Occupation	Farmer
Married	Ida Mary Mason Carter
Notes	Married on Saturday, September 22, 1894, a marriage of 20 years. He held a Draft Registration Card from the United States Army during WWI on Wednesday, September 19, 1917. He was buried on Tuesday, July 8, 1930, a widower. His parents were Amanda Clement Carter (b. May 1850, and – d. Monday, November 5, 1928, age 78) and Warren L. Carter (b. 1846 – d. 1916, age 69 – 70), buried at Oakdale Union Hill in Salisbury, North Carolina – Rowan County. Ida, Amanda, and Lueco were all buried at Cedar Grove Baptist Church Cemetery. His parents were married on Saturday, September 21, 1872, a marriage of 44 years.

Jettie Ann Hairston Mason Brown - See Entry Page 161-162
Jesse James Brown [I] - See Entry Page 162

The Family Line of Emerline Hairston Mason and William B. Mason [I]

The connection to the family line was William, the son of Lucinda Mason Mason and Burrell T. Mason.

The Third Generation

Emerline Hairston Mason - See Entry Page 180
William B. Mason [I] - See Entry Page 179-180

Their (2) Children

Name	William B. Mason II
Date Of Birth	1874
Place Of Birth	Mocksville, North Carolina – Davie County
Date Of Death	Sunday, April 30, 1916

My Family Tree

Age At Death	41-42
Place Of Death	Salisbury Township, North Carolina – Rowan County
Occupation	Hotel Waiter
Married	Ola Winford Mason
Notes	He was a widower when he died. He was buried on Tuesday, May 2, 1916, at Cedar Grove Baptist Church Cemetery, but his body was not there. Married on Tuesday, February 7, 1905, in Winston Township, North Carolina – Davie County. Ola was of Native-American descent. Her adoptive parents were Adelia "Delia" Hairston (b. Tuesday, June 12, 1860, and – d. Wednesday, May 19, 1926, age 65) and Sabe Hairston (b. 1853, and – d. Monday, November 5, 1928, age 74 –75), who was buried on Sunday, November 11, 1928. Sabe's parents were Louisa Hairston and Bush Hairston. Ola's parents' place of birth and place of death was North Carolina – Davie County. Adelia and Sabe were both buried at Cedar Grove Baptist Church Cemetery.

Name	**Emerline Wachovia Mason Hawkins**
Date Of Birth	Thursday, December 2, 1897
Place Of Birth	Mocksville, North Carolina – Davie County
Date Of Death	Tuesday, August 6, 1968
Age At Death	70
Place Of Death	Concord, North Carolina – Cabarrus County
Occupation	School Teacher
Married	Henderson Hulbert Hawkins
Notes	She was buried on Thursday, August 8, 1968. Their children: James William Hawkins II (b. 1914, and – d. 1984, age 69-70), Samuel Maye Hawkins (b. 1922, and – d. 1991, age 68 – 69), and Florence Hawkins Cofield (b. 1925, and – d. 1958, age 32 – 33). Their children were born and died in North Carolina.

Name	**Henderson Hulbert Hawkins**
Date Of Birth	Sunday, April 17, 1892

My Family Tree

Place Of Birth	Mocksville, North Carolina – Davie County
Date Of Death	Tuesday, September 3, 1974
Age At Death	82
Place Of Death	Salisbury Township, North Carolina – Rowan County
Occupation	Minister
Married	Emerline Wachovia Mason Hawkins
Notes	He was buried in September 1974, a widower. Emerline and Henderson were both buried side-by-side at St. Luke Baptist Church Memorials in Salisbury, North Carolina – Rowan County. They lived at 57 Chestnut Street in S.W. Concord at the time of their death, homeowners. His parents were Elizabeth "Bettie" Clingman Hawkins (b. 1858 – d. 1917, age 58–59) and James William Hawkins [1] (b. 1848 – d. 1898, age 49–50). Henderson's parents were slaves, and they were married Thursday, April 10, 1879, in North Carolina – Forsyth County, married for 38 years.

The Family Line of Wyvonnia M. Mason Ables and Eddie Lee Ables [1]

The connection to the family line was Wyvonnia, the daughter of Elizabeth O. Winford Mason and Dennis De Quincy Mason [1].

The Fifth Generation

Wyvonnia M. Mason Ables - See Entry Page 195
Eddie Lee Ables [1] - See Entry Page 195

Their (3) Children

Name	**Demetrius Lee Ables**
Date Of Birth	Monday, April 15, 1968
Place Of Birth	Fulton Township, North Carolina – Guilford County
Date Of Death	N/A
Age At Death	N/A
Place Of Death	N/A
Occupation	N/A
Married	N/A

My Family Tree

Notes	

Name	**Edith Elaine Ables McLeod**
Date Of Birth	Saturday, April 7, 1973
Place Of Birth	Fulton Township, North Carolina – Guilford County
Date Of Death	N/A
Age At Death	N/A
Place Of Death	N/A
Occupation	N/A
Married	Darrell McLeod
Notes	Her twin brother is Eddie [II]. Their children: Nyema McLeod and Ernest McLeod.

Name	**Eddie Ables II**
Date Of Birth	Saturday, April 7, 1973
Place Of Birth	Fulton Township, North Carolina – Guilford County
Date Of Death	N/A
Age At Death	N/A
Place Of Death	N/A
Occupation	N/A
Married	N/A
Notes	His twin sister is Edith.

The Family Line of Brownie Younger Bassett and Daniel Benjamin Bassett [I]

The connection to the family line was Brownie, the daughter of Henrietta Hatchett Cunningham Younger and Henderson Younger.

The Fourth Generation

My Family Tree

Brownie Younger Bassett   -   See Entry Page 49
Daniel Benjamin Bassett [1]   -   See Entry Page 49-50

Their (5) Children

Name	Helen W. Bassett
Date Of Birth	Wednesday, August 9, 1922
Place Of Birth	Winston-Salem, North Carolina – Forsyth County
Date Of Death	February 1984
Age At Death	61
Place Of Death	Winston-Salem, North Carolina – Forsyth County
Occupation	Unknown
Married	Unknown
Notes	

Name	Walter A. Bassett
Date Of Birth	Tuesday, March 19, 1929
Place Of Birth	Winston-Salem, North Carolina – Forsyth County
Date Of Death	Saturday, August 24, 1929
Age At Death	5 Months Old
Place Of Death	Winston-Salem, North Carolina – Forsyth County
Occupation	None
Married	Single
Notes	He was buried on Saturday, August 24, 1929.

Name	Golden F. Bassett Wall
Date Of Birth	Tuesday, October 25, 1921

My Family Tree

Place Of Birth	Winston-Salem, North Carolina – Forsyth County
Date Of Death	Sunday, February 5, 2006
Age At Death	84
Place Of Death	Winston-Salem, North Carolina – Forsyth County
Occupation	Retired – School Teacher – PhD
Married	(1) Ephraim Coleman Byrd (2) Grover Cleveland Wall
Notes	She was buried on Thursday, February 9, 2006, in Winston-Salem, North Carolina – Forsyth County. Mrs. Wall has an obituary that talks about her life. (1) Married on Saturday, February 10, 1940, in Henry County, Virginia. (1) b. Wednesday, May 8, 1918, POB. South Carolina – Darlington County – d. Wednesday, September 11, 1954, age 36), POD. Winston-Salem, North Carolina – Forsyth County. (1) He was buried in September 1954 at Evergreen Cemetery. (1) His parents were Ada Coleman Byrd and William Byrd. (1) He served in WWII.

Name	Grover Cleveland Wall
Date Of Birth	Monday, November 17, 1919
Place Of Birth	Pembroke, North Carolina – Forsyth County
Date Of Death	Thursday, February 23, 2006
Age At Death	86
Place Of Death	Winston-Salem, North Carolina – Forsyth County
Occupation	Barbershop Owner
Married	Golden F. Bassett Wall
Notes	Married on Monday, October 13, 1952, in Winston-Salem, North Carolina – Forsyth County, a marriage of 53 years. His parents were Flossie Wall and Lawrence Wall. They had no children together – his son was Earnest Wall.

Name	Daniel Benjamin Bassett II
Date Of Birth	Tuesday, December 16, 1924

My Family Tree

Place Of Birth	Winston-Salem, North Carolina – Forsyth County
Date Of Death	October 1981
Age At Death	56
Place Of Death	Oskaloosa, Iowa – Mahaska County
Occupation	Firefighter
Married	Betty Jane Gilbert Bassett
Notes	Their daughters: Angela E. Bassett Vance and D'nette B. Bassett.

Name	**Betty Jane Gilbert Bassett**
Date Of Birth	Saturday, August 3, 1935
Place Of Birth	Saint Petersburg, Florida – Pinellas County
Date Of Death	Saturday, June 22, 2014
Age At Death	78
Place Of Death	Saint Petersburg, Florida – Pinellas County
Occupation	Retired – Social Worker
Married	Daniel Benjamin Bassett II
Notes	Married on Wednesday, June 24, 1959, and divorced on Thursday, April 29, 1971, in Florida – Pinellas County after 12 years of marriage. Her parents were Emma Jean Stokes Gilbert and LeRoy Gilbert. Her grandparents were Minnie Lee Jackson Stokes (b. Saturday, December 16, 1893 – d. Saturday, October 1, 1977, age 83) and Slater Samuel Stokes (b. Saturday, April 1, 1893 – d. Thursday, January 3, 1980, age 86).

Name	**Jethro Benjamin Bassett**
Date Of Birth	Thursday, September 30, 1926
Place Of Birth	Winston-Salem, North Carolina – Forsyth County
Date Of Death	Thursday, April 7, 2013

My Family Tree

Age At Death	86
Place Of Death	Fayetteville, North Carolina – Cumberland County
Occupation	Day Laborer
Married	Vera Mae McDaniel Bassett
Notes	His stepdaughter: Cheryl Vernette McDaniel. Grandson: LaQuan Hampton. His nickname was "Jerry." He was buried on Monday, April 11, 2013, at Hillside Memorial Park Cemetery in Laurinburg, North Carolina – Scotland County, but his body was not buried there.

The Family Line of Emma Jean Stokes Gilbert and LeRoy Gilbert

The Fourth Generation

Name	**Emma Jean Stokes Gilbert**
Date Of Birth	Thursday, March 22, 1917
Place Of Birth	Quitman, Georgia – Brooks County
Date Of Death	Tuesday, June 3, 2003
Age At Death	86
Place Of Death	Saint Petersburg, Florida – Pinellas County
Occupation	Housewife
Married	Leroy Gilbert
Notes	Her parents were Minnie Lee Jackson Stokes and Slater Samuel Stokes. Her grandparents were Emily Stokes and Henry Stokes.

Name	**Leroy Gilbert**
Date Of Birth	Thursday, May 23, 1907
Place Of Birth	Dawson, Georgia – Terrell County
Date Of Death	Sunday, March 30, 1969
Age At Death	61

My Family Tree

Place Of Death	Saint Petersburg, Florida – Pinellas County
Occupation	Day Laborer
Married	Emma Jean Stokes Gilbert
Notes	Married on Monday, January 14, 1935, in Florida – Pinellas County. His parents were Annie Lee Gilbert (b. November 1876) and Jimmie T. Gilbert (b. Tuesday, February 4, 1872 – d. Saturday, December 30, 1933, age 60).

The connection to the family line was Betty Jane Gilbert Bassett, the daughter of Emma Jean Stokes Gilbert and Leroy Gilbert.

The First Generation

Emily and Henry Stokes Story:

Dr. Henry Louis Gates, Jr. and his team tracked Angela Bassett's mother's side of the family back to the slave master. Angela's great-great-grandparents were Emily Stokes, born in 1827, and Henry Stokes, born in 1825. Their place of birth was in Quitman, Georgia – Brooks County on a Georgia plantation, where they lived most of their lives there as slaves. J.W. Stokes was Angela's great-great-grandparents' slave master. Census records noted that he owned 35 slaves on his plantation before the Civil War. J.W. Stokes was the first in his county to assist the Confederate Army in upholding the institution of slavery for Southern states. Emily and Henry had four children: Judge Stokes, born in 1860 (his wife – Henrietta Stokes, born in 1860 in Quitman, Georgia – Brooks County); Gordon Stokes, born in 1862; Elizabeth Stokes, born in 1866 and Slater Samuel Stokes (his wife – Minnie Lee Jackson Stokes born in Georgia). Angela's great-grandparents on her mother's (father) side were Annie Lee Gilbert and Jimmie T. Gilbert; they were married in 1897 in Georgia. Angela's great-grandfather, Slater Samuel Stokes, was born Saturday, April 1, 1893, in Quitman, Georgia – Brooks County; and later he became a preacher after slavery ended. The Civil War ended Monday, December 18, 1865, in the United States, and the 13th Amendment was officially passed abolishing slavery, which delivered freedom to all slaves throughout the United States. When Henry was told that he was free because of the 13th Amendment, he had to grasp the idea that he was a free man, and he registered to vote in the State of Georgia on Tuesday, June 25, 1867. With no education Henry stood as a proud black man as he made his X on the dotted line on the Voting Registration Card. The 13th Amendment was signed in 1865, then the 14th Amendment was signed in 1868, and the last one to be signed was the 15th Amendment in 1870. It was documented in the United States Census in the 1920s that Minnie and Slater were literate.

The Family Line of Betty Jane Gilbert Bassett and Daniel Benjamin Bassett [II]

The connection to the family line was Daniel, the son of Brownie Younger Bassett and Daniel Benjamin Bassett [1].

The Fifth Generation

My Family Tree

Betty Jane Gilbert Bassett - See Entry Page 204
Daniel Benjamin Bassett II - See Entry Page 203-204

Their (2) Children

Name	Angela Evelyn Bassett Vance
Date Of Birth	Saturday, August 16, 1958
Place Of Birth	Harlem, New York – Manhattan County
Date Of Death	N/A
Age At Death	N/A
Place Of Death	N/A
Occupation	American Actress
Married	Courtney Bernard Vance
Notes	Angela has three other sisters: Martha Jean Bassett, Linda Bassett, and Lisa Carter. Married Wednesday, October 12, 1997. Angela and Courtney had one set of twins – Bronwyn Golden Vance and Slater Josiah Vance (b. Friday, January 27, 2006). Public knowledge testimony.

Name	Courtney Bernard Vance
Date Of Birth	Thursday, March 17, 1960
Place Of Birth	Detroit, Michigan – Wayne County
Date Of Death	N/A
Age At Death	N/A
Place Of Death	N/A
Occupation	American Actor
Married	Angela Evelyn Bassett Vance
Notes	His parents were Leslie Antia Daniels Vance (b. Monday, October 22, 1934) and Conroy Bernard Vance (b. Monday, February 6, 1933 – d. Wednesday, December 19, 1990, age 56–57). Public knowledge testimony.

My Family Tree

Name	D'nette Belinda Bassett
Date Of Birth	Saturday, August 16, 1958
Place Of Birth	N/A
Date Of Death	N/A
Age At Death	N/A
Place Of Death	N/A
Occupation	N/A
Married	N/A
Notes	

The Family Line of Jinny "Jin" Ingram and George Ingram

The connection to the family line was William Henry Bassett, the son of Jinny and George, Angela's great-great-grandparent on her father's side.

The First Generation

Jinny and George Ingram Story:

Dr. Henry Louis Gates, Jr., and his team tracked Angela Bassett's father's side of the family back to the slave master. Angela's great-great grandparents were Jinny Ingram, born in 1810, and George Ingram, born in 1803. According to the United States Federal Census, they were born on James Ingram's plantation in Virginia. Jinny and George were married in 1816 at an incredibly young age on their master's plantation, but their marriage was not recognized because of the slave codes that were in place at that time. James Ingram left a living WILL for his children. When James died his children would have ownership over two of his slaves, one named Jinny (for his daughter) and the other named George (for his son). Jinny and George had a son named William Henry, born in 1846 in Martinsville, Virginia – Henry County. William was Angela's great-grandfather. The Ingram family had William's name on their inventory listed as a slave at the age of three, and then he totally disappeared. Jinny and George knew their master, James, sold their son and there was nothing they could do about it but accept the fact that their son was sold. After their only son was sold, the couple had two more children named Sally, born 1855-1856, and Fleming, born 1860-1861, in Martinsville, Virginia, on James's plantation. Eleven years later, William Henry's name appeared on the Census records in Martinsville, Virginia, in 1860 as a slave on the Bassett's plantation. The Ingram family sold William to John Henry Bassett and his wife, 20 miles away from his parents. Monday, December 18, 1865, in Virginia, William was 16 years old when the 13th Amendment was officially passed abolishing slavery. After slavery was abolished, all former slaves had the right to choose their own legal name because they were free, and he kept his first name and chose Bassett as his last name. Later, William Henry Bassett became a preacher and General Farmer after gaining his freedom. During slavery, it was impossible to preserve family ties because

My Family Tree

slave masters would use slave codes to their advantage to buy, trade, or sell, separate families as punishment for slaves who disobeyed orders, or make a profit and use them for cheap labor, among other things. He met and married a lady named Martha Jane Price Bassett, born in March 1860 in Virginia and her occupation – a launderer. They were married Thursday, October 29, 1885, in Virginia – Henry County, and they were married for 33 years. Martha's parents were Charlotte Price and Oscar Price. Martha and William's children were John Henry Bassett, Daniel Benjamin Bassett [1], Franklin Bassett, George Washington Bassett [1], and Theodore Roosevelt Bassett. William's life ended Sunday, October 6, 1918, at the age of 71 – 72 in Princeville, North Carolina – Edgecombe County. Martha's life ended Wednesday, July 15, 1931, at the age of 70 – 71 in Winston-Salem, North Carolina – Forsyth County. Martha's siblings were Daniel W. Price (b. 1861), Frank Price (b. 1863), Mary A. Price (b. 1866-1867), John Price (b.1868), Mollie Price (b.1870), Lucy Hettie Price (b.1870) and Mary Price (b.1877). Three of her siblings grew up in slavery with her on the Duke Price plantation in Henry County, Virginia.

The Family Line of Martha Jane Price Bassett and William Henry Bassett

The Second Generation

Martha Jane Price Bassett - See Entry Above
William Henry Bassett - See Entry Above

Their (5) Children

Name	John Henry Bassett
Date Of Birth	Thursday, December 30, 1875
Place Of Birth	Preston, Virginia – Henry County
Date Of Death	Sunday, December 1, 1935
Age At Death	59
Place Of Death	Martinsville, Virginia – Henry County
Occupation	United States – Army/Farm Hand
Married	(1) Mattie Green Price Bassett (b. 1881 – d. 1960, age 79) (2) Mary Travis Bassett (b. 1885 – d. 1975, age 90)
Notes	His mother was Lucy Jane Staples Bassett (b. 1850 – d. 1907, age 56–57), a slave. He served in the United States Army during WWI from (1917–1918) and was honorably discharged. According to official records, he had a pension from the United States General Index, and in the 1920 Census, he was literate. His children: Countess L. Bassett (her mother Mattie), William E. Bassett, and Carrie Francis Bassett Dillard (their mother Mary) (b. 1911 – d. 1988, age 77), POB. Martinsville, Virginia, occupation – Domestic Worker (husband – Horace William Dillard (b. 1909 – d. 1976, age 67), POB. Ridgeway, Virginia – Henry County, occupation – Albert

My Family Tree

	Bros – Construction Worker). Carrie and Horace were married Monday, July 13, 1942, in Martinsville, Virginia – Henry County. Mary's children before her marriage to John – Sarah E. Mitchell, Katie L., Obe D., Alice A., Matthew M., Eva P., and Mildred J. He accepted her children as his own. The 1920 Census in Virginia had them all listed Mulatto. John was buried Tuesday, December 3, 1935, at Watkins Cemetery in Martinsville City, Virginia – Henry County.

Name	**Franklin Bassett**
Date Of Birth	Tuesday, October 13, 1885
Place Of Birth	Martinsville, Virginia – Henry County
Date Of Death	Unknown
Age At Death	Unknown
Place Of Death	Unknown
Occupation	Farm Hand – Prison/R. J. Reynolds – Tobacco Industry – Worker
Married	Unknown
Notes	

Name	**George Washington Bassett I**
Date Of Birth	Friday, April 6, 1888
Place Of Birth	Martinsville, Virginia – Henry County
Date Of Death	Unknown
Age At Death	Unknown
Place Of Death	Winston-Salem, North Carolina – Forsyth County
Occupation	Ground Porter
Married	Ada Dillard Bassett
Notes	He held a Draft Registration Card from the United States Army during WWI (1917–1918), having registered in Winston-Salem, North Carolina – Forsyth County.

My Family Tree

Name	Ada Dillard Bassett
Date Of Birth	Wednesday, July 15, 1891
Place Of Birth	Martinsville, Virginia – Henry County
Date Of Death	Thursday, February 14, 1985
Age At Death	93
Place Of Death	Winston-Salem, North Carolina – Forsyth County
Occupation	Retired – R. J. Reynolds – Tobacco Industry – Stemmer Worker
Married	George Washington Bassett [I]
Notes	Married Wednesday, December 27, 1916, in Martinsville, Virginia – Henry County. She was buried in February 1985. Her mother was Lucy Dillard. Their children: Edna Dillard Bassett Allen, George Washington Bassett [II], Frank Bassett, and Douglas Bassett.

Daniel Benjamin Bassett [I] - See Entry Page 49-50
Brownie Younger Bassett - See Entry Page 49

Name	Theodore Roosevelt Bassett
Date Of Birth	Monday, April 1, 1901
Place Of Birth	Martinsville, Virginia – Henry County
Date Of Death	Wednesday, May 18, 1994
Age At Death	93
Place Of Death	New York
Occupation	Retired – R. J. Reynolds – Tobacco Industry Worker/Harlem Activist and Writer
Married	Grace Colwell Thornton Bassett
Notes	His nickname was "Ted."

My Family Tree

Name	**Grace Colwell Thornton Bassett**
Date Of Birth	Sunday, December 17, 1916
Place Of Birth	New Orleans, Louisiana
Date Of Death	Sunday, November 10, 2013
Age At Death	96
Place Of Death	New York
Occupation	Civil Rights Activist/SYNC/PhD
Married	Theodore Roosevelt Bassett
Notes	Census noted that their marriage was in 1952, lasting 42 years. She was a member of the Delta Sigma Theta Sorority while in New Orleans at Dillard University. She was a lifelong drum major for "Justice." She was a widow when she died. Mrs. Bassett has an obituary and a live testimony that talks about her life.

The Family Line of Ada Dillard Bassett and George Washington Bassett [1]

The connection to the family line was George, the son of Martha Jane Price Bassett and William Henry Bassett.

The Third Generation

Ada Dillard Bassett - See Entry Page 211
George Washington Bassett [1] - See Entry Page 210

Their (4) Children

Name	**George Washington Bassett II**
Date Of Birth	1919
Place Of Birth	Virginia – Henry County
Date Of Death	Unknown
Age At Death	Unknown
Place Of Death	Unknown
Occupation	Unknown
Married	Unknown

My Family Tree

Notes	

Name	**Edna Dillard Bassett Allen**
Date Of Birth	Tuesday, April 20, 1920
Place Of Birth	Virginia – Henry County
Date Of Death	Thursday, March 6, 2014
Age At Death	93
Place Of Death	North Carolina – Forsyth County
Occupation	Housewife
Married	Willie Taylor Allen
Notes	A marriage of 47 years, working together in love.

Name	**Willie Taylor Allen**
Date Of Birth	Monday, January 22, 1923
Place Of Birth	Boykin, South Carolina – Kershaw County
Date Of Death	Monday, November 29, 2004
Age At Death	81
Place Of Death	Winston-Salem, North Carolina – Forsyth County
Occupation	Day Laborer
Married	Edna Dillard Bassett Allen
Notes	Married Friday, January 25, 1957, in Winston-Salem, North Carolina – Forsyth County. He was buried in December 2004 at Evergreen Cemetery. His parents were Janie Taylor Allen and Abraham Allen.

My Family Tree

Name	Frank Bassett
Date Of Birth	1923
Place Of Birth	Virginia – Henry County
Date Of Death	Unknown
Age At Death	Unknown
Place Of Death	Unknown
Occupation	Unknown
Married	Unknown
Notes	

Name	Douglas Bassett
Date Of Birth	1924
Place Of Birth	Virginia – Henry County
Date Of Death	Unknown
Age At Death	Unknown
Place Of Death	Unknown
Occupation	Unknown
Married	Unknown
Notes	

The Family Line of Cora Perrell Mason and Sherlie H. Mason

The connection to the family line was Sherlie, the son of Lucinda Mason Mason.

The Third Generation

Sherlie H. Mason - See Entry Page 181
Cora Perrell Mason - See Entry Page 181-182
Their (3) Children

My Family Tree

Name	**Buxton F. Mason**
Date Of Birth	Thursday, September 22, 1904
Place Of Birth	Fulton Township, North Carolina – Davie County
Date Of Death	May 1973
Age At Death	68
Place Of Death	Maryland
Occupation	Day Laborer
Married	Viola A. Scales Mason
Notes	

Name	**Viola A. Scales Mason**
Date Of Birth	Monday, December 12, 1910
Place Of Birth	Madison, North Carolina – Rockingham County
Date Of Death	Tuesday, January 14, 1997
Age At Death	86
Place Of Death	South Carolina
Occupation	Housewife/Domestic Worker
Married	Buxton F. Mason
Notes	Married Monday, November 30, 1931, in Danville, Virginia – Pittsylvania County, and they were married for 42 years. Her parents were Frances Martin Scales and Luther Scales.

Name	**Lucille Mason Hamilton**
Date Of Birth	Saturday, July 8, 1911
Place Of Birth	Fulton Township, North Carolina – Forsyth County

My Family Tree

Date Of Death	Thursday, March 15, 1973
Age At Death	61
Place Of Death	Charlotte, North Carolina – Mecklenburg County
Occupation	School Teacher
Married	John David Hamilton
Notes	She was buried on Tuesday, March 20, 1973. Lucille and John were both buried at York Memorial Park Cemetery in Charlotte, North Carolina – Mecklenburg County. She lived at 701 Grandin Road in Charlotte at the time of her death, a widow and homeowner.

Name	John David Hamilton
Date Of Birth	Thursday, September 20, 1906
Place Of Birth	South Carolina – Spartanburg County
Date Of Death	Tuesday, August 24, 1965
Age At Death	58
Place Of Death	Charlotte, North Carolina – Mecklenburg County
Occupation	Minister
Married	Lucille Mason Hamilton
Notes	Married on Saturday, July 11, 1936, in North Carolina – Mecklenburg County, a marriage of 29 years. He was buried on Sunday, August 29, 1965. He lived at 1617 N. McCall Street in Charlotte at the time of his death. His parents were Annie Belle Woodward Hamilton and Henry Hamilton.

Name	Thelma Mason
Date Of Birth	1910
Place Of Birth	Fulton Township, North Carolina – Forsyth County
Date Of Death	Unknown

My Family Tree

Age At Death	Unknown
Place Of Death	Unknown
Occupation	Unknown
Married	Unknown
Notes	She lived at 1743 McKean Avenue in Baltimore, Maryland – Baltimore County, a homeowner. Her cousins on her mother's side were Matthew Perrell (b. 1900 – d. 1913, age 12–13) and Nancy "Nicie" A. Perrell Payne (b. Monday, August 6, 1906, POB. North Carolina – d. Tuesday, May 1, 1973, POD. Baltimore, Maryland – Baltimore County, age 66), occupation – Housewife. Nicie was buried Saturday, May 5, 1973, at Cedar Grove Baptist Church Cemetery. Nancy's husband was William Payne. Nancy's and Matthew's father was Bud Perrell.

The Family Line of Ella Audrey Orr and Washington A. "Wash" Orr II

The connection to the family line was Washington II, the son of Caroline Elliott Orr and Washington A. Orr I.

The Third Generation

Ella Audrey Orr	-	See Entry Page 33
Washington A. "Wash" Orr II	-	See Entry Page 32-33

Their (10) Children

Name	Lillian Orr Burton
Date Of Birth	August 1892
Place Of Birth	Crab Orchard Township, Precinct 1, North Carolina – Mecklenburg County
Date Of Death	Unknown
Age At Death	Unknown
Place Of Death	North Carolina – Mecklenburg County
Occupation	Housewife/Domestic Worker
Married	Raymond Burton (b. 1884), POB. Charlotte, North Carolina – Mecklenburg County
Notes	According to the 1910 Census, she was literate. Married on Monday, June 18, 1923, in Manhattan, New York – New York City. His parents were

My Family Tree

	Lottie Rush Burton and Calvin Burton. According to the records, Calvin's name was spelled Calven.

Name	**Emma Orr McCombs**
Date Of Birth	September 1896
Place Of Birth	Charlotte, North Carolina – Mecklenburg County
Date Of Death	Wednesday, November 28, 1951
Age At Death	55
Place Of Death	Charlotte, North Carolina – Mecklenburg County
Occupation	Domestic Worker/Housewife
Married	Cliff McCombs
Notes	According to the 1920 Census, she was literate. She was buried on Sunday, December 2, 1951, at Jonesville Cemetery in Charlotte, North Carolina – Mecklenburg County.

Name	**Cliff McCombs**
Date Of Birth	Wednesday, December 30, 1891
Place Of Birth	Shelby Township, North Carolina – Cleveland County
Date Of Death	Saturday, February 23, 1935
Age At Death	43
Place Of Death	St. Louis, Missouri
Occupation	United States – Army/Farmer
Married	Emma Orr McCombs
Notes	He served in the United States Army during WWI on Saturday, July 27, 1918, and was honorably discharged. His parents were Pricilla McCombs and John McCombs.

My Family Tree

Name	Enzelia Orr
Date Of Birth	January 1898
Place Of Birth	Charlotte, North Carolina – Mecklenburg County
Date Of Death	Unknown
Age At Death	Unknown
Place Of Death	Unknown
Occupation	Private Domestic Worker
Married	Unknown
Notes	According to the 1910 Census, noted that she was literate and her first name was spelled as Uheal.

Name	Jessie B. Orr McCain
Date Of Birth	Wednesday, December 22, 1886
Place Of Birth	Charlotte, North Carolina – Mecklenburg County
Date Of Death	Tuesday, August 30, 1988
Age At Death	101
Place Of Death	Charlotte, North Carolina – Mecklenburg County
Occupation	Retired – School Teacher
Married	Milton Walker McCain
Notes	According to the 1910 Census, she was literate. She was buried on Saturday, September 3, 1988, and she was a widow when she died. Jessie and Milton were both buried side-by-side at York Memorial Park Cemetery in Charlotte, North Carolina – Mecklenburg County.

Name	Milton Walker McCain
Date Of Birth	Wednesday, August 1, 1888
Place Of Birth	Charlotte, North Carolina – Mecklenburg County

My Family Tree

Date Of Death	Friday, March 13, 1959
Age At Death	70
Place Of Death	Charlotte, North Carolina – Mecklenburg County
Occupation	Retired – Postal Office Worker/Cement Finishing Worker
Married	Jessie B. Orr McCain
Notes	He was buried on Tuesday, March 17, 1959. His parents were Mary Alexander McCain and Jack McCain

Name	**Ella Mae Orr Watts**
Date Of Birth	January 1894
Place Of Birth	Crab Orchard, Precinct 1, Township 7, North Carolina – Mecklenburg County
Date Of Death	Unknown
Age At Death	Unknown
Place Of Death	North Carolina
Occupation	Domestic Worker/Housewife
Married	Charles Watts (b. 1891)
Notes	According to the 1910 Census, noted that she was literate, and her first name was spelled Allice May. Married on Wednesday, June 26, 1912, in Charlotte, North Carolina – Mecklenburg County.

Name	**Eunice Orr Oden**
Date Of Birth	Tuesday, January 22, 1907
Place Of Birth	Crab Orchard Township, Precinct 1, North Carolina – Mecklenburg County
Date Of Death	Saturday, February 6, 1982
Age At Death	75
Place Of Death	Morganton, North Carolina – Burke County

My Family Tree

Occupation	School Teacher
Married	Sylvester Oden
Notes	According to the 1910 Census, she was literate. She lived at 1000 S. Sterling Street in Morganton, a widow and homeowner. She was buried on Friday, February 12, 1982. Eunice and Sylvester were both buried at York Memorial Park Cemetery in Charlotte, North Carolina – Mecklenburg County, but her body was not buried there.

Name	**Sylvester Oden**
Date Of Birth	Sunday, December 22, 1907
Place Of Birth	Birmingham, Alabama – Jefferson County
Date Of Death	Friday, April 1, 1966
Age At Death	58
Place Of Death	Charlotte, North Carolina – Mecklenburg County
Occupation	Retired – United States – Army/Charlotte Fire Department
Married	(1) Charley Mae Oden (2) Eunice Orr Oden
Notes	Charley and Sylvester lived in Washington, DC, in 1930, where they were servants for the Owen Howestein family. He served during WWII in the Army in September 1942 and was honorably discharged (TEC 481 Port BN TC). He was buried in April 1966. His parents were Delia Oden and Thomas A. Oden.

Name	**Jane Orr**
Date Of Birth	February 1899
Place Of Birth	Crab Orchard Township, Precinct 1, North Carolina – Mecklenburg County
Date Of Death	Unknown
Age At Death	Unknown
Place Of Death	Unknown
Occupation	Unknown

My Family Tree

Married	Unknown
Notes	According to the 1910 Census, she was literate.

Name	**Lolo Orr**
Date Of Birth	January 1900
Place Of Birth	Crab Orchard Township, Precinct 1, North Carolina – Mecklenburg County
Date Of Death	Unknown
Age At Death	Unknown
Place Of Death	Unknown
Occupation	Unknown
Married	Unknown
Notes	According to the 1910 Census, she was literate.

Name	**James B. Orr**
Date Of Birth	Saturday, February 4, 1899
Place Of Birth	Crab Orchard Township, Precinct 1, North Carolina – Mecklenburg County
Date Of Death	Monday, July, 1929
Age At Death	30
Place Of Death	Richmond, Virginia – Henrico County
Occupation	Baker
Married	Mary Orr
Notes	According to the 1910 Census, he was literate. He lived at 215 Nicholson Street in Richmond at the time of his death, a homeowner. He was buried on Wednesday, July 3, 1929, at Woodland Cemetery in Richmond, Virginia – Henrico Count.

My Family Tree

Name	George Anna Hyatt
Date Of Birth	1914
Place Of Birth	Sharon, North Carolina – Mecklenburg County
Date Of Death	Unknown
Age At Death	Unknown
Place Of Death	Unknown
Occupation	Unknown
Married	Unknown
Notes	Adopted daughter

The Family Line of Lula Senie Mae Mason Clement and George Washington Clement [1]

The connection to the family line was Lula, the daughter of Elizabeth O. Winford Mason and Dennis De Quincy Mason [1].

The Fifth Generation

Lula Senie Mae Mason Clement - See Entry Page 187-188
George Washington Clement [1] - See Entry Page 188

Their Child

Name	George Washington Clement II
Date Of Birth	Tuesday, May 1, 1945
Place Of Birth	Fulton, North Carolina – Davie County
Date Of Death	Wednesday, April 27, 1988
Age At Death	42
Place Of Death	Mocksville, North Carolina – Davie County
Occupation	Testing Machines Technician
Married	Mattie Arwilda Steelman Clement (b. Thursday, April 25, 1946)
Notes	He was buried Monday, May 2, 1988, at Cedar Grove Baptist Church Cemetery. Their child: George La Van Clement (b. Friday, December 12, 1969), POB. Iredell, North Carolina – Statesville County. She got

My Family Tree

remarried to Dewey Arnold Parks in Winston-Salem, North Carolina – Forsyth County. Her parents were Addie Vaughters Steelman and Abraham Steelman.

The Family Line of Addie Mason Haizlip and U Grant Haizlip

The connection to the family line was Addie, the daughter of Elizabeth Mason and Samuel M. Mason.

The Fifth Generation

Addie Mason Haizlip - See Entry Page 58
U Grant Haizlip - See Entry Page 58-59

Their Child

Name	Lillie Mae Haizlip Warren
Date Of Birth	1904
Place Of Birth	Winston-Salem, North Carolina – Forsyth County
Date Of Death	Unknown
Age At Death	Unknown
Place Of Death	Winston-Salem, North Carolina – Forsyth County
Occupation	Housewife/Domestic Worker
Married	Jon W. Warren II
Notes	Census records noted that she was listed Mulatto, and her first name was spelled Lillie May.

Name	Jon W. Warren II
Date Of Birth	Wednesday, January 23, 1907
Place Of Birth	Winston-Salem, North Carolina – Forsyth County
Date Of Death	August 1984
Age At Death	77
Place Of Death	Winston-Salem, North Carolina – Forsyth County
Occupation	Day Laborer

My Family Tree

Married	Lillie Mae Haizlip Warren
Notes	His parents were Catherine Warren and Jon W. Warren [1]. Married on Saturday, July 6, 1929, in Clemmons, North Carolina – Forsyth County.

The Family Line of LaKeisha Renee Thues Stiff and William Stiff

The connection to the family line is LaKeisha, the daughter of Venus Renee Mason-Thues and Jerome Anthony Thues (she was the granddaughter of William Anthony Mason).

The Seventh Generation

LaKeisha Renee Thues Stiff - See Entry Page 90-91
William Stiff - See Entry Page 91

Their (2) Children

Name	Madison Rene Stiff
Date Of Birth	Friday, March 7, 2008
Place Of Birth	Southfield, Michigan – Oakland County
Date Of Death	N/A
Age At Death	N/A
Place Of Death	N/A
Occupation	N/A
Married	N/A
Notes	

Name	Jordan Jewel Stiff
Date Of Birth	Friday, November 17, 2006
Place Of Birth	Southfield, Michigan – Oakland County
Date Of Death	N/A
Age At Death	N/A
Place Of Death	N/A

My Family Tree

Occupation	N/A
Married	N/A
Notes	

The Family Line of Sukie Turner Mason, Phyllis Ann Brown Hairston Mason, and Burrell Mason

The First Generation

Sukie Turner Mason - See Entry Page 179
Phyllis Ann Brown Hairston Mason - See Entry Page 179
Burrell Mason - See Entry Page 179

Their (10) Children

Name	John Henry Mason
Date Of Birth	Saturday, August 30, 1845
Place Of Birth	Virginia – Halifax County
Date Of Death	Tuesday, August 28, 1917
Age At Death	71
Place Of Death	Fulton Township, North Carolina – Davie County
Occupation	General Farmer
Married	(1) Mary Jane Brown Mason (2) Naomi Bailey Mason (3) Alice Gaither Mason
Notes	He was born a slave. According to the 1880 Census, he was illiterate. He was buried Wednesday, August 29, 1917, at Cedar Grove Baptist Church Cemetery. His mother was Sukie Turner Mason. (1) Marriage Tuesday, December 22, 1868, in Mocksville, North Carolina – Davie County. (1) Her parents were Catherine Brown and Cary Brown. Mary and John's children: Bessie C. Mason Hairston and Walter Mason. (2) Marriage Saturday, October 18, 1884, in Mocksville, North Carolina – Davie County.

Name	Alice Gaither Mason

My Family Tree

Date Of Birth	1841
Place Of Birth	North Carolina
Date Of Death	Wednesday, March 26, 1919
Age At Death	77 – 78
Place Of Death	Fulton Township, North Carolina – Davie County
Occupation	Housewife/Domestic Worker
Married	John Henry Mason
Notes	She was born a slave. Married on Thursday, September 28, 1899, in Mocksville, North Carolina – Davie County. She was buried in March 1919 at Piney Grove United Methodist Church Cemetery in Advance, North Carolina – Davie County, as a widow. Their children: Julia Ellen Mason Pebbles and Lula M. Mason Goolsby.

Lucinda Mason Mason - See Entry Page 178-179
Spencer Mason - See Entry Page 179
Colwell Mason - See Entry Page 179
Clayborn Mason - See Entry Page 179
Burrell T. Mason - See Entry Page 179

Name	Mack Mason
Date Of Birth	1851
Place Of Birth	North Carolina
Date Of Death	Unknown
Age At Death	Unknown
Place Of Death	Unknown
Occupation	Unknown
Married	Unknown
Notes	

Name	Celia Mason

My Family Tree

Date Of Birth	1853
Place Of Birth	North Carolina
Date Of Death	Unknown
Age At Death	Unknown
Place Of Death	Unknown
Occupation	Unknown
Married	Unknown
Notes	

Name	Martha Mason
Date Of Birth	1856
Place Of Birth	North Carolina
Date Of Death	Unknown
Age At Death	Unknown
Place Of Death	Unknown
Occupation	Unknown
Married	Unknown
Notes	

According to the United States Freedmen's Bureau Records for 1865 – 1872… the prominent Hairston family of North Carolina and slave owners were Samuel Hairston and his son, Major Peter Wilson Hairston. The Hairstons owned over 400 slaves in North Carolina and Virginia. The Hairston family were the largest slave owners in the South, and they were also involved in the Slave Trade. The Hairstons owned 40 plantations and enslaved around 10,000 people of color. Their partners in running these plantations were General Jesse A. Pearson, John Goolsby, and the Wilson family. One of their plantations in North Carolina – Davie County was Cooleemee Plantation. Most of my father (father's side of the family) were enslaved to the Hairston family.

My Family Tree

Name	**Susan Mason Hairston**
Date Of Birth	September 1857
Place Of Birth	North Carolina
Date Of Death	Saturday, April 27, 1912
Age At Death	54
Place Of Death	North Carolina
Occupation	Housewife/Domestic Worker
Married	Wiseman H. Hairston
Notes	Her nickname was "Susie." Susan and Wiseman were born slaves and were married for 37 years. In the 1910 Census, she was the mother of 17 children, of which 8 were still living at that time. The Census also listed her and her husband with four single children living in their home: Effie Hairston (age 22), Robert Baxter Hairston (age 21), Martha Hairston Barron (age 18), Bernis Hairston (age 9); and their other children were: Wanne Hairston (age 25), in jail, Noah Hairston (age 19), Margaret Hairston (age 23), Mack Hairston (age 17), in jail, John Thomas Hairston, Iseral H. Hairston (age 27), in jail, Perley Hairston, Nancy Lois Hairston Young, and Vance Wiseman Hairston. She was buried in April 1912.

Name	**Wiseman H. Hairston**
Date Of Birth	1850
Place Of Birth	North Carolina
Date Of Death	Tuesday, October 8, 1929
Age At Death	79
Place Of Death	Winston-Salem, North Carolina – Forsyth County
Occupation	Minister/Farmer
Married	Susan Mason Hairston
Notes	His parents were Bashie Hairston (b. 1812) and Adam Hairston (b. 1807). His parents' POB. was Virginia. Married Sunday, November 1, 1874, in North Carolina. He was the Founder of two churches – Pastor of Cedar Grove Baptist Church and Pine Hall Baptist Church in 1905. He was

My Family Tree

	buried on Saturday, October 12, 1929. Susan and Wiseman were both buried at Cedar Grove Baptist Church Cemetery. He was a widower when he died. A short biography of Wiseman and (their son) John Thomas Hairston were interviewed by Editor A. B. Caldwell, who wrote about him in his book "History of the American Negro and His Institutes," Volume IV, in 1921.

Name	**William Mason**
Date Of Birth	1861
Place Of Birth	North Carolina
Date Of Death	Unknown
Age At Death	Unknown
Place Of Death	Unknown
Occupation	Unknown
Married	Unknown
Notes	He was born into slavery.

Name	**Lizzie Mason**
Date Of Birth	1863
Place Of Birth	North Carolina
Date Of Death	Unknown
Age At Death	Unknown
Place Of Death	Unknown
Occupation	Unknown
Married	Unknown
Notes	She was born into slavery.

My Family Tree

Name	William A. Mason
Date Of Birth	1867
Place Of Birth	North Carolina
Date Of Death	Unknown
Age At Death	Unknown
Place Of Death	Unknown
Occupation	Unknown
Married	Unknown
Notes	

Name	Henry P. Mason
Date Of Birth	1870
Place Of Birth	Fulton Township, North Carolina – Davie County
Date Of Death	Unknown
Age At Death	Unknown
Place Of Death	Unknown
Occupation	Unknown
Married	Unknown
Notes	

The Family Line of Mary Jane Brown Mason, Alice Gaither Mason, and John Henry Mason

The connection to the family line was John, the son of Sukie Turner Mason and Burrell Mason.

The Third Generation

Mary Jane Brown Mason - See Entry Page 226
Alice Gaither Mason - See Entry Page 226-227

My Family Tree

John Henry Mason - See Entry Page 226

Their (4) Children

Name	**Lula M. Mason Goolsby**
Date Of Birth	Saturday, April 11, 1896
Place Of Birth	Fulton Township, North Carolina – Davie County
Date Of Death	Saturday, May 18, 1957
Age At Death	61
Place Of Death	Lexington, North Carolina – Davidson County
Occupation	Domestic Worker/Homemaker
Married	John Hairston Goolsby [I]
Notes	According to the 1910 Census, she was literate. Her mother was Alice Gaither Mason. She was buried on Wednesday, May 22, 1957. Their children: Lettie F. Goolsby Brown, Alice Goolsby Benson, Fannie Elizabeth Goolsby Hudson, Annie Lucille Goolsby Burke, and John Hairston Goolsby [II].

Name	**John Hairston Goolsby I**
Date Of Birth	Monday, April 11, 1898
Place Of Birth	Advance, North Carolina – Davie County
Date Of Death	Sunday, September 15, 1974
Age At Death	76
Place Of Death	Mocksville, North Carolina – Davie County
Occupation	General Farmer/Retired – Reed Elementary – School Teacher
Married	Lula M. Mason Goolsby
Notes	He was buried on Tuesday, September 17, 1974. Lula and John were both buried at Cedar Grove Baptist Church Cemetery, and he was a widower when he died. Lula and John both lived at 103 Village Drive in Lexington at the time of their death; they were homeowners. Married on Tuesday, February 1, 1916, in North Carolina – Davie County, married for 41 years.

My Family Tree

	His parents were Mary Goolsby and Horace Goolsby. He held a United States Draft Registration Card during WWI from (1917–1918).

Walter Mason - See Entry Page 176
Effie Neely Mason - See Entry Page 175

Name	Julia Ellen Mason Peebles
Date Of Birth	Tuesday, April 22, 1873
Place Of Birth	North Carolina – Davie County
Date Of Death	Thursday, December 8, 1960
Age At Death	87
Place Of Death	Lexington, North Carolina – Davidson County
Occupation	Domestic Worker/Homemaker
Married	George Washington Peebles
Notes	She was buried in December 1960, a widow when she died. Her mother was Alice Gaither Mason. Their child: Lucinda Jane Peebles Ellis.

Name	George Washington Peebles
Date Of Birth	Saturday, February 22, 1868
Place Of Birth	North Carolina – Davie County
Date Of Death	Thursday, February 24, 1938
Age At Death	70
Place Of Death	North Carolina – Davie County
Occupation	School Teacher
Married	Julia Ellen Mason Peebles
Notes	Married on Friday, April 26, 1895, in North Carolina – Davie County. He was buried on Sunday, February 27, 1938. His parents were LeAnn Haynes Peebles (b. Thursday, October 1, 1840 – d. Saturday, September 4, 1915, age 74) and Adam Peebles (b. Thursday, February 23, 1832 – d. Wednesday, October 12, 1898, age 66). His parents' place of birth and death: North Carolina – Davie County. Julia, George, and his parents were

My Family Tree

	all buried at Piney Grove United Methodist Church Cemetery in Advance, North Carolina – Davie County. His parents were slaves.

Name	**Bessie C. Mason Hairston**
Date Of Birth	December 1872
Place Of Birth	Fulton Township, North Carolina – Davie County
Date Of Death	Wednesday, August 4, 1926
Age At Death	53
Place Of Death	Fulton Township, North Carolina – Davie County
Occupation	House Cook/Homemaker
Married	Ivory Shack Hairston
Notes	She was buried on Thursday, August 5, 1926. Her mother was Mary Jane Brown Mason. Her children: Wise Hairston and Nume Hairston.

Name	**Ivory Shack Hairston**
Date Of Birth	1864
Place Of Birth	North Carolina – Davie County
Date Of Death	Monday, August 22, 1927
Age At Death	62 – 63
Place Of Death	Fulton Township, North Carolina – Davie County
Occupation	Domestic Worker/Homemaker
Married	(1) Hester Hairston (2) Bessie C. Mason Hairston
Notes	He was buried in August 1927. Bessie and Ivory were both buried at Cedar Grove Baptist Church Cemetery. (1) Married on Monday, August 14, 1893, in North Carolina – Davie County, married for 11 years. (2) Married on Thursday, September 15, 1904, in North Carolina – Davie County, married for 22 years.

My Family Tree

The Family Line of Julia Ellen Mason Peebles and George Washington Peebles

The Fourth Generation

Julia Ellen Mason Peebles	-	See Entry Page 233
George Washington Peebles	-	See Entry Page 233

Their Child

Name	**Lucinda Jane Peebles Ellis**
Date Of Birth	Sunday, August 25, 1907
Place Of Birth	North Carolina – Davie County
Date Of Death	Tuesday, December 17, 1985
Age At Death	78
Place Of Death	Winston-Salem, North Carolina – Forsyth County
Occupation	Retired – Domestic Worker/Housewife
Married	George Adam Ellis
Notes	She was buried Saturday, December 21, 1985, at Mount Sinai AME Zion Church Cemetery in Advance, North Carolina – Davie County. She lived at 9524 Reynolds Street in Tobaccoville, a widow and homeowner.

The Family of Lula M. Mason Goolsby and John Hairston Goolsby [I]

The connection to the family line was Lula, the daughter of Alice Gaither Mason and John Henry Mason.

The Fourth Generation

Lula M. Mason Goolsby	-	See Entry Page 232
John Hairston Goolsby [I]	-	See Entry Page 232-233

Their (6) Children

Name	**Annie Lucille Goolsby Burke**
Date Of Birth	1920
Place Of Birth	North Carolina
Date Of Death	Tuesday, September 25, 2007

My Family Tree

Age At Death	86 – 87
Place Of Death	Columbia, South Carolina – Richland County
Occupation	Housewife
Married	Widow
Notes	She was buried on Saturday, September 29, 2007, at Cedar Grove Baptist Church Cemetery. Annie was buried side-by-side with her sister-in-law, Brenda Ann Burke (b. 1945 – d. 1964, age 18–19).

John Hairston Goolsby II - See Entry Page 167
Ida Doreatha Brown Goolsby - See Entry Page 166-167

Lettie F. Goolsby Brown - See Entry Page 165
Jesse James Brown II - See Entry Page 164-165

Name	Alice Goolsby Benson
Date Of Birth	Unknown
Place Of Birth	North Carolina – Davie County
Date Of Death	Unknown
Age At Death	Unknown
Place Of Death	North Carolina
Occupation	Day Laborer
Married	Widow
Notes	

Name	Nancy Goolsby Hairston
Date Of Birth	1922
Place Of Birth	North Carolina – Davie County
Date Of Death	Unknown

My Family Tree

Age At Death	Unknown
Place Of Death	North Carolina
Occupation	Day Laborer
Married	Widow
Notes	

Name	**Fannie Elizabeth Goolsby Hudson**
Date Of Birth	Saturday, October 13, 1923
Place Of Birth	North Carolina – Davie County
Date Of Death	Tuesday, March 14, 2017
Age At Death	93
Place Of Death	Trinity, North Carolina – Randolph County
Occupation	Housewife
Married	R. J. Hudson
Notes	She was buried on Saturday, March 18, 2017. Fannie and R. J. were both buried side-by-side at Cedar Grove Baptist Church Cemetery.

Name	**R. J. Hudson**
Date Of Birth	Saturday, January 17, 1925
Place Of Birth	Mocksville, North Carolina – Davie County
Date Of Death	Tuesday, March 4, 2003
Age At Death	78
Place Of Death	North Carolina – Randolph County
Occupation	Served in WWII – PVT – U.S. Army/Day Laborer
Married	Fannie Elizabeth Goolsby Hudson

My Family Tree

Notes	Married on Wednesday, August 3, 1949, in North Carolina, Davie County, a marriage for 53 years. He was buried in March 2002. His parents were Cornelia Goren Hall Hudson (b. 1898 – d. 1970, age 71 – 72) and William McKinley Hudson (b. 1896 – d. 1974, age 77 – 78).

The Family Line of Fannie M. Bryant Mason and Fisher Robert Mason

The connection to the family line was Fisher, the son of Lucinda Mason Mason and Colwell Mason.

The Third Generation

Fannie M. Bryant Mason - See Entry Page 182-183
Fisher Robert Mason - See Entry Page 182

Their (3) Children

Name	Everett H. Mason
Date Of Birth	1905
Place Of Birth	Salisbury, North Carolina – Rowan County
Date Of Death	1909
Age At Death	4
Place Of Death	Salisbury, North Carolina – Rowan County
Occupation	None
Married	Single
Notes	She was buried in 1909 at Oakdale Union Hill Cemetery in Salisbury, North Carolina – Rowan County.

Frank Edward Bryant Mason II - See Entry Page 183
Gladys Beatrice Haith Mason - See Entry Page 183

Name	Lillie Mae Mason Davis
Date Of Birth	Wednesday, July 7, 1909
Place Of Birth	Salisbury, North Carolina – Rowan County
Date Of Death	Thursday, June 13, 1991
Age At Death	81

My Family Tree

Place Of Death	Guilford, North Carolina – Guilford County
Occupation	Retired – Public School – Elementary Teacher
Married	Benjamin F. Davis II (b. 1911 – d. 1966, age 54–55)
Notes	According to the 1920 Census, she was literate. She was buried on Wednesday, June 19, 1991, as a widow. Lillie and Benjamin were both buried at Green Hill Cemetery in High Point, North Carolina – Guilford County – a widow. He served in WWII as a Tec4 3588 QM Truck Co. They both lived at 531 Radford Street in High Point, homeowners.

The Family Line of Geraldine Tatum Brown and Jesse James Brown III

The connection to the family line was Jesse, the son of Lettie F. Goolsby Brown and Jesse James Brown II.

The Sixth Generation

Geraldine Tatum Brown - See Entry Page 171
Jesse James Brown III - See Entry Page 171

Their (7) Children

Name	**Michael Arnelle Brown I**
Date Of Birth	Friday, March 4, 1955
Place Of Birth	Salisbury, North Carolina – Rowan County
Date Of Death	Monday, February 13, 2012
Age At Death	56
Place Of Death	Winston-Salem, North Carolina – Forsyth County
Occupation	Retired – R. J. Reynolds – Tobacco Industry Worker
Married	Single
Notes	His children: Michael A. Brown II, NeKeith Brown, and Michaela Brown. He was buried on Sunday, February 18, 2012, at Cedar Grove Baptist Church Cemetery. Mr. Brown has an obituary that talks about his life.

Name	**Jessica Darlene Brown**
Date Of Birth	Wednesday, August 30, 1961
Place Of Birth	Mocksville, North Carolina – Davie County

My Family Tree

Date Of Death	Friday, January 15, 1982
Age At Death	20
Place Of Death	Winston-Salem, North Carolina – Forsyth County
Occupation	Secretary
Married	Single
Notes	She was buried on Sunday, January 17, 1982, at Cedar Grove Baptist Church Cemetery.

Name	Lawrence Clayton
Date Of Birth	N/A
Place Of Birth	Salisbury, North Carolina – Rowan County
Date Of Death	N/A
Age At Death	N/A
Place Of Death	N/A
Occupation	N/A
Married	Linda Clayton
Notes	

Name	Christopher Brown
Date Of Birth	Monday, August 17, 1959
Place Of Birth	Salisbury, North Carolina – Rowan County
Date Of Death	N/A
Age At Death	N/A
Place Of Death	N/A
Occupation	N/A

My Family Tree

Married	Jeri Brown
Notes	

Name	**Derrick Brown**
Date Of Birth	N/A
Place Of Birth	Salisbury, North Carolina – Rowan County
Date Of Death	N/A
Age At Death	N/A
Place Of Death	N/A
Occupation	N/A
Married	Christy Brown
Notes	

Name	**Lucy Michelle Brown Jones**
Date Of Birth	Saturday, April 11, 1970
Place Of Birth	Salisbury, North Carolina – Rowan County
Date Of Death	N/A
Age At Death	N/A
Place Of Death	N/A
Occupation	N/A
Married	Jock Jones
Notes	

Name	**Cynthia Brown West**

My Family Tree

Date Of Birth	Monday, August 17, 1959
Place Of Birth	Salisbury, North Carolina – Rowan County
Date Of Death	N/A
Age At Death	N/A
Place Of Death	N/A
Occupation	N/A
Married	Herman West
Notes	

The Family Line of Catherine Bailey Mason and Charlie Mason

The connection to the family line was Charlie, the son of Maggie Fowler Mason and Robert M. Mason [II].

The Fifth Generation

Catherine Bailey Mason - See Entry Page 126-127
Charlie Mason - See Entry Page 126

Their Child

Name	Joseph Bailey Mason
Date Of Birth	Saturday, May 17, 1924
Place Of Birth	Mocksville, North Carolina – Davie County
Date Of Death	Thursday, March 10, 2016
Age At Death	91
Place Of Death	Mocksville, North Carolina – Davie County
Occupation	Day Laborer
Married	(1) Unknown (2) Minnie Lee Johnson Rivers Mason
Notes	According to his marriage license, he was illiterate, and there were no records found of any form of education during or after his marriage. He was divorced from his first wife in 1954 in North Carolina. He was buried in March 2016. Minnie and Joseph were both buried side-by-side at Cedar Grove Baptist Church Cemetery, and he was a widower when he died.

My Family Tree

Name	**Minnie Lee Johnson Rivers Mason**
Date Of Birth	Sunday, May 15, 1932
Place Of Birth	Georgia, Franklin County
Date Of Death	Saturday, January 19, 2008
Age At Death	75
Place Of Death	Mocksville, North Carolina – Davie County
Occupation	Housewife/ Davie County Department of Social Service from (1972-1997)
Married	Joseph Bailey Mason
Notes	She was divorced from her first husband in March 1971. Her parents were Luvie Scott Rivers and Boyd Rivers. She got re-married to Joseph on Friday, September 10, 1971, in Mocksville, North Carolina – Davie County. Minnie loved to sew and became self-employed as a seamstress. She used her talent to sew home furniture, crafts, and upholstery for automobiles for different companies, family members, friends, and neighbors. She was buried in January 2008. Minnie and Joseph both lived at Route 3, Box 157 in Mocksville when they both died, homeowners.

The Family Line of Esther Chaplin Doulin and John Thomas Doulin [I]

The connection to the family line was John Thomas Doulin [I], the grandson of Lucinda Mason Mason.

The Fourth Generation

Name	**Esther Chaplin Doulin**
Date Of Birth	Friday, May 16, 1902
Place Of Birth	North Carolina – Davie County
Date Of Death	Thursday, August 10, 1989
Age At Death	87
Place Of Death	North Carolina – Davidson County
Occupation	Housewife
Married	John Thomas Doulin [I]

My Family Tree

Notes	Esther and John were married on Sunday, March 24, 1929, in Fork, North Carolina – Davie County. She was buried in August 1989. They were both buried side-by-side at Cedar Grove Baptist Church Cemetery. Her parents were Louisiana Hairston Chaplin and Thomas Jonas Chaplin.

Name	**John Thomas Doulin I**
Date Of Birth	Sunday, November 15, 1896
Place Of Birth	North Carolina – Davie County
Date Of Death	Saturday, August 24, 1968
Age At Death	71
Place Of Death	Mocksville, North Carolina – Davie County
Occupation	Farmer
Married	Esther Chaplin Doulin
Notes	His parents were Mary Mason Doulin and Robert Doulin. John was buried on Wednesday, August 28, 1968.

Their (2) Children

Name	**Garfield Sylvester Doulin**
Date Of Birth	Friday, December 9, 1927
Place Of Birth	Mocksville, North Carolina – Davie County
Date Of Death	Monday, April 16, 2018
Age At Death	90
Place Of Death	North Carolina
Occupation	Retired – United States Army/Tool and Die Maker/MTA Supervisor – Power Distribution
Married	Frankie Marie Hargraves Doulin
Notes	He served in the United States Army during WWII, registering in North Carolina-Davie County, and earned an honorable discharge. Married on Sunday, April 5, 1953, in North Carolina – Davie County, married for 62 years. He was buried in December 2018. They were both buried side-by-

My Family Tree

	side at Forest Hill Memorial Park in Lexington, North Carolina – Davidson County. Mr. Doulin has an obituary that talks about his life.

Name	**Frankie Marie Hargraves Doulin**
Date Of Birth	Sunday, December 11, 1932
Place Of Birth	Mocksville, North Carolina – Davie County
Date Of Death	Sunday, February 14, 2016
Age At Death	83
Place Of Death	Lexington, North Carolina – Davidson County
Occupation	Housewife
Married	Garfield Sylvester Doulin
Notes	Frankie was buried in February 2016. Her mother was Veola Parker Hargraves, born on Wednesday, November 2, 1910, in North Carolina – Davidson County, and died on Saturday, December 21, 1991 (age 81), in Brooklyn, New York – Kings County. Veola was buried in December 1991 at the same cemetery as her daughter Frankie and her son-in-law Garfield. Veola's parents were Wilson Cooper Parker and Walter Parker.

Name	**James Roosevelt Doulin**
Date Of Birth	Sunday, July 16, 1944
Place Of Birth	Mocksville, North Carolina – Davie County
Date Of Death	Monday, July 27, 1959
Age At Death	15
Place Of Death	Advances, North Carolina – Davie County
Occupation	None
Married	Single
Notes	He was buried on Saturday, August 1, 1959, at Cedar Grove Baptist Church Cemetery.

My Family Tree

The Family Line of Alice Foster Doulin and Fisher S. Doulin

The connection to the family line was Fisher S. Doulin, the son of Mary Mason Doulin and Robert Doulin.

The Fourth Generation

Name	**Alice Foster Doulin**
Date Of Birth	Tuesday, June 9, 1908
Place Of Birth	North Carolina – Davie County
Date Of Death	Tuesday, April 21, 1987
Age At Death	78
Place Of Death	Mocksville, North Carolina – Davie County
Occupation	Housewife
Married	Fisher S. Doulin
Notes	Alice and Fisher were both buried side-by-side at Shiloh Baptist Church Cemetery in Mocksville, North Carolina – Davie County. Her parents were Fannie Harris Foster (born March 1859, and died Saturday, June 3, 1939, in North Carolina – Davie County, age 80) and Alexander Davis Foster (born 1866 in North Carolina, and died 1920 in Mocksville, North Carolina – Davie County, age 53 – 54; Alexander went by "Alec or Alex"). Fannie's second marriage was on Thursday, September 14, 1911, to Alexander Davis Foster. Fannie's parents were Jane Frohop Harris and Frank Harris. Fannie's first marriage was on Thursday, November 29, 1877, to Levi Mitchell Van Easton. Fannie was buried on Monday, June 5, 1939. Alice's siblings included Estell Foster Knox (born in March 1891, and died on Wednesday, August 30, 1922, in Cooleemee, North Carolina – Davie County, age 31; occupation – R. J. Reynolds – Tobacco Industry – Worker; buried on Thursday, September 1, 1922, at Second Presbyterian Church Cemetery in Mocksville, North Carolina – Davie County; husband – Osee Knox; Estell's parents were Lula Malone Foster and Alexander Davis Foster, born in North Carolina – Davie County and Rufus C. Foster (born Monday, March 6, 1893, and died on Saturday, February 12, 1955, in Salisbury, North Carolina – Rowan County, age 62); wife – Eula Van Easton Foster (born on Tuesday, July 9, 1895, and died on Monday, January 18, 1965, age 69; buried in January 1965); Eula and Rufus were both buried side-by-side, at Fairfield Baptist Church Cemetery in Mocksville, North Carolina – Davie County.

My Family Tree

Name	Fisher S. Doulin
Date Of Birth	Sunday, July 2, 1905
Place Of Birth	Mocksville, North Carolina – Davie County
Date Of Death	Monday, November 27, 1950
Age At Death	45
Place Of Death	Mocksville, North Carolina – Davie County
Occupation	Night Watchman
Married	Alice Foster Doulin
Notes	Married on Wednesday, September 27, 1922, in Mocksville, North Carolina – Davie County. Although Fisher and his siblings were buried at different cemeteries, there is a headstone bearing his name and those of his siblings, at Cedar Grove Baptist Church Cemetery. His parents were Mary Mason Doulin and Robert Doulin.

Their (3) Children

Name	John C. Charlie Doulin
Date Of Birth	Sunday, May 6, 1923
Place Of Birth	Mocksville, North Carolina – Davie County
Date Of Death	Saturday, February 15, 2003
Age At Death	79
Place Of Death	Mocksville, North Carolina – Davie County
Occupation	Day Laborer
Married	Lillian Mae Dalton Doulin
Notes	He was buried in February 2003. Lillian and John were both buried side-by-side at Saint John's AME Zion Church Cemetery in Mocksville, North Carolina – Davie County.

Name	Lillian Mae Dalton Doulin

My Family Tree

Date Of Birth	Tuesday, January 22, 1924
Place Of Birth	Mocksville, North Carolina – Davie County
Date Of Death	Wednesday, July 24, 2019
Age At Death	95
Place Of Death	Mocksville, North Carolina – Davie County
Occupation	Housewife
Married	John C. Charlie Doulin
Notes	

Name	**Walter Manuel Doulin**
Date Of Birth	Saturday, June 14, 1924
Place Of Birth	Mocksville, North Carolina – Davie County
Date Of Death	Tuesday, October 21, 2008
Age At Death	84
Place Of Death	Mocksville, North Carolina – Davie County
Occupation	Retired – United States Army
Married	Single
Notes	He served during WWII as Tec5 in the United States Army. He was buried in 2008 at Calverton National Cemetery in Calverton, New York – Suffolk County.

Name	**Mary Doulin Holman**
Date Of Birth	Thursday, December 10, 1925
Place Of Birth	Mocksville, North Carolina – Davie County
Date Of Death	Wednesday, December 14, 2016

My Family Tree

Age At Death	91
Place Of Death	Mocksville, North Carolina – Davie County
Occupation	Housewife
Married	Walter Holman
Notes	She was buried in December 2016 as a widow. Mary and Walter were both buried side-by-side at Shiloh Baptist Church Cemetery in Mocksville, North Carolina – Davie County.

Name	**Walter Holman**
Date Of Birth	Thursday, October 15, 1925
Place Of Birth	Mocksville, North Carolina – Davie County
Date Of Death	Thursday, March 11, 1993
Age At Death	67
Place Of Death	Mocksville, North Carolina – Davie County
Occupation	Day Laborer
Married	Mary Doulin Holman
Notes	He was buried in March 1993. His parents were Jettie E. C. Holman (born 1899 – and died in 1983, age 83) and Holloway Holman (born in 1896 – and died in 1950, age 54). His parents were married on Sunday, August 20, 1916, in North Carolina.

The Family Line of Millie Barber Orr and Charley Orr

The connection to the family line was Charley, the son of Caroline Elliott Orr and Washington A. Orr[1].

The Third Generation

Millie Barber Orr - See Entry Page 34
Charley Orr - See Entry Page 33

Their (6) Children

Name	Cora Orr McLaughlin
Date Of Birth	Friday, June 7, 1889

My Family Tree

Place Of Birth	Charlotte Township, North Carolina – Mecklenburg County
Date Of Death	Sunday, March 4, 1917
Age At Death	27
Place Of Death	Charlotte Township, North Carolina – Mecklenburg County
Occupation	Domestic Worker/Housewife
Married	John McLaughlin
Notes	Cora was buried on Monday, March 5, 1917, at Pinewood Cemetery in Charlotte Township, North Carolina – Mecklenburg County.

Name	Walter Orr
Date Of Birth	February 1897
Place Of Birth	Sharon, North Carolina – Mecklenburg County
Date Of Death	Saturday, February 1, 1913
Age At Death	16
Place Of Death	Charlotte Township, North Carolina – Mecklenburg County
Occupation	Farm Laborer
Married	Single
Notes	Walter was buried in February 1913 at Pinewood Cemetery in Charlotte Township, North Carolina – Mecklenburg County.

Name	Lillie Orr
Date Of Birth	Unknown
Place Of Birth	Charlotte Township, North Carolina – Mecklenburg County
Date Of Death	Unknown
Age At Death	Unknown
Place Of Death	Unknown

My Family Tree

Occupation	Unknown
Married	Unknown
Notes	

Name	**Infant Orr**
Date Of Birth	Unknown
Place Of Birth	Charlotte Township, North Carolina – Mecklenburg County
Date Of Death	Unknown
Age At Death	0
Place Of Death	Unknown
Occupation	None
Married	Single
Notes	

Name	**Ione Orr**
Date Of Birth	June 1888
Place Of Birth	Charlotte Township, North Carolina – Mecklenburg County
Date Of Death	Unknown
Age At Death	Unknown
Place Of Death	Unknown
Occupation	Unknown
Married	Unknown
Notes	

My Family Tree

Name	Joe Orr
Date Of Birth	1906
Place Of Birth	Charlotte Township, North Carolina – Mecklenburg County
Date Of Death	Unknown
Age At Death	Unknown
Place Of Death	Unknown
Occupation	Unknown
Married	Unknown
Notes	

The Family Line of Louisa Sadler Orr Alexander and Jefferson Alexander

The connection to the family line was Louisa, the daughter of Caroline Elliott Orr and Washington A. Orr [1].

The Third Generation

Louisa Sadler Orr Alexander - See Entry Page 37
Jefferson Alexander - See Entry Page 37-38

Their (4) Children

Cornelius Vanderbilt Alexander - See Entry Page 37
Mary Elizabeth Alexander - See Entry Page 37

Name	Sarah Alexander McVey
Date Of Birth	1889
Place Of Birth	Charlotte Township, North Carolina – Mecklenburg County
Date Of Death	Sunday, June 22, 1924
Age At Death	34-35
Place Of Death	Charlotte Township, North Carolina – Mecklenburg County
Occupation	Domestic Worker
Married	Thomas J. McVey (b. 1858 – d. Sunday, June 26, 1927, age 68 – 69)

My Family Tree

Notes	Sarah was buried on Tuesday, June 24, 1924, at Antioch Missionary Baptist Church Cemetery in Charlotte, North Carolina – Mecklenburg County.

Name	**Dorothy L. Alexander Webber**
Date Of Birth	Thursday, August 3, 1905
Place Of Birth	Kings Mountain, North Carolina – Cleveland County
Date Of Death	Monday, October 25, 2010
Age At Death	105
Place Of Death	Charlotte, North Carolina – Mecklenburg County
Occupation	Teacher
Married	Spurgeon Willard Webber [I]
Notes	Dorothy was buried in October 2010, a widow. Their children: Loretta Jean Hill Webber (b. 1936 – and died unknown) and Spurgeon Willard Webber [II] (b. Friday, January 26, 1934 – d. Tuesday, December 6, 2011, age 77), POD. Spurgeon [II] was buried in December 2011. Dorothy, Spurgeon [I], Loretta, and Spurgeon [II] were all buried at Forest Lawn West Cemetery in Charlotte Township, North Carolina – Mecklenburg County. Their children were born in Kings Mountain, North Carolina – Cleveland County, and died in Charlotte Township, North Carolina – Mecklenburg County.

Name	**Spurgeon Willard Webber I**
Date Of Birth	Friday, March 24, 1905
Place Of Birth	Gaston, North Carolina – Gaston County
Date Of Death	Monday, September 25, 1978
Age At Death	73
Place Of Death	Charlotte Township, North Carolina – Mecklenburg County
Occupation	Day Laborer
Married	Dorothy L. Alexander Webber

My Family Tree

Notes	Dorothy and Spurgeon were married on Thursday, May 11, 1933, in Gaston, North Carolina – Gaston County, and were married for 45 years. Spurgeon [1] was buried in September 1978. Spurgeon's parents were Elizabeth Roberts Webber and Tolston Webber.

The Family Line of Alice Wallace Orr and Alexander Orr

The connection to the family line was Alexander, the son of Caroline Elliott Orr and Washington A. Orr[1].

The Third Generation

Alice Wallace Orr - See Entry Page 38
Alexander Orr - See Entry Page 38

Their (3) Children

Name	Lawrence Orr
Date Of Birth	Sunday, May 14, 1882
Place Of Birth	North Carolina – Mecklenburg County
Date Of Death	Wednesday, September 25, 1946
Age At Death	64
Place Of Death	Crab Orchard, North Carolina – Mecklenburg County
Occupation	Farmer
Married	Addie Dennis Orr (b. 1891 – d. Saturday, December 15, 1928, age 36 – 37), POD. Crab Orchard, North Carolina – Mecklenburg County
Notes	In the 1900s Census, her name was spelled as Allie. They were married on Sunday, May 26, 1907, in Crab Orchard 7 Township, North Carolina – Mecklenburg County, and married for 39 years. Addie's parents were Susan Ann Dennis and Elias Dennis. Lawrence was buried on Sunday, September 29, 1946. Addie was buried in 1928. They were both buried side-by-side at St. Paul Presbyterian Church Cemetery in Charlotte, North Carolina – Mecklenburg County. He was a widower.

Name	Thomas Orr
Date Of Birth	1892
Place Of Birth	North Carolina – Mecklenburg County
Date Of Death	Monday, June 14, 1920

My Family Tree

Age At Death	27 – 28
Place Of Death	Winston-Salem, North Carolina – Forsyth County
Occupation	Minister/Cement Worker
Married	Single
Notes	Thomas was buried on Tuesday, June 15, 1920, in Charlotte Township, North Carolina – Mecklenburg County.

Name	Annie Orr Walker
Date Of Birth	Saturday, May 2, 1885
Place Of Birth	North Carolina – Mecklenburg County
Date Of Death	Monday, March 18, 1974
Age At Death	88
Place Of Death	Winston-Salem, North Carolina – Forsyth County
Occupation	Housewife/Domestic Worker
Married	Widow
Notes	Annie was buried in March 1974, at Evergreen Cemetery, a widow.

The Family Line of Esther Lee Springs and Samuel Springs

The connection to the family line was Samuel, the son of Isabela Elliott.

The Second Generation

Esther Lee Springs - See Entry Page 29
Samuel Springs - See Entry Page 28-29

Their (2) Children

Name	James Springs
Date Of Birth	1873
Place Of Birth	North Carolina – Mecklenburg County
Date Of Death	Thursday, August 6, 1914

My Family Tree

Age At Death	40-41
Place Of Death	Charlotte, North Carolina – Mecklenburg County
Occupation	House Man (Male Servant)
Married	Rosanne Witherspoon Springs
Notes	He had a common school education. His nickname was "Jim." They lived at 704 S. Meyers Street in Charlotte at the time of their deaths, homeowners, and he was a widower when he died. He was buried on Friday, August 7, 1914. Both Rosanna and James were buried at Pinewood Cemetery in Charlotte, North Carolina – Mecklenburg County.

Name	**Rosanne Witherspoon Springs**
Date Of Birth	1875
Place Of Birth	North Carolina – Mecklenburg County
Date Of Death	Saturday, June 13, 1914
Age At Death	38-39
Place Of Death	Charlotte, North Carolina – Mecklenburg County
Occupation	Nurse
Married	James Springs
Notes	Her nickname was "Rosa." Her parents were Galva L. Williams Witherspoon and H. W. Witherspoon. According to the 1880 Census, they were both illiterate. They were married on Sunday, December 20, 1893, in North Carolina – Mecklenburg County, and married for 20 years. She was buried on Sunday, June 14, 1914. Their child: Annie Springs Wilson.

Name	**Amos Springs**
Date Of Birth	1866
Place Of Birth	North Carolina – Mecklenburg County
Date Of Death	Unknown
Age At Death	Unknown

My Family Tree

Place Of Death	Unknown
Occupation	Farmer
Married	Mattie Heath Springs
Notes	According to the 1880 Census, he could read but could not write. Her father was Westley Heath. They were married on Sunday, November 11, 1888, in North Carolina – Mecklenburg County.

The Family Line of Rosanna Witherspoon Springs and James Springs

The Fourth Generation

Their Child

Name	Annie Springs Wilson
Date Of Birth	March 1900
Place Of Birth	North Carolina – Mecklenburg County
Date Of Death	Friday, January 3, 1936
Age At Death	35
Place Of Death	Charlotte, North Carolina – Mecklenburg County
Occupation	Domestic Worker/Housewife
Married	John Wilson (b. 1890), POB. South Carolina
Notes	She lived at 633 Cherry Street in Charlotte at the time of her death as a homeowner. She was buried on Sunday, January 5, 1936, in Charlotte, North Carolina – Mecklenburg County. In 1930, her father (Amos) was a boarder at their home until he died. Their child: Margaret Wilson (b. 1914), POB. North Carolina – Mecklenburg County.

The Family Line of Molly A. Hairston Hairston and Samuel H. Hairston

Name	Molly A. Hairston Hairston
Date Of Birth	Friday, December 25, 1874
Place Of Birth	North Carolina – Davie County
Date Of Death	Sunday, August 16, 1942

My Family Tree

Age At Death	67
Place Of Death	Fulton Township, North Carolina – Davie County
Occupation	Laundress/Housewife
Married	Samuel H. Hairston
Notes	As a child, she was raised on a farm. According to the 1910 Census, Molly and Samuel were both illiterate. She was a widow when she died. Her mother was Louise Hairston.

Name	**Samuel H. Hairston**
Date Of Birth	March 1864
Place Of Birth	North Carolina – Davie County
Date Of Death	Friday, April 14, 1922
Age At Death	58
Place Of Death	Fulton Township, North Carolina – Davie County
Occupation	Day Laborer
Married	Molly A. Hairston Hairston
Notes	He was born into slavery. Their granddaughter, Helen M. Hairston (b. 1919), was a boarder at their house. His wife and two of their children, Otis D. and Stella W., were all buried side-by-side at Cedar Grove Baptist Church Cemetery.

Their (6) Children

The connection to the family line was Ernest I., the son of Maggie Fowler Mason and Robert M. Mason ^{II}.

Mary Hairston Mason - See Entry Page 121
Ernest I. Mason - See Entry Page 120-121

Name	**Savannah Hairston Payne**
Date Of Birth	Wednesday, April 26, 1905
Place Of Birth	Cooleemee, North Carolina – Davie County

My Family Tree

Date Of Death	Monday, November 5, 2001
Age At Death	96
Place Of Death	North Carolina – Davie County
Occupation	Domestic Worker
Married	Delos Dewitt Payne
Notes	She was buried in November 2001. Savannah and Delos were both buried at Erwin Temple CME Church in North Carolina – Rowan County.

Name	**Delos Dewitt Payne**
Date Of Birth	Wednesday, December 2, 1903
Place Of Birth	Cooleemee, North Carolina – Davie County
Date Of Death	Wednesday, June 22, 1966
Age At Death	62
Place Of Death	North Carolina – Davie County
Occupation	Ervin Cotton Mill – Worker
Married	Savannah Hairston Payne
Notes	His sister, – Elizabeth Payne Neely. Married on Saturday, February 13, 1926, in North Carolina, a marriage of 40 years. His parents were Lula Malone Payne and William Henry Payne. He was buried on Saturday, June 25, 1966.

Name	**Stella W. Hairston**
Date Of Birth	1905
Place Of Birth	Fulton Township, North Carolina – Davie County
Date Of Death	1954
Age At Death	48-49
Place Of Death	Fulton Township, North Carolina – Davie County

My Family Tree

Occupation	Servant – Private House
Married	Single
Notes	She was buried in 1954 at Cedar Grove Baptist Church Cemetery.

Name	**Thurman Roscoe Hairston**
Date Of Birth	Thursday, September 15, 1898
Place Of Birth	Fulton Township, North Carolina – Davie County
Date Of Death	Unknown
Age At Death	Unknown
Place Of Death	North Carolina – Davie County
Occupation	Farming Laborer
Married	Seaila Wilson Hairston
Notes	He held a United States Draft Registration Card during WWI from (1917 – 1918).

Name	**Seaila Wilson Hairston**
Date Of Birth	1897
Place Of Birth	North Carolina – Davie County
Date Of Death	Friday, June 9, 1933
Age At Death	35 – 36
Place Of Death	Calahaln, North Carolina – Davie County
Occupation	Servant – Private House
Married	Thurman Roscoe Hairston
Notes	She was known by her nickname, "Ila," and her nickname was on her death record. Married on Wednesday, November 28, 1923, in North Carolina – Davie County. She was buried in June 1933 at Cedar Grove Baptist Church Cemetery. Her parents were Rebecca Clement Wilson (d. Thursday,

My Family Tree

	March 19, 1936) and Obadiah H. Wilson (b. 1849 – d. Sunday, February 19, 1939, age 89 – 90).

Name	**Otis D. Hairston**
Date Of Birth	Sunday, April 27, 1913
Place Of Birth	Fulton Township, North Carolina – Davie County
Date Of Death	Thursday, August 7, 1941
Age At Death	28
Place Of Death	Winston-Salem, North Carolina – Forsyth County
Occupation	Service Station – Laborer
Married	Pauline Hairston
Notes	He was buried on Sunday, August 10, 1941, at Cedar Grove Baptist Church Cemetery. His headstone has his birth year as 1908.

Name	**Beatrice Hairston Hairston**
Date Of Birth	Monday, April 1, 1901
Place Of Birth	Fulton Township, North Carolina – Davie County
Date Of Death	Wednesday, October 4, 1934
Age At Death	33
Place Of Death	North Carolina – Rowan County
Occupation	Domestic Worker/Housewife
Married	Paschal Hairston
Notes	She was buried in October 1934. Their children: Dest Hairston (b. Saturday, January 6, 1934, POB. North Carolina – Davie County – d. Wednesday, October 30, 1940, age 6), POD. Winston-Salem, North Carolina – Forsyth County, she was buried November 1940, at Evergreen Cemetery – Smith Reynolds Airport, Flora Hairston Bowman (b. Saturday, May 1, 1920 – d. Thursday, February 21, 1952, age 31), Flora's husband – Clarence Bowman (b. 1908 – d. 1963, age 54 – 55), Bernice Hairston (b. 1922), Louise Hairston Springs (b. Thursday, July 26, 1923 –

My Family Tree

	d. Thursday, August 18, 1988, age 65), William Hairston (b. 1926), Willard H. Hairston (b. 1927), and Thomas C. Hairston (b. 1929 – d. 1981, age 51 – 52).

Name	**Paschal Hairston**
Date Of Birth	Monday, January 1, 1872
Place Of Birth	North Carolina – Davie County
Date Of Death	Sunday, October 10, 1937
Age At Death	65
Place Of Death	North Carolina – Rowan County
Occupation	General Farmer
Married	(1) Maggie Doulin Hairston (2) Beatrice Hairston Hairston
Notes	(1) Married on Saturday, April 9, 1898. (2) Married on Monday, February 16, 1920, and both marriages took place in North Carolina. He was buried on Sunday, October 11, 1937. Beatrice and Paschal were both buried side-by-side at Cedar Grove Baptist Church Cemetery. Paschal's parents were Mary Hairston and William P. "Bud" Hairston. He was a widower when he died.

The Family Line of Louisiana Hairston Chaplin and Thomas Jonas Chaplin

The Fourth Generation

Name	**Louisiana Hairston Chaplin**
Date Of Birth	Friday, June 8, 1877
Place Of Birth	North Carolina
Date Of Death	Monday, May 19, 1941
Age At Death	63
Place Of Death	North Carolina
Occupation	Housewife
Married	Thomas Jonas Chaplin

Notes	She was buried on Thursday, May 22, 1941. Her parents were Hester Doulin Hairston and Henry Hairston. Louisiana's sister was Maggie Hairston (b. 1870, POB. and POD. Winston-Salem, North Carolina – Forsyth County – d. Thursday, May 29, 1919, age 48 – 49), and her occupation was a farmer. Maggie, Louisiana, and Thomas were all buried at Cedar Grove Baptist Church Cemetery. Louisiana and Maggie had the same father.

Name	**Thomas Jonas Chaplin**
Date Of Birth	Wednesday, September 13, 1876
Place Of Birth	North Carolina
Date Of Death	Tuesday, September 27, 1927
Age At Death	51
Place Of Death	North Carolina
Occupation	Farmer
Married	Louisiana Hairston Chaplin
Notes	He was buried on Thursday, September 29, 1927. Married on Wednesday, August 3, 1966 in North Carolina. His parents were Celia Atkinson Chaplin (b. 1846) and Thomas "Tom" Chaplin (b. 1836 POB. Virginia – d. Tuesday, March 7, 1916, age 79 – 80), POD. North Carolina – Davie County. Celia and Tom could not read or write, according to the Census records.

Their (13) Children

Name	**McDuff Chaplin**
Date Of Birth	1907
Place Of Birth	North Carolina
Date Of Death	Monday, June 30, 1975
Age At Death	67 – 68
Place Of Death	North Carolina
Occupation	Farmer

My Family Tree

Married	Marie Chaplin
Notes	He was buried on Friday, July 4, 1975, at Cedar Creek Baptist Church Cemetery in Mocksville, North Carolina – Davie County. He held a United States Drafted Registration Card during WWII.

Name	Abraham Chaplin
Date Of Birth	1910
Place Of Birth	North Carolina
Date Of Death	Unknown
Age At Death	Unknown
Place Of Death	North Carolina
Occupation	Farmer
Married	Single
Notes	

Name	Samuel Chaplin
Date Of Birth	Unknown
Place Of Birth	North Carolina
Date Of Death	Unknown
Age At Death	Unknown
Place Of Death	North Carolina
Occupation	Farmer
Married	Single
Notes	

My Family Tree

Name	Thessalonia Chaplin
Date Of Birth	Unknown
Place Of Birth	North Carolina
Date Of Death	Unknown
Age At Death	Unknown
Place Of Death	North Carolina
Occupation	Day Laborer
Married	Single
Notes	

Name	Roosevelt Chaplin
Date Of Birth	Unknown
Place Of Birth	North Carolina
Date Of Death	Unknown
Age At Death	Unknown
Place Of Death	North Carolina
Occupation	Farner
Married	Single
Notes	

Name	Thelma Chaplin
Date Of Birth	Unknown
Place Of Birth	North Carolina
Date Of Death	Unknown

My Family Tree

Age At Death	Unknown
Place Of Death	North Carolina
Occupation	Day Laborer
Married	Single
Notes	

The connection to the family line was Catherine, the daughter of Maggie Fowler Mason and Robert M. Mason [II].

Robert Bob Chaplin [I] - See Entry Page 127-128
Catherine Mason Chaplin - See Entry Page 127

Name	**Columbus Sylvester Chaplin**
Date Of Birth	Tuesday, October 24, 1916
Place Of Birth	North Carolina – Davie County
Date Of Death	Saturday, November 18, 1916
Age At Death	25 Days Old
Place Of Death	Fork Township, North Carolina – Wayne County
Occupation	None
Married	Single
Notes	He was buried on Sunday, November 19, 1916, at Cedar Grove Baptist Church Cemetery.

The connection to the family line was John Thomas Doulin [I], the son of Mary Mason Doulin and Robert Doulin.

Esther Chaplin Doulin - See Entry Page 243-244
John Thomas Doulin [I] - See Entry Page 244

Name	**John Henry Chaplin**
Date Of Birth	Wednesday, April 6, 1904
Place Of Birth	North Carolina – Davie County
Date Of Death	Thursday, October 31, 1974

My Family Tree

Age At Death	70
Place Of Death	Black Mountain, North Carolina – Forsyth County
Occupation	Barber
Married	Widower
Notes	He lived at 1026 N. Trade in Winston-Salem and was a widower when he died and a homeowner. He was buried on Wednesday, November 6, 1974, at Cedar Grove Baptist Church Cemetery.

Name	Rosco Corklin Chaplin
Date Of Birth	Saturday, November 7, 1914
Place Of Birth	North Carolina – Davie County
Date Of Death	Thursday, May 6, 1915
Age At Death	5 Months Old
Place Of Death	Fork Township, North Carolina – Wayne County
Occupation	None
Married	Single
Notes	His twin brother was Frederick Talmage Chaplin. Both twin brothers were buried on Friday, May 7, 1915, at Cedar Grove Baptist Church Cemetery.

Name	Frederick Talmage Chaplin
Date Of Birth	Saturday, November 7, 1914
Place Of Birth	North Carolina – Davie County
Date Of Death	Thursday, May 6, 1915
Age At Death	5 Months Old
Place Of Death	Fork Township, North Carolina – Wayne County
Occupation	None

My Family Tree

Married	Single
Notes	His twin brother was Rosco Corklin Chaplin. Both twin brothers were buried on Friday, May 7, 1915, at Cedar Grove Baptist Church Cemetery.

Name	**Ella T. Chaplin Bryson**
Date Of Birth	Wednesday, June 6, 1900
Place Of Birth	North Carolina – Davie County
Date Of Death	Monday, July 5, 1926
Age At Death	26
Place Of Death	Fork Township, North Carolina – Wayne County
Occupation	Farmer/Housewife
Married	Willie Bryson
Notes	She was buried on Wednesday, July 7, 1926. Ella and (her son) Columbus were both buried at Cedar Grove Baptist Church Cemetery. Her sons' father was John Bryson. Their sons: James L. Bryson and Columbus Bryson (b. Saturday, July 22, 1922 – d. Thursday, May 31, 1923, age 10 Months), POB. and POD. North Carolina – Davie County. Columbus was buried on Friday, June 1, 1923.

The Family Line of Grace Virginia Hargraves Bryson and James L. Bryson

The connection to the family line was James L., the son of Ella T. Chaplin Bryson and John Bryson.

The Fifth Generation

Name	**James L. Bryson**
Date Of Birth	Thursday, April 28, 1921
Place Of Birth	North Carolina – Davie County
Date Of Death	Thursday, November 8, 1962
Age At Death	41
Place Of Death	Lexington, North Carolina – Davidson County

My Family Tree

Occupation	Self-Employed – Junk
Married	Grace Virginia Hargraves Bryson
Notes	He was buried on Wednesday, November 11, 1962. Grace and James L. were supposed to be buried side-by-side. Her name was on the headstone, but her body was not buried there. Their child: James Thomas Bryson (b. Sunday, April 21, 1945, POB. North Carolina – Rowan County – d. Monday, May 21, 1945, age 29 Days Old), POD. Lexington, North Carolina – Davidson County and James T. lived at 319 Pugh Street in Lexington at the time of his death; he was buried on Monday, May 22, 1945. James L. and their son, James Thomas Bryson, were both buried at Cedar Grove Baptist Church Cemetery. James L. lived on Edna Street in Lexington at the time of his death.

Name	**Grace Virginia Hargraves Bryson**
Date Of Birth	Sunday, April 3, 1927
Place Of Birth	North Carolina – Davie County
Date Of Death	Unknown
Age At Death	Unknown
Place Of Death	Lexington, North Carolina – Davidson County
Occupation	Housewife
Married	James L. Bryson
Notes	

According to Census records for the period of 1828 covering Forsyth County – North Carolina, West Virginia, and Virginia, the Native Americans traveling in the region included: (Commerce, 1832).

The Eastern Band Cherokees

The Creek

The Shawnee (Saunee)

The Iroquois

The Saponi

The Saponi – were known for sheltering fugitive slaves. It has been reported that the inhabitants of *Native American* villages welcomed fugitive slaves, and many of their encampments were known as active stations along the *Underground Railroad* (Richardson, 2016). The *Underground Railroad* had safe houses to hide fugitives, and sometimes, the houses were invaded by slave catchers looking for fugitive slaves. It has been reported that the white communities of West Virginia, Virginia, and North Carolina called the natives "**Blackfoot.**" Some say the reason might have been because of the name of a particular band or a leader's name sounded or translated to the term (Setting, n.d.).

The Family Line of Ellen Clement Winford, Mary Belle Doulin Winford, Rebecca Ellis-Young Winford, and Alexander Winford

The Third Generation

Name	**Mary Belle Doulin Winford**
Date Of Birth	November 1875
Place Of Birth	Jerusalem, North Carolina – Davie County
Date Of Death	1906
Age At Death	31
Place Of Death	Jerusalem, North Carolina – Davie County
Occupation	Domestic Worker/Housewife
Married	Alexander Winford
Notes	Mary was a full-blooded Native American descent. It was written on her headstone at Cedar Grove Baptist Church Cemetery. Married December 1892 in North Carolina – Davie County, married for 14 years.

Name	**Alexander Winford**
Date Of Birth	June 1846
Place Of Birth	North Carolina – Davie County
Date Of Death	Saturday, October 20, 1928
Age At Death	82
Place Of Death	Jerusalem, North Carolina – Davie County
Occupation	Farmer
Married	(1) Ellen Clement Winford

My Family Tree

	(2) Mary Belle Doulin Winford
	(3) Rebecca Ellis-Young Winford
Notes	Alexander's name appeared on the Census Slave Schedule on Thursday, September 5, 1850, at the age of 4. He was going to Tennessee – Wilson County, but plans changed because the ship did not sail out. His nickname was "Alex." Alexander was buried on Tuesday, October 23, 1928, at Boxwood Baptist Church Cemetery in Jerusalem, North Carolina – Davie County. Alexander's parents were Annie Winford, POB. Kentucky and Henry Darr. (1) b. 1865 – d. 1892, age 27 – 28). (1) Married on Thursday, December 24, 1885. His first wife – Ellen, was born into slavery. (3) Married on Monday, September 6, 1909, in Fulton Township, North Carolina – Davie County. (3) b. 1871 – d. 1962, age 90–91). His parents were slaves, and his first wife was born into slavery.

His (12) Children

Edna Bell Winford Mason	-	See Entry Page 147-148
John Bunyon Mason	-	See Entry Page 147
Elizabeth O. Winford Mason	-	See Entry Page 158
Dennis DeQuincy Mason [1]	-	See Entry Page 157-158

Name	**Dorsey Winford**
Date Of Birth	April 1887
Place Of Birth	North Carolina – Davie County
Date Of Death	Unknown
Age At Death	Unknown
Place Of Death	North Carolina – Davie County
Occupation	Domestic Worker
Married	Unknown
Notes	His mother was Ellen Clement Winford.

Name	**Fallie Winford Foster**
Date Of Birth	Wednesday, June 4, 1919

My Family Tree

Place Of Birth	Jerusalem, North Carolina – Davie County
Date Of Death	Wednesday, February 11, 1998
Age At Death	78
Place Of Death	Winston-Salem, North Carolina – Forsyth County
Occupation	Domestic Worker/Housewife
Married	Lafayette "Fate" Foster (b. 1899 – d. 1962, age 62 – 63)
Notes	Married Monday, June 28, 1926, in North Carolina – married for 36 years. Her mother was Rebecca Ellis-Young Winford. Their children: Edna Lee Foster-Williams (b. 1928 – d. 2003, age 74-75), Helen M. Foster (b. 1930 – d. 1991, age 60-61), and Annie Frances Foster-Revel (b. June 1932 – d. 1966, age 33 – 34). Fallie was buried in February 1998 at Mainville AME Zion Church Cemetery in Mocksville, North Carolina – Davie County.

Name	Mary Winford Hairston
Date Of Birth	Friday, September 14, 1888
Place Of Birth	North Carolina – Davidson County
Date Of Death	Sunday, June 29, 1919
Age At Death	30
Place Of Death	North Carolina – Davie County
Occupation	Domestic Worker/Housewife
Married	James Hairston
Notes	Mary was buried on Sunday, June 29, 1919. Her mother was Ellen Clement Winford.

Name	James Hairston
Date Of Birth	1886
Place Of Birth	North Carolina – Davidson County
Date Of Death	Monday, November 28, 1938

My Family Tree

Age At Death	51 – 52
Place Of Death	Clemmons, North Carolina – Forsyth County
Occupation	Day Laborer
Married	(1) Mary Winford Hairston (2) Laura Florence Winfred Hairston
Notes	(1) Married on Saturday, March 9, 1907 in North Carolina. He was buried in November 1939. His parents were Hester Hairston and Andy Rorie. Mary and James were both buried at Cedar Grove Baptist Church Cemetery.

Name	**Laura Florence Winfred Hairston**
Date Of Birth	November 1896
Place Of Birth	North Carolina – Davie County
Date Of Death	Tuesday, February 15, 1983
Age At Death	86
Place Of Death	Winston-Salem, North Carolina – Forsyth County
Occupation	Domestic Worker
Married	James Hairston
Notes	She had eleven children who preceded her in death. She was buried in February 1983. Their two daughters were Sarah Maggie Hairston (b. Tuesday, October 14, 1930 – d. Sunday, January 24, 2021, age 90). She died in Winston-Salem and was buried at Parklawn Memorial Park in Winston-Salem, North Carolina – Forsyth County. Marian Hairston Lewis Harris (b. Wednesday, September 24, 1938 – d. Thursday, July 25, 2019, age 80). Both of her daughters were born in Clemmons, North Carolina – Forsyth County. Marian's son is Rodney Kenneth Lewis. Laura and her daughter Marian were both buried at Evergreen Cemetery.

Name	**Ella Winford Furlow**
Date Of Birth	August 1890
Place Of Birth	North Carolina – Davie County

My Family Tree

Date Of Death	Unknown
Age At Death	Unknown
Place Of Death	North Carolina – Davie County
Occupation	Domestic Worker
Married	Tommy Furlow (b. 1889)
Notes	Married on Sunday, April 19, 1908, in North Carolina – Davie County. Her mother was Ellen Clement Winford.

Name	Laura Winford
Date Of Birth	November 1895
Place Of Birth	North Carolina – Davie County
Date Of Death	Unknown
Age At Death	Unknown
Place Of Death	North Carolina – Davie County
Occupation	Domestic Worker
Married	Unknown
Notes	Her mother was Mary Belle Doulin Winford.

Name	Emma Winford
Date Of Birth	August 1898
Place Of Birth	North Carolina – Davie County
Date Of Death	Unknown
Age At Death	Unknown
Place Of Death	North Carolina – Davie County
Occupation	Domestic Worker

My Family Tree

Married	Unknown
Notes	Her mother was Mary Belle Doulin Winford.

Name	**Celesta Winford**
Date Of Birth	March 1897
Place Of Birth	North Carolina – Davie County
Date Of Death	Unknown
Age At Death	Unknown
Place Of Death	North Carolina – Davie County
Occupation	Domestic Worker
Married	Unknown
Notes	Her mother was Mary Belle Doulin Winford.

Name	**Maggie Winford**
Date Of Birth	1906
Place Of Birth	North Carolina – Davie County
Date Of Death	Unknown
Age At Death	Unknown
Place Of Death	North Carolina – Davie County
Occupation	Domestic Worker
Married	Unknown
Notes	Her mother was Mary Belle Doulin Winford.

Name	**Tallie Winford**

My Family Tree

Date Of Birth	1911
Place Of Birth	North Carolina – Davie County
Date Of Death	Unknown
Age At Death	Unknown
Place Of Death	North Carolina – Davie County
Occupation	Domestic Worker
Married	Unknown
Notes	Her mother was Rebecca Ellis-Young Winford.

Name	**Charlie Robert Winford**
Date Of Birth	Monday, April 22, 1912
Place Of Birth	Jerusalem, North Carolina – Davie County
Date Of Death	Saturday, January 2, 1971
Age At Death	58
Place Of Death	Winston-Salem, North Carolina – Forsyth County
Occupation	Plumber
Married	(1) Elouise Margaret Darr Henley Winford (2) Susie Shannon Glenn Winford
Notes	His mother was Rebecca Ellis-Young Winford. He was listed as Mulatto in the Census records. (1) Married in 1938. (2) Married on Saturday, July 20, 1968, married for 2 years. He was buried in January 1971 at Boxwood Baptist Church Cemetery in Mocksville, North Carolina – Davie County. Susie's parents were Maggie Stover Glenn and Tom Glenn. Susie was buried in 1972 at Evergreen Cemetery. (1) b. 1914 – d. 2002, age 87–88). (2) b. 1899 – d. 1972, age 72–73). Both marriages took place in Winston-Salem, North Carolina – Forsyth County.

My Family Tree

The Family of Mary Ann Ijames Neely and George Washington Neely

The connection to the family line was George, the son of Elsie Hawkins Neely and Henry Neely.

The Fourth Generation

Mary Ann Ijames Neely - See Entry Page 177
George Washington Neely - See Entry Page 176-177

Their (8) Children

Name	Joshua S. Neely
Date Of Birth	Monday, June 5, 1899
Place Of Birth	Jerusalem, North Carolina – Davie County
Date Of Death	Thursday, November 30, 2000
Age At Death	101
Place Of Death	Lexington, North Carolina – Davidson County
Occupation	Boiling Room Attendant
Married	(1) McIver Holman Neely (2) Winnie Lee Thomas Neely
Notes	He was buried in December 2000 at Carolina Biblical Gardens Cemetery in Jamestown, North Carolina – Guilford County. (1) Married in 1917 and (2) married in 1947; both marriages took place in North Carolina. (1) b. 1901 – d. 1938, age 37). (2) b. 1908 – d. 1964, age 56).

Name	James K. Neely
Date Of Birth	Monday, July 29, 1899
Place Of Birth	Jerusalem, North Carolina – Davie County
Date Of Death	Sunday, December 8, 1935
Age At Death	36
Place Of Death	Jerusalem, North Carolina – Davie County
Occupation	Textile Factory
Married	Ossie Holman Wilson Neely (b. 1905 – d. 1985, age 79 – 80)

My Family Tree

Notes	He had a Registration Card for WWI that had his middle name as "Camillis." Married on Saturday, March 20, 1920, in North Carolina. He was buried on Monday, December 9, 1935, at Liberty A.M.E. Zion Cemetery in Davie County, North Carolina. Ossie was a Domestic Worker.

Name	Joseph Frank Neely
Date Of Birth	Thursday, May 15, 1902
Place Of Birth	Jerusalem, North Carolina – Davie County
Date Of Death	Thursday, September 5, 1985
Age At Death	83
Place Of Death	Salisbury, North Carolina – Rowan County
Occupation	Operated Press Machine – Janitor – Erwin Cotton Mill Rowan County Schools
Married	Elizabeth Payne Neely
Notes	He was buried on Sunday, September 8, 1985, at Calahaln Friendship Baptist Church Cemetery in Cooleemee, North Carolina – Davie County.

Name	Elizabeth Payne Neely
Date Of Birth	Monday, August 28, 1905
Place Of Birth	North Carolina – Davie County
Date Of Death	Tuesday, November 10, 1992
Age At Death	87
Place Of Death	Salisbury, North Carolina – Rowan County
Occupation	Cook – School Cafeteria
Married	Joseph Frank Neely
Notes	Her brother was Delos Dewitt Payne. She was buried on Thursday, November 19, 1992, at Friendship Baptist Church Cemetery in Cooleemee, North Carolina – Davie County. Her parents were Lula Malone Payne (b. 1867 – d. Thursday, September 20, 1928, age 60–61). She was buried Friday, September 21, 1928, at New Bethel Baptist Church

My Family Tree

	Cemetery in Mocksville, North Carolina – Davie County, a widow, and William Henry Payne. Lula and William had 12 children together. Lula and William were married on Sunday, January 3, 1886, in North Carolina. Lula was the daughter of Milly Malone. Elizabeth and Joseph had two sons: Clyde Eugene Neely (b. 1923 – d. 1955, age 31–32), who served as a GM2 in the United States Navy during WWII, and DeWhitt Clinton Neely (b. 1925 – d. 2014, age 88–89), who served as an SGT in the United States Army in the Korean War. His nickname was "Dee." DeWhitt's wife was Margaret Sturdevant Neely (b. Tuesday, June 15, 1933 – d. Tuesday, December 3, 2019, age 86).

Name	Zelma Thomas Neely
Date Of Birth	Monday, March 9, 1914
Place Of Birth	Mocksville, North Carolina – Davie County
Date Of Death	Sunday, July 28, 1963
Age At Death	49
Place Of Death	North Carolina – Davie County
Occupation	Domestic Worker
Married	Lois Rebecca Turner Neely (b. 1916 – d. 1998, age 81 – 82)
Notes	Married on Monday, July 11, 1938, in Mocksville, North Carolina – Davie County.

Name	Beulah Irene Neely
Date Of Birth	Sunday, November 2, 1906
Place Of Birth	Salisbury, North Carolina – Rowan County
Date Of Death	Monday, February 16, 1976
Age At Death	69
Place Of Death	Salisbury, North Carolina – Rowan County
Occupation	Domestic Worker
Married	Single

My Family Tree

Notes	She was buried on Thursday, February 19, 1976. She was buried side-by-side with her mother at Calahaln Friendship Baptist Church Cemetery in Cooleemee, North Carolina – Davie County.

Name	**Norman Eugene Neely**
Date Of Birth	Monday, April 16, 1917
Place Of Birth	Jerusalem, North Carolina – Davie County
Date Of Death	Friday, August 21, 1959
Age At Death	42
Place Of Death	Durham, North Carolina – Durham County
Occupation	Steel Worker
Married	Ora Mae Holman Neely (b. October 1914)
Notes	Married in October 1933 in North Carolina. He lived at Route 4 in Durham at the time of his death and was a homeowner. Norman was buried on Wednesday, August 26, 1959, at Calahaln Friendship Baptist Church Cemetery in Cooleemee, North Carolina – Davie County. Her parents were Maggie Holman and Albert Holman.

Name	**William Odell Neely**
Date Of Birth	Monday, August 29, 1910
Place Of Birth	Jerusalem, North Carolina – Davie County
Date Of Death	Sunday, November 18, 1984
Age At Death	74
Place Of Death	Mocksville, North Carolina – Davie County
Occupation	Retired – Hyster Operator – Burlington Mills Company
Married	(1) Lillie Doulin Neely (2) Savannah Latner Myers Neely
Notes	(1) b. 1909 – d. 1949, age 39–40) (2) b. 1912 – d. 2005, age 92–93). (1) Married on Saturday, September 5, 1931, and (2) Married on Monday, April 21, 1952. Both marriages took place in North Carolina. William was buried on Wednesday, November 21, 1984. Savannah and William were

My Family Tree

	both buried side-by-side at Calahaln Friendship Baptist Church Cemetery in Woodleaf, North Carolina – Rowan County. They lived at 1128 Oak Street in Mocksville at the time of their deaths and were homeowners. Lillie and William had children: George Henry Neely (b. 1936 – d. 1994, age 57–58), Ethel Leona Neely (b. 1931 – d. 1944, age 12–13), and Annie Ruth Neely Hairston (b. Friday, August 23, 1939, POB. and POD. North Carolina – d. Tuesday, November 12, 1991, age 52). Annie was buried on Monday, December 16, 1991, at Erwin Temple Church in North Carolina – Rowan County. Annie's first husband was LeRoy Thurmon Cowan, married on Wednesday, November 27, 1963, and her second husband was John Westly Hairston. Annie's occupation was Garment Manufacturer Company – Presser. She lived at 114 Cotton Street in Mocksville at the time of her death, was a widow, and was a homeowner.

Name	**Mattie Louise Neely Wilson**
Date Of Birth	Monday, January 27, 1919
Place Of Birth	Jerusalem, North Carolina – Davie County
Date Of Death	Wednesday, December 16, 1959
Age At Death	40
Place Of Death	Mocksville, North Carolina – Davie County
Occupation	Housewife
Married	Glenn Thomas Wilson (b. Wednesday, September 8, 1915 – d. Friday, September 21, 2007, age 92), occupation – Reverend
Notes	She was buried on Sunday, December 20, 1959, at Calahaln Friendship Baptist Church Cemetery in North Carolina – Davie County. She lived at Route 1 Box 145 in Woodleaf, North Carolina. He was buried Saturday, September 22, 2007, at Redland Church of Christ Cemetery in Advance, North Carolina – Davie County. Their children: Richard Wilson, George Willson (Cuttie), James Wilson (Deborah), Mildred Delores Wilson Bares (b. 1940 –d. 2011, age 70–71), Mary Elizabeth Wilson Lassiter (b. 1944 – d. 2013, age 68–69), Glenna Wilson Latten, Dr. Patricia Wilson Copeland, Claudine Wilson Clark (Larry), and Vonnie Wilson Cunningham (Edward).

The Family Line of Mary Mason Doulin and Robert Doulin

The connection to the family line was Mary, the daughter of Lucinda Mason Mason.

My Family Tree

The Third Generation

Mary Mason Doulin	-	**See Entry Page 183**
Robert Doulin	-	**See Entry Page 184**

Their (4) Children

Esther Chaplin Doulin	-	**See Entry Page 243-244**
John Thomas Doulin [1]	-	**See Entry Page 244**
Alice Foster Doulin	-	**See Entry Page 246**
Fisher S. Doulin	-	**See Entry Page 247**

Name	Martha Doulin Wallace
Date Of Birth	June 1895
Place Of Birth	North Carolina – Davie County
Date Of Death	Sunday, June 18, 1939
Age At Death	44
Place Of Death	Mocksville, North Carolina – Davie County
Occupation	Laundry Worker
Married	(1) Robert Hairston (2) Howard Wallace
Notes	Martha was buried on Tuesday, June 20, 1939. Martha and Robert's child: William Hairston (b. Tuesday, June 10, 1924, POB. North Carolina – Davie County – d. Wednesday, February 1, 1939, age 13–14) POD. North Carolina – Rowan County. William was buried on Thursday, February 2, 1939. (2) Married on Wednesday, February 28, 1934 in North Carolina. Martha, Robert, and William were all buried at Cedar Grove Baptist Church Cemetery.

Name	Robert Hairston
Date Of Birth	1897
Place Of Birth	North Carolina – Davie County
Date Of Death	Thursday, August 8, 1929
Age At Death	31 – 32

My Family Tree

Place Of Death	Mocksville, North Carolina – Davie County
Occupation	Laundry Worker
Married	Martha Doulin Hairston
Notes	Married on Monday, December 20, 1915, in North Carolina – Davie County, married for 13 years. He was buried on Friday, August 9, 1929. His parents were Judy Wilson Hairston and Patrick Hairston (b. April 1859 – d. Saturday, April 16, 1921, age 61–62). Patrick was buried on Saturday, April 16, 1921, at Cedar Grove Baptist Church Cemetery. Judy and Patrick were married in 1895 in North Carolina. Robert's siblings were Mary Hairston Van Easton (b. 1900 – d. 1967, age 66), Samuel Hairston (b. 1903 – d. 1920, age 16–17), and George Hairston (b. 1910 – d. 1957, age 46–47).

Name	**Mosella Doulin Neely Grant**
Date Of Birth	Monday, December 25, 1899
Place Of Birth	North Carolina – Davie County
Date Of Death	Saturday, January 25, 1969
Age At Death	69
Place Of Death	North Carolina – Davie County
Occupation	Domestic Worker/Housewife
Married	(1) Grant Neely (2) Gaston Neely (3) Grover Grant
Notes	Her nickname was "Mossie." (1) b. 1895 – d. 1933, age 37 – 38), he served in the United States Army during WWI. They were married in 1920. (2) b. 1896 – d. 1933, age 36 – 37), married Wednesday, December 29, 1920. Gaston was buried at Liberty A. M. E. Zion Cemetery in North Carolina – Davie County. (3) b. 1913 – d. 1988, age 74 – 75), married Tuesday, August 29, 1939, and married for 30 years. Her husband's POB. and POD. North Carolina and all three marriages took place in Mocksville, North Carolina – Davie County. Mosella children with Thomas Hairston: Fred Neely (b. 1936) and John Henry Neely (b. June 1938). Mosella and Gaston children: Robert Junior Neely (b. 1920 – d. 1981, age 60), George Cornelius Neely (b. August 1923), Ernest Lee Neely (b. August 1925), Josie Ann Neely (b.

My Family Tree

	1928 – d. 1994, age 65 – 66), and Sarah Georganna Neely (b. Friday, September 14, 1928 – d. Thursday, November 14, 1996, age 68). All Mossie's children POB. Fulton Township, North Carolina – Davie County. Mossie was buried on Wednesday, January 29, 1969. Mossie, Robert, and Sarah were all buried at Second Presbyterian Cemetery in Mocksville, North Carolina – Davie County. Mosella's headstone has her first and maiden name spelled as Mozella Dulin.

The Family Line of Eliza Little Workman and Franklin Workman

The Second Generation

Name	**Eliza Little Workman**
Date Of Birth	March 1830
Place Of Birth	South Carolina
Date Of Death	Tuesday, August 6, 1912
Age At Death	82
Place Of Death	Spartanburg, South Carolina – Spartanburg County
Occupation	Farmer Laborer
Married	Franklin Workman
Notes	According to the 1870 Census, Eliza's first name was spelled Ailsie, and they were illiterate.

Name	**Franklin Workman**
Date Of Birth	January 1822
Place Of Birth	Scuffletown, South Carolina – Laurens County
Date Of Death	Unknown
Age At Death	Unknown
Place Of Death	Spartanburg, South Carolina – Spartanburg County
Occupation	General Farmer
Married	Eliza Little Workman

My Family Tree

Notes	They were both slaves. Franklin went by the nickname "Frank." They were married in 1866 in South Carolina

Their (5) Children

Name	**Emma Workman**
Date Of Birth	April 1876
Place Of Birth	Paris Mountain, South Carolina – Greenville County
Date Of Death	Unknown
Age At Death	Unknown
Place Of Death	South Carolina
Occupation	Domestic Worker
Married	Unknown
Notes	According to the 1910 Census, Emma was literate and attended school.

Name	**James J. Workman**
Date Of Birth	February 1870
Place Of Birth	Laurens, South Carolina – Laurens County
Date Of Death	Monday, April 23, 1945
Age At Death	75
Place Of Death	Newberry, South Carolina – Newberry County
Occupation	General Farmer
Married	Lucinda Williams Workman
Notes	According to the 1910 Census, he was literate.

Name	**Lucinda Williams Workman**

My Family Tree

Date Of Birth	1886
Place Of Birth	South Carolina – Greenville County
Date Of Death	Unknown
Age At Death	Unknown
Place Of Death	Laurens, South Carolina – Laurens County
Occupation	Farmer Laborer/Housewife
Married	James J. Workman
Notes	Lucinda and James were married in 1899 in Scuffletown, South Carolina – Laurens County. Lucinda's mother was Fannie Williams (b. 1864). Their sons: James W. Workman (b. 1903) and Mack Charles Workman (b. Sunday, September 18, 1910 – d. Tuesday, May 13, 1952, age 41). Both sons' POB and POD were in South Carolina.

The connection to the family line was Henry Workman, the father of William Essix Workman, who married Euphonia Bernice Orr Workman.

Henry Workman - See Entry Page 56-56
Carrie Green Workman - See Entry Page 57

Name	Essex Workman
Date Of Birth	Saturday, December 25, 1875
Place Of Birth	Laurens, South Carolina – Laurens County
Date Of Death	Monday, September 26, 1949
Age At Death	73
Place Of Death	South Carolina – Greenville County
Occupation	General Farmer
Married	Single
Notes	According to the 1910 Census, he was literate.

Name	Edgar Workman

My Family Tree

Date Of Birth	September 1873
Place Of Birth	Paris Mountain, South Carolina – Greenville County
Date Of Death	Friday, August 3, 1934
Age At Death	60
Place Of Death	Spartanburg, South Carolina – Spartanburg County
Occupation	General Farmer
Married	Willimina Workman (b. January 1878 – d. 1934, age 55–56)
Notes	According to the 1910 Census, he was literate.

The Family Line of Hester Hairston, Bessie C. Mason Hairston, and Ivory Shack Hairston

The connection to the family line was Bessie C., the daughter of Mary Jane Brown Mason and John Henry Mason.

The Third Generation

Hester Hairston	-	See Entry Page 234
Bessie C. Mason Hairston	-	See Entry Page 234
Ivory Shack Hairston	-	See Entry Page 234

Hester (2) Children with Ivory

Name	Wise Hairston
Date Of Birth	Wednesday, September 19, 1894
Place Of Birth	North Carolina – Davie County
Date Of Death	Friday, July 16, 1915
Age At Death	20
Place Of Death	North Carolina – Davie County
Occupation	Day Laborer
Married	Mary Cornelia Martin Hairston
Notes	Married on Sunday, March 7, 1915, in North Carolina – Davie County. He was buried in July 1915 at Cedar Grove Baptist Church Cemetery. Their children: Willie Wise Hairston and Willie Martin Hairston. His mother was Hester.

My Family Tree

Name	**Nume Hairston**
Date Of Birth	Tuesday, May 26, 1896
Place Of Birth	Advance, North Carolina – Davie County
Date Of Death	Tuesday, April 7, 1964
Age At Death	67
Place Of Death	North Carolina – Davie County
Occupation	R. J. Reynolds – Tobacco Industry – Worker/Military Services
Married	Single
Notes	He registered on Tuesday, June 5, 1917, in Winston-Salem, North Carolina – Forsyth County, in WWI, as PVT, and was honorably discharged on Monday, July 7, 1919. He was buried in April 1964 at Piney Grove United Methodist Church Cemetery in Advance, North Carolina – Davie County. His mother was Bessie C.

The Family Line of Mary Cornelia Martin Hairston and Wise Hairston

The Fourth Generation

Mary Cornelia Martin Hairston - See Entry Page 287
Wise Hairston - See Entry Page 287

Their (2) Children

Name	**Willie Wise Hairston**
Date Of Birth	Tuesday, April 20, 1915
Place Of Birth	Winston-Salem, North Carolina – Forsyth County
Date Of Death	Thursday, June 24, 1915
Age At Death	2 Months Old
Place Of Death	Winston-Salem, North Carolina – Forsyth County
Occupation	None
Married	Single
Notes	He was buried on Thursday, June 24, 1915, at Foy Cemetery in Winston-Salem, North Carolina – Forsyth County.

My Family Tree

Name	**Willie Martin Hairston**
Date Of Birth	1920
Place Of Birth	Winston-Salem, North Carolina – Forsyth County
Date Of Death	Monday, May 2, 1983
Age At Death	62-63
Place Of Death	Winston-Salem, North Carolina – Forsyth County
Occupation	Day Laborer
Married	Princess Irene Tatum Hairston
Notes	He was buried on Thursday, May 5, 1983.

Name	**Princess Irene Tatum Hairston**
Date Of Birth	Saturday, February 1, 1919
Place Of Birth	Virginia
Date Of Death	Wednesday, November 5, 1986
Age At Death	67
Place Of Death	Winston-Salem, North Carolina – Forsyth County
Occupation	Domestic Worker/Homemaker
Married	Willie Martin Hairston
Notes	Her parents were Cora Scales Tatum and Ballard Tatum. She was buried in November 1986. Princess and Willie were both buried at Evergreen Cemetery.

The Family Line of Susan Mason Hairston and Wiseman H. Hairston

The connection to the family line was Susan, the daughter of Phyllis Ann Brown Hairston Mason and Burrell Mason.

The Second Generation

Susan Mason Hairston - See Entry Page 229
Wiseman H. Hairston - See Entry Page 229-230

My Family Tree

Susan had 17 children, but only 12 were listed according to the 1910 Census records.

Their (12) Children

Name	**Vance Wiseman Hairston**
Date Of Birth	Monday, September 12, 1881
Place Of Birth	North Carolina – Davie County
Date Of Death	Monday, April 14, 1952
Age At Death	70
Place Of Death	Winston-Salem, North Carolina – Forsyth County
Occupation	Merchant
Married	(1) Sadie Long Hairston (2) Sallie Weaver Hairston
Notes	According to the Census records for 1910, he was literate. He was buried in April 1952. Sallie and Vance were both buried at Evergreen Cemetery. He was a widower when he died.

Name	**Sadie Long Hairston**
Date Of Birth	1881
Place Of Birth	North Carolina
Date Of Death	Thursday, November 3, 1932
Age At Death	50-51
Place Of Death	North Carolina – Forsyth County
Occupation	Merchant Helper
Married	Vance Wiseman Hairston
Notes	Married on Wednesday, July 16, 1902, in Winston-Salem, North Carolina – Forsyth County. Her mother was Divie Long. She was buried in November 1932 at Evergreen Cemetery – Smith Reynolds Airport. Their children: Nellie Hairston Pauling, Mildred B. Hairston, Nathaniel H. Hairston, Richard Aubrey Hairston, Lucile Hairston, and Ophelia Hairston.

My Family Tree

Name	Sallie Weaver Hairston
Date Of Birth	Tuesday, September 4, 1883
Place Of Birth	Wadesboro, North Carolina – Anson County
Date Of Death	Saturday, January 28, 1950
Age At Death	66
Place Of Death	Winston-Salem, North Carolina – Forsyth County
Occupation	Domestic Worker
Married	Vance Wiseman Hairston
Notes	She was buried in 1950. Their children: Wallace C. Hairston and Thelma Hairston.

Name	Martha Hairston Barron
Date Of Birth	Saturday, March 11, 1893
Place Of Birth	North Carolina – Davie County
Date Of Death	Wednesday, November 22, 1961
Age At Death	68
Place Of Death	Winston-Salem, North Carolina – Forsyth County
Occupation	Housewife
Married	Charles J. Barron
Notes	According to the Census records for 1910, she was literate. Martha was buried on Sunday, November 26, 1961, at Evergreen Cemetery. Martha and Charles both lived at 1445 W. 27th Street in Winston-Salem at the time of their death and were homeowners. Her child: Eulia Hairston (b. Wednesday, April 15, 1915 – d. Tuesday, May 18, 1915, age 1 Month Old) POB. and POD. Winston-Salem, North Carolina – Forsyth County. Eulia was buried in May 1915 at Cedar Grove Baptist Church Cemetery.

My Family Tree

Name	Charles J. Barron
Date Of Birth	Tuesday, February 2, 1892
Place Of Birth	North Carolina – Gaston County
Date Of Death	Thursday, January 30, 1958
Age At Death	68
Place Of Death	Winston-Salem, North Carolina – Forsyth County
Occupation	Retired Hospital Worker
Married	Martha Hairston Barron
Notes	Married on Saturday, December 19, 1953, in North Carolina, married for 5 years. He was buried on Sunday, February 2, 1958, at Odd Fellows Cemetery. His parents were Laura Witherspoon Barron and Charles A. Barron.

Name	Robert Baxter Hairston
Date Of Birth	Tuesday, May 8, 1888
Place Of Birth	North Carolina – Davie County
Date Of Death	Wednesday, December 23, 1964
Age At Death	76
Place Of Death	Winston-Salem, North Carolina – Forsyth County
Occupation	Custodian – Winston-Salem City Hall
Married	Beulah Watt Shoaf Hairston
Notes	According to the Census records for 1910, he was literate. Married on Saturday, October 13, 1956, in North Carolina – Forsyth County. He was buried on Wednesday, December 26, 1964, at Evergreen Cemetery. He lived at 2050 N. Cherry Street in Winston-Salem when he died as a widower and homeowner. Her parents were Marjorie Watt and Jim Watt.

My Family Tree

Name	John Thomas Hairston
Date Of Birth	Friday, September 8, 1876
Place Of Birth	North Carolina – Davie County
Date Of Death	Thursday, February 25, 1960
Age At Death	83
Place Of Death	Greensboro, North Carolina – Guilford County
Occupation	Farmer/Minister
Married	(1) Lucille Ingram Hairston (2) Nancy Alice Wright Hairston (3) Martha Y. Jordan Hairston
Notes	According to the Census records for 1910, he was literate. He was buried on Tuesday, March 1, 1960, at Maplewood Cemetery in Greensboro, North Carolina – Guilford County. He lived at 836 Austin in Greensboro at the time of his death. His other children: Warren G. Hairston (b. Tuesday, November 2, 1920 – d. Friday, September 27, 2013, age 92) and Nancy Lois Hairston Young (b. Saturday, March 4, 1922 – d. Tuesday, April 16, 2002, age 80), occupation – Domestic Worker/Housewife. Nancy's husband – Cecil Thomas Young [1] (b. 1920 – d. 1988, age 67). According to the Census records for 1930, Nancy was literate. Nancy was buried in April 2002 at Lakeview Memorial Park Cemetery in Greensboro, North Carolina – Guilford County, as a widow. Mr. Hairston has an obituary that talks about his life.

Name	Lucille Ingram Hairston
Date Of Birth	Tuesday, April 13, 1886
Place Of Birth	North Carolina
Date Of Death	Thursday, December 14, 1911
Age At Death	25
Place Of Death	Greensboro, North Carolina – Guilford County
Occupation	Housewife
Married	John Thomas Hairston

My Family Tree

Notes	Married on Thursday, October 8, 1908, in North Carolina, married for 2 years. She was buried in December 1911 at Union Cemetery in Greensboro, North Carolina – Guilford County. Their children: George Thomas Hairston (b. 1912) and Jasper Roland Hairston (b. Sunday, August 15, 1909, in Greensboro, North Carolina – Guilford County – d. Friday, December 29, 1959, age 50), in Philadelphia, Pennsylvania, buried in 1959, at Maple Cemetery in Greensboro, North Carolina – Guilford County. Jasper was a WWII Veteran enlisting as a PVT in the United States Army on Wednesday, June 17, 1942, in Philadelphia. Jasper separated from active service on Saturday, October 20, 1945, in Newark, New Jersey – Essex County. Jasper's wife was Esther Hairston.

Name	Nancy Alice Wright Hairston
Date Of Birth	Monday, December 10, 1883
Place Of Birth	South Carolina
Date Of Death	Thursday, July 16, 1931
Age At Death	47
Place Of Death	Greensboro, North Carolina – Guilford County
Occupation	Housewife
Married	John Thomas Hairston
Notes	Married on Tuesday, October 21, 1913, married for 17 years. She was buried in July 1931 at Maple Cemetery in Greensboro, North Carolina – Guilford County. Her parents were J. T. Hairston Wright and Julian Wright. Their children: Rev. Otis L. Hairston (b. Sunday, April 28, 1918 – d. Tuesday, July 18, 2000, age 82) and Elmer Howitt Hairston (b. Tuesday, July 29, 1919 – d. Tuesday, December 31, 1991, age 72).

Name	Martha Y. Jordan Hairston
Date Of Birth	Saturday, June 22, 1889
Place Of Birth	Raleigh, North Carolina – Wake County
Date Of Death	Greensboro, North Carolina – Guilford County
Age At Death	78

My Family Tree

Place Of Death	Monday, June 17, 1968
Occupation	Housewife
Married	John Thomas Hairston
Notes	Married in 1933 in North Carolina, married for 27 years. Her parents were Elizabeth Gordon Jordan and Jacob Jordan. She was buried in June 1968 at Evergreen Cemetery.

Name	Perley Hairston
Date Of Birth	November 1880
Place Of Birth	North Carolina – Davie County
Date Of Death	Unknown
Age At Death	Unknown
Place Of Death	Unknown
Occupation	Unknown
Married	Unknown
Notes	According to the Census records for 1910, she was literate.

Name	Effie Hairston
Date Of Birth	July 1888
Place Of Birth	North Carolina – Davie County
Date Of Death	Unknown
Age At Death	Unknown
Place Of Death	Unknown
Occupation	Domestic Worker
Married	Unknown

My Family Tree

Notes	According to the Census records for 1910, she was literate.

Name	**Bernis Hairston**
Date Of Birth	1901
Place Of Birth	North Carolina – Davie County
Date Of Death	Unknown
Age At Death	Unknown
Place Of Death	Unknown
Occupation	Unknown
Married	Unknown
Notes	According to the Census records for 1910, he was literate

Name	**Israel H. Hairston**
Date Of Birth	Saturday, July 3, 1886
Place Of Birth	North Carolina – Davie County
Date Of Death	Saturday, April 21, 1945
Age At Death	58
Place Of Death	Bethania, North Carolina – Forsyth County
Occupation	Minister
Married	Gertrude Crump Hairston
Notes	According to the Census records for 1910, he was literate. He was buried on Wednesday, April 25, 1945. Gertrude and Israel were both buried at Odd Fellows Cemetery. They both lived at 1443 Pittsburg in Winston-Salem at the time of their death and were homeowners.

My Family Tree

Name	**Gertrude Crump Hairston**
Date Of Birth	Saturday, July 3, 1884
Place Of Birth	North Carolina – Davie County
Date Of Death	Thursday, June 8, 1916
Age At Death	21-22
Place Of Death	Winston-Salem, North Carolina – Forsyth County
Occupation	Domestic Worker/Housewife
Married	Israel H. Hairston
Notes	She was buried in June 1916. Her parents were Ruthie Bailey Crump and Nat Crump.

Wanne Hairston	-	**See Entry Page 229**
Margaret Hairston	-	**See Entry Page 229**
Mack Hairston	-	**See Entry Page 229**
Noah Hairston	-	**See Entry Page 229**
Notes		According to the Census records for 1910, they were literate.

The Family Line of Sadie Long Hairston and Vance Wiseman Hairston

The connection to the family was Vance, the son of Susan Mason Hairston and Wisemen H. Hairston.

The Third Generation

Sadie Long Hairston	-	**See Entry Page 290**
Vance Wiseman Hairston	-	**See Entry Page 290**

Their (6) Children

Name	**Ophelia Hairston**
Date Of Birth	Thursday, October 23, 1902
Place Of Birth	Winston Township, North Carolina – Forsyth County
Date Of Death	Sunday, October 6, 1918
Age At Death	15
Place Of Death	Winston-Salem, North Carolina – Forsyth County

My Family Tree

Occupation	None
Married	Single
Notes	She was buried in October 1918 at Odd Fellows Cemetery.

Name	**Nellie Hairston Pauling**
Date Of Birth	Sunday, February 14, 1904
Place Of Birth	North Carolina – Forsyth County
Date Of Death	Saturday, February 2, 1957
Age At Death	52
Place Of Death	Winston-Salem, North Carolina – Forsyth County
Occupation	Housewife
Married	Alonzo Pauling [I]
Notes	She was buried Thursday, February 7, 1957, at Evergreen Cemetery.

Name	**Alonzo B. Pauling I**
Date Of Birth	Friday, July 3, 1896
Place Of Birth	North Carolina – Forsyth County
Date Of Death	Wednesday, July 31, 1974
Age At Death	79
Place Of Death	Winston-Salem, North Carolina – Forsyth County
Occupation	Day Laborer
Married	Nellie Hairston Pauling
Notes	They both lived at 1454 Clark Avenue in Winston-Salem at the time of their death and were homeowners. He was buried in August 1974 at Piedmont Memorial Gardens Cemetery in Winston-Salem, North Carolina – Forsyth County.

My Family Tree

Name	Richard Aubrey Hairston
Date Of Birth	Tuesday, May 7, 1912
Place Of Birth	North Carolina – Davie County
Date Of Death	Saturday, October 16, 1943
Age At Death	31
Place Of Death	Old Town, North Carolina – Forsyth County
Occupation	Truck Driver Tobacco Company
Married	Bessie Hooper Hairston
Notes	He was buried on Wednesday, October 20, 1943, at Odd Fellows Cemetery. He lived at RFD # 7 in Winston-Salem at the time of his death as a homeowner and a widower.

Name	Mildred B. Hairston
Date Of Birth	Monday, March 4, 1907
Place Of Birth	North Carolina
Date Of Death	Thursday, November 6, 1969
Age At Death	62
Place Of Death	Winston-Salem, North Carolina – Forsyth County
Occupation	Housewife/Domestic Worker
Married	Widow
Notes	She was buried on Monday, November 10, 1969, at Evergreen Cemetery. She lived at 1331 Oak Street in Winston-Salem at the time of her death, a homeowner.

Name	Nathaniel H. Hairston
Date Of Birth	Tuesday, April 6, 1909
Place Of Birth	Winston Township, North Carolina – Forsyth County

My Family Tree

Date Of Death	Saturday, August 31, 1963
Age At Death	54
Place Of Death	Winston-Salem, North Carolina – Forsyth County
Occupation	Day Laborer
Married	Jessie Mae Collie Hairston (b.1916)
Notes	Married on Friday, May 10, 1935, in North Carolina. He was buried on Thursday, September 5, 1963, at Evergreen Cemetery.

Name	Lucile Hairston
Date Of Birth	Friday, April 11, 1913
Place Of Birth	Winston Township, North Carolina – Forsyth County
Date Of Death	Tuesday, October 29, 1918
Age At Death	5 Years Old
Place Of Death	Winston-Salem, North Carolina – Forsyth County
Occupation	None
Married	Single
Notes	She was buried on Wednesday, October 30, 1918, at Odd Fellows Cemetery. She lived at 1327 Derby Street in Winston-Salem at the time of her death.

The Family Line of Letitia Goolsby Hairston and Winston Hairston

Name	Letitia Goolsby Hairston
Date Of Birth	March 1860
Place Of Birth	Virginia – Henry County
Date Of Death	Thursday, June 18, 1914
Age At Death	54
Place Of Death	North Carolina – Davie County

My Family Tree

Occupation	Private Cook
Married	Winston Hairston (b. 1857) POB. Beaver Island, North Carolina – Stokes County POD. Sauratown, North Carolina – Stokes County
Notes	She was born into slavery. According to the Census records for 1910, she was literate. She was buried in June 1914 at Cedar Grove Baptist Church Cemetery as a widow. The daughter of Bethany "Thany" Hairston Goolsby (b. 1835) and John Goolsby (b. 1828 – d. 1918, age 90), they both died in Sauratown, North Carolina – Stokes County. Bethany and John were married Sunday, October 21, 1877, in Sauratown, North Carolina – Stokes County. Her father, John Goolsby, was a slave and a coachman for the Hairston family. According to John, he was a descendant of an African King. He hid a tea set and other valuables in the woods when Union troops passed through the area during the Civil War. When Peter W. Hairston left the plantation to serve the Confederacy, John Goolsby accompanied him. Letitia was a cook and servant for Peter W. and Fannie Hairston and her children (Agnes Hairston and Ruth Hairston) in the 1900s through 1910s Census at the Cooleemee Plantation House in North Carolina – Davie County on Yadkin River. The Cooleemee Plantation House is a United States National Historical Landmark. Winston's parents were Sophia Anna Hairston (b. 1831 – d. 1926, age 94 – 95) and Salem Hairston (b. 1827), and they were slaves. Winston's parents died in North Carolina.

Her (3) Children

Name	**Robert Lee Hairston**
Date Of Birth	1882
Place Of Birth	North Carolina – Stokes County
Date Of Death	Monday, September 19, 1932
Age At Death	50
Place Of Death	Winston-Salem, North Carolina – Forsyth County
Occupation	Factory Worker/Janitor
Married	Rosa E. Williams Hairston
Notes	According to the Census records for 1910, he was listed as literate. In the 1930 Census in Winston-Salem, at the age of 45, Robert was a boarder at the house of Madison D. Stockton. He was a Janitor at an office building and his wife Rosa was a Servant (Cook) in the Stockton home, too. Rosa and Robert had been married for 22 years. He was buried on Tuesday, September 20, 1932, at Sunset Cemetery in Asheville, North Carolina –

My Family Tree

	Buncombe County. He lived at 1422 Jackson Street in Winston-Salem at the time of his death, a homeowner.

Name	Rosa E. Williams Hairston
Date Of Birth	Monday, December 6, 1880
Place Of Birth	North Carolina – Forsyth County
Date Of Death	Friday, January 8, 1954
Age At Death	73
Place Of Death	Winston Salem, North Carolina – Forsyth County
Occupation	Cook
Married	She was buried on Monday, January 11, 1954, at Lewisville Cemetery in Lewisville, North Carolina – Forsyth County. She lived at 2041 N. Cherry Street in Winston-Salem at the time of her death, a homeowner. Her parents were Febby Williams and Anderson Williams.
Notes	

The connection to the family line was Annie Geneva Mason Hairston, the daughter of Nancy Jane Crump Mason and John Henry Mason. Annie's husband, Winston Ervin Hairston, was the son of Ruth W. Hairston Hairston and William Thomas Hairston. Ruth W. Hairston was married to William Thomas Hairston, the son of Peter Wilson Hairston. Peter and his father Samuel were Ruth's parents and grandparents former slave masters. Ruth and William stayed married well-into their 90s and lived on the Cooleemee Plantation in North Carolina.

Ruth W. Hairston Hairston - See Entry Page 160
William Thomas Hairston - See Entry Page 160

Name	John Winston Hairston I
Date Of Birth	Tuesday, June 4, 1878
Place Of Birth	North Carolina – Stokes County
Date Of Death	Friday, May 9, 1947
Age At Death	68
Place Of Death	Asheville, North Carolina – Buncombe County

My Family Tree

Occupation	Minister
Married	(1) Mary C. Chambers Hairston (2) Annie Mae Miller Hairston Bolden
Notes	He had a Draft Registration Card during WWI from (1917-1918). He was buried on Tuesday, May 13, 1947. He lived at Route 2 Box 214 in Emma, North Carolina – Buncombe County, as a homeowner. He was the son of former slaves and graduated from Livingstone College with a Doctor in Divinity. He was a minister with the largest number of Baptist members in North Carolina. He was interviewed by Editor A. B. Caldwell, who wrote about him in his book name, "History of the American Negro and his institutes," Volume IV, in 1921. (1) b. 1874 – d. 1938, age 65 – 66). Mary and John were married on Monday, May 2, 1904, in North Carolina. Mary and John's children: Roy Charles Hairston (b. 1904 – d. 1970, age 66 – 67), James Edison Hairston (b. 1914 – d. 1972, age 58 – 59) and John Winston Hairston ^{II} (b. 1913).

Name	**Annie Mae Miller Hairston Bolden**
Date Of Birth	Monday, March 19, 1894
Place Of Birth	North Carolina
Date Of Death	Monday, March 4, 1996
Age At Death	102
Place Of Death	Asheville, North Carolina – Buncombe County
Occupation	Housewife
Married	John Winston Hairston ^{I}
Notes	She was buried in March 1996. Annie and John were both buried at Sunset Cemetery in Asheville, North Carolina – Buncombe County.

My Family Tree

Bishop, {Rev.} Gary Marcus Simpson

Bishop Gary Marcus Simpson has maintained a significance in our family life, interacting with generations of both the **Carey and Mason** contingents. While my parents were active members of the **Temple of I AM**, other members of the family have also maintained their own relationship with him. Early in his ministry, church services were held in his basement on Joy Road.

On my mother's side, my grandmother, *Levonia M. Carey Cowan*, knew the young *Minister Simpson* and was his housekeeper for several years. Having observed his dedication to GOD, she was convinced of his calling and worked to help him build his church. She provided three pulpit chairs and a podium (used yet today) for the temple. Although she was not a member of the temple, my grandmother would bring my aunts (my mother's sisters) *Elise Cowan, Judy Cowan, and Toni Cowan* to hear him speak. She loved hearing him teach the word. My aunts joined the temple and sang in the choir. *Reverend Simpson* would officiate at the wedding ceremonies for my aunts *Elise and Judy*.

My grandparents *(Hazel and Napoleon)* also maintained a close relationship with *Reverend Simpson* until they passed. Their longstanding Southern Baptist background precluded them from joining the temple, but they, too, loved the manner in which he delivered the message of GOD. Other family members in the South who heard of him shared a positive opinion of his dedication and skill in delivering the word.

Active in the temple, my parents were among the original *Charter Members* of the church corporation. Today, more than fifty years later, my mother stands with *Reverend Simpson* as one of the last two of the group.

Through the good times and the bad, *Reverend Simpson* has been close to our family. *Rev. Simpson* had instructed my mother through inspiration from **I AM** what to do after the death of her firstborn, *Rodney Allen Mason*. He was there when my father got sick and passed away on Wednesday, October 11, 1989. *Rev. Simpson* was right by my mother's side. He spoke at my father's funeral about how my parents met and how their marriage was the first at the temple on Friday, July 1, 1966. He recounted the marriage vows that my parents faithfully maintained. *Rev. Simpson* was there and spoke at my grandmother's *(Levonia)* funeral Monday, September 27, 1999. At both funerals, there was no one in the room who was not touched by the love and compassion expressed in his words for them.

He officiated the wedding ceremony of my sister *Iris A. Mason and James R. Nicholas III* on Saturday, June 23, 2012. Their son, *James IV*, now represents the fourth generation of the family's interaction with *Reverend Simpson*.

Rev. Simpson has touched the lives of members of my family in so many ways. We love you so much for your dedication to GOD and your love for GOD's children. We would like to say thank you for your love, dedication, and support for our family. Thank you for saying *"Yes"* to **I AM.** May **I AM** continue to bless you for doing HIS will, and He will continue to bless your life.

Rev. Gary Marcus Simpson moved on to the next level of life with the **Great I AM,** on Monday, October 5, 2020, in Southfield, Michigan – Oakland County.

My Family Tree

Introduction

Virginia

Based on its settlement history, Virginia has generally been recognized as the birthplace of American slavery. Yet, it is recognized that Virginia was not the focal point of secession for the slave states that would become the Confederacy. Some might find it ironic that the first southern state to secede was South Carolina, while North Carolina was the last.

States joining the ranks of the Confederacy included South Carolina, Mississippi, Florida, Alabama, Georgia, Louisiana, and Texas, making their determination in 1860. Following the attack on Fort Sumter in 1861, Virginia, Arkansas, Tennessee, and North Carolina joined the Confederacy. The original capital was Montgomery, Alabama, but Richmond, Virginia, would become the historic seat of the ill-fated Confederate effort.

While historians argue about the causes leading to the rift that split the Union, the underlying cause, of course, was slavery. Even those who argue that economics and/or state's rights were the root of the dispute acknowledge that slavery was the economic backbone of the South.

West Virginia

Following the secession of Virginia from the union, internal political upheaval set into opposition from the eastern and western portions of the state against one another. Slavery was just one of the issues under dispute. The Western portion of the state was more concerned with the levying of taxes that unduly impacted mining operations. A significant portion of the western population was committed to remaining with the union in the face of the coming violent conflict. Some thirty-nine counties in the western part of the state looked to secede from the state, increasing to fifty by the time a Constitutional Convention was called to apply for separate statehood.

While West Virginia was one of two states established during the turmoil of the Civil War, it was the only state that came into existence as a result of secession from the Confederacy. Some historians argue that secession was illegal because the United States Constitution notes that no state can secede without the approval of the original state. Even the admissions process for West Virginia contravened the normal order, as statehood was granted by presidential caveat as opposed to Congressional approval.

The Underground Railroad

Although abolitionist efforts date back to the time of *George Washington* in the late 1700s, the term *Underground Railroad* did not find voice until sometime in the 1830s, and less than a decade later, the term was part of the national lexicon.

The *Fugitive Slave Acts* precipitated the establishment of clandestine efforts to assist slaves seeking to escape the indignities of American slavery. The United States Supreme Court struck down efforts to legally suppress efforts aimed at reclaiming escaped slaves, and the business of returning slaves to their owners flourished.

My Family Tree

Persons providing aid, shelter, and comfort to escaping slaves were generally referred to as *Stationmasters.* The locations in which slaves sought temporary rest were referred to as *Depots or Stations*, and those who assisted in guiding slaves along the path to freedom were known as *Conductors*. Among the most famous conductors was *Harriet Tubman,* an escaped slave from Maryland. It has been reported that *Tubman* led three hundred escaped slaves to freedom. *Frederick Douglass,* a former Maryland slave who escaped, lent his voice and efforts to oppose slavery, becoming a well-known abolitionist. It was also reported that *Douglass* assisted more than four hundred escaped slaves to reach freedom. It is noted that Wheeling, West Virginia, was an active port for the *Underground Railroad*. It is from these roots that members of the family began their trek into the pages of history and into this volume.

⌘

My Family Tree

Editor's Note

Please keep in mind that because of the eras (Pre- and post-Civil War), information was sometimes sparse because of poor records – documentation and maintenance. Sometimes, the information provided by family members had gaps due to memory loss, reticence, and personal preference. We have tried to respect their wishes to every extent possible. It is our hope that the information provided will help those other members to develop closer family ties, inspire new relationships, and bring us together. We are diverse, we are survivors, we are achievers – we are family!

Mount Tabor Presbyterian Church Cemetery in Cleveland, North Carolina – Rowan County and Mount Ulla Township, North Carolina – Rowan County is a resting place for African–Americans of the region. The first church was organized by a group of newly freed slaves. *Mount Tabor United Presbyterian Church* is one of the oldest colored churches west of Yadkin. It was organized around 1866 in the remote area of Western Rowan County. It is about three-fourth miles east of the Iredell County line, in the Mount Ulla Township, in Cleveland, North Carolina, and it was reorganized Saturday, September 7, 1867, and was listed in Rowan County Registry. In 1868, the first building, a log cabin, was established on the east side of the cemetery and is a Historical Landmark for African – Americans (find-a-grave.com, 2018). It serves as the final resting place for one-half of our family members:

- **Cornelius**
- **Cowan**
- **Rankin**
- **White**
- **Witherspoon**

Whitman Cemetery in Holden, West Virginia – Logan County is a resting place for African – Americans of the region. *Whitman Cemetery* is a Historical Landmark for African – Americans; it was founded in the early 1900s in Holden, West Virginia – Logan County. It is still in use today and is being preserved by the *Whitman Cemetery Association* (find-a-grave.com, 2018). It serves as the final resting place for one-fourth of our family members as well:

- **Bass**
- **Carey**
- **Morrison**

Antioch Baptist Church Cemetery in Cleveland, North Carolina – Iredell County, a resting place for African – Americans and the largest and oldest of the region. It is a Historical Landmark for African – Americans and was founded in the latter part of the 1890s (find-a-grave.com, 2018). It serves as the final resting place for one-third of our family members:

- **Glaspy**
- **Mills**

My Family Tree

- **Pearson**
- The *Carey* side consists of 16 main branches of the family tree: *Alison, Anderson, Bass, Beverly, Carey, Carrington, Cornelius, Cowan, Cunningham, Faulkner, McCrary, Moore, Palmer, Summers, White, and Witherspoon:*
- Each of these main branches includes members who were slaves or the immediate descendants of slaves
- Many established Boarding Houses as a means of economic survival through unstable times
- The jobs they held after slavery included Coal Miners, Domestic Workers, Factory Workers, Homemakers, Farmers and/or Farmer Laborers (Sharecroppers), Laundress, served in the military, or held – United States Draft Registration Cards.

My Family Tree

The Carey Bloodline

The bloodlines (on the *Masons*) with the same last names are italicized, but only a few families have had convergence.

Alison	*Allen*	Allison	Anderson	Avery	Awanna
Baity	*Baker*	Barber	Barnes	Bass	Baxter
Beverly	Blackmon	Blyden	*Bolden*	Bradley	Bradshaw
Bratcher	Brauch	Brooks	*Brown*	*Bruce*	Bruce-Wilson
Burney	Burns	Burwell	Caldwell	Cameron	*Carey*
Carrington	Cats	Causer	Childs	Clarke	*Clement*
Copeland	Cornelius	Constans	*Cowan*	Craft	Cram
Crawford	Crummie	*Cunningham*	Dalton	Davidson	*Davis*
Day	Dickerson	Dingess	Dobyne	Donaldson	Douglas
Dunbar	Faber	Falls	Farmer	Faulkner	Fennel
Ferguson	Ferron	Fetterson	Forest	*Freeman*	Galloway
Gamble	Gardner	Garner	Gibson	Gilbreath	Glass
Glaspy	*Glenn*	Goode	Goodman	Graham	*Grant*
Gray	Green	Griffith	Guyse	*Hall*	*Harris*
Harris-Johnson	*Hawkins*	*Haynes*	Heaggans	Hicklen	Higgins
Hill	*Holmes*	*Howard*	Hrobowski	Hyde	Irby
Irvin	*Jackson*	Jacobs	*Johnson*	*Jones*	Kittler
Knott	*Knox*	Langhorne	Lashley	Leaser	Leazer
Lee	Lewis	*Lipscomb*	*Lockhart*	Lomax	Love
Lydick	Lyerly	Lynard	*Lyons*	*Malone*	Marlin
Martin	Mason	McCall	McClain	McCluney	McCoy
McCrary	*McDaniel*	McElmore	McHenry	McNeely	*Miller*
Mills	Moody	*Moore*	*Morrison*	Morsen	Morton
Moss	Muwwakkil	Nancy	Neal	Nicholas	Owens
Palmer	*Parker*	Parks	Partee	*Patterson*	*Pearson*
Pennington	Penry	Perry	Person	Peters	Polk
Pollard	Pulliam	Ramsey	Rankin	Rankin-Ramsey	Reid
Richardson	Richerson	*Roberson*	Robertson	*Robinson*	Rogers
Rose	Salahuddin	Saliba	Sanders	Sbinowitz	*Scott*
Settles	Sharpe	Siegel	*Simpson*	Sloan	Stewart
Stinson	Stockton	Stylin	Summer	Summers	Sylvester
Taylor	Teasley	*Tillman*	Timbers	Trent	Tucker
Turner	Vance	Vaughn	Wade	*Walker*	Walton
Ward	*White*	Whiteside	Wilbur	Willett	*Williams*
Wilson	Winston	*Witherspoon*	Woods	Wyatt	*Young*

My Family Tree

The Great - Great Grandparents of Norma Jean Carey Mason–Maternal (Her Mother's Side)

The Family Line of Laura Palmer Carey and Charles Carey

According to the United States Freedmen's Bureau Records for 1865-1872… Charles Carey was loaned out to work at Julia Gardner – Gardner Plantation in Virginia – Montgomery County, and he continued working for her after he was free.

The Second Generation

Name	**Laura Palmer Carey**
Date Of Birth	Sunday, December 25, 1853
Place Of Birth	Virginia – Roanoke County
Date Of Death	Tuesday, January 10, 1933
Age At Death	79
Place Of Death	Virginia – Roanoke County
Occupation	Housewife/Domestic Worker
Married	Charles Carey
Notes	She was born a slave. The 1880 Census noted that her first name was spelled two different ways: Laura or Lania. Laura and Charles were both illiterate. Her parents were Jane White Palmer and Joshua Palmer.

Name	**Charles Carey**
Date Of Birth	Tuesday, September 4, 1855
Place Of Birth	Virginia – Goochland County
Date Of Death	Unknown
Age At Death	Unknown
Place Of Death	Virginia – Roanoke County
Occupation	Day Laborer
Married	Laura Palmer Carey

My Family Tree

Notes	Charles and his parents were born slaves. The 1880 Census noted that Charles's siblings were illiterate. His brother (Rufus) was born in 1864 into slavery. His other siblings: James Carey (b. 1866), Iza Carey (b. 1876), Miles Carey II (b. 1872), and Lucy Carey (b. 1868). His parents were Louise Constans Carey (b. 1840), occupation – Housekeeper/Housewife and Miles Carey I (b. 1831), occupation – Farmer. His parents were married in 1866 in Virginia – Goochland County.

Their Child

Name	James A. Carey
Date Of Birth	March 1873
Place Of Birth	Holden, West Virginia – Logan County
Date Of Death	Saturday, October 9, 1948
Age At Death	75
Place Of Death	Logan, West Virginia – Logan County
Occupation	Retired – Miner – Coal Company
Married	Lillie Belle Carrington Carey
Notes	The 1910 Census noted that James turned his home into a boarding house with 5 boarders living with his family, and in 1930, they had 6 boarders. He was buried on Sunday, October 17, 1948, at Whitman Cemetery as a widower. His headstone has his birth year as 1895, but his death certificate documented his birth year as 1873. The elders of the family stated that his death certificate has the correct year.

Name	Lillie Belle Carrington Carey
Date Of Birth	Friday, June 27, 1884
Place Of Birth	Charlotte, Virginia – Roanoke County
Date Of Death	Wednesday, January 8, 1941
Age At Death	56
Place Of Death	Holden, West Virginia – Logan County
Occupation	Domestic Worker/Housewife

My Family Tree

Married	James A. Carey
Notes	The records also noted that her name was spelled in various ways: Lilobelle, Corrington, Lillebelle, Lulu, or Lilly. Her parents were Susan Beverly Carrington and Abraham Carrington. The 1910 Census noted that Lillie and James were literate, and it was reported that Lillie had a child from a previous relationship named Bettie Louise Jones. Their children: Charles Alexander Carey, William Bryant Carey, Elizabeth Carey Dickerson, George A. Carey, Joseph David Carey, and John Carey. Lillie was buried on Friday, January 10, 1941, in West Virginia – Logan County.

The Great- Great Grandparents of Norma Jean Carey Mason–Maternal (Her Mother's Side)

A bit of information that was found out about the Carrington family from Virginia Freedmen's Bureau Field Office Records from 1865-1872 ... Census; Returns of Colored Population of Mecklenburg County, State of Virginia noted that Susan and Abraham identified their former slave masters: William Carrington (slaves – Flora – mother, Abe – father, and Abraham – son) and Mr. Mason (slave – Susan Beverly).

The Family Line of Susan Beverly Carrington and Abraham Carrington

The Second Generation

Name	**Susan Beverly Carrington**
Date Of Birth	March 1831
Place Of Birth	Virginia – Mecklenburg County
Date Of Death	Unknown
Age At Death	Unknown
Place Of Death	Big Lick, Virginia – Roanoke County
Occupation	Cook/Housekeeper
Married	Abraham Carrington
Notes	She was born a slave. In the 1880 Census, it was noted that Susan and Abraham were illiterate.

Name	**Abraham Carrington**
Date Of Birth	November 1830

My Family Tree

Place Of Birth	Virginia
Date Of Death	1920
Age At Death	89 – 90
Place Of Death	Big Lick, Virginia – Roanoke County
Occupation	Farmer Laborer
Married	Susan Beverly Carrington
Notes	He was born a slave. Census records noted their marriage in 1845 in Big Lick, Virginia – Roanoke County, a marriage of 55 years. The records also noted that his first name was spelled Abram. He was a widower when he died. His parents were Flora Carrington and Abe Carrington. According to the 1880 Census, Flora and Abe were illiterate.

Their (8) Children

Name	**Anna Carrington Settles**
Date Of Birth	Saturday, February 15, 1868
Place Of Birth	Big Lick, Virginia – Roanoke County
Date Of Death	Wednesday, October 26, 1898
Age At Death	30
Place Of Death	Virginia
Occupation	Farmer
Married	Monroe Walker Settles
Notes	According to the 1880 Census, she was illiterate.

Name	**Monroe Walker Settles**
Date Of Birth	1841
Place Of Birth	Virginia – Botetourt County
Date Of Death	Unknown

My Family Tree

Age At Death	Unknown
Place Of Death	Virginia
Occupation	Farmer Laborer
Married	(1) Caroline Settles (2) Anna Carrington Settles
Notes	Monroe and his parents were slaves. (1) b. 1843, POB. Virginia, her occupation – Keeping House. Caroline and Monroe had a son named James Carr Settles (b. Wednesday, June 27, 1866), POB. Virginia – Roanoke County, his occupation – Farm Laborer. Census records for 1880 noted James was illiterate. (2) Married on Saturday, December 18, 1886, in Amsterdam, Virginia – Botetourt County. He was a widower when he married Anna. His parents were Dinah Settles (b. 1810), POB. Virginia and David Settles. Dinah was listed as a widow in the 1880 Census. The report also noted that his mother and cousin, Willie A. Burwell, were boarders at their home.

Name	Levina T. Carrington
Date Of Birth	1865
Place Of Birth	Big Lick, Virginia – Roanoke County
Date Of Death	Unknown
Age At Death	Unknown
Place Of Death	Unknown
Occupation	Unknown
Married	Unknown
Notes	She was born into slavery. Census records for 1880 noted her as illiterate.

Name	Samuel C. Carrington I
Date Of Birth	May 1859
Place Of Birth	Big Lick, Virginia – Roanoke County

My Family Tree

Date Of Death	Unknown
Age At Death	Unknown
Place Of Death	Unknown
Occupation	General Farmer
Married	(1) Mary Langhorne Carrington (2) Eliza Morton Carrington
Notes	He was born a slave. His nickname was "Sam." His name was found on the Virginia Freedmen's Bureau Field Office Record (1865 – 1872) – Labor Contacts, Indenture, and Apprenticeship Record in Petersburg, Virginia – Fauquier County, on Wednesday, August 9, 1865, making $8.00 a month (as a Quartermaster in the United States Army) and was honorably discharged. Census records for 1910 noted that he was literate, and his father (Abraham) was a boarder at his house at the age of 80 and remained in residence until he died.

Name	**Mary Langhorne Carrington**
Date Of Birth	October 1860
Place Of Birth	Virginia – Roanoke County
Date Of Death	Wednesday, July 12, 1916
Age At Death	55
Place Of Death	Botetourt, Virginia – Roanoke County
Occupation	Laundress/Housewife
Married	Samuel C. Carrington [I]
Notes	She was born into slavery. Census records for 1900 noted that Mary was literate. They were married on Thursday, March 6, 1884, in Cloverdale Amsterdam, Virginia – Botetourt County, a marriage of 15 years. Their children: Lillie B. Carrington, Lovvenia Carrington, Ida N. Carrington, Beatrice Langhorne, Caroline Carrington Morsen, and Samuel C. Carrington [II]. Her parents were Caroline Langhorne (b. 1841), occupation – Keeping House and Henry Langhorne (b. 1835), occupation – General Farmer. The 1880 Census had listed her parents as illiterate. Her siblings: Charles Langhorne (b. 1863), occupation – Farmer, Benjamin Langhorne (b. 1867), John Langhorne (b. 1870), James Langhorne (b. 1874), Bettie

My Family Tree

	Langhorne (b. 1877), and Houston Langhorne (b. 1879). Mary's parents and her siblings' POB. Virginia

Name	Eliza Morton Carrington
Date Of Birth	Saturday, July 28, 1866
Place Of Birth	Virginia – Roanoke County
Date Of Death	Wednesday, January 28, 1948
Age At Death	81
Place Of Death	Hollins, Virginia – Roanoke County
Occupation	Laundress/Housewife
Married	Samuel C. Carrington [1]
Notes	Her parents were Rebektah Morton Bolden and Clem Bolden. She was buried on Sunday, February 1, 1948, at Green Ridge Baptist Church Cemetery in Virginia – Roanoke County. Married Wednesday, September 18, 1918, in Virginia – Roanoke County.

Name	Amelia Carrington
Date Of Birth	Sunday, February 4, 1866
Place Of Birth	Glade Spring, Virginia – Roanoke County
Date Of Death	Unknown
Age At Death	Unknown
Place Of Death	Unknown
Occupation	Unknown
Married	Unknown
Notes	Census records for 1880 listed her as being in school, and her nickname was "Anna."

My Family Tree

Name	**Fleming Carrington**
Date Of Birth	1868
Place Of Birth	Cloverdale, Virginia – Roanoke County
Date Of Death	Thursday, November 15, 1888
Age At Death	19 – 20
Place Of Death	Cloverdale Amsterdam, Virginia – Botetourt County
Occupation	Day Laborer
Married	Single
Notes	Census records for 1880 listed him as being in school.

Name	**John W. Carrington**
Date Of Birth	Thursday, December 12, 1872
Place Of Birth	Big Lick, Virginia – Roanoke County
Date Of Death	Unknown
Age At Death	Unknown
Place Of Death	Virginia – Halifax County
Occupation	Day Laborer
Married	Eliza Palmer Carrington
Notes	Census records for 1880 listed him as being in school.

Name	**Eliza Palmer Carrington**
Date Of Birth	1886
Place Of Birth	Virginia – Halifax County
Date Of Death	Thursday, February 16, 1922

My Family Tree

Age At Death	35 – 36
Place Of Death	Virginia – Halifax County
Occupation	Housewife/Domestic Worker
Married	John W. Carrington
Notes	Married on Monday, December 23, 1895, in Virginia – Halifax County. Her parents were Carris Brauch Palmer and Daniel Palmer.

Name	**Mary E. Carrington**
Date Of Birth	Tuesday, March 3, 1874
Place Of Birth	Big Lick, Virginia – Roanoke County
Date Of Death	Sunday, January 9, 1966
Age At Death	91
Place Of Death	Richmond, Virginia – Henrico County
Occupation	Retired – Domestic Worker
Married	Single
Notes	Census records for 1880 do not have her listed as being in school.

The connection to the family line was James A., the son of Laura Palmer Carey and Charles Carey, and James's wife – Lillie, the daughter of Susan Beverly Carrington and Abraham Carrington.

Lillie Belle Carrington Carey - See Entry Page 311-312
James A. Carey - See Entry Page 311

The Civil War – Slaves, Soldiers, Spies…...

There are many stories about roles played by slaves, former slaves, and free men of color when it comes to the Civil War. Some stories are true. Some are myths, and some have a grain of truth that somehow has blossomed into legends. What remains a fact is that during the Civil War, there were blacks serving on both sides, some voluntarily and some involuntarily.

Although there were many blacks (mostly slaves) active in southern encampments, there are no known records of a black Confederate combat unit. Military reports that have survived indicate

My Family Tree

that there were blacks firing on Union troops. There are records of captured black southern soldiers. There is also a credible report of observing a Confederate officer holding a pistol to the heads of blacks, forcing them to man a battle cannon.

Dating back to 1792, Federal Law prohibited blacks from being armed in the military. The efforts of General John C. Fremont in Missouri and General David Hunter in South Carolina to encourage Blacks' enlistments were officially rejected. In 1862, Congressional action freed any slave whose master served in the Confederate Army. Among the first three Black Regiments were those in South Carolina, Tennessee, and Massachusetts. The 54th Massachusetts gained later fame through the film "Glory." Today, the unit serves as an Honor Guard. The Confederate Congress forestalled any action to arm blacks until March 1865, with the provision that they would remain slaves. The war ended three weeks later.

Official records indicate that by the end of the Civil War, blacks made up almost 10% of the Union Army, but less than 1% of the number attributed to General Robert E. Lee's Army of Northern Virginia. Although most blacks served in auxiliary roles in both the North and the South, records indicate the Union Army had almost eighty black commissioned officers.

The activities of black men and women during the Civil War were not restricted to formal battle lines. Intelligence operations were vital to the war effort, including the success of not just a few strategic battles. At least two black Intelligence Operatives were actively providing vital information from inside the Jefferson headquarters in Richmond, Virginia.

One slave stole the plans for upgrading the South's Merrimac to the ironclad Virginia and presented them to the North. The information was vital to advancing the development of the Monitor. Among the most famous black spies was **Harriet Tubman,** *who was buried Monday, March 10, 1913, at Fort Hill Cemetery in Auburn, New York, with military honors. Another slave,* **Mary Elizabeth Bowser,** *for her intelligence efforts (of having a photographic memory and could repeat word for word and recapture each event as they took place), was inducted into the United States Army Intelligence Hall of Fame at Fort Huachuca, Arizona in 1995.*

The Great Grandparents of Norma Jean Cary Mason–Paternal (Her Father's Side)

The Second Generation

Name	George R. White
Date Of Birth	Tuesday, September 7, 1830
Place Of Birth	North Carolina
Date Of Death	Monday, July 14, 1913
Age At Death	82
Place Of Death	Chambersburg Township, North Carolina – Iredell County

My Family Tree

Occupation	Farmer/Retired – United States – Army
Married	Mary C. Summers White
Notes	He was born a slave. He served during the Civil War as a soldier, registered in the Confederate Army, First Lieutenant 8th Battalion, North Carolina – Cumberland County Junior Reserves from (1861–1865). He was honorably discharged. Census records for 1910 noted that he could read but could not write. He had a Will in Probate Court on Thursday, June 7, 1917, in North Carolina – Iredell County. He was buried in July 1913 at Cameron Presbyterian Church Cemetery in Statesville, North Carolina – Iredell County. His parents were Jane E. Alison White (b. 1805) and George White (b. 1800). The inscription on his headstone read 83 years old.

Name	Mary C. Summers White
Date Of Birth	1846
Place Of Birth	North Carolina
Date Of Death	Sunday, March 28, 1915
Age At Death	68 – 69
Place Of Death	Troutmans, North Carolina – Iredell County
Occupation	Domestic Worker/Homemaker
Married	George R. White
Notes	She was born a slave. Census records for 1910 noted her as illiterate. The record also spelled her name as Marey. Married on Wednesday, August 15, 1866, in North Carolina – Iredell County, married for 47 years. She was buried on Friday, April 2, 1915, at Cameron Elmrose Church Cemetery in Statesville, North Carolina – Iredell County, a widow. Census records for 1910 noted that they had a nephew living with them named Manuel Gray (b. May 1892), POB. Chambersburg Township, North Carolina – Iredell County), he attended school and worked as a Day Laborer. She had one set of twins from a previous relationship – John M.A. White and Henry White. Jay adopted her sons. Her parents were Adaline Summers McCrary and Newton McCrary. Her sister was Laura Summers (b. 1865).

Their (4) Children

My Family Tree

Name	**Frank George White**
Date Of Birth	Sunday, September 18, 1870
Place Of Birth	Chambersburg Township, North Carolina – Iredell County
Date Of Death	Sunday, December 27, 1942
Age At Death	72
Place Of Death	Chambersburg Township, North Carolina – Iredell County
Occupation	Farmer/Retired – United States – Army
Married	Florence Miller White
Notes	He was listed as a Private 1st Regiment in the Confederate Army, having registered in Chambersburg Township, North Carolina – Iredell County, and was honorably discharged. Census records for 1910 noted him as literate. He was buried on Wednesday, December 30, 1942.

Name	**Florence Miller White**
Date Of Birth	1886
Place Of Birth	North Carolina – Rowan County
Date Of Death	Monday, November 27, 1950
Age At Death	63 – 64
Place Of Death	Salisbury, North Carolina – Rowan County
Occupation	Domestic Worker/Homemaker
Married	Frank George White
Notes	Married in 1912 in North Carolina – Iredell County, married for 30 years. She was buried in November 1950. Florence and Frank were both buried side-by-side at Cameron Presbyterian Church Cemetery in Statesville, North Carolina – Iredell County. Her headstone had her maiden name as Knox, but her death certificate has Miller. Their children: Forest White (b. 1916) and Rowan White (b. 1920); their POB. Chambersburg, North Carolina – Iredell County.

My Family Tree

Name	Jay Hugh White
Date Of Birth	Sunday, February 19, 1882
Place Of Birth	Chambersburg Township, North Carolina – Iredell County
Date Of Death	Saturday, April 9, 1960
Age At Death	78
Place Of Death	Statesville, North Carolina – Iredell County
Occupation	Retired – Farm Laborer/Retired – United States Army
Married	(1) Maggie McCall White (2) Annie Lee Cornelius White
Notes	Census records for 1910 noted him as literate, and his middle name was spelled Huge. (2) Married on Wednesday, October 26, 1910, in Chambersburg Township, North Carolina – Rowan County. Jay had turned his home into a Boarding House. Jay had permission from his wife (Annie) to go after Grace E. White, to have kids by her to help with the farming. Grace lived in their household from (1920 – 1940). Grace E. White (b. 1890), POB. Chambersburg Township, North Carolina – Iredell County, her occupation – Domestic Worker. Census records for 1930 noted that Grace E. was literate, and she had two children by Jay: Nathaniel White and Isaac E. White. Jay served in the United States Army during WWI from (1917 – 1918), registered in Chambersburg Township, North Carolina – Iredell County, and was honorably discharged. The report also noted that as of 1960, he had a Living Will recorded in the Superior Probate Court in North Carolina – Iredell County, and he had Joseph L. White (his older son, as executor) of his estate. His wife (Annie) and all his children were listed. He was buried on Wednesday, April 13, 1960. He owned his farm and was mortgage-free, according to the Census records.

Name	Annie Lee Cornelius White
Date Of Birth	Saturday, October 26, 1889
Place Of Birth	Mount Ulla Township, North Carolina – Rowan County
Date Of Death	Monday, October 11, 1965
Age At Death	75
Place Of Death	Morganton, North Carolina – Burke County

My Family Tree

Occupation	Retired – Farmer Laborer/Homemaker
Married	Jay Hugh White
Notes	Her parents were Susan Jane (Sookey), Cowan Cornelius, and Augustus (Gus) Cornelius. Census records for 1940 noted her as literate. Their children: Mary Bell White Whiteside, Walter White, Rayford Odell White, Anne Lou White Awanna, DeWitt Shuford White, Grace Vivian White, Andrew Wilson White, Vernie Matilda White, Jay Roger White, and John Carl White. She was buried on Friday, October 15, 1965, as a widow. Annie and Jay were both buried side-by-side at Mount Tabor Presbyterian Church Cemetery.

Name	John M.A. White
Date Of Birth	1864
Place Of Birth	North Carolina
Date Of Death	Sunday, June 23, 1929
Age At Death	64 – 65
Place Of Death	Asheville, North Carolina – Buncombe County
Occupation	Common Laborer
Married	Widower
Notes	He was born into slavery and was literate. His twin brother was Henry. He was buried on Wednesday, June 26, 1929, at South Asheville Cemetery in Asheville, North Carolina – Buncombe County. He lived at 28 Brooklyn Alley in Asheville at the time of his death.

Name	Henry White
Date Of Birth	1864
Place Of Birth	North Carolina
Date Of Death	Thursday, January 23, 1913
Age At Death	48 – 49
Place Of Death	Asheville, North Carolina – Buncombe County

My Family Tree

Occupation	Laborer – Railway Shop
Married	Widower
Notes	He was born into slavery, and he was literate. Their father was Cy Davidson. He was buried on Saturday, January 25, 1913, at Riverside Cemetery in Asheville, North Carolina – Buncombe County.

According to the United States Freedmen's Bureau Records for 1865-1872 ... the prominent Witherspoon family of North Carolina – Rowan County became one of the largest slaveowners in Rowan County, owning 113 slaves. The Witherspoon's and Cowan's were one big family in North Carolina – Rowan County. Elizabeth was re-sold to John Cowan (a family member), her new slave master. Charles Cowan was a slave master of North Carolina – Rowan County. He fathered a son, who was his slave, named Charles.

The Great-Great-Grandparents of Norma Jean Carey Mason – Paternal (Her Father's Side)

The Family Line of Elizabeth Witherspoon Cowan and Charles Cowan [I]

The Second Generation

Name	Elizabeth Witherspoon Cowan
Date Of Birth	1836
Place Of Birth	Salisbury Township, North Carolina – Rowan County
Date Of Death	Tuesday, July 13, 1897
Age At Death	60-61
Place Of Death	Cleveland, North Carolina – Rowan County
Occupation	Domestic Worker
Married	Charles Cowan [I]
Notes	She was born a slave. Census records for 1880 reported that Elizabeth and Charles were illiterate. She was listed as Mulatto and went by her nickname, "Lizzie." She was buried in July 1897.

Name	Charles Cowan I
Date Of Birth	Saturday, November 6, 1824

My Family Tree

Place Of Birth	Salisbury Township, North Carolina – Rowan County
Date Of Death	Monday, December 3, 1900
Age At Death	76
Place Of Death	Cleveland, North Carolina – Rowan County
Occupation	Farmer
Married	Elizabeth Witherspoon Cowan
Notes	He was born a slave, and his father was his slave master. He was buried in December 1900. Elizabeth and Charles were both buried at Mount Tabor Presbyterian Church Cemetery.

Their (8) Children

Name	**Susan Jane Cowan Cornelius**
Date Of Birth	January 1860
Place Of Birth	Mount Ulla Township, North Carolina – Rowan County
Date Of Death	Saturday, May 9, 1914
Age At Death	54
Place Of Death	Mount Ulla Township, North Carolina – Rowan County
Occupation	Domestic Laborer/Homemaker
Married	Augustus Cornelius (William Guess Cornelius)
Notes	Born into slavery. She was literate in the 1880 Census and Mulatto. Known by many nicknames, including "Sookey." Married on Thursday, February 6, 1879, in Statesville, North Carolina – Iredell County. Buried on Sunday, May 10, 1914, at Mount Tabor Presbyterian Church Cemetery. The 1870 Census noted that her husband's name was William Guess Cornelius, and his last name was documented as his wife's maiden name. She was a widow in the early 1900s. Had nine children, seven surviving; their children were Locke A. Cornelius, Jay Lawrence Cornelius, Vernie Mae Cornelius Partee, Annie Lee Cornelius White, Eugenia B. Cornelius Goodman, Mary E. Cornelius, and Johnnie Augustus Cornelius.

My Family Tree

Name	**John H. Cowan**
Date Of Birth	Sunday, January 12, 1851
Place Of Birth	Mount Ulla Township, North Carolina – Rowan County
Date Of Death	Tuesday, January 7, 1930
Age At Death	78
Place Of Death	Mount Ulla Township, North Carolina – Rowan County
Occupation	Farm Laborer
Married	Emma H. Griffith Cowan
Notes	He was born a slave. He was literate in the 1900 Census. Buried in January 1930.

Name	**Emma H. Griffith Cowan**
Date Of Birth	Saturday, May 15, 1858
Place Of Birth	Mount Ulla Township, North Carolina – Rowan County
Date Of Death	Tuesday, January 16, 1940
Age At Death	81
Place Of Death	Cleveland, North Carolina – Rowan County
Occupation	Retired Housekeeper/Homemaker
Married	John H. Cowan
Notes	Born a slave, illiterate in 1880 but literate by 1900. Married in 1878 in Mount Ulla Township, North Carolina – Rowan County, lasting 52 years. The report noted that she had nine children with eight surviving. Their children were Charles Edward Cowan [I], Lillie D. Cowan Rankin, William Lee Cowan, Henry Caldwell Cowan, Nancy E. Cowan Cameron, Robert N. Cowan, Mary N. Cowan Marlin, Martha Elizabeth Cowan, and John Thomas Monroe Cowan. Their grandchildren: Preneet Cowan (b. 1913) and Allie Cowan (b. 1912) and their POB. Mount Ulla Township, North Carolina – Rowan County, and they were boarders at their home. She was a widow, buried in January 1940 at Mount Tabor Presbyterian Church Cemetery alongside her husband.

My Family Tree

Name	Rhody Isabella Cowan Rankin
Date Of Birth	May 1854
Place Of Birth	Mount Ulla Township, North Carolina – Rowan County
Date Of Death	1910
Age At Death	55-56
Place Of Death	Cleveland, North Carolina – Rowan County
Occupation	Farmer Laborer/Homemaker
Married	Pinkney C. Rankin
Notes	Born a slave, listed as Mulatto. Notes in the 1880 Census, her name was spelled Rhodie. Her and Pinkney were illiterate in 1900. Mother of nine children, with eight surviving, their children were James Francis Rankin, Edward Caldwell Rankin[1], Clarence C. Rankin, Thomas C. Rankin, Espy Lee Rankin, Earl Green Rankin, Estella Ina Rankin Mills, William Henry Rankin, and Mary Ann Rankin Neal. She was buried in 1910.

Name	Pinkney C. Rankin
Date Of Birth	December 1853
Place Of Birth	Mount Ulla Township, North Carolina – Rowan County
Date Of Death	Thursday, September 28, 1916
Age At Death	62
Place Of Death	Cleveland, North Carolina – Rowan County
Occupation	General Farmer
Married	Rhody Isabella Cowan Rankin
Notes	Born a slave. Son of Phyllis L. Kittler Rankin and Eli Barr Rankin. Married Rhody on Thursday, January 25, 1877, in Mount Ulla Township, North Carolina – Rowan County, lasting for 23 years. He was a widower at the time of his death, buried in October 1916, alongside his wife, at Mount Tabor Presbyterian Church Cemetery.

My Family Tree

Name	Lucinda Cowan
Date Of Birth	1856
Place Of Birth	Mount Ulla Township, North Carolina – Rowan County
Date Of Death	Unknown
Age At Death	Unknown
Place Of Death	Unknown
Occupation	Farm Laborer
Married	Unknown
Notes	She was born a slave. Listed as Mulatto in the 1880 Census and illiterate.

Name	Charles Cowan II
Date Of Birth	1861 – 1862
Place Of Birth	Mount Ulla Township, North Carolina – Rowan County
Date Of Death	Unknown
Age At Death	Unknown
Place Of Death	Unknown
Occupation	Farm Laborer
Married	Unknown
Notes	Born into slavery. Listed as Mulatto and illiterate in the 1880 Census.

Name	Eliza Elizabeth Cowan Barber
Date Of Birth	Saturday, June 10, 1865
Place Of Birth	Mount Ulla Township, North Carolina – Rowan County
Date Of Death	Thursday, July 11, 1935

My Family Tree

Age At Death	70
Place Of Death	Cleveland, North Carolina – Rowan County
Occupation	Retired Domestic Worker/Homemaker
Married	John L. Barber (b. July 1860), POD. North Carolina – Rowan County
Notes	Born into slavery. Listed as Mulatto and not being in school. Married in 1894 in North Carolina and buried under her maiden name in July 1935, at Mount Tabor Presbyterian Church Cemetery. Mother of 11 children, John Gaither Barber, Philo Barber, Genola Cowan, Milton McKinley Barber, Henry Barber, Lura L. Barber, Dwight Barber, Lino Barber, Jura Barber, Alice M. Barber, and Allen Cowan. John's parents were Mary Barber (b. 1837 – d. 1869, age 31 – 32) and Alfred Barber (b. 1819 – d. 1882, age 62 – 63).

Name	William A. Cowan
Date Of Birth	Saturday, October 15, 1864
Place Of Birth	Mount Ulla Township, North Carolina – Rowan County
Date Of Death	Thursday, October 21, 1920
Age At Death	56
Place Of Death	Pittsburgh, Pennsylvania – Allegheny County
Occupation	Farm Laborer/Waiter
Married	Mary Jane Taylor Cowan (b. 1866)
Notes	Born into slavery. Listed as Mulatto and illiterate in the 1880 Census. Married Mary on Thursday, May 9, 1895, in Mount Ulla Township, North Carolina – Rowan County. Mary's father was Thomas Taylor. Their child was Martha Jane Cowan Howard (b. Tuesday, August 4, 1908, POB. South Carolina – d. Saturday, June 30, 1973, age 64) POD. Winston-Salem, North Carolina – Forsyth County; her occupation – R. J. Reynolds – Tobacco Industry – Worker. Martha lived at 1500 Gholston Street at the time of her death, a widow and homeowner; she was buried in July 1973, at Evergreen Cemetery.

My Family Tree

Name	Mary Ann Cowan
Date Of Birth	Thursday, February 17, 1870
Place Of Birth	Mount Ulla Township, North Carolina – Rowan County
Date Of Death	Saturday, August 8, 1896
Age At Death	26
Place Of Death	Mount Ulla Township, North Carolina – Rowan County
Occupation	Domestic Worker
Married	Single
Notes	Listed as Mulatto in the 1880 Census and not attending school. Buried in August 1896 at Mount Tabor Presbyterian Church Cemetery.

The Great Grandparents of Norma Jean Carey Mason–Paternal (Her Father's Side)

The connection to the family line was Susan Jane (Sookey), the daughter of Elizabeth Witherspoon Cowan and Charles Cowan [1].

The Third Generation

Susan Jane (Sookey) Cowan Cornelius - See Entry Page 325
Augustus (Gus) Cornelius - See Entry Page 325

Their (7) Children

Name	Locke A. Cornelius
Date Of Birth	Tuesday, August 7, 1883
Place Of Birth	Mount Ulla Township, North Carolina – Rowan County
Date Of Death	Thursday, April 29, 1915
Age At Death	31
Place Of Death	Cleveland, North Carolina – Rowan County
Occupation	Farmer Laborer
Married	Single

My Family Tree

Notes	According to the 1900 Census, he was listed as literate. He was buried on Wednesday, April 30, 1915, at Mount Tabor Presbyterian Church Cemetery.

Name	**Jay Lawrence Cornelius**
Date Of Birth	September 1887
Place Of Birth	Mount Ulla Township, North Carolina – Rowan County
Date Of Death	Thursday, April 21, 1927
Age At Death	39
Place Of Death	Cleveland, North Carolina – Rowan County
Occupation	Farmer Laborer
Married	Florence Gray Cornelius (b. 1887)
Notes	According to the Census reports of 1900, he was listed as literate. Married on Monday, September 28, 1908, in Salisbury, North Carolina – Rowan County. He was buried in April 1927 at Mount Tabor Presbyterian Church Cemetery, but on his headstone, his middle name was spelled as Laurence.

Name	**Vernie Mae Cornelius Partee**
Date Of Birth	Friday, July 7, 1848
Place Of Birth	Mount Ulla Township, North Carolina – Rowan County
Date Of Death	Saturday, April 24, 1937
Age At Death	88
Place Of Death	Salisbury, North Carolina – Rowan County
Occupation	Domestic Worker/Housewife
Married	Miles Harrison Partee
Notes	She was born a slave. Vernie and Miles were listed as literate in the 1900 Census records. Their children: Miles Allen Partee, Ida Mae Partee Willett, Genie Elizabeth Partee Avery, Jonnie E. Partee (b. 1912), Alexander Miles Partee, Clarence Anderson Partee, Vernie Edith Partee Person, Esther Naomi Partee Baker, Samuel J. Partee, Martha Lucille

My Family Tree

	Partee Witherspoon, Robert Partee, and Margaret Ruth Partee Wyatt. Vernie was cremated on Tuesday, April 27, 1937, in Salisbury, North Carolina – Rowan County, and she was a widow when she died. They lived at 1315 West Horah Street in Salisbury, homeowners.

Name	**Miles Harrison Partee**
Date Of Birth	Monday, March 17, 1884
Place Of Birth	Salisbury, North Carolina – Rowan County
Date Of Death	Wednesday, February 6, 1935
Age At Death	50
Place Of Death	Salisbury, North Carolina – Rowan County
Occupation	Laborer – Railway Shop Worker
Married	Vernie Mae Cornelius Partee
Notes	Married on Tuesday, October 3, 1906, in Salisbury Township, North Carolina – Rowan County, a marriage of 30 years. The Census report listed the spelling of their names as Vivia and Milas. He held a United States Draft Registration Card during WWI from (1917 – 1918). He registered in Salisbury Township, North Carolina – Rowan County. His siblings: Arthur Partee, Emery J. Partee, Robert Partee [II], Clarence D. Partee, Charles Partee, David Partee, Bessie Partee Wilson, Mary Ella Partee Pennington, Frank Partee, Nettie Langton Partee, Louisa Partee, and Milton Partee. His parents were Margaret Summer Partee (b. Friday, November 16, 1855 – d. Wednesday, January 26, 1938, age 82) and Robert Partee [I] (b. October 1847 – d. Sunday, November 14, 1926, age 79). His parents POB. North Carolina and their POD. Salisbury, North Carolina – Rowan County. Miles's parents were slaves.

The connection to the family line was Jay, the son of Mary C. Summers White and George R. White.

Annie Lee Cornelius White - See Entry Page 322-323
Jay Hugh White - See Entry Page 322

Name	**Eugenia B. Cornelius Goodman**
Date Of Birth	September 1894
Place Of Birth	Mount Ulla Township, North Carolina – Rowan County

My Family Tree

Date Of Death	Unknown
Age At Death	Unknown
Place Of Death	Unknown
Occupation	Housewife
Married	William Goodman (d. Tuesday, April 10, 1917)
Notes	According to the 1900 Census, both Eugenia and William were literate.

Name	**Mary E. Cornelius**
Date Of Birth	Monday, September 7, 1896
Place Of Birth	Mount Ulla Township, North Carolina – Rowan County
Date Of Death	Unknown
Age At Death	Unknown
Place Of Death	Unknown
Occupation	Domestic Worker
Married	Unknown
Notes	According to the 1900 Census listed her as literate.

Name	**Johnnie Augustus Cornelius**
Date Of Birth	Monday, August 15, 1892
Place Of Birth	Mount Ulla Township, North Carolina – Rowan County
Date Of Death	Friday, December 14, 1917
Age At Death	25
Place Of Death	Chapel Hill, North Carolina – Orange County
Occupation	Waiter

My Family Tree

Married	Single
Notes	According to the 1900 Census listed him as literate. He was buried on Sunday, December 16, 1917, at Mount Tabor Presbyterian Church Cemetery.

According to the United States Freedmen's Bureau Records for 1865 – 1872 ... the prominent Cunningham family of Petersburg, Virginia – Person County and (Rubin and Lucia) slave owners were Alexander Cunningham and then his son, John Wilson Cunningham, owners of the Waverly Plantation.

The Great – Great Grandparents of Norma Jean Carey Mason–Maternal (Mother's Side)

The Second Generation

Name	Lucia Cunningham
Date Of Birth	1838
Place Of Birth	Cunningham Township, North Carolina – Person County
Date Of Death	Unknown
Age At Death	Unknown
Place Of Death	Mount Carmel, Virginia – Halifax County
Occupation	Domestic Worker/Housewife
Married	Rubin Cunningham (b. 1820)
Notes	They were both slaves. According to the 1900 Census, both Lucia and Rubin were illiterate. Rubin POB. Mount Carmel, Virginia – Halifax County.

Their (5) Children

Name	Kate Cunningham
Date Of Birth	1865
Place Of Birth	Cunningham Township, North Carolina – Person County
Date Of Death	1880
Age At Death	15 – 16

My Family Tree

Place Of Death	Cunningham Township, North Carolina – Person County
Occupation	Domestic Worker
Married	Single
Notes	She was born into slavery. According to the Census for 1880 in Mount Carmel, Virginia – Halifax County noted that she was illiterate. Her name was listed on the United States Federal Census Mortality Schedule in North Carolina, ranging from 1855 to 1880.

Name	**Sarah Cunningham Wade**
Date Of Birth	1867
Place Of Birth	Cunningham Township, North Carolina – Person County
Date Of Death	Unknown
Age At Death	Unknown
Place Of Death	Mount Carmel, Virginia – Halifax County
Occupation	Domestic Worker
Married	Armstead Wade (b. 1860)
Notes	According to the 1880 Census in Mount Carmel, Virginia – Halifax County, she was literate. Married on Wednesday, February 25, 1885 in Cunningham Township, North Carolina – Person County, she was 17 years old when she got married.

Name	**Harriett Cunningham**
Date Of Birth	1869
Place Of Birth	Cunningham Township, North Carolina – Person County
Date Of Death	Wednesday, September 8, 1880
Age At Death	11-12
Place Of Death	Mount Carmel, Virginia – Halifax County
Occupation	Domestic Worker

My Family Tree

Married	Single
Notes	According to the Census for 1880 noted that she was literate. Her name was listed on the United States Federal Census Mortality Schedule in North Carolina, ranging from 1855 to 1880.

Name	**Martha Cunningham Bass**
Date Of Birth	June 1871
Place Of Birth	Cunningham Township, North Carolina – Person County
Date Of Death	Unknown
Age At Death	Unknown
Place Of Death	Holden, West Virginia – Logan County
Occupation	Domestic Worker/Homemaker
Married	Joseph Bass
Notes	The 1880 Census in Mount Carmel, Virginia – Halifax County noted that she was listed as illiterate, and then the 1900 report in Cunningham Township listed her as literate. The 1920 Census listed her as having had nine children, with seven surviving. Their children: Pattie Bass Howard, Lottie Bass Walker, Helen Bass Carey, Mary E. Bass, Maud JW Bass, Marian Bass Roberson, Etta Bass Lewis, Walter Joe Bass, and Floyd Cordest Bass.

Name	**Joseph Bass**
Date Of Birth	May 1867
Place Of Birth	Virginia
Date Of Death	Friday, January 20, 1928
Age At Death	60
Place Of Death	Holden, West Virginia – Logan County
Occupation	Coal Miner/Farmer
Married	Martha Cunningham Bass

My Family Tree

Notes	According to the Census report for 1900, he was listed as literate, and they were married in 1888 in North Carolina – Person County, a marriage of 12 years. The Census report for 1910 listed his home as a Boarding House with eight persons in residence including James's Aunt Rebecca Bass, her child: Martha Allen Bass (b. Tuesday, February 14, 1911), POB. West Virginia – Logan County. His parents were Elvira Anderson Bass (b. 1845, POB. North Carolina – d. February, Friday, 15, 1929, age 83–84) POD. Coaldale, West Virginia – McDowell County, her occupation – House Worker. Elvira was buried on Sunday, February 17, 1929, in Algoma, West Virginia – McDowell County, a widow, and James Bass (b. 1850, POB. Virginia – d. 1910, age 59 – 60) POD. West Virginia. James's nickname was "Jimmie." James's mother was Debby Bass (b. 1825), POB. Virginia. Elvira's father was Jim Anderson. Debby, James, Rebecca, Elvira, and Jim were all slaves.

Name	Edmon Cunningham
Date Of Birth	1874
Place Of Birth	Cunningham Township, North Carolina – Person County
Date Of Death	Unknown
Age At Death	Unknown
Place Of Death	Unknown
Occupation	Unknown
Married	Unknown
Notes	According to the 1880 Census, he was listed as literate.

The Great Grandparents of Norma Jean Carey Mason–Maternal (Her Mother's Side)

The Family Line of Martha Cunningham Bass and Joseph Bass

The connection to the family line was Martha, the daughter of Lucia Cunningham and Rubin Cunningham, and Martha's husband – Joseph, the son of Elvira Anderson Bass and James Bass.

The Third Generation

Martha Cunningham Bass - See Entry Page 336
Joseph Bass - See Entry Page 336-337

Their (9) Children

My Family Tree

Name	Pattie Bass Howard
Date Of Birth	November 1888
Place Of Birth	Cunningham Township, North Carolina – Person County
Date Of Death	Unknown
Age At Death	Unknown
Place Of Death	North Carolina – Person County
Occupation	Domestic Worker/Housewife
Married	Edward Daniel Howard
Notes	According to the 1910 Census, she was listed as literate.

Name	Edward Daniel Howard
Date Of Birth	Sunday, March 16, 1879
Place Of Birth	Virginia – Nelson County
Date Of Death	Saturday, December 5, 1925
Age At Death	46
Place Of Death	Holden, West Virginia – Logan County
Occupation	Day Laborer
Married	Pattie Bass Howard
Notes	His parents were Susan Winston Howard and Matt Howard. According to the 1900 Census, his parents and he were listed as literate. He held a United States Draft Registration Card during WWI from (1917 – 1918) in Holden, West Virginia – Logan County. Married Wednesday, May 14, 1913, in Holden, West Virginia – Logan County.

Name	Lottie Bass Walker
Date Of Birth	Thursday, April 7, 1892

My Family Tree

Place Of Birth	Cunningham Township, North Carolina – Person County
Date Of Death	Sunday, February 10, 1918
Age At Death	25
Place Of Death	Holden, West Virginia – Logan County
Occupation	Domestic Worker/Housewife
Married	Emanuel Jr. Walker II
Notes	According to the 1910 Census, they were listed as literate.

Name	**Emanuel Jr. Walker II**
Date Of Birth	Friday, April 10, 1885
Place Of Birth	Prospect, Virginia – Prince Edward County
Date Of Death	Friday, March 3, 1944
Age At Death	58
Place Of Death	Maloney, West Virginia – Logan County
Occupation	Machinist Helper – Railroad Company
Married	Lottie Bass Walker
Notes	His parents were Mary Francis Brown Walker and Emanuel Jr. Walker I. The 1920 Census noted that he was 23 years old, living as a boarder at Joseph Bass's home in Holden, West Virginia – Logan County, and that his first name was spelled Manuel. Married on Wednesday, June 22, 1910, in Holden, West Virginia – Logan County, married for 7 years. He was buried on Thursday, March 9, 1944, in Prospect, Virginia – Prince Edward County. He held a Draft Registration Card from the United States Army during WWII – Monday, April 27, 1942, registered in Keystone, Virginia – McDowell County.

Name	**Helen Bass Carey**
Date Of Birth	April 1893

My Family Tree

Place Of Birth	Cunningham Township, North Carolina – Person County
Date Of Death	Friday, December 10, 1920
Age At Death	27
Place Of Death	Holden, West Virginia – Logan County
Occupation	Domestic Worker/Homemaker
Married	(1) George Beamon Faulkner (2) Charles Alexander Carey
Notes	According to the 1910 Census, she was listed as literate and Mulatto. It was noted that both of her married names were spelled Frattini and Cary. Her children with Charles were Levonia M. C. Cowan, Vereece C. Carey Sanders Gant, Wilbur C. Carey [1], Isabelle Carey Morrison, and James Arthur Carey. She died from complications of a self-induced abortion. She was buried on Saturday, December 11, 1920, in Holden, West Virginia – Logan County. Jetta Malinda Faulkner's father was George Beamon Faulkner.

Name	**George Beamon Faulkner**
Date Of Birth	Thursday, September 1, 1892
Place Of Birth	Halifax, Virginia – Halifax County
Date Of Death	Sunday, August 1, 1954
Age At Death	61
Place Of Death	Halifax, Virginia – Halifax County
Occupation	Day Laborer
Married	Helen Bass Carey
Notes	He was literate in the 1910 Census. Married on Monday, August 2, 1909, in Cunningham, North Carolina – Person County. They got a divorce before she and her family moved to Holden, West Virginia – Logan County. He wanted to keep their daughter, Jetta Malinda Faulkner Childs. The 1910 Census noted that George was 19 years old, living as a boarder at Joseph Bass's home. The report identifies George as Beameon Frattini. His middle and last names were spelled wrong; the correct spelling was Beamon Faulkner. His parents were Louise Mason Faulkner and Isaac Faulkner. Louise's parents were Lucy Mason and John Mason.

My Family Tree

Name	Charles Alexander Carey
Date Of Birth	Thursday, April 4, 1895
Place Of Birth	Cloverdale, Virginia – Botetourt County
Date Of Death	Monday, January 31, 1944
Age At Death	48
Place Of Death	Holden, West Virginia – Logan County
Occupation	Coal Miner – Machine Operator/Janitor – Grocery Store
Married	Helen Bass Carey
Notes	According to the 1910 Census, he was listed as literate. He held a Draft Registration Card from the United States Army during WWI from 1917–1918. He registered in Holden, West Virginia – Logan County, and his military card listed his birth on Saturday, July 13, 1895, but his death record stated on April 4, 1895. His parents were Lillie Belle Carrington Carey and James A. Carey. Married on Monday, August 3, 1914, in Holden, West Virginia – Logan County, a marriage of 5 years. After his wife Helen died, his family helped him raise his children. According to the 1930 Census, his home was listed as a Boarding House. He was buried on Wednesday, February 2, 1944, at Whitman Cemetery.

Name	Mary E. Bass
Date Of Birth	August 1896
Place Of Birth	Cunningham Township, North Carolina – Person County
Date Of Death	Unknown
Age At Death	Unknown
Place Of Death	Unknown
Occupation	Domestic Worker
Married	Unknown
Notes	According to the 1910 Census, she was listed as literate.

My Family Tree

Name	Maud J W Bass
Date Of Birth	December 1897
Place Of Birth	Cunningham Township, North Carolina – Person County
Date Of Death	Unknown
Age At Death	Unknown
Place Of Death	Unknown
Occupation	Domestic Worker
Married	Unknown
Notes	According to the 1910 Census, she was listed as literate.

Name	Marian Bass Roberson
Date Of Birth	April 1895
Place Of Birth	Cunningham Township, North Carolina – Person County
Date Of Death	Unknown
Age At Death	Unknown
Place Of Death	Unknown
Occupation	Domestic Worker/Homemaker
Married	Alex Roberson (POB. Alabama – Calhoun County)
Notes	According to the 1910 Census, she was listed as literate. Married on Thursday, May 15, 1913, in Holden, West Virginia – Logan County.

Name	Etta Bass Lewis
Date Of Birth	November 1898
Place Of Birth	Cunningham Township, North Carolina – Person County
Date Of Death	Unknown

My Family Tree

Age At Death	Unknown
Place Of Death	Unknown
Occupation	Domestic Worker/Homemaker
Married	Ed Lewis (b. 1892), POB. Ohio
Notes	His parents were Florence Ferguson Lewis and Dan Lewis. According to the Census, she was listed as literate. The Census record has his name as Edd. Married on Tuesday, July 14, 1914, in Holden, West Virginia – Logan County. Their children: Hazel Lewis (b. 1905) and Oscar Lewis (b. 1907) and their children POB. Holden, West Virginia – Logan County.

Name	**Walter Joe Bass**
Date Of Birth	Tuesday, August 14, 1900
Place Of Birth	South Boston, Virginia – Halifax County
Date Of Death	Saturday, August 15, 1959
Age At Death	59
Place Of Death	Holden, West Virginia – Logan County
Occupation	Disabled – Coal Miner Worker – Island Creek Coal Company
Married	Henrietta Lee Bass
Notes	According to the Census, he was listed as literate. He held a Draft Registration Card during WWII on Monday, February 16, 1942 in Holden, West Virginia – Logan County. The card stated that his POB. Milton, North Carolina – Caswell County but his death certificate stated that his POB. South Boston, Virginia – Halifax County. He preferred to use his middle name. He was buried Sunday, August 23, 1959, at Whitman Cemetery.

Name	**Henrietta Lee Bass**
Date Of Birth	Thursday, November 3, 1898
Place Of Birth	Tennessee
Date Of Death	Monday, November 26, 1973

My Family Tree

Age At Death	75
Place Of Death	Holden, West Virginia – Logan County
Occupation	Housewife
Married	Walter Joe Bass
Notes	Married on Wednesday, November 20, 1918, in Holden, West Virginia – Logan County; they were married for 40 years. Her first name on her marriage license was documented as Henry, but on her headstone, her name was spelled Henrietta. Their children: William Joe Bass and Eddie Bass [1]. She was buried in November 1973 at Forest Lawn Cemetery in Pecks Mill, West Virginia – Logan County. Her parents were Agnes Knott Lee and Henry Lee. Her grandfather was Elijah (Gadson) Knott.

Name	**Floyd Cordest Bass**
Date Of Birth	Wednesday, August 6, 1902
Place Of Birth	West Virginia
Date Of Death	Friday, September 24, 1948
Age At Death	46
Place Of Death	Den Mar, West Virginia – Pocahontas County
Occupation	Janitor – Coal Miner Worker
Married	Bertha Jackson Bass
Notes	According to the Census, he was listed as literate. He held a Draft Registration Card from the United States Army during WWII – Monday, February 16, 1942, registered in Holden, West Virginia – Logan County.

Name	**Bertha Jackson Bass**
Date Of Birth	Monday, February 3, 1902
Place Of Birth	North Carolina
Date Of Death	Saturday, January 7, 1989

My Family Tree

Age At Death	86
Place Of Death	Raleigh, North Carolina – Wake County
Occupation	Domestic Worker/Housewife
Married	Floyd Cordest Bass
Notes	Married in 1943 in Holden, West Virginia – Logan County; married for 5 years.

The Family Line of Henrietta Lee Bass and Walter Joe Bass

The connection to the family line was Walter, the son of Martha Cunningham Bass and Joseph Bass.
The Fourth Generation

Henrietta Lee Bass - See Entry Page 343-344
Walter Joe Bass - See Entry Page 343

Their (2) Children

Name	William Joe Bass
Date Of Birth	Wednesday, January 1, 1919
Place Of Birth	Holden, West Virginia – Logan County
Date Of Death	Tuesday, April 1, 1969
Age At Death	50
Place Of Death	Holden, West Virginia – Logan County
Occupation	Coal Miner
Married	Ethel Perry Martin Bass
Notes	Their child: Mattie Bass Ward (married in 1938). Ethel's parents were Ella Martin and Phil Martin. His headstone has his birth year as 1920; however, his brother Eddie stated that William's birth year was 1919.

Name	Eddie Bass I
Date Of Birth	Wednesday, November 30, 1921

My Family Tree

Place Of Birth	Holden, West Virginia – Logan County
Date Of Death	Monday, August 2, 1999
Age At Death	77
Place Of Death	Holden, West Virginia – Logan County
Occupation	Retired – Coal Miner Worker
Married	(1) Dorothy Jones Harris Bass (2) Joyce Lavern Donaldson Bass
Notes	Buried in August 1999 at Forest Lawn Cemetery in Pecks Mill, West Virginia – Logan County.

Name	**Dorothy Jones Harris Bass**
Date Of Birth	Thursday, March 24, 1927
Place Of Birth	Holden, West Virginia – Logan County
Date Of Death	Wednesday, November 29, 1950
Age At Death	23
Place Of Death	Holden, West Virginia – Logan County
Occupation	Housewife
Married	Eddie Bass [1]
Notes	Married on Tuesday, August 26, 1947, in Holden, West Virginia – Logan County; married for 3 years. Her parents were Eva Day Harris and Prince Harris. She was buried on Sunday, December 3, 1950, at Whitman Cemetery.

Name	**Joyce Lavern Donaldson Bass**
Date Of Birth	Saturday, October 15, 1932
Place Of Birth	Holden, West Virginia – Logan County
Date Of Death	Saturday, December 18, 2010
Age At Death	78

My Family Tree

Place Of Death	Holden, West Virginia – Logan County
Occupation	Homemaker
Married	Eddie Bass [1]
Notes	Married on Thursday, August 18, 1951, in Holden, West Virginia – Logan County; married for 47 years. Joyce was buried on Tuesday, December 21, 2010, as a widow. She and Eddie were both buried side-by-side at Forest Lawn Cemetery in Pecks Mill, West Virginia – Logan County. Her parents were Lillian Lynard Donaldson and Jack Donaldson. Their children include Jesse Lanei Bass, Eddie Bass [II] (b. Wednesday, January 15, 1958), Kenneth S. Bass (b. Friday, October 18, 1957), Dorothy Bass Forest (b. Friday, April 23, 1948), Sandra Bass Moss (b. Monday, June 22, 1959), (Jeff Moss), Kim Bass, Jacqueline Bass (Johnny Richardson), Melissa Bass, Katherine Bass, Walter Bass (b. Thursday, February 7, 1952 – d. Tuesday, January 4, 1983, age 30), and Harry Edward Bass (b. Tuesday, January 26, 1954 – d. Wednesday, August 17, 2016, age 62), POD. Price Bottom, West Virginia – Logan County, occupation – Maintenance and retired from Navy service, his wife – Martha Ann Bratcher Bass (b. Wednesday, May 29, 1946). Their children were born in Holden, West Virginia – Logan County.

The Great – Great- Grandparents of Norma Jean Carey Mason–Maternal (Her Mother's Side)

The Family Line of Lille Belle Carrington Carey and James A. Carey

The Third Generation

Lillie Belle Carrington Carey - See Entry Page 311-312
James A. Carey - See Entry Page 311

<u>**Their (7) Children**</u>

Charles Alexander Carey - See Entry Page 341
Helen Bass Carey - See Entry Page 339-340

Name	**Bettie Louise Jones Carey Peters**
Date Of Birth	November 1892
Place Of Birth	Unknown
Date Of Death	Unknown

My Family Tree

Age At Death	Unknown
Place Of Death	Unknown
Occupation	Homemaker/Housewife
Married	(1) Dock White (2) Austin Hicklen (3) Robert Peters
Notes	Listed as literate in the 1910 Census. Robert was born on Monday, January 30, 1888, in West Virginia – Kanawha County. Robert held a Draft Registration Card during WWI (1917 – 1918), listed as a Day Laborer.

Name	**Dock White**
Date Of Birth	1883
Place Of Birth	Virginia
Date Of Death	Wednesday, July 9, 1947
Age At Death	64
Place Of Death	Fayette, West Virginia – Logan County
Occupation	Coal Miner
Married	Bettie Louise Jones Carey White
Notes	His nickname was "Doc." Married in 1927 in Raleigh, West Virginia – Wake County.

Name	**Austin Hicklen**
Date Of Birth	Wednesday, July 4, 1888
Place Of Birth	South Carolina – Chester County
Date Of Death	Unknown
Age At Death	Unknown
Place Of Death	Holden, West Virginia – Logan County
Occupation	Coal Miner

My Family Tree

Married	Bettie Louise Jones Carey Hicklen
Notes	He held a Draft Registration Card during WWI (1917 – 1918), registered in Holden, West Virginia – Logan County.

Name	**William Bryant Carey**
Date Of Birth	Thursday, August 31, 1899
Place Of Birth	Holden, West Virginia – Logan County
Date Of Death	Wednesday, January 15, 1975
Age At Death	75
Place Of Death	Detroit, Michigan – Wayne County
Occupation	Retired – United States – Army/Coal Miner
Married	Maude Martin Carey
Notes	Listed as literate in the 1910 Census. Held a Draft Registration Card during WWI (1917 – 1918), registered in Dunbar, West Virginia – Kanawha County. Married on Wednesday, December 18, 1918, in West Virginia – Logan County. Their children: James Carey (b. 1920 – d. Thursday, January 2, 1930, age 10) and Thomas Ray Carey (b. Saturday, January 27, 1923 – d. Monday, January 17, 1977, age 53). Both children POB. and POD. Holden, West Virginia – Logan County. Thomas's wife was Vernell Mae Baxter Carey. Maude's parents were Effie Gilbreath Martin and Charles Martin.

Name	**Elizabeth Carey Dickerson**
Date Of Birth	1901
Place Of Birth	Virginia – Roanoke County
Date Of Death	Tuesday, October 9, 1945
Age At Death	43 – 44
Place Of Death	Holden, West Virginia – Logan County
Occupation	Housewife

My Family Tree

Married	Woodrow Wilburn Dickerson
Notes	Listed as literate in the 1910 Census. Married on Monday, August 30, 1915, in Virginia – Roanoke County. Buried on Sunday, October 14, 1945, in Holden, West Virginia – Logan County. His parents were Ella Wilson Dickerson and Mac Dickerson. The Census records showed two spellings of Woodrow's last name: Dickerson and Dockery; the correct spelling was Dickerson.

Name	George A. Carey
Date Of Birth	July 1895
Place Of Birth	Amsterdam, Virginia – Botetourt County
Date Of Death	Unknown
Age At Death	Unknown
Place Of Death	Unknown
Occupation	Unknown
Married	Unknown
Notes	Listed as literate in the 1920 Census.

Name	Joseph David Carey
Date Of Birth	Sunday, October 27, 1907
Place Of Birth	Holden, West Virginia – Logan County
Date Of Death	Unknown
Age At Death	Unknown
Place Of Death	Unknown
Occupation	Unknown
Married	Unknown
Notes	Listed as literate in the 1910 Census.

My Family Tree

Name	John Carey
Date Of Birth	1909
Place Of Birth	Holden, West Virginia – Logan County
Date Of Death	Unknown
Age At Death	Unknown
Place Of Death	Unknown
Occupation	Unknown
Married	Unknown
Notes	Listed as literate in the 1910 Census; named Johnie Cary in the 1920 Census.

The Grandparents of Norma Jean Carey Mason–Maternal (Her Mother's Side)

The Family Line of Helen Bass Carey, George Beamon Faulkner, and Charles Alexander Carey

The connection to the family line was Helen, the daughter of Martha Cunningham Bass and Joseph Bass, and Helen's second husband – Charles, was the son of Lillie Belle Carrington Carey and James A. Carey, and first husband – George Beamon Faulkner, was the son of Louise Mason Faulkner and Isaac Faulkner.

The Fourth Generation

Helen Bass Carey	-	See Entry Page 339-340
Charles Alexander Carey	-	See Entry Page 341
George Beamon Faulkner	-	See Entry Page 340

Helen's daughter with George Beamon Faulkner

Name	Jetta Malinda Faulkner Childs
Date Of Birth	Saturday, March 19, 1910
Place Of Birth	Holden, West Virginia – Logan County
Date Of Death	Tuesday, February 29, 2000

My Family Tree

Age At Death	89
Place Of Death	Fayetteville Magisterial, West Virginia – Fayette County
Occupation	Retired – Domestic Worker/Homemaker
Married	George Edward Childs
Notes	Jetta and her younger sister Levonia Margaret Carey Cowan did not grow up together and met later in life. Mattie Mason was Jetta's father's aunt, and Louise Mason was her grandmother on her father's side, who cared for her while her father worked. Listed as Mulatto in the 1920 Census, where her name was spelled Jette Melinda Frattini. Children include Elise Childs Sylvester, Edvern Dallas Childs, Doris Alorie Childs Grant, Quince Childs, Gladys Childs, and Mary Childs. Her father was George Beamon Faulkner.

Name	George Edward Childs
Date Of Birth	Sunday, January 6, 1907
Place Of Birth	Mount Carmel, Virginia – Halifax County
Date Of Death	Thursday, August 5, 1965
Age At Death	58
Place Of Death	Petersburg, Virginia – Dinwiddie County
Occupation	Retired – New River and Pocahontas Coal Company – Coal Miner
Married	Jetta Malinda Faulkner Childs
Notes	Listed as Mulatto in the United States Federal Census. He had a Draft Registration Card for WWII from Wednesday, October 16, 1940, to 1945, registered in Garten, West Virginia – Fayette County. Married on Tuesday, July 27, 1926, in Virginia – Halifax County. They were legally separated before his death. His parents were Hallie Bell Owens Childs and William Childs.

Helen (5) Children with Charles Alexander Carey

Name	Levonia Margaret Carey Cowan

My Family Tree

Date Of Birth	Tuesday, May 20, 1919
Place Of Birth	Holden, West Virginia – Logan County
Date Of Death	Monday, September 27, 1999
Age At Death	80
Place Of Death	Detroit, Michigan – Wayne County
Occupation	Retired – Aviation Factory Worker / Retired – Domestic Worker/ Homemaker
Married	James Avery Cowan
Notes	Levonia was a member of the Eastern Star. Listed as Laroanie Cary in the 1930 Census. During WWII, she worked at the Willow Run Aviation Factory located between Ypsilanti Township and Belleville in Michigan. She had two daughters from a previous relationship, Roxie Lee Carey and Norma J. Carey, who were raised in different boarding houses. With James, she had daughters Elise Cowan Love, Judy Carol Cowan Brown, and Toni Sue Cowan. She divorced James in Detroit. Buried on Friday, October 1, 1999, at Detroit Memorial Park West Cemetery in Livonia, Michigan – Wayne County. Ms. Cowan has an obituary detailing her life.

Name	**James Avery Cowan**
Date Of Birth	Saturday, January 1, 1916
Place Of Birth	Cleveland, North Carolina – Rowan County
Date Of Death	Saturday, July 5, 1997
Age At Death	81
Place Of Death	Tuscaloosa, Alabama – Tuscaloosa County
Occupation	United States Armed Forces – Retired / Retired – Ford Motor
Married	(1) Levonia Margaret Carey Cowan (2) Ella Wilson Crummie Cowan
Notes	His parents were Ana Barber Cowan and John Cowan. He joined the Freemasons and served honorably in the United States Armed Forces during WWII, registered in Cleveland, North Carolina – Rowan County and was honorably discharged. Siblings include Roy Cowan, Ferrell Cowan, Castle Cowan Irvin, Mary Cowan Vance, Kathy Cowan Galloway, and Dorothy Cowan. Married Levonia on Wednesday, October

My Family Tree

| | 30, 1945, in Detroit, Michigan – Wayne County. Mr. Cowan has an obituary about his life. |

The connection to the family line was Walter, the son of Annie Lee Cornelius White and Jay Hugh White.

Name	**Walter White**
Date Of Birth	Friday, February 12, 1915
Place Of Birth	Cleveland, North Carolina – Rowan County
Date Of Death	Wednesday, October 19, 1983
Age At Death	68
Place Of Death	Cleveland, Ohio – Cuyahoga County
Occupation	Retired – Coal Miner / Retired – Assembly Line Worker – White Motors
Married	Lucille Bruce-Wilson White
Notes	His parents were Annie Lee Cornelius White and Jay Hugh White. His daughter with Levonia is Norma J. Carey Mason. His nickname was "Bill." Buried on Sunday, October 23, 1983, at Highland Park Cemetery in Cleveland, Ohio – Cuyahoga County. Mr. White has an obituary about his life.

Name	**Lucille Bruce-Wilson White**
Date Of Birth	Friday, July 6, 1923
Place Of Birth	Jackson, Mississippi – Hinds County
Date Of Death	Saturday, July 30, 1994
Age At Death	68
Place Of Death	Cleveland, Ohio – Cuyahoga County
Occupation	Housekeeper / Homemaker
Married	Walter White
Notes	Their child: Randy White, wife – Donna White; Donna and Randy's children: Bryan Walter White and Jonathan White. Siblings: Nellie Bruce

My Family Tree

	McDaniel, Ida Bruce Woods, Jesse Bruce Turner, and Allen Bruce. Buried on Thursday, August 4, 1994, at Highland Park Cemetery in Highland Hills, Ohio – Cuyahoga County. Her parents were Virginia Bruce and Wardell Bruce. Mrs. White has an obituary about her life.

Name	**Newell Virgil Moore**
Date Of Birth	Monday, May 24, 1920
Place Of Birth	Huntington, Alabama – Madison County
Date Of Death	Monday, December 10, 1973
Age At Death	53
Place Of Death	Detroit, Michigan – Wayne County
Occupation	Day Laborer
Married	Widower
Notes	His daughter with Levonia is Roxie Lee Carey. His parents were Lucy Nancy Moore and Archie Moore [I]. Siblings: Frank Lee Moore I, Ellen Moore Burns, Pearline Moore Bass, Archie Moore [II], Lowell Moore, Otis Moore, and Christine Moore Crawford. Enlisted in the United States Army during WWII – Tuesday, February 18, 1941, registered in Huntington, West Virginia – Logan County as a Private (Branch Immaterial – Warrant Officer) from (1938 – 1946) and was honorably discharged. Attended college for one year before returning to work full-time.

Name	**Vereece Carolyn Carey Sanders Gant**
Date Of Birth	Saturday, May 4, 1918
Place Of Birth	Holden, West Virginia – Logan County
Date Of Death	Sunday, March 28, 1999
Age At Death	80
Place Of Death	Cleveland, Ohio – Cuyahoga County
Occupation	Homemaker
Married	(1) Arvella Levis Farmer (2) Percy Sanders

My Family Tree

	(3) Gant
Notes	Married Arvella in Lorado, West Virginia – Logan County. Listed as Verice Cary in the 1930 Census. Children: Audradella Carey Grant and Wilbur Carey.

Name	Percy Sanders
Date Of Birth	Sunday, September 30, 1917
Place Of Birth	Holden, West Virginia – Logan County
Date Of Death	March 1980
Age At Death	62
Place Of Death	Holden, West Virginia – Logan County
Occupation	Day Laborer
Married	**Vereece Carolyn Carey Sanders**
Notes	Married in 1937 in West Virginia – Logan County. Percy was a boarder in North Fork, West Virginia – McDowell County, at age 12.

Name	Wilbur C. Carey I
Date Of Birth	Wednesday, April 9, 1913
Place Of Birth	Holden, West Virginia – Logan County
Date Of Death	Tuesday, May 23, 1995
Age At Death	82
Place Of Death	Holden, West Virginia – Logan County
Occupation	Retired – United States Army / Retired – Retail Maintenance
Married	Bertha Martin Carey
Notes	He had 3 years of high school education. Enlisted in the Army on Tuesday, November 23, 1943, serving as a private, registered in Huntington, West Virginia – Logan County; was honorably discharged. They were married on Wednesday, August 8, 1934, in Cora, West Virginia – Logan County. He was listed as Nibert Cary in Census records.

My Family Tree

Name	Bertha Martin Carey
Date Of Birth	Saturday, June 7, 1913
Place Of Birth	Sprotts, Alabama – Perry County
Date Of Death	Sunday, September 6, 2015
Age At Death	102
Place Of Death	Holden, West Virginia – Logan County
Occupation	Retired Commercial Cook/Domestic Worker
Married	Wilbur C. Carey [I]
Notes	Their children: June L. Carey Parker, Donna Jean Carey McCoy, Malva J. Carey, Elbert James Carey, Albert Martin Carey, Henry F. Carey, Wilbur C. Carey [II], and Joseph C. Carey. Her parents were Estella Young Martin and Jim Martin.

Name	James Arthur Carey
Date Of Birth	Sunday, May 5, 1912
Place Of Birth	Holden, West Virginia – Logan County
Date Of Death	Saturday, October 13, 1990
Age At Death	78
Place Of Death	Columbus, Ohio – Franklin County
Occupation	Retired – US – Army/Chilton Block Coal Construction Supervisor
Married	Luna Carey
Notes	Census records noted him as Mulatto. He never went past the eighth grade; he had to help his father during the harvest seasons. He joined the Armed Forces on Wednesday, October 16, 1940, registered in Ethel, West Virginia – Logan County, and was honorably discharged. His nickname was, "Buster." He was buried in October 1990 in Columbus, Ohio – Franklin County.

Name	Isabelle Carey Morrison

My Family Tree

Date Of Birth	Sunday, November 26, 1916
Place Of Birth	Holden, West Virginia – Logan County
Date Of Death	Saturday, October 4, 2008
Age At Death	91
Place Of Death	Concord, North Carolina – Cabarrus County
Occupation	Retired – Domestic Worker / Homemaker
Married	Roscoe Morrison [I]
Notes	Children: Alfrederick Morrison [I], Irene Morrison Richardson, and Roscoe Morrison [II]. Buried on Saturday, October 11, 2008, at Highland Memory Gardens Pecks Mill Cemetery in Holden, West Virginia, but laid to rest at Guyan Memorial Gardens in Godby Heights, West Virginia – Logan County. Mrs. Morrison has an obituary detailing her life.

Name	**Roscoe Morrison I**
Date Of Birth	Monday, April 27, 1914
Place Of Birth	Hartwell, Georgia – Hart County
Date Of Death	Friday, October 30, 1959
Age At Death	45
Place Of Death	Holden, West Virginia – Logan County
Occupation	Coal Miner
Married	Isabelle Carey Morrison
Notes	Married in 1937 in West Virginia. Siblings: Sara Morrison (b. 1919), Cordeline Morrison (b. 1922), and Thelma Morrison Teasley (b. 1913). His parents were Iredle Morrison and Oliver Morrison. The 1940 Census noted they had 4 boarders – his sister Sara, sister-in-law Levonia, niece Norma, and Cousin Joseph Cromwell Peters. Buried on Sunday, November 8, 1959, at Whitman Cemetery, but his body is not buried there.

The Family Line of Mary Langhorne Carrington and Samuel C. Carrington [I]

The connection to the family line was Samuel [I], the son of Susan Beverly Carrington and Abraham Carrington.

My Family Tree

The Third Generation

Mary Langhorne Carrington - See Entry Page 315-316
Samuel C. Carrington [1] - See Entry Page 314-315

Their (6) Children

Name	Beatrice Langhorne
Date Of Birth	Wednesday, December 31, 1879
Place Of Birth	Virginia – Roanoke County
Date Of Death	Sunday, December 9, 1956
Age At Death	76
Place Of Death	Virginia – Roanoke County
Occupation	Domestic Worker
Married	Divorced
Notes	According to the 1910 Census, she was listed as being in school. Her mother, Mary, had her from a previous relationship, and her father was not listed on her death certificate. She was supposed to be buried on Wednesday, December 12, 1956, at Green Ridge Baptist Church Cemetery in Hollins, Virginia – Roanoke County, but her body was not buried there.

Name	Lillie B. Carrington
Date Of Birth	Unknown
Place Of Birth	Charlotte, Virginia – Roanoke County
Date Of Death	Unknown
Age At Death	Unknown
Place Of Death	Cloverdale Amsterdam, Virginia – Botetourt County
Occupation	Hotel – Waitress
Married	Single
Notes	According to the 1910 Census, she was listed as being in school. The Census records noted various spellings of her name: Lilobelle Corrington, Lillebelle, Lulu, or Lilly.

My Family Tree

Name	Lovvenia Carrington
Date Of Birth	August 1888
Place Of Birth	Cloverdale Amsterdam, Virginia – Botetourt County
Date Of Death	Unknown
Age At Death	Unknown
Place Of Death	Virginia – Botetourt County
Occupation	Private Family Cook
Married	Unknown
Notes	According to the 1910 Census, she was listed as being in school.

Name	Ida N. Carrington
Date Of Birth	January 1891
Place Of Birth	Cloverdale Amsterdam, Virginia – Botetourt County
Date Of Death	Unknown
Age At Death	Unknown
Place Of Death	Virginia – Botetourt County
Occupation	Unknown
Married	Unknown
Notes	According to the 1910 Census, she was listed as being in school.

Name	Caroline Carrington Morsen
Date Of Birth	October 1892
Place Of Birth	Cloverdale Amsterdam, Virginia – Botetourt County
Date Of Death	Unknown

My Family Tree

Age At Death	Unknown
Place Of Death	Virginia – Botetourt County
Occupation	Unknown
Married	Widow
Notes	According to the 1910 Census, she was listed as being in school.

Name	**Samuel C. Carrington II**
Date Of Birth	Monday, March 4, 1907
Place Of Birth	Cloverdale Amsterdam, Virginia – Botetourt County
Date Of Death	Monday, December 21, 1942
Age At Death	35
Place Of Death	Johnstown, Pennsylvania – Cambria County
Occupation	Barber
Married	Single
Notes	According to the United State Federal Census on Friday, April 22, 1910, in Cloverdale Amsterdam, Virginia – Botetourt County, he was not in school.

The Family Line of Bertha Martin Carey and Wilbur C. Carey [1]

The connection to the family line was Wilbur C. [1], the son of Helen Bass Carey and Charles Alexander Carey.

The Fifth Generation

Bertha Martin Carey	-	**See Entry Page 357**
Wilbur C. Carey [1]	-	**See Entry Page 356**

Their (8) Children

June L. Carey Parker	-	**See Entry Page 357**
Donna Jean Carey McCoy	-	**See Entry Page 357**
Malva J. Carey	-	**See Entry Page 357**
Elbert James Carey	-	**See Entry Page 357**

My Family Tree

Albert Martin Carey - See Entry Page 357

Name	Henry F. Carey
Date Of Birth	Monday, December 17, 1934
Place Of Birth	Cora, West Virginia – Logan County
Date Of Death	Saturday, July 7, 2007
Age At Death	72
Place Of Death	Columbus, Ohio – Franklin County
Occupation	Spiegel Distributors (Retail)
Married	Widower
Notes	He lived at 303 Oakland Park Avenue in Ohio at the time of his death. He was cremated on Thursday, July 12, 2007, in Columbus.

Name	Wilbur C. Carey II
Date Of Birth	1937
Place Of Birth	Cora, West Virginia – Logan County
Date Of Death	N/A
Age At Death	N/A
Place Of Death	N/A
Occupation	N/A
Married	N/A
Notes	Currently living in Odenton, Maryland – Anne Arundel County.

Name	Joseph C. Carey
Date Of Birth	Friday, September 16, 1938
Place Of Birth	Cora, West Virginia – Logan County

My Family Tree

Date Of Death	N/A
Age At Death	N/A
Place Of Death	N/A
Occupation	N/A
Married	Patricia Carey
Notes	His nickname is "Teddy." Currently living in Merced, California – Merced County.

The Family Line of Bettie Louise Jones Carey Peters, Dock White, Austin Hicklen, and Robert Peters

The connection to the family line was Bettie Louise Jones Carey, the daughter of Lille Belle Carrington Carey and James A. Carey.

The Fourth Generation

Bettie Louise Jones Carey Peters	-	**See Entry Page 347-348**
Robert Peters	-	**See Entry Page 348**
Dock White	-	**See Entry Page 348**
Austin Hicklen	-	**See Entry Page 348-349**

Their (6) Children

Name	Nona Bell Hicklen Malone
Date Of Birth	Monday, August 5, 1918
Place Of Birth	Holden, West Virginia – Logan County
Date Of Death	Tuesday, February 28, 2012
Age At Death	93
Place Of Death	Charleston, West Virginia – Kanawha County
Occupation	West Virginia State – Tax Department / Housewife
Married	(1) Reginald Timbers (2) Otis C. Malone
Notes	(1) Married on Wednesday, December 27, 1939, in Virginia – Tazewell County. Reginald Timbers' parents were Arie E. Green Timbers and Warren Timbers. (b. 1915), POB. East Beckley, West Virginia – Raleigh

My Family Tree

	County. Otis Malone (b. Saturday, April 5, 1913, in Charleston, West Virginia – Kanawha County). Both husbands were coal miners. Her father was Austin Hicklen. Otis Malone is alive at the age of 111 years old.

Name	James Edward Peters
Date Of Birth	Monday, March 2, 1925
Place Of Birth	West Virginia
Date Of Death	Thursday, September 9, 1926
Age At Death	1 Year, 6 Months, 7 Days
Place Of Death	Holden, West Virginia – Logan County
Occupation	None
Married	Single
Notes	He was buried on Saturday, September 11, 1926, in Holden, West Virginia – Logan County. His father was Robert Peters. Bettie adopted him, but his biological mother's name was listed as unknown on his death record.

Name	Charles Hicklen
Date Of Birth	Unknown
Place Of Birth	Holden, West Virginia – Logan County
Date Of Death	Unknown
Age At Death	Unknown
Place Of Death	Unknown
Occupation	Unknown
Married	Unknown
Notes	His father was Austin Hicklen.

My Family Tree

Name	David White
Date Of Birth	1930
Place Of Birth	Sewell Mountain, West Virginia – Fayette County
Date Of Death	Unknown
Age At Death	Unknown
Place Of Death	Holden, West Virginia – Logan County
Occupation	Retired – Coal Miner
Married	Unknown
Notes	His father was Dock White.

Name	Joseph Crombwell Peters
Date Of Birth	Saturday, April 25, 1925
Place Of Birth	Holden, West Virginia – Logan County
Date Of Death	Friday, July 21, 2006
Age At Death	81
Place Of Death	Charleston, West Virginia – Kanawha County
Occupation	U.S. Army – Retired / Retired – Budget Analyst
Married	(1) Ida Octavia Hawkins Peters (2) Jean Freeman Barnes Peters (b. Thursday, November 29, 1928), POB. Virginia
Notes	Served in the U.S. Army during WWII, registered in Holden, West Virginia – Logan County, and honorably discharged. Married (1) in 1955 in Charleston, West Virginia – Kanawha County. Married (2) on Saturday, July 2, 1977, in Richmond, Virginia – Henrico County. Jean's parents were Mae Eva Cram Freeman and Joseph Freeman. Their child: Karl Anthony Peters and his two stepsons – Joseph Barnes [II] and Kelvin Barnes. His father was Robert Peters. His body was donated to the Human Gift Registry at West Virginia State University on Tuesday, July 25, 2006 in Charleston, West Virginia – Kanawha County. Mr. Peters has an obituary that details his life.

My Family Tree

Name	Robert White
Date Of Birth	Unknown
Place Of Birth	Holden, West Virginia – Logan County
Date Of Death	Unknown
Age At Death	Unknown
Place Of Death	Unknown
Occupation	Unknown
Married	Unknown
Notes	His father was Dock White.

The Family Line of Jetta Malinda Faulkner Childs and George Edward Childs

The connection to the family line was Jetta, the daughter of Helen Bass Carey and George Beamon Faulkner.

The Fifth Generation

Jetta Malinda Faulkner Childs - See Entry Page 351-352
George Edward Childs - See Entry Page 352

<u>**Their (6) Children**</u>

Name	Elise Childs Sylvester
Date Of Birth	Sunday, April 3, 1927
Place Of Birth	Fayetteville, West Virginia – Fayette County
Date Of Death	Tuesday, February 29, 2000
Age At Death	72
Place Of Death	Ohio, Cuyahoga County
Occupation	Housewife
Married	Raymond Bundrant Sylvester
Notes	

My Family Tree

Name	**Edvern Dallas Childs**
Date Of Birth	Wednesday, March 27, 1929
Place Of Birth	Kaymoor, West Virginia – Fayette County
Date Of Death	Thursday, March 12, 1987
Age At Death	57
Place Of Death	West Virginia
Occupation	Day Laborer
Married	Madeline Allen Childs
Notes	He held a Draft Registration Card during WWII (Friday, March 29, 1946) from the United States Army in Fayetteville, West Virginia – Fayette County. Married in 1949, divorced on Wednesday, October 16, 1968 (19 years of marriage).

Name	**Doris Alorie Childs Grant**
Date Of Birth	Saturday, April 4, 1931
Place Of Birth	Fayetteville, West Virginia – Fayette County
Date Of Death	Monday, July 24, 2017
Age At Death	86
Place Of Death	Detroit, Michigan – Wayne County
Occupation	Housewife
Married	Virgil Eugene Grant
Notes	Married on Saturday, August 5, 1950, in Raleigh, West Virginia – Wake County, 35 year marriage. Virgil (b. Saturday, September 27, 1930, Osaka, Virginia – Wise County – d. Saturday, December 14, 1985, Detroit, Michigan – Wayne County, age 55). Both are buried at Westland Cemetery, Wayne, Michigan – Wayne County. Virgil's parents were Jessie Durham Grant and Robert Grant.

My Family Tree

Name	Quince Childs
Date Of Birth	Tuesday, February 21, 1933
Place Of Birth	Fayetteville, West Virginia – Fayette County
Date Of Death	Friday, December 1, 1962
Age At Death	29
Place Of Death	Bloomfield, New Jersey – Essex County
Occupation	Day Laborer
Married	Single
Notes	Buried in December 1996 at Glendale Cemetery in Bloomfield, New Jersey.

Name	Gladys Childs
Date Of Birth	Wednesday, February 13, 1935
Place Of Birth	Fayetteville, West Virginia – Fayette County
Date Of Death	N/A
Age At Death	N/A
Place Of Death	N/A
Occupation	N/A
Married	N/A
Notes	

Name	Mary Childs
Date Of Birth	Saturday, December 11, 1937
Place Of Birth	Fayetteville, West Virginia – Fayette County
Date Of Death	N/A

My Family Tree

Age At Death	N/A
Place Of Death	N/A
Occupation	N/A
Married	N/A
Notes	

The Grandparents of Norma Jean Carey Mason –Maternal (Her Father's Side)

The Family Line of Annie Lee Cornelius White, Maggie McCall White, Grace E. White, and Jay Hugh White

The connection to the family line was Annie, the daughter of Susan Jane (Sookey) Cowan Cornelius and Augustus Cornelius, and Annie's husband – Jay, the son of Mary C. Summers White and George R. White.

The Fourth Generation

Annie Lee Cornelius White - See Entry Page 322-323
Jay Hugh White - See Entry Page 322

His (13) Children

Name	Joseph Linzie White
Date Of Birth	Tuesday, April 16, 1901
Place Of Birth	Chambersburg Township, North Carolina – Iredell County
Date Of Death	Tuesday, March 7, 1978
Age At Death	76
Place Of Death	Gaston, North Carolina – Iredell County
Occupation	Scrap Iron Worker
Married	Widower
Notes	His mother was Maggie McCall White. Census records from 1910 noted him as being in school. He was buried on Saturday, March 11, 1978, at Antioch Baptist Church Cemetery in North Carolina – Iredell County. His son was Donald R. White [1].

My Family Tree

Walter (Bill) White - See Entry Page 354
Lucille Bruce-Wilson White - See Entry Page 354-355

Name	Mary Bell White Whiteside
Date Of Birth	Tuesday, November 5, 1918
Place Of Birth	Cleveland, North Carolina – Rowan County
Date Of Death	Monday, May 24, 1999
Age At Death	80
Place Of Death	Cleveland, North Carolina – Rowan County
Occupation	Retired – Domestic Worker/Housewife
Married	Otho Whiteside
Notes	The couple had no children together. She was buried in May 1999 at Mount Tabor Presbyterian Church Cemetery. Her mother was Annie Lee.

Name	Andrew Wilson White
Date Of Birth	Saturday, October 14, 1922
Place Of Birth	Cleveland, North Carolina – Rowan County
Date Of Death	Wednesday, June 12, 1996
Age At Death	73
Place Of Death	New York, New York – Queens County
Occupation	Day Laborer
Married	Jane White
Notes	Annie was his mother. The couple had no children. His nickname was "Andy." He lived at 205-14 110th Avenue, St Albans, in New York, at the time of his death. He held a United States Draft Registration Card during WWII in 1942 in Chambersburg Township, North Carolina – Iredell County.

My Family Tree

Name	Jay Roger White
Date Of Birth	Tuesday, March 31, 1925
Place Of Birth	Cleveland, North Carolina – Rowan County
Date Of Death	Saturday, February 22, 1986
Age At Death	60
Place Of Death	Cleveland, Ohio – Cuyahoga County
Occupation	White Motors – Assembly Line Worker
Married	Gloria White (d. Thursday, January 22, 1976)
Notes	Annie was his mother. He was buried on Friday, February 28, 1986. Their child: Stanley Eric White (b. Monday, May 18, 1959 – d. Saturday, December 19, 1998, age 39), occupation – Unemployed – Disabled. Stanley POB. and POD. Cleveland, Ohio – Cuyahoga County and he was buried in December 1998. Jay and Stanley were both buried side-by-side, at Highland Park Cemetery in Cleveland, Ohio – Cuyahoga County.

Name	Anne Lou White Awanna
Date Of Birth	Wednesday, August 26, 1925
Place Of Birth	Cleveland, North Carolina – Rowan County
Date Of Death	Saturday, July 5, 1997
Age At Death	71
Place Of Death	Cleveland, North Carolina – Rowan County
Occupation	Housewife
Married	John Awanna
Notes	Annie was her mother. Their children: Bernice Awanna and Elaine Awanna. She was buried on Tuesday, July 8, 1997, at Mount Tabor Presbyterian Church Cemetery.

My Family Tree

Name	DeWitt Shuford White
Date Of Birth	Sunday, July 7, 1929
Place Of Birth	Cleveland, North Carolina – Rowan County
Date Of Death	Thursday, July 15, 2010
Age At Death	81
Place Of Death	New York, New York – Queens County
Occupation	Day Laborer
Married	Carolyn Mack Lipscomb White
Notes	His mother was Annie. They did not have any children. He was buried in July 2010, at Mount Tabor Presbyterian Church Cemetery. Carolyn and DeWitt are supposed to be buried side-by-side. Mr. White has an obituary that talks about his life.

Name	Carolyn Mack Lipscomb White
Date Of Birth	Saturday, June 24, 1944
Place Of Birth	New York, New York – Queens County
Date Of Death	N/A
Age At Death	N/A
Place Of Death	N/A
Occupation	Protective Services Official/Social Worker/Teacher
Married	DeWitt Shuford White
Notes	Married on Sunday, April 3, 1977 in New York. Carolyn's parents were Bertha Mack and McKenzie Mack. Mrs. White has a living testimony that talks about her life.

Name	John Carl White
Date Of Birth	Friday, March 11, 1927

My Family Tree

Place Of Birth	Cleveland, North Carolina – Rowan County
Date Of Death	Monday, December 7, 2009
Age At Death	82
Place Of Death	Dearborn Heights, Michigan – Wayne County
Occupation	Retired – United States Army/Retired – Assembly Line Worker – Daimler Chrysler
Married	Eloise Rankin White
Notes	He served in the United States Army during WWII, registered in Cleveland, North Carolina – Rowan County, and was honorably discharged. His children: Lenore Heaggans Reid (b. 1948 – d. 2024, age 76), Marion White Hrobowski, and Thouston Conrad Heaggans (b. 1950 – d. 1970, age 20), and service in Vietnam. He has an obituary that talks about his life. He was buried on Saturday, December 12, 2009, at Mount Tabor Presbyterian Church Cemetery. His mother was Annie.

Name	**Eloise Rankin White**
Date Of Birth	Wednesday, December 21, 1927
Place Of Birth	Cleveland, North Carolina – Rowan County
Date Of Death	Tuesday, December 27, 2022
Age At Death	95
Place Of Death	Dearborn Heights, Michigan – Wayne County
Occupation	Housewife
Married	John Carl White
Notes	Married in 1954, married for 55 years. Her parents were Essie Mae Ellis Rankin and David Rankin. She has an obituary that talks about her life. Her body was shipped back to North Carolina to be laid to rest with her husband.

Name	**Rayford Odell White**
Date Of Birth	Tuesday, June 26, 1917

My Family Tree

Place Of Birth	E. Statesville, North Carolina – Iredell County
Date Of Death	Wednesday, February 26, 1947
Age At Death	29
Place Of Death	Chambersburg Township, North Carolina – Iredell County
Occupation	United States Army
Married	Widower
Notes	He served in the United States Army as PFC Trans Corps in WWII, registering in Cleveland, North Carolina – Rowan County, honorably discharged. He was buried on Sunday, March 2, 1947, at Mount Tabor Presbyterian Church Cemetery. His mother was Annie.

Name	**Nathaniel White**
Date Of Birth	Friday, March 24, 1911
Place Of Birth	Chambersburg Township, North Carolina – Iredell County
Date Of Death	Saturday, March 24, 1990
Age At Death	79
Place Of Death	Arkansas
Occupation	Day Laborer
Married	Hazel Dell McElmore White (b. 1913)
Notes	Grace E. White was his biological mother. Married on Saturday, March 26, 1932, in Pine Bluff, Arkansas – Jefferson County.

Name	**Isaac E. White**
Date Of Birth	1916
Place Of Birth	Chambersburg Township, North Carolina – Iredell County
Date Of Death	Unknown
Age At Death	Unknown

My Family Tree

Place Of Death	Unknown
Occupation	Unknown
Married	Unknown
Notes	Grace E. White was his biological mother.

Name	**Grace Vivian White**
Date Of Birth	Tuesday, April 25, 1916
Place Of Birth	Chambersburg Township, North Carolina – Iredell County
Date Of Death	Saturday, February 27, 1971
Age At Death	54
Place Of Death	Troutman, North Carolina – Iredell County
Occupation	Farmer
Married	Merle Inay Gamble Polk White
Notes	He was buried in February 1971 at Mount Tabor Presbyterian Church Cemetery. His mother was Annie.

Name	**Merle Inay Gamble Polk White**
Date Of Birth	Thursday, November 18, 1915
Place Of Birth	North Carolina – Iredell County
Date Of Death	Sunday, December 2, 2001
Age At Death	86
Place Of Death	Troutman, North Carolina – Iredell County
Occupation	Retired – Domestic Worker/Housewife
Married	Grace Vivian White
Notes	Married on Tuesday, November 13, 1934 in Statesville, North Carolina – Iredell County, a marriage of 37 years. According to the Census records,

My Family Tree

	her full name was spelled Myrtle Inez Gamble White. Her parents were Martha Gamble and Samuel Gamble. She was buried in December 2001, a widow when she died. Her nickname was "Nellie." Their children: Samuel Jay "Jimmie" White (b. Sunday, October 2, 1938 – d. Monday, December 7, 2020, age 82) and Vernie Grace White (b. Sunday, April 13, 1935 – d. Saturday, November 6, 2010 age 75). Both of their children POB. and POD. is North Carolina – Iredell County. Vernie was buried in November 2010, and Samuel was buried in December 2020. Merle, Vernie, and Samuel were all buried at Glenwood Memorial Park in Mooresville, North Carolina – Iredell County. Samuel served in the United States Army from 1957 to 1959.

Name	Vernie Matilda White
Date Of Birth	Wednesday, June 30, 1920
Place Of Birth	North Carolina – Iredell County
Date Of Death	Wednesday, April 6, 1921
Age At Death	10 Months Old
Place Of Death	Chambersburg Township, North Carolina – Iredell County
Occupation	None
Married	Single
Notes	She was buried in April 1921 at Mount Tabor Presbyterian Church Cemetery. Her mother was Annie.

The Family Line of Emma H. Griffin Cowan and John H. Cowan

The connection to the family line was John, the son of Elizabeth Witherspoon Cowan and Charles Cowan [1].

The Third Generation

Emma H. Griffith Cowan - See Entry Page 326
John H. Cowan - See Entry Page 326

Their (9) Children

Name	Lillie D. Cowan Rankin
Date Of Birth	Sunday, December 16, 1877

My Family Tree

Place Of Birth	Mount Ulla Township, North Carolina – Rowan County
Date Of Death	Saturday, September 11, 1965
Age At Death	87
Place Of Death	Salisbury, North Carolina – Rowan County
Occupation	Housewife
Married	Cornelius Alexander Rankin
Notes	Their children: Thelma M. Rankin (b. 1911 – d. 2005, age 93 – 94), Claude DeWitt Rankin (b. 1902 – d. 1972, age 69 – 70), Emma Rankin Heaggans (b. 1898 – d. 1968, age 69 – 70), Ollie Rankin Irby (b. 1900 – d. 1983, age 82-83), Albert Alexander Rankin (b. 1903 – d. 1966, age 62 – 63), William Theodore Rankin (b. 1907 – d. 1981, age 73–74), Raymond Wilford Rankin (b. 1908 – d. 1978, age 69 – 70), Leroy Wilson Rankin (b. 1913 – d. 1988, age 74 –75), Richard Elihue Rankin (b. 1915 – d. 1987, age 71-72), Lillie Mae Rankin Wilson (b. 1917 – d. 1978, age 60 –61), and Johnny Cornelius Rankin (b. 1920 – d. 1995, age 74). It was reported to the United States Federal Census on Wednesday, June 23, 1880 in Mount Ulla Township, North Carolina – Rowan County, that Lillie was not in school and her first name was spelled as Aleay. She was buried on Wednesday, September 15, 1965, a widow. Lillie and Cornelius were both buried side-by-side, at Mount Tabor Presbyterian Church Cemetery. Her headstone has the wrong year when she was born in 1878.

Name	**Cornelius Alexander Rankin**
Date Of Birth	Friday, January 10, 1875
Place Of Birth	North Carolina – Rowan County
Date Of Death	Monday, March 5, 1962
Age At Death	87
Place Of Death	Salisbury, North Carolina – Rowan County
Occupation	Day Laborer
Married	Lillie D. Cowan Rankin
Notes	Married on Sunday, May 29, 1898, in North Carolina – Rowan County – a marriage of 64 years. His parents were Lillie C. Rankin and Cornelius Rankin. He was buried in March 1962.

My Family Tree

Name	**Charles Edward Cowan I**
Date Of Birth	Sunday, January 22, 1882
Place Of Birth	Mount Ulla Township, North Carolina – Rowan County
Date Of Death	Thursday, February 21, 1935
Age At Death	53
Place Of Death	Braeholm, West Virginia – Logan County
Occupation	Farm Laborer
Married	Carrie Mozella Clement Cowan
Notes	His twin brother was William. According to Census records of 1900, he was listed as literate. He held a Draft Registration Card during WWI from the United States Army from 1917 to1918. He was buried on Saturday, February 23, 1935, at Mount Tabor Presbyterian Church Cemetery.

Name	**Carrie Mozella Clement Cowan**
Date Of Birth	Saturday, September 10, 1881
Place Of Birth	North Carolina – Rowan County
Date Of Death	Sunday, September 8, 1968
Age At Death	86
Place Of Death	Man, West Virginia – Logan County
Occupation	Farm Labor/Housewife
Married	Charles Edward Cowan ^{I}
Notes	Married on Sunday, August 7, 1904 in West Virginia – Logan County – a marriage of 31 years. Carrie's parents were Emma Ferron Clement and Alexander Clement. Their children: Leslie Cowan, Lou Cowan (b. 1906), Allen Dewitt Cowan (b. 1907 – d. 1986, age 79 – 80), Mildred Cowan Walton (b. 1908), Mellon Cowan (b. 1908), Gilbert Cowan (b. 1911), and Charles Edward Cowan ^{II} (b. Thursday, July 6, 1916, POB. West Virginia – Logan County – d. Monday, April 12, 1999, POD. Amherstdale, West Virginia – Logan County age 82), Charles's ^{II} wife – Emma L. Lyons Cowan (b. Tuesday, May 30, 1916, POB. Virginia – d. Sunday, July 11, 2010, age 94), POD. Lancaster, California – Los Angeles County, buried

My Family Tree

	on Saturday, July 17, 2010, at Guyan Memorial Gardens in Godby Heights, West Virginia – Logan County. Emma's child: Donald Cowan (Janet), and her sister was Ann Lyons Richerson (Robert). Emma's parents were Rachel Bradley Lyons (b. 1891 – d. 1969, age 77) and William Jacob Lyons (b. 1889 – d. 1969, age 80).

Name	**William Lee Cowan**
Date Of Birth	Sunday, January 22, 1882
Place Of Birth	Mount Ulla Township, North Carolina – Rowan County
Date Of Death	Friday, May 23, 1947
Age At Death	65
Place Of Death	Mount Ulla Township, North Carolina – Rowan County
Occupation	Farm Laborer
Married	Addie Lee Ferron Cowan
Notes	According to the Census records for 1900, he was listed as literate. His twin brother was Charles. His nickname was "Will, Willie, or Bill." Married on Thursday, December 18, 1902, married for 13 years. He was buried in May 1947. Addie and William were both buried, at Mount Tabor Presbyterian Church Cemetery.

Name	**Addie Lee Ferron Cowan**
Date Of Birth	Sunday, February 1, 1885
Place Of Birth	Mount Ulla Township, North Carolina – Rowan County
Date Of Death	Wednesday, December 29, 1915
Age At Death	30
Place Of Death	Mount Ulla Township, North Carolina – Rowan County
Occupation	Farm Laborer
Married	William Lee Cowan
Notes	She was buried in January 1916. Their children: Mitchell Lewis Cowan (b. 1929 – d. 1981, age 51– 52), Irdee Cowan Dixon (b. 1907 – d. 1980

My Family Tree

	age 72–73), Murlee Cowan Falls (b. 1907 – d. 1956, age 50– 49), and Josephine Cowan Anderson (b. 1910 – d. 1975, age 64–65). Irdee and Murlee were twins.

Name	**Henry Caldwell Cowan**
Date Of Birth	Wednesday, November 24, 1886
Place Of Birth	Mount Ulla Township, North Carolina – Rowan County
Date Of Death	Saturday, December 19, 1964
Age At Death	78
Place Of Death	Salisbury, North Carolina – Rowan County
Occupation	Retired – United States Army / Retired – Farm Laborer
Married	Tinsie Mae C. Baity Cowan
Notes	According to the Census records for 1900, he could read but could not write. He served during WWI as a PFC in the United States Army and was honorably discharged. He was buried in December 1964.

Name	**Tinsie Mae C. Baity Cowan**
Date Of Birth	Sunday, August 11, 1907
Place Of Birth	Mount Ulla Township, North Carolina – Rowan County
Date Of Death	Saturday, March 11, 2006
Age At Death	98
Place Of Death	Mount Ulla Township, North Carolina – Rowan County
Occupation	Retired – Domestic Worker / Housewife
Married	Henry Caldwell Cowan
Notes	Married on Wednesday, November 25, 1936 in Lumberton, North Carolina – Robeson County – a marriage of 28 years. She was buried in March 2006. Tinsie and Henry were both buried side-by-side, at Mount Tabor Presbyterian Church Cemetery. Her parents were Mamie Baity and Bud Baity.

My Family Tree

Name	Nancy E. Cowan Cameron
Date Of Birth	Monday, April 18, 1898
Place Of Birth	Mount Ulla Township, North Carolina – Rowan County
Date Of Death	Monday, August 3, 1981
Age At Death	83
Place Of Death	Greensboro, North Carolina – Guilford County
Occupation	Retired – Domestic Worker / Housewife
Married	Widow
Notes	According to the Census records for 1900, she could read but could not write. She was buried in August 1981, at Guilford Memorial Garden Cemetery in Greensboro, North Carolina – Guilford County.

Name	Robert N. Cowan
Date Of Birth	Monday, January 11, 1892
Place Of Birth	Mount Ulla Township, North Carolina – Rowan County
Date Of Death	Saturday, April 23, 1988
Age At Death	96
Place Of Death	Fayetteville, North Carolina – Cumberland County
Occupation	Minister / Farmer
Married	Ethel Baker Burney Cowan (b. 1903 – d. 1971, age 68)
Notes	According to the Census records for 1900, he could read but could not write. Married on Saturday, December 20, 1952, in Fayetteville, North Carolina – Cumberland County. Her parents were Rebecca Burney and George W. Burney. Her and her parents POB. North Carolina.

Name	Mary N. Cowan Marlin
Date Of Birth	Saturday, September 9, 1893

My Family Tree

Place Of Birth	Mount Ulla Township, North Carolina – Rowan County
Date Of Death	Wednesday, January 27, 1982
Age At Death	88
Place Of Death	Philadelphia, Pennsylvania – Philadelphia County
Occupation	Housewife
Married	Marshall Marlin (b. 1898 – d. 1977, age 79)
Notes	According to the Census records for 1900, she could read but could not write. Married in 1924 in North Carolina.

Name	Martha Elizabeth Cowan
Date Of Birth	Sunday, April 12, 1896
Place Of Birth	Mount Ulla Township, North Carolina – Rowan County
Date Of Death	Sunday, November 16, 1967
Age At Death	71
Place Of Death	Statesville Township, North Carolina – Iredell County
Occupation	Retired – Domestic Worker
Married	Single
Notes	The Census records for 1900 show she was not listed as being in school. Her children include Nancy Cinora Cowan Haynes, Vivian Catherine Cowan Hyde, Grover Cowan, Russell Alberta Cowan, and Lula Virginia Cowan. Martha was buried in November 1967, at Mount Tabor Presbyterian Church Cemetery.

Name	John Thomas Monroe Cowan
Date Of Birth	Friday, June 25, 1880
Place Of Birth	Cleveland, North Carolina – Rowan County
Date Of Death	Tuesday, March 16, 1954

My Family Tree

Age At Death	73
Place Of Death	Cleveland, North Carolina – Rowan County
Occupation	Retired – Farmer / Retired – United States Army
Married	Margaret A. McHenry Cowan
Notes	Married on Sunday, January 10, 1904, in Cleveland, North Carolina – Rowan County, marriage lasting 49 years. He served in the United States Army during WWI from 1917–1918, registered in Chambersburg Township, North Carolina – Rowan County, and was honorably discharged. He was buried on Thursday, March 18, 1954.

Name	**Margaret A. McHenry Cowan**
Date Of Birth	Tuesday, January 15, 1884
Place Of Birth	Mount Ulla Township, North Carolina – Rowan County
Date Of Death	Tuesday, October 25, 1955
Age At Death	71
Place Of Death	Cleveland, North Carolina – Rowan County
Occupation	Retired – Domestic Worker / Housewife
Married	John Thomas Monroe Cowan
Notes	According to the Census records for 1900, Margaret and John were listed as literate. Her nickname was "Maggie." She was buried in October 1955. They were both buried side-by-side, at Mount Tabor Presbyterian Church Cemetery.

The Family Line of Levonia Margaret Carey Cowan, Newell Virgil Moore, Walter White, and James Avery Cowan

The connection to the family line was Levonia, the daughter of Helen Bass Carey and Charles Alexander Carey, and Walter, the son of Annie Lee Cornelius White and Jay Hugh White, and Newell, the son of Lucy Nancy Moore and Archie Moore[1], and Levonia's husband – James, the son of Ana Barber Cowan and John Cowan.

The Fifth Generation

Levonia Margaret Carey Cowan	-	See Entry Page 352-353
Walter White	-	See Entry Page 354

My Family Tree

| Newell Virgil Moore | - | See Entry Page 355 |
| James Avery Cowan | - | See Entry Page 353-354 |

Her (5) Children

| Norma Jean Carey Mason | - | See Entry Page 75 |
| Eugene Napoleon Mason | - | See Entry Page 74 |

Name	Roxie Lee Carey Muwwakkil
Date Of Birth	Thursday, October 1, 1936
Place Of Birth	Holden, West Virginia – Logan County
Date Of Death	N/A
Age At Death	N/A
Place Of Death	N/A
Occupation	Retired – Administration – State of California Corrections Dept.
Married	Marvin Guyse
Notes	Roxie and Marvin changed their names to their Muslim faith – Muslimah Muwwakkil and Abdul Muwwakkil. Her father was Newell Virgil Moore. Married on Monday, August 19, 2002, in Hanford, California – Kings County. Their children: Abdul Rafeeq Salahuddin, Ebony Latifah Salahuddin Saliba, Sabreen Lavonia Salahuddin, Marvinah Nyderah Salahuddin Sbinowitz, and Ameerah Salahuddin Lydick. Mrs. Muwwakkil has a living testimony about her life.

Name	Elise Cowan Love
Date Of Birth	Friday, May 4, 1951
Place Of Birth	Detroit, Michigan – Wayne County
Date Of Death	N/A
Age At Death	N/A
Place Of Death	N/A
Occupation	Retired – Detroit Free Press Worker / Homemaker / Caretaker
Married	(1) Eddie Andrew Trent [1] (2) Gene Edward Love

My Family Tree

Notes	Her father was James Avery Cowan. Their children: Lisa Ann Trent and Eddie Andrew Trent [II], who are twins. Mrs. Love has a living testimony about her life.

Name	**Eddie Andrew Trent I**
Date Of Birth	Monday, August 16, 1948
Place Of Birth	Tallahassee, Florida – Leon County
Date Of Death	Thursday, October 14, 2021
Age At Death	73
Place Of Death	Jacksonville, Florida – Duval County
Occupation	Retired – General Motors – UAW
Married	Elise Cowan Trent
Notes	Married on Saturday, March 22, 1969, in Detroit, Michigan – Wayne County. The first wedding performed by Bishop, Rev. Gary M. Simpson at the **Temple of I AM** at the church's new location on Hamilton in Detroit. Elise and Eddie [1], got a divorce in Michigan. His mother was Mary Johnson. He was cremated in Jacksonville, Florida – Duval County. Mr. Trent [1] has an obituary that talks about his life.

Name	**Gene Edward Love**
Date Of Birth	Friday, May 4, 1951
Place Of Birth	Dumas, Arkansas – Desha County
Date Of Death	N/A
Age At Death	N/A
Place Of Death	N/A
Occupation	Furniture Repair / Auto Repair / Handyman
Married	Elise Cowan Love
Notes	Married on Sunday, July 29, 1984, in Detroit, Michigan –Wayne County.

My Family Tree

Name	**Judy Carol Cowan Brown**
Date Of Birth	Friday, October 2, 1953
Place Of Birth	Detroit, Michigan – Wayne County
Date Of Death	N/A
Age At Death	N/A
Place Of Death	N/A
Occupation	Retired – Make-up Artist / Homemaker / Caterer
Married	(1) Elco Jr. Brown II (2) Kenneth D. Pollard
Notes	Her father was James Avery Cowan. Their children: Maria Antoinette Brown and Nakia LeMone Brown. Ms. Brown has a living testimony about her life. (2) b. Monday, June 22, 1953, POB. Johnstown, Pennsylvania – Cambria County, his occupation – Security Guard – Ford Field. Judy and Kenneth were divorced in Detroit, Michigan – Wayne County. His nickname is "Kenny."

Name	**Elco Jr. Brown II**
Date Of Birth	Sunday, November 2, 1947
Place Of Birth	Greensboro, North Carolina – Guilford County
Date Of Death	N/A
Age At Death	N/A
Place Of Death	N/A
Occupation	Retired – United States Army / Retired – United States Postal Worker
Married	Judy Carol Cowan Brown
Notes	His parents were Bessie Brown and Elco Jr. Brown I. He served in the United States Army, registered in Greensboro, North Carolina – Guilford County, and received an honorable discharge. Married on Friday, July 14, 1972, in Detroit, Michigan – Wayne County. Their wedding was performed by Bishop, Rev. Gary M. Simpson at the **Temple of I AM** on Hamilton in Detroit. Judy and Elco were divorced in Detroit, Michigan – Wayne County.

My Family Tree

Name	Toni Sue Cowan
Date Of Birth	Monday, February 6, 1956
Place Of Birth	Detroit, Michigan – Wayne County
Date Of Death	N/A
Age At Death	N/A
Place Of Death	N/A
Occupation	Retail Store – Floor Manager
Married	N/A
Notes	Census records noted that in 1980 she had three children, with two that survived. Her father was James Avery Cowan. Her children: Stephen Idel Cowan [1], Keith Jerome Cowan, and AnRico Celete Levonia Cowan Lockhart [1]. Ms. Cowan has a living testimony about her life.

The Family Line of Isabelle Carey Morrison and Roscoe Morrison [1]

The connection to the family line was Isabelle, the daughter of Helen Bass Carey and Charles Alexander Carey.

The Fifth Generation

Isabelle Carey Morrison - See Entry Page 357-358
Roscoe Morrison [1] - See Entry Page 358

Their (3) Children

Name	Alfrederick Morrison I
Date Of Birth	Tuesday, January 24, 1939
Place Of Birth	Holden, West Virginia – Logan County
Date Of Death	Sunday, September 1, 2013
Age At Death	74
Place Of Death	Winter Park, Florida – Orange County
Occupation	Retired – Air Force/Retired – United States Government – Computer Specialist
Married	(1) Gloria Jean Harris-Johnson Morrison (2) LeAnn Jacobs Morrison (b. Saturday, September 7, 1957)

My Family Tree

Notes	(2) Marriage in 1984 – a marriage of 29 years. His nickname was "Moe or Pond." He served in the United States Air Force, registered in West Virginia – Logan County, and was honorably discharged. He was cremated on Friday, September 6, 2013, in Winter Park, Florida – Orange County. Mr. Morrison has an obituary that talks about his life. LeAnn's son – Eric James Wilson (b. Friday, March 31, 1978), and after Alfrederick married LeAnn, he adopted Eric as his son.

Name	**Gloria Jean Harris-Johnson Morrison**
Date Of Birth	Wednesday, June 18, 1941
Place Of Birth	Fayetteville, Tennessee – Lincoln County
Date Of Death	N/A
Age At Death	N/A
Place Of Death	N/A
Occupation	Homemaker
Married	Alfrederick Morrison ^{I}
Notes	(1) Marriage in 1962 in Holden, West Virginia – Logan County. She is of Native-American descent – Black foot. Their children: Valeria Jean Harris-Johnson Morrison, Electra Jean Morrison Holmes, Alfrederick Morrison ^{II}, Shawn Manuel Morrison, Prentice Tayvon Morrison ^{I}, and Eureka Jean Morrison Dunbar.

Name	**Irene Morrison Richardson**
Date Of Birth	1938
Place Of Birth	Holden, West Virginia – Logan County
Date Of Death	N/A
Age At Death	N/A
Place Of Death	N/A
Occupation	Homemaker
Married	Wilbur Richardson

My Family Tree

Notes	Their children: Renee Richardson, Terry Richardson, and Randy Richardson. Their children were born in Camp Springs, Maryland – Prince George's County. Living in Concord, North Carolina – Cabarrus County.

Name	**Roscoe Morrison II**
Date Of Birth	Monday, September 9, 1940
Place Of Birth	Holden, West Virginia – Logan County
Date Of Death	Saturday, May 11, 2013
Age At Death	72
Place Of Death	White Plains, New York – Westchester County
Occupation	Retired – Accountant – Banking Industry
Married	Connie Morrison
Notes	Married on Friday, October 5, 1962, in White Plains, New York – Westchester County. His nickname was "Babe." Their child: Deborah Michelle Morrison Davis. He was on buried Saturday, May 18, 2013, at Kensico Cemetery in Valhalla, New York – Westchester County. Mr. Morrison has an obituary that talks about his life.

The Family Line of Gloria Jean Harris-Johnson Morrison and Alfrederick Morrison [I]

The connection to the family line was Alfrederick[I], the son of Isabelle Carey Morrison and Roscoe Morrison[I].

The Sixth Generation

Gloria Jean Harris-Johnson Morrison - See Entry Page 388
Alfrederick Morrison [I] - See Entry Page 387-388

Their (7) Children

Name	**Valeria Jean Harris-Johnson Morrison**
Date Of Birth	Saturday, December 29, 1956
Place Of Birth	Holden, West Virginia – Logan County
Date Of Death	July 2002
Age At Death	45

My Family Tree

Place Of Death	Holden, West Virginia – Logan County
Occupation	Disabled
Married	Single
Notes	

Name	**Electra Jean Morrison Holmes**
Date Of Birth	Saturday, July 11, 1964
Place Of Birth	San Bernardino, California – San Bernardino County
Date Of Death	N/A
Age At Death	N/A
Place Of Death	N/A
Occupation	Real Estate Management Team
Married	Sebastian Holmes
Notes	Their child: Grace Kristen Holmes.

Name	**Fred Blyden**
Date Of Birth	Wednesday, July 13, 1960
Place Of Birth	The Philippines
Date Of Death	N/A
Age At Death	N/A
Place Of Death	N/A
Occupation	N/A
Married	Nermaryha Blyden

My Family Tree

Notes	Their children: Raphael Santi Pasamonte Blyden, Zsa Zsa Nicole Pasamonte Blyden, and Giovanni Alexavier Blyden, born in Corona, California – Riverside County.

Name	**Alfrederick Morrison II**
Date Of Birth	Sunday, December 2, 1962
Place Of Birth	Dayton, Ohio – Montgomery County
Date Of Death	N/A
Age At Death	N/A
Place Of Death	N/A
Occupation	Home Improvement Design Services
Married	Kim Morrison
Notes	Their children: Eric Todd Morrison, Theresa Jean Morrison, and Malik Morrison, born in Oxon Hill, Maryland – Prince George's County.

Name	**Shawn Manuel Morrison**
Date Of Birth	Wednesday, January 12, 1966
Place Of Birth	Riverside, California – Riverside County
Date Of Death	N/A
Age At Death	N/A
Place Of Death	N/A
Occupation	N/A
Married	N/A
Notes	His daughter: Gelia Jean Morrison.

Name	**Prentice Tayvon Morrison I**

My Family Tree

Date Of Birth	Tuesday, November 12, 1968
Place Of Birth	Camp Springs, Maryland – Prince George's County
Date Of Death	N/A
Age At Death	N/A
Place Of Death	N/A
Occupation	N/A
Married	Tanya Morrison
Notes	Their child: Prentice Tayvon Morrison II.

Name	**Eureka Jean Morrison Dunbar**
Date Of Birth	Sunday, March 15, 1970
Place Of Birth	Camp Springs, Maryland – Prince George's County
Date Of Death	N/A
Age At Death	N/A
Place Of Death	N/A
Occupation	Homemaker
Married	Michael Dunbar
Notes	Their children: JaVon Dunbar and Aaron DeVanta Dunbar.

Alfrederick Morrison I   Great Granddaughter

Name	Heaven Morrison
Date Of Birth	N/A
Place Of Birth	N/A
Date Of Death	N/A
Age At Death	N/A

My Family Tree

Place Of Death	N/A
Occupation	N/A
Married	N/A
Notes	

The Family Line of Tanya Morrison and Prentice Morrison [1]

The connection to the family line is Prentice [1], the son of Gloria Jean Harris-Johnson Morrison and Alfrederick Morrison [1].

The Seventh Generation

Tanya Morrison	-	See Entry Page 392
Prentice Tayvon Morrison [1]	-	See Entry Page 391-392

Their Child

Name	**Prentice Tayvon Morrison II**
Date Of Birth	Thursday, September 13, 2001
Place Of Birth	Camp Springs, Maryland – Prince George's County
Date Of Death	N/A
Age At Death	N/A
Place Of Death	N/A
Occupation	N/A
Married	N/A
Notes	

The Family Line of Eureka Jean Morrison Dunbar and Michael Dunbar

The connection to the family line is Eureka, the daughter of Gloria Jean Harris-Johnson Morrison and Alfrederick Morrison [1].

The Seventh Generation

Eureka Jean Morrison Dunbar	-	See Entry Page 392
Michael Dunbar	-	See Entry Page 392

Their (2) Children

My Family Tree

Name	JaVon Dunbar
Date Of Birth	Monday, March 18, 1985
Place Of Birth	Camp Springs, Maryland – Prince George's County
Date Of Death	N/A
Age At Death	N/A
Place Of Death	N/A
Occupation	N/A
Married	N/A
Notes	

Name	Arron DeVanta Dunbar
Date Of Birth	Friday, July 24, 1992
Place Of Birth	Jacksonville, North Carolina – Onslow County
Date Of Death	N/A
Age At Death	N/A
Place Of Death	N/A
Occupation	N/A
Married	N/A
Notes	

The Family Line of Vereece Carolyn Carey Sanders Gant

The connection to the family line was Vereece, the daughter of Helen Bass Carey and Charles Alexander Carey.

The Fifth Generation

Vereece Carolyn Carey Sanders Gant - **See Entry Page 355-356**

Her (2) Children

My Family Tree

Name	**Audradella Carey Grant**
Date Of Birth	Monday, May 11, 1936
Place Of Birth	Loredo, West Virginia – Logan County
Date Of Death	N/A
Age At Death	N/A
Place Of Death	N/A
Occupation	N/A
Married	LeRoy Grant
Notes	Her nickname is "Pinky."

Name	**Wilbur Carey**
Date Of Birth	N/A
Place Of Birth	Loredo, West Virginia – Logan County
Date Of Death	N/A
Age At Death	N/A
Place Of Death	N/A
Occupation	N/A
Married	N/A
Notes	His nickname is "Bucky." His sons: Eric Craft (b. Wednesday, April 6, 1966, works at Ohio State University) and Mark Craft (retail sales). Both children were born in Columbus, Ohio – Franklin County. His granddaughter: Kaiyela Craft.

The Family Line of Vernie Mae Cornelius Partee and Miles Harrison Partee

The connection to the family line was Vernie, the daughter of Susan Jane (Sookey) Cowan Cornelius and Augustus Cornelius.

The Fourth Generation

Vernie Mae Cornelius Partee - **See Entry Page 331-332**

My Family Tree

Miles Harrison Partee - See Entry Page 332

Their (12) Children

Name	Miles Allen Partee
Date Of Birth	Wednesday, June 28, 1916
Place Of Birth	Salisbury Township, North Carolina – Rowan County
Date Of Death	Sunday, July 23, 1989
Age At Death	73
Place Of Death	Salisbury Township, North Carolina – Rowan County
Occupation	Retired – Stapler – Chemical Factory
Married	Sadie Marie Miller Partee
Notes	Sadie and Miles both lived at 1309 West Horah Street at the time of their death; they were homeowners. He was buried in July 1989, a widower. Sadie and Miles were both buried side-by-side at Oakwood Cemetery in Salisbury, North Carolina – Rowan County. In the Census and on his headstone his name was spelled Milas but the death certificate had his name as Miles.

Name	Sadie Marie Miller Partee
Date Of Birth	Monday, November 18, 1918
Place Of Birth	Salisbury Township, North Carolina – Rowan County
Date Of Death	Monday, February 21, 1994
Age At Death	75
Place Of Death	Salisbury Township, North Carolina – Rowan County
Occupation	Domestic Worker/Housewife
Married	Miles Allen Partee
Notes	Married on Saturday, June 28, 1941, in Salisbury, North Carolina – Rowan County – a marriage of 48 years. She was buried in February 1994.

My Family Tree

Name	**Ida Mae Partee Willett**
Date Of Birth	Tuesday, November 14, 1911
Place Of Birth	Salisbury Township, North Carolina – Rowan County
Date Of Death	Sunday, December 15, 1974
Age At Death	63
Place Of Death	Salisbury Township, North Carolina – Rowan County
Occupation	Practical Nurse
Married	Charles Carroll Willett (b. 1896 – d. 1993, age 96 – 97)
Notes	They lived at 424 S. Partee Street at the time of their death, homeowners. She was buried on Wednesday, December 18, 1974, at Oakdale Union Hill Cemetery in Salisbury, North Carolina – Rowan County.

Name	**Genie Elizabeth Partee Avery**
Date Of Birth	Friday, November 8, 1912
Place Of Birth	Spencer, North Carolina – Rowan County
Date Of Death	Wednesday, April 18, 2001
Age At Death	88
Place Of Death	Chesapeake, Virginia
Occupation	Retired – School Teacher/Deaconess
Married	William Henry Avery
Notes	Genie and William both lived at 815 Partridge Ave until they died in Chesapeake, Virginia, where they were homeowners. Her nickname was "Jonnie." She was buried on Friday, April 20, 2001, as a widow. Genie and William were both buried side-by-side at Oakwood Cemetery in Salisbury, North Carolina – Rowan County.

Name	**William Henry Avery**
Date Of Birth	Saturday, July 6, 1912

My Family Tree

Place Of Birth	Salisbury Township, North Carolina – Rowan County
Date Of Death	Thursday, December 16, 1999
Age At Death	87
Place Of Death	Salisbury, North Carolina – Rowan County
Occupation	Day Laborer
Married	Genie Elizabeth Partee Avery
Notes	His parents were Mary Belle Sharpe Avery and Samuel R. Avery. Married on Thursday, September 15, 1938, in Salisbury, North Carolina – Rowan County; a marriage of 61 years. He was buried in December 1999.

Name	**Alexander Miles Partee**
Date Of Birth	Friday, November 6, 1914
Place Of Birth	Salisbury Township, North Carolina – Rowan County
Date Of Death	Unknown
Age At Death	Unknown
Place Of Death	Unknown
Occupation	Unknown
Married	Unknown
Notes	

Name	**Clarence Anderson Partee**
Date Of Birth	Sunday, October 12, 1919
Place Of Birth	Salisbury Township, North Carolina – Rowan County
Date Of Death	Sunday, June 28, 1981
Age At Death	61

My Family Tree

Place Of Death	Salisbury, North Carolina – Rowan County
Occupation	Retired – United States Army/Truck Driver
Married	Lowell Goode Partee
Notes	He was enlisted in the United States Army during WWII on Wednesday, January 12, 1944, as a Private, registered in Salisbury, North Carolina – Rowan County, and honorably discharged. He saw action in the Philippines and was awarded the Bronze Star. He was buried on Thursday, July 2, 1981, in the United States National Cemetery in Salisbury, North Carolina – Rowan County, a widower when he died.

Name	**Lowell Goode Partee**
Date Of Birth	Sunday, June 26, 1921
Place Of Birth	Salisbury Township, North Carolina – Rowan County
Date Of Death	Monday, June 12, 1967
Age At Death	45
Place Of Death	Salisbury Township, North Carolina – Rowan County
Occupation	Domestic Worker/Housewife
Married	Clarence Anderson Partee
Notes	Married on Tuesday, October 5, 1937, in Salisbury, North Carolina – Rowan County – a marriage of 30 years. Her parents were Mary Causer Goode and Walker Goode. Their child: Barbara Elenola Partee Dalton (b. Tuesday, January 25, 1938 – d. Wednesday, March 3, 1999, age 61). Barbara's husband – Robert Dalton [II] (b. Sunday, April 29, 1934 – d. Tuesday, April 29, 1997, age 63). Barbara and Robert POB. and POD. in Salisbury, North Carolina – Rowan County, married on Saturday, June 13, 1959 – a marriage of 38 years. Robert's father was Robert Dalton [I].

Name	**Vernie Edith Partee Person**
Date Of Birth	Sunday, January 6, 1918
Place Of Birth	Salisbury Township, North Carolina – Rowan County
Date Of Death	Thursday, February 15, 2001

My Family Tree

Age At Death	83
Place Of Death	Salisbury, North Carolina – Rowan County
Occupation	Domestic Worker/Housewife
Married	Robert Person
Notes	Son: Ernest Elmore Person (b. Sunday, March 29, 1931), POB. is Salisbury, North Carolina – Rowan County).

Name	Esther Naomi Partee Baker
Date Of Birth	Monday, October 19, 1925
Place Of Birth	Salisbury, North Carolina – Rowan County
Date Of Death	Saturday, August 21, 2004
Age At Death	78
Place Of Death	Salisbury, North Carolina – Rowan County
Occupation	Housewife
Married	Widow
Notes	

Name	Samuel J. Partee
Date Of Birth	Monday, June 13, 1927
Place Of Birth	Salisbury, North Carolina – Rowan County
Date Of Death	Unknown
Age At Death	Unknown
Place Of Death	North Carolina – Rowan County
Occupation	Day Laborer
Married	Christine Tucker Partee

My Family Tree

Notes	Their child: Samuel Allen Partee (b. June 9, 1947), POB. Salisbury, North Carolina – Rowan County.

Name	**Martha Lucille Partee Witherspoon**
Date Of Birth	Wednesday, December 18, 1929
Place Of Birth	Salisbury, North Carolina – Rowan County
Date Of Death	Monday, April 30, 2007
Age At Death	77
Place Of Death	Salisbury, North Carolina – Rowan County
Occupation	Retired – Nurse Assistant
Married	(1) Ernest O. Sloan (2) Harold Adron Witherspoon [I] (b. 1925)
Notes	(1) Married Saturday, November 23, 1940, in Salisbury, North Carolina – Rowan County. (2) Married Friday, February 6, 1948, in Salisbury, North Carolina – Rowan County. She was buried Monday, May 7, 2007, at Oakwood Cemetery in Salisbury, North Carolina – Rowan County. Mrs. Witherspoon has an obituary that talks about her life.

Name	**Robert Partee**
Date Of Birth	1908
Place Of Birth	Salisbury Township, North Carolina – Rowan County
Date Of Death	Monday, October 18, 1937
Age At Death	29
Place Of Death	Durham, North Carolina – Rowan County
Occupation	Day Laborer
Married	Single
Notes	Census records listed him as Mulatto.

My Family Tree

Name	**Margaret Ruth Partee Wyatt**
Date Of Birth	Saturday, February 16, 1924
Place Of Birth	Salisbury Township, North Carolina – Rowan County
Date Of Death	Wednesday, November 26, 1969
Age At Death	45
Place Of Death	Salisbury, North Carolina – Rowan County
Occupation	United States Army – Air Forces Fighter – Pilot
Married	John Ottus Wyatt
Notes	She served in the United States Army during WWII. She made a career out of the Army. She was an NC Private First Class (PFC) in the 4121 Base Unit – Army Air Forces (AAF) and was registered in Salisbury Township, North Carolina – Rowan County. Married on Sunday, November 4, 1951, in Salisbury Township, North Carolina – Rowan County. Margaret and her husband were legally separated when she died. Her military records were sealed. She was buried on Wednesday, November 26, 1969.

Name	**John Ottus Wyatt**
Date Of Birth	Wednesday, September 27, 1922
Place Of Birth	Salisbury, North Carolina – Rowan County
Date Of Death	Thursday, January 9, 1992
Age At Death	69
Place Of Death	Lexington, North Carolina – Davidson County
Occupation	United States Army
Married	Margaret Ruth Partee Wyatt
Notes	He was buried on Tuesday, January 14, 1992. Margaret and John were both buried at the United States National Cemetery in Salisbury Township, North Carolina – Rowan County.

Jonnie E. Partee - See Entry Page 331

My Family Tree

The Family Line of Judy Carol Cowan Brown and Elco Jr. Brown II

The connection to the family line is Judy, the daughter of Levonia Margaret Carey Cowan and James Avery Cowan.

The Sixth Generation

Judy Carol Cowan Brown	-	See Entry Page 386
Elco Jr. Brown II	-	See Entry Page 386

Their (2) Children

Name	**Nakia LeMone Brown**
Date Of Birth	Monday, January 13, 1975
Place Of Birth	Detroit, Michigan – Wayne County
Date Of Death	N/A
Age At Death	N/A
Place Of Death	N/A
Occupation	United States Navy/Minister
Married	Merisa Douglas Brown
Notes	Married on Sunday, January 14, 2018, in Northeast Washington DC – Prince George's County. Mr. Brown has a living testimony about his life. Merissa is an Elementary School Teacher.

Name	**Maria Antoinette Brown**
Date Of Birth	Wednesday, June 30, 1976
Place Of Birth	Detroit, Michigan – Wayne County
Date Of Death	N/A
Age At Death	N/A
Place Of Death	N/A
Occupation	Business Analyst – Accountant/Retail Sales
Married	N/A
Notes	Ms. Brown has a living testimony about her life.

My Family Tree

The Family Line of Toni Sue Cowan

The connection to the family line is Toni, the daughter of Levonia Margaret Carey Cowan and James Avery Cowan.

The Sixth Generation

Toni Sue Cowan - See Entry Page 387

Her (3) Children

Name	Stephen Idel Cowan I
Date Of Birth	Tuesday, February 26, 1974
Place Of Birth	Detroit, Michigan – Wayne County
Date Of Death	Thursday, June 9, 2011
Age At Death	37
Place Of Death	Detroit, Michigan – Wayne County
Occupation	Owner – Transportation Service/Volunteer – Homeless Centers/ Handyman/Auto Repair
Married	Single
Notes	His children: Stephen Idel Cowan II, Destiny Tiara Robinson, and Trevon Deonte Cowan. His children POB. Detroit, Michigan – Wayne County. He was cremated Monday, June 20, 2011, in Detroit, Michigan – Wayne County. Mr. Cowan has an obituary and a letter written to the court about his life.

Name	AnRico Celete Levonia Cowan Lockhart I
Date Of Birth	Thursday, April 24, 1975
Place Of Birth	Detroit, Michigan – Wayne County
Date Of Death	N/A
Age At Death	N/A
Place Of Death	N/A
Occupation	City Detroit Worker – 911 Dispatcher
Married	(1) Sean Scott (2) Al Lockhart

My Family Tree

Notes	Their children: Monique Anthony Cowan (b. Monday, March 5, 1990) her occupation – Make-up Artist; her father is Victor Richard Robinson. AnRico Celete Levonia Scott II (b. Monday, June 5, 2000): her father is Sean Scott. Both daughter's POB. is Detroit, Michigan – Wayne County.

Name	**Keith Jerome Cowan**
Date Of Birth	Wednesday, November 10, 1976
Place Of Birth	Detroit, Michigan – Wayne County
Date Of Death	Wednesday, November 10, 1976
Age At Death	0
Place Of Death	Detroit, Michigan – Wayne County
Occupation	None
Married	Single
Notes	

The Family Line of Connie Morrison and Roscoe (Babe) Morrison II

The connection to the family line was Roscoe II, the son of Isabelle Carey Morrison and Roscoe Morrison[1].

The Sixth Generation

Connie Morrison - See Entry Page 389
Roscoe (Babe) Morrison II - See Entry Page 389

Their Child

Name	**Deborah Michelle Morrison Davis**
Date Of Birth	Sunday, October 2, 1966
Place Of Birth	Bronx, New York – Westchester County
Date Of Death	N/A
Age At Death	N/A
Place Of Death	N/A

My Family Tree

Occupation	N/A
Married	N/A
Notes	Her child is Jonathan Darrell Davis.

The Family Line of Elise Cowan Trent and Eddie Andrew Trent [I]

The connection to the family line is Elise, the daughter of Levonia Margaret Carey Cowan and James Avery Cowan.

The Sixth Generation

Elise Cowan Trent - See Entry Page 384-385
Eddie Andrew Trent [I] - See Entry Page 385

Elise (2) Children with Eddie [I]

Name	Lisa Ann Trent, (R. Ph.)
Date Of Birth	Monday, September 22, 1969
Place Of Birth	Detroit, Michigan – Wayne County
Date Of Death	N/A
Age At Death	N/A
Place Of Death	N/A
Occupation	Pharmacist – VA Healthcare
Married	N/A
Notes	Her twin brother is Eddie [II]. Ms. Trent has a living testimony about her life.

Name	Eddie Andrew Trent II
Date Of Birth	Monday, September 22, 1969
Place Of Birth	Detroit, Michigan – Wayne County
Date Of Death	N/A
Age At Death	N/A

My Family Tree

Place Of Death	N/A
Occupation	Flight Control Attendant/Luggage Department
Married	N/A
Notes	His twin sister is Lisa. Mr. Trent has a living testimony about his life.

Elise and Eddie A. Trent [1] Granddaughter

Name	**Deidre Marie Trent Lashley**
Date Of Birth	Wednesday, May 25, 1988
Place Of Birth	Detroit, Michigan – Wayne County
Date Of Death	N/A
Age At Death	N/A
Place Of Death	N/A
Occupation	Retail Store Manager
Married	Corey Lashley
Notes	Her parents are Lisa Ann Trent and Kevin Harris. Mrs. Lashley has a living testimony about her life. Corey's daughter: Kouri Lashley.

The Family Line of Roxie Lee Carey (Muslimah Muwwakkil) and Marvin Guyse (Abdul Muwwakkil)

The connection to the family line is Roxie, the daughter of Levonia Margaret Carey Cowan and Newell Virgil Moore.

The Sixth Generation

Muslimah Muwwakkil - See Entry Page 384
Abdul Muwwakkil - See Entry Page 384

Their (5) Children

Name	**Abdul Rafeeq Salahuddin**
Date Of Birth	Tuesday, May 7, 1957
Place Of Birth	Los Angeles, California – Los Angeles County

My Family Tree

Date Of Death	Wednesday, April 4, 1984
Age At Death	26
Place Of Death	Los Angeles, California – Los Angeles County
Occupation	Physician Assistant
Married	Single
Notes	

Name	**Ebony Latifah Salahuddin Saliba**
Date Of Birth	Monday, January 18, 1960
Place Of Birth	Los Angeles, California – Los Angeles County
Date Of Death	N/A
Age At Death	N/A
Place Of Death	N/A
Occupation	Hairstylist – Entrepreneur
Married	N/A
Notes	

Name	**Sabreen Lavonia Salahuddin**
Date Of Birth	Saturday, January 8, 1966
Place Of Birth	Los Angeles, California – Los Angeles County
Date Of Death	N/A
Age At Death	N/A
Place Of Death	N/A
Occupation	Substance Abuse Director – State of California Dept. of Corrections Facility

My Family Tree

Married	N/A
Notes	

Name	**Marvinah Nyderah Salahuddin Sbinowitz**
Date Of Birth	Wednesday, May 23, 1973
Place Of Birth	Los Angeles, California – Los Angeles County
Date Of Death	N/A
Age At Death	N/A
Place Of Death	N/A
Occupation	License – Radiologist Assistant/Medical Assistant
Married	N/A
Notes	

Name	**Ameerah Salahuddin Lydick**
Date Of Birth	Monday, January 29, 1968
Place Of Birth	Los Angeles, California – Los Angeles County
Date Of Death	N/A
Age At Death	N/A
Place Of Death	N/A
Occupation	Accountant/Homemaker
Married	Tariq Lydick
Notes	Their children: Hamazah Lydick (b. Thursday, July 27, 1989); Safadin Lydick (b. Monday, January 25, 1993); Mustafa Lydick (b. Tuesday, July 2, 1996); Ridhwana Lydick (Girl) (b. Saturday, July 13, 1991); and Melik Lydick (b. Saturday, August 24, 2013). Ameerah and Tariq's children: POB. Los Angeles, California – Los Angeles County.

My Family Tree

The Family Line of Rhody Isabella Cowan Rankin and Pinkney C. Rankin

The connection to the family line was Rhody, the daughter of Elizabeth Witherspoon Cowan and Charles Cowan [1].

The Third Generation

Rhody Isabella Cowan Rankin - See Entry Page 327
Pinkney C. Rankin - See Entry Page 327

Their (9) Childre

Name	James Francis Rankin
Date Of Birth	Saturday, December 25, 1880
Place Of Birth	Mount Ulla Township, North Carolina – Rowan County
Date Of Death	Monday, April 18, 1955
Age At Death	74
Place Of Death	North Carolina – Rowan County
Occupation	Retired – Farmer
Married	Ada R. Bradshaw Rankin
Notes	According to the Census records for 1900, Ada and James were listed literate. Married on Sunday, March 25, 1906, in Mount Ulla Township, North Carolina – Rowan County; married for 45 years. He was buried in April 1955.

Name	Ada R. Bradshaw Rankin
Date Of Birth	Saturday, July 16, 1887
Place Of Birth	North Carolina – Rowan County
Date Of Death	Thursday, August 2, 1951
Age At Death	64
Place Of Death	North Carolina – Rowan County
Occupation	Domestic Worker/Housewife
Married	James Francis Rankin

My Family Tree

Notes	Their children: Hilda Rankin Ramsey, Ethel Mae Rankin Baity, Robert Lewis Rankin, Howard V. Rankin, Clara Clementine Rankin Glaspy, Sylvester R. Rankin, Willie Lee Rankin, Frank Edward Rankin, Ruth Rankin Faber, and Elmer Rankin. Ada was buried in August 1951. Ada and James were both buried, at Mount Tabor Presbyterian Church Cemetery.

Name	**Edward Caldwell Rankin I**
Date Of Birth	1884
Place Of Birth	Mount Ulla Township, North Carolina – Rowan County
Date Of Death	1931
Age At Death	46 – 47
Place Of Death	North Carolina – Rowan County
Occupation	Farmer
Married	Fannie L. Parks Rankin
Notes	According to the Census records for 1900, he was listed as literate.

Name	**Fannie L. Parks Rankin**
Date Of Birth	Saturday, August 11, 1888
Place Of Birth	Mount Ulla Township, North Carolina – Rowan County
Date Of Death	Thursday, February 15, 1968
Age At Death	79
Place Of Death	North Carolina – Rowan County
Occupation	Domestic Worker/Housewife
Married	Edward Caldwell Rankin I
Notes	According to the Census records for 1900, she was listed as literate. Their children: Edward Caldwell Rankin II (b. Saturday, November 5, 1927 – d. Wednesday, April 7, 1982, served during WWII–TEC 5 Army, age 54), Elva Rankin, and Geneva Rankin.

My Family Tree

Name	Clarence C. Rankin
Date Of Birth	Sunday, January 13, 1884
Place Of Birth	Mount Ulla Township, North Carolina – Rowan County
Date Of Death	Thursday, July 20, 1905
Age At Death	21
Place Of Death	Mount Ulla Township, North Carolina – Rowan County
Occupation	Farmer
Married	Single
Notes	According to the Census records for 1910, he was listed as literate. He was buried in July 1905, at Mount Tabor Presbyterian Church Cemetery.

Name	Thomas C. Rankin
Date Of Birth	April 1885
Place Of Birth	Mount Ulla Township, North Carolina – Rowan County
Date Of Death	1909
Age At Death	23 – 24
Place Of Death	Mount Ulla Township, North Carolina – Rowan County
Occupation	Farmer
Married	Single
Notes	According to the Census records for 1910, he was listed as literate. He was buried in 1909, at Mount Tabor Presbyterian Church Cemetery.

Name	Espy Lee Rankin
Date Of Birth	Monday, July 8, 1889
Place Of Birth	Mount Ulla Township, North Carolina – Rowan County
Date Of Death	Tuesday, April 24, 1962

My Family Tree

Age At Death	72
Place Of Death	Mount Ulla Township, North Carolina – Rowan County
Occupation	Retired – Farmer
Married	Gertrude Cowan Rankin
Notes	Married on Wednesday, January 14, 1914, in North Carolina – Rowan County – married for 48 years. He was buried in May 1962, at Mount Tabor Presbyterian Church Cemetery. His headstone had his name spelled as Espie.

Name	**Gertrude Cowan Rankin**
Date Of Birth	Wednesday, March 13, 1889
Place Of Birth	Virginia
Date Of Death	Wednesday, November 9, 1966
Age At Death	77
Place Of Death	Mount Ulla Township, North Carolina – Rowan County
Occupation	Domestic Worker/Housewife
Married	Espy Lee Rankin
Notes	Married on Wednesday, January 14, 1914, in North Carolina – Rowan County. According to the Census records for 1910, they both were listed as literate. She was a widow when she died.

Name	**Earl Green Rankin**
Date Of Birth	Tuesday, July 7, 1891
Place Of Birth	Mount Ulla Township, North Carolina – Rowan County
Date Of Death	Friday, May 14, 1982
Age At Death	90
Place Of Death	Mount Ulla Township, North Carolina – Rowan County

My Family Tree

Occupation	Retired – Farmer/Deacon/Trustee
Married	Odena Allison Rankin
Notes	According to the Census records for 1900, he was listed as illiterate. He was buried on Wednesday, May 19, 1982. Odena and Earl were both buried side-by-side, at Mount Tabor Presbyterian Church Cemetery. Mr. Rankin had an obituary about his life.

Name	**Odena Allison Rankin**
Date Of Birth	Wednesday, April 23, 1902
Place Of Birth	North Carolina – Iredell County
Date Of Death	Monday, January 7, 1974
Age At Death	71
Place Of Death	Salisbury, North Carolina – Rowan County
Occupation	Housewife/ Domestic Worker
Married	Earl Green Rankin
Notes	According to the Census records for 1900, she was listed as illiterate. Married on Wednesday, June 3, 1925 in North Carolina – Rowan County – married for 48 years. Her parents were Julia Higgins Allison and Walter Allison. Their child: Walter Earl Rankin. Her siblings: Everett Allison, Fletcher Allison, and Ernest Allison. She was buried on Friday, January 11, 1974. Mrs. Rankin had an obituary about her life.

Name	**Estella Ina Rankin Mills**
Date Of Birth	Saturday, February 13, 1892
Place Of Birth	Mount Ulla Township, North Carolina – Rowan County
Date Of Death	Wednesday, February 14, 1951
Age At Death	59
Place Of Death	North Carolina – Rowan County
Occupation	Housewife/Domestic Worker

My Family Tree

Married	Richard DeWitt Mills
Notes	According to the Census records for 1900, she was listed as illiterate. Her nickname was "Ina." She was buried in February 1951.

Name	**Richard DeWitt Mills**
Date Of Birth	Friday, August 17, 1900
Place Of Birth	North Carolina – Rowan County
Date Of Death	Tuesday, September 10, 1991
Age At Death	91
Place Of Death	North Carolina – Rowan County
Occupation	Day Laborer
Married	Estella Ina Rankin Mills
Notes	His nickname was "R.D." Married on Thursday, December 24, 1925, in North Carolina – Rowan County – married 25 years. He was buried in September 1991. Estella and R. D. were both buried side-by-side, at Mount Tabor Presbyterian Church Cemetery.

Name	**Mary Ann Rankin Neal**
Date Of Birth	Monday, May 25, 1896
Place Of Birth	Mount Ulla Township, North Carolina – Rowan County
Date Of Death	Saturday, November 30, 1991
Age At Death	95
Place Of Death	North Carolina – Rowan County
Occupation	Housewife/Domestic Worker
Married	(1) Henry Luther Neal (2) Chester Vaughn
Notes	According to the Census records for 1900, she was listed as illiterate. She was a widow when she died. She was buried in December 1991. Mary and Henry were both buried side-by-side, at Mount Tabor Presbyterian Church Cemetery. Their child: Hollan Reid Neal (b. Friday, October 19, 1923 – d.

My Family Tree

	Thursday, July 18, 1974, age 50), POB. and POD. Cleveland, North Carolina – Rowan County. Hollan was buried in July 1974 at Belmont Cemetery in Statesville, North Carolina – Iredell County. Hollan's wife – Bessie Lee Stockton Neal Vaughn (b. Monday, January 11, 1926, POB. North Carolina – Iredell County – d. Saturday, June 27, 2015, POD. Lexington, North Carolina – Davidson County, age 89). Bessie was buried on Tuesday, July 7, 2015, at the Church of Christian Belmont Cemetery in Statesville, North Carolina – Iredell County. Bessie's parents were Mildred Inez Stockton Sloan and Will Stewart.

Name	Henry Luther Neal
Date Of Birth	Wednesday, January 3, 1894
Place Of Birth	North Carolina – Rowan County
Date Of Death	Thursday, February 14, 1971
Age At Death	77
Place Of Death	North Carolina – Rowan County
Occupation	Day Laborer
Married	Mary Ann Rankin Neal
Notes	He was buried in February 1971. His parents were Aggie Gibson Neal (b. 1861 – d. 1945, age 83 – 84) and Samuel Neal (b. 1863 – d. 1949, age 85 – 86).

Name	William Henry Rankin
Date Of Birth	Monday, November 19, 1877
Place Of Birth	Mount Ulla Township, North Carolina – Rowan County
Date Of Death	Wednesday, September 28, 1960
Age At Death	82
Place Of Death	North Carolina – Rowan County
Occupation	Farm Laborer
Married	(1) Loula Bradshaw Rankin (2) Julia Lyerly Rankin (b. 1889 – d. 1968, age 78 – 79)

My Family Tree

Notes	(1) Married on Thursday, January 28, 1897, and (2) Married in 1933, both marriages took place in North Carolina – Rowan County. Loula and William child: Walter Ellmore Rankin (b. Friday, August 17, 1900) POB. Mount Ulla Township, North Carolina – Rowan County. He was buried in October 1960 at Mount Tabor Presbyterian Church Cemetery.

The Family Line of Eliza Elizabeth Cowan Barber and John L. Barber

The connection to the family line was Eliza, the daughter of Elizabeth Witherspoon Cowan and Charles Cowan[1].

The Third Generation

Eliza Elizabeth Cowan Barber - See Entry Page 328-329
John L. Barber - See Entry Page 329

Their (11) Children

Name	John Gaither Barber
Date Of Birth	Monday, October 15, 1888
Place Of Birth	Mount Ulla Township, North Carolina – Rowan County
Date Of Death	Wednesday, December 28, 1977
Age At Death	89
Place Of Death	Wilkesboro, North Carolina – Wilkes County
Occupation	Day Laborer
Married	Single
Notes	

Name	Philo Barber
Date Of Birth	Friday, October 11, 1889
Place Of Birth	Wilkesboro, North Carolina – Wilkes County
Date Of Death	Sunday, October 10, 1937
Age At Death	47
Place Of Death	Wilkesboro, North Carolina – Wilkes County

My Family Tree

Occupation	Farm Laborer
Married	Single
Notes	

Name	Genola Cowan
Date Of Birth	1898
Place Of Birth	North Carolina – Rowan County
Date Of Death	Unknown
Age At Death	Unknown
Place Of Death	North Carolina – Rowan County
Occupation	Farm Laborer
Married	Unknown
Notes	

Name	Milton McKinley Barber
Date Of Birth	1898
Place Of Birth	North Carolina – Rowan County
Date Of Death	Unknown
Age At Death	Unknown
Place Of Death	North Carolina – Rowan County
Occupation	Farm Laborer
Married	Unknown
Notes	

My Family Tree

Name	Henry Barber
Date Of Birth	Monday, March 5, 1894
Place Of Birth	Wilksbarre, North Carolina – Wilkes County
Date Of Death	Unknown
Age At Death	Unknown
Place Of Death	North Carolina – Rowan County
Occupation	Farm Laborer
Married	Margaret Harris Barber (b. Saturday, September 15, 1900)
Notes	

Name	Lura L. Barber
Date Of Birth	1900
Place Of Birth	North Carolina – Rowan County
Date Of Death	Sunday, December 5, 1982
Age At Death	81-82
Place Of Death	Brooklyn, New York – Kings County
Occupation	Domestic Worker
Married	Single
Notes	

Name	Dwight Barber
Date Of Birth	Wednesday, March 5, 1902
Place Of Birth	Wilkesboro, North Carolina – Wilkes County
Date Of Death	Wednesday, September 9, 1933

My Family Tree

Age At Death	28
Place Of Death	Wilkesboro, North Carolina – Wilkes County
Occupation	Farm Laborer
Married	Single
Notes	

Name	Lino Barber
Date Of Birth	Sunday, July 5, 1903
Place Of Birth	Cleveland, North Carolina – Rowan County
Date Of Death	Monday, June 22, 1992
Age At Death	88
Place Of Death	Salisbury, North Carolina – Rowan County
Occupation	Farm Laborer
Married	Single
Notes	

Name	Jura Barber
Date Of Birth	Sunday, April 7, 1907
Place Of Birth	Wilkesboro, North Carolina – Wilkes County
Date Of Death	Monday, July 31, 1950
Age At Death	43
Place Of Death	Wilkesboro, North Carolina – Wilkes County
Occupation	Farm Laborer
Married	Widower

My Family Tree

Notes	

Name	Alice M. Barber
Date Of Birth	1908
Place Of Birth	North Carolina – Rowan County
Date Of Death	Tuesday, October 7, 1958
Age At Death	49-50
Place Of Death	Wilkesboro, North Carolina – Wilkes County
Occupation	Domestic Worker
Married	Single
Notes	

Name	Allen Cowan
Date Of Birth	1909
Place Of Birth	North Carolina – Rowan County
Date Of Death	Unknown
Age At Death	Unknown
Place Of Death	Wilkesboro, North Carolina – Wilkes County
Occupation	Day Laborer
Married	Unknown
Notes	

The Family Line of Margaret Summer Partee and Robert Partee[1]

The connection to the family line was Vernie, the daughter of Susan Jane (Sookey) Cowan Cornelius and Augusta (Gus) Cornelius.

The Third Generation

My Family Tree

Margaret Summer Partee - See Entry Page 332
Robert Partee [1] - See Entry Page 332

Their (13) Children

Miles Harrison Partee - See Entry Page 332
Vernie Mae Cornelius Partee - See Entry Page 331-332

Name	Arthur Partee
Date Of Birth	January 1875
Place Of Birth	Salisbury Township, North Carolina – Rowan County
Date Of Death	December 1974
Age At Death	99
Place Of Death	Bridgeville, Pennsylvania – Allegheny County
Occupation	Day Laborer
Married	Single
Notes	

Name	Emery J. Partee
Date Of Birth	1876
Place Of Birth	Salisbury Township, North Carolina – Rowan County
Date Of Death	Thursday, July 26, 1900
Age At Death	23 – 24
Place Of Death	Salisbury Township, North Carolina – Rowan County
Occupation	Day Laborer – Railway Shop
Married	M. Angeline Penry Partee (b. 1877)
Notes	Married on Saturday, March 11, 1899, in North Carolina – Rowan County. According to the Census records, they were listed as literate.

My Family Tree

Name	Robert Partee II
Date Of Birth	1878
Place Of Birth	Salisbury Township, North Carolina – Rowan County
Date Of Death	1919
Age At Death	40 – 41
Place Of Death	North Carolina – Rowan County
Occupation	Day Laborer
Married	Single
Notes	

Name	Clarence D. Partee
Date Of Birth	Thursday, May 20, 1880
Place Of Birth	Salisbury Township, North Carolina – Rowan County
Date Of Death	Friday, January 3, 1913
Age At Death	32
Place Of Death	Salisbury Township, North Carolina – Rowan County
Occupation	Day Laborer
Married	Single
Notes	

Name	Charles Partee
Date Of Birth	Thursday, April 15, 1886
Place Of Birth	Spencer, North Carolina – Rowan County
Date Of Death	Tuesday, May 17, 1960

My Family Tree

Age At Death	73
Place Of Death	Salisbury Township, North Carolina – Rowan County
Occupation	Badin Aluminum Plant Rowan Company / United States Army
Married	Single
Notes	He served in the United States during WWI as PVT-QMC. He was buried on Monday, May 23, 1960, at the National Cemetery in Salisbury, North Carolina – Rowan County.

Name	David Partee
Date Of Birth	April 1886
Place Of Birth	Spencer, North Carolina – Rowan County
Date Of Death	Wednesday, February 6, 1935
Age At Death	48
Place Of Death	North Carolina
Occupation	Day Laborer
Married	Single
Notes	

Name	Bessie Partee Wilson
Date Of Birth	Sunday, September 23, 1888
Place Of Birth	Spencer, North Carolina – Rowan County
Date Of Death	Sunday, October 26, 1986
Age At Death	98
Place Of Death	Linden, New Jersey – Union County
Occupation	Domestic Worker

My Family Tree

Married	Andrew Alexander Wilson (b. Saturday, June 15, 1929 – d. Thursday, January 20, 2004, age 74)
Notes	She was buried in October 1986. He was buried in January 2004. They were buried side-by-side, at Rosedale and Rosehill Cemetery in Linden, New Jersey – Union County.

Name	**Mary Ella Partee Pennington**
Date Of Birth	Friday, September 5, 1890
Place Of Birth	Spencer, North Carolina – Rowan County
Date Of Death	Unknown
Age At Death	Unknown
Place Of Death	Unknown
Occupation	Domestic Worker
Married	Guy William Pennington (b. 1892)
Notes	Married on Monday, March 6, 1916, in North Carolina – Rowan County.

Name	**Frank Partee**
Date Of Birth	1894
Place Of Birth	Spencer, North Carolina – Rowan County
Date Of Death	Unknown
Age At Death	Unknown
Place Of Death	Unknown
Occupation	Day Laborer
Married	Unknown
Notes	

My Family Tree

Name	Nettie Langston Partee
Date Of Birth	Saturday, March 23, 1895
Place Of Birth	Spencer, North Carolina – Rowan County
Date Of Death	November 1900
Age At Death	5
Place Of Death	Salisbury Township, North Carolina – Rowan County
Occupation	None
Married	Single
Notes	

Name	Milton Partee
Date Of Birth	September 1898
Place Of Birth	Spencer, North Carolina – Rowan County
Date Of Death	Unknown
Age At Death	Unknown
Place Of Death	Unknown
Occupation	Day Laborer
Married	Unknown
Notes	

Name	Louisa Partee
Date Of Birth	Thursday, February 23, 1882
Place Of Birth	Spencer, North Carolina – Rowan County
Date Of Death	Unknown

My Family Tree

Age At Death	Unknown
Place Of Death	Salisbury Township, North Carolina – Rowan County
Occupation	Domestic Worker
Married	Unknown
Notes	

The Family Line of Lucy Nancy Moore and Archie Moore [1]

The Fourth Generation

Name	**Lucy Nancy Moore**
Date Of Birth	1904
Place Of Birth	Harvest, Alabama – Madison County
Date Of Death	Unknown
Age At Death	Unknown
Place Of Death	Unknown
Occupation	Domestic Worker
Married	Archie Moore I (b. 1898), POB. Harvest, Alabama – Madison County
Notes	Married on Thursday, March 28, 1918, in Harvest, Alabama – Madison County.

The connection to the family line is Roxie, the daughter of Levonia Margaret Carey Cowan and Newell Virgil Moore.

Their (8) Children

Newell Virgil Moore - See Entry Page 355

Name	**Frank Lee Moore I**
Date Of Birth	Thursday, September 5, 1918
Place Of Birth	Harvest, Alabama – Madison County
Date Of Death	Friday, October 5, 2012

My Family Tree

Age At Death	93
Place Of Death	Charleston, West Virginia – Kanawha County
Occupation	Day Laborer
Married	Mary Dingess Moore
Notes	Frank's nickname was, "Rail." Frank was buried on Friday, October 12, 2012, at Forest Lawn Cemetery in Pecks Mill, West Virginia – Logan County. He has an obituary that talks about his life.

Name	**Mary Dingess Moore**
Date Of Birth	Friday, July 13, 1923
Place Of Birth	West Virginia – Logan County
Date Of Death	Tuesday, July 17, 1973
Age At Death	50
Place Of Death	West Virginia – Logan County
Occupation	Housewife/Domestic Worker
Married	Frank Lee Moore [I]
Notes	Mary and Frank were married on Saturday, June 25, 1949 – married for 24 years. Mary's parents were Josephine Glass Dingess and James Dingess. Their children: Deborah Moore (Frank Walker), Shelia Moore, Frank Lee Moore [II], and Gregory Moore. Their children's place of birth is Holden, West Virginia – Logan County.

Name	**Ellen Moore Burns**
Date Of Birth	Friday, February 18, 1921
Place Of Birth	Harvest, Alabama – Madison County
Date Of Death	Saturday, August 1, 1987
Age At Death	66
Place Of Death	Detroit, Michigan – Wayne County

My Family Tree

Occupation	Domestic Worker/Housewife
Married	Emmett Jake Burns
Notes	

Name	**Emmett Jake Burns**
Date Of Birth	Wednesday, August 7, 1918
Place Of Birth	Huntsville, Alabama - Madison County
Date Of Death	Thursday, June 19, 1952
Age At Death	33
Place Of Death	Allen Park, Michigan – Wayne County
Occupation	Day Laborer
Married	Ellen Moore Burns
Notes	Married on Thursday, June 11, 1942, married for 14 years. Emmett's parents were Mary Wilbur Burns and Aaron Burns. He was on buried Thursday, June 26, 1953, at Center Grove Cemetery in Huntsville, Alabama – Madison County. He served in WWII as PVT – 1853 SVC COMD Unit.

Name	**Pearline Moore Bass**
Date Of Birth	Wednesday, January 13, 1926
Place Of Birth	Holden, West Virginia – Logan County
Date Of Death	Friday, February 9, 2007
Age At Death	81
Place Of Death	San Antonio, Texas – Bexar County
Occupation	Housewife
Married	Garland Bass

My Family Tree

Notes	

Name	**Garland Bass**
Date Of Birth	Wednesday, September 10, 1919
Place Of Birth	West Virginia – Logan County
Date Of Death	Monday, September 28, 2015
Age At Death	96
Place Of Death	San Antonio, Texas – Bexar County
Occupation	Day Laborer
Married	Pearline Moore Bass
Notes	Married on Wednesday, May 29, 1946, in Detroit, Michigan, a marriage lasting 60 years. Garland's parents were Congera Bass and Roy Bass.

Name	**Archie Moore II**
Date Of Birth	Saturday, October 31, 1925
Place Of Birth	Harvest, Alabama – Madison County
Date Of Death	Saturday, August 10, 1974
Age At Death	48
Place Of Death	Detroit, Michigan – Wayne County
Occupation	Day Laborer
Married	Mildred Mason Moore
Notes	Married on Saturday, May 27, 1950. Mildred's parents were Ola Moody Mason and Herbert Mason.

Name	**Lowell Moore**
Date Of Birth	1933

My Family Tree

Place Of Birth	Harvest, Alabama – Madison County
Date Of Death	Unknown
Age At Death	Unknown
Place Of Death	West Virginia – Logan County
Occupation	Day Laborer
Married	Unknown
Notes	Unknown

Name	**Otis Moore**
Date Of Birth	Sunday, March 4, 1928
Place Of Birth	Holden, West Virginia – Logan County
Date Of Death	February 1978
Age At Death	49
Place Of Death	West Virginia – Logan County
Occupation	Day Laborer
Married	Margaret Moore
Notes	

Name	**Christine Moore Crawford**
Date Of Birth	Unknown
Place Of Birth	West Virginia – Logan County
Date Of Death	Unknown
Age At Death	Unknown
Place Of Death	Unknown

My Family Tree

Occupation	Domestic Worker
Married	Widow
Notes	

The Family Line of Martha Elizabeth Cowan

The connection to the family line was Martha, the daughter of Emma H. Griffith Cowan and John H. Cowan.

Martha Elizabeth Cowan - See Entry Page 382

The Fifth Generation

Their (5) Children

Name	**Russell Alberta Cowan**
Date Of Birth	Tuesday, July 4, 1916
Place Of Birth	Cleveland, North Carolina – Rowan County
Date Of Death	Friday, June 25, 1999
Age At Death	82
Place Of Death	Cleveland, North Carolina – Rowan County
Occupation	Day Laborer
Married	Virginia Catherine Glaspy Cowan
Notes	Russell was buried on Tuesday, June 29, 1999. Virginia and Russell were both buried side-by-side, at Mount Tabor Presbyterian Church Cemetery. They lived at 1130 Shinnville Road in Cleveland at the time of their deaths and homeowners. Their daughter: Virginia Theodoric Cowan Witherspoon.

Name	**Virginia Catherine Glaspy Cowan**
Date Of Birth	Tuesday, February 11, 1919
Place Of Birth	Cleveland, North Carolina – Rowan County
Date Of Death	Sunday, May 31, 1998

My Family Tree

Age At Death	79
Place Of Death	Brooklyn, New York – Kings County
Occupation	Housewife
Married	Russell Alberta Cowan
Notes	She was buried in June 1998. Virginia's parents were Margaret Lula Allison Glaspy and David Lee Glaspy. Mrs. Cowan has an obituary that talks about her life.

Name	**Lula Virginia Cowan**
Date Of Birth	Thursday, February 19, 1925
Place Of Birth	North Carolina – Rowan County
Date Of Death	Sunday, November 20, 1994
Age At Death	69
Place Of Death	Brooklyn, New York – Kings County
Occupation	Homemaker
Married	Single
Notes	Her daughter: Phyllis A. Stockton Copeland. Lula lived at 3930 Powell Street in Brooklyn at the time of her death and a homeowner. She was buried in November 1994, at Mount Tabor Presbyterian Church Cemetery. Mrs. Cowan has an obituary that talks about her life.

Name	**Nancy Cinora Cowan Haynes**
Date Of Birth	Monday, November 11, 1940
Place Of Birth	North Carolina – Rowan County
Date Of Death	Monday, October 5, 1998
Age At Death	57
Place Of Death	Brooklyn, New York – Kings County

My Family Tree

Occupation	Homemaker
Married	Widow
Notes	Their children: David Haynes (Bobbie), Lisa Haynes, and Mary Haynes Wilson (Jerell). She was buried on Saturday, November 10, 1998, at Mount Tabor Presbyterian Church Cemetery. Mrs. Haynes has an obituary that talks about her life. Her grandchildren: Olympic Nicole Harris, Freddie Haynes, and Jerryl Jairus Wilson.

Name	**Vivian Catherine Cowan Hyde**
Date Of Birth	Thursday, March 29, 1923
Place Of Birth	North Carolina – Rowan County
Date Of Death	Monday, October 18, 1999
Age At Death	76
Place Of Death	Cleveland, North Carolina – Rowan County
Occupation	Housewife/ Flight Stewardess
Married	Widow
Notes	She was buried on Wednesday, March 20, 1999, at Third Creek AME Zion Church Cemetery in Cleveland, North Carolina – Rowan County. She lived at 103 Phifer ST. in Charlotte at the time of her death.

Name	**Grover Cowan**
Date Of Birth	1939
Place Of Birth	North Carolina – Rowan County
Date Of Death	N/A
Age At Death	N/A
Place Of Death	Cleveland, North Carolina – Rowan County
Occupation	Day Laborer
Married	Widower

My Family Tree

Notes	

The Family Line of Ada R. Bradshaw Rankin and James Francis Rankin

The connection to the family line was James, the son of Rhody Isabella Cowan Rankin and Pinkney C. Rankin.

The Third Generation

Ada R. Bradshaw Rankin	-	See Entry Page 410-411
James Francis Rankin	-	See Entry Page 410

Their (10) Children

Name	Elmer Rankin
Date Of Birth	Tuesday, August 26, 1913
Place Of Birth	Mount Ulla Township, North Carolina – Rowan County
Date Of Death	Thursday, October 20, 1983
Age At Death	69
Place Of Death	Cleveland, North Carolina – Rowan County
Occupation	Day Laborer
Married	Rosa Williams Rankin
Notes	Their children: Chester Leaser, Jerry McNeely, Ruth Rankin Hall, Marie Rankin Stylin, Margie Rankin, Hallie Jane Rankin Davidson, and Ada Rankin. He was buried on Monday, October 24, 1983, at Mount Tabor Presbyterian Church Cemetery.

Name	Ruth Rankin Faber
Date Of Birth	Monday, April 25, 1920
Place Of Birth	Mount Ulla Township, North Carolina – Rowan County
Date Of Death	Unknown
Age At Death	Unknown
Place Of Death	Cleveland, North Carolina – Rowan County

My Family Tree

Occupation	Domestic Worker/ Housewife
Married	Widow
Notes	

Name	**Frank Edward Rankin**
Date Of Birth	Sunday, December 25, 1927
Place Of Birth	Mount Ulla Township, North Carolina – Rowan County
Date Of Death	Wednesday, October 25, 1978
Age At Death	50
Place Of Death	Troutman, North Carolina – Iredell County
Occupation	Retired – Veteran/Niemand Industries
Married	Lacy Belle Everline Gray Graham Rankin
Notes	He was buried on Saturday, October 28, 1978.

Name	**Lacy Belle Everline Gray Graham Rankin**
Date Of Birth	Monday, March 13, 1922
Place Of Birth	North Carolina – Iredell County
Date Of Death	Monday, February 6, 2006
Age At Death	83
Place Of Death	Troutman, North Carolina – Iredell County
Occupation	Retired – Cosmetologist/Owner of Bells Beauty Shop
Married	Frank Edward Rankin
Notes	She was buried on Saturday, February 11, 2006. Lacy and Frank were both buried, at Shinnville United Church of Christ Cemetery in Troutman, North Carolina – Iredell County. Her parents were Dora Ramsey Gray and Melvin Gray. Their children: Félix Graham, Cozette Graham Ramsey,

My Family Tree

	Wendy Brown, Hallie Rankin Ramsey, Charmaine Ramsey, and Juanita L. Graham Glaspy.

Name	Willie Lee Rankin
Date Of Birth	Saturday, January 12, 1907
Place Of Birth	Mount Ulla Township, North Carolina – Rowan County
Date Of Death	Sunday, May 18, 1969
Age At Death	62
Place Of Death	Cleveland, North Carolina – Rowan County
Occupation	Day Laborer – Yadkin Hotel
Married	Single
Notes	He was buried on Thursday, May 22, 1969, at Mount Tabor Presbyterian Church Cemetery.

Name	Sylvester R. Rankin
Date Of Birth	Saturday, March 26, 1910
Place Of Birth	Mount Ulla Township, North Carolina – Rowan County
Date Of Death	Wednesday, August 1, 1945
Age At Death	35
Place Of Death	Statesville, North Carolina – Iredell County
Occupation	Farmer
Married	Single
Notes	He was buried on Saturday, August 4, 1945, at Mount Tabor Presbyterian Church Cemetery.

Name	Howard V. Rankin
Date Of Birth	1922

My Family Tree

Place Of Birth	Mount Ulla Township, North Carolina – Rowan County
Date Of Death	Unknown
Age At Death	Unknown
Place Of Death	Cleveland, North Carolina – Rowan County
Occupation	Day Laborer
Married	Unknown
Notes	

Name	**Hilda Rankin Ramsey**
Date Of Birth	Monday, August 9, 1915
Place Of Birth	Mount Ulla Township, North Carolina – Rowan County
Date Of Death	Saturday, September 18, 1954
Age At Death	39
Place Of Death	Cleveland, North Carolina – Rowan County
Occupation	Domestic Worker/Housewife
Married	Joseph Knox Ramsey
Notes	Their children: Tommy Lee Rankin (Marie P.), Nathaniel Ramsey, James Ramsey, Kent Ramsey, Chris Robertson, and Annie Delois Rankin-Ramsey (b. Monday, January 7, 1946 – d. Tuesday, February 12, 1946, age 1). Hilda was buried in September 1954, at Mount Tabor Presbyterian Church Cemetery.

Name	**Robert Lewis Rankin**
Date Of Birth	Thursday, March 15, 1923
Place Of Birth	Mount Ulla Township, North Carolina – Rowan County
Date Of Death	Sunday, November 26, 1995

My Family Tree

Age At Death	72
Place Of Death	Cleveland, North Carolina – Rowan County
Occupation	Veteran/Retired Grinnell Fire Protection Systems
Married	Eldora Knox Rankin
Notes	He was buried on Wednesday, November 29, 1995, at Mount Tabor Presbyterian Church Cemetery. He served in the United States WWII.

Name	Eldora Knox Rankin
Date Of Birth	Saturday, November 18, 1922
Place Of Birth	Mount Ulla Township, North Carolina – Rowan County
Date Of Death	Cleveland, North Carolina – Rowan County
Age At Death	Unknown
Place Of Death	Unknown
Occupation	Domestic Worker/ Housewife
Married	Robert Lewis Rankin
Notes	

Name	Ethel Mae Rankin Baity
Date Of Birth	Sunday, January 14, 1917
Place Of Birth	Mount Ulla Township, North Carolina – Rowan County
Date Of Death	Friday, December 30, 2005
Age At Death	88
Place Of Death	Cleveland, North Carolina – Rowan County
Occupation	Domestic Worker/ Housewife
Married	Garfield Alexander Baity

My Family Tree

Notes	Ethel Mae was buried on Thursday, January 5, 2006, as a widow. They were both buried, at Mount Tabor Presbyterian Church Cemetery. Their children: Marshall Rankin Baity and Annie Mae Baity Blackmon.

Name	**Garfield Alexander Baity**
Date Of Birth	Friday, January 12, 1917
Place Of Birth	Cleveland, North Carolina – Rowan County
Date Of Death	Thursday, May 3, 1979
Age At Death	62
Place Of Death	Cleveland, North Carolina – Rowan County
Occupation	Day Laborer
Married	Ethel Mae Rankin Baity
Notes	Married on Saturday, March 12, 1938, in Mooresville, North Carolina – Rowan County. He was buried on Thursday, May 3, 1979.

Name	**Clara Clementine Rankin Glaspy**
Date Of Birth	Saturday, August 26, 1911
Place Of Birth	Mount Ulla Township, North Carolina – Rowan County
Date Of Death	Tuesday, March 11, 1986
Age At Death	74
Place Of Death	Statesville, North Carolina – Iredell County
Occupation	Domestic Worker/Housewife
Married	John Lee Glaspy
Notes	She was buried in March 1986. Clara and John were both buried side-by-side, at Antioch Baptist Church in North Carolina – Iredell County, as a widow. Their children: Francis Lee Glaspy, Scott Reid Rankin, William Olly Glaspy, Donald Ray Glaspy, Jay Allen Glaspy, Robert Lewis Glaspy, Ada G. Glaspy Graham, Virginia Ruth Glaspy, and Katie Geneva Glaspy Pearson. Mrs. Glaspy had an obituary that talks about her life.

My Family Tree

Name	**John Lee Glaspy**
Date Of Birth	Saturday, May 16, 1914
Place Of Birth	Cleveland, North Carolina – Rowan County
Date Of Death	Tuesday, May 14, 1985
Age At Death	70
Place Of Death	Statesville, North Carolina – Iredell County
Occupation	Farmer
Married	Clara Clementine Rankin Glaspy
Notes	His parents were Margaret Lula Allison Glaspy and David Lee Glaspy. He was buried on Saturday, May 18, 1985. Clara and John both lived at Route 7, Box 264 in Statesville, and they were homeowners. Mr. Glaspy had an obituary that talked about his life.

The Family of Margaret Lula Allison Glaspy and David Lee Glaspy

Name	**Margaret Lula Allison Glaspy**
Date Of Birth	Sunday, October 9, 1887
Place Of Birth	North Carolina
Date Of Death	Wednesday, July 31, 1957
Age At Death	69
Place Of Death	North Carolina – Iredell County
Occupation	Domestic Worker/Housewife
Married	David Lee Glaspy
Notes	

Name	**David Lee Glaspy**
Date Of Birth	Sunday, April 12, 1885

My Family Tree

Place Of Birth	North Carolina – Iredell County
Date Of Death	Friday, October 26, 1934
Age At Death	49
Place Of Death	North Carolina – Rowan County
Occupation	Day Laborer
Married	Margaret Lula Allison Glaspy
Notes	Census records noted that they got married in 1909 in North Carolina.

Their (8) Children

The connection to the family line was Clara, the daughter of Ada R. Bradshaw Rankin and James Francis Rankin.

John Lee Glaspy	-	See Entry Page 441
Clara Clementine Rankin Glaspy	-	See Entry Page 440

The connection to the family line was Russell, the son of Martha Elizabeth Cowan.

Virginia Catherine Glaspy Cowan	-	See Entry Page 432-433
Russell Alberta Cowan	-	See Entry Page 432

Name	Otha David Glaspy
Date Of Birth	Sunday, October 15, 1905
Place Of Birth	North Carolina – Iredell County
Date Of Death	Thursday, January 8, 1976
Age At Death	70
Place Of Death	North Carolina – Rowan County
Occupation	Day Laborer
Married	Elizabeth Patterson Glaspy
Notes	He was buried in January 1976. Elizabeth and Otha were both buried, at Antioch Baptist Church Cemetery in North Carolina – Iredell County a widower.

My Family Tree

Name	Elizabeth Patterson Glaspy
Date Of Birth	Tuesday, June 9, 1903
Place Of Birth	North Carolina
Date Of Death	Sunday, September 29, 1974
Age At Death	71
Place Of Death	North Carolina – Rowan County
Occupation	Domestic Worker/Housewife
Married	Otha David Glaspy
Notes	Elizabeth's parents were Mary McClain Patterson and J. S. Patterson. Her nickname was "Lizzie." She was buried October 1974.

Name	Joseph Franklin Glaspy
Date Of Birth	Wednesday, September 1, 1915
Place Of Birth	North Carolina – Iredell County
Date Of Death	Wednesday, October 5, 1988
Age At Death	73
Place Of Death	Mooresville, North Carolina – Iredell County
Occupation	Day Laborer
Married	(1) Mamie Clarke Glaspy (2) Mattie Odessa Leazer Glaspy
Notes	(1) Married on Wednesday, November 27, 1935, in North Carolina – Iredell County. (2) b. 1918 – d. 1994, age 75 – 76). Mattie and Joseph were both buried side-by-side, at Sills Creek AME Zion Church Cemetery in Mount Ulla, North Carolina – Rowan County.

Name	Curtis William Glaspy
Date Of Birth	Tuesday, December 26, 1922

My Family Tree

Place Of Birth	North Carolina – Iredell County
Date Of Death	Friday, November 8, 2002
Age At Death	79
Place Of Death	Winston-Salem, North Carolina – Forsyth County
Occupation	Reverend
Married	Eloise R. Garner Glaspy
Notes	His twin brother was Carlton. Married on Saturday, November 22, 1975, in Winston-Salem, North Carolina – Forsyth County. He was buried in 2002.

Name	Eloise R. Garner Glaspy
Date Of Birth	1925
Place Of Birth	North Carolina – Iredell County
Date Of Death	2009
Age At Death	83 – 84
Place Of Death	Winston-Salem, North Carolina – Forsyth County
Occupation	Housewife
Married	Curtis William Glaspy
Notes	She was buried in 2009; they were both buried side-by-side, at Parklawn Memorial Park in Winston-Salem, North Carolina – Forsyth County.

Name	Carlton James Glaspy
Date Of Birth	Tuesday, December 26, 1922
Place Of Birth	North Carolina – Iredell County
Date Of Death	Monday, June 10, 2002
Age At Death	79

My Family Tree

Place Of Death	Salisbury, North Carolina – Rowan County
Occupation	Retired – United States Army
Married	Martha Louise Rogers Glaspy
Notes	He served in the United States Army during WWII as TEC5. He was buried in June 2002, at Salisbury National Cemetery Annex in Salisbury, North Carolina – Rowan County. His twin brother was Curtis.

Name	**Martha Louise Rogers Glaspy**
Date Of Birth	Friday, June 18, 1926
Place Of Birth	North Carolina – Iredell County
Date Of Death	Wednesday, November 20, 1963
Age At Death	37
Place Of Death	Statesville, North Carolina – Iredell County
Occupation	Housewife
Married	Carlton James Glaspy
Notes	Her parents were Marie Waddell Williams (b. 1903 – d. 1993, age 90) and Marvin Rogers. She was buried in November 1963, at Cameron Presbyterian Church Cemetery in Statesville, North Carolina – Iredell County.

Name	**Cora Pauline Glaspy Mills**
Date Of Birth	Friday, October 1, 1909
Place Of Birth	North Carolina – Iredell County
Date Of Death	Sunday, January 29, 1967
Age At Death	57
Place Of Death	Mooresville, North Carolina – Iredell County
Occupation	Domestic Worker/Housewife

My Family Tree

Married	Wurdy James Mills
Notes	She was buried in February 1967. Cora and Wurdy were both buried side-by-side, at Antioch Baptist Church Cemetery in North Carolina – Iredell County. Their child was Effie Mills Fetterson (b. Friday, October 4, 1946, POB. North Carolina – Iredell County – d. Friday, June 2, 2000, age 53, POD: Mooresville, North Carolina – Iredell County.

Name	**Wurdy James Mills**
Date Of Birth	Sunday, July 18, 1909
Place Of Birth	North Carolina
Date Of Death	Tuesday, June 30, 1985
Age At Death	75
Place Of Death	North Carolina
Occupation	Day Laborer
Married	Cora Pauline Glaspy Mills
Notes	Wurdy's parents were Lissie Ramsey Mills (b. 1879 – d. 1962, age 82 – 83) and Richard L. Mills (b. Wednesday, March 22, 1876, POB. North Carolina – Rowan County – d. Sunday, April 13, 1941, age 65, POD. Barringer Township, North Carolina; buried Wednesday, April 16, 1941). Lissie and Richard were both buried side-by-side, at Shinnsville United Church of Christ Cemetery in Troutman, North Carolina – Iredell County. Richard's parents were Phoebe Cats Mills (b. 1845 – d. 1908, age 62 – 63; headstone says Oats) and Andrew Mills (b. 1832 – d. 1905, age 72 – 73), married in 1860 in North Carolina. Wurdy's sibling was Sylvorn Eugene Mills.

Name	**Mary Glaspy Mills**
Date Of Birth	Saturday, March 18, 1911
Place Of Birth	North Carolina – Iredell County
Date Of Death	Friday, February 18, 2000
Age At Death	88

My Family Tree

Place Of Death	North Carolina – Rowan County
Occupation	Day Laborer
Married	Sylvorn Eugene Mills
Notes	Mary and Sylvorn were both buried, at Antioch Baptist Church Cemetery in North Carolina – Iredell County.

Name	**Sylvorn Eugene Mills**
Date Of Birth	Sunday, September 10, 1911
Place Of Birth	North Carolina – Iredell County
Date Of Death	Saturday, May 21, 1966
Age At Death	54
Place Of Death	Mooresville, North Carolina – Iredell County
Occupation	Retired – Mill Worker
Married	(1) Mary Glaspy Mills (2) Mary Rose Mills
Notes	(1) Married in 1928 in North Carolina. He was buried on Wednesday, May 25, 1966.

The Family Line of Clara Clementine Rankin Glaspy and John Lee Glaspy

The connection to the family line was Clara, the daughter of Ada R. Bradshaw Rankin and James Francis Rankin.

Clara Clementine Rankin Glaspy - See Entry Page 440
John Lee Glaspy - See Entry Page 441

Their (9) Children

Name	**Francis Lee Glaspy**
Date Of Birth	Friday, March 10, 1933
Place Of Birth	North Carolina – Iredell County
Date Of Death	Saturday, December 17, 1960
Age At Death	27

My Family Tree

Place Of Death	Statesville, North Carolina – Iredell County
Occupation	North Carolina – City Worker
Married	Single
Notes	He was buried on Wednesday, December 21, 1960, at Antioch Baptist Church Cemetery in North Carolina – Iredell County. He lived at Route 1 in Statesville at the time of his death, as a homeowner.

Name	**Scott Reid Rankin**
Date Of Birth	Thursday, May 7, 1931
Place Of Birth	North Carolina – Rowan County
Date Of Death	N/A
Age At Death	N/A
Place Of Death	N/A
Occupation	N/A
Married	Ruth D. Sanders Rankin
Notes	His father was Herman Wilson. Their children include Margaret S. L. Rankin (b. Sunday, December 16, 1956), Sharon Rankin (b. Wednesday, September 21, 1966), and Ernestine Lavawn Rankin (b. Thursday, September 14, 1961 – d. Tuesday, October 24, 1961, age 1 Month and 10 Days Old). Their children were born in Mooresville, North Carolina – Iredell County. Ernestine was buried on Wednesday, October 25, 1961, in North Carolina – Iredell County. Ernestine lived at Route 3 in Mooresville at the time of her death, as a homeowner.

Name	**William Olly Glaspy**
Date Of Birth	Thursday, November 1, 1934
Place Of Birth	North Carolina – Rowan County
Date Of Death	Friday, August 3, 2001
Age At Death	67

My Family Tree

Place Of Death	Frankfort, Kentucky – Franklin County
Occupation	Retired Employee of the State of Kentucky
Married	Single
Notes	His nickname was "Bill." His children include Diane Caldwell, Monika Moore, Edward Tillman, Monica Garner, Rodney Garner, David Rankin, Eugene Hyde, and Gregory Pulliam. He was buried in August 2001, at Antioch Baptist Church Cemetery in Cleveland, North Carolina – Iredell County.

Name	**Donald Ray Glaspy**
Date Of Birth	Saturday, August 15, 1936
Place Of Birth	North Carolina – Iredell County
Date Of Death	Thursday, August 31, 2023
Age At Death	87
Place Of Death	Statesville, North Carolina – Iredell County
Occupation	Superintendent of Sunday School /Teacher
Married	Juanita L. Graham Glaspy
Notes	He was affectionately known as "Duke" and "The Original Car Doctor." Buried on Friday, September 8, 2023, at Antioch Baptist Church Cemetery in Cleveland, North Carolina – Iredell County.

Name	**Juanita L. Graham Glaspy**
Date Of Birth	Sunday, May 21, 1939
Place Of Birth	North Carolina – Iredell County
Date Of Death	N/A
Age At Death	N/A
Place Of Death	N/A
Occupation	N/A

My Family Tree

Married	Donald Ray Glaspy
Notes	Their children include Donna Glaspy, Ray Glaspy, Youorra Glaspy, and Teresa Laverne Glaspy (b. Wednesday, February 14, 1962, POB. North Carolina – Iredell County – d. Friday, December 24, 1982, age 20), POD. Morganton, North Carolina – Burke County. Teresa was buried on Monday, December 27, 1982, at Antioch Baptist Church Cemetery in North Carolina – Iredell County.

Name	Jay Allen Glaspy
Date Of Birth	Wednesday, August 17, 1938
Place Of Birth	North Carolina – Iredell County
Date Of Death	N/A
Age At Death	N/A
Place Of Death	N/A
Occupation	N/A
Married	Doris Amentia Siegel Glaspy
Notes	Married on Sunday, March 1, 1959, in North Carolina – Rowan County.

Name	Robert Lewis Glaspy
Date Of Birth	Wednesday, April 19, 1950
Place Of Birth	North Carolina – Iredell County
Date Of Death	N/A
Age At Death	N/A
Place Of Death	N/A
Occupation	N/A
Married	N/A
Notes	

My Family Tree

Name	Ada G. Glaspy Graham
Date Of Birth	Wednesday, June 4, 1941
Place Of Birth	North Carolina – Iredell County
Date Of Death	N/A
Age At Death	N/A
Place Of Death	N/A
Occupation	N/A
Married	N/A
Notes	

Name	Virginia Ruth Glaspy
Date Of Birth	Sunday, April 11, 1948
Place Of Birth	Mooresville, North Carolina – Iredell County
Date Of Death	Thursday, June 10, 1948
Age At Death	2 Months and 29 Days Old
Place Of Death	Mooresville, North Carolina – Iredell County
Occupation	None
Married	Single
Notes	She was buried on Thursday, June 10, 1948, at Antioch Baptist Church Cemetery in North Carolina – Iredell County.

Name	Katie Geneva Glaspy Pearson
Date Of Birth	Tuesday, November 13, 1951
Place Of Birth	North Carolina – Iredell County
Date Of Death	N/A

My Family Tree

Age At Death	N/A
Place Of Death	N/A
Occupation	N/A
Married	Widow
Notes	

The Family Line of Ethel Mae Rankin Baity and Garfield Baity

The connection to the family line was Ethel, the daughter of Ada R. Bradshaw Rankin and James Francis Rankin.

The Fourth Generation

Ethel Mae Rankin Baity - See Entry Page 439-440
Garfield Alexander Baity - See Entry Page 440

Their (2) Children

Name	**Marshall Rankin Baity**
Date Of Birth	Saturday, September 5, 1936
Place Of Birth	Cleveland, North Carolina – Rowan County
Date Of Death	Tuesday, July 13, 1982
Age At Death	45
Place Of Death	Cleveland, North Carolina – Rowan County
Occupation	Self-employed
Married	Single
Notes	Marshall was buried on Friday, July 16, 1982, at Mount Tabor Presbyterian Church Cemetery. He lived at Route 2 Box 335 in Cleveland at the time of his death, a homeowner.

Name	**Annie Mae Baity Blackmon**
Date Of Birth	Monday, April 2, 1934
Place Of Birth	Cleveland, North Carolina – Rowan County

My Family Tree

Date Of Death	Saturday, March 15, 2014
Age At Death	79
Place Of Death	Cleveland, North Carolina – Rowan County
Occupation	Housewife
Married	Charles E. Blackmon (b. 1943 – d. 2019, age 75 – 76)
Notes	Their children are Martha Lucille Blackmon and Patricia Ann Blackmon. Annie was buried Thursday, March 20, 2014, in Cleveland, North Carolina – Rowan County.

The Family Line of Annie Mae Baity Blackmon and Charles E. Blackmon

The connection to the family line was Annie, the daughter of Ethel Mae Rankin Baity and Garfield Baity.

The Fifth Generation

Annie Mae Baity Blackmon - See Entry Above
Charles E. Blackmon - See Entry Above

<u>**Their (2) Children**</u>

Name	**Martha Lucille Blackmon**
Date Of Birth	Monday, August 10, 1959
Place Of Birth	Cleveland, North Carolina – Rowan County
Date Of Death	N/A
Age At Death	N/A
Place Of Death	N/A
Occupation	N/A
Married	N/A
Notes	

Name	**Patricia Ann Blackmon**
Date Of Birth	Sunday, July 28, 1957

My Family Tree

Place Of Birth	Cleveland, North Carolina – Rowan County
Date Of Death	N/A
Age At Death	N/A
Place Of Death	N/A
Occupation	N/A
Married	N/A
Notes	

Life was extremely hard back then for people of color, trying to raise their families and keep them together during and after slavery. Combining both families, I have tracked over two thousand family members on both mother's and father's side. The family members listed here I was trying to give you a glimpse of their lives. Some of the stories are incomplete due to a lack of available documents, or some by reason of memories growing dim over time. Sometimes, due to run-ins with the law when danger was upon them (where people of color had to disappear by changing their names or move out of the area to hide). Some family members did not feel comfortable participating in the United States Federal Census back then. Here are their names:

McQueene Ables	Rilla Ables	Isabel Adams	Jack Adams
Joseph Aikens	Amanda Alexander	Jackson Alexander	Abraham Allen
Janie Taylor Allen	Ralph Q. Allen	Ernest Allison	Everett Allison
Fletcher Allison	Julia Higgins Allison	Walter Allison	Jake Jacob Alston
Olivia Mills Alston	Jim Anderson	Edward Anthony	Martha Douthit Anthony
Pearl Brandon Anthony	Emily Robinson Audrey	Joe Audrey	Mary Belle Sharpe Avery
Samuel R. Avery	John Awanna	Griffin Bailey	Lillie Bailey
Bud Baity	Mamie Baity	Alice M. Barber	Charlotte Barber
Effie Fisher Barber	Henry Barber	John L. Barber	Lie Barker
Lura L. Barber	Margaret Harris Barber	Milton McKinley Barber	Eliza Downs Barksdale
Tobe Barksdale	Doc Barnett	Sue Morrow Barnett	Venus Orr Barnett
Charles A. Barron	Laura Witherspoon Barron	Congera Bass	Debby Bass
Ethel Perry Martin Bass	Martha Allen Bass	Martha Cunningham Bass	Mary E. Bass
Maud JW Bass	Rebecca Bass	Roy Bass	Countless L. Bassett
Douglas Bassett	Frank Bassett	Franklin Bassett	George Washington Bassett I
George Washington Bassett II	Vera Mae McDaniel Bassett	William E. Bassett	Alice Goolsby Benson
Albert Berry	Anna Whitfield Berry	Clem Bolden	Rebektah Motron Bolden
Fannie Boyd	Preston Boyd	Washington Boyd	Augusta Brandon
Walter Brandon	Willie Lee Britton	Bessie Brown	Cary Brown
Catherine Brown	Elco Jr. Brown I	Isabella Brown	James I. Brown
Odell Brown	Priscilla Mason Brown	Wyatt Brown	Alma Davis Browning
Charles Browning	Virginia Bruce	Wardell Bruce	Bettye Meroney Bryant

My Family Tree

William Bryant	Grace Virginia Hargraves Bryson	John Bryson	Willie Bryson
George W. Burney	Rebecca Burney	Aaron Burns	Mary Wilbur Burns
Calvin Burton	Lillie Orr Burton	Lottie Rush Burton	Raymond Burton
Clarence Burrs	Emerline Butler Burrs	Willie A. Burwell	Ada Coleman Byrd
William Byrd	Hattie Cain	Julius Cain	Maggie M. Davis Cain
William Cain	Charles Carey	George A. Carey	
Iza Carey	John Carey	Joseph David Carey	Louise Constans Carey
Lucy Carey	Luna Carey	Maude Martin Carey	Miles Carey I
Miles Carey II	Nancy Carey	Rufus Carey	Vernell Mae Baxter Carey
Abe Carrington	Amelia Carrington	Flora Carrington	Ida N. Carrington
John W. Carrington	Levina T. Carrington	Lillie B. Carrington	Lovvenia Carrington
Samuel C. Carrington I	Susan Beverly Carrington	Mary Leak Carter	Nash Carter
Abraham Chaplin	Celia Atkinson Chaplin	Marie Chaplin	Roosevelt Chaplin
Samuel Chaplin	Thelma Chaplin	Thessalonia Chaplin	Hallie Bell Owens Childs
Madeline Allen Childs	William Childs	Dixie Ware Chubbs	Raymond Chubbs
Selman Clabona	Ada C. Pate Clement	Alexander Clement	Emma Ferron Clement
Matt Conrad	Phyllis A. Stockton Copeland	Augustus Cornelius	Florence Gray Cornelius
Mary E. Cornelius	Allen Cowan	Allie Cowan	Ana Barber Cowan
Charles Cowan II	Charles Edward Cowan II	Emma Wilson Crummie Cowan	Genola Cowan
Gilbert Cowan	John Cowan	Leslie Cowan	Lou Cowan
Lucinda Cowan	Mary Jane Taylor Cowan	Mellon Cowan	Mildred Cowan
Preneet Cowan	Christine Moore Crawford	Mary Crump	Nat Crump
Ruthie Bailey Crump	Stimson Crump	E. C. Gan Cunningham	Edmon Cunningham
Rubin Cunningham	Robert Dalton I	Henry Darr	Hallie Jane Rankin Davidson
Cleveland Davis	Grace Davis	John Davis	Mary Smith Davis
Caroline Tomlin Denison	George Denison	Eilas Dennis	Susan Ann Dennis
Ella Wilson Dickerson	Mac Dickerson	Woodrow Wilburn Dickerson	Lucy Dillard
James Dingess	Josephine Glass Dingess	Jack Donaldson	Lillian Lynard Donaldson
Lucy B. Steele Doulin	George Adam Ellis	Mary Mason Doulin	Frederick Doulin
Isabela Elliott	Lethia Elliott	Alex Ervin	Pansy Harris Ervin
Ruth Rankin Faber	Arvella Levis Farmer	Isaac Faulkner	Louise Mason Faulkner
Ben Fields	Eula Van Easton Foster	Lula Malone Foster	Alex Fowler I
Alex Fowler II	Connie Hairston Fowler	Emerline Lord Fowler	Isaac Fowler
Margaret Fowler	Mary Fowler	Willie Mae Fowler	Joseph Freeman
Mae Eva Cram Freeman	C. F. Friday	Clarence Friday	Zulla Friday
Ella Winford Furlow	Tommy P. Furlow	Alice Gaither	Thomas A. Gaither
Martha Gamble	Samuel Gamble	Annie Lee Gilbert	Callie Gilliam
George Gilliam I	George Gilliam II	Priscilla E. Holton Gilliam	Essre Myricle Gillon
Doris Amentia Siegel Glaspy	Mamie Clarke Glaspy	Maggie Stover Glenn	Tom Glenn
Mary Causer Goode	Walker Goode	Eugenia B. Cornelius Goodman	William Goodman
Bethany Hairston Goolsby	Horace Goolsby	John Goolsby	Mary Goolsby
Grover Grant	Jessie Durham Grant	Robert Grant	Virgil Eugene Grant
Dora Ramsey Gray	Manuel Gray	Melvin Gray	Anne Green
Edwin Green	Ilar Grier	John Grier	Carrie Green Workman Griffith
MG Griffith	Adam Hairston	Bashie Hairston	Beatrice Hairston Hairston

My Family Tree

Bernice Hairston	Bernis Hairston	Bessie Hooper Hairston	Beulah Watt Shoaf Hairston
Bush Hairston	Effie Hairston	Esther Hairston	Fannie Hairston
Frank Hairston	Helen M. Hairston	Henry Hairston	Hester Hairston
Hester Hairston	Hester Doulin Hairston	Jessie Collie Hairston	Judy Wilson Hairston
Louisa Hairston	Maggie Doulin Hairston	Mary Hairston	Mary Clodfelter Hairston
Mary Cornelia Martin Hairston	Mollie Ellis Hairston	Nancy Goolsby Hairston	Pauline Hairston
Perley Hairston	Righteous Hairston	Salem Hairston	Salem Hairston
Thomas Hairston	Tom Hairston	Thurman Roscoe Hairston	Wanne Hairston
Willard H. Hairston	William P. Hairston	Winston Hairston	Mary Ann Lash Haizlip
Ruth Rankin Hall	Annie Belle Woodward Hamilton	Henry Hamilton	LaQuana Hampton
Henry M. Hargraves	Laura J. Hargraves	Louise Hargraves	Osborn Hargraves
Eva Day Harris	Frank Harris	Jane Frohop Harris	Prince Harris
Effie Lyons Hawkins	Richmond Hawkins	Westley Heath	Anderson Hege
Arabelle Hege	Cora Young Hege	Eliza Wilson Hege	Julia White Hege
Leah Hege	Louise Hairston Hege	Margaret Hege	Roscoe Hege
Thomas Hege	James A. Herrin	Rufus Herrin	Susie Herrin
Austin Hicklen	Charles Hicklen	Albert Holman	Maggie Holman
Creolla Ann Mason Holmes	Lee Thomas Holmes	Ophelia Tillman Holmes	Bruce E. Holton
Harry Holton	Icy Holton	James Holton II	John Holton
Ona Holton	Paul Holton	Thelma Holton	Matt Howard
Pattie Bass Howard	Susan Winston Howard	George Anna Hyatt	Alice Holman Ijames
George Ijames	Fleming Ingram	Jinny Ingram	Sally Ingram
Louise Johnson Jackson	Willie Gladden Jackson	Anthony James	Benjamin James
Dora Wallace James	Mariah Holmes James	Glenn Jefferson	Mary Bell Jefferson
Roxie Martin Jefferson	Walter Jefferson I	Haywood Johnson	Houston Johnson
Laura Johnson	Mary Johnson	Lillie Mae Webster Jones	Marie Mason Jones
Mary A. Simms Jones	Elizabeth Gordon Jordan	Jacob Jordan	Elijah Gadson Knott
Osee Knox	Benjamin Langhorne	Bettie Langhorne	Caroline Langhorne
Charles Langhorne	Henry Langhorne	Houston Langhorne	James Langhorne
John Langhorne	Robert Law	John Lay	Lula Shields Lay
Chester Leaser	Agnes Knott Lee	Henry Lee	Oberian Lee
Alice Patricia Parker Lewis	Dan Lewis	Ed Lewis	Etta Bass Lewis
Florence Ferguson Lewis	George Lewis	Hazel Lewis	Leonard Radney Lewis
Oscar Lewis	Abram Lindsay	Levenia Moore Lindsay	Divie Long
Aurelia Person Mack	John Mack	Milly Malone	Allen Martin
Caroline Austin Martin	Charles Martin	Effie Gilbreath Martin	Ella Martin
Estella Young Martin	Jim Martin	Phil Martin	Sid Martin
Aaron Mason	Alice Roberson Mason	Bettie Click Mason	Blanche Lucille Vaughters Mason
Burleson Mason	Burrell Mason	Burrell T. Mason	Celia Mason
Clayborn Mason	Cleophus Mason	Colwell Mason	Cora Patterson Mason
Elizabeth Mason	Elizabeth Mason	Emma Mason	Eugene Mason
Fannie P. Mason	G. G. Mason	Henry P. Mason	Herbert Mason
Isabella Dubose Mason	Janet Secreca Britton Mason	John Mason	Lizzie Mason
Lizzie Mason	Lois Mason	Lucy Mason	Mack Mason
Marguerite Mason	Marie Mason	Martha Mason	Mary Jane Brown Mason
Mary Taylor Mason	Mildred Mason	Nanna Mason	Naomi Bailey Mason
Nebraska Mason	Nevada Mason	Ola Mason	Ola Moody Mason
Ola Winford Mason	Penix M. Mason	Phyllis Ann Brown Hairston Mason	Priscilla Hargraves Mason

My Family Tree

Robert Mason	Robert Mason	Robert M. Mason [1]	Sukie Turner Mason
Sally Mae Jones Mason	Silla Bruce Mason	Spencer Mason	Sylvia Ijames Mason
Thelma Mason	William Mason	William A. Mason	William T. Mason
Jake McCain	Mary Alexander McCain	Duncan McCall	Hattie Ivory McCall
Margaret Mason McCall	John McCombs	Priscilla McCombs	Adaline Summers McCrary
Newton McCrary	Cheryl Vernette McDaniel	John McLaughlin	Jerry McNeely
Estee McQueen	Kinney M. McQueen [1]	Alice M. Johnson Miller	Almeta Robinson Miller
Errie Miller [1]	Isiah Miller	Mary Rose Mills	Nannie B. Mason Mock
Odell Mock	Pearl Mock	Rudolph Mock	Archie Moore [1]
Lucy Nancy Moore	Margaret Moore	Mildred Mason Moore	Connie Morrison
Cordeline Morrison	Iredle Morrison	Oliver Morrison	Sara Morrison
Caroline Carrington Morsen	Alsey Lyons Neely	Ernest Lee Neely	George Neely
George Cornelius Neely	Josie Ann Neely	Ora Mae Holman Neely	Sallie May Farris Neely
Annie Nelson	Eddie Nelson	James Russell Nicholas [1]	Charley Mae Oden
Delia Oden	Thomas A. Oden	Alexander Orr	Alice Wallace Orr
Charley Orr	Enzelia Orr	Ione Orr	James A. Orr
Jane Orr	Joe Orr	Lee Orr	Lillie Orr
Lolo Orr	Maggie Tate Orr	Marry Orr	Mary E. Whitworth Orr
Millie Barber Orr	Robert Orr	Stella Orr	Violet Orr
Washington A. Orr [1]	Carris Brauch Palmer	Jane White Palmer	Joshua Palmer
Daniel Parker	Elizabeth Gay Parker	George Parker	Walter Parker
Wilson Cooper Parker	Allen Parks	Ophelia Gray Parks	Alexander Miles Partee
Christine Tucker Partee	Frank Partee	Louisa Partee	Gloria White
M. Angeline Penry Partee	Milton Partee	George White	George White
Grace E. White	Forest White	Isaac E. White	Hazel Dell McElmore White
Jane White	Jane E. Alison White	Maggie McCall White	Robert White
Rowan White	Zepha White	Otho Whiteside	Titus Whitworth
Anderson Williams	Fannie Williams	Febby Williams	Otis Livingston Williams
Herman Wilson	John Wilson	Margaret Wilson	Annie Winford
Celesta Winford	Ella Winford	Ellen Clement Winford	Dorsey Winford
Maggie Winford	Laura Winford	Tallie Winford	Galva L. Williams Witherspoon
H. W. Witherspoon	Harold Adorn Witherspoon [1]	Virginia Theodoric Cowan Witherspoon	J. T. Wright
Julian Wright	Earnest Wooden	Eliza Herron Woody	Roosevelt Woody
Emma Workman	Evelyn T. Workman	Franklin Workman	James W. Workman
Lucinda Williams Workman	Charlotte Hodge Younger	Jeff Younger	Jeff Younger
Henderson Younger	Martha Younger	Nelly J. Carey Younger	Priscilla Younger

My Family Tree

The Storm

It seems every time you turn around, life or man has pushed you down

And you cannot take it anymore, and you try to figure out why your face is on the ground

You tell yourself I be damn and as soon as you dust yourself off

You are back on the ground again

Life is full of surprises, and you must watch out for the pros and cons

Life is like a roller coaster

Do not laugh at me

Do not cut your eyes my way

Do not mock me

You know I'm right

This world is not my home

I have a job to do while I'm down here

To find my reason

Maybe your storm has not knocked you down hard enough

Do believe it's coming, and you will say I be damn

Like the ones who appear on these pages before you

They got right back up, pushing through their storm with God on their side

Everybody will go through trials and tribulations

But knowing when you are in your storm

It does not matter why, how, or when the storm is coming

It's how you handle yourself through the storm

Just remember it's only a test

Are you going to pass or fail

Do you have God on your side while you go through your storm

That's what matters

Take your hands off it, and do not reach back

Then watch God move, and things will workout

Life is hard

People act funny most of the time

My Family Tree

Things not going your way

Jobs are hard to find and keep

Most of the time, people are full of jealousy and envy toward you and others.

Your money is not right, or your color is not right

Or they feel that you are not intelligent enough or funny to be around

Hell, do not give up

God is on your side if you let Him

Take God everywhere you go and most definitely through your storms

He can guide you through it

Life is one big game, and you must play to win

The women and men whose names appear on these pages did; why not you

By Stephanie M. Mason © 2024

My Family Tree

Living Testimonies

Editor's Note: Living Testimonies seek to capture the heart and soul of those we love. These are their stories, in their own words, describing their adventure called life. These testimonies express the highs and lows of life, a recounting of their time with us, providing a glimpse of their struggles and victories.

Theodore Cornelius Mason   **b. Thursday, April 4, 1967**

This is the testimony of my life so far:

I was a gift of life from GOD. I was born into the union of the late *William Anthony (Tony) Mason* [the son of the late *Napoleon Jefferson Mason and Hazel Lorraine Workman Mason*] and his wife, *the late Litha Ruth Walker Mason,* in Detroit, Michigan – Wayne County. My first and middle names are expressions of respect to the pastor of their church at that time, Theodore Cornelius Simmons, who had no male children.

In June 1985, I graduated from Renaissance High School in Detroit, Michigan – Wayne County and went on to earn a Bachelor of Arts degree with honors from Wayne State University in 1989. Since 1993, I have been working for Chrysler as an Assembly Line worker.

I was married on Friday, October 14, 1994 (and divorced – damn it, not soon enough!) to *Audrey F. Holloway Mason*. I have two wonderful children born in Redford, Michigan – Wayne County – my daughter, *Amber Rose Mason,* was born on Friday, June 19, 1998, and my son, *Anthony Jefferson Mason* (named from the middle names of his grandfather, great grandfather, and great-great-grandmother maiden name on my dad's side of the family), was born on Thursday, January 18, 2007.

I am a firearms enthusiast and a sports fan; especially the Red Wings and Tigers. It seems that I inherited my passion for baseball from my grandfather, *Napoleon Jefferson Mason,* nicknamed *"Poppy."* I love to cook, exercising, lifting weights, the outdoors and walking outside, writing and politics. I am often called a *smart ass*. I dispute that as an oxymoron since *asses* are generally considered dumb. Therefore, am I a smart ass or a dumb ass? But I am very knowledgeable and a well-rounded individual.

Now I have moved on with my life ".... I broke out of hell, meaning I got a divorce from the DEVIL HERSELF." Now, I am remarried to my very best friend, the love of my life, *Suzanne Maria Zeglen Mason*. *Suzanne* and I got married on Friday, September 1, 2017, in Novi, Michigan – Oakland County. 📖

My Family Tree

Stephanie Michele Mason   b. Friday, June 20, 1975

This is the testimony of my life so far:

In more ways than one I was a gift of life to my parents from GOD, whom we call by His Great Name *"I AM."* The gift was a two-way street, as I was blessed to have two loving, caring, and understanding parents – *Norma Jean Carey Mason and* the late *Eugene Napoleon Mason*. I was born in the **Temple of I AM** and anointed by our Pastor and Founder *(Bishop) Reverend Gary M. Simpson*. As of this statement, I am still an active member of the temple, sing regularly in the choir every Sunday and I am practicing becoming one of the lead singers in the church choir.

I am a product of the Detroit Public School System. From elementary through high School, I was in Special Education classes, as I had difficulties with reading and learning comprehension. I have struggled throughout my life with some difficulties more than most. At that time, it was very disheartening to have your teachers that were supposed to help you learn, but they really did not care about me. They did not try to encourage me to do better. I have been teased so badly by my peers and teachers they would put me down because I was left-handed and had a problem with reading, learning, and retaining information that I was ready to give up on school all together. Through elementary and middle school, the teachers would have me read aloud in class, so everyone could laugh at me including them. After my parents found out what was going on, they got my sister, my grandparents *(Hazel and Napoleon)*, my godparents *(Earlene Ray and Lee Ray)* and *Rev. Simpson* involved (my support team). My support team always stood by me and continually nudging me to strive to do my best. I had a very hard time dealing with it, but, with **I AM** helping me every step of the way, I knew I would be okay. I did not allow my learning and reading difficulties to deter me and continually looked for new ways to push through to achieve. After my dad passed, I was determined to be more pro-active with respect to my studies. I buckled down and kept my promise to all of them. All that teasing from my teachers and peers stopped when I started high school. I demanded respect like a normal student, and I got it.

Our godparents asked my parents if we (my sister – *Iris* and I) could call them uncle and aunt. They said, "It was fine by them." My godparents were a big part of our lives, all the way until they passed. My parents, godparents, and **I AM** always made sure my sister and I had everything we needed and more, and I truly do thank them, and I love you so much. My first car was given to me by my (godmother) *Aunt Earlene. Rev. Simpson* was a big part of my life, and I love him for the love he shows, the way he cares about people, and his passion for teaching about **I AM**. Thank you, Mommy, for loving, teaching and caring for me. My baby girl.

I graduated from J. R. King Elementary School, moving on to Winship Middle School and then to Redford High School. In my junior year at Redford, I also attended Crockett Vocational, Career, and Technical Center, because the school offered free classes in their Dental Assisting Program. I would go to vocational school in the morning and come back to Redford at noon for my regular classes. I graduated with a 3.6 GPA from Redford and a 4.0 GPA from Crockett in June 1995, with

My Family Tree

a Dental Assistant certification. In my senior year at Crockett, I served as an unpaid intern - Dental Assistant at the office of Dr. Eric Smith, DDS, on the west side of Detroit. At the same time, I entered a Dental Assisting competition for only high school students.

I competed in local, regional, state, and national levels. Among the tasks that were evaluated in my competition were Dental Terminology, Teeth charting, Periodontal charting, taking dental impressions and pour up models, mixing dental materials, mounting x-rays, naming instruments and what they were used for and setting-up for dental procedures. Shifting to a high focus on my studies and paying attention to everything in detail that was thrown my way, really paid off. I won at all four levels in my competitions. At graduation, I received from Crockett Academic Awards, Special Recognition Awards, Attendance Awards, Certificate of Appreciation and Participation in Mentoring to Middle School Students Awards, Certificate of Participation Awards, The WAVE Award, won a Scholarship and Certificate of Completion of the Dental Assistant Program. When I was in my senior year of high school, I only had one Special Ed class. In high school and after high school, I had a total of five surgeries done on my right eardrum (now I have an artificial eardrum), and sometimes I have problems hearing things because of too much background noise or recurring ear infections. I have loss some hearing in my right ear without having to use a hearing aid.

I began my college education at Wayne County Community College (WCCC). My intent was a career as a Radiologist. However, I was not comfortable at (WCCC) and left after a year and a half. While I was at (WCCC) I discovered my inner world and ability for poetry. I was still determined to get an education, so I enrolled at Baker College of Allen Park, on my birthday in 2007. Baker provided a much more comfortable and conducive atmosphere for learning than Wayne County Community College. I liked the way the staff members interacted with the students and the passion the instructors displayed in the classrooms. Their work experience provided a learning advantage. I graduated from Baker College June 2010 with an Associate of Applied Science degree in Health Information Technology with a 3.75 GPA. I wasted no time in my educational pursuits and enrolled again that fall to pursue a Bachelor of Science degree in Health Services Administration; graduating June 2012 with a 3.82 GPA. Each semester at Baker College I either made the Dean's List or the President's List. There was, for me, a sense of urgency, so I worked harder so that my name appeared on the President's List more than the Dean's List. There was also the incentive of a $20 gift card for making the President's List. At Baker I won three scholarships. I did not know at that time when I started at Baker College, that it was a high accelerated learning institution. What I mean by that is Baker's term was ten weeks during the winter and fall semesters, and nine weeks during the summer semesters to pass or fail. There is no doubt in my mind that **I AM** was with me every step of the way through my collegiate experience. Because of this there was no special treatment, even though in each class, I made sure to sit in the first row to hear my lessons better.

While at Baker College, I worked full-time and went to school full-time. Part of my degree requirement was volunteer services, for practical experience. I had to complete 340 hours of an externship that covered both of my degrees. The total hours were reduced by 60 hours because I worked in the dental field. Dr. Ben Go, MD, in Riverview, provided me with the opportunity to work in his office as a volunteer, working as a Receptionist and Medical Biller to gain more work experience. I updated and completed the diagnosis and procedure codes (ICD-9-CM and CPT codes) for their encounter fees ticket. I participated in a State of Michigan-mandated audit consisting of over 150 patients' database records with the pharmacist in Dr. Go's building for controlled substances. I utilized their E. Thomas database system to post insurance claims, prepared invoices for over 200 patients, and assisted in the preparation of an insurance company audit. Dr. Stuart Kirschenbaum, DPM in Detroit, provided me with the opportunity to work in his office as a volunteer; as Receptionist, working alongside Ms. Deborah Rose. I organized patient's medical records for the hospital submittal and reviewed them prior to surgical procedures. I also volunteered at Team Mental Health Services (TMHS) at all three locations – Dearborn Clinic, Southgate Clinic, and Eastern Market Clinic as an unpaid Administrative Assistant. Among my responsibilities was the development of an electronic tracking process system to monitor employees' work projects and volunteer hours. I also participated in a second audit, a State of Michigan-mandated audit, consisting of over 250 medical records. I created a newsletter using Microsoft Word that addressed healthy heart, healthy living, and healthy diet for their workers and patients. The Administrator at (TMHS) in Southgate stated, I was the first volunteer and student to perform a State of Michigan audit because I was willing to work, I learned their system very quickly, and because of the grades that I was receiving at Baker College. The Administrator at the Southgate Clinic stated that she wanted to offer me a job as an Administrative Assistant because of my work, but they were in a union, and the position had to be offered to a union person first before me. It was hard and I was tired at the end, but I did it.

One of my classmates *(Andrea Martin)* asked me, "How are you able to work full-time and go to school full-time and keep up in your classes, plus do your homework, have time to do your externships and find time to go to church and keep up with your house duties, go grocery shopping too and being on high pain medication and muscle relaxer too, taking them three times a day for your Thoracic Outlet Syndrome?" My response was, "…GOD keeps me going, and He keeps me focused on the things I need to get done. I was always taught to believe in GOD and His glorious works. I was taught that, if you take one step, GOD will take two steps with you."

I obtained certification through Detroit-Wayne County Community Mental Health Agency for the Health Insurance Portability Accountability and Act (HIPAA). I am a member of Health Information Management Association since 2008. I earned a Cardiopulmonary Resuscitation (CPR) with Basic Life Support (BLS), certified through American Safety and Health Institute. I maintain certification through Detroit-Wayne County for (HIPAA) in all three levels, Infection Control and Standard Precaution, I am certified through the Michigan Dental Association for Dental Radiographer, and certifications through VIVA Learning for Sexual Harassment Training, Harassment Training, Occupational Safety and Health Administration (OSHA) and Hazard Safety, Biochemical and Toxic Substances.

Since 1990, my work experience has included that of a Police Cadet (summer job), White Castle Restaurant, Northland Dental Center, and Eastland Dental Center as a full-time Dental Assistant. I also worked full-time as a Security Guard for American Axle, full-time at Guardian Armored Truck Security as a driver and nighttime Balancer, working on ATM machines at night and pick-up night drops in the banks. From there, I was hired at AIMCO Court Reporting as full-time Office Manager/Secretary. I have worked at seven different private dental offices, plus for a temporary

My Family Tree

service. I am currently working full-time as a Dental Assistant. I have been a Dental Assistant for over twenty years, and I had helped a few dentists built their practices from scratch. I started putting together my family tree in July 2000 and some of my family members call me the *Navigator* or *Historian* of the family. You can imagine that this is not the easiest project to take on, as some family members on both sides have been reluctant to provide assistance and information. It was a little disheartening to be rejected by some family members. Even though I told them who I was and explained what I was doing, some of them acted as if I wanted their social security number, credit card number or their banking information; or I was trying to get them to reveal a dark, dirty secret about themselves or others. All I wanted to do was show the history of each family member so we could learn from one another and learn our collective family history.

In 2004, my *Uncle Tony* (my dad's middle brother) directed me to one of his older cousins on his father's side, *Cousin Frances*, because he only knew his uncle's and aunt's names on his mother's and father's side. He felt that she could be more helpful with the family information since she knew more about them. *Cousin Frances* and her two oldest daughters *(Mildred and Maria)* and granddaughter *(Joneice),* who all hail from Winston-Salem, North Carolina – Forsyth County, started helping me. Before I had a chance to visit *Cousin Frances* and her family in Winston-Salem, I would call her all the time, asking questions about family members, ones that I knew little of or nothing at all. We would stay on the phone for hours at a time. When I got vacation time, I went down to the Greyhound Station to purchase a ticket to go see them. It was two weeks before Christmas, my early Christmas gift to myself. I was so excited to get a chance to see them and start my journey of learning about my family tree. The trip to Winston-Salem took about sixteen and a half hours, and I loved every minute of it. After I left Winston-Salem, I was full of information from both sides of the family and glad to receive the information and to see my dad's side of the family.

I got a chance to see the house my dad grew up in before my grandparents moved the family to Detroit and to see my great-grandparents' *(Big Grandmamma Hazel's* parents) house. The house was old but still standing as of today, which is a Historical Landmark. I also got a chance to read my great-grandfather's (*Grandpa Samuel*) big journal. The book was made from brown paper (from his time-period). While I was there, *Cousin Frances and Maria* (her second oldest daughter) took me to visit an old church on a long dirt road in the Fork Community within Mocksville, Davie County and behind this very old church was (Cedar Grove Baptist Church Cemetery) a cemetery full of *Masons* that were buried there on my dad's father and grandfather side.

Mildred took me to the old part of Salem and told me the history of the town. In the old part of Salem, white men sold and killed slaves. *Maria and Cousin Frances* took me to an Old Country Store where they sold fresh fruits, nuts, and vegetables and (old but good) candy in barrels, and the store cured their own meats. They took me to church with them and a gospel concert in downtown Winston-Salem. I really enjoyed myself with my cousins and learned a lot from them about the *Mason's*, the *Hege's*, the *Strickland's,* the *Peppers's,* the *Pledger's,* the *Sawyer's* and even the *Workman's* side of the family, which is my dad's mother's side of the family. I came home with a lot of homework to do. *Mildred* made some copies of old pictures from their family photo album, plus *Mildred* made copies of some of their recipes. *Maria* can cook and bake her butt off.

My Family Tree

Her food tastes like she has been cooking all day long, and it does not take her long to put a meal together.

This Southern family (in Winston-Salem) really surprised me by holding onto family traditions and passing them from generation to generation. They are a very close-knit family, and they talk to each other daily and if someone is in need, they would all come or call to see what they can do to help. These cousins are active in the same church and hold different duties within their church. They have Sunday dinners together after church every Sunday and have a Fish Fry every Friday as a family. The cousins told me, "This is one way which we keep the family close together." They go to each other's events, including the children's sporting events and hang out together too.

Part of the experience, of course, were family stories. One was about the night *Joneice* spent the night at her dad parents' house. She told us that she went to bed by herself and woke up with an old man sitting in a rocking chair next to the window looking at her, and she ran out the bedroom. She emphasized the story with the fact that she "…would never spend the night over there again."

Another story was one in which the three of them shared an experience *(Mildred, Joneice, and Ronnie)*. It took place in a small town where *Ronnie's* parents lived at. They told me the name of this town, but I could not remember it to save my life. In this town was an old cemetery where slaves and some of their families were laid to rest. Of course, it was just down the street from *Ronnie's* parents' house. Sometimes when it rains, the cemetery is the only place it rains, and no were else, most of the time. At night you could see black people, young and old, walking the streets, with some of them hollering, singing, working around their homes, dressed in old clothes like slaves wore back then. Cars would ride down the street, and the cars would go right through them. Since this strange experience happened twice, when they came to visit *Ronnie's* parents in the evening, they decided it would be best to leave before dark. *Joneice's* grandmother would "…say to them don't let the night catch you on your back." They all knew what she was saying.

My first travel coming from Winston-Salem to Detroit had its own moment of dread. The trip home was terrifying. The Greyhound bus stopped somewhere in Virginia off the highway, and it was dark. I overheard a black male passenger riding with us get into an altercation with a white female worker at McDonald's over his food not being ready. He pulled a knife on her in the restaurant. The manager saw what happened and call the police. The man left the scene before the police arrived.

Standing outside, by the bus, I overheard the driver talking as he was locking the door. He went into the restaurant. A few of us were waiting to get back on the bus when the man came up, asking where the driver was. We looked back towards McDonald's and we did not see the bus driver at all. He was in a hurry and needed his things. None of us could answer because we did not know. So, the man left, and a few minutes later, the driver showed up. The driver let us back on the bus, and before the driver could shut the door to the bus, both state and local police showed up, with a canine unit. We were asked to step off the bus again. One officer with a dog began a search of the bus because two other passengers reported that they had seen (the black male passenger) shifting through his bags, and they saw a lot of money and a lot of small bags with pills stuffed inside two big clear bags, before he got into an altercation with the McDonald's employee. I called the cousins and told them what was happening. My cousins said, "…if that bus has not moved in the next hour

My Family Tree

to call back, and they were praying for my safety." They would contact other family members in Virginia, which is an hour way from my location, to come and retrieve me. Either way, I was to call and let them know. Luckily, we would be on our way again, in less than 45 minutes. The officer and dog did find the man's bags with the items in there. I never did find out if the police caught up with the man, but he did not get back on our bus.

And to top the night off, I did not see them at first until we got back on the bus the second time. I spotted them as soon as I took my seat and lost my cookies (a form of not so mild hysteria). I told myself I cannot miss this bus, plus it was dark as hell out here, even with the golden arches lit up, and I have to be to work Monday. This bus has a lot of bugs! I do mean bigggg roaches crawling around and hissing at us. The other people on the bus did not care that the roaches were on the bus. I could not fall asleep, and I was glad I had some Kleenex in my coat pocket. I stuffed the Kleenex in my ears and pulled my winter hat down over my ears and tied my scarf around my mouth and nose. I pulled my socks over my blue jeans. Then I tucked my coat around me, and I pulled my sleeves in around my fingers tight. Yes, I looked crazy as hell but, as I said to myself, "…hey no entering here guys." I didn't want to be caught off guard if I fell asleep with them crawling in my mouth or in my clothes. I could not wait to get off that bus. Dammit I am sitting here riding with other people's unwanted family members. They need to control their family members and keep them in their damn section. They should have left them home this time. By the time I got off the bus, my damn fingers were hurting so bad from being balled up for such a long time, it was not funny.

June 19, 2014, I received an early birthday gift from my sister *Iris* and my brother-in-law, *James*. My nephew *James Russell Nicholas* ^{IV} was born the day before my birthday. He was only three pounds and seventeen inches long. A preemie, he was born a month and four days ahead of schedule. His nickname is *"Little Man"* or *"Yam Yam,* now it's *JJ."* Every time I see or hear my *Little Man,* I will say to him, "You are handsome, beautiful, intelligent, smart, a gentleman and an **I AM**. And he would smile at me every time. Now I see what *Rev. Simpson* meant when he told us that our dad wanted to come back through *Iris* or me. Dad chose *Iris*.

Just about every time *Little James* would cry, *Iris* would say, "…Dad, please stop crying. I do not feel well or what's wrong with you," and he would stop crying and just smile at *Iris* and me. Sometimes, I would say, "*Eugene,* please stop crying," and he would stop crying and just smile at *Iris*, Mommy, and me. We all have noticed that *Little James* would stop crying and just smile his little butt off at us. When he is not crying, he would be laughing like crazy, and he would be staring in one direction. We all knew it was Dad playing with him.

At first, his parents were going to name him, *Anthony Eugene,* or *Eugene Anthony*, but *Iris and James* changed his name at the last minute. *Anthony* was to represent *James'* brother who passed, and *Eugene* was to represent our dad – but they named him after *James*. I love that little boy like he is my son, too. I will make sure *Little Man* will be brought up in *("Thy Name")* the doctrine of **I AM**. *Little Man* is my heart. I love him like crazy, and sometimes I forget he is *Iris'* and *James's* child, because I treat him just like he is mine – and I hate to see or hear him cry; it breaks my heart or sees him getting in trouble with his parents. *Iris and Little James* look like twins, and sometimes, he displays my mean personality. *Iris* cannot stand it, but I love to watch him display my

My Family Tree

personality towards others. If someone gets after him for it, I am on their butts for it, because he is doing it for a reason, and I understand why.

Mrs. Tess Haney was the one who showed me how to do the family tree the right way. I changed the game on her a little bit, and she loves it because I am not doing a traditional family tree. Whenever *Mrs. Tess Haney* had a chance to help me out with tracking down family members, she would tell me when she was going to Washington, DC. She would go to the Congressional Library, or the Department of Commerce to search Federal Census records. She made copies and brought them back to me. I truly appreciate *Mrs. Haney's* help with this big project. *Mrs. Haney* is my Mentor and Co-Researcher. My sister *Iris, Mrs. Haney, and Mr. William C. Roberson* were invaluable, help with proofreading and other areas.

I did worked full-time for a full-service organization center with *Dr. Gloria J. Smith, DDS*. I was her personal Dental Assistant. *Dr. Smith* is an excellent dentist to work for and with, plus she is a true friend. I have other certifications through Detroit-Wayne County for Abuse and Neglect of Children, Dependent Adults, and Elder Adults; Anti-Harassment and Non-Discrimination Training for Employees; Anti-Harassment and Non-Discrimination Training for Leaders; Case Management and Supports Coordination for Service Providers to Adults with Medicaid; Case Management and Supports Coordination for Service Providers to Children with Medicaid; Child Sex Trafficking in America; Cultural Competence: A Foundational Course, Emergency Preparedness, Limited English Proficiency, Medicaid Fair Hearings, Local Appeals and Grievances; Medicare and Medicaid General Compliance Training; Medicare Fraud and Abuse; Person-Centered Planning and Individual Plan of Service for Direct support Professionals (Direct Care Workers); Person-Centered Planning with Children, Adults and Families; Recipient Rights, and Recovery-Enhancing Environment.

My previous location, we offer the community a full scale of services: Medical, Dental, Behavioral Health, Housing Services, donations- food, clothes, school supplies, women's personal hygiene products, baby formula and bottles, baby and adult diapers and shoes, Health Education, Clubhouse, Re-entry Support, Transportation Services, vouchers for bus tickets, transportation shuttle and the Pharmacy, they offer employment and school programs for adults. One food truck comes to deliver food, but not on Wednesday's. Wednesday's, another organization comes to feed the community while playing gospel music for the people. Once a week a truck drops off free diabetes testing strips and needles to the community. At the health center, 'No patients are turn away because they can't afford their treatments.' I did work for an organization that gives back to the community in so many ways. The people in the community were grateful that we are there to help them, and I came across a few friends there too.

I AM remove me from my full-time job to come back home to be my mother's full-time caregiver, her business manager, and be a part of her health care team. As I look at my life, I can truly say that I have a testimony. I am so thankful that **I AM** sit at the center of my life. I am trying my best to do God's work. I have been truly blessed and all praises are due unto **The Great I AM**. I will always praise **I AM** until I am back in **HIS** arms. I am currently working on my (Doctor of Philosophy) – PhD in history. I am so proud of my sister and our mother for always loving and caring. They are both my very best friends, and I love you both, sis and Mommy. 📖

My Family Tree

Iris Althea Mason Nicholas   b. **Monday, November 1, 1976**

This is the testimony of my life so far:

I was the second gift of life to my parents from **I AM,** and I, too, was blessed to have loving, caring, and understanding parents – *Norma Jean Carey Mason and the late Eugene Napoleon Mason.* I too, was born in the **Temple of I AM**, anointed by *(Bishop) Reverend Gary M. Simpson,* and remain an active member.

My education was through the Detroit Public Schools System. I graduated from J. R. King Elementary School, Edward Cerveny Middle School, and then Thomas M. Cooley High School. At J. R King Elementary I played the violin. At Cooley, I was on the Track and Field Team, Cross Country Team, but I was best known for my shot-put/disc efforts. I competed in the female division in local, regional, state and nationals and won all four levels. My secret was that I trained with the male division in high school and in college. I was a member of the swim team, with a mean backstroke and joined the Junior Reserve Officers Training Corps (JROTC). My Drill Team and I competed in local, regional, state and nationals and won all four levels. My Drill Team and I traveled to Washington D.C. to see the White House and the museums – Smithsonian National Air and Space Museum, National Museum of African American History and Culture, The National Archives Museum, National Gallery of Art, International Spy Museum, National Portrait Gallery, National Geographic Museum, National Museum of American History and United States Holocaust Memorial Museum.

At Cooley High I rose in rank, serving as Sergeant in my junior year. In my senior year I was a Lt. Colonel. The United States Army wanted me to enlist because of my rank in high school and because I scored very high on the military placement test. My recruiter at that time told me that if I joined the Army, I would enter as a Sergeant. He told me he needed my mother to sign a waiver, to allow me to go. My mother's reaction was "Hell no! Have you lost your mind?" I had not yet reached my 18th birthday. I graduated Cooley High School June 1994 in Detroit.

My godparents *(Earlene and Lee Ray)* were a big part of my sister and my life all the way until they passed. Our parents, godparents and **I AM** worked together to make sure we had everything we needed and more. And I thank them for it. *Rev. Simpson* was a big part of my life and I love him for the love he shows, the way he cares and his teaching about **I AM** and my mother is my heart. I love her so much for loving and teaching me, too.

Before I left to go to Wilberforce University in Dayton, Ohio – Greene County, *Stephanie* and I agreed to become Morticians. After I left for school *Stephanie* changed her mind and went in another direction. I was hoping she would come along for the ride. I enrolled at Wilberforce University in 1994, to pursue a master's degree in business and a Management degree to go along with a master's degree in Mortuary Science. It was my plan to become a Mortician, owning my own business. After, I started at Wilberforce, they did not offer the Mortuary Science Program anymore, so I knew I would have to transfer to another school to earn my degree. My Financial

My Family Tree

Aid did not come in time for my next set of classes. Now my plans had to change, and I returned home the following year.

Still on track somewhat, I enrolled at Wayne County Community College (WCCC) in 1998, to become a Paramedic. I had two classes with *Stephanie* at (WCCC). One of my classes with *Stephanie* was a math class. The teacher like me but hated *Stephanie*. *Stephanie* hated that teacher with a passion because he had a smart mouth when it came to her. The teacher found out that we were sisters. When it came time to have a test the teacher would move *Stephanie* or me away from each other and give us different tests. The teacher claimed that she was cheating off me. How was this so… if we had different tests? Now who the dumb ass? *Stephanie* stated, to me, the teacher, and the whole class, "…you sound like a fool, accusing me of cheating. If you were on fire, I would not spit on you to put you out. I would add more gasoline to watch you burn some more." The whole class start laughing at the teacher, and he was mad about it. But she had every right to go off on him. I am proud of her for standing up for herself because he accused her of cheating in front of the whole class and he was wrong for that. Like I said, who the dumb ass? She had witnesses concerning his behavior towards my sister and the way he handles things. As *Stephanie* and I was leaving the classroom, everybody stood up in class and walked out, and we all stood in line to drop his class that day.

The other class I had with my sister was a Paramedic class. The teacher liked both of us and told us that we had great personalities. "You ladies would make a great team and plus, you ladies have a weird sense of humor about yourselves to handle the job as Paramedics." We both did not like Wayne County Community College because a lot of the teachers did not give a damn about the students and how we were progressing in the class or how they presented their lessons to their students. Later, I attended Everett Institute and earned a certification in Medical Billing and Coding. I worked full-time while going to school part-time and completed a 200-hour externship at Providence Hospital in Southfield, Michigan. I graduated from Everett Institute in 2007, with two terms on the Dean's List. Providence had a hiring freeze that prevented me from joining their staff there.

Since 1995, I have worked various jobs – full-time at White Castle, as an Assistant Manager, full-time at TCF Bank as a Lead Teller, full-time as a Truck Driver for Panther local and out-of-state driving, full-time at Orkin as a Pest Control Technician, full-time as a Vault Teller for Guardian Armored Security and as a Security Officer at Metro Airport in Romulus. Currently, I serve as a Retail Clothing Manager, shifting between two suburban stores. Oh, I finally retired as a part-time Pantry Supervisor at Ford Field in Detroit. I had worked at Ford Field for over 12 years. Now I can spend more time with my family. Ford Field did send me to Ohio for catering events and it was good money to earn before I got pregnant with *Little James*.

In my early twenties, *Rev. Simpson* made a statement to my sister and me about our dad wanting to come back through one of us. I met *James* in 2007, at Ford Field, and we became good friends. Shortly after we started dating, he got the opportunity to advance his career at Motor City Casino and Hotel as a Lead Chef. We dated four years before he asked my mother, my *Uncle Tony* and me for my hand in marriage. We were married Saturday, June 23, 2012 at the **Temple of I AM,** *Bishop Gary Simpson* officiating.

My Family Tree

I told *James* that we were the second generation to be married by *Bishop Simpson*, in the name of **I AM**. *James* asked, "What I meant by that." I explained that my parents were the first couple to be married at the temple, by *Bishop Gary Simpson*; our friend, father figure, our pastor, and founder. For me, "…it would be an honor and a pleasure to take our vows before GOD and him." "We have known *Bishop Simpson* all our lives; he treats us like his own daughters, and it would do my heart good for him to marry us." *James*, of course said, "Yes."

You can imagine my joy being married to a wonderful man, my best friend, *James Russell Nicholas III*. Adding to that has been yet another blessing from **I AM**, nothing less than a beautiful, intelligent little gentleman and an absolute joy. He was born a preemie Thursday, June 19, 2014 in Royal Oak, Michigan – Oakland County. He was an early birthday gift to my big, but little sister. *James Russell Nicholas IV* was named after his father and grandfather. We call him *Yam* or *JJ*. I now see what *Bishop Simpson* meant when he said that dad wanted to come back through *Stephanie* or me.

I had a very hard pregnancy with my *Yam,* and **I AM** was with me. I had pre-eclampsia, and my cervix started shrinking, so the doctors had a hard time measuring my cervix. I was on bed rest throughout my whole pregnancy. Every time I turned around, I was in the hospital for this or that. One time they kept me for all most two months. I tried my best to persuade the nurses at the hospital to let me out or get me some food from outside the hospital with my credit card and for one of them to buy themselves something, too. The answer was always, "No, *Mrs. Nicholas* that would be going against hospital policies to do that for you and we can lose our job too."

Mom and *Stephanie* would come to visit me every day. I was glad when the doctor said I could leave my room for a few hours, but I had to stay in the wheelchair. When my few hours were up, I was brought back to my room. *Stephanie* took my only transportation out of my room and the hospital, too; I was mad as hell at her. The whole time, I would ask the nurses to bring me extra sheets, blankets, and towels to use for a rope to leave out my bedroom window of the hospital and use the wheelchair to make my get away. The night nurse would only make one round to my room at night, and no one would have to know I was gone until morning. My plan would have worked out well if *Stephanie* did not take the damn wheelchair back to the nurse's station. She knew I was up to something, so that is why she did it, to keep me there.

Every time *Little James* would cry, I would say, "…dad please stop crying, I do not feel well." The crying would stop, replaced by a smile. Other times I would say, "…*Eugene*, please stop crying," and that smile would appear. We *(Mom, Stephanie, Big James, and I)* have all noticed that his tears were replaced by a smiling face.

When *Yam* was a baby, *Stephanie* would hover over him like *Mother Hen* all the time. *James,* our cousin *Maria* (from Detroit) and me, we would tease her about acting like *Mother Hen.* She would say, "So, he is my baby, too." *Stephanie* would hover over other people who held *Yam* all the time and she would watch them like a *hawk*. And if she was over and *Yam* was laying down taking his nap, she was right there with him. Half of the time I could not even hold or feed my own baby because of her. *Stephanie* would have a fit if she were not spending enough time with him and she still acts like that now. *Yam* acts just like my sister - bad, hardheaded, and evil sometimes, but he is my baby. Damn you, *Stephanie!* (ROFL). *Stephanie* would run *James* and me over just to get to him every time, especially when he is crying or if he hurt himself or if he does not feel well and

My Family Tree

she spoils him too much. When *Yam* gets in trouble, he looks for her to save him, and *Stephanie* would save him most of the time. As *Little James* is getting older, she still watches over him like *Mother Hen*, she needs to know what school he is attending. I found out that Thomas M. Cooley is on the United States National Register of Historic place. To my first my best friend, my sister. Love you. 📖

James Russell Nicholas III   **b. Tuesday, March 16, 1977**

This is the testimony of my life so far:

I, too, was a gift of life from GOD, I was born to the union of *AlFreda Elaine Williams Nicholas and James Russell Nicholas II* (deceased). It has been a blessing to have loving, caring, and understanding parents like them. I am the oldest of the boys. I was born on March 16, 1977, in Detroit, Michigan - Wayne County.

I am the second oldest of their five children: I have an older sister, *Lashonia Williams* and three younger brothers born in order – *Anthony Nicholas, DeAndre Nicholas, and Donzel Murphy*. After my dad passed, my mother re-married to *Willie James Parker (aka Daddy Will)*, who has been a positive role model for each of us. *Anthony Nicholas* preceded us in death.

I am a product of the Detroit Public School System. I graduated from Louis Pasture Elementary School, Remus Robinson Middle School, and John J. Pershing High School in June 1994 in Detroit, Michigan – Wayne County. I did attend Oakland Community College to pursue a degree in Fine Cuisine, as a Sous Chef.

The jobs I have held from high school and after include working on the auto assembly line parts at a few hotels, part-time at a law firm, full-time at Ford Field as a Line Chef, and full-time at Motor City Casino and Hotel as a Lead Chef and as a Union Steward.

I met *Iris Althea Mason* at Ford Field in 2007 and we became good friends. While we were dating, I was fortunate enough to get an opportunity for advancement, working at Motor City Casino and Hotel in Detroit as a Lead Chef. We dated four years before I asked her mother, her *Uncle Tony, and Iris* for her hand in marriage. I found out that we would be the second generation to be married by *Bishop Gary M. Simpson* at the **Temple of I AM**. There is no question that I would do anything to make *Iris* happy, and we were married on Saturday, June 23, 2012, at the **Temple of I AM**.

Needless to say, I am married to a beautiful woman, who is also my best friend and the love of my life. We have been blessed by the addition to our lives with a handsome young man, *James Russell Nicholas IV*. He was an early birthday gift to my sister-in-law *Stephanie*. He was born a preemie on Thursday, June 19, 2014 (the day before her birthday).

The family and I were concerned about my wife's well-being while she was pregnant because she was diagnosed with pre-eclampsia along with having high blood pressure, and she was told to stay on total bed rest. *Iris* was constantly in the hospital for this or that. Every time she was admitted to the hospital, I stayed with her even when I had to go to work. I would come back to be with her.

My Family Tree

There were very high concerns that we could lose the baby or my wife or them both. The whole entire family on both sides, close friends, neighbors, co-workers, my wife's church family and the doctors working with her started praying for my wife and my son to make it through. I was there when the doctors decided to do an emergency C-section because my wife's blood pressure went up very high when they tried to induce her labor. My son's blood pressure dropped very low, almost off the monitor, and I was in the delivery room when my wife was having the emergency C-section. I am very thankful to GOD to have both of them here with us and doing very well. We would like to have one more child, but I would not like her to go through that again. I would rather have her and the little guy. I am currently working as a full-time Executive Chef, trying to provide for my family. 📖

Norma Jean Carey Mason   b. Wednesday, October 18, 1939

This is the testimony of my life so far:

I was born October 18, 1939, in Holden, West Virginia – Logan County to the late *Levonia Margaret Carey Cowan and Walter (Bill) White*. I was a gift of life from GOD, the **Great "I AM"** that works two ways – I for them and them for me. I am the second oldest of my siblings. My mother, my sisters, and nieces and nephews all call me *Jean*.

My mother was pregnant with me while she was living with her second oldest sister, *Isabelle Carey Morrison* and her husband, *Roscoe Morrison*[1]. They lived in Holden, West Virginia – Logan County. My mother asked her sister *(Isabelle)* if she would take care of me while she looked for work in Detroit. They treated me as if I were one of their daughters. Eventually, my mother found work at an airplane factory making parts for the military. During my stay with my aunt, uncle, and her family we became so close that sometimes I joined in with her children in calling her Mama. Yet, *Aunt Isabelle* would always gently correct me so that I would not forget my mother.

We lived in Post-Depression in the South. It was no walk in the park. We only had cold water running in the kitchen. Dirt roads (which we call country roads) were the norm. We had a pot-belly stove that was used for cooking, heating laundry water, bathing, and cleaning. We used a wash tub for baths, with all the children using the same water. The younger kids would bathe first, and then the older kids. When it was your turn, you could only hope and pray that the water was still warm enough and not too dirty. If not, you were crap out of luck! The kids bathed in the kitchen, and in the winter months, we bathe near the stove to keep warm. The adults moved the wash tub to their bedroom for their baths. We lived right next to the mountains. Looking at the mountains every morning and at night was breathtaking.

My Family Tree

The bathroom, of course, was the "outhouse." We went to the outhouse during the daytime, only. Us children were not allowed to go to the outhouse at night, and the adults were advised not to go to the outhouse at night, too, because you could fall in. Plus, there was always the danger of animals lurking around the house and outhouse – snakes, coyotes, and wolves. Since we were in the country, they roamed at will. The outhouse was about 150 feet away from the house, there were four steps to enter the outhouse, and it was the size of a small kitchen. Before night fall a pail (used for waste) would be brought into the house and placed in our parents' room. If your parents had boarders living with them, a pail would be place in their room, too. Every morning, the pails would be taken back to the outhouse, emptied out, washed out and left on the back porch to dry out.

The outhouse had one door with a moon shape carved in it to let in the sunlight and air. There were several seat sizes, from child to adult, carved into a flat board. Underneath the flat board were large holes dug out to hold the waste. Privacy was out of the question, as you could readily see the person sitting next to you. Plus, it was used by your neighbors as well as your family and boarders. The only time the outhouse did not smell so bad was in the wintertime.

Every three weeks, some men would come by in a big truck and remove the flat boards in the outhouse to reach the human waste. They had boots that came up to their knees. They had thick gloves and a lot of pails with thick ropes tied to the handles of the pails to collect the waste.

Back then, funerals were held at the house of a family member. The body was placed on ice to preserve the body. The body would be placed in the living room for viewing until time for burial. The undertaker would only hold the body no more than three days tops. Neighbors and family members would take turns sitting up with the body while the body was out for viewing. The main reason was to keep the vermin's (rats or other animals) from disfiguring the body. We did not have screens at the windows back then to keep them out. The houses back then were made of wood, so vermin's could squeeze or eat their way through. Besides, somebody had to keep adding ice underneath the body to preserve the body. When it was time for burial, the (wooden) coffin would be conveyed to the cemetery in a wagon with a horse pulling the wagon (later, the coffin was transported into the back of a pick-up truck).

It was not uncommon to have boarders living with your family. They would stay on the same floor or second floor only depending on the size of the house. The children were not allowed on the second floor or beyond the area where the boarder's room began for any reason. Usually, the boarder was someone who worked in the mines or had a job in town.

Once a week a man would come in our neighborhood selling fruits and vegetables from his truck. We also had a meat man who would stop by once a week, too. The milk man would sell us milk, butter, cheese, and eggs once a week. The ice man would deliver blocks of ice three times a week to the house. And if your parents did not want to buy from them, we had a small Country Store in the middle of town.

Back then, we had an Old Country Store that sold everything you needed, and today, it is known as a grocery store or Walmart. In my day, we had a medium size icebox, made of wood. The block of ice was placed at the top of the icebox to keep things cold. We had a pan in the icebox that would collect the water from the melted ice and used for cold drinking water.

My Family Tree

As a child, I do not know if it was just a working-class thing, but every Monday in the working-class homes in the North and South was wash day, and that is how (black and white) women made extra money for their household by washing other people's laundry. My *Aunt Isabelle* and other women in the area would get up early in the morning and start washing laundry. For us, Mondays meant cold leftovers from Sunday dinner, sometimes with chips, and that was our dinner because it was the quickest and easiest meal to prepare because wash day was hard labor and long hours. We used Chamber Lye or Black Soap to wash our clothes, and that soap would eat our skin up. We did not have washers or dryers at that time. We had to wash our laundry in boiling water over the pot-belly stove. We used a long wooden stick to move the laundry around in the water while it was boiling. Then, we had to transfer them to a washboard with a long wooden stick. The washboard was used to scrub the clothes, towels, blankets, and sheets. All items had to be rinsed twice. All clothes, towels, blankets, and sheets had to be hung on a line to dry out and then ironed. The iron was placed over the pot-belly stove to be heated up. We had to iron everything because our clothes were made from hard fabric, not the cheap stuff we have today.

Movies were an experience all its own. Yes, we could go to the movies, but with restrictions. We had to buy our tickets, then walk around to the back of the theater, up the stairs, and sit on the balcony. The nice thing was that the movies were only a quarter.

Walking or riding the bus was sometimes our main form of transportation. Very few blacks had cars in those days. We could step on the bus to pay our fare, then turn around, step off the bus, and walk to the back of the bus to get a seat. We had to sit in the back of the bus. If there were not enough seats for the white passengers, the driver would re-arrange the seats to accommodate the white passengers, and sometimes, you could be put off the bus. And if that happened, you had to wait for the next bus, or you walked to your destination. It was not uncommon for us (blacks) to be put off the bus with no refund. If you refused to get off the bus, the driver would not move the bus and he would not hesitate to call the cops on you.

Sometimes, we could sit in the back of white-owned restaurants. In contrast, other white owners refused to let us in. If we wanted something to eat from that particular restaurant, we would have to walk around to the back door to place our order and pick-up our food there, and then we had to leave. You did not stand around once you got your food. If you did, the restaurant owner did not hesitate to call the police to remove you from the premises or sometimes, they would arrest you just for the hell of it. And if the police officers did not arrest you, you were told not to come back, otherwise there would be trouble.

I was six years old when I moved to Highland Park, Michigan – Wayne County, to live with my mother and older sister. It was my first time meeting my mother, my older sister, *Roxie,* and my father. My dad introduced me to his side of the family. My sister and I were raised in two different households in Holden. My sister was raised in the Boarding House (like a hotel) with *Aunt Vesta Carey*, her father, and his family in Holden, West Virginia. They had running water throughout the whole house. The showers were in the basement or outside behind the house for the miners or other people living there (the showers outside in those days were made using a medium-height wooden fence with a door, a pail with a lid filled with water on a platform above your head and a

My Family Tree

rope to control the water flow from the pail), but the showers were not to be used by family members.

My mom used to work as a Domestic Worker at the Boarding House in Holden. That is where she met my dad. When she became pregnant with me, the owner of the Boarding House wanted to fire her because she was missing so many days at work. She told *Aunt Isabelle* that she did not like working there and that the job did not pay enough to support herself, now with two children. It was always a struggle to keep food on the table, put clothes on our backs and pay bills too. Once she stopped working at the Boarding House, my mom lost contact with my dad until she ran into one of his friends (a former co-worker) who told her that he had found a job in Cleveland, Ohio.

My education was through the Detroit Public Schools – Crosman Elementary, Hutchins Middle School, and Central High School in Detroit, Michigan – Wayne County. While I was at Central High, I was interested in and joined the tennis team. I graduated from Central High School in June 1956 in Detroit.

My first job was as a Domestic Worker working with my mother at Catholic Social Services for two years. I also worked at Carl's Diner as a Dishwasher for two years. While working at Carl's Diner for a year and a half, I applied for a Nursing Assistant job at the United States Department of Veteran's Affairs Health System (VA Health System) in Ann Arbor, Michigan. It took a while for the VA to contact me by mail. I went in for the interview, and I was hired right there on the spot as a full-time Nursing Assisting. I started training as a Nursing Assistant the following week.

While I was working at Carl's Diner, I experienced racial cruelty from the owner's niece. The owner's (*Carl's*) niece waited until I bent down to pick up a large container of soap off the floor in the kitchen of the diner when she poured boiling HOT water on my back. She told me she did it because she "…just wanted to see if a light-skinned nigger could turn red." *Carl* came into the kitchen just in time to hear and see what his niece had said and done to me. *Carl's* niece tried to lie about what happened, and her statement was, "…it was an accident because I thought my customer was trying to leave without paying their bill." *Carl* told her to "…stop lying because he had heard and seen what his niece did." I was not thinking when this happened because I was in total shock and in a lot of pain (my back was on fire). I did not care it was in the dead of winter (I just needed to cool off and stop my back from hurting). I was trying to run out of the back door of the kitchen, when *Carl* ran and caught me before I exited out of the back door. *Carl* told his niece to get his wife. He was fussing and cussing at his niece because of her behavior towards me. *Carl* stated to his niece, "…after you get my wife, go directly to my office and stay there." His wife came running into the kitchen and found out what happened; she was mad as hell at her niece for what had happened. They both looked at my back and told me that my back was deep red and "…needs medical attention right now." *Carl* told his wife to get me to their doctor. Their doctor had an office right above the restaurant. *Carl* stated to me, "…we will talk to your mother later and tell her what happened to you." When I was able to come back to work, *Carl* told me they had fired their niece for her behavior towards me. He apologized and informed me that my medical bills were being taken care of and that he would pay me for the whole time I was off from work, and he did.

My Family Tree

In my youth, children were never allowed to be around adults when they were talking because it was a sign of disrespect (in their minds, at that time, a child needed to stay in a child's place). Children had no business in adult conversations, so we did not know anything about adult business. In my day, there were only two classes of society: the rich (today's society, more than not means, middle class) and the poor. Back then, there was no middle-class society. The poor made do with what we had, trying to make life as comfortable as possible, and we were thankful for getting through each day. We only got new dresses on our birthdays or at Christmas time; other than that, it was always hand-me-downs. Our Christmas gift usually consisted of one toy, three pieces of fruit or nuts, one pair of new shoes, and one dress.

My parents did not have the money to send us to college. There was no such thing as Financial Aid or Government Grants to help us with college fees. There was only money available for important things like paying the rent and buying food. A lot of blacks back then did not own their homes or had cars. So, I decided to work for the VA Health System because they were providing for me to go back to school as a Nursing Assistant, which was both an opportunity and a blessing rolled into one. They sent me to school to study Nursing Assisting, and then they sent me back to school again for advanced training as a Nurse. I moved up steadily, serving in the Surgical Unit and Recovery Unit, then later became Head Nurse in the Intensive Care Unit.

The Detroit riots began on Sunday, July 23, 1967. My supervisor and her boss asked my co-workers and me, who lived in Detroit, to stay at the hospital because they were worried about our safety. I told both of them that I had to pick up my younger sisters because our mother was still working, and they were waiting for me. I told my boss that I would see her in the morning. She begged me to stay. The next day, the VA made it mandatory that all workers who lived in Detroit and the surrounding area of Detroit could not leave the hospital for any reason and that the hospital would board and feed us.

My mother used to work for *Rev. Gary Simpson* as his housekeeper when I was younger. Before I got married to *Eugene*, I would visit the **Temple of I AM** with my mother and my sisters after I got off from work on Sunday afternoons. One Sunday, *Rev. Simpson* came to me and told me that he would like for me to "...come to church dressed up" one Sunday. For whatever reason, I did as he asked and joined the temple in the summer of 1965, three years after the doors of the church were opened. The temple was then on Joy Road and Livernois in Detroit. In the winter of that same year, I met *Eugene Napoleon Mason*. We courted for several months before he asked for my hand in marriage. We were married Saturday, July 1, 1967, in the backyard of *Rev. Simpson's* home on Joy Road and Livernois (church services were held in his basement at that time). Ours was the first wedding ceremony performed in the temple, in the name of **I AM**, with *Reverend Gary Marcus Simpson* officiating.

After I got married, my dad called me and told me that I had two half-brothers that he would like me to meet. I got the chance to meet one of my half-brothers, *Randy White,* at my dad's house in Cleveland, Ohio - Cuyahoga County. My other half-brother, I did not get a chance to meet him before he passed. My dad stayed in touch with me until he passed. He asked one of his younger brothers *(Uncle John)* to check on me and my family since we both lived in Detroit. *Uncle John* also came by the house once a week to check on us.

My Family Tree

During my first pregnancy, I took time off from work at the VA. Our first child, *Rodney Allen Mason,* was born *on* Saturday, January 12, 1974. He was born with Newborn Respiratory Distress Syndrome and only survived four days because his lungs were not fully developed. In my heart, I felt that there would be no other children in our lives. *Rev. Simpson* came to me and said,…"I want you to lay your maternity clothes on the throne of **I AM**." He went on to explain, "…you will bear more children." Eight months later, I was pregnant with our second child, *Stephanie Michele Mason,* born Friday, June 20, 1975. After she was born, I retired from the VA Hospital in Ann Arbor, Michigan – Washtenaw County. One year and five months later, our third pregnancy resulted in the birth of *Iris Althea Mason*, born on Monday, November 1, 1976. Our children were born in Detroit, Michigan –Wayne County.

I worked for the VA for eleven years and retired to be there for my family. I would not go back to work until both girls were in school full-time. It was then I began to work at Gesu Private School part-time and then move to full-time, where I have been working there for thirty – eight years; now, I am retired, enjoying my golden years not punching someone's clock.

We sent *Stephanie and Iris* to the **Temple of I AM** for Pre-Kindergarten School before they entered Kindergarten at J. R. King Elementary School in Detroit. Our goal was to get the girls used to being away from home, to learn new things, to be around other children, and to get a good head start in school.

As of this writing, I have survived my husband *(Eugene)*, our only son *(Rodney)*, my three sisters-in-law *Peggy Mason, Euphonia C. Mason Jackson, and Litha Ruth Walker Mason*, my children's grandparents on both sides, my parents – *Levonia and Walter,* and *Eugene* parents – *Hazel and Napoleon,* and my two gifted and full-hearted nephews *Abdul Rafeeq Salahuddin and Stephen Idel Cowan[1] (Steve)* and my children's godparents *(Earlene Jackson Ray and Lee Ray)*, my brother-in-law's *William Anthony Mason (Tony) and Robert Stanley Mason (Bobby)*. The girls' two spiritual godmothers from the **Temple of I AM**, *Shirley Jeane Sims and Flora Mae Tilley-Thomas,* and all my aunts and uncles, grandparents, and a handful of cousins on both sides of the family have also departed from our midst.

Earlene and Lee were a blessing to my family in so many ways; only **I AM**, *Eugene*, the girls, and I knew. **I AM** sent us angels to help us along the way. They were always there for us through thick and thin. I thank them and love the times they shared with my family. They were more than just godparents to our daughters, for they were dear friends; they were family – our family.

When *Eugene* passed, and *Steve* was much older, he would come by to help me fix little things around the house, and he helped me when I had problems with my car. *Steve* even talked to the girls like a big brother would, about staying street smart, staying in school, and watching out for these guys out here, "….and I quote dead beats, so and so." *Stephanie* and I were at the **Temple of I AM** on a Sunday afternoon when *Steve* gave his life to **I AM** in the summer of 2009 when he became a member of the temple. *Steve* loved working with his hands on any project, even if it wasn't his project. What I had seen and heard from my neighbors and at church was that he was a loving, caring, very dependable individual who loved being around positive-spirited people. He always had been a very good listener, a problem solver, and a very good thinker. My neighbors called him *Mrs. Mason's* nephew, who knew how to fix it or knew someone who could fix it at a

My Family Tree

low price." *Steve* loved to sit and talk to his elders, especially my neighbors (*The Fords and Mr. Wayne (Bob) Outley),* all day long. My church family reports that he knew the Bible front and backward. He would not hesitate to quote scriptures from the Bible right there on the spot. He has shown me how to fix things I did not know how to fix, using less money. *Steve* developed a gift that was passed from his grandmother *(Levonia)* to his grandson on how to read people. I miss talking and working with him.

Yes, you should be aware that I have been blessed in so many ways, not the least of which I have been able to see both of my daughters grow into beautiful, well-adjusted, and positive young ladies. I watched the girls graduate from high school and college with good grades. I am proud of my daughters and very thankful that they have traveled down a positive path in life, guided by the grace of **I AM** and His mercy. My love for them is made even greater by their devotion and attention to me in my life. My daughters come forth to help me in any way they can, and my love for them is without measure.

In my life, I have been a witness to many of their achievements and celebrate their advancement as they move through life. I stood a witness to my older daughter, *Stephanie's* purchase of her first property in the Downriver area. I stood to witness my younger daughter *Iris* get married on Saturday, June 23, 2012, to a good man, *James Russell Nicholas ^{III}*. I stood a witness to the birth of an absolute bundle of joy, my grandson, *James Russell Nicholas ^{IV}* and I am thankful knowing that he will be brought up in the name of **I AM**. *Little James* was originally named *Anthony Eugene Nicholas*, but *Iris and James* changed his name at the last minute. I stood a witness to *Iris and James'* purchase of their first property in Detroit.

There was a tense moment for all of us – *Stephanie, James, and* me. We were concerned because of the problems *Iris* was experiencing with her pregnancy. The doctors did not know if the baby would survive through the pregnancy or if she would have any more children, and there was the added concern for her own well-being, too. The combined prayers of our families, our **I AM** family, close friends, and neighbors were raised on behalf of the mother and child. The blessings of **I AM** has them both with us, happy and healthy today.

When it concerns the **Temple of I AM,** I took notice that I am one of the oldest living members, next to our pastor, *Bishop Gary M. Simpson.* I am the *"Mother of the Church"* not because of my age but because I hold the distinction of being the last remaining original *"Charter Member"* of the church corporation. I still serve as one of the Offering Collection Clerks, happy in my continued service to GOD in any way I can (**The Great "I AM"**). Since *Bishop Simpson* passed Monday, October 5, 2020, now **I AM** is the last living Charter member of the temple.

My hobbies include working in my garden and making repairs around the house (hanging ceiling fans, drop-down ceilings, painting, laying tile, grout work, minor plumbing work, minor cement work, snaking out the main drains in the basement, building cabinets, and drawers, or re-leveling the kitchen floor). I love working outside in the spring and summertime. I take joy in cutting the grass, re-shaping the bushes, pulling weeds, and edging the grass. In the fall, one might find me cleaning out the gutters around the house and the garage or raking leaves. In the wintertime do not be surprised to see me shoveling the snow. I also love helping my neighbors with their projects with *Steve* as my helper when he is not too busy doing his thing. There is also my love of sewing

My Family Tree

and leather work, making purses, belts, wallets, and coin purses of varies sizes, Bible covers, house shoes, and upholstery work – and do not forget I love shopping! I love shopping period on good sales!

I find joy in helping others. At work, if there is any food left after lunch, we must throw it out. It cannot be saved for later use. I have asked for permission to give the food to my family members, church members, and my elderly neighbors to help them out. I shared my garden produce with my church members, my family members, and my neighbors. We are all struggling to get through this life, and I do not mind helping in any way I can. I have always been taught that if you are blessed, pass it on, and GOD will bless you tenfold. My sisters, girlfriends at church, my neighbors, and sister-in-law *(Litha)* have all come to call me *"The Handy Lady." Litha and I* are close like sisters and we consider each other as sisters.

As I said before, I have been blessed in so many ways. When *Eugene* got sick, I got a part-time job at Gesu Private School to help with the bills and groceries. *Eugene's* pension from Ford Motor Company was stretched very thin. After he passed, the company reduced his pension amount for the family. Two months later I asked the School Principal, *Sister Stella,* if there might be a full-time job there for me. Her response was, "…yes, just for you!" When the girls were old enough, the pension checks shifted into their names. The girls would take $50 from their checks and give me the rest, saying, "…Mommy, use the rest of the money to pay the bills and anything else you need. We all have to live, and we are willing to help out." *Stephanie* got a summer job as a Police Cadet in middle school and then started working at White Castle. Every month *Stephanie* would sign over the whole pension check to me, and she would add money in to help with the bills. *Stephanie* helped me by buying *Iris* and her school clothes and school supplies. *Iris* got a job at White Castle and started doing the same thing as *Stephanie*. To this day, they both give me extra money just because, and I thank them for their love and help. I was asked why I didn't remarry; my statement was, "…*Eugene* was my partner for life, and he was my first and last love.

We work together as a team, even though *Stephanie and Iris* have their own place to maintain. *Stephanie* lives an hour away, and both of the girls work full-time. Yet, Stephanie spends every weekend with me until Monday morning. *Stephanie and Iris* check up on me every day, and throughout the day since now, I am retired and getting older. *Stephanie and Iris* help me with house chores, buying my medicines and groceries, paying for all my doctor's visits, plus cooking and baking. *Stephanie* even helps *Iris and James* and loves to babysit *Little James* for them. *Iris* is married with a child, and she works a full-time job, too. Between the three of them *(Stephanie, Iris, and Big James),* they make sure I get to my doctor's appointments, remind me to take my daily medications, drive me to church, pay for my hair to be done, and drive me to family events and shopping too. Both girls stated to me every time, "…that my money is no good to them when I'm with them or with anyone else and for me not to worry that they have me cover on everything I need or want." Even *Little James* keeps an eye on me too, and he would tell on me, too. If they are unable to take me somewhere they would arrange for help through family members, neighbors, or close friends. As I am getting older the people in my life that are irreplaceable dear friends besides my daughters, my grandson and my son-in-law *(Big James) –* (Rev. Gary M. Simpson – *deceased), Karen Boyd, Helen Gross, Michele Lipscomb, Mrs. Ethel Jones and Mr. Lawrence Jones, Mrs. Tess Haney, Mrs. Velma Thweatt, Mrs. Druel Outley, and Mr. Wayne Outley, (Mrs.*

My Family Tree

Frankie Ford and Mr. Cleophas Ford – deceased), (Mrs. Earlen J. Ray and Mr. Lee Ray – deceased), (Minister, William C. Roberson – deceased), Mrs. Hattie Lue Carpenter – deceased), Barbara Brown – deceased), Bob Lenning, Gloria Jean Smith, Courtney Dillard, Valerie Beavers, Linda Tibbs, Chantelle Hearns– my Caregivers and *(Mrs. Doris Mullins – deceased),* just to mention a few. Words cannot express the depth of my love and joy they bring and brought to my life. With help from them, I am ever thankful to **I AM** to have daughters, *Big James and* my grandson, *Little James,* and dear friends who give love and a helping hand, always showing love and compassion, true concern, and true friendship towards my family and me.

Iris and James got slick on me; they had an alarm company come out here to install cameras around the front and backyard to keep a close eye on me and my four-legged friend *(Ikey Jr)* to see what we were doing and what direction did we go in on foot. The alarm system talks to me, and the damn thing has the nerve to call help for me. They do not play fair. All three of them can watch *Ikey Jr* and me on their cell phones, and if I get locked out of the house, they can use their cell phones to open the doors. Plus, they can answer the door for me, play music for me, and they can control the temperature in the house, too. Thank you, and I love you girls, *James and Little James.* Even *Little James* talks to the alarm system and the system answers him back. Now, since I am in my late golden years, my daughters do everything for me – like making sure everything runs smoothly around the house; all I have to do is put on my clothes, eat, take my meds, and enjoy myself, plus do what I want to. The girls and *Big James* cook for me and fix things around the house, too. *Stephanie* is my live-in caregiver, a part of my health team, PCT – trained by my doctors, ground-keeper, and business manager. Thank you, Tesiley Ash, RN, and Jigar Shah, PT, for all of your services. All three of them got slick on me again. Iris, James, and Stephanie had cameras installed in the house to keep a very close eye on me. I found out the schools I graduated from are on the United States National Register of Historic Places. 📖

Muslimah Muwwakkil (Aunt Roxie)   b. Thursday, October 1, 1936

This is the testimony of my life so far:

I was a gift of life from GOD, born to the late *Levonia Margaret Carey Cowan and Newell Virgil Moore.* I was born October 1, 1937, in Holden, West Virginia – Logan County. I am the oldest of my siblings.

When I was eight years old, I moved to Highland Park, Michigan, to meet my mother and my younger sister *(Jean)*. My early years (until age 8) were spent with my father, his family, and *Aunt Vesta Carey* in a Boarding House, knowing nothing of my mother and younger sister, *Jean.* I learned she lived with other relatives – *Aunt Isabelle and Uncle Roscoe* until she was six years old.

Life in the Boarding House was something of a fantasy world. I was dressed in beautiful dresses with shoes to match. My hair was always done up beautifully every day. I had everything I wanted living with my *Aunt Vesta,* my dad, and his family.

My Family Tree

When I was eight, I was told that I would be moving to live with my mother and younger sister, in Highland Park, Michigan. Life was different living with my mother. My sister *(Jean)* and I grew close. Life had taken a turn from being okay to being difficult when my mother got married to *James Avery Cowan*. I did not get a chance to see or talk to my dad and *Aunt Vesta* as much as I wanted to, since momma had married *Mr. Cowan*. He was a mean and selfish man towards *Jean* and me, because we were not his daughters.

I was educated through the Detroit Public School System - Crosman Elementary, Hutchins Middle school, and I graduated Central High school June 1954 in Detroit. Before the age of eighteen I moved out. I asked my mother for *Jean* to come with me and she said, "No." I wish I could have taken *Jean* with me, so she did not have to deal with our stepfather's foolishness. I could not live with them anymore because of his behavior towards me, but I wish I could have taken *Jean* with me. I prayed for my sister every night that she would be okay, and I could not wait until she was old enough to move away from him. I started living with other family members until I had enough money to move on my own. Later, I moved to Los Angeles, California, to start a new chapter in my life.

I met and got married to *Marvin Guyse* Monday, August 19, 2002, in Hanford, California – Kings County. Based on our conversion to Islam, my husband and I changed our names in 1976 to *Muslimah Muwwakkil and Abdul Muwwakkil*. My life was blessed with five beautiful children, one of whom has departed this plane of life.

Our first child, *Abdul Rafeeq Salahuddin* was born Tuesday, May 7, 1957. GOD took him home at the age of 26, due to complications from *Sickle Cell Anemia*. He was a Physician's Assistant. Our second child, *Ebony Latifah Salahuddin Saliba* was born Monday, January 18, 1960. She owns her own hair salon – Xtentsion Connection. Our third child, *Sabreen Lavonia Salahuddin* was born Saturday, January 8, 1966. She works at the State of California Department of Corrections as a Substance Abuse Director for over twenty years. Our fourth child, *Ameerah Salahuddin Lydick* was born Monday, January 29, 1968. She is a Homemaker and Accountant. Our fifth child, *Marvinah Nyderah Salahuddin Sbinowitz* was born Wednesday, May 23, 1973. She is a Radiology Technician and Medical Assistant. Our children were born in Los Angeles, California. *Ameerah* and her husband *Tariq Lydick* have four children – *Hamazah Lydick,* was born Thursday, July 27, 1989; *Ridhwana Lydick* was born Saturday, July 13, 1991; *Safadin Lydick* was born Monday, January 25, 1993 and *Mustafa Lydick* was born Saturday, July 2, 1996 and my great-grandchild, *Melike Lydick* was born Saturday, August 24, 2013. All my children, grandchildren and great-grandchild were born in Los Angeles, California. My son-in-law, *Tariq,* is in the Insurance Business.

I don't know anything about going to college until I was in my late 20's. Our parents did not have the money to send us to college. We had to work hard to get things done, with tough love and challenging times facing us. Life was hard back then, but we survived, and it made us better people. I wish our children were raised a little more around my mother's side of the family because our children know so little about my side of the family. My niece *Stephanie* (from Michigan) one day sent my husband and I a rough draft of the family tree she was doing, and that got us started with Ancestry.com, looking for family members. After a few years later, I found out that I have two other brothers. One brother talks to me, and the other brother has no desire to communicate; but that is fine with me. I found out that I had two stepbrothers because my husband and I start doing the family tree.

I retired in 1992 from the State of California Department of Corrections as an Administrator and presently enjoy life with my husband in Jacksonville, Florida – Duval County. Life is good, all because of GOD being in my life. I found out that the schools I graduated from are on the United States National Register of Historic place. 📖

Angela Evelyn Bassett Vance   **b. Saturday, August 16, 1958**

This is the testimony of my life so far:

Angela was born August 16, 1958 in Harlem, New York – Manhattan County. She was a gift from GOD; she was born into the union of her parents, the late *Betty Jane Gilbert Bassett and Daniel Benjamin Bassett II*. The blessing was a two-way street, as she was blessed with loving, caring, and understanding parents. She is the oldest of her siblings.

Her education included Jordan Park Elementary School and then Disston Middle School. *Angela* was bussed to Azalea Middle School and went on to Boca Ciega High School. Her higher education included a bachelor's degree in African-American Studies from Yale University in 1980 and a master's in fine arts degree in 1983.

While at Yale, she met the man with whom she desired to spend the rest of her life with, *Courtney Bernard Vance.* Needless to say, they took some time to get to know one another before he asked for her hand in marriage. They were married Sunday, October 12, 1997. She has a sister – *D'nette Bassett,* and three other- sisters - *Martha Jean Bassett, Linda Bassett, and Lisa Carter. Angela and Courtney* have a beautiful set of twins – *Bronwyn Golden Vance and Slater Josiah Vance* was born Friday, January 27, 2006.

As an actress, it seems she has become known for her roles portraying some of life's most resilient, progressive and well-known black women, including *Tina Turner* in *"What's Love Got To Do With It,"* as well as *Betty Shabazz* in *Malcolm X and Panther, Rosa Parks* in *"The Rosa Parks Story," Katherine Jackson* in *"The Jacksons: An American Dream,"* and *Voletta Wallace* in *"Notorious. Angela* began her film career in the mid-80s after graduating from Yale. She did not find any stability in the industry until the 1990's when she appeared in films nearly every year. As of 2000 there seemed to be a progression, over the next ten years, as *Angela* appeared in a film nearly every year. In 2010, her contribution to the industry was recognized with an *Oscar nomination*. She is presently featured in the NBC series, "911," She is an avid supporter of programs for the Arts, particularly in support of youth. *Angela and Courtney* annually attend events for children with diabetes and those in foster homes. *Angela* is an active *Ambassador* for *UNICEF* for the USA. *Angela and Courtney* are big supporters of the *Royal Theater Boys and Girls Club* in her mother's hometown of St. Petersburg, Florida – Pinellas County.

My Family Tree

Dr. Henry Louis Gates Jr. and his team *(Finding your Roots by PBS.org)* worked on her family tree. They track *Angela's* DNA to her great-great grandparents on the *Bassett and Stokes* side. *Angela* found out that her DNA has traces to the Sub-Saharan Africa, 32% Nigeria, 15% Benin, 9% Cameroon Congo, 8% Mali, 6% Southeastern Bantu, 4% Ivory Coast/Ghana, 2% Senegal and 1% South Central hunter gatherers. There is a definite Pan-African genome, with emphasis on what is now Nigeria. At this time, the family members had a hard time contacting her, due to her work schedule about documenting her living testimony for the family tree. The information gather on *Angela* is all public knowledge. 📖

Courtney Bernard Vance   **b. Saturday, March 12, 1960**

This is the testimony of my life so far:

Courtney was a gift of life from GOD, he was born into the union of his parents to *Leslie Anita Daniels Vance and the late Conroy Vance*. He was born March 12, 1960, in Detroit, Michigan – Wayne County. *Courtney's* father was a Grocery Store Manager/Benefits Administrator for Chrysler Corporation, and his mother was a Librarian.

His early education was through the Detroit Country Day School, a private college preparatory institution in Michigan. *Courtney* would go on to Harvard University. At Harvard University, he was already working in a Boston Shakespeare Company, graduated in 1983 with a Bachelor of Arts degree. He got his Master of Fine Arts degree through the Yale School of Drama graduated in 1986. It was at Yale that he met his future wife and fellow artist, *Angela Evelyn Bassett*.

Their courtship advanced and transitioned to marriage October 12, 1997. They have two lovely children (twins) – *Bronwyn Golden Vance, and Slater Josiah Vance* was born Friday, January 27, 2006.

As an actor, *Courtney* have been nominated for two *Tony* (stage performance) awards. His first was for his role in August Wilson's Pulitzer Prize winning play, *"Fences."* He was later nominated for his role in John Guare's *"Six Degrees of Separation."* *Courtney* has been recognized for his work in film and presently is featured in the NBC series, *"Law and Order: Criminal Intent."* *Angela and Courtney* are big supporters of the *Royal Theater Boys and Girls Club* in her mother's hometown of St. Petersburg. Their original date was Friday, September 12, 1997, but they pushed the wedding date back to Sunday, October 12, 1997. At this time, the family members had a hard time contacting *Courtney*, due to his work schedule about documenting his living testimony for the family tree. The information gather on *Courtney* is all public knowledge. 📖

My Family Tree

Elise Cowan Love   b. Friday, May 4, 1951

This is the testimony of my life so far:

I was a gift of life from GOD. I was born into the union of my parents, the late *Levonia Margaret Carey Cowan and James Avery Cowan*. I was born on May 4, 1951, in Detroit, Michigan – Wayne County. I am the third oldest of my siblings.

I graduated from Crosman Elementary School in Detroit and attended Highland Park High School. Graduated in June 1968 in Highland Park and then transferred to Central High School in Detroit, Michigan – Wayne County.

As a teen I joined the choir at the **Temple of I AM**. My first husband was the late *Eddie Andrew Trent [1]*, he was from Tallahassee, Florida – Leon County. Ours was the first wedding ceremony performed by *Rev. Simpson* at the **Temple of I AM** after the church moved to its new location on Hamilton Avenue in Highland Park, Michigan. We were married Saturday, March 22, 1969. Our union was blessed with the birth of twins, *Lisa Ann and Eddie Andrew [II]* born Monday, September 22, 1969. My daughter blessed our lives with the birth of her child, *Deidre Marie Trent,* born Monday, May 2, 1988. Yet, our marriage did not last long, and after some time we got a divorce. I was yet blessed again to find love. After some time, I met and married my current husband, *Gene Edward Love*. Once my children were grown, I returned back to school and attended Wayne County Community College and Detroit Institute Commerce College.

My work career includes the Detroit Free Press, a Bank Teller and I had worked at 5 different banks in the surrounding area of Detroit. I retired from my last employer and enjoyed life as a Homemaker. My family sees me as one who knows the "system" and can navigate it to help them get through demanding times. I am knowledgeable on a few things that can help people. My sister *Jean* and my nieces, *Iris and Stephanie* stated, that I "…could con someone out of their underwear and talk a lot of mess." My family keeps me laughing all the time, especially *Iris*, who talks a lot of mess and *Maria*, who relates the drama from her workplace. I thought I could talk a lot of mess, but my niece *Iris* has me beat, hands down. *Jean* always loves messing with me by calling me early in the morning talking junk to me and *Stephanie* too. Early to me is before 12 o'clock, and she gets me every time by disguising her voice. She would say that she had found me some roadkill for me to cook or she wanted me to cook chitterlings or beef tongue or pig feet for her and my neighbors. My response to her is always the same, "…Sh-it" and we start laughing. We always talk about good sales on groceries, other sales, and medical things. Good food is a joy with me, with strawberries being my favorite. I will cut a person over some watermelon. Among my other favorites are fried chicken, BBQ ribs, steak, lobster, and crab meat. I still love to eat with my feet on the table, like I did when I was a little girl. I love reading anything I can put my hands on. I had the opportunity to babysit my sisters' children and my friends' children too. I am a Homemaker; sometimes I am a Caretaker and Babysitter for family and friends. 📖

My Family Tree

Eddie Andrew Trent II   b. Monday, September 22, 1969

This is the testimony of my life so far:

I was a gift of life from GOD, I was born into the union of *Elise Cowan Love and* the late *Eddie Andrew Trent [1]*. I was born September 22, 1969 in Detroit, Michigan – Wayne County. I am the youngest of my twin.

My education was through the Canton Public School System, graduating from John Glenn High School June 1987 in Canton, Michigan – Wayne County. From middle school and high school, I played on the football team until I got badly hurt and stopped playing, but I still love football. Thereafter, I attended Henry Ford Community College in Dearborn, Michigan – Wayne County, to study to become a Disc Jockey. I also attended Eastern Michigan University Ypsilanti, Michigan – Washtenaw County. I love to eat good food. I am not a good cook but can make some damn good ice. I love to work out, eat healthy, watch sports, and hanging out with my family, friends, and just plain old good fun. I love playing cards, love to talk junk and playing board games. I am known for telling good stories and love making people laugh. I work at Detroit Metro Airport (DTW) in Romulus. I have been working there for over twenty years, and I am into Boot Camp in Michigan, plus work there too.

Lisa Ann Trent   b. Monday, September 22, 1969

This is the testimony of my life so far:

I was a gift of life from GOD, I was born into the union of *Elise Cowan Love and* the late *Eddie Andrew Trent [1]*. I am the oldest of my twin. I was born September 22, 1969 in Detroit, Michigan – Wayne County.

I was educated in the Canton Public School System, graduated from John Glenn High School June 1987 in Canton, Michigan – Wayne County. I completed my coursework in Cosmetology and was licensed in 1995, and I have continued my efforts for many years. I graduated from Davenport University in 1998 with a bachelor's in business administration degree. I worked at BoRics Hair Salon in Canton, Michigan – Wayne County for many years until I moved to Jacksonville, Florida – Duval County, where I attended Florida A and M University to become a pharmacist. I graduated in May 2012 with a Doctor of Pharmacology (PhD) and passed my Florida Boards that same summer. I also graduated from Baker College (online) in May 2014 with a master's in healthcare administration degree (MBA). I currently work as a Clinician Specialist and licensed Pharmacist at the Veterans' Affairs Healthcare System in Jacksonville, Florida – Duval County.

My daughter *Deidre Marie Trent* was born Monday, May 2, 1988 in Detroit, Michigan – Wayne County. Her father is *Kevin Harris*. I am the first doctor in my family. I love to read, play cards, and talk junk. I am excellent in all levels of math and science. I like working out, traveling, hanging out with family and friends, love to eat good food, shopping, watching good movies, and sports. My father came to live with me, and I was my father's caregiver before he passed. I enjoyed every minute spending time with him, all the way to the end.

My Family Tree

Deidre Marie Trent Lashley   **b. Monday, May 2, 1988**

This is the testimony of my life so far:

I was a gift of life from GOD to my parents *Lisa Ann Trent and Kevin Harris*. I was born May 2, 1988 in Detroit, Michigan – Wayne County; their only child.

I was educated in the Canton Public School System and graduated from John Glenn High School in June 2006 in Canton, Michigan – Wayne County (the same schools my mother and *Uncle Eddie* graduated from). I graduated with a Minor in Marketing of Arts degree from the Art Institute of Chicago, Illinois – Cook County in May 2010. Currently I am working at Vonmaur Department Store in Chicago, Illinois – Cook County. I met and married *Corey Lashley*. I adopted his daughter's name – *Kouri* when we got married. I am driven when it comes to fashion, hair styling, make-up, clothes, shoes, shopping, and jewelry. I like playing cards, traveling, board games, working out, and watching sports. 📖

Nakia LeMone Brown   **b. Monday, January 13, 1975**

This is the testimony of my life so far:

I was the gift of life from GOD to my parents *Judy Carol Cowan Brown and Elco Jr Brown ^{II}*. I was born into their union on January 13, 1975, in Detroit, Michigan – Wayne County. I am the oldest of my siblings.

I graduated from Gesu Catholic School and Cass High School June 1993 in Detroit, Michigan – Wayne County. I am incredibly good at drawing pictures; a good writer, and I write music. I played the piano/keyboard, and I think I am a particularly good DJ. I joined the United States Navy and was assign to the Navy Base in Chicago in 2001. The Navy moved me around a lot. While I was on the Navy Base, the guys in my unit often asked me to write letters or poems to their wives or girlfriends for them. I earned a Bachelor of Science in Technical Management in 2020.

In February 2015, I decided to get baptized and join a church. I attended a service at World Changer Church in Washington, D.C. and immediately connected with the word that was being preached, after attending service for a couple weeks. I was approached by a member of the praise and worship team to audition at a rehearsal. To say the most about the audition I could at least hold a note.

Merissa Douglas, who had been a member of World Changers Church for 11 years, was the praise and worship team leader at the time. Through fellowship events and conference calls, and us being members of the team we developed a dear friendship. After a few months of talking with *Merissa* on a consistent basis, I asked her to go out on a date with me in November 2016. After that date we became really good friends. Our friendship grew in trust and love for one another. In January of that next year, I asked *Merissa* if we could date one another exclusively. She answered, "Yes!" From that, a year and eleven months later, our relationship progressed into a decision that I made Saturday, October 21, 2017, to ask *Merissa* for her hand in marriage. She answered, "Yes!" I was

My Family Tree

very, very pleased with her answer! We are both anticipating a marriage blessed in the manifestation of the love of GOD in every area of it! We got married Sunday, January 14, 2018, in Northeast Washington, DC – Prince George's County. 📖

Maria Antoinette Brown   b. Wednesday, June 30, 1976

This is the testimony of my life so far:

I was a gift of life from GOD to my parents, *Judy Carol Cowan Brown and Elco Jr. Brown II*. I was born into their union on June 30, 1976, in Detroit, Michigan – Wayne County. I am the youngest of their children.

I was educated at Gesu Catholic School and graduated from Cass High School June 1994 in Detroit, Michigan – Wayne County. I took classes at Wayne County Community College because the classes were cheaper and then I transferred my credits to Davenport University to continue my education for a degree in Business Accounting. I graduated from Davenport University in 2005.

Even though *Lisa* and I are first cousins on our mother's side, we are close like sisters. I am currently employed as Business Accounting Analyst and Retail Sales. I enjoy family gatherings at my house or other family members' houses. I like playing cards board games, love reading good books and listening to books on Audible, love to watch good television shows and movies. I can cook my butt off, and I am a good hostess for parties and love to decorate things. 📖

Judy Carol Cowan Brown   b. Friday, October 2, 1953

This is the testimony of my life so far:

I was born into the union of the late *Levonia Margaret Carey Cowan and James Avery Cowan*. I was yet another gift from GOD on October 2, 1953, in Detroit, Michigan – Wayne County, the fourth eldest child.

I graduated from Crosman Elementary School in Detroit and then attended Highland Park High School in Highland Park, Michigan. I later transferred to Detroit's Central High School June 1970. I graduated from Wayne County Community College with an Associate of Science degree.

As a teen I joined the choir at the **Temple of I AM**. I met my husband, *Elco Jr. Brown II,* from Greensboro, North Carolina – Guilford County in Detroit. We were married by *Rev. Simpson* at the **Temple of I AM** while it was still on Hamilton Avenue. Our union produced two beautiful children, a boy, *Nakia LeMone Brown* – born Monday, January 13, 1975, in Detroit and *Maria Antoinette Brown* – born Wednesday, June 30, 1976, in Detroit. I eventually re-married; this time to *Kenneth Dwight Pollard* from Johnstown, Pennsylvania – Cambria County. Yet, our marriage did not last long, and after some time we got a divorce. I have been blessed to watch both of my children grow into positive young people. My son (*Nakia*) is coming into his own as a married man with his beautiful wife in Maryland. My daughter *(Maria)* purchased her first property, works two jobs and is coming into her own as a young lady and doing very well for herself. It goes without saying that I am proud of them.

I love being around children, teaching them and taking a hand in their growth. I should have been a teacher. I love to sing, act in plays, and dancing, as well as doing signing. I have a passion for sewing clothes and making praise flags. I attended Wayne County Community College and have taken classes in Sign Language. I have a deep passion for the Mime Ministry, flag ministry, and singing in the choir. I am a loving member of the Metro Detroit Area Fellowship Choir. I am one of the children Sunday school teachers and one of the church nurses at my church. I am over the Culinary Arts Department at my church, Lake Ridge Ministry. My greatest passion is cooking and baking for my family and friends. I am a Homemaker and often bake for different organizations around my community, schools, and church events. I enjoy watching good movies, reading, and board games, as well as listening to gospel music. I love playing the piano/keyboard and guitar too. At one time, I owned a big black piano for many years. I retired from Cosmetic Retail Department Store at Northland Mall as a Counter Manger/Beauty Advisor in Southfield, Michigan, where I worked at for twenty years.

Suzette De-Carroll Strickland Willis  **b. Thursday, November 3, 1966**

This is the testimony of my life so far:

I was a gift of life from GOD, and I was born into the union of the late *Frances Rebecca Hege Strickland and Samuel Lay Strickland* *III*. I was born November 3, 1966, in Winston-Salem, North Carolina – Forsyth County.

I graduated from East Forsyth High School in June 1985 in Winston-Salem, North Carolina – Forsyth County, graduated from Winston-Salem State University in 1989 with a Bachelor of Science degree in accounting. I graduated from Wake Forest University in Winston-Salem, North Carolina – Forsyth County in 2001 with a Master of Business Administration degree.

I met and eventually married *Joel Stephen Willis* from High Point, North Carolina – Guilford County. We were married Tuesday, February 25, 2003, at Emmanuel Baptist Church in Winston-Salem, North Carolina – Forsyth County, where we made it our home. I am a Business Planning Analyst. I love watching football, watching good movies, and doing Crosswords with my family and friends.

My Family Tree

Joel Stephen Willis b. Saturday, February 8, 1964

This is the testimony of my life so far:

I was a gift of life from GOD. I was born into the union of *Mary Willis and Joe V. Willis*. I was born on February 8, 1964, in High Point, North Carolina – Guilford County.

I graduated from Ragsdale High School in June 1982 in Jamestown, North Carolina – Guilford County, and from Appalachian State University in Boone, North Carolina – Watauga County in 1988. My degree is in Printing Production Management. I have a beautiful daughter named *Raven Willis*.

I met and married *Suzette DeCarroll Strickland* Tuesday, February 25, 2003 at Emmanuel Baptist Church in Winston-Salem, North Carolina – Forsyth County, and we are now living in Winston-Salem, North Carolina – Forsyth County. Living in God's love for each other and enjoying life together. Previously I was a Purchasing Manager in Winston-Salem and am currently working as a Category Manager Distributor in Winston-Salem. I studied at Appalachian State University for Graphic Arts/Printing. Always moving up. I love watching sports and good movies with family and friends. 📖

Lakeisha Renee Thues-Stiff b. Saturday, March 25, 1978

This is the testimony of my life so far:

I was a gift of life from GOD. I was born to the union of *Venus Renee Mason-Thues and Barry Allen Floyd*. I was born March 25, 1978, in Detroit, Michigan – Wayne County. In 1989, *Jerome (Rick) Anthony Thues* adopted me as his daughter.

I graduated from Mumford High School June 1996 in Detroit, with honors and from Specs Howard School of Broadcast Arts in 2000, with a certification in Television Broadcasting. I also attended Eastern Michigan University in Ypsilanti, Michigan and University of Phoenix in Southfield, Michigan, with a concentration in Marketing Management. Over the years, I completed various video production projects and started my first company *Kiwi Media Productions*. I met and married *William Stiff* Monday, December 5, 2005, in Detroit.

I deferred my education and the production company in order to focus on my family. Our first child, *Jordan Jewel Stiff* was born Friday, November 17, 2006, and *Madison Rene' Stiff* was born Friday, March 7, 2008. During my time as a stay-at-home mom and with my husband working out of town, I found myself with time on my hands and took a deeper look into entrepreneurship. As a result, I launched my web design and social media marketing business. The *Kiwi Media Group* was established in 2009. Over the years, I have become a *Serial Entrepreneur*, starting other businesses for family members, and launching businesses for others. I most recently established

My Family Tree

Elite Entrepreneurs Magazine. My husband launched a clothing line, and our daughters began a clothing and accessory line. We live in Southfield, where I serve as an ambassador for the city. 📖

Maria Jeanette Stricklandb. Thursday, January 12, 1950

This is the testimony of my life so far:

I was a gift of life from GOD, I was blessed to have had two loving and caring parents, like the late *Frances Rebecca Hege Strickland and Samuel Lay Strickland III*. I was born to their union on January 12, 1950 in Winston-Salem, North Carolina – Forsyth County. I am the second oldest of my siblings.

I graduated from Lilly Preparatory Kindergarten, Columbus Heights Elementary School, and Anderson Senior High School June 1967 in Winston-Salem. I attended Winston-Salem State University for two years. I graduated from Beauty School for Cosmetology in Winston-Salem in the early 1970's. I attached my business to my mother's house, so I could be close to her and be her caretaker. I have been a licensed Cosmetologist for over thirty years.

There is a philosophy behind me not being married; *why mess up a good thing?* I take pride in my cooking, baking, and cleaning the home. I make everything from scratch for my family and friends. I do not mind eating out occasionally, but I prefer home cooked meals. People constantly ask me to cook or bake something for them, even family members and friends that live out of state. I guess people loves my cooking and baking.

My family in North Carolina is a close-knit family. We talk daily, and if one is in need, we all come together to find out what we can do to help. I am active in my church and sing in the choir every Sunday. We sing old slave songs with no music, using our hands and feet to hold the rhythm. I take pleasure in the fact that my family members in Winston-Salem all attend the same church. We have Sunday dinners every Sunday after church and a Fish Fry every Friday at one of our homes. This is one way in which we keep the family close together. I am currently living and working in Winston-Salem, North Carolina, as a Hairdresser. 📖

Toni Sue Cowanb. Monday, February 6, 1956

This is the testimony of my life so far:

I was a gift of life from GOD, born to the union of the late *Levonia Margaret Carey Cowan and James Avery Cowan*. I was born February 6, 1956 in Detroit, Michigan – Wayne County. I am the youngest of my siblings.

I graduated from Crosman Elementary School in Detroit, and Highland Park High School June 1973 in Highland Park. At the time Highland Park was combined as a middle and senior high school.

My Family Tree

As a teen, I joined the choir at the **Temple of I AM.** I left the temple as an adult. My first child, *Stephen Idel Cowan [1]* was born Tuesday, February 26, 1974, but preceded us in death. My second child, *AnRico Celete Levonia Cowan Lockhart [1]* was born Thursday, April 24, 1975. My third child, *Keith Jerome Cowan,* was born (stillborn) Wednesday, November 10, 1976. All my children were born in Detroit. I have four beautiful grandchildren and they were all born in Detroit. My daughter's two children are *Monique Anthony Cowan*, born Friday, March 9, 1990 (with *Victor Robinson)*. *AnRico Celete Levonia Scott [II]* was born Monday, June 5, 2000 (with *Sean Scott)*. My son (*Stephen [1]*) has three children – *Stephen Idel Cowan [II]*, *Destiny Tiara Robinson and Trevon Deonte Cowan*. In my younger days I worked as a Barmaid for over ten years. I am currently working as a Retail Manager.

Litha Ruth Walker Mason   b. Saturday, March 20, 1937

This is the testimony of my life so far:

I was a gift of life from GOD, I was the first child to be born into the union of the late *Estella Lewis Walker and Theortic Calvin (T.C.) Walker*. I was born March 20, 1937, in Locust Grove, Georgia – Henry County.

Our family moved to Detroit, Michigan, in 1938. We settled in Highland Park. The family joined the Russell Street Missionary Baptist Church in Detroit. In 1940, my mother was pregnant with twins, *Catherine Walker and Calvin Walker*. Unfortunately, she had a bad fall during her pregnancy, and the twins were born stillborn.

I attended school in Highland Park. I remember the teacher at Frances E. Willard School telling my mother that I should be in kindergarten because of my age. My mother informed her that I could read and print. So, I was given a piece of chalk and printed some words, not just letters. I was then placed in the first grade.

In the latter part of 1940s, my parents separated, divorcing in 1954. My mother re-married a few years later. Her first husband was *Raymond Ware*. Her second husband was *Theortic Calvin (T.C.) Walker,* and later she was married to *Sidney Lewis*, all three husbands preceding her in death. There were no children from her first and third marriage. My mother departed this life Saturday, January 28, 1992, and was buried at Westland Cemetery in Wayne, Michigan – Wayne County.

I graduated from Highland Park High School June 1955. After I graduated, I got a job at Winkelman's Brothers Warehouse as a Secretary in the Clothing Distribution Department. I attended Highland Park Junior College for one year. The college was next door to the high school. I could not finish school because my mother could not afford to help me go any farther. So, I saved my money for my schooling and went back to Highland Park Junior College, a year and half later, I graduated from Highland Park Junior College. I was told by my teachers I was an excellent student and was awarded for my typing skills, as I could type 120 words a minute.

My Family Tree

I was busy at my home church, Messiah Missionary Baptist Church, which was under the leadership of *Rev. Theodore C. Simmons*. I am one of the lead soprano in my church choir and Pianist and Director of the Children's Choir. My signature song is *"I must tell Jesus."*

I later met *William (Tony) Anthony Mason*, who worked in the building across the street as part of the property's maintenance crew. I made *Tony* wait about six months before agreeing to a date with me. Our first date was on a Sunday, and I told him to meet me at the corners of Humbolt and Poplar Street. He did not have a clue until he got there that the intersection was the location of Messiah Missionary Church, and our first date would be at my church.

We dated for about a year or so and got married Saturday, March 19, 1960. His brothers *Gene and Bobby* were in our wedding party. The little kids from my Sunday school class hosted our reception in the church basement. We were married at Messiah Missionary Church, by *Rev. Theodore Cornelius Simmons*, our pastor, and friend.

We lived on Monterey in Highland Park with my mother, who owned the house. Winkelman's had a rule that married couples could not work for the same company. Couples had six months to decide which one would leave the job. Since I had the better job, we decided that I would stay at Winkelman's.

We have celebrated fifty-seven years of marriage. In that time, we have had three beautiful children and four beautiful grandchildren. Our first child, *Anthony Troy Mason* was born Friday, January 6, 1961. Our second child, *Jenean Evette Mason,* was born Wednesday, December 30, 1964 and our third child, *Theodore (Ted) Cornelius Mason*, was born Tuesday, April 4, 1967. Our children were born and raised in Detroit.

We have three daughters-in-laws. *Theodore's* first wife was *Audrey F. Holloway Mason* "…not anymore thank you, *Jesus*." Their children are *Amber Rose Mason* was born Friday, June 19, 1998, and *Anthony Jefferson Mason* was born Thursday, January 18, 2007, both born in Redford Township. *Tony* and I love *Ted's* second wife *Suzanne Maria Zeglen Mason and Suzanne's* daughter *Alyssa.*

Anthony's wife is *Sandar Lewin Mason* (b. Tuesday, April 4, 1967). Their children are *Austin Shane Mason* was born Friday, February 26, 1999 and *Ashley Sherrin Mason* was born Sunday, September 24, 2000. *Anthony's* children were born in Falls, Virginia – Fairfax County. I have a "bonus of three daughters" *Venus R. Mason Thues, Stephanie M. Mason, and Iris A. Mason Nicholas.*

I retired as a seamstress for Winkelman's warehouse and became a homemaker when we started our family. While my husband attended Baker College, I was his secretary, proofreader, and the disciplinarian of our church circle. I made sure everyone did their homework, including him. I typed his assignments while he was working or doing research for his other classes, checking their homework, or just trying to get some sleep.

I like to help the elderly whenever I go shopping or when I am out and about. I enjoy helping family members and friends, driving them to doctor's appointments. I enjoy cooking for my family, but I have slowly retired from kitchen duties, allowing my husband to take over to show off his cooking skills. He can really cook and is a master with barbecue. I just come in to do the baking when I feel like it or help when he needs me.

I participate in different organizations within the church – choir member, Sunday school teacher, and a member of the Usher Board. I enjoy hanging out and talking with family and friends. As a youth I was fascinated with the piano and learned how to play. I love fishing with my husband and just hanging out on the water, soaking up the warm breeze, the quietness and sunshine. We both enjoy traveling, some leisure time at the casino and visiting our grandchildren. My husband took me to the gun range. I had no idea that I'd be so good at shooting a gun. I did not even miss my targets. My younger nieces – *Iris and Stephanie,* I enjoy talking and hanging out with them. They are so much fun. You can say I love life - both its small and big moments. Even though *Norma Jean* is my sister-in-law we act like sisters, love you. 📖

NOTE: ***Litha*** *passed Monday, April 22, 2019, at home in Detroit, Michigan – Wayne County, with her family at her bedside.*

Jenean Evette Mason   b. Wednesday, December 30, 1964

This is the testimony of my life so far:

I was a gift of life from GOD, the second child born to the union of the late *Litha Ruth Walker Mason and William (Tony) Anthony Mason.* I was born on December 30, 1964, in Detroit, Michigan — Wayne County.

I graduated from St. Mary of Redford High School June 1983 in Detroit and from Detroit Mercy College in 1989 with a Bachelor of Science degree in Information Technology. I did not allow my hearing problem to hinder my education or keep me from learning new things. After I graduated from Detroit Mercy College, I began working for Trillium Teamologies, Inc. as an Administrative Assistant. I was there for fifteen years before I was laid off permanently. I then began working at Hartford Memorial Baptist Church in a similar capacity.

I began my new journey four years ago with Baker College of Clinton Township and was transferred to their other location in Allen Park, Michigan, as a Health Sciences Administrative Assistant for the Nursing Department. I have some degree of proficiency in navigating the computer world, surfing the internet, and creating Power Point Presentations. I enjoy reading, watching television, playing games on the computer, shopping, and doing my hair. I am a proud aunt of two nieces and two nephews. Yes, I am a homebody, and I love it. I am a resident in Detroit. 📖

My Family Tree

Mildred Elizabeth Strickland Peppers   b. Saturday, June 12, 1948

This is the testimony of my life so far:

I was a gift of life from GOD. I was born into the union of my parents, the late *Frances Rebecca Hege Strickland and Samuel Lay Strickland* ^{III}. I was born on June 12, 1948, in Winston-Salem, North Carolina — Forsyth County. I am the oldest of my siblings.

I graduated from Lilly Preparatory Kindergarten, Columbus Heights Elementary School, and Anderson Senior High School in June 1965 in Winston-Salem, North Carolina — Forsyth County. I graduated from Winston-Salem State University with a Major in Education. I have been teaching at the high school and college level for over thirty years.

I met my future husband at Winston-Salem State University the day I was pledging in the yard for Zeta Phi Beta Sorority. I married *Ronald (Ronnie) Carl Peppers* on Thursday, November 22, 1973, in Winston-Salem, and we had three beautiful daughters who were born into our union. Our first child, *Blanche Yvonne Peppers Sawyer,* was born on Monday, October 15, 1962. She met and married *Darren A. Sawyer* on Saturday, April 27, 1991. Our second child, *Frances Vencelia Peppers,* was born on Friday, August 9, 1963. Our third child, *Joneice Conchetta Peppers Pledger,* was born on Wednesday, September 3, 1975. She met and married *Willie Lee Pledger* ^{II} on Saturday, May 22, 1999, in Winston-Salem. Our three daughters were born and raised in Winston-Salem, North Carolina — Forsyth County. We have four beautiful grandchildren. Our first grandson, *Xavier J. Sawyer,* was born on Wednesday, October 5, 1994. The second grandson, *Alexander J. Sawyer,* was born on Wednesday, October 15, 1997. *Xavier and Alexander* were born in Portsmouth, Virginia. Our third grandson, *Jadon Carl Pledger,* was born on Thursday, September 13, 2001 and our only granddaughter, *Carrington Sabory Pledger,* was born on Friday, November 17, 2006. *Jadon and Carrington* were born and raised in Winston-Salem, North Carolina.

My family here in North Carolina is a close-knit family. We talk to one another on a daily basis, and if one is in need, we all come running to help. I am active in the church choir. We sing old slave songs with no music, using our hands and feet to hold the rhythm. Our family group here all belong to the same church because we know a family that prays together will always stay together. We have Sunday dinner together after church every Sunday and a Fish Fry every Friday — at somebody's house. This way we remain close and be involved with each other lives. I have been blessed to witness my sisters *(Maria and Suzette)* grow up into very dependable, strong women with a loving heart, their education achievements, and their careers. My daughters had grown up into strong and beautiful young ladies with their own families, their education achievements, and their careers. I will say again I have also witnessed my grandchildren starting on their journeys in life as young adults. They each have a passion for life in their hearts and GOD on their side; they will beat the devil running.

We had family reunion every other year at Thanksgiving time, and then we would go to our homeplace, which is Fork, North Carolina. GOD has always been the center of our family life, my grandma and momma made sure we knew GOD for our self and our family history.

My Family Tree

North Carolina News Journal

A review from the UJIMA Community Development Corporation concerning *Mildred*, as a treasurer at Winston-Salem State University reads: *Upon completing Neighbors for Better Neighborhoods 2006 weekend seminar, Mildred and her husband's (Ronnie now deceased) interest in nonprofits was ignited. January 2009 was the official date of her acceptance letter to the board. A retired teacher, her skills include strong speaking, writing, and listening skills, as well as organizational skills. A team player, she has a basic understanding of board governance and accountability. She believes that the City View project will put new life into the area.* 📖

NOTE: *Mildred* passed Tuesday, November 7, 2016, in Winston-Salem, at home surrounded by her immediate family.

Blanche Y. Peppers Sawyer   b. **Monday, October 15, 1962**

This is the testimony of my life so far:

I was a gift of life from GOD, born into the union of the late *Mildred Elizabeth Strickland Peppers and Ronald (Ronnie) Carl Peppers*. I was born on October 15, 1962, in Winston-Salem, North Carolina — Forsyth County. I am the oldest of my siblings.

I graduated from East Forsyth High School in June 1979 in Winston-Salem, North Carolina — Forsyth County. My concentration was in Interior Design. As a design professional, I serve as the Chief Executive Officer of *Sawyer's Design*, the company I started in 1991.

I met and married *Darren A. Sawyer* on Saturday, April 27, 1991. He graduated from West Forsyth High School in Winston-Salem, North Carolina — Forsyth County in June 1979. After High school, my husband spent thirty years in the United States Navy was honored in (ISCM Dillard Retirement Ceremony).

Our union was blessed with two sons. *Xavier J. Sawyer* was born on Wednesday, October 5, 1994, in Portsmouth, Virginia — Norfolk County. He went to Triton High School and transferred with him and graduated from Maurice J. McDonough High School in Portsmouth, Virginia — Norfolk County in June 2010. He graduated from North Carolina State University, studying Accounting in 2016. *Xavier* is currently living in Raleigh, North Carolina — Wake County. Our other son, *Alexander J. Sawyer,* was born on Wednesday, October 15, 1997, in Portsmouth, Virginia — Norfolk County; he graduated from Benjamin Stoddert High School in Portsmouth, Virginia — Norfolk County in June 2014. *Alexander* lives in Waldorf, Maryland — Charles County.

My family group in North Carolina is close-knit, maintaining daily communications. If one of us needs help, we all come running. We belong to the same church and enjoy the family gathering every Sunday for Sunday dinners and the Fish Fry every Friday. This activity helps keep us close. My husband and I live in Dunn, North Carolina — Forsyth County. 📖

My Family Tree

Venus Renee Mason Thues   **b. Saturday, September 29, 1956**

This is the testimony of my life so far:

I was a gift of life from GOD, born to the late *Mary Frances Clinkscales Harris and William (Tony) Anthony Mason*. I was born on September 29, 1956, in Detroit, Michigan — Wayne County. My maternal grandparents were *Maddie Mae Wright (Ne'e Jordan) and George Wright*.

I graduated from Mumford High School in June 1973 and graduated from the University of Detroit Mercy with an Associate of Arts degree in Legal Assistant/Paralegal Assistant in 1994.

My first marriage was to *Barry Allen Floyd on* Saturday, October 15, 1977, in Detroit, Michigan — Wayne County, and we got a divorce in 1984. We had one daughter together, *Lakeisha Renee Floyd (N'ee),* born on Saturday, March 25, 1978, in Detroit, Michigan — Wayne County. My second marriage was to *Jerome Anthony Thues (aka — Rick) on* Wednesday, April 3, 1985, in Detroit, Michigan – Wayne County. *Jerome* adopted *LaKeisha (N'ee)* in 1989 as his daughter. *(N'ee Floyd,* later changed her last name to *Thues*). We had one daughter together, *Jessica Marie Thues,* born on Monday, October 27, 1986 Detroit, Michigan – Wayne County.

I am an author and full-time family manager; which means I did provide around-the-clock care for my mother when she was alive, in addition to being a wife for over twenty-eight years. I am a mother and a grandmother to the smartest, most talented grandchildren in the world. I am supposed to say that. It is my duty as a NaNa!

I have always LOVED books. I love the way the paper feels as I turn the pages. I believe that a thoughtful and beautifully crafted book cover is as much a work of art as a museum exhibit. I love visiting bookstores and libraries, but I must admit that eBooks are growing on me. Becoming a published author of my first *"Faith-Based"* novel has been the beginning of my dream come true. I am also passionate about all things in marriage. I am a coach and mentor to wives and single women who are preparing for marriage. I have only just begun my journey. I know that GOD has in store for me. *Jerome (Rick)* and I serve as the Co-Directors of the Uplift Family Ministry at our home church and Greater Grace Temple in Detroit. The platform of Joyfully-Ever-After Marriage offers hope, healing, and assurance that contrary to popular belief, monogamous, joyful marriage is indeed alive and well. I have had five books published: *Breached Father and Child Relationship?, Brown Paper Bag, Sistah Talk, Getting Ready for the Ring* and *Faith-Based.*

Jerome and I had witnessed *LaKeisha Rene Thues-Stiff* get married to *William Stiff* on Monday, December 5, 2005, in Detroit, Michigan. I have watched both of my daughters grow into their own and live life well. We have three beautiful granddaughters – *Ramiyah Kimberly White* was born on Friday, May 28, 2004; *Jordan Jewel Stiff* was born on Friday, November 17, 2006; and *Madison Rene' Stiff* was born on Friday, March 7, 2008. I love spending time with my King (my husband – *Rick*), cooking, and baking. Plus, trying new recipes to fix for us. I love gardening. I love to feed my family knowledge and good home meals. My husband and I love to listen to the gospel, gospel music, and good jazz. 📖

My Family Tree

Jerome (Rick) Anthony Thues   b. Thursday, August 7, 1952

This is the testimony of my life so far:

I was a gift of life from GOD, and I was adopted into the union of *Jessie Mae Thues and Willie Thues.* I was born on August 7, 1952 in Detroit, Michigan — Wayne County.

I graduated from Murray Wright High School in June 1971 in Detroit and graduated from Macomb Community College with a degree in Education Community Administration Management in 1990, a Bachelor of Arts in general and Technical Studies, an Associate of Arts in General Business Management in 1994, Industrial Relations in 1995, and graduated from Wayne State University with a double Master's in Mental Health Counseling and Labor Relations in 2000. I maintain a private Consulting and Counseling practice, operating for the last thirty years. I am a License Professional Counselor.

I met and married *Venus Renee Mason Thues* on Wednesday, April 3, 1985, in Detroit, Michigan — Wayne County. We had one daughter together, *Jessica Marie Thues,* born on Monday, October 27, 1986, in Detroit, Michigan — Wayne County. In 1989, I adopted *LaKeisha* as my daughter. So, now I have two beautiful daughters and two sons, *James Thues and Royale Thues.*

Venus (Renee) and I serve as the Co-Directors of the Uplift Family Ministry at our home church and Greater Grace Temple in Detroit. The platform of Joyfully-Ever-After Marriage offers hope, healing, and assurance that contrary to popular belief, monogamous, joyful marriage is indeed alive and well.

Renee and I witnessed *LaKeisha Rene Thues* marry *William Stiff* on Monday, December 5, 2005, in Detroit, Michigan — Wayne County. We have three granddaughters — *Ramiyah Kimberly White, Jordan Jewel Stiff,* and *Madison Rene' Stiff.* I miss fishing and good conversations with my father-in-law - *Tony* and his wife *Litha.* I also love family gatherings and cookouts. I truly love spending time with my lovely wife out on the town for good food, listening to jazz, and long rides in the car. I love these precious moments with my Queen. 📖

Joneice Conchetta Peppers Pledger   b. Wednesday, September 3, 1975

This is the testimony of my life so far:

I was a gift of life from GOD, born in the union of the late *Mildred Elizabeth Strickland Peppers and Ronnie Carl Peppers.* I was born on September 3, 1975, in Winston-Salem, North Carolina — Forsyth County, the youngest of my siblings.

I am now married to *Willie Lee (Will) Pledger [II].* *Willie* and I met and got married on May 22, 1999 in Winston-Salem. We have two beautiful children, *Jaden Carl Pledger,* born on Thursday, September 13, 2001, and *Carrington Sabory Pledger,* born on Friday, November 17, 2006. Both of our children were born and raised in Winston-Salem, North Carolina.

My Family Tree

I grew up in Winston-Salem, where I still live with my family. I went to college NCA and T State University in Greensboro where I received a bachelor's degree of Science in Chemistry.

My *Mason* connection is through my great grandmother on my mother's side, *Mildred Ann Mason Hege*, who was very instrumental in raising me and my two sisters. Through her, I was able to have a relationship with *Uncle Napoleon Mason, Aunt Hazel Mason, Aunt Veada, Aunt Peggy, Cousin Euphonia, Cousin Gene, Cousin Tony, Cousin Bobby* and the rest of the *Mason* clan. We had family reunions every other year at Thanksgiving, and then we would go to our homeplace, which is Fork, North Carolina. GOD has always been the center of our family life, my great grandmother, grandmother and mother made sure that we knew GOD for our self and our family history. During my upbringing, my grandmother, who I referred to as *Mama Frances (*the daughter of *Mildred Ann Mason Hege*), was a great cook, and during our family reunions, she was the organizer and made sure my grandma *(great grandma Mildred Ann Mason Hege)* was surrounded by her brothers and sisters during her later years in life. Then she taught us about her other brothers and sisters that had already gone to glory. Now, I continue the *Mason* family tradition. My husband and I continue to raise our children in church and make sure that they have a relationship with GOD for their self and they know our family history.

Willie Lee (Will) Pledger II   b. Sunday, December 31, 1972

This is the testimony of my life so far:

I was a gift of life from GOD, born to the union of *Whilhelmenia Jackson Pledger (deceased) and Willie Lee Pledger [1]*. I was born December 31, 1972 in Winston-Salem, North Carolina – Forsyth County. I am the fourth oldest of my siblings.

I have two sisters and two brothers living, and one sister that is deceased. I grew up in Winston-Salem, North Carolina – Forsyth County, where I met and married *Joneice Conchetta Peppers* May 22, 1999 in Winston-Salem, North Carolina. We are High School Sweethearts.

Joneice and I have two children. *Jaden Carl Pledger and Carrington Sabory Pledger.* Both of our children were born and raised in Winston-Salem, North Carolina. I served five years in the United State Navy, and I also have been in law enforcement, where I served as a Correction Officer here in Winston-Salem. I am now listed as a Disabled Veteran. *Joneice* and I currently live in Winston-Salem. My father's people come from Elizabeth City, North Carolina — Pasquotank County, and my mother's people are from here in Winston-Salem.

My Family Tree

William Anthony (Tony) Mason   b. Wednesday, January 22, 1938

This is the testimony of my life so far:

I was a gift of life from GOD, born to the union of the late *Hazel Lorraine Workman Mason and Napoleon Jefferson Mason*. I was born on January 22, 1938 in Winston-Salem, North Carolina — Forsyth County. I am the second oldest of my siblings.

Growing up in Winston-Salem, North Carolina, at 808 Marcenia was fun. We looked up to my older brother *Eugene (Gene)* because he went to school all day. I only went to school half a day, and my younger brother *Robert (Bobby)* was too young to go to school.

Bobby and I played in the red dirt — and sometimes red mud. We played all afternoon, and we watched for *Gene* to come down the dusty road with his sweater tied around his waist. We would run to meet him every day. We would have a snack, fresh fruit, or dried fruit, and then the three of us would play until supper time. In those days, we lived with our grandma, *Euphonia Bernice Orr Workman* and grandpa, *William Essix Workman*, momma's parents. They, along with our *Uncle James (June) and Uncle Richard* were the world to us. We lived a dream life growing up in Winston-Salem. They raised us for three years while our momma and daddy were in Detroit. They went to Detroit to get jobs in the auto plants and find a place for all of us to live together. I do not recall much about them before coming to Detroit.

A neighbor, *Miss Honey,* often took care of us when our parents, grandma and grandpa were at work. At one time, grandma, grandpa, daddy, momma, *Aunt Grace, Uncle Richard, and Uncle William*, all worked at R. J. Reynolds Tobacco factory, at the same time. Grandma worked at the church and did "day work" at the Tobacco factory. Our good life got better when daddy came back and told us that we were going back with him and momma to Detroit, Michigan. We had never been more than ten miles away from the home before. Daddy had rented a big truck. Daddy and his friend drove the truck to Winston-Salem to get us and the furniture they had left behind. We were so excited to see momma and about going to Detroit. We had never heard of Detroit and had no idea of where it was. After a few days, everything was loaded in the truck, and it was time to go. Grandma fixed the food we would need for the trip. She had made us fried chicken and packed bags of apples and peaches too. There were a lot of tears of happiness and sadness, but it was time to go. We rode from Winston-Salem to Detroit on the mattress from our beds, placed on top of our stuff in the back of an open truck. It was a great adventure to see cars, streetlights, tall buildings, gas stations and long winding highways. Riding in the back of the truck, we had a perfect view of places and things we had never seen before. As we went through the mountains and looked down, we saw people, houses and animals that looked so small. Little did we know that this would be the best road trip and the best time of our lives. The trip took about a day and a half to arrive to Detroit. Actually, we arrived in Royal Oak Township to a housing project built by the auto companies to house black workers coming up from the south. *Gene, Bobby,* and I went to George Washington Carver School. *Euphonia* was born a couple of years later. She was a beautiful baby and a sweet child. We lived in the project until 1952. Daddy and momma said, we had to move "…because the

My Family Tree

house was too small, and the neighborhood had become too violent." When we moved to Alden Street, mama made the house our home in Detroit. For the first time, the *Masons* were buying and not renting.

I accepted Christ at an early age and united with The New Mt. Vernon Baptist Church under the pastorate of the late *Reverend R. J. Cunningham*. *Gene* went to Northern High School. I went to Post Intermediate School, *Bobby and Euphonia* went to Custer Elementary School on Linwood. I later went to Central High School and then transferred to Northwestern. *Gene* graduated from Northern High School in June 1954. I graduated from Northwestern in June 1955, and *Euphonia* later graduated from Central High School in June 1960. *Barbara Ware* lived down the street from us on Alden. We dated for a couple of years, and our son, *Gregory Ware,* was born on Monday, October 17, 1955, in Detroit, Michigan. Then, I met *Mary Frances Clinkscales Harris* at Prophet Jones' mansion on Arden Park. We dated for about a year and a half, and our daughter, *Venus Renee Mason,* was born on Saturday, September 29, 1956.

In late 1958, I got a job at Winkelman's through an employment agency. I had to pay them 5% for the first six months. It was worth it, because I had not been able to find a job on my own. It was at Winkelman's that I met *Litha*. She was a secretary in the office across the street from where I worked. It took me about six months to get a date with her. Our first date was on a Sunday, and she invited me to meet her on Humbolt and Poplar. I did not know until I got there that this was the corner where Messiah Missionary Church was located. Our first date was at her church. We dated for about a year or so and got married on Saturday, March 19, 1960. Her birthday is on Saturday, March 20, 1937. My brothers *Gene* and *Bobby* were in our wedding party. The little kids in *Litha's* Sunday school did our reception in the church basement. We got married at Messiah Missionary Church by the *Pastor, Theodore Cornelius Simmons*, our pastor, and friend. *Troy* was born on Friday, January 6, 1961. *Litha's* mother was very excited, even though she had hoped for a girl. He became her first grandchild as well as her favorite grandchild.

We lived on Monterey in Highland Park with *Litha's* mother, who owned the house. Winkelman's had a rule that married couples could not work for the company. Couples had six months to decide which one would leave the job. Since *Litha* had the better job, we decided that she would stay at Winkelman's.

I worked a number of different jobs. I sold *Encyclopedia Britannica* from door to door in Lincoln Park, Michigan. I also sold Fuller Brush products and Kirby Vacuums. Somewhere around 1962, I started working for James Crystal Manufacturing on 12th Street, near I-94, making light fixtures. Two years later, I began working at Chrysler, at the Hamtramck Assembly Plant. I worked both jobs for about a year. The two jobs got to be too much, so I quit Chrysler. The foreman asked me not to quit, but I told him I had to. He told me if I ever needed a job and Chrysler was hiring, I could use his name to get back in. Several years later, we bought a three-bedroom house on Hedge, near Mt. Elliot. I quit the job at James Crystal Manufacturing and was hired back at Chrysler's Huber Avenue Foundry, which was three blocks from the house. *Jenean* was born on Wednesday, December 30, 1964. We were hoping that she would be born before the end of the year so we could get a tax deduction. I called her my "…tax break baby."

My Family Tree

Pastor Simmons, asked *Litha* and me if we had another boy could we name him *Theodore Cornelius* in his honor. We had another boy, and we name him, *Theodore Cornelius Mason (Ted)* to represent the pastor because he wanted a boy really bad, but he had girls. *Ted* was born on Tuesday, April 4, 1967.

At the Foundry I started shoveling sand, driving a high-low (forklift) and stock chasing. I worked the afternoon and midnight shifts most of the time. I held a series of salaried jobs in the following order — Janitor Foreman, Production Foreman, Production General Foreman, and Production Superintendent. I was laid off in 1979 when the Foundry shut down. I looked for a job for almost a year before I was called back to Chrysler. I was hired at the small Chrysler Winfield Foundry, where I had to start again near the bottom as a foreman. During this time, I was also going to school. I started at Central Michigan University, working on a bachelor's degree in management and Supervision. I would write my homework out, and *Litha* would type it out for me. She was also my proofreader. When I graduated, *Litha* and I went to the Central Michigan University campus in Mount Pleasant, Michigan. I graduated again in 1983 with an MBA. Chrysler was building a new car Assembly Plant in Sterling Heights, Michigan. The plant became known as SHAP. I was offered a promotion as the Second Shift Chief Inspector. I helped train the inspection workforce. The plant was launched in 1985. In 1987, I was promoted to Quality Control Executive at Chrysler's World Headquarters in Highland Park. I was there for about a year. In 1998, I was promoted to Production Manager at Chrysler's Detroit American Axle Plant. During this time, I was also Professor of Leadership Strategies at Baker College in Clinton Township. I later became a member of the Baker College System Board of Regents. In 1992, I was promoted to Plant Manager of Chrysler's at American Axle Plant.

Litha and I loved going to Las Vegas. We bought a Time Share Condo, which we used about every two months. We sold it in 2006 because air travel became a hassle after "…911," also by then, Detroit had three great new casinos. I became a member of Baker College Board of Trustees. After thirty-one years of service, I retired from Chrysler in July 1996. I set up a small consulting company. My primary clients were Tyssen Steel, American Axle, Manufacturing and Baker College. For the past eleven years I have served as the Chairman of Baker College of Allen Park Board of Regents. For the last eight years I have been a member of the Baker College System Board of Trustees. In 2011, Baker College of Allen Park awarded me an honorary PhD in Humane Letter. The college also created the *Annual William Anthony Mason Service Award*, presented to the graduating student "In Recognition of Outstanding Citizenship, Activism and Scholarship." I presented *Alisha Marie Harden* with the first award. To date, every year, I personally present the award to the student selected by the college.

I talked to *Bobby* several times by phone before he passed on Monday, August 11, 2014, in Garfield Heights, Ohio — Cuyahoga County.

My wife and I have four beautiful grandchildren — *Amber Rose Mason* was born on Friday, June 19, 1998; *Anthony Jefferson Mason* was born on Thursday, January 18, 2007, in Redford Township, Michigan; *Austin Shane Mason* was born on Friday, February 26, 1999, and *Ashley Sherrin Mason* was born on Sunday, September 24, 2000, in Falls, Virginia. *Litha* and I enjoy traveling and visiting our grandchildren. I have taken *Litha* to the Gun Range. She did not know

My Family Tree

how good she was. She did not miss her targets. *Litha* and I had adopted our younger nieces, *Iris and Stephanie,* as our daughters and we enjoy their company with my promise to my brother*(Eugene)* that I will keep a close eye on *Iris and Stephanie.* This brief account of my life is being written on Saturday, February 28, 2015. At this time, *Litha* and I are 77 years old and in good health. As of Thursday, March 19, 2015, we will be celebrating our 55th wedding anniversary. 📖

Note: William passed Monday, August 3, 2020, in Michigan. He was surrounded by his children.

Grace Colwell Thornton Bassett   **b. Sunday, December 17, 1916**

Grace Bassett Has a Story to Tell

(Reported by Dan Margolis from People's Weekly World Friday, February 17, 2006)

Grace Bassett Foot Soldier for Justice — approaching 90, *Grace*, a lifelong activist for African-American equality, is going strong. Like anyone her age, she has seen many changes, but *Bassett*, perhaps more than most, has taken an active part in shaping those changes, and continues to do so. Originally from New Orleans, Louisiana, the current destruction of the Crescent City distresses her profoundly.

In a recent interview, she spoke about her early years. "We were very active in the church. She said, and activities like the Girl Scouts, but at the time, they were not receptive to Blacks." So, *Bassett* joined the YWCA. But it was on a camping trip with the Methodist Church that she realized she liked helping people. She met a woman, a Social Worker, who took her on home visits. "That was my beginning. My whole life began there," she said. She realized that she wanted to be a social worker. In church and high school, *Bassett* became involved in all sorts of activities — chorus, acting, counseling other youth, and dating. "I always had my boyfriends, but I had my activities."

At Dillard University *Bassett* went on a trip organized by her teacher. It was a lunch with students from a white college. "It was my first interracial experience," she said. *Bassett* became active in the Southern Negro Youth Congress, founded in 1937, just before she graduated Dillard with a Bachelor of Arts in Social Work. *Bassett* said SNYC's main focus was registering Black people to vote and voter education drives among Whites and Blacks. "Sometimes we went into unreceptive places," she said, describing how the SNYC and a white student group went to a white neighborhood to do voter education.

While many were friendly "somebody reported us, *Bassett* said. Interracial groups at that time were targets of sheriff departments and the Klan. "So, we ran to our car, jumped in and left. Our program wasn't just for Black people. It was for White people, too, working-class White. We tried to get them to vote and educate them on what to vote for." The activities of the SNYC helped give birth to the modern Civil Rights Movement, she noted.

World War II came, and many men went into the services. *Bassett* assumed leadership roles in the New Orleans SNYC. Later, *Bassett* went to Atlanta to further her education. She traveled to SNYC, organizing meetings in Mississippi. She met and developed friendships with SNYC leaders like

My Family Tree

Dorothy Burnham and James and Ester Jackson. In 1984, *Bassett* was among those interviewed on the SNYC for New York University's (NYU) Tamiment Library.

Bassett moved to Chicago around 1942 with her first husband. *McCarthy* had cost him his job with the transport workers union. *Bassett* got a job with the Daily Worker and later became editor of its Du Sable edition, in which she campaigned for the integration of the White Sox and Cubs baseball teams. At this time, *Bassett* and her husband divorced. It was in New York at a convention when *Grace* met Harlem organizer, activist and writer *Theodore (Ted) Bassett.* They were married in 1952, and *Grace* moved to New York. She joined the ongoing grassroots and electoral struggles there for Civil Rights, peace, low rents, and health care. *Bassett* returned to Social Work at New York hospitals until she turned 70 when *Ted* took ill, and she retired to care for him. *Theodore Roosevelt (Ted) Bassett* died in 1994. *Bassett* is a member of the People's Weekly World's editorial board and volunteers her skills on a weekly basis. She is now a community activist in Manhattan. "I can't stand to just sit around," *Bassett* said. 📖

Note: Grace Colwell Thornton Bassett *passed Sunday, November 10, 2013, with her family at her side.*

Monique Anthony Cowan   b. Monday, March 5, 1990

This is the testimony of my life so far:

When I was born, my *Uncle Stephen [1] (Fee)* named me. My parents are *AnRico Celete Levonia Cowan Lockhart [1] and Victor Richard Robison.* I was raised and lived in Detroit most of my life. I was raised by my grandmother *(Toni Sue Cowan)*, a.k.a. *Nana*. Along with my *Nana*, I had two more strong women in my life, which was my great-grandmother *(Levonia Cowan), a.k.a . Grandma* and my *Nana's* second older sister *(Norma Mason), a.k.a. Aunt Jean, plus godmother.* I am the oldest of my siblings, and my younger sister is *AnRico Celete Levonia Scott [II].*

I spend my days laughing and listening to family stories from these three women more of *Aunt Jean* who always had me laughing until my stomach was hurting. These women shape me into being the woman I am today. When I hung out with *Aunt Jean*, we spend a lot of time working in her garden with her dog who was named *Milana*, who was my best friend at that time. She told me how she played a role in raising her younger sisters, how life was like in her time and taught me how to grow plants and now that I am older I know how to take care of plants. *Aunt Jean* show me how to pick fresh green beans from her garden. My *Grandma* and *Aunt Jean* always watch me when my *Nana* had to work. These women made sure that I ate good, that we did fun things together, and that I was comfortable. *Grandma* was always cooking for me and she show me how to cook as a little girl. I remember the first time I spend the night at *Aunt Jean* house in the winter as a little girl, I didn't know that she put so many blankets on me until I was trying to turn over on my side and couldn't, I prayed until I fell asleep that I didn't have to go to the bathroom, because I would have to call out for help and hope someone heard me. The next

My Family Tree

morning, I told *Aunt Jean* about the blankets and she start laughing, she told me sorry that she was trying to keep me warm.

My *Nana* has supported me every step of the way on my dreams, and she made sure I had everything I need to excel in this life, but she was no joke, she meant business. I graduated from Cody High School in June 2008 with honors in Detroit. I started traveling the world, perfecting my talent as a professional Cosmetic Artist. From the time I was born, my uncle always kept a close eye on me and who was around me, especially when I had to walk to and from school. My *Uncle Fee* will always come up to me out of nowhere when a guy walks up to me and tell me to get in the car. *My Uncle Fee* made sure that I knew that I was loved, his hugs was breathtaking, he was always encouraging me to do my best, and he would show that he cares. To be honest my *Uncle Fee* was my father figure, my *Uncle Fee* and I talk all the time until he passed. *My Uncle Fee* was cool as hell, but he was no joke and he kept it real with me about getting a good education, watching out for these dead-beat guys, don't let nobody use me and how life was on the streets, and to stay off of them. My *Nana*, my sister *AnRico,* and I have a great relationship, and we hang out together. Now, I am part-owner of a Beauty, Cosmetic and Personal Care Company. I would like to say thank you and love you — *Nana, Grandma, Uncle Fee, and Aunt Jean*. I miss my *Uncle Fee and Grandma,* I wish both of you was still here with me, I miss both of you dearly. 📖

Jessica Marie Thues  **b. Monday, October 27, 1986**

This is the testimony of my life so far:

I was a gift of life from GOD, born to *Venus Renee Mason Thues and Jerome Anthony Thues*. I have an older sister — *Lakeisha Renee Thues-Stiff*. I graduated from Mumford High School in June 2005 in Detroit with honors and moved on to higher learning at Everest Institute in Dearborn and graduated in 2014 as a Medical Assistant. I love the medical field; my next step is to study for the State Boards for Nursing. Plus, I have a background in marketing.

I am a mother to my beautiful daughter *Ramiyah Kimberly White* was born on Friday, May 28, 2004, in Detroit. I love to dance and hang out with family and friends. I am into fashion — hair styling, make-up, clothes, shoes, shopping, and jewelry. I love my life, my family and caring for people. 📖

My Family Tree

Darren Antwon Sawyer   b. Friday, August 9, 1963

This is the testimony of my life so far:

I was a gift of life from GOD, born into a union of the late *Alva Jean Davis Sawyer and Donald R. Sawyer* in Virginia Beach, Virginia — Virginia Beach County. I graduated from West Forsyth High School in June 1979 in Winston-Salem, North Carolina — Forsyth County. After High school, I spent thirty years in the United States Navy (ISCM Dillard Retirement Ceremony).

I am a former Navy Captain — Intelligent Information Systems and studied at Virginia Military Institute in Virginia. I currently work for the United States Federal Government. I met and married *Blanche Y. Peppers Sawyer* on Saturday, April 27, 1991. We were blessed with two sons. *Xavier J. Sawyer* was born on Wednesday, October 5, 1994, in Portsmouth, Virginia — Norfolk County. Our other son, *Alexander J. Sawyer,* was born on Wednesday, October 15, 1997, in Portsmouth, Virginia — Norfolk County. 📖

Frances Vencelia Peppers   b. Friday, August 9, 1963

This is the testimony of my life so far:

I was a gift of life from GOD, born into the union of the late *Mildred Elizabeth Strickland Peppers and Ronnie Carl Peppers*. I was born on August 9, 1963, in Winston-Salem, North Carolina — Forsyth County, the second oldest of my siblings.

I graduated from East Forsyth High School in June 1981 in Winston-Salem, North Carolina — Forsyth County, moving on to North Carolina Agricultural and Technical State University NCA and TSU (Aggies), receiving an MBA in Electrical Engineering in 1985 in Greensboro, North Carolina – Guilford County. I grew up in Winston-Salem with my family. I currently live in Newport News, Virginia, with my best friend *Dallas (my dog)*. Living a full life with love and happiness with my family and friends. God, family, and dear friends mean everything to me. 📖

Carolyn Mack Lipscomb White   b. Saturday, June 24, 1944

This is the testimony of my life so far:

I was a gift of life from GOD, born in the union of the late *Bertha Mack and McKenzie Mack.* I was born on June 24, 1944, in New York. I graduated from New York City Public School.

In 1970, I earned a Bachelor of Arts at City College in New York, and in 1972 earning a Master of Social Worker at Columbia University in New York. I am an American Protective Services Official, Social Worker, and Certified teacher — both in New York and a Peace Officer. I am also a member of the Columbia University Alumni and Probation Officer Association. A member of the Democratic Black Caucus, Mount Vernon, since 1995 and an Advisory of the board Community

My Family Tree

Service Council since 1993. I have been a busy-bee. I was a College Counselor at City University in New York, Bayside, and New York from 1972-1975. I was also in Sales and Marketing for Xerox in New York City from 1975-1980. I was an Escort Interpreter for the United States Department of Washington from 1972-1990. A Probation Officer Gang Related Intervention Program of Westchester County (New York) Department Probation, White Plains, since 1990. I am a proud owner and contractor of C and D Update Interiors, Mount Vernon, and New York from 1980-1990.

Between all my work, I met and married the love of my life on Sunday, April 3, 1977, in New York City, the late *DeWitt Shuford White*; he passed in July 2019.

When God Calls

With a heavy heart and a bowed down head when God has called for one of his angels to come home to rest. All the life experiences we shared with them, while they were setting examples for us, their love, joy, happiness, laughter, and their work ethics. They have walked with each of us through life's ups and downs with God helping to guide us along the way. They have always shown us to put God first and always put our hands in God's hands while keeping God at the center of our table. I wrote this poem for them.

By Stephanie M. Mason © 2024

My Family Tree

The Journey

Why Do You Creep So Softly Into My Conscious

Telling Me That It's Time To Go

I Ask You Why

You Didn't Say a Word

I Question Myself

I Don't Remember Having Any Plans

The Voice Comes Again, Saying I Have To Go

The Voice Said You Don't Have Time To Do What You Want To Do

You Come Creeping So Softly Into My Conscious

The Voice Comes To Me With A Warm Feeling

Like You Know Me

I Have Things To Show You

It Will Be Different

Things You Wouldn't Imagine

But Before I Show You

You Have To End To Begin

Don't Be Afraid My Child

Now I Understand That I Have To Travel This Journey By Myself

I'm Sorry

I Don't Mean To Leave You Behind

When I'm Gone, I Know Your Eyes Will Weep, And Your Heart Will Feel Heavy

Just Remember The Good Times We Had Together

I Feel So Free

But I Will See You Again

I Love You So Much

By Stephanie M. Mason © 2024

My Family Tree

A Word of Inspiration

GOD has taught us the GOLDEN RULE — to "LOVE" ye one another; and that we are bone of one bone, and flesh of one flesh; when one hurts, we all hurt, when one needs, we all need;

That when two or three come together on one accord in "**I AM's**" name, touching and agreeing, there **I AM** is in the midst to bless and satisfy the needy ones. (…words spoken by **I AM** through the mouth of ***Bishop Reverend Gary M. Simpson***)

We are that family that loves, plays, laughs, helps each other, and prays together to stay together, even when a family member has gone from this world to be with the ***Holy Father***.

- *Take your notes while you are down here and watch out how you treat people and how you live your life, or you will be back down here with your bookbag back in school.*
- *{Our main purpose in life is to*
-
- *Live Life - To the fullness*
-
- *Learn - God's ways*
-
- *Help - God's children and yourself*
-
- *Witness - God's unchanging hand*
-
- *Testify - of God's glorious works.*
-
- *And praise God's Holy Name}*

- *By Stephanie M. Mason © 2024*

⌘

My Family Tree

Will The Circle Be Unbroken

Their ancestors, our ancestors, endured strange lands

Separated from their families, customs, worship, and language

These dark-skinned people survived, grew strong, and established new families

They long to see their loved ones who was left behind, sold off, or killed

They fought and dreamed for the day to see freedom

Free from separation, racism, slavery, abuse, and our women being raped

Their ancestors, our ancestors, struggled through slavery

They had run and fought for their freedom, our freedom

A lot of them died along the way, and most survived

We as a people always strive to achieve higher

By watching, listening, and learning from the old ones

On how they better themselves and their families to come

There were always hard times living in the south

Long days and a lot of hard work facing them

In the north was a given back then

The north was a hard road to travel

But were you really free

Not knowing if the beast was going to drag you back or worse

Trying to be one step ahead of the beast

Sometimes, they helped along the way to freedom

It was scary and dangerous to travel with or without the beast or the native tribes.

Always trying to keep the family together

These loved ones whose names appear on these pages

Read their testimonies, see how they lived their lives

They went through so much to pave the way for our future

Never let their memories grow dim with the passage of time

May their memory of sacrifices ever be with us as a guide into our tomorrows

My Family Tree

Just remember their spirit is always with us

Their memories lie in our hearts and in our minds

No, the circle will never be unbroken with our love for them

By Stephanie M. Mason © 2024

⌘

My Family Tree

In Loving Memory

It is here that we re-produce some of the obituaries of the family. It is our tribute to the contributions of their lives, the love they shared, the lessons taught and the memories we ever hold dear.

Editor's Note: As these are reproductions, care has been taken to maintain fidelity to the original statements, including grammar, spelling, and names. We have tried not to change what was written — to the best of our ability. ∞

Rev. John Thomas Hairston   Friday, September 8, 1876 – Friday, February 26, 1960

…83 years of age. Son of *Susan Mason Hairston and Wiseman Hairston*. Husband of *Martha Y. Jordan Hairston*. He had been a minister and lived at 836 Austin St. at the time of his death. He had been pastor of Shiloh Baptist church for 53 years and a former president of the General Baptist State Convention. The forgoing bio was posted by Find-A-Grave Member Sleeping Dog in 2012.

A short biography of *John Thomas Hairston* was published in the 1921 book "History of the American Negro and His Institutes." That bio provides birth date and place, father *(Wiseman Hairston)*, mother *(Susan "Susie" Mason)*, paternal grandparents *(Bashie Hairston and Adam Hairston)*, and maternal grandparents *(Phyllis Ann Brown Hairston Mason and Burrell Mason)*. The bio notes, "They were all slaves, and hence, he cannot trace his ancestry further back."

John Thomas Hairston attended public schools in Davie County before graduating from Livingstone College in 1904. He then attended Shaw University, graduating with the degree of B. Th. [Theology] in 1908. *Dr. Hairston* married *Lucille Ingram* of Rockwell, North Carolina, on Thursday, October 8, 1908. They had two children, *Jasper Roland Hairston and George Thomas Hairston,* before *Lucille Ingram Hairston* died on Thursday, December 14, 1911. *Dr. Hairston* married again to *Nancy Alice Wright* of Asheville on Tuesday, October 21, 1913. As of 1921, they had two children, *Otis L. Hairston and Elmer Howitt Hairston*.

In the 1930 United States Census (Greensboro, North Carolina – Guilford County), *Dr. Hairston* listed his children as *George T. Hairston* (18 years old), *Otis L. Hairston* (11 years old), *Elmer H. Hairston* (10 years old), *Warren G. Hairston* (9 years old) *and Nancy L. Hairston* (8 years old). *Dr. Hairston's* wife, *Nancy*, died soon after the Census was completed. She died in July 1931 following a " …bad fall down the stairway." *Nancy* was a teacher in the Greensboro City Schools at the time of the accident. In the 1940 United States Census (Greensboro, North Carolina – Guilford County), *Dr. Hairston* reveals he married a third time following the death of his second wife, *Nancy*. The Census lists his wife as *Martha Y. Jordan Hairston*, age 54, born in North Carolina, occupation — teacher in city schools. Marriage Records lists the marriage of *John*

My Family Tree

Thomas Hairston, age 56, and *Martha Y. Jordan*, age 47, on Tuesday, July 25, 1933. Her parents were *Elizabeth Gordon Jordan and Jacob Jordan.*

Rev. Fisher Robert Mason   Monday, September 9, 1878 – Tuesday, November 23, 1965

The story of the life arid work of *Rev. Fisher Robert Mason*, was a pastor of Mt. Zion Baptist church of Salisbury, was more like romance than biography. He was one of a large family of small children. Losing his father when only a child and brought up in poverty and obscurity, his early years could have given but little promise of the important work he was to do in life. Fortunately for a lad, his mother was spared to him. She was a godly woman and her prayers and the words of encouragement which she gave him in early life started him in the right direction and held him steady during the years. Another fortuitous circumstance in his life was his marriage to a capable and willing Christian woman who has entered heartily and cheerfully into all his plans. He was born at Fork in Davie County Monday, September 9, 1878. His father, *Spencer Mason*, was a farmer. His mother's name was *Lucinda Mason Mason*, and her father *Burleson (Burrell) Mason*, was brought from Virginia to North Carolina in the sixties.

Mr. Mason was married on Wednesday, May 18, 1904, to *Miss Fannie M. Bryant,* daughter of *Elizabeth Meroney Bryant and Rev. William H. Bryant*. Three children have been born to them — *Everett H. Mason*. Two survives. Their names was *Lillie May Mason Davis and Frank Edward Bryant Mason[II]*.

Speaking of his education, *Dr. Mason* says, "He left home to enter the State School at Salisbury in 1898." He had eighty cents with which to begin his studies. His mother gave him the last five cents she had and said, "He might use it for ferry money, and to save the amount he had, instead of using it." He enrolling in the school, he began looking for a job. Work was scarce then, so he got a job cutting wood after school at twenty-five cents a cord at the wood pile of residences. So, he kept his self in school, bought his books and board, and at the close of the term, he had paid all his expenses and purchased his mother some little articles and carried her six dollars in money. That was an opening for him. So, he continued year in and year out until 1900, when he went North to work. He kept in touch with his mother needs and returned and resumed his studies. He began preaching in the country in 1898. Through the summer months he worked on the farm during the week and went to his church on Sunday. His mother permitted him to go to his church on Friday and return to work on Tuesday, since it was forty miles to his church and had to be made on foot."

Dr. Mason's mother survived until 1915 and had the sweet satisfaction of seeing her son firmly established in his work. In February of that year, while he was engaged in evangelistic work at Greenwood, South Carolina, he was called to her bedside, but she passed to her reward before he could reach her.

"Then in 1902 at the close of the year while he was in school, the church of which he pastor called him for its pastor and for sixteen years. He had served it, bringing it from a membership of about fifty to more than six hundred; property valued at that time at about $700.00 was now worth more

My Family Tree

than $30,000.00. During pastorate here, he served as principal of the city graded school for four years, from 1908 to 1912."

In 1917, *Dr. Mason's* report showed that since the beginning of the Salisbury pastorate, he had married more than two hundred couples, baptized five hundred candidates, and conducted one hundred and eighty funerals. *Dr. Mason* experienced the new birth at the early age of ten, was called to preach at eighteen, and was ordained to the full work of the ministry in 1902. His has been a fruitful ministry not only in his own church but in his evangelistic work at well. The meetings which he has held have resulted in the conversion of more than three thousand. He did stand high in denominational circles. He was Vice President of the State Sunday School Convention and President of the Western North Carolina Sunday School Convention. He did belong to Odd Fellows. *Dr. Mason* advocates a closer association of his people with the churches and educational institutes. The story of such a life should be a source of helpful inspiration to all struggling youth. Biography taken from "History of the American Negro and his institutes," edited by *A. B. Caldwell,* Volume IV, 1921.

Rev. Brachelor Kelly Mason   Friday, September 2, 1881 – Saturday, March 16, 1968

Among the younger men who was doing excellent work the *Rev. Brachelor Kelly Mason*, now of Charlotte, North Carolina, had made a great record of accomplishment in his chosen vocation, the ministry. He was in his early prime, born near Fork Church, Davie County, North Carolina, on Friday, September 2, 1881, son of *Lucinda Mason Mason and Colwell Mason.* His mother was the daughter of *Phyllis Ann Brown Hairston Mason and Burrell (Burleson) Mason*, and his father was the son of *G. G. Mason* and, all of them having been brought from Virginia to Carolina in old slave days.

Colwell Mason was a farmer and his son had the usual rearing of a farmer's boy. At the age of 13 he was converted and joined the Cedar Grove Baptist Church. *Mr. Mason* received his elementary training from the country school at Fork Church and arriving at manhood, feeling the call to the ministry, he was licensed by his home church and ordained to the ministry.

His first call was to First Baptist Church, West Raleigh, North Carolina, serving next the Mt. Zion Baptist Church of Reidsville, North Carolina. Coincidentally with these early pastorates, he pursued his college studies first at Livingstone College, Salisbury, North Carolina, and then at Shaw University, Raleigh, North Carolina.

He graduated in Theology in 1911, and college degrees in 1914, holding the degrees of Bachelor of Theology and Bachelor of Arts, both from Shaw University. After four years of service at Reidsville, North Carolina, he was called to the White Rock Baptist Church of Lynchburg, Virginia. This Lynchburg pastorate began in 1914 and terminated in the summer of 1920.

Those six years were years of splendid success. He secured the building of a new church at a cost of $35,000 with modern equipment and conveniences, and far greater than his material success, he added six hundred members to his church. In September 1920, he accepted a call to the Friendship

My Family Tree

Baptist Church at Charlote, North Carolina, thus coming again in close touch with his home state and home people. While in Virginia, he served as a member of the Educational Board of Virginia Baptist State Convention.

Mr. Mason had the usual difficulties to overcome in securing and education, which seems to be the lot of the small farmer's boy. He attended college without a month's tuition ahead and made himself a mail boy for other students and professors, then his early pastorates helped him out. He credits as the most potent factors in shaping his life his faith in God, and the prayers of a godly and sainted mother.

He has been a man of one work, a pastor, and the results so far achieved appear to fully justify his concentration on and consecration to his work. With the Bible and religious literature as the foundation of his reading he has added such a range of secular reading as well serve to keep him in close touch with current events and modern topics. He was a Republican in politics and held membership in the Odd Fellows and Masons. *Mr. Mason* was of the opinion that the best interest of the race was best promoted by racial confidence and self-help, which was mighty good doctrine. He has accumulated some property, now valued at over $30,000, which proves that he was not lacking business qualifications.

Mr. Mason was married on Thursday, October 9, 1913, to *Miss Marie Antoinette Alston,* daughter of *Olivia Mills Alston and Jack Jacob Alston*, of Weldon, North Carolina, and they have one son, *William T. Mason. Mrs. Mason* was educated at Hartshorn College, Richmond, Virginia, and prior to her marriage, was an accomplished teacher. With 14 years of experience in the pastorate, with fine natural ability, with good educational equipment, with large success already won and not yet forty years old, *Brachelor Kelly Mason* bids fair to do a great work if he was spared to the length of days. Biography taken from "History of the American Negro and his institutes," edited by *A. B. Caldwell*, Volume IV, 1921.

Carrie Mozella Clement Cowan   Saturday, September 10, 1881 – Sunday, September 8, 1968

Mrs. Carrie Mozella Clement Cowan, 87, of Man, West Virginia — Logan County, died at Appalachian Regional Hospital, Man. Native of Cleveland, North Carolina – Rowan County to the late *Charles Edward Cowan* [I]. She was born into the union of the late *Emma Ferron Clement and Alexander Clement.* Surviving; *sons, Gilbert Cowan* of Man, North Carolina, *Charles Edward Cowan* [II] of Braeholm, North Carolina; *Allen Cowan* of Chicago, Illinois; *Leslie Cowan* of New York City, New York; daughter, *Mrs. Mildred Cowan Walton* of Huntington, West Virginia.

Odena Allison Rankin   Wednesday, April 23, 1902 – Monday, January 7, 1974

Salisbury — *Mrs. Odena Allison Rankin,* 71, of Route 2, Cleveland, died at Rowan Memorial Hospital Monday. She had been seriously ill for three weeks. She was born April 23, 1902, in Iredell County and was the daughter of the later *Julia Higgins Allison and Walter Allison.* She was educated in Iredell County public schools and was a member of Mount Tabor Presbyterian Church. Survivors include her husband, *Earl Green Rankin; one son, Walter Earl Rankin* of Route 2,

My Family Tree

Cleveland; three brothers, *Everett Allison* of Jamaica, Long Island — New York, *Fletcher Allison* of New York City, New York, and *Ernest Allison* of Troutman.

Frank Edward Rankin   Sunday, December 25, 1927 – Wednesday, October 25, 1978

Troutman — *Frank Edward Rankin*, 60, of Route1, Troutman, died Wednesday at Iredell Memorial Hospital after a brief illness. He was born in Rowan County on December 25, 1927, the son of the late *Ada R. Bradshaw Rankin and James Francis Rankin*. He was a Veteran and was employed at Niemand Industries in Statesville. Surviving — *his wife, Mrs. Lacy Belle Evelina Gray Rankin; one foster son, Felix Graham,* of the home; *two foster daughters, Juanita L. Glaspy* of Route 7, Statesville, and *Cozetta Graham Ramsey* of Route 1, Troutman; *three brothers*, Egg 5:13 an of Route 2, Cleveland, *Elmer Rankin* of Route 1, Troutman and *Howard V. Rankin* of Marina, Florida; *three sisters Clara Clementine Rankin Glaspy* of Route 7, Statesville and *Ethel Mae Rankin Baity and Ruth Rankin Faber*, both of Route 2, Statesville.

Grace Louise Workman Browning   Saturday, January 28, 1922 – Tuesday, July 7, 1981

Grace Louise Workman Browning was born on January 28, 1922, to *Euphonia Bernice Orr Workman and to the late William Essix Workman* in Winston-Salem, North Carolina — Forsyth County. *Grace* was the third oldest child to be born into her family and the second girl.

She joined Waughtown Baptist Church at an early age. She spent most of her young adult life in Winston-Salem, North Carolina, and she then moved to Detroit, Michigan – Wayne County in 1944. Her father, *William Essix Workman* and her three siblings that preceded her in death were *Edward Ray Workman, Treva Mae Workman, and Eugene N. Workman.*

Grace was united in Holy matrimony to *Elwood B. Browning* on Friday, September 13, 1946, in Detroit, Michigan — Wayne County. To this union were born two daughters, *Marva Lorraine Browning and Mona Louise Browning*. In the early nineteen-sixties, she became a devoted member of Good Shepherd Lutheran Church. She was a member of T. U. L. C., 1st District Democratic Party, and was active in the community.

Mrs. Browning was a former employee of the Wayne County Auditors Department and the City of Detroit Employee and Training Department. *Mrs. Grace Browning* was a devoted wife, mother, sister, and grandmother until her passing on Tuesday, July 7, 1981, in Detroit.

She leaves to mourn: *her husband, Elwood B. Browning;* two daughters, *Marva Lorraine Browning Benoit Grant and Mona Louise Browning McMiller*; one grandchild, *LaShawn Maria McMiller*; her mother, *Euphonia Bernice Orr Workman,* and *one sister, Hazel Lorraine Workman Mason (Napoleon Jefferson)* of Detroit, Michigan — Wayne County and *her three brothers, William Robert Workman*[1] *(Melba Elizabeth Thompson), Richard LeRoy Workman*[1] *(Mildred Delores*

My Family Tree

Cherry) of Winston-Salem, North Carolina — Forsyth, *and James Leonard Workman (Evelyn T.)* of South Carolina, and *a host of loving nieces, nephews, in-laws, cousins, family, and friends.*

Earl Green Rankin Tuesday, July 7, 1891 – Friday, May 14, 1982

Mr. Rankin died at 10:55 am on Friday at Rowan Memorial Hospital and had been in declining health for several months. He was born on July 7, 1891, in Mount Ulla Township, North Carolina — Rowan County, the son of the late *Rhody Isabella Cowan Rankin and Pinkney C. Rankin*. He was educated in Rowan public schools and was a retired farmer and a member of Mount Tabor Presbyterian Church, where he was a deacon and trustee. Surviving is a *son, Walter Earl Rankin*, of Route 2, Cleveland; a sister, *Mrs. Mary Ann Rankin Neal* of Mooresville; and four grandchildren.

Walter White Friday, February 12, 1915 – Wednesday, October 19, 1983

Walter White was the loving son of the late *Annie Lee Cornelius White* and *Jay Huge White.* He was born in Cleveland, North Carolina — Rowan County, on Friday, February 12, 1915.

Walter worked in the coal mines in West Virginia, Logan County, for 17 years. In 1953, he moved to Cleveland, Ohio — Cuyahoga County, where he became an Assembler for White Motors. He retired at the age of 62 years old. He was the second oldest out of his twelve siblings. His five siblings who preceded him in death were *Rayford Odell White, Vernie Matilda White, Grace Vivian White, Joseph Linzie White, Isaac E. White, and grandson Rodney Allen Mason.*

In his passing, he leaves to mourn a loving wife, *Lucille Bruce-Wilson White*; one daughter, *Norma J. Mason (Eugene N. Mason)* of Detroit, Michigan; one son, *Randy White (Donna)* of Cleveland, Ohio — Cuyahoga County; two sisters, *Mary Bell White Whiteside (Otho)* and *Anne Lou White Awanna (John)* of North Carolina, five brothers, *Andrew Wilson White (Jane)*, and *Dewitt Shuford White (Carolyn Mack Lipscomb)* of New York City, *John Carl White (Eloise Rankin)* of Detroit, Michigan, *Nathaniel White (Hazel Dell McElmore), and Jay Roger White (Gloria)* of Cleveland, Ohio — Pitty County; *two beautiful granddaughters Stephanie M. Mason and Iris A. Mason* of Detroit, Michigan; five nephews, six nieces and many other relatives and friends.

Elmer Rankin Tuesday, August 26, 1913 – Thursday, October 20, 1983

Elmer Rankin, 70, lived at Route 1 in Troutman, North Carolina. He died Thursday night in Iredell Memorial Hospital following a brief illness. He was born on Tuesday, August 26, 1913, in Rowan County, the son of the late *Ada R. Bradshaw Rankin and James Francis Rankin*. He retired from Mooresville Iron Works. His wife, *Rosa Williams Rankin,* of the home. Other survivors include *two sons, Chester Leaser* of Elizabeth City, New Jersey and *Jerry McNeely* of New York, New

My Family Tree

York; *five daughters, Ada Rankin* of Patterson, New Jersey, *Miss Margie Rankin* of Troutman, North Carolina, *Hallie Jane Rankin Davidson* of Statesville, North Carolina, *Ruth Rankin Hall* of Los Angeles, California, *and Marie Rankin Stylin* of Spencer, North Carolina; *two brothers, Robert Lewis Rankin* of Rowan County and *Howard V. Rankin* of Miami, Florida; *two sisters Ethel Mae Rankin Baity* of Cleveland, North Carolina and *Clara Clementine Rankin Glaspy* of Route 7 of Statesville, North Carolina; 21 grandchildren and nine great-grandchildren.

John Lee Glaspy　　　　　　　　　　　　　Sunday, August 16, 1914 – Tuesday, May 14, 1985

He was born on August 16, 1914, in Iredell County, North Carolina, the son of the late *Margaret Lula Allison Glaspy and David Lee Glaspy*. He was employed as a farmer by Edmiston Farm in Rowan County and was a member of Antioch Baptist Church, where he served as a Sunday School supervisor, a deacon, and a member of the senior choir. *Mr. Glaspy* was survived by *his wife, Mrs. Clara Clementine Rankin Glaspy*; *five sons, Scott Reid Rankin* of Mooresville, *William Olly Glaspy* of Frankfort, Kentucky, *Donald Ray Glaspy* of Statesville, *Jay Allen Glaspy* of Plainville, New Jersey, and *Robert Lewis Glaspy* of Troutman; *two daughters, Ada G. Glaspy Graham and Katie Geneva Glaspy Pearson* of Statesville; *three brothers, Joseph Franklin Glaspy* of Mooresville, *Curtis William Glaspy* of Winston-Salem, North Carolina, and *Carlton James Glaspy* of Cleveland; sister *Virginia Catherine Glaspy Cowan* of Cleveland; 54 grandchildren and 27 great-grandchildren.

Euphonia C. Mason Jackson　　　　　　　Sunday, June 13, 1943 – Thursday, January 16, 1986

Euphonia C. Mason Jackson was born on June 13, 1943, to the union of her parents, *Hazel Lorraine Workman Mason and Napoleon Jefferson Mason,* in Winston-Salem, North Carolina — Forsyth County. She was the youngest of four children and the only daughter.

At the age of one, *Euphonia,* her parents, and three brothers moved to Detroit, Michigan — Wayne County. *Euphonia* brothers are *Eugene Napoleon Mason, William Anthony Mason, and Robert Stanley Mason.* She received her formal education in the Detroit Public Schools System. She graduated from Central High School in June 1960.

She accepted Christ in her early teens and was united with The New Mt. Vernon Baptist church during the pastorate of the late *Pastor R. J. Cunningham.* She served on the Young People's Usher Board for quite a few years.

Euphonia met and was united in matrimony to *Sgt. Horace. R. Jackson* by *Pastor J. L. Webb,* on Saturday, September 16, 1961, in Detroit. To this union was, three children were born *one daughter, Euphonia Tracy Jackson* and *two sons, Horace Reginale Jackson and Eric Creighton Jackson.*

My Family Tree

Mrs. Jackson worked for Chrysler Corporation for fifteen years. *Mrs. Jackson* was a loving daughter, sister, a devoted and loving wife, mother, and grandmother.

Mrs. Euphonia C. Mason Jackson departed this life Thursday, January 16, 1986, in the Henry Ford Hospital in Detroit after a two-year illness.

She leaves to mourn her passing and to cherish her memories: her loving husband, *Horace R. Jackson* ; *one daughter, Euphonia Tracy Jackson, and two sons, Horace R. and Eric C.; one grandson, Trevor Anthony Jackson, her parents, Hazel Lorraine Workman Mason and Napoleon Jefferson Mason,* her grandmother *Euphonia Bernice Orr Workman,* her *three brothers, Eugene Napoleon (Norma J. C.), William Anthony (Litha Ruth Walker) and Robert Stanley (Peggy)*, aunts, uncles, *a host of loving nieces, nephews, cousins, and friends.*

Clara Clementine Rankin Glaspy   Saturday, August 26, 1911 – Tuesday, March 11, 1986

Mrs. Clara Clementine Rankin Glaspy, 73, of Route 7, Statesville, died at Iredell Memorial Hospital. She was born in Rowan County, North Carolina, on August 26, 1911, and was the daughter of the late *Ada R. Bradshaw Rankin and James Francis Rankin.* She was a farmer most of her life. *Her husband, John Lee Glaspy,* preceded her in death on May 14, 1985. Surviving are *five sons, Scott Reid Rankin* of Mooresville, *William Olly Glaspy* of Frankfort, Kentucky, *Donald Ray Glaspy* of Statesville, *Jay Allen Glaspy* of Plainville, New Jersey, and *Robert Lewis Glaspy* of Troutman, North Carolina; *two daughters, Ada G. Glaspy Graham and Katie Geneva Glaspy Pearson* of Statesville, North Carolina; of the home; *two brothers, Howard V. Rankin* of Miami, Florida *and Robert Lewis Rankin* of Cleveland; *one sister Ethel Rankin Baity* of Cleveland, North Carolina; 57 grandchildren and 29 great-grandchildren.

Euphonia Bernice Orr Workman   Wednesday, October 1, 1902 – Saturday, January 17, 1987

Euphonia Bernice Orr Workman departed this life Saturday afternoon, January 17, 1987, at Forsyth

Memorial Hospital in Winston-Salem, North Carolina. She was born on October 1, 1902, in Columbus, Ohio — Franklin County, and was adopted into the union of the late *Annie Cornelius Hege Orr and Isaac Orr* as an infant.

Mrs. Workman had spent most of her time in Winston-Salem, North Carolina - Forsyth County. *Mrs. Workman* worked and raised her children with her husband in Winston-Salem. She was a faithful member of the Waughtown Baptist Church until her death. At the Waughtown Church, she was a member of the Senior Choir, the Senior Gospel Choir and on the Deaconess Board. She was also a member of the Belview Community Club and was an active member of the Meridian Chapter #308 O. E. S., Prince Hall Affiliate of Winston-Salem.

Mrs. Workman was a former employee of R. J. Reynolds Tobacco Company and she worked there for twelve faithful years with the E.S.R. of Winston-Salem and the Senior Citizens. She worked diligently with the Sunday school for many years and enjoyed coordinating different plays and

My Family Tree

programs for the church, namely *"The Pathway To Heaven."* She also planned and directed numerous weddings near and far.

She was united in Holy Matrimony to the late *William Essix Workman* on Friday, June 20, 1919, in Lexington, North Carolina — Davidson County, and to this union, eight children were born: *Hazel Lorraine, William Robert [1], Grace Louise, Edward Ray, Treva Mae, Richard LeRoy [1], James Leonard, and Eugene N.* They all played a role in raising *Hazel's* children until they moved to Detroit. She was a full-blooded Cherokee. Euphonia and her oldest daughter (Hazel) always spoke their Native-American tongue fluently in each other's presence.

She leaves to mourn her passing and to cherish her loving memories of her *three sons, William Robert Workman [1] (Melba Elizabeth Thompson) and Richard LeRoy Workman [1] (Mildred Delores Cherry)* of Winston-Salem, North Carolina — Forsyth County, *and James Leonard Workman (Evelyn T.)* of Charleston, South Carolina — Charleston County, *one daughter, Hazel Lorraine Workman Mason (Napoleon Jefferson), and son-in-law, Elwood B. Browning* of Detroit, Michigan — Wayne County; thirteen grandchildren; twenty-one great-grandchildren and nine great-great grandchildren. Relatives and friends will greatly miss *Mrs. Euphonia Workman.* We all loved her, but **GOD** loved her the best.

Eugene Napoleon Mason Monday, November 23, 1936 – Wednesday, October 11, 1989

Eugene Napoleon Mason was born on November 23, 1936, to the union of *Hazel Lorraine Workman Mason and Napoleon Jefferson Mason* in Winston-Salem, North Carolina — Forsyth County. He was the eldest of their four children.

At the age of nine, *Eugene*, his parents, and siblings moved to the west side of Detroit, Michigan — Wayne County. He was educated in the Detroit Public Schools System and graduated from Northern High School in June 1953. He was baptized at an early age at New Mt. Vernon Baptist Church.

Mr. Mason was employed at the Ford Motor Company until he retired on disability in 1980.

Mr. Mason found his temple family while they yet gathered in the basement on Joy Road and Livernois. He served in various capacities of the church. An active member of the body, he served on the Council and the Usher Board, serving terms as president of both. He was also actively involved with the Men's Board. When the church moved to Hamilton and then Conner Avenue, he took it upon himself to serve as caretaker and made sure the church was a clean facility in which to worship.

It was at the **Temple of I AM** that he met *Norma Jean Carey* and became united in Holy matrimony on Friday, July 1, 1967. The marriage was officiated by *Rev. Gary Marcus Simpson* in his backyard on Joy Road and Livernois. Theirs would be the first ceremony performed in the name of **I AM**.

My Family Tree

To this union was born three children, *Rodney Allen Mason, Stephanie Michele Mason, and Iris Althea Mason.*

Active not only in the church but equally in his community, *Eugene Mason* also served for a period as president of the Lesure Street Block Club.

Eugene was a loving son, devoted, loving, caring, and dependable husband, father, brother and friend. The marriage between *Eugene Napoleon Mason and Norma Jean Mason* was the first wedding performed by *Rev. Gary M. Simpson* in the **Temple of I AM**, but also stands as the longest lasting marriage in the temple.

Mr. *Eugene Napoleon Mason* departed this life on Wednesday, October 11, 1989, in Henry Ford Hospital in Detroit after many years of illness.

He leaves to cherish his memories: a loving and devoted wife; *Norma J. Mason, two daughters, Stephanie M. Mason and Iris A. Mason, his parents; Hazel L. Workman Mason and Napoleon J. Mason* and *two brothers, William A. Mason (Litha Ruth Walker) and Robert S. Mason (Peggy)*; his two uncles *Elwood B. Browning, and William Robert* Workman I; his *four sisters-in-laws and four brothers-in-laws; Muslimah Muwwakkil (Abdul Muwwakkil), Elise Love (Eddie A. Trent [I]), (Gene E. Love), Judy C. Cowan Brown (Elco Jr. Brown [II]), and Toni S. Cowan* and a host of loving nieces and nephews; *Gregory Ware, Venus R. Mason-Thues (Jerome A.), Troy A. Mason (Sandar Lewin), Jenean E. Mason, Theodore C. Mason (Audrey F. Holloway), Tyrone Mason, Terrence Mason (Patricia), Linda Mason Gill, Euphonia T. Jackson, Horace Jackson, Eric Jackson, Lisa A. Trent, Eddie A. Trent [II], Stephen I. Cowan [I], AnRico C. Cowan [I], Nakia L. Brown, Maria A. Brown, Abdul R. Salahuddin, Marvinah N. Salahuddin, Sabreen L. Salahuddin, Ebony L. Salahuddin, Ameerah Salahuddin, his great niece; Deidre M. Trent, family, cousins, friends and his **I AM** family.*

Mr. Eugene Napoleon Mason has a story to tell:

Monday, November 23, 1936, was a special day, as it marked my arrival as the first gift of life to my parents — *Hazel Lorraine Workman Mason and Napoleon Jefferson Mason.* My birth took place in Winston-Salem, North Carolina — Forsyth County.

For nine years, life at 808 Marcenia was a time of happiness. As the eldest, mine was a full day at school. *Tony* had a half day. Poor *Bobby* was too young for school. He wanted to hang with the big boys, but "…yet he was always happy when we were all together."

During their time at home (while I was in school), *Tony and Bobby* enjoyed playing in the red clay — and, of course, mud. They would play and watch for me to come down the dusty road with my sweater tied around my waist. After I got home, we would snack on fresh fruit or dried fruit. Then, it was playtime again until supper.

We lived with our grandparents — *Euphonia Bernice Orr Workman and William Essix Workman* (my mother's parents). Our family was a tobacco plant household — the adults all worked for R. J. Reynolds Tobacco Company. My parents worked the same shift. My grandmother worked the morning shift, and my grandfather worked the evening shift. Included in our happy gathering were my Uncles *James (June) and Richard.* They helped to make our lives a dream and joy, something like heaven on earth for little black boys in the post-depression South. My parents moved to

My Family Tree

Michigan to find better jobs — and a home for us. The children remained behind for the time being because they knew we were surrounded by love. Grandma worked at Waughtown Baptist Church when she wasn't at the tobacco factory.

My grandmother was an easy-going woman, but firm in her caring. How often would we listen to her low-toned singing as she cooked or cleaned around the house. My grandfather, although firm and a no-nonsense type, always showed just how much he loved us. But he was not averse to correction. His favorite phrase was that he would have to "tune us up." Sometimes, it was so that we "…wouldn't grow out of our brains." *Bobby* became Grandpa's favorite because he was tongue-tied and had trouble with his speech. The man looked out for him, watched over him, and — young or old — Grandpa would put a whooping on anybody who teased or laughed at *Bobby*. He was also a man who believed in standing up for yourself and your family. As long as he felt a person was trying, he was right there to help. He always stated to us boys, "…that GOD and family come first."

One of Dad's sisters — *Aunt Mildred,* and *her daughter*, *Frances,* also helped take care of us boys. *Aunt Mildred* was nice, but she was also strict. She had a habit of *dipping snuff* (peach snuff, to be exact), and when she *fussed* at us, the juices would fly out of her mouth, landing all over us – face, arms, and clothes. She would get mad if we complained about her juiciness. When she whipped us, part of the indignity was that we would have to go out and select a green switch from her Weeping Willow tree in the backyard. Her warning was, "…if you don't get me a good switch, you are gonna get beat more, you hear me." She would back that up with, "…don't you play with me boy." You just know we hated her fussing at us, plus with tobacco juice flying around, and we couldn't say a word. And it looked and smelled nasty, too. Fussing, tobacco juice and a whipping – but we still loved our life with them.

Miss Honey, one of our neighbors, would often take care of us, helping when the adults of the house all had to be at work at the same time. For the life of me, I can't remember being in want of anything in those days, especially love.

You can imagine that life changed when dad came back and told us we'd be moving to Detroit, Michigan. We'd never been more than ten miles from home. The year was 1944 when dad rented a big truck. Dad and his friend drove the truck to Winston-Salem to get us and the furniture they left behind. We were happy to see momma and going on a road trip to Michigan. We had never heard of Michigan, and we had no idea of where it was. We were so excited to be going on an adventure like this. After a few days everything was loaded in the truck, and it was time to go. Grandma fixed the food we would need for our trip to Michigan. She cooked fried chicken, a loaf of bread and packed bags of apples and peaches. There were a lot of tears – both happy and sad, but it was time to go.

We rode from Winston-Salem to Michigan on the mattress from our beds, placed on top of our stuff in the back of an open truck. It was a great adventure to see cars, streetlights, tall buildings, gas stations, and other sights along the windy highways. Riding in the back of the truck, we had a perfect view to see everything, things we had never seen before. As we went through the mountains and looked down, we saw people, houses, and animals that looked so small. My brothers

My Family Tree

and I couldn't stop talking, laughing, and pointing at different things that one of us had seen. We had a ball.

We had the best time of our lives on this road trip as young boys. The trip took about a day and a half for us to arrive in Michigan. When we arrived, we found that we would be living in the projects of Royal Oak Township. Dad's job (Chrysler) had a housing project built for the black auto workers coming up from the South. We lived in a two-bedroom apartment.

Our parents decided that we all needed to save up for a house. On the third week of the month, momma, my brothers and I would buy food and small things, and dad would put his check in the bank. On the fourth week dad would pay the rent and buy big things. With all of us working together, it didn't take long for us to save up for a house.

Chrysler was acting crazy when dad was laid off for a week. He would work a week and then was off again. There was no compensation unless you were laid off for thirty days or more in a row. Money was tight around the house, but we made it with God's help.

In fact, I put up my age to get a paper route part-time. My brothers got part-time jobs as soon as they were old enough. *Tony* didn't want to carry Newspaper, so he got a part-time job at Duke Theater on west 8 Mile Road and *Bobby* worked part-time as a paper boy, with a big paper route. *Bobby* loved to treat his friends when it was time to collect on his paper route.

When Chrysler went on strike dad went to work at General Motors in Pontiac, Michigan. He worked there for 105 days. When he did go back to work at Chrysler things got much better because he stated that he, "…made more money there." Dad worked twelve hours a day, seven days a week. I got a job at Big Bear, and *Tony* and *Bobby* got better jobs too.

We were the first family in the project to get a car. We were the second family in the project to get a television. *Tony* would always tell his friends, "…that we were poor as dirt," and those knuckleheads would believe him every time. One-time momma heard him, and she said, "boy we are not poor.… stop telling them lies." *Tony's* friends start laughing at him.

Tony, Bobby, and I went to George Washington Carver School for elementary and junior high in Highland Park. *Euphonia* was born a couple of years later. She was a beautiful baby girl.

We went house hunting for the first time as a family in 1951. We found Momma's dream house on Monday, December 3, 1951. Our parents made the down payment; however, we didn't move in until March 1952 because the house wasn't finished. Dad worked two jobs so that we could get the things we needed. He worked at Dodge Main for eight hours and then eight hours at the Brigg Plant, too. Dad and Momma said we had to move out of the projects because "…the apartment was getting too small for us, plus the neighborhood had become too violent." We lived in the projects until 1952 and moved into a house on Alden Street. For the first time, the *Masons* were buying and not renting.

I was baptized at an early age and united with The New Mt. Vernon Baptist Church with my family under the pastorate of the late *Reverend R. J. Cunningham*. I went to Northern High School. *Tony* went to Post Intermediate School, *and Bobby and Euphonia* went to Cluster Middle School on Linwood. Later *Tony* went to Central High School and then transferred to Northwestern. I

My Family Tree

graduated from Northern in June 1954. *Tony* graduated from Northwestern in June 1955, and *Euphonia* later graduated from Central High School in June 1960. I don't remember if *Bobby* graduated from high school with him also working.

I took *Tony* to an interview, and I ended up with the job, just a few months out of school. I got offered a job as an Assembly Line worker for Ford Motor Company. *Tony* always wanted to drive everywhere because he thought he was the better driver. He would speed all the time, trying to scare the living crap out of me. If I didn't let him drive, he would tell on me; then I was in trouble.

Bobby was the first one to get married to *Peggy*. Then *Tony* got married to *Litha* on Saturday, March 19, 1960, in Detroit. *Euphonia* got married to *Horace* on Saturday, September 16, 1961, and I was the last to get married to *Norma* on Friday, July 1, 1967.

When I first became aware of the **Temple of I AM,** they were holding service in the basement on Joy Road and Livernois. I liked what I heard from *Rev. Simpson* and joined in 1965. I am one of the original *"Charter Members"* of the church corporation.

I met *Norma* at the temple. She would accompany her mother *(Mrs. Levonia Cowan)* to service. We dated for several months before I asked for her hand in marriage. We were united in Holy matrimony by *Rev. Gary Simpson* on Friday, July 1, 1967, in Detroit, Michigan. The wedding ceremony took place in *Rev. Gary Marcus Simpson's* backyard. Ours was the first wedding ceremony performed in the temple. After *Norma* and I got married we moved in above *Rev. Simpson* on Joy Road and Livernois — a two-family flat. Before we had any children, we both agreed to get a house of our own. In the early 1970's we bought our home.

To our union, three children were born, *Rodney A. Mason, Stephanie M. Mason, and Iris A. Mason*. Our son, *Rodney,* only survived four days. His death was heart breaking for us and our family. *Norma* didn't know if she could have any more children.

Rev. Simpson instructed *Norma*, saying…"I want you to lay your maternity clothes on the throne of **I AM**." He went on to explain…"you will bear more children." Eight months later she was pregnant with our second child, *Stephanie*, born on Friday, June 20, 1975. After she was born, *Norma* retired from the VA Hospital. One year and four months later, the third pregnancy resulted in the birth of *Iris* on Monday, November 1, 1976. Our two daughters were born and raised in Detroit, Michigan. Our daughters were baptized by *Rev. Simpson* and raised at the **Temple of I AM** on Conner.

I was employed at the Ford Motor Company until I retired on disability in 1980. *Norma* would not go back to work until both girls were in school full-time. With me having to retire at an early age (on medical disability) money was tight. I never counted on my wife's money to pay the bills but now I do, and I am not pleased with it. My wife and daughters are supposed to depend on me, not the other way around. I know **GOD** will make away for us. I put my trust in **I AM**. *Norma* went back to work at Gesu Private School part-time to help with the bills. *Norma* and I made sure the girls were well taken care of with the help from the girls' godparents, *Earlene Jackson Ray and Lee Ray. Lee Ray* worked at the plant (Ford Motor Company) with me. *Earlene and Lee* lived three doors down from us. With their help and the grace and mercy of **I AM**, we made it through.

My Family Tree

I served in various capacities of the church. I was the president of the Usher Board, president of the Council and involved with the Men's Board. I am the President of the Lesure Street Block Club. I help my pastor and the men of the church with the building and orchestrate various activities at *I AM Showcase Supper Club* in Highland Park, Michigan. I attended every *Creator's Day Service,* which takes place on the first Saturday of August until I was not able to go. I had retired on disability in 1980 because of surgery that went wrong, and slowly but surely, my health started to decline.

Before I took **I AM** hand, I asked six people to come to my hospital bedside. I asked my two brothers, my parents, and the girls' godparents to please step up and help my family in any way they can. They all gave me their word that they would. Then I asked, **I AM** to please watch over them and guide their footsteps and please let them know I love them so much and I will see them again in GOD's many mansions.

⌘

Postscript: A very special word of appreciation is extended to *Earlene Jackson Ray and Lee Ray* for the exceptional amount of love, caring and assistance they have provided in the ensuing years. I also extended my hand to my brother *William Anthony Mason (Tony)* and his wife *Litha Ruth Walker Mason* in love for their guidance, reassuring my girls and my wife – *Norma,* on their life experiences, always handling them with the loving care of my family in my absence. Know that the *Masons – Norma, Stephanie, Iris*, and I are eternally grateful, and we love you. Thank you so much from the bottom of our hearts!

Mary Ann Rankin Neal   Monday, May 25, 1896 – Saturday, November 30, 1991

Mary Ann Rankin Neal, 95, lived at 521 W. McClellan Avenue in Mooresville, North Carolina, at the time of her death. She died on November 30, 1991, at Lake Norman Regional Medical Center in Mooresville. She was the daughter of the late *Rhody Isabella Cowan Rankin and Pinkney C. Rankin.* She was a member of the Mount Tabor Presbyterian Church. *Mrs. Neal* was a homemaker and was a Rowan County native. *Mrs. Neal's husband, Henry Luther Neal,* preceded her in death. The survivors are her *daughter-in-law (Bessie Lee Stockton Neal)* and 10 grandchildren, 22 great-grandchildren, and two great-great-grandchildren.

Dorthea M. Mason White   Thursday, August 4, 1927 – Thursday, November 15, 1990

Doretha was born on August 4, 1927, in Chatham County, North Carolina, to *Roxanna S. Smith Mason and Raymond D. Mason [1]*. She departed this life on November 15, 1990, in Columbus, Ohio – Franklin County. *Her husband Abney* preceded her in death; they were married for 43 years.

My Family Tree

Elwood B. Browning   Tuesday, November 22, 1910 – Monday, January 18, 1993

Elwood B. Browning was born in Bowling Green, Kentucky – Warren County, son of the late *Alma Davis Browning and Charles Browning on* November 22, 1910. At an early age, he was reunited with his father in Detroit, Michigan – Wayne County.

Elwood proudly served in the United States Armed Forces during World War II and was honorably discharged. He attended Michigan University. *Elwood* was united in Holy matrimony on Friday, September 13, 1946, to *Grace Louise Workman* from Winston-Salem, North Carolina – Forsyth County. His beloved wife preceded him in death on Tuesday, July 7, 1981.

Elwood was a member of the International Masons. He was very active in the Congressional District and was a Precinct Delegate for many years. He was also active in the U. A. W. Union. *Elwood* joined Good Shepherd Lutheran Church in the 1960s and was very active and a member of the Men's Club until his illness.

Survivors include *two daughters, Marva Lorraine Browning Grant (Tommy Grant)* of Detroit, Michigan and *Mona L. Browning Cooper (Willie Cooper)* of Fort Lauderdale, Florida, *two grandchildren, Lashawn M. McMiller and Justin Merrick Malone,* devoted *sister-in-law, Hazel Lorraine Workman Mason (Napoleon Jefferson),* and great niece – his caretaker, *Euphonia Tracy Jackson* and *a host of loving nieces, nephews, cousins, family and friends.*

Lucille Bruce-Wilson White   Friday, July 6, 1923 – Saturday, July 30, 1994

Mrs. *Lucille White* was born in Jackson, Mississippi, on June 6, 1923, to the late *Virginia Bruce and Wardell Bruce*. She was united in holy matrimony to the late *Walter White*. From this union *one son* was born *Randy White*. She confessed Christ at an early age and was baptized at Hope Springs Missionary Church in Jackson, Mississippi. She leaves to cherish loving memories of her, her *only son, Randy, and daughter-in-law, Donna*; one *step-daughter, Norma, and her daughters, Stephanie and Iris* of Detroit, Michigan; two grandsons, *Bryan and Johnathan*; *three sisters: Nellie Bruce McDaniel* of Cleveland, Ohio, *Ida Mae Bruce Woods* of Chicago, Illinois and *Jesse Bruce Turner* of Jackson, Mississippi; *one brother, Allen Bruce*; *one sister-in-law; Frankie Lee Bruce* of Gary, Indiana; two *uncles, Abraham Jones* of Cleveland, Ohio and *Elijah Jones* of Jackson, Mississippi; *one aunt, Benella Arnold* of Chicago, Illinois, and a host of other relatives and friends. She always expressed love, goodness, kindness, and compassion. She was a lovable person. The family humbly submitted to the family and friends: In life, we loved you dearly; in death, we love you still; in our hearts, you hold a place No one else could ever fill.

Lula Virginia Cowan   Wednesday, February 19, 1925 – Sunday, November 20, 1994

Lula Virginia Cowan, 69, of 393 Powell St., Brooklyn, New York – Kings County, died Sunday, November 20, 1994 at Brooklyn Medical Center. *Mrs. Cowan* was born in Rowan County, the daughter of the late *Martha E. Cowan*. She was educated in the Iredell County school system and joined Mount Tabor Presbyterian Church at an early age. Survivors include one daughter, *Phyllis A. Stockton Copeland* of Bronx, New York – New York City Borough; *two brothers, Russell Alberta Cowan* of Cleveland *and Grover Cowan* of Philadelphia, Pennsylvania; *two sisters, Vivian C. Cowan Hyde* of Cleveland *and Nancy Cinora Cowan Haynes* of Brooklyn, New York – Kings County; and two grandchildren.

Hazel Lorraine Workman Mason   Sunday, October 27, 1918 – Wednesday, September 13, 1995

Hazel Lorraine Workman Mason was born October 27, 1918, in Winston-Salem, North Carolina – Forsyth County, to the late Euphonia Bernice Orr Workman and William Essix Workman. She was the eldest of eight children.

Her siblings included (in order) William Robert Workman[1], Grace Louise Workman Browning, Edward Ray Workman, Treva Mae Workman, Richard LeRoy Workman[1], James Leonard Workman, and Eugene N. Workman.

Hazel accepted Christ at the age of seven and was baptized in the creek at Wartown Baptist Church. She attended the Atkins School in Winston-Salem.

She started working at R. J. Reynolds Tobacco Company when she was fifteen years of age. While working at R. J. Reynolds, she met *Napoleon Jefferson Mason*. *Hazel and Napoleon* were married Friday, June 12, 1936, in Winston-Salem, North Carolina. From this union three sons and one daughter were born: *(Gene) Eugene Napoleon Mason, (Tony) William Anthony Mason, (Bobby) Robert Stanley Mason and (Phonia) Euphonia C. Mason.*

In 1944, the family moved to Detroit, Michigan where she worked at Chrysler Jefferson Plant; Packard Motors and Stouffers until she retired. She joined New Mt. Vernon Baptist Church in 1945, and she joined the Usher Board in 1946. She served the church and Usher Board faithfully until her health failed.

Hazel took pride in her family and devoted herself to their well-being. Her wisdom and soft-spoken voice provided wise counsel and guidance for her family. Those who knew her often stated, "Behold, how she loves everybody, even the unloved." She demonstrated unselfish, unchanging, and unconditional love. Her family and all that knew her are better because she was a part of their lives for a short period of time, or nearly seventy-seven years.

In times of trouble and chaos her voice calmed fears, her prayers delivered, and her pleading and begging GOD sustained. She taught us to walk by faith not by sight and told us that "…if you get lost, I know a man who will be your lamp; he will send an angel to guide you to safety." She taught us that success was often disguised as hard work, and barriers and roadblocks were opportunities waiting to be discovered. She was a sweet, fun-loving person with a warm sense of humor. Although she is physically gone from us, she left a store house of love, sense of purpose, the Wisdom of Solomon, patience of Job and love for GOD.

My Family Tree

Wednesday, September 13, 1995, she peacefully departed this earth as her husband, *Napoleon*, son, *Tony*, and daughter-in-law, *Litha*, witnessed her spirit transcend into the arms of *Jesus*.

She leaves to mourn her home going *her husband, Napoleon Jefferson Mason*, of fifty-nine years; *her sons (Tony) William Anthony Mason (Litha R. Walker), (Robert Stanley (Annette); daughter-in-law (Norma J. Mason)*, and *three brothers, William R. Workman (Melba E. Thompson), Richard L. Workman (Mildred Delores Cherry), and James L. Workman (Evelyn T.)*; *thirteen grandchildren*; *Gregory Ware, Venus R. Mason-Thues (Jerome A.), Troy A. Mason (Sandar Lewin), Jenean E. Mason, Theodore C. Mason (Audrey F. Holloway), Tyrone Mason, Euphonia T. Jackson, Horace R. Jackson, Eric C. Jackson, Terrance Mason (Patricia), Linda Mason Gills, Stephanie M. Mason, and Iris A. Mason;* she also leaves ten great-grandchildren, one great-great-grandchild, nieces, nephews, cousins, a number of adopted daughters, family and a host of friends.

"Big Grand Mommy has a story to tell."

– Hazel Lorraine Workman Mason

I was the oldest of eight children born to the union of the late *Euphonia B. Orr Workman and William E. Workman*. There were five boys – *William Robert Workman, Edward Raymond Workman, Richard Leroy Workman, Eugene N. Workman, and James Leonard Workman*. There were three girls - *Grace Louise Workman, Treva Mae Workman,* and me. *Treva Mae* died when she was five days old, and *Eugene N.* died when he was eight months old. As a little girl my mother taught me how to speak her language. My mother was a full-blooded Native-American. We both spoke her native tongue and English fluently until she died. At the age of thirteen I was my parents personal babysitter. That is until my dad got me a job at R. J. Reynolds Tobacco Company at the age of 15.

When I was seven years old, I started cooking for my family. I didn't know how to make biscuits, so I asked my mother, who was ill at that time, to show me. I took the ingredients to her sick bed, and she showed me how to measure everything and how much to use.

In the wintertime, the buttermilk was frozen in a pail that was put in a well on the back porch, so I had to break the ice to get the buttermilk out. We kept things cool in the summertime by putting extra pails in the well on the back porch. We had a wooden stove with a big water tank on the back porch. The water was used for cooking, cleaning, bathing, and doing laundry. The water had to be heated throughout the day and night.

Before we could wash the clothes, we had to scrub out the dirt using a rub board. Clothes were washed in lye soap. All white clothes were placed in a large iron pot with three-legged pot, filled with boiling water to boil them. The clothes were rinsed twice so that they were sparkling clean. In the south, every Monday was wash day. Black and White women would wash other people's laundry for extra money for their households. The labor was intensive from washing laundry all day long. The women back then made sure they cooked a lot of food on Sunday afternoon because they didn't have time to cook on Mondays. Mondays was leftovers day.

When I was not babysitting my siblings, I was cooking, washing, and ironing clothes sheets, cleaning the house, and went shopping at the Country Store for my mother because she was sick a

My Family Tree

lot. I was expected to help with the housework, babysit and go to work at night, too. I didn't have much time for playing. It seems that I have been grown all my life.

I accepted Christ and was baptized in a creek at the age of seven. We went up to the creek for spring and summer baptizing, and we also baptized people in cold weather. All the soil was red clay or sand. It was a long time before we had running water and electric lights. Before that, we had oil lamps.

I started school in Belleville. Belleville had four rooms, and the school grades were from one to six. I attended sixth grade at Columbia Heights Elementary. We had to walk three miles to go to school. When they closed Columbia Heights Elementary, I went to eighth grade at Atkins School. I got as far as the tenth grade before my dad got me a job at R. J. Reynolds Tobacco Company No. #12, making Camel cigarettes at the age of fifteen years old. I had to stop going to school because of my daddy. He stated, "…that this is not the time for you to be going to school because we need money to pay the bills and plus, your mother is sick." I was only fifteen years old, but I could pass for eighteen years old, because I was tall.

As I said before, my mama was very ill when I was growing up. My dad told me that "…if I worked and helped out with the bills until September, I could go back and finish high school." That never happened. I was hoping that I could go back in January, unfortunately I had to keep on working. When I was working in the afternoons, my daddy would come up to my job to collect my pay every Thursday night. We got paid in cash instead of checks. He paid a man to bring me home every night, and sometimes daddy would pay for my lunch. Sometimes I got a few dollars to keep to myself, and sometimes I didn't.

By this time, I met and had start dating *Napoleon*. We wanted to get married at Christmas, but daddy said, "No!" *Napoleon* and I made plans on June 12th when we went to Davie County, where he had been living. The laws were as strict as they were in Winston-Salem about being married under eighteen without your parents' permission. They had to attend. I had to say that I was eighteen and had a friend say she was my older sister. My mother knew about the marriage to *Napoleon,* and she knew I was four months pregnant with our first child. Daddy wasn't happy about my marriage to *Napoleon* when he found out. I told my daddy I would continue to help with the bills around the house. After I got married, I joined Emmanuel Baptist Church where *Napoleon* and his family attended.

We were living with *Napoleon's* sister *Mildred* and her three children. He would pay the rent and help with the food. We lived there until *(Gene) Eugene* was a year old, and my sister-in-law *(Mildred)* had a job, and she started helping us out with *Gene.* Mama kept *Gene* after I went back to work. Fourteen months later, *Tony* was born. *Napoleon and Gene* had Chickenpox. I don't think *Tony* ever had them, and he was very sickly until he was seven years old. *Tony* had pneumonia every October until he was five years old. *Tony* was two years old when *Robert* was born. I wanted a girl so badly that we called him *Bobby*. He had beautiful hair, so I didn't cut his hair until he was two years old. When folks would say, "…what a cute little girl," *Bobby* would say, "…I'm not a girl," and then smile at them. So, we cut his hair.

Euphonia was born June 13, and *Bobby* was four years old. *Bobby* didn't like her at all because he had been the baby for so long. He would take her bottles away from her and drink them. One day,

My Family Tree

I was watching him, and I saw what he had been doing. I had always wondered why she would cry so much. Now I know why.

By the time *Euphonia* was born, *Napoleon* was working at Dodge Main, and I was still working at R. J. Reynolds Tobacco Company. *Napoleon* would move from his siblings' houses and other family members' homes because he didn't want to join the Army. The Army was looking for him, but they couldn't find him at that time. After staying there for a year, he quit his job and came back to stay. Then he got a telegram to report to Dodge Main or the Draft Board for the Army. Needless to say, he went back to Detroit and started looking for a place for us to live. It was hard to find a place to rent if you had more than one child.

In April 1944, *Euphonia* and I moved to Detroit, and the boys stayed with my parents in Winston-Salem. Two days later, *Grace Thornton Bassett and Golden Bassett Wall* came to live in Michigan. We all got jobs in the factory. I worked at Chrysler Jefferson Plant for a few weeks, then I quit and went to work at Packard Motor Plant. *Grace and Golden* worked at Desoto Chrysler. We all worked in the afternoons except *Napoleon and Golden's* brother, *Daniel B. Bassett ^{II}*, so they helped with the babysitting. We put in for a housing project in Royal Oak Township, but it was taking a long time to get in, so we decided to move back to Winston-Salem because the war was almost over.

In June, they called us and told us that there was a building project we should see in Michigan. If we saw it, we would like it. We were told it would be a year before it would be ready. Imagine our surprise when they called us back two weeks later and said the place was ready. We moved in. *Napoleon* was going to get the furniture and boys as soon as possible.

I got ahead of my story. We had such a hard time finding a good babysitter that when Dodge Main went on strike in 1945, *Napoleon* took *Euphonia* back home to Winston-Salem, North Carolina. One week after the war ended, I was laid off for good, and *Napoleon* was off from Dodge Main for the changeover. So, *Napoleon* went to get the kids. Once again, we were all together again. We then began our life on the west side of Detroit.

The boys went to George Washington Carver School. *Euphonia* was too young to go to school. The projects were nice. We had a large playground and plenty of room. I went to work on the midnight shift so that I could be home in the daytime for the kids. When *Euphonia* was old enough to attend school, I got a job at Stouffer's.

Chrysler was acting crazy when *Napoleon* was laid off for a week. Then, he worked one week and was laid off again. There was no compensation unless you were laid off for thirty days or more in a row. Money was tight, but we made it with GOD's help.

The boys got part-time jobs as soon as they were old enough. In fact, *Gene* put his age up to get a paper route. *Tony* didn't want to carry papers, so he got a job at Duke Theater on 8 Mile Road. *Bobby* had a big paper route, but he liked to treat his friends when he collected. We were doing pretty well then.

When Chrysler went on strike again, *Napoleon* went to work at General Motors in Pontiac. He worked there for a hundred and five days when Chrysler was on strike. When they went back to work, things got much better and we all were happy. He worked twelve hours a day, seven days a week. *Gene* got a job at Big Bear Grocery, and *Tony and Bobby* got better jobs.

My Family Tree

We decided to save up for a house, we need more room. Three weeks a month, the boys and I would buy food and small things, and *Napoleon* would put his checks in the bank. On the fourth week he would pay the rent and buy big things. With all of us working, it didn't take long to save the money for a house.

We were the first one in the project to get a car and the second family to get a television. So, at last, in 1951, we went house hunting, due to the neighborhood becoming violent. We found this house on Alden Street in Detroit on Monday, December 3, 1951, and made a down payment. However, we didn't move in until March 1952 because the house wasn't finished. *Napoleon* worked two jobs so that we could get the things we needed. He worked at Dodge Main for eight hours and eight hours at Brigg Plant.

Gene went to Northern High School, *and Tony and Bobby* went to Central High School. *Gene* graduated from Northern High School in June 1954. *Tony* graduated from Northwestern High School in June 1955. *Bobby* quit school and continued working. We were disappointed in him, but I can say this… "he kept his head down and his nose clean, so it did work out." *Euphonia* graduated from Central High School in June 1960. *Bobby* was the first to get married, and then *Tony* got married to *Litha. Euphonia* got married to *Horace*, and *Gene* was the last to get married to *Norma*. I've been married to *Napoleon* for over forty years, and I have thirteen grandchildren and one great-grandson. Life is good.

⌘

Robert Lewis Rankin　　　　　　　　　Thursday, March 15, 1923 – Sunday, November 26, 1995

Cleveland – *Mr. Robert Lewis Rankin*, 72, lived at 1130 Rankin Road in Cleveland. He died at the Veterans Administration Medical Center in Salisbury, North Carolina. He had been in declining health for two years and seriously ill for one month. He was born Thursday, March 15, 1923, in Rowan County and was the son of the late *Ada R. Bradshaw Rankin and James Francis Rankin.* He attended Rowan County schools, and he retired from Grinnell Fire Protection Systems. He was a member of Mount Tabor Presbyterian Church, where he was on the Deacon Board. He was a Veteran of WWII and was a member of J. C. Price American Legion Post No. 107. Survivors include *his wife, Eldora K. Knox Rankin,* of the home; *one brother, Howard V. Rankin* of Miami, Florida; and *one sister, Ethel Mae Rankin Baity* of Cleveland, North Carolina.

Frank Edward Bryant Mason II　　　　　Thursday, March 4, 1920 – Wednesday, April 10, 1996

HIGH POINT - *Frank Edward Bryant Mason, Jr.*, 76, a resident of 1022 Barbee Avenue, died on Wednesday, April 10, 1996, at Starmount Villa Nursing Center, Greensboro, where he had been a patient for six months. He had been in declining health for two years. *Mr. Mason* was born in Orange County, New Jersey, *the son* of the late *Fannie M. Bryant Mason and Rev. Fisher Robert Mason.* He was a graduate of William Penn High School and a member of Temple Memorial Baptist Church. He was a member of the Deacon Board. *Mr. Mason* was self-employed as a barber and was also a retired employee of Reliance Universal. He was a veteran of the United States Army and a member of the Masonic Lodge and Furniture City Elk Lodge. Survivors include *his wife, Mrs. Gladys Beatrice Haith Mason* of the home; *daughter, Mrs. Delores Mason Sieber and*

530

My Family Tree

husband Hal of Greensboro; *son, Frank Edward Bryant Mason III and wife, Delores* of Cincinnati, Ohio; nine grandchildren, among them, *Keith Lipscomb and wife Sharon*, and *Ms. Sequita Renee-Lipscomb* of High Point, *Dwayne Mason and wife Lisa*; 17 great-grandchildren; one great-great-granddaughter; two step-grandchildren; six step-great-grandchildren; a nephew, *Robert (Bobby) F. Davis and wife, Marie* of High Point; *niece, Mrs. Faye Davis Gill and husband, Wilson* of New Jersey.

Napoleon Jefferson Mason   Thursday, July 6, 1911 – Saturday, May 11, 1996

Napoleon was the sixth child born to the union of the late *Ellen Jefferson Mason and Samuel M. Mason* – he was a grandson of slaves. His father was born into slavery as a baby. His grandparents - *Elizabeth Dubose Mason and Robert Mason (Bud)*, were slaves. He was born on July 6, 1911, in Mocksville, North Carolina – Davie County. *Napoleon* was preceded in death by his parents, grandparents, and all his siblings.

Napoleon was baptized at the age of twelve and joined the Baptist Youth Training Union (BYTU). As a youth, he was selected to attend the National Bible Convention in Charlotte, North Carolina – Mecklenburg County.

He moved to Winston-Salem and joined the Emmanuel Baptist Church. At about the same time, he went to work at R. J. Reynolds Tobacco Company, where he met *Hazel Lorraine Workman*.

Napoleon and Hazel courted for nearly two years before they were married on Friday, June 12, 1936. From this union, three sons and one daughter were born: *(Gene) Eugene Napoleon Mason, (Tony) William Anthony Mason, (Bobby) Robert Stanley Mason, and (Phonia) Euphonia C. Mason.*

In 1944, he loaded his family and belongings into a rented truck and moved to Detroit. He was hired by the Chrysler Corporation after he moved from Winston-Salem. He worked at the Jefferson Assembly Plant, Hamtramck Foundry, and Hamtramck Assembly in Hamtramck, Michigan. He was a loyal and faithful employee as well as a reliable and dedicated member of the United Automobile Workers of America. Because of his devotion to his family, he would work double shifts, two jobs at times, and even part-time jobs to provide for his wife, *Hazel,* and his children. Because he lived for the joy and well-being of his family, no sacrifice was too great. After thirty years of service at Chrysler, he retired in good health.

He joined the New Mount Vernon Baptist Church in 1946 and began to serve in many capacities, such as maintenance of the church building and lawn; he served two terms as President of the Usher Board, chairman of the Finance Committee, member of the Male Chorus and as a Deacon and Trustee. *Napoleon* was a member of the Prince Hall Free Mason Lodge, Alden Street Block Club Corporation for twenty years as well as precinct delegate for twenty years and was still serving at the time of his death. During his retirement, *Napoleon* and his beloved *wife, Hazel,* loved to travel all over the world. They went everywhere they wanted and did everything they wanted to do together.

My Family Tree

In addition to their four children, the couple adopted many sons and daughters, including *Maizie, Debbie, Dorothy, Shirley, Jessie, Karen, Olympia, Cynthia, Beverly, and Peggy*. Napoleon was a good neighbor and friend. The neighborhood children loved to sit on his porch and "play" with him. He was also the neighborhood repairman. He willingly "fixed" his neighbor's washers, dryers, stoves, automobiles, lawnmowers, etc. *Napoleon* was known affectionately by many names, especially *"Daddy," "Pops," and "Poppie."* He taught all who would listen to the power of loving someone in spite of their shortcomings, the power of forgiving the unforgivable, and the power of serving others instead of being served. His life demonstrated his wisdom.

Napoleon Jefferson Mason lived a full life. He worked hard, he loved and cared for his family. He shared all that he had with others. He served GOD for over seventy-two years, and it was time for him and *his wife, Hazel*, to be together again in the presence of GOD. On Saturday, May 11, 1996, *Napoleon Jefferson Mason* peacefully departed this earth as his son, *Tony*, and daughter-in-law, *Litha*, witnessed his spirit transcend into the arms of *Jesus*.

He leaves to celebrate his homegoing: *two sons, William Anthony Mason (Litha Ruth Walker), Robert Stanley Mason (Annette), daughter-in-law, Norma Mason, and brothers-in-law: William Robert Workman [1] (Melba Elizabeth Thompson), Richard LeRoy Workman [1] (Mildred Delores Cherry), and James Leonard Workman (Evelyn T.); thirteen grandchildren: Gregory Ware, Renee Mason-Thues (Jerome A.), Troy Mason (Sandar Lewin), Jenean E. Mason, Theodore C. Mason (Audrey F. Holloway), Tyrone Mason, Euphonia T. Jackson, Horace R. Jackson, Eric C. Jackson, Terrance Mason (Patricia), Linda Mason Gills, Iris A. Mason and Stephanie M. Mason;* he also leaves twelve great-grandchildren, five great-great-grandchildren, *a host of loving nieces, nephews, cousins, "adopted" sons and daughters and friends.*

"Poppie has a Story to Tell" (Napoleon Jefferson Mason)

I was the sixth child born to the union of the late *Ellen Jefferson Mason and Samuel M. Mason* and was a grandson of slaves. My father was born into slavery as an infant, and when slavery ended, my father was still an infant. My grandparents — Isabelle *Dubose Mason and Robert Mason (Bud)* were slaves. I was born on July 6, 1911, in Mocksville, North Carolina — Davie County.

My parents and grandparents struggled through a dangerous era in their lives, keeping their heads down and their mouths shut to stay alive, but they saw glory in the end. My dad and his father were sharecroppers (known as – farmers), and they were able to own their own land. We lived on a farm. We had horses, cows, chickens, ducks, geese, hogs, and genies. Genies were a cross between chicken and pheasant. We would feed the chickens and genies and then put them in a pen and clipped their wings so they could not fly away. The genies served as watchdogs because even if a cricket would go by the barn, they would start a chattering and screeching sound. The neighbors didn't like the sounds of the genies at all. The meat was all dark, and we had plenty to eat. I started to work at the age of six, carrying water to the fields for my father. With my dad being a Farmer, we sometimes were unable to go to school(during the harvest months) for the whole year because my dad had us working – plowing the fields, growing crops, and storing the processed crops in the barn, so we could bring money in the house. When we did go to school it was from November until March each year. My dad said, "…only the girls needed an education because they couldn't

My Family Tree

help us out in the fields, and the girls had housework to do, and they had time to get an education." I walked three miles to school and had to walk past a white school just to get to school. We all worked to send my oldest sister *(Mildred)* to college. All of us had to pull our weight to make things run smoothly. *Etta* got married to a man named G. O. *Webster,* and he wouldn't let her work far away from the house.

I went to church every Sunday with my mother and my siblings. My mother made all of our clothes from flour and cotton seed bags. I was baptized at the age of twelve. I joined the Baptist Youth Training Union (BYTU). As a youth, I was selected to attend the National Bible Convention in Charlotte, North Carolina — Mecklenburg County.

My dad's first marriage was to *Elizabeth Mason* in 1883 in North Carolina, and the child they had together was *Addie Mason Haizlip*. Then, he married *Mary Mason* in 1896 in Winston Township, North Carolina – Forsyth County. *Mary Mason* was born on Wednesday, November 5, 1873, in Mocksville, North Carolina – Davie County. *Mary* passed away at the age of 27 on Thursday, July 26, 1900, in Winston-Salem. They had five children – *Etta Mason Webster, Green Mason, Ella M. Mason Neely, Nebraska Mason, and Nevada Mason*. With *Mary's* children living in the house with us, I was the 12th child.

My dad married my mother *(Ellen Jefferson Mason)* on Saturday, October 13, 1901, in Mocksville, North Carolina – Davie County. My mother was born on Saturday, February 28, 1880, in Milton, North Carolina – Caswell County. She passed away at the age of 48 on Thursday, January 26, 1928, in Mocksville, North Carolina – Davie County. She was buried at Cedar Grove Baptist Church Cemetery on Sunday, January 29, 1928, in Mocksville, North Carolina. My mother had nine children. All three of Dad's wives were Domestic Workers cleaning white people's homes.

When my brothers got old enough to make some money, my father would take their money from them. Therefore, as soon as they found another place to stay, they left home. When I got old enough to make some money, my mother got sick. I didn't want her to be alone with my three baby sisters who my father spoiled them rotten. My mother had died, and I left my dad and sisters in Mocksville.

I got a job washing dishes for three dollars a week, and I paid $1.50 a week for a room. I saved $35.00 and put it in the bank. Then the Great Depression came, and I lost all my money like everyone else. When the banks went broke, I went to Philadelphia, and no one was working. In Philadelphia, I joined Liberty Baptist Church and the Secret Order of Woodsmen of the World.

After Roosevelt became President, he put everyone back to work. I went back to Winston-Salem and got a new job at R. J. Reynolds Tobacco Company, and I worked for that company for nine years. In Winston-Salem, I joined Emmanuel Baptist Church. When I was old enough, the military was looking for a few good men to service in World War II. At that time, I was 29 years old. When the U. S. Army sent out draft cards to me in 1940-1947, I started moving among my siblings who lived out of state to run from the military and finally moved to Detroit.

I met and married *Hazel Loraine Workman* on Friday, June 12, 1936, in Winston-Salem, North Carolina – Forsyth County. When *Hazel* and I got married, I was taking care of my sister *Mildred*, who we helped to pay for her education and her three children. Her husband had a car accident and

My Family Tree

killed some white people, so he went to jail. *Hazel* and I had four children: *Eugene Napoleon, William Anthony, Robert Stanley,* and *Euphonia C.*

One of my siblings called and told me that our dad had passed. My dad *(Samuel M. Mason)* was born on Tuesday, January 5, 1864, in Mocksville. He passed away at the age of 73 on Tuesday, March 29, 1937, in Mocksville. His occupation was a General Farmer, and he owned his land. He was buried at Cedar Grove Baptist Church Cemetery Sunday, April 4, 1937, in Mocksville, right next to my mother.

In Detroit, I got a job with Chrysler, and I worked at the Jefferson Assembly Plant, Hamtramck Foundry and Hamtramck Assembly in Hamtramck, Michigan. I had to take the midnight shift to make a dollar an hour more. We had to go on strike to get pension, vacation, overtime pay, and blacks could only get work in the foundry and janitorial work. We went on strike so that black women could work in the plant and for black people to work on the assembly lines. *Walter Reuther* was the head of the unions for automobiles.

I joined New Mount Vernon in 1946 in Detroit, Michigan. I was the President of two (2) Usher Boards, Vice President of the Usher Board, Chairman of the Trustee Board, Chairman of the Finance Committee, Member of the Deacons Board, member of the Male Chorus, a member of the Prince Hall Free Mason Lodge, Alden Block Club President for twenty years and precinct delegate for twenty years.

In the order of my sibling's birth's, included: *Addie Mason Haizlip, Etta Mason Webster, Ella M. Mason Neely, Green Mason, Nebraska Mason, Nevada Mason, Raymond D. Mason I, Mildred Ann Mason Hege, Cornelius Mason, Cleophus Mason, Margaret Mason McCall,* (me) *Napoleon Jefferson Mason, Veada Mason Pittman, Suphonia M. Mason Lewis (Peggy),* and *Brownie Mae Mason Ryder.*

⌘

James Avery Cowan Sunday, January 2, 1916 – Wednesday, July 5, 1997

James Avery Cowan was born into their union January 2, 1916, in Cleveland, North Carolina – Rowan County to the late *Ana Barber Cowan and John Cowan.* He served in the United Stated Armed Forces in World War II in 1943, became 33rd degree Mason and worked at Ford Motor Corporation in Michigan until retirement.

He leaves to cherish his loving memories, *his wife, Mrs. Ella Wilson Crummie Cowan* of Tuscaloosa, Tuscaloosa County, Alabama, and three daughters from Detroit, Michigan: *Judy Carol Brown (Elco Jr. Brown [II]), Elise Love (Eddie Trent [I]), (Gene Edward Love)* and *Toni Sue Cowan* and ex-wife, *Levonia Margaret Carey Cowan;* two brothers *Roy Cowan* and *Ferrell Cowan* of Pittsburgh, Pennsylvania. *Four sisters: Castle Cowan Irvin, Mary Cowan Vance, Kathy Cowan Galloway,* and *Dorothy Cowan,* all of Pittsburgh, Pennsylvania; *six grandchildren* all from Detroit, Michigan: *Lisa A. Trent, Eddie A. Trent [II], Stephen I. Cowan [I], AnRico C. Scott [I] (Sean Scott), Nakia L. Brown, Maria A. Brown* and two great-grandchildren all from Detroit, Michigan, *Deidre M. Trent, Monique A. Cowan,* and *a host of relatives and friends.*

My Family Tree

Virginia Catherine Glaspy Cowan Tuesday, February 11, 1919 – Wednesday, May 31, 1998

Virginia Catherine Glaspy Cowan, 48, Negro, the late *Margaret Lula Allison Glaspy and David Lee Glaspy, her husband Russell Alberta Cowan* and *siblings Otha David Glaspy, Cora Pauline Glaspy Mills, and John Lee Glaspy*, Route 2, Cleveland, who had been hospitalized at Iredell Memorial Hospital since September 12 as the result of an automobile accident died Wednesday at Iredell Memorial Hospital. *Bill Baynard*, county coroner, said he would wait for the results of an autopsy before determining if she died of wreck injuries. If the death is ruled a highway fatality, it will raise the Iredell County Highway death count to 23 persons killed on county roads this year. *Mrs. Cowan* was driving a 1960 Chevrolet, which was struck in the rear by a 1968 GMC truck driven by *Ralph Summers*, 38, of Route 4, Mooresville. The accident occurred on U.S. 21 South of Statesville in front of O.K. Tire Recapping Company. *Baynard* said the attending physician at Iredell Memorial Hospital has requested an autopsy, and he will wait for the report to make an official ruling.

Nancy Cinora Cowan Haynes Monday, November 11, 1940 – Monday, October 5, 1998

Mrs. Nancy Cinora Cowan Haynes, of New York, departed this life on October 5, 1998, at her home in Brooklyn, New York – Kings County. She had had failing health in the past years before being called home by the Lord. At an early age, she joined Mount Tabor Presbyterian Church. She was born on November 11, 1940, to the late *Martha E. Cowan*. She joined Holy Dove Church. She was a member there for 25 years. She leaves behind which she loved and cherished: *her two daughters, Lisa Haynes and Mary Haynes (Jerell Wilson)*; *one son, David Haynes*, and *daughter-in-law, Bobbie Haynes*, all from Brooklyn, New York; *one granddaughter, Olympia Nicole Harris, and two grandsons, Freddie Haynes and Jerryl Jairus Wilson*, all from Brooklyn, New York; *one sister Vivian C. Cowan Hyde* of Cleveland, North Carolina; *two brothers, Russell Alberta Cowan* of Cleveland, North Carolina *and Grover Cowan* of Philadelphia, Pennsylvania, and *a host of nieces and nephews, cousins, and friends.*

Charles Edward Cowan II Thursday, July 6, 1916 – Monday, April 12, 1999

Charles E. Cowan II, 82, of Amherstdale, died on Monday, April 12, 1999, in Logan General Hospital after a long-time illness. He was born in West Virginia – Logan County, to the late *Carrie Mozella Clement Cowan and Charles Edward Cowan I*. He was a member of Mount Olivet Missionary Baptist Church, a retired Miner, and a former owner of Exxon Service Station in Amherstdale. Surviving: *wife, Emma L. Lyons Cowan*; *one son, Donald Cowan* of California City, California; four grandchildren; four great-great-grandchildren.

Russell Alberta Cowan Tuesday, July 4, 1916 – Friday, June 25, 1999

Mr. Russell Alberta Cowan, 82, of 1130 Shinnville Road, Cleveland, North Carolina., died Friday, June 25, 1999, at Forsyth Memorial Hospital. He was born in Rowan County to the late *Martha E. Cowan. Mr. Cowan* attended Rowan County schools. He was a lifetime member and elder of

My Family Tree

Mount Tabor Presbyterian Church and served on the board of directors at Crescent Electric. He also served on the board of trustees at Iredell Memorial Hospital and was a member of Masonic Lodge #395 of Mooresville. His *wife, Virginia Catherine Glaspy Cowan,* also preceded him in death. Survivors include *a daughter, Virginia Theodoric Cowan Witherspoon,* of Cleveland, North Carolina; four grandchildren; three great-grandchildren; a brother, *Grover Cowan,* of Philadelphia, Pennsylvania, and *one sister, Vivian C. Cowan Hyde,* of Cleveland, North Carolina.

Euphonia Tracy Jackson Monday, February 26, 1962 – Sunday, July 18, 1999

Euphonia Tracy Jackson was born on February 26, 1962, in Detroit, Michigan – Wayne County, to the proud parents of the late *Euphonia C. Mason Jackson and Horace R. Jackson. Tracy* made her final transition from the physical world to the spiritual world on Sunday, July 18, 1999; she was 37.

Even as a toddler, this beautiful bundle of "joy" was filled with excitement and adventure. She enjoyed camping, boating, and "playing" the motherly role to her younger *siblings, Horace R. and Eric C.*

As a teenager, because of *Tracy's* beauty certainly kept the phone ringing because of her many male suitors. The watchful eyes of her dad *(Horace R.)* kept them at bay. *Tracy*, however, was not daunted by this inordinate amount of attention. Her passion for reading and zest for learning assisted her in graduating with honors from Cooley High School in Detroit in June 1980. Shortly thereafter, *Tracy* attended and graduated from Lewis College of Business with a degree in Cosmetology. Her final place of employment was with Daimler Chrysler on the Assembly Line. *Tracy* later bores two beautiful children, a son, *Trevor Anthony Jackson,* and a beautiful daughter, *Trina Thomas,* who resembles her "ma."

Tracy saw *Stephanie and Iris* as her little sisters and watched them on the weekends to give *Aunt Jean* a break after their dad *(Uncle Eugene)* passed. She loved doing hair, cooking, and cleaning and loved hosting parties at her house.

Tracy will be dearly missed. There are also many who will cherish her precious memory, including an adoring son, *Trevor,* and a "vivacious" daughter, *Trina.* A loving *father, Horace;* her two brothers, *Horace and Eric;* a "doting" Grandma *Ruth, David Thomas, Aunt (Jean) Norma Mason, Iris Mason, and Stephanie Mason;* a host of loving uncles, aunts, nieces, nephews, cousins, and friends.

My Family Tree

Levonia Margaret Carey Cowan   Tuesday, May 20, 1919 – Monday, September 27, 1999

Levonia Margaret Carey Cowan departed her life on September 27, 1999. She was born to the union on May 20, 1919, of the late *Helen Bass Carey and Charles Carey* in Holden, West Virginia – Logan County. She was the youngest of six *siblings* - *Wilbur C. Carey[I], James A. Carey, and Vereece Carey Gant* (each of whom preceded her in passing). She was survived by her sisters *Isabelle Carey Morrison and Jetta Malinda Faulkner Childs.*

As a child, *Levonia* only knew she had two older sisters, and she had an older sister she never met but heard so much about *Jetta Faulkner Childs. Levonia* accepted Christ as a young child.

She attended public schools in West Virginia. In Holden, she worked in the Boarding House as a Domestic Worker. Later, after leaving the Boarding House, *Levonia* found a job working in a factory as an Assembly Line Worker at Aviation Factory during World War II, building airplane parts for the military in Detroit. Until the men return from the war and took the factory back over, then she found a full-time job as a Domestic Worker for Catholic Social Services after the war. She worked for Catholic Social Services for 30 years, retiring in 1970.

In the late 1940s, she sent for her two older daughters, *Roxie and Norma,* to move to Detroit with her. She also found a part-time job as a Domestic Worker in private homes to earn extra money for her household. She married in the early 1950s — *James Avery Cowan* from Cleveland, North Carolina – Rowan County. *Levonia and James* had three daughters born into their union – *Judy, Elise, and Toni.*

She met *Rev. Simpson* in the late 1950's, and she start working for him part-time as his housekeeper. In the early 1960's she would visit the **Temple of I AM** with her daughters. *Levonia* had observed *Rev. Simpson's* dedication to GOD and in which he delivery his message to the people. It was through her love, dedication, and commitment to the temple that there are the three pulpit chairs and podium that grace the chapel of the temple.

After she retired from the workforce, she lived in the Herman Garden projects in Detroit. She had a chance to meet her older sister, *Jetta Malinda Faulkner Childs,* who was born in Holden, Logan County, West Virginia and was moved as a child to North Carolina to be raised by her father side, which were *Masons. Levonia* was also a member of the Eastern Stars for over 30 years.

She was a loving mother of *five daughters*, *Roxie – Muslimah Muwwakkil* (Abdul Muwwakkil), *Norma Mason, Elise Cowan Love (Gene Edward Love), Judy Carol Cowan Brown, and Toni Sue Cowan,* and two sons-in-law, *Elco Jr. Brown[II], and Eddie Andrew Trent[I], her fifteen grandchildren, Ebony Salahuddin Salibs, Sabreen Salahuddin, Ameerah Salahuddin(Tariq) Lydick, Marvinah Salahuddin Sibinowitz, Lisa Trent, Eddie Trent[II], Stephen Cowan[I], AnRico Scott (Sean), Nakia Brown, Maria Brown, Stephanie Mason, and Iris Mason, ten great-grandchildren Stephen Cowan[II], Destiny Robinson, Trevon Cowan, Deidre Trent, Hamazah Lydick, Safadin Lydick, Mustafa Lydick, Ridhwana Lydick, and Monique Cowan* and *a host of loving cousins, nieces, and nephews. Levonia* was dearly loved and will be missed by all.

My Family Tree

Genie Elizabeth Partee Avery   Friday, November 8, 1912 – Wednesday, April 18, 2001

Genie Elizabeth Partee Avery, 88, formerly of 815 Partridge Ave, Chesapeake, Virginia, died Wednesday, April 18, 2001, at Spencer Health Care Center, Spencer, after a period of declining health. Born November 8, 1912, in Salisbury, *Mrs. Avery* was the daughter of the late *Vernie Mae Cornelius Partee and Miles H. Partee*. She was educated in the Salisbury schools and graduated from J. C. Price High School and Booker T. Washington Night School, Norfolk, Virginia. She retired from the Virginia schools. A former member of Church Street, now Trinity Presbyterian Church, she was previously affiliated with First United Presbyterian Church, Norfolk, Virginia. She was a member of Covenant Presbyterian Church, Norfolk, Virginia, where she was an ordained deacon and a member of the choir. Her husband, *William Henry Avery*, died December 16, 1999. Survivors include sisters *Esther Naomi Partee Baker* of Prairie View, Texas –Waller County, and *Martha Lucille Partee Witherspoon* of Salisbury, North Carolina – Rowan County.

William Olly Glaspy   Thursday, November 1, 1934 – Friday, August 3, 2001

He was born in Rowan County, North Carolina, to the late *Clara Clementine Rankin Glaspy and John Lee Glaspy*. His nickname was *Bill*. He retired as an employee of the State of Kentucky. He died on August 3, 2001, at Frankfort Regional Medical Center in Frankfort, Kentucky, at the age of 66. His siblings who preceded him in passing were *Francis Lee Glaspy and Virginia Ruth Glaspy. Bill* will be dearly missed. There are also many who will cherish his precious memory, including his special friend *Elizabeth Matney* of Frankfort, Kentucky; his children *Diane Caldwell*, of Mooresville, North Carolina; *Monika (Richard) Moore and Edward Tillman*, both of Frankfort, Kentucky; *Monica Garner and Rodney Garner*, both of Statesville, North Carolina; *David Rankin* of Cleveland, North Carolina and *Eugene Hyde and Gregory Pulliam* of Salisbury, North Carolina. His siblings are *Scott Reid Rankin* of Mooresville, North Carolina; *Ada G. Glaspy Graham and Donald Ray Glaspy* of Statesville, North Carolina; *Jay Allen Glaspy* of Newark, New Jersey; *Katie Geneva Glaspy Pearson* of Plainville, New Jersey and *Robert Lewis Glaspy* of Troutman, North Carolina.

Tommy Lee Rankin   Friday, August 25, 1933 – Monday, August 13, 2001

Winston-Salem – *Tommy Lee Rankin*, 67, lived at 418 W. 25th Street at the time of his death. He died on Monday, August 13, 2001, at his home. Born on Friday, August 25, 1933 in Rowan County. Mr. Rankin was the son of the late *Hilda Rankin Ramsey and Joseph Knox Ramsey*. He worked in the textile industry in New York and was a member of Mount Tabor Presbyterian Church. His wife, *Marie P. Rankin,* preceded him in death. Survivors include *his brothers, James Ramsey and Nathaniel Ramsey*, both of Troutman, North Carolina, *Kent Ramsey* of Statesville, North Carolina, and *Chris Robertson* of Winston-Salem, North Carolina.

My Family Tree

Mary Elizabeth Holmes Brown   Friday, December 21, 1928 – Wednesday, July 9, 2003

Elizabeth was born on December 21, 1928, to *Ophelia Tillman Holmes and Lee Thomas Holmes.* She was educated in the public systems of Davidson County and Lexington City Schools. She made her home in Lexington with her husband of 52 years, *Thomas Frank Brown.* She dedicated most of her life to raising her children. In the early years, she worked locally at the Diana Shop and Manhattan Shirt Co. In her later years, she found pleasure in working with children as a school crossing guard. She was baptized at First Baptist Church in Southmont at the age of 12. She later moved her membership to First Baptist Church, Village Drive. She was preceded in death by her husband; her parents; *three brothers, Manuel Odell Holmes, Thomas Brice Holmes, and Robert Willard Holmes; and one sister, Mildred Holmes Michael.*

She leaves to cherish her memory for *her children, Dr. Raynorda Faye Brown* of Jefferson, Louisiana., *Rhonda Kaye Brown Brock* and *her husband, Luther II,* of Winston-Salem and *Reginald Thomas Brown and his wife, Rhonda,* of Raleigh; *three grandchildren, Morgan Elizabeth Brown, Thomas Christopher Brown and Luther G. Brock III*, three sisters, *Bettie Holmes Neely,* her husband, *John I, Eugina Holmes Hargraves* of Lexington and *Gail Holmes Winton* of Durham; *two brothers, Joseph Lee Holmes and his wife Melvina, of Lexington and Eugene Holmes* of Norfolk, Virginia.; and *a host of nieces, nephews and other relatives and friends.*

Thelma Mayfield Rankin   Sunday, February 12, 1911 – Sunday, January 23, 2005

Cleveland – *Thelma Mayfield Rankin*, 93, lived at 4020 Amity Hill Road, died on Sunday, January 23, 2005, at Brain Center Health and Rehabilitation, Salisbury, North Carolina, after two weeks of serious illness. Born on Sunday, February 12, 1911, in Rowan County, *Miss Rankin* was the daughter of the late *Lillie D. Cowan Rankin and Cornelius Alexander Rankin.* She was a graduate of Rowan County schools and Barber-Scotia College and formerly an examiner with the Lillie of France Foundation in New York. A member of Mount Tabor Presbyterian Church. She was a former member of Siloam Presbyterian Church in Brooklyn, New York. At both churches, she served as a deaconess and elder and was a member of the choir and Presbyterian women. Survivors include a number of nieces and nephews.

William Robert Workman I   Thursday, August 5, 1920 – Thursday, March 10, 2005

William Robert Workman I, 84, died on March 10, 2005, at Forsyth Medical Center. He was born into the union of the late *Euphonia Bernice Orr Workman and William Essix Workman* in Winston-Salem, North Carolina – Forsyth County, on Thursday, August 5, 1920. He was preceded in death by *his brothers, Eugene N. Workman, and Edward R. Workman and three sisters, Treva Mae Workman, Hazel Lorraine Workman Mason, and Grace Louise Workman Browning.* He retired from Sherwood Treating Company after 45 years of service. In 1973, he was baptized as a Jehovah's Witness, and he served as ministerial servant in the East Congregation on Northampton Drive.

My Family Tree

He is survived by his devoted *wife of 63 years*, Melba Thompson Workman; *his three loving children*, William Robert Workman[II] *and wife Alice* of Hickory, Melba Louise Lindsay Workman Bostic *and husband Delmar* of Winston-Salem, and Lenora W. Cochran *and husband Donald* of Raleigh; *his four cherished grandchildren*, Robert V. Workman *and wife Coleen* of Raleigh, Rickey E. Workman of Hickory, Velesha Edwards Baker *and husband Kenneth*, and Paris Ashley Lindsay of Winston-Salem; *his three adorable great-grandchildren*, Ryan Mathes, Quinn Baker *and* Collin Baker of Winston-Salem, *his brothers*, James Leonard Workman and Richard LeRoy Workman[I]; nieces Theola W. (Fred) Miller and Shirley W. Means, and nephew Michael Workman, all of Darlington, South Carolina; William Anthony (Tony) Mason and wife Litha and nieces Marva Lorraine Browning Grant and Mona Browning Cooper of Detroit; *his brothers-in-law*, Benjamin *and* Maynard Thompson; *sister-in-law* Mary Alice (James[I]) Cason, *nephews* James (Ivory) Cason[II], *and* Oliver (Sara) Thompson of Winston-Salem; *niece* Debbie C. Williams of Oxnard, California; other nieces and nephews and *a host of friends, including his spiritual sisters and brothers at the Kingdom Hall.*

Golden F. Bassett Wall　　　　　　　　　Tuesday, October 25, 1921 – Sunday, February 5, 2006

Dr. Golden F. Bassett Wall departed this life on Sunday, February 5, 2006, at Oakdale Heights in Winston-Salem, North Carolina – Forsyth County. She was born on October 25, 1921, in Winston-Salem, the daughter of the late *Brownie Younger Bassett and Reverend Daniel Benjamin Bassett[I]*.

Dr. Wall attended public schools in Winston-Salem and was an honor graduate of Winston-Salem State University. She earned a master's degree from New York University and Ph.D. from Southern Illinois University (Carbondale). Her love and enthusiasm for teaching, which began in the classroom and continued throughout her career, led her to an assignment as an elementary school principal in Thomasville. In 1966, she joined the faculty of Winston-Salem State University. She became a director of student teaching proudly served in that position until her retirement in 1985.

Her various honors include the award for Outstanding Teacher of Thomasville City Schools, President of North Carolina Association of Teacher Educators, President and campus advisor for Phi Delta Kappa and an award for Excellence in teaching at Winston-Salem State University. She was also an evaluator of education programs for the State of North Carolina and for the Southern Association of colleges and schools. *Dr. Wall* was an active supporter of her community, including social organizations, the Winston-Salem State Alumni Association and Goler Metropolitan AME Zion Church, where she was a faithful member for over 35 years.

In addition to her parents, *Dr. Wall* was preceded in death by *her brother*, Daniel Benjamin Bassett[II]. She leaves to cherish her memory *her loving husband of 53 years*, Grover C. Wall; *her dear brother*, Jethro B. Bassett (Vera); *adoring* nieces, Jean B. Fenwick (Victor), Linda D. Askew (Alphonso), Angela E. Bassett Vance (Courtney), D'nette B. Bassett, and Lisa Carter; great-nieces and nephews Robin Fenwick, Jonathan Fenwick, Brian Askew, Elise Askew, Alexandra Askew, Slater Vance, and Bronwyn Vance and *a host of other family members and friends.*

My Family Tree

Lacy Belle Everlina Gray Graham Rankin Monday, March 13, 1922 – Monday, February 6, 2006

Lacy B. Gray Rankin of Troutman died on Monday, February 6, 2006, at her home. She was born on Monday, March 13, 1922, in Iredell County to the late *Dora Ramsey Gray and Melvin Gray*. *Mrs. Rankin* was a retired Cosmetologist and was owner of Bells Beauty Shop in Mooresville. A member of Shinnville United Church of Christ in Troutman, she served as the church secretary and was a member of the Singing Stars Choir and on the Usher Board. *Mrs. Rankin* was active in the community and was a member of the Progressive Beautician Club. She was married to *Frank Edward Rankin,* who preceded her in death in 1978. Survivors include children she raised in her home, *Juanita L. Graham Glaspy and Wendy Brown* of Statesville, *Felix Graham and Cozette Graham Ramsey,* both of Troutman and *Charmaine Ramsey and Hallie Ramsey* of the home; nine grandchildren, 13 great-grandchildren; and *a host of nieces, nephews, and other relatives.*

Joseph Cromwell Peters   Saturday, April 25, 1925 – Friday, July 21, 2006

Joseph Cromwell Peters, who was born on April 25, 1925, and was the son of the late *Bettie Louise Carey Peters and Robert Peters*, succumbed to decades of physical challenges on Friday, July 21, 2006, with of 29 years, *his wife Jean Freeman Barnes Peters,* by his side. In addition to his wife, he is survived by *his son, Karl Anthony Peters* of St. Albans, West Virginia – Kanawha County; *stepsons, Joseph Barnes II and Kelvin Barnes* of Richmond, Virginia – Richmond County; *sister, Nona Bell Hicklen Malone and brother Dave White* both of Charleston, West Virginia – Kanawha County; special caregiver, *Carl Hickman* and nieces, nephews, and cousins.

Peters' keen intellect and talent for administrative work surfaced immediately when, as a young boy just out of Aracoma High School, Logan, he volunteered for the Army. At Camp Davis in North Carolina, he was made acting sergeant major, an administrative non-commissioned officer. As manager of five military movie theatres, he supervised personnel and developed a record keeping system for sales and banking, prepared correspondence and pay vouchers and kept a staff journey and policy file. After more than four years in the Army, including a stint in the Pacific Theatre, he enrolled in West Virginia State College, now West Virginia State College and received a Bachelor of Science degree in business administration. In 1950, he earned a master's degree in business administration from the University of Wisconsin.

In 1952, *Peters* began a distinguished career in West Virginia State Government when he was assigned the job of assistant clerk of the House of Delegates Finance Committee. In 1953, he became the first African American to serve as budget analyst for the West Virginia Budget Office, a job he held until his appointment as research analyst for the Board of Public Works in 1959. In 1968, he received the top state job in his field, Commissioner of Finance and Administration. That position was followed by an appointment as Vice President for Business Affairs at Marshall University. As the school's financial officer, he administered the memorial fund for the families of the university plane crash in 1971. After 11 years at Marshall, he resigned. *Peters* retired from the position of Director of Operations for the state Tax Department in 1986.

My Family Tree

Peters participated in many churches civic and social organizations. He was a member of the National Association of College and University Business Officers. He was a member and chairman of the Trustee Board of the First Baptist Church. He was once a member and President of the International Optimist Club of Charleston. As a member of the Secondary Schools and the Intercollegiate Football and Basketball Associations, he was an official for high school and college football basketball for 27 years.

Governor Gaston Caperton appointed *Peters* to the Study Committee on Public School Education and to the West Virginia State College System Board of Directors in 1989. He served on that committee with distinction and its chairman for two terms. Honors received by *Peters* include: The Past Polemarch Award and Kappa Alpha Psi Fraternity; he was a life member of the fraternity. He was inducted into the West Virginia State University Sports Hall of Frame for his exceptional record as a baseball player. Upon the recommendation of *Dr. Hazo W. Carter [II]*, President of West Virginia State University, he received a citation for exemplary experiences that honor you Alma Mater from the National Association for Equal Opportunity in Higher Education. *Peters* was a life member of the West Virginia State University Alumni Association and received the Alumnus of the Year Award in 1975. *Dr. Jerry Beasley*, President of Concord University, established the *Joseph C. Peters* Scholarship Fund in honor of *Peters* in 1997. In recognition of his exemplary record of community service, Alpha Phi Alpha Fraternity Inc. presented the 2001 Alpha Community Service Award to *Joseph C. Peters,* a true gentleman of West Virginian.

When the Board of Directors of Higher Education was dissolved, *Peters* was appointed to the Board of Governors of Glenville State College. On December 21, he was presented with a Proclamation of Appreciation by Glenville's President, *Robert Freeman,* and the school's Board of Governors. To top off that day, held in honor of *Joseph's* long career and public service to the state, he was presented by Governor *Joe Manchin* with the Distinguished West Virginian Award for Outstanding Achievement and Meritorious Service. *Peter's* body had been donated to the Human Gift Registry at West Virginia State University.

Martha Lucille Partee Witherspoon   Wednesday, December 18, 1929 – Monday, April 30, 2007

Salisbury – *Martha Lucille Partee Witherspoon*, 77, passed away on Monday, April 30, 2007, in Durham, North Carolina, after several years of declining health. She was born December 18, 1929, in Salisbury to the late *Vernie Mae Cornelius Partee and Miles H. Partee* as part of a close and loving family. She graduated from Price High School and received an AB degree from Livingstone College in 1948. Raised in Trinity Presbyterian Church USA (formerly Church Street Presbyterian Church), which was co-founded by her father, she later found a spiritual family at Southern City AME Zion Church, East Spencer, North Carolina. Surviving are *five children, Naomi Voncille Witherspoon* of Burke, Virginia, *Adrienne Witherspoon, Kathy Witherspoon, Gary Witherspoon (Beverly)* of Durham, North Carolina, *Harold Adron Witherspoon [II]* of Raleigh, North Carolina, *and six grandchildren, Christine Witherspoon, Stephanie McCluney Fennell (Allen), Willie McCluney, Sean Lomax, Tamika Witherspoon, and Jonathan Witherspoon;* and three great-grandchildren.

My Family Tree

Ronald Carl Peppers "Ronnie"   Thursday, January 12, 1950 – Saturday, April 12, 2008

Ronnie's Play.... A Love Story

Final Curtain Call: *Ronnie Carl Peppers*, affectionately known as *"Pepp,"* was an old-fashioned awesome husband, no nonsense, belt toting, loveable father, a loyal, trustworthy, committed son, brother, in-law, friend, and a warrior for Jesus with dignity, honor and grace with his family and loves ones by his bedside, he peacefully transitioned to his heavenly reward on April 12, 2008.

Act I: The scene was set on January 12, 1950, when *Sarah Lee Peppers and Jonnie Peppers* welcomed into the world a bouncing baby boy in South Carolina – Dillon County. *Ronnie* was educated in the public-school system in Wilson, North Carolina, where he graduated from Fike Senior High School.

Act II: *Ronnie Peppers* left small town America for the big city to attend Winston-Salem State University, there he earned his B. A. in History. While on the yard, he pledged Omega Psi Phi Fraternity, Inc. and met the love of his life, *Mildred Strickland*. After numerous failed attempts, *Mildred* finally accepted his invitation to the dance. As a commissioned officer in the United States Marine Corps, the two were off on adventure of a lifetime.

Act III: The love birds produced "The Girls" – *Frances Valencia, Blanche Yvonne, and Joneice Conchetta*. After an honorable discharge from the Marines, he worked as a production supervisor at Schlitz Container Plant and R.J. Reynolds Tobacco Company. In 2004, *Ronnie* retired from the United States Postal Service.

Act IV: The Peppers' family Circle of Love grew with the marriages of *Blanche* to Captain *Darren A. Sawyer*, United States Navy *and Joneice* to *Willie L. Pledger II*, an Untied States Navy Soldier. After 1993, *Ronnie and Mildred* became *Nana and Grandma Peppers* with the births of *four grandchildren – Xavier and Alexander Sawyer and Jaden and Carrington Pledger.*

Act V: *Ronnie* loved the Lord and served Him faithfully at Emmanuel Baptist Church for 32 years, serving on the Deacon Board, Sunday School, Laymen League and MAAFA committee. With a deeply committed love for his community, he was both a Hospice and Guardian Ad Litem volunteer and a member of the American Legion.

Act VI: *Ronnie* said goodbye to *his brother Harvey Lee Peppers,* who departed life's play in early 2003. *Ronnie's* stellar performance has been characterized as knowledgeable, honorable, faithful, committed, dependable, and wise. His sudden departure from the stage will leave a void in future acts for his wife, children, grandchildren, parents, *sister Rugina Peppers*, brother *James A. (Belinda) Peppers*; mother-in-law, *Frances H. Strickland*; *four sisters-in-law: Maria J. Strickland, Suzette S. (Joel) Willis, and Linda Peppers* along with five nieces, one nephew and *a host of other relatives and friends. Lovingly submitted, Mildred and "The Girls"*

My Family Tree

Isabelle Carey Morrison　　　　　　　　Sunday, November 26, 1916 – Saturday, October 4, 2008

Isabelle Morrison, 91, of Concord, North Carolina, formerly of Holden, West Virginia – Logan County, passed away peacefully to be with the Lord Saturday, October 4, 2008, in Concord, North Carolina – Cabarrus County. She was born to her parent's union on November 26, 1916, at Holden, Logan Avenue, a daughter of the late *Helen Bass Carey and Charles A. Carey.*

In addition to her parents, she was preceded in death by her loving *husband, Roscoe Morrison* [1]; *two brothers, James (Bus) and Wilbur Carey* [1]*; three sisters, Jetta Malinda Faulkner Childs, Vereece Carey Gant, and Levonia Margaret Carey Cowan.*

Mrs. Morrison was a devoted wife, mother, grandmother, cousin, friend, and, above all, a Christian lady. She was a member of the Greater Mt. Zion Missionary Baptist Church of Holden, where she served faithfully until declining health would not permit her to serve. She sang in the choir and was active in many of the organizations.

Mrs. Morrison lived a long, full, and loving life and was a well-respected person in the community. She was an excellent cook, having worked for the former Island Greek Coal Company for years, preparing delicious meals at the Holden Club House. Everyone near and far enjoyed her cooking. As a homemaker, she was very creative, especially loving designing and making quilts, which she shared with her family and friends.

Survivors include *one daughter, Irene (Wilbur) Richardson* of Concord, North Carolina; *two sons, Alfrederick Morrison (Moe) (LeAnn) Morrison* of Winter Garden, Florida, and *Roscoe Morrison* [II] of White Plains, New York; *her niece Norma J. Mason* of Detroit, Michigan; 12 grandchildren, *Nona Bell Hicklen Malone* of Durbar, West Virginia, a devoted friend *Frank Moore* of Holden, West Virginia, *other extended family members and friends.*

John Carl White　　　　　　　　Friday, March 11, 1927 – Monday, December 7, 2009

John Carl White moved to Detroit, Michigan. *John* was age 82 when he died. *Mr. White* lived at 3770 Whitney Street, Detroit, Michigan, a former member of Rowan County, and passed away on Monday, December 7, 2009, at Imperial Health Care Center in Dearborn Heights, Michigan. *Mr. White* was born on March 11, 1927, in Iredell County to the late *Annie Lee Cornelius White and Jay Hugh White.* He was a member of Mt. Tabor Presbyterian Church and a member of Calvary Presbyterian Church. *Mr. White* was a retired employee of General Motors after 39 years of service and served in the United States Army. In addition to his parents, he was preceded in death by *a son, Thurston Heaggans,* and 6 brothers and 2 sisters. Survivors include a *wife of 55 years, Eloise Rankin White* of the home, *2 daughters Marion Hrobowski* of Detroit, Michigan, *and Lenora Heaggans Reid* of Troutman.

My Family Tree

Emma L. Lyons Cowan Tuesday, May 30, 1916 – Sunday, July 11, 2010

Lancaster, California – Los Angeles – *Mrs. Emma L. Lyons Cowan, 94, of Lancaster, formerly of Braeholm, was welcomed by the angels on Sunday, July 11, 2010. Born on May 30, 1916 in Inman, Virginia. She was the daughter of the late Rachel Bradley Lyons and William Lyons.* Also preceding her death was *her husband of 62 years, Charles Edward Cowan ^{I}, one son, Charles Edward Cowan ^{II}*, six sisters, and two brothers. *Emma* was a long-time member of the Mount Olivet Missionary Baptist Church at Braeholm, serving faithfully in many offices of the church. She spent the last seven years living in California with her son and family. She leaves to cherish her memories *one son, Donald (Janet) Cowan of California City, California; one sister, Ann (Robert) Richerson of Akron, Ohio;* four granddaughters, many grand-grandchildren; *a nephew, Hillary Brooks of Amherstdale; other nieces, nephews and extended family and a host of friends.*

Dewitt Shuford White Sunday, July 7, 1929 – Thursday, July 15, 2010

Dewitt Shuford White, 81, of Mooresville, died Thursday, July 15, 2010, at Lake Norman Regional Hospital. He was born on Sunday, July 7, 1929, in Iredell County, the omega of twelve siblings born to the late *Annie Lee Cornelius White and Jay Hugh White. Mr. White* is survived by *his loving wife, Carolyn Mack Lipscomb White,* of the home, *nieces, nephews, and a host of other family members and friends.*

Grace Colwell Thornton Bassett Sunday, December 16, 1917 – Sunday, November 10, 2013

Honoring Grace Bassett, lifelong drum major for justice

Reported Wednesday, November 27, 2013, by Jarvis Tyner at People's World News

[Editors' note: CPUSA Executive Vice Chair Jarvis Tyner delivered the following eulogy for Grace Bassett, a lifelong activist for Civil Rights and Socialism, at the celebration of her life held at Benta's Funeral Home in Harlem, New York, on November 15. Bassett was a member of the People's World editorial board and volunteer copy editor for many years, as well as the editor of Chicago's DuSable edition of The Daily Worker during the 1940s. The entire staff, editorial board, and network of volunteer reporters extend our deepest condolences to Grace's family.]

Grace Colwell Thornton Bassett was born on Sunday, December 17, 1916, in New Orleans. *Grace* died Sunday, November 10, 2013, at the age of 96; next month, she would have been 97, just three years shy of 100. I have known *Grace* and husband, *Ted,* for over 40 years. She was all *Grace* to me; then I married her great-niece, and she became *Aunt Grace*. She was a member of Delta Sigma Theta Sorority while a student at Dillard University in New Orleans. She was a social activist all of her life. She was a lifelong member of the Communist Party USA. *Grace* didn't see a contradiction in being active in both the sorority and party – and neither do we.

In an interview with People's World, *Grace*, speaking of her growing up years, said, "We were very active in the church and activities like the Girl Scouts, but at that time, they were not receptive to blacks." That led *Grace* to join the YWCA. But it was on a camping trip with her Methodist

My Family Tree

Church that she realized she liked helping people. We had just heard a beautiful rendition of "If I can help somebody, then my living shall not be in vain." It is a very fitting song for *Aunt Grace*.

Back then, she met a woman Social Worker who took her on home visits. "That was my beginning. "My whole life began there, "she said." She realized then she wanted to be a Social Worker. In church and high school, she became involved in all sorts of activities: chorus, acting, counseling other youth, and she added, "Dating too." "I always had my boyfriends, but I had my activists," she said. At Dillard University, *Grace* went on a trip organized by her teacher. It was a lunch with students from a white college. "It was my first interracial experience," she said. In time, *Grace* became active in the Southern Negro Youth Congress (SNYC), founded in 1937, just before she graduated Dillard with a Bachelor of Arts in Social Work. SNYC, like the Student Nonviolent Coordinating Committee (SNCC) which followed SNYC, was registering black people to vote. It was an organization of 100,000 active young people that carried out voter registration and education campaigns among blacks and whites in the Deep South.

"Sometimes," said *Grace*, "we went to unreceptive places." She described how SNYC, and a white student group went to a white neighborhood to do voter education. "While many were friendly, somebody reported us," she said. Interracial groups at that time were targeted by the Sheriff Departments and the Klan. "So, we ran to our car, jumped in and left. Our program wasn't just for Black people. It was for white people, too, working class whites. We tried to get them to vote and educate them on what to vote for." The activities of SNYC helped give birth to the modern Civil Rights Movement, she noted. World War II came, and many men went into the service. *Grace* assumed a leadership role in the New Orleans SNYC.

Later, she went to Atlanta to further her education. She traveled to SNYC, organizing meetings in Mississippi. She met and developed friendships with SNYC leaders like *Dorothy Burnham and, James and Esther Jackson*. In 1984, Bassett was among those interviewed about SNYC for New York University's (NYU) Tamiment Library. NYU was where she got her master's in social work.

SNYC, in addition to voter registration, organized tobacco and other workers into unions. *Grace* and her pioneering colleagues were active in fighting various violations of Civil Rights, all done at great personal risk.

In 1941, *Mildred McAdory*, a domestic worker and SNYC activist, refused to give up her seat on a bus to a white person in Birmingham, Alabama and was arrested. That was 14 years before *Rosa Parks* did just that in Montgomery. Mildred was arrested, and SNYC led the struggle on her behalf. *Mildred, or Millie* as many knew her, had to leave the South and came to Harlem, where she became a member of the CPUSA's National Committee.

Rosa Parks, the heroine of Montgomery Bus Boycott and the Civil Rights Movement, later credited the role of both the NAACP and SNYC for leading the way to breaking segregation. *Grace* moved to Chicago around 1942 with her husband. *McCarthyism* had cost him his job with the transport workers union. She got a job with the Daily Worker and later became editor of its DuSable edition, in which she campaigned for the integration of the White Sox and Cubs baseball teams. She and her husband later divorced. It was in New York, at a party convention, where *Grace* met *Basset*t, the Harlem organizer of the party, political activist, and writer. *Grace and Ted* were married in 1952, and *Grace* moved to New York. She joined the ongoing grassroots and electoral

My Family Tree

struggles there for Civil Rights, peace, low rents, and health care. In the 1970s, *Ted and Grace* lived in Cuba. *Ted* was from Virginia but spoke Spanish and was the correspondent for the Daily World. *Grace* was very active in the movement to free *Angela Davis*, the anti-apartheid movement in the 1980's and the Ben Davis Club of the Communist Party here in Harlem.

Grace Bassett returned to Social Work and was an active member of Local II 99 union as well as Social Workers' professional organizations. She worked in New York hospitals, including Harlem's Sydenham hospital, until it was closed by *Mayor Ed Koch*, despite community protests of which *Grace* was a part. She worked until she turned 70, and Ted took ill. She retired to care for him. *Ted* died in 1994.

Grace was a journalist and a member of the People's World editorial board. Once a week, she would get on the subway at her advanced age and travel from the Washington Heights neighborhood downtown to Chelsea to volunteer her considerable editing skills and help get the paper out. She would say, "I can't stand just sitting around." Remarkable.

When *Grace* spoke in our club, everybody listened. We listened to her when she was wrong. Like when Obama ran for President in 2008 and we were talking optimistically about the campaign: *Grace* interrupted and said, "You comrades are leading with your heart and not your head. This country is not ready to elect a Black President." In the broad sweep of history, change is constant. The *Rev. Martin Luther King Jr.* said the moral arc of the universe was "Long, but it bends towards justice." *Frederick Douglass* said, "Power concedes nothing without a demand. It never did, and it never will."

But where do the great demands and struggle that make great change come from? They come from PEOPLE! The first to speak up. The first to say, "Let's go." The first to sit down and strike and the first to pick up a picket sign. They know they can't do it alone, and they know how to effectively get others involved. Why did this beautiful young black woman college student end up in Birmingham registering black voters under the thread of the Klan? After all, everybody who was opposed to Jim Crow didn't all jump out there first.

It was the heroes and sheroes like *Grace Bassett* - special people who have a deep understanding and are highly motivated to struggle against injustice. That's why I joined the Communist Party. Our dear *Grace* was one of those drum majors for freedom and peace, and we loved her for that. We love her for who she was and the great things she did and her beliefs in a socialist future. She couldn't stand to sit around.

Mrs. Bassett is survived by her nieces, nephews, *Angela E. Bassett, Courtney B. Vance, Bronwyn G. Vance Slater J. Vance, D'nette B. Bassett, Martha J. Bassett, Linda Bassett, Lisa Carter, Jean B. and Victor Fenwick, Robin Fenwick, Jonathan Fenwick, Linda D. and Alphonso Askew, Elise Askew, Alexandra Askew, and Brain Askew and a host of other family members and friends.*

My Family Tree

Stephen Idel Cowan I   Tuesday, February 26, 1974 – Thursday, June 9, 2011

Editor's Note: *Those who knew Stephen ever remember and are inspired by the essence of his spirit, his understanding heart, and his sense of camaraderie. His life serves as an example of selflessness, of caring, of sharing, of humility and love. As he remains in our hearts and memories, we might all learn how to be better to ourselves and one another.*

Stephen Idel Cowan[1] was born in Highland Park, Michigan – Wayne County, on February 26, 1974, to *Toni Sue Cowan,* the eldest of three children. He was educated through the Detroit Public School System. Who had preceded him in God's glory were his brother *Keith Jerome Cowan*, a good friend/father figure, *Darnell Woods,* and his grandmother, *Levonia Margaret Carey Cowan.*

A caring and dependable person, he loved being around family and friends. The unity and closeness of family were important to his very being. He was known to be a good listener and was ever ready with a word of encouragement, comfort, and advice. Quick of thought and wit (he loved to laugh), he enjoyed being in the company of his elders, exchanging ideas, and thoughts and absorbing the wisdom of experience. One cannot ignore the fact that he also knew his way around the kitchen.

Part of his passion for life was biblical study, as he often amazed those around him with his knowledge of scripture. It seems that one of the genetic gifts passed along from *his grandmother (Levonia)* was his ability to read the essence of others. His sense of spirit came through in 2009 when he joined the **Temple of I AM.**

A fixture in both the Highland Park and Lesure Block, he was that person who knew how to fix something or knew someone. He had a talented hand in remodeling, drawing pictures, carpentry, and auto repair. He also volunteered at the homeless shelters and provided rides for area shoppers in the Highland Park community. He made himself readily available to help neighbors with their work around the house and yard.

In the midst of his efforts, the will of God was made evident as he was called to his rest on Thursday, June 9, 2011. Among those to cherish his memory are *his mother, Toni Sue Cowan; sister, AnRico Lockhart (Al Lockhart); his three children, Stephen Idel Cowan*[II], *Destiny Tiara Robinson, and Trevon Deonte Cowan; two nieces, Monique Anthony Cowan and AnRico Celete Levonia Scott*[II], *brother-in-law Sean Scott, his aunts and uncles, Roxie Lee Carey (Marvin Guyse), Norma Jean Mason, Judy Carol Cowan (Kenneth Dwight Pollard), Elise Cowan, (Gene Edward Love), Elco Jr. Brown*[II], *Eddie Andrew Trent*[1], *and a host of loving cousins, as well as his best friend, Edward Foster, and his **I AM** family and friends.*

Wednesday, November 16, 2011, a letter was written to the Wayne County Circuit Court Judge in Detroit, Michigan, about Stephen I. Cowan[1] *from his first cousin Stephanie on his mother's side.*

To whom it may concern:

My Family Tree

My name is *Stephanie Mason*; I am *Stephen Idel Cowan [1]*. *I was the first* cousin on his mother's side. On June 9, 2011, I knew something was wrong but unfortunately, I could not figure out the reason behind my foreboding feeling. I honestly kept thinking it had to do with my final test in my Health Ethics course at Baker College of Allen Park. While I was taking the test, I felt angry and could not sit still; then I felt "a pull." The next day, I was informed by my mother that *Stephen [1]* had been murdered the day prior. I could not think straight the entire time I was at work; my mind kept going in circles. However, I told my mother and myself that it was not so, there was no possible way that the news could be true. I kept telling myself that they had the wrong person, and it was not *Stephen [1]*.

After his death, I felt irritated because I also lost my cousin, who acted like a big brother toward my sister and me. The reality of the matter was that he was abruptly taken from our family. It breaks my heart that he is no longer around the family that he desperately loved. The chains were broken among his children, his mother, his sister, cousins, and other family members. I will miss *Stephen [1]'s* beautiful mind and the way he viewed the world. Also, I will miss the beautiful smile that accompanied his demeanor. It saddens me that I can never talk to him again about anything that was going on in my life, how to fix things around my house, what's going on with my car, or the world in general.

Now, every time my birthday comes around, I will always remember *Stephen [1]'s* homecoming; his funeral was held on my birthday. Every time *Stephen [1]* saw the family, he always had a hug and a kiss for his mother, sister, his two children, his two nieces, aunts, and female cousins, and a hug and a handshake for his male cousins. I am never going to have the opportunity to play card games with him or "crack" jokes with him ever again due to this tragedy. Each time I think about the fact that he is not here, it makes me angry, and I want to cry. His death has disturbed the entire family and the church family as well. *Stephen* would have still been here but because of someone else's foolish act. Instead of him looking towards the future filled with possibilities for him, all we have now is just memories of him.

Out of my male cousins on my mother's side, *Stephen [1]* was the one who always had my and the rest of our family's best interests at heart. *Stephen [1]* always made sure that I was on the right track because he always exemplified moral values when it came to family, friends, and even people that he did not know. It has been extremely hard not having *Stephen [1]* around. In addition to his kindness, he was very handy with repairing items around the house and very good at fixing automobiles. He consistently gave good advice to those who were in need and always had compassionate conversations with family, friends, and others. *Stephen [1]* was the type of person who would literally give the shirt off his back or go without just to make someone else's day, and he would not mind helping anyone who was in need; it did not matter if he knew the person or not.

When I was living in a certain area of Detroit that turned unsafe and when my ex-fiancé was stalking me, *Stephen [1]* always made sure that I got into my apartment safely and called a few hours later to see if I was still okay. Every morning, he stood outside by my car, ensuring that I left my residence safely, told me "…to have a good day at work and he would see me later." I remember when I told *Stephen [1]* that I was moving to a safer neighborhood, he was so happy for me.

My Family Tree

I remember when I told *Stephen¹* that I was going back to school, he was so happy for me. Every time *Stephen¹* saw me at my mother's house, he would ask me how school was going. After I began to show him my report cards, I did not realize that my efforts also encouraged *Stephen¹* to go back to school to obtain his GED. He was extremely happy and proud of the fact that he had chosen to go back to school. Every weekend, he would bring his clothes over to my mother's house to wash and press them for school the next week. He loved learning new things and new ways to accomplish tasks.

I remember when I had problems with a couple of women in my class who did not want to do their portions for a group project that was assigned to us. *Stephen¹* told me this, and I quote, "...*Stephanie,* whatever you do, do not let anyone knock you off your block." What he was trying to tell me was that it does not matter what your classmates do or say; just keep your head in the books and do the best you know how to do. Every time I wanted to give up because a class was stressing me to the breaking point, I just remembered what he said and pushed harder to do better. Finally, when graduation was upon me, I can recall the look of pride on *Stephen¹'s* face as he watched from the audience with the rest of the family. He was beaming from ear to ear with tears streaming down his face when I walked passed him and other family members at the moment that the announcer called my name. Through the noise I could still make out what he was saying, "...we are so proud of you." I was so proud of *Stephen¹* when he joined the **Temple of I AM** in the summer of 2009. Both of us were crying and hugging each other and praising that GOD had sent him to the **Temple of I AM**. I was very shocked to find out that he knew the Holy Bible from front to back. In my eyes and heart, *Stephen¹* was the big brother that I always wanted. He knew without us (my sister and I) "...saying it to him" that we had adopted him as our big brother. He will be forever missed and loved by all who knew him. After *Stephen¹* died, he received his GED in the mail in June 2011. He was planning to go to college to get his degree in home remodeling and carpentry work.

⌘

Michael Arnelle Brown I Friday, March 4, 1955 – Monday, February 13, 2012

Winston-Salem, North Carolina – Davie County – *Michael Arnelle Brown*, age 56, died on February 13, 2012, at Wake Forest University Baptist Medical Center. He retired from R. J. Reynolds Tobacco Company. He is survived by his parents, *Geraldine Tatum Brown and Jesse James Brown III* of Mocksville, North Carolina; *two sons, Michael Arnelle Brown II* of Greensboro *and NeKeith Brown* of Dallas, Texas; *one daughter, Michaela Brown* of Winston-Salem, North Carolina; *three brothers, Lawrence (Linda) Clayton* of New Jersey, *Christopher (Jeri) Brown* of Mocksville, North Carolina, *and Derrick (Christy) Brown* of Mocksville; *two sisters, Cynthia (Herman) West* of Mocksville, North Carolina *and Lucy Michelle (Jock) Jones* of Richmond Virginia; a special friend, *Ann Nickerson.*

My Family Tree

Raymond A. Mason II Friday, January 2, 1931 – Friday, July 13, 2012

Raymond A. Mason II was born January 2, 1931, to the late *Roxanna S. Smith Mason and Raymond D. Mason I* in Columbus, Ohio. He retired from the Columbus Public School System and served during the Korean Conflict in the United States Army. At age 81, *Raymond* went home to be with the Lord on July 13, 2013, at OSU (Wexner) Hospital.

He is preceded in death by his parents, *daughter Ramona L. Mason Morrison*, and siblings *Alberta Mason Samuels, Doretha Mason White, and Melvin Mason*.

Ray leaves to cherish his memories, *Gay Mason-Mote; children Raymond (Barbara) Mason III, Evelyn Mason (John) Boyce, Gwendolyn Mason (Sam) McMillan, Pamela Mason Lewis, Lessee Mason, and Gayle Mason (Eric) Troy;* 17 grandchildren, 22 great-grandchildren; *sisters, Lois Mason (Kennard) Croston and Ella Mason*; and *a host of other relatives and friends.*

Frank Lee Moore I Thursday, September 5, 1918 – Friday, October 5, 2012

Frank Lee "Rail" Moore I, 94, of Holden, passed away on Friday, October 5, 2012, following a long illness. He lived and raised his children "on the hill," but for the past couple of years, he resided with his oldest daughter in the Institute.

Born on September 5, 1918, in Harvest, Alabama, he was the son of the late *Lucy Nancy Moore and Archie Moore I*.

Frank accepted Christ as his Savior earlier this year and was glad to become a child of God. He graduated from Aracoma High School, where he was active on both the basketball and baseball teams. He also entered the workforce at the tender age of 18 for the Island Creek Coal Company before retiring in 1981. During his 43 years of dedicated service, *Frank* was promoted to the position of a mine foreman. He held the position during the latter years of his employment. He also enjoyed playing amateur baseball for the Holden Bearcats, where he traveled to many states. He was a dedicated husband and father and loved watching his grandchildren and great-grandchildren grow into young adults. *Frank* was gifted in electronics and worked well with his hands by repairing cars, televisions, and small appliances. He loved life and enjoyed helping people. He also loved taking care of his cats and feeding the birds, watching them come and go from the window. *Frank* liked to watch and discuss all topics, especially sports and politics. Some things he would say were, *"You are born to die," "I am here beyond my time,"* and *"I want to live just two more years."*

Also preceding him in death was *his wife, Mary Dingess Moore; sisters, Ellen Moore Burns and Pearline Moore Bass; and his brothers, Newell Moore, Lowell Moore, and Archie Moore II*. *Frank* passed the torch and leaves his legacy to *two daughters, Deborah Moore (Frank Walker)* of Institute and *Sheila Moore (Jesse Jones)* of Atlanta, Georgia; *two sons, Frank Moore II*, of Thailand and *Gregory Moore* of Huber Heights, Ohio, as well as a beloved *daughter-in-law, Denise Moore*.

My Family Tree

He leaves to mourn *his siblings, Otis Moore (Margaret), Christine Moore Crawford* and *sisters-in-law, and brother-in-law, Emmett Burns, Mildred Mason Moore, and Inez Moore*; 12 grandchildren; six great-grandchildren and a host of nieces, nephews, family, and friends to cherish his memories. Special thanks *to Frank Walker* [1], as well as caregiver and friend *Monty McCrary*.

Roscoe Morrison II　　　　　　　　　　　Sunday, September 8, 1940 – Saturday, May 11, 2013

Roscoe Morrison [II] was born into his parent's union on September 8, 1940, in Holden, West Virginia – Logan County. He was the son of the late *Isabelle Carey Morrison and Roscoe Morrison* [I]. He was the younger brother of *Irene Morrison Richardson and Alfrederick Morrison* [I].

Growing up in a small town in West Virginia was one of the greatest personal joys of *Roscoe's* life. He would often reminisce on his fond memories of his childhood. As a child, *Roscoe* was a member of Greater Mount Zion Baptist Church. It was at Great Mount Zion that he accepted the Lord as his personal savior, being baptized at the age of nine. In June 1958, *Roscoe* graduated from Aracoma High School, where he relished and excelled at sports, his favorite being football. That same year, at the age of 17, he ventured out to make his imprint on the world. He would first go to Boston, Massachusetts, and then later to Brooklyn, New York.

As a young man, one of the first professional positions *Roscoe* held was at Klein's Department store, in their accounting department. This assignment would be the beginning of his successful and distinguished career in the computer industry. It was also at Klein's where he met his beloved wife, *Connie*. It was from this beginning that the couple set out on the course of their lives together, married on Friday, October 5, 1962. Their partnership lasted for 35 years until God told her to come home in 1998.

In 1974, *Roscoe* began working in the banking industry for Chemical Bank in the Wall Street section of New York City. He was employed in their Information Technology division. After many years of exemplary and exceptional work, he was promoted to a supervisory role. Twenty-four years later, in 2001, *Roscoe* decided to enter a new facet of his life and retired. In his semi-retirement, *Roscoe* became employed with the Avis Enterprise Car Rental Company. Being an enterprising man himself, he developed an informal taxi service where he would drive the elderly to and from their appointments. He enjoyed gardening, sowing, and harvesting a variety of flowers and vegetables, which he readily shared. He found extreme pleasure in maintaining an aquarium of various fish, playing the keyboard, attending street fairs, and painting.

Roscoe departed this life and went on to be with the Lord for his final reward on Saturday, May 11, 2013. He is survived by his loved ones and special friends. *Roscoe Morrison* [II] fought a good fight and will truly be missed, but we know that he is safe and may finally rest in peace.

My Family Tree

Alfrederick "Moe" Morrison I Tuesday, January 24, 1939 – Sunday, September 1, 2013

Alfrederick Morrison [I] was born into his parent's union on Tuesday, January 24, 1939, in the small coal mining town of Holden, West Virginia – Logan County. He was the son of the late *Isabelle Carey Morrison* and *Roscoe Morrison* [I]. He was the second of three children, having an older sister, *Irene Morrison Richardson,* and a younger brother, the late *Roscoe Morrison* [II].

Alfrederick, as he was growing up, was nicknamed *"Pon"* by a next-door neighbor, and that name stuck with him during his years in West Virginia. He attended Durbar Grade School in Holden, West Virginia, and he graduated from Aracoma High School in June 1956 in Logan, West Virginia. He excelled in sports, lettering in varsity football and baseball in his Junior and Senior years.

In 1956, after graduating from Aracoma High School he immediately joined the United States Air Force. He was trained as a Communication Specialist and served until 1965, when he retired with a service-connected disability.

He served overseas in Korea, Japan, the Philippines, Vietnam, and Thailand. While stationed in the Philippines, he had his first child, *Alfrederick "Fred" Blyden.* He later established a relationship with him in Florida. While stationed at Wright-Patterson AFB, *Alfrederick* picked up the name *"Moe,"* and it remained with him until the end.

In 1962, while stationed at Wright-Patterson AFB - Dayton, Ohio, he met and married *Gloria Jean Harris-Morrison.* The marriage lasted twenty-two years, ending in a divorce in 1984. Children resulting from the marriage are a stepdaughter, the late *Valeria Jean Harris-Johnson Morrison, Alfrederick Morrison* [II], *Electra Jean Morrison (Sebastian Holmes), Shawn Morrison, Prentice Morrison* [I]*(Tanya), and Eureka Jean Morrison (Michael Durbar).*

In 1984, *Moe* met and married *LeAnn Wilson Morrison* and took on the responsibility of stepfather to her young son, *Eric James Wilson. Moe* was trained as a Computer Specialist and managed several computer operations for the government and the City of Washington, D.C. *Moe* had a very successful career with the government, and in 1991, he retired as a Supervisory Computer Specialist. In 1992, the family moved to Orlando, Florida, where *Moe* worked as a salesman for several companies. He enjoyed selling Home Security Systems, Insurance, Mortgages, Real Estate, and automobiles. *Moe* often said he would sell anything to keep from getting a 9 to 5 job.

In 2010, *Moe* and his wife joined the Buffalo Soldiers Motorcycle Club of Orlando. He really enjoyed the comradely of motorcyclists and ex-servicemen. *Moe* worked for charity causes assigned to him by the Buffalo Soldiers M/C and he prided himself on projecting a good positive image while giving back to the communities. In 2010, *Moe* was baptized by the *Rev. Frankie Massey* of the St. Paul A.M.E. at Winter Garden, Florida, and enjoyed attending church there. He only missed church services when he was out of town or attending another church. Even though he was not a member of St. Paul A.M.E., he supported the church in any way he could.

My Family Tree

He leaves behind to cherish his memories *his wife, LeAnn Wilson Morrison,* and *his children: Alfrederick "Fred" Blyden* (Nermaryah), *Alfrederick Morrison II, Electra Jean Morrison Holmes* (Sebastian Holmes), *Shawn Morrison, Prentice Morrison I* (Tanya Morrison), *Eureka Jean Morrison Durbar* (Michael Durbar), *and stepson Eric James Wilson. Grandchildren: Raphael Santi Pasamonte Blyden, Zsa Zsa Nicole Pasamonte Blyden, Giovanni Alexavier Blyden, Eric Todd Morrison, Theresa Jean Morrison, Malik Morrison, Gelia Jean Morrison, Prentice Tayvon Morrison II, Javon Dunbar, Aaron DeVanta Dunbar, and Grace Kristen Holmes, great grandchild: Heaven Morrison, his cousin Norma J. Mason, in-laws: Sally Carol Jacobs, (mother-in-law), Carolyn Harris (sister-in-law) (Cornel), Gabrielle Jacobs (sister-in-law), Lauren Jacobs (sister-in-law) and a host of loving of other nieces, nephews, cousins, family members, friends and his beloved dog "Sophie"*

Frances Rebecca Hege Strickland   Tuesday, May 25, 1926 – Thursday, September 19, 2013

Frances Rebecca Hege was the fourth child born to the union of the late *Mildred Ann Mason Hege and Jesse Lee Hege,* born Tuesday, May 25, 1926, in Fork, North Carolina – Forsyth County. Her siblings include *James, Charlie,* and *John.* She made her transition to her heavenly home on Thursday, September 19, 2013.

Her family moved to Winston-Salem, North Carolina, in 1932 and resided in the Columbia Heights Community. She graduated from Atkins High School in June 1943. Married to *Samuel Strickland* III on November 2, 1946, in Winston-Salem, this union produced *three daughters, Mildred Elizabeth, Maria Jeanette,* and *Suzette De-Carroll.*

Frances was a member of Emmanuel Baptist Church, serving in the Missionary Circle, the Sunday school, and the Cancer Survivor ministries. She was an active member of the American Legion Auxiliary Post 220 and 453, a member of the Zion Memorial Senior Citizens Club, and an avid bowler with the North Carolina Baptist Hospital League at Major League Lanes. She retired from Wake Forest Baptist Medical Center with over 20 years of service.

Frances was preceded in death by her parents, brothers, *her husband – Samuel Lay Strickland* III, and her sons-in-law- *Ronnie Carl Peppers and James D. Patterson.*

Surviving to cherish her memory are *her daughters – Mildred Elizabeth Strickland Peppers, Maria Jeanette Strickland, and Suzette De-Carroll Strickland Willis;* her good-looking *son-in-law, Joel S. Willis; four granddaughters - Frances Vencelia Peppers, Blanche Yvonne Peppers (Darren A.) Sawyer, Joneice Conchetta Peppers (Will L.) Pledger II* and *Raven Willis; four great-grandchildren – Xavier J. Sawyer, Alexander J. Sawyer, Jaden Carl Pledger, and Carrington Sabory Pledger;* and a host of loving nieces, nephews, and cousins. In addition to all these, dear friends *Mrs. Almenia Little, Mrs. Julia Hill, Mrs. Elizabeth Fields, Mrs. Pearline Howard,* and *Mrs. Mary Ann Blue. Frances Rebecca Hege Strickland* was known for her jokes, laughter, and exuberance! Though she will be missed. We will forever carry her memory in our hearts and spirits.

My Family Tree

Ida Doretha Brown Goolsby   Wednesday, August 22, 1920 – Tuesday, November 19, 2013

Ida Doretha Brown Goolsby, born August 22, 1920, in Davie County, North Carolina, was one of nine children born to the late *Jettie Ann Hairston Mason Brown and Jesse James Brown [I]*. She peacefully departed this life on Tuesday, November 19, 2013. She was educated in the Davie and Davidson County schools, graduating as valedictorian of Davie County Training School, Mocksville, North Carolina. She was also awarded a scholarship to North Carolina Agricultural and Technical College, Greensboro, North Carolina. From her infancy, *Jettie and Jesse* brought her to the Cedar Grove Baptist Church.

At an early age, she accepted Christ, was baptized into the fellowship, and was an active member for over 85 years. *Sister Goolsby* was instrumental in every area of the church, serving as a Deaconess, President of the Choir, Secretary of the Missionary Circle, Sunday School teacher, and Officer and Member of the Best Yet Club for 50 years, and Davie County Missionary Union.

She was a woman of great character, with a calm, meek, and quiet spirit, a sense of humor, and a ready smile. Her life was an example and inspiration to her family as she exhibited the "Fruit of the Spirit:" love, joy, peace, longsuffering, self-control, faithfulness, gentleness, goodness, and kindness. *Ida* was known in her family and community for many things: her delicious chicken n' dumplings, chess pies, and her caramel pound cake. She was a meticulous homemaker and a wonderful gardener. She had a green thumb and always had beautiful plants growing year-round. Her skillful hands and brilliant mind blessed the family and carried forth the legacy of her grandmother, *Hanna Brown Michael*, as she made quilts for each of her children and grandchildren. She also loved reading and studying. Though she gave birth to only four children, she was a 'mother' to the community. As a woman of faith who showed her love for Christ and others, she was one with whom you could share your problems and concerns and know that they would be held in confidence. She never judged others but always gave the benefit of the doubt. She was industrious and worked until she was 90 years old.

She was preceded in death by *her husband of 34 years, John Hairston Goolsby [II]*. Also preceding her in death were *her five sisters, Eva Mae Brown Hairston, Alberta Brown Hairston, Hannah Elizabeth Brown Hairston, Leona Brown Mason, and Addie B. Mae Brown, and her three brothers: Odell Brown, Jesse James Brown [II], and Thomas Frank Brown*. She loved and was deeply devoted to her family. She leaves to cherish and carry on her legacy *three daughters*: *Lula Goolsby (Milton, deceased), Williams, Gwendolyn Goolsby (Leroy) Reynolds, Linda Goolsby (Dellwyn) Johnson; and one son John Hairston Goolsby [III] (Betty, deceased)*; 11 grandchildren and 16 great-grandchildren; *three sisters-in-law, Alice Goolsby Benson, Juanita Cuthrell Brown, and Fannie Elizabeth Hudson Goolsby;* and a host of nieces, nephews, other relatives and friends. She was a selfless mother, grandmother, companion, and friend to all who knew and loved her. When she departed this life, one of her favorite songs filled the room. 'Somehow, Someway', we're going to make it to the other side.

My Family Tree

Robert Stanley Mason Friday, February 2, 1940 – Sunday, August 10, 2014

Robert Stanley Mason affectionately known as *Bobby* to most of his family and friends. He felt the warmth of his mother's kiss touch his forehead and her warm embrace on February 2, 1940. He was the third child born to *the late Hazel Lorraine Workman Mason and Napoleon Jefferson Mason* in Winston-Salem, North Carolina – Forsyth County.

As a child and well into his adult years, he has always looked up to his two older brothers, and he adored their baby sister. *Bobby* was never a stranger when it came down to hard work and family values. *Bobby* followed in his brother *Tony's* footsteps by working at Daimler Chrysler, working his way up to the ladder and retired from Chrysler as a supervisor. Two of his siblings preceded him in death: *his brother Eugene Napoleon Mason and sister Euphonia C. Mason Jackson.*

He leaves to cherish his life three sons, Terrence Mason, Tyrone Mason, Rashad Mason, and one daughter, Linda Mason Gill; his brother William Anthony Mason; two sisters-in-law, Litha Ruth Mason and Norma Jean Mason; his nieces and nephews – Gregory Ware, Venus R. Mason-Thues (Jerome A.), Troy A. Mason (Sandar Lewin), Jenean E. Mason, Theodore C. Mason, Stephanie M. Mason, and Iris A. Mason Nicholas (James R. [III]), and great nephew James R. Nicholas [IV] and; a host of great – nieces, nephews, cousins and other family members and friends.

Bertha Martin Carey Saturday, June 7, 1913 – Sunday, September 6, 2016

Bertha Martin Carey was born June 7, 1913, in Sprotts, Alabama. The daughter of the *late Estella Young Martin and Jim Martin*. She moved with her family to West Virginia at the age of three.

Bertha Transitioned this life on Sunday, September 6th, at C.A.M.C. General Division. She was a Beloved resident at the Dunbar Care-Genesis Long-Term Care Facility.

She was also preceded in death by *her husband, Wilber C. Carey [1] and their son Henry F. Carey, six brothers, Willie Matin, Jeff Martin, Memphis, O.D., James Martin and Ernest Martin, five sisters; Cornelia Martin Perry, Pearl Martin Stinson, Clemistine Martin Glenn and Addie Martin Ward. Bertha* was a long-time member of the Greater Mt Zion Baptist Church in Holden, serving as *"Mother of the Church"* for many years and a faithful choir member. She was a retired Commercial cook and Domestic Worker. A Aracoma High School graduate where, she was Inducted into the Aracoma High School's Sports Hall of Fame as a Cheerleader. A Member of the Federated Woman's Club of Logan, daughter of Isis Lodge and Past President of West Virginia's Chapter of the Martin Family Reunion. Bertha enjoyed cooking, sewing and reading her Bible. She was often asked by family members the secret to her good cooking. Bertha

My Family Tree

loved to dance and won many dance contests. She said, her father said to her one day, " if anything will keep you out of heaven, it would be your dancing.

Thank God for Salvation Survivors left to cherish her memory include *three loving daughters, Mrs. June L. Carey Parker* of Columbus, Ohio, *Mrs. Donna Jean Carey McCoy* of Huntington, West Virginia, and *Ms. Malva J. Carey* of Institute West Virginia, *four loving sons, Wilber C. Carey [II]* of Odenton, Maryland, *Joseph C. Carey* of Merced, California, *Elbert James Carey* of Detroit, Michigan and *Albert Martin Carey* of Merced, California. *Two sisters, Jamie Martin Lewis* of Detroit, Michigan and *Mahaley Martin Dobyne* of Columbus, Ohio., 15 grandchildren, 16 great-grandchildren and 10 great-great-grandchildren, and a host of nieces, nephews, cousins, other relatives, and friends, her special caregiver *Doretta Hairston* and the Caring Staff at Dunbar Care Center.

Harry Edward Bass Tuesday, January 26, 1954 – Wednesday, August 17, 2016

Harry Edward Bass, 62, of Price Bottom, departed this life Wednesday, August 17, 2016 in CAMC Memorial Division Hospital in Charleston, West Virginia. He was born in Holden to the late *Joyce Lavern Donaldson Bass and Eddie Bass [1].* He had been employed by the Logan County Board of Education in the Maintenance Department. In addition to his parents, he was also preceded in death by his grandparents and *one brother, Walter Bass.* Those left to cherish his memories are *his beloved wife, Martha Bratcher Bass* of Price Bottom*; one step-son, Douglass Bratcher* of Logan; *one step-daughter, Hope Marie Bass Hill* of Tennessee; *his brothers, Jesse Lanie Bass* of Michigan, *Kenneth Bass and Eddie Bass [II],* both of Holden; *six sisters; Dorothy Bass Vern (Allen) Forest* of Ohio, *Sandra Bass (Jeff) Moss and Kim Bass* both of Charleston West Virginia, *Jackie (Johnny) Richardson, Melissa Bass* of Florida, *Kathy Bass* of Charleston, West Virginia, eight grandchildren, and five great-grandchildren.

Mildred Elizabeth Strickland Peppers Wednesday, June 12, 1946 – Tuesday, November 7, 2016

Mildred Strickland Peppers, a God fearing and deeply devoted wife, mother, sister, and friend, met her bridegroom November 7, 2016. *Mildred* was born June 12, 1948, to the late *Frances Rebecca Hege Strickland and Samuel Lay Strickland [III]* in Winston-Salem, North Carolina – Forsyth County.

She was educated in the Winston-Salem Public School System and graduated from Albert H. Anderson High School June 1968. *Mildred* attended Winston-Salem State University (WSSU), where she received her B.S. in History. While at WSSU, she pledged Zeta Phi Beta Sorority, where she became affectionately known as *"Skinner."* On the yard, she also met her *"Diamond,"* the late *Ronnie Carl "Pepp" Peppers.*

My Family Tree

The *Skinner and Pepp* union produced three beautiful girls: *Frances Valencia, Blanche Yvonne,* and *Joneice Conchetta*. Out of this love grew the marriages of *Blanche* to Captain *Darren A. Sawyer* (Retired from the) United States Navy and *Joneice* to *Will L. Pledger [II]* (Retired from the) United States Navy.

After 1994, *Skinner and Pepp* became proud grandparents with the birth of four grandchildren, *Xavier, Alexander Sawyer, Jadon and Carrington Pledger*. *Mildred* was blessed again in 2010 with her only *grand dog, Dallas*.

Mildred, an educator at heart dedicated nearly 29 years of her life as a teacher at Newton-Conover Junior High School Hickory, North Carolina – Catawba County and at Winston-Salem, North Carolina. She retired in 2001. Her calling was teaching, and she was very active at her home church, Emmanuel Baptist, for over 40 years, where she served as a Deaconess, Missionary, and she was a teacher for the New Members Class, Sunday school and Vacation Bible School. Spreading the gospel beyond the walls of Emmanuel, she wrote the Sunday school lesson for The Chronicle for over 17 years.

Her heavenly reward leaves cherished memories for her girls, *Frances Valencia Peppers, Blanche Yvonne Peppers Sawyer (Darren A.), and Joneice Conchetta Peppers Pledger (Willie L.); sons-in-law;* grandchildren; *sisters, Maria Strickland and Suzette D. (Joel) Willis; sisters-in-law, Rugina Peppers and Linda Peppers; brother-in-law, James (Belinda) Peppers;* along with five nieces; one nephew; and a host of other loved ones and friends.

Fannie Elizabeth Goolsby Hudson   Saturday, October 13, 1923 – Tuesday, March 14, 2017

Fannie Elizabeth Goolsby Hudson, 93, died Tuesday, March 14, 2017, at Gray Brier Nursing and Rehabilitation in Trinity. She was born in Davie County on October 13, 1923, to *Lula M. Mason Goolsby and John Hairston "Jack" Goolsby [I]*. She was preceded in death by her parents, *R. J. Hudson;* a *brother, John Hairston Goolsby [II];* and *three sisters: Lettie F. Goolsby Brown, Nancy Goolsby Hairston, and Annie Goolsby Burke*. She leaves to cherish her memory *her sister, Alice Goolsby Benson* of South Carolina, a devoted niece and caregiver, *Judy Richards,* and a host of nieces and nephews, cousins, and extended family.

Garfield Sylvester Doulin   Friday, December 9, 1927 – Monday, April 16, 2018

Garfield Sylvester Doulin was the son of *Esther Chaplin Doulin and John Thomas Doulin [I],* both deceased. He had five brothers and two sisters. He graduated from Davie County High School in 1947 and was drafted into the United States Army. He served during the Korean War. He married *Frankie Hargraves* Sunday, April 5, 1953. He worked at Manhattan Shirt Factory in Lexington, North Carolina, as a Tool and Die Maker in Brooklyn, New York; and for MTA New York City as a Special Machinist. He retired 20 years later as a Transit Supervisor of Power Distribution.

My Family Tree

He was preceded in death by *his brothers, William Doulin, John Thomas Doulin II, Adam Doulin, and James Roosevelt Doulin*, and by *his sisters, Queen Doulin and Marion Doulin*. He was survived by his daughters, his grandchildren, and great-grandchildren.

Litha Ruth Walker Mason   Saturday, March 20, 1937 – Monday, April 22, 2019

Saturday, March 20, 1937, *Litha Ruth Walker* entered this world, the most beautiful baby born to *Estella Lewis Walker and Theortic Calvin (T.C.) Walker,* who lived in Locust Grove, Georgia – Henry County.

Six months later, they decided to relocate to Michigan in 1938 and settled in Highland Park. The family joined the Russell Street Missionary Baptist Church in Detroit. In those days, Highland Park was filled with tree-lined streets and lovely brick homes. It was a delightful place to reside.

In 1940, her mother was pregnant with *twins, Catherine Walker and Calvin Walker*. Unfortunately, she had a bad fall during her pregnancy, and the twins were born stillborn.

Litha was a cute little girl, full of love and promise. She had many friends and dreamed about what her life would be when she grew up. She attended school in Highland Park. *Litha* could remember the teacher at Frances E. Willard School telling her mother that she should be in kindergarten because of her age. Her mother informed her that *Litha* could read and print. So, *Litha* was given a piece of chalk and printed some words, not just letters. *Litha* was then placed in the first grade. She graduated from Highland Park High School and Highland Park Junior College. She was an excellent student and was awarded for her typing skills, as she could type 120 words a minute. She worked as a Secretary at Winkelman's Brothers Warehouse and was busy in her church, Messiah Missionary Baptist Church, which was under the leadership of *Rev. Theodore C. Simmons*. She was lead soprano in the church choir and Pianist and Director of the Children's Choir. Her signature song was "I must tell Jesus." *Rev. Simmons* was her Mentor and was like a father to her. *Litha* always had a love for dogs and cats. All her dogs lived for 14 years or more. She loved and cared for them, and they guarded her. One day, she was spied on by a young man named *William "Tony" Mason*. He loves to say that she chased him until he let her catch him, but the truth was that it took him six months to get a date with her. They became fast friends and remained so even until this day. They got married 59 years ago on Saturday, March 19, 1960.

They had *three children: Anthony Troy (Troy), Jenean Evette, and Theodore Cornelius (Ted)*. Raising their children together brought them much joy, and she loved them all. Later in life, *Litha and Tony* adopted their nieces *Tony's* older brother *Eugene's* daughters as their own, but her greatest love was her *"T-Bird."* She was his fishing partner for 40 years, and they both loved casino gambling and traveling. Ask him sometimes; he has many stories to tell.

Once he was trying to tell her how to tie up a boat, and it was a windy day. He was showing her exactly how to place her feet when the wind suddenly stopped blowing, and he ended up in the water. She said, "Are you sure that is how you want me to do that?"

My Family Tree

Litha was such a loving and caring person. She was known to go out shopping and would come home, bringing a new friend. Life for her and *Tony* was chock full of love, laughter, friends, food, friendship, and fun. They eventually joined Fellowship Chapel and found new family members and friends there. Early Monday morning, April 22, 2019 she took on her angel's wings and went to be with GOD and the heavenly choir where her lead soprano voice can be appreciated again.

Litha leaves to cherish her memory, *her loving husband Tony (T-Bird)*; *sons Anthony (Troy) and Theordore (Ted)*; daughter *Jenean Mason*; *daughters-in-laws Sandar Lewin and Suzanne Zeglen(Suzanne's daughter Alyssa Zeglen); nieces Stephanie M. and Iris A. (James R. Nicholas III)*; *sister-in-law sister Norma Jean Mason; grandchildren Amber Mason, Anthony Jefferson Mason (AJ), Austin Mason, and Ashely Mason; "bonus daughter" Venus Mason Thues (Rick) and their two daughters LaKeisha (William Stiff) and Jessica Thues; great nephew James R. Nicholas IV, great-granddaughter Ramiyah White, Jordan Stiff and Madison Stiff;* best friend *Bea Brown*, many good friends and folks she loved and who loved her. She was a blessing to this world, and her kind and loving ways will always be remembered.

Margaret Sturdevant Neely Thursday, June 15, 1933 – Tuesday, December 3, 2019

Margaret Sturdevant Neely peacefully accepted her call on December 3, 2019. She was born on June 15, 1933, to the late *Margaret and Richard Sturdevant.* She was an honors grad in Davie County Training School and Bennett College where she earned a BA degree in French and English. She taught English and French in the Virginia School System, the High Point School System, and the Winston-Salem Forsyth County School System. She did further studies at City College in New York, A and T College in Greensboro, Women's College in Milledgeville, GA, and UNC at Chapel Hill, NC. *Margaret* was the founding president of the Rural Hall Chapter of National Women of Achievement Inc. She was selected twice for the President of the Year award. She was also selected as Chaplain for the Southeastern region and later inducted into the Hall of Fame for NWOA, Inc. She was an avid basketball fan, which she shared with her grandson. Waiting to greet her were her mother and father, her *husband, DeWitt Clinton Neely, and nephew, Richard,* who preceded her in transition.

My Family Tree

Edna Elizabeth Ijames Mason Allen   Thursday, June 6, 1918 – Tuesday, April 21, 2020

Edna Elizabeth Ijames Mason Allen passed away at 101, Tuesday, April 21, 2020, at Holden Heights Senior Living and Memory Care in Greensboro, North Carolina. She lived a beautiful full life of faithful service to God, family, church, and community for 101 years and 10 months. Born in Davie County on June 6, 1918, she was the fourth of seven children born to the late *Columbia Veatrice Sturdevant Ijames and John "Johnnie" Alexander Ijames.*

She started her Christian journey at an early age in the Clement Grove Church of God 7th Day. She was educated in the Davie County School System in Mocksville, North Carolina – Davie County, where she met and married the love of her life to the late *Rev. Baxter Sherman Mason.* They were married for 33 years, and to this union was born *three children, Sylvester Mason* (died at birth), *William S. Mason, and Columbia DeAnn Mason Stanton.* After working in New York for many years, she and *Baxter* purchased and returned to live in the old *Mason* place in Mocksville. Along with her husband became a lifelong member of Cedar Grove Baptist Church, where she was lovingly called *"Mother of the Church."*

After the passing of *Baxter* in 1971, she married the late *Rev. Ralph Q. Allen* in 1981.

Some of her involvements include the following: she served as: First Lady at Boxwood, Old Smith Grove, Goodwill, and Chestnut Grove Baptist Churches. When age and health did not allow her to live alone, she worshipped under watch care at New Bethel Baptist Church in High Point, North Carolina – Guilford County, and at Grant AME Church in Chesilhurst, New Jersey – Camden County. She was an active member of the Eagle Network for the Widows, sponsored by Graham Funeral Home in Mocksville, North Carolina. She received a lifetime member plaque from the local NAACP of Mocksville. She served as treasurer for a number of years for Davie County Agriculture Extension Service. She also served as Band Booster President at William Penn High School for three years, President of the Best Yet Club at Cedar Grove Baptist in Mocksville for many years, President of the Cedar Grove Missionary Circle for 15 years, served as Chairperson of District 3, Group 2 of the Woman's Home and Foreign Missionary Convention and was currently a member of the Scarlet Dames (Red Hatters) of Greensboro, North Carolina.

She leaves to cherish her memories *one son, William S. Mason [I] (Mary)* of Greensboro, North Carolina; *one daughter, Columbia DeAnn Mason Stanton* of Warterford Works, New Jersey; *one brother, John Lester Ijames (Peggy)* of Walnut Cove, North Carolina; *two brothers-in-law, Rev. John Mason (Margaret) and Peter E. Mason (Irma)* of High Point, North Carolina; *four grandchildren, Rev. William S. Mason [II] (Stephanie), Matthew Lewis, DeAnnette E. Cross (Clyde), and Karma L. Mason;* six great-grandchildren; two great-great-grandchildren; and a host of nieces, nephews, relatives, and friends.

My Family Tree

William Anthony Mason Wednesday, January 22, 1938 – Monday, August 3, 2020

Humble Beginnings

William Anthony Mason, affectionately known as *Tony* to most of his friends, took his first breath on January 22, 1938, the second of four children born to *the late Hazel Lorraine Workman Mason and Napoleon Jefferson Mason,* in Winston-Salem, North Carolina – Forsyth County. *Napoleon,* modeling a work ethic that inspired *Tony,* spent more than three years away from home, working in the auto factories in the north to make a better life for his family and saved enough to move them to Detroit. *Tony* was never afraid of working and wanted a job to buy nice clothes, as his was tired of wearing hand-me-downs from his older brother, *Eugene.* While working at Winkelman's Department store, one of the secretaries caught his eye. But she had a reputation for being a serious young lady. So, *Tony* took a bet that he could get a date. It was a bet that, much to his chagrin, he lost. He persisted and eventually gained the love of his life, *Litha.* They were joined in marriage March 19, 1960, and remained joyous partners for 59 years until her passing on April 22, 2019.

Preparation and Determination Paid Off

Tony's faith in the Lord and the work ethic he learned from his parents equipped him the determination to persevere during difficult times, as he worked as a shoes salesman, made lamps at James Crystal Manufacturing, sold encyclopedias, Kirby vacuum cleaners and Fuller Brush products, door-to-door, no easy feat for a black man in the 1960's. *Tony's* perseverance carried him far after he began a career at Chrysler Corporation. Beginning with a position shoveling sand, he worked his way up into executive level management.

Steadfast, Unmovable Faith

Despite excellent performance reviews, it appeared he had reached a plateau. Not *Tony.* He continued to work six days a week and began night school. The next time he was told that a promotion was beyond his grasp due to the lack of a degree, he calmly replied, "You mean one of these?" And produced his Bachelor of Science in Management and Supervision from Central Michigan, received in 1982. He went on to earn a Master of Science in Management and Supervision from Central Michigan in 1983 as well. With the official education married to his experience, he continued to rise through the ranks at Chrysler, culminating with his promotion to Plant Manager at Detroit Axel in 1993 until his retirement in 1996.

The Latter Years

For Tony, the term "retirement" was used loosely, as he started a management consulting company, *Tony Mason and Associates,* with himself as the president and only employee. He also began to teach graduate school classes at Baker College, eventually joining the Board of Regents and becoming a vital part of the School of Nursing. He was honored with a Doctorate of Humane Letters from Baker College in 2011. If I can help somebody along the way…

My Family Tree

Generosity was an integral part of *Tony's* philosophy and life. Not only giving monetarily, but gifting time and knowledge, helping others in their journeys in their careers and their lives. He continued to serve at his church, Fellowship Chapel, as an usher and in other capacities. Even during his "semi-retirement," *Tony* found time to pursue his passion for fishing, hit the casinos and travel with his beloved *Litha*. He also came to enjoy cooking, sitting outside in his "backyard office," grilling and his famous love of "mindless action" movies and video games. Blessed is the man whose quiver is filled…

Tony leaves a legacy of cherished memories and invaluable life's lessons *to sons Troy (Sandar) and Theodore (Ted) (Suzanna); daughters Jenean Mason (Boots) and Venus Rene Mason (Rick Thues); grandsons Austin Mason and Anthony Mason, granddaughters LaKeisha (William Stiff) Jessica Thues, Amber Mason, Ashley Mason, and Alyssa Zeglen (Peter Engstrom); great-granddaughters Jordan, Madison, and Ramiyah White; sister-in-law Norma Jean Mason and nieces Iris Mason (James R. Nicholas III) and Stephanie Mason; and great nephew James R. Nicholas IV; and a host of cousins in North Carolina, as well as many friends, neighbors and church family who loved him.* The *Mason* family is grateful to *Ms. Courtney Dillard* for providing outstanding care and personal assistance during *Tony's* illness. The man affectionately dubbed *"The Smartest Man in the Universe"* by his son *Ted* is now a citizen of Heaven. Until we meet again…

Eddie Andrew Trent I Monday, August 16, 1948 – Thursday, October 14, 2021

Tallahassee, Florida – *Eddie A. Trent I*, 73, passed in Jacksonville, Florida, on October 14, 2021. Memorial services will be held at 12 noon Saturday on the grounds of TILLMAN OF TALLAHASSEE. A Leon County native, *Eddie* was a 1967 graduate of Tallahassee's original Lincoln High School. He settled in Detroit, where he worked for General Motors. He ascended to Union Representative for the United Auto Workers (UAW), a position he held for many years. In Detroit, he continued his education at Wayne State University. Survivors include *his twins, Lisa Ann and Eddie Andrew Trent II granddaughter, Deidre (Corey) Lashley; great-granddaughter, Kouri Lashley; life partner Letty Torres; sisters, Betty Trent Young, Debbie Trent, and Helen Trent (Buster) Leon; brother, John D. (Reverend Jimmie) Dickey; and a host of nieces, nephews, other relatives, and friends.*

My Family Tree

Eloise Rankin White   Wednesday, December 21, 1927 – Tuesday, December 27, 2022

Mrs. Eloise Rankin White, age 95, transitioned to her heavenly home on Tuesday, December 27, 2022, in Dearborn, Michigan. She was born to the late *Essie Mae Ellis Rankin and David Rankin* on December 21, 1927, in Rowan County.

Mrs. White, formerly of Cleveland, attended R.A. Clement School, Cleveland. At a young age, she was a member of Third Creek A.M.E. Zion Church before she moved to Detroit, Michigan, where she attended Calvary Presbyterian Church. In addition to her parents, she was preceded in death by *her husband, John Carl White; brothers, Theodore Rankin, John Rankin, Powell Rankin and David Rankin; sisters, Jenette Rankin, Jean Rankin, Eva Rankin Lee, Vivian Rankin; step-mother, Annie Ellis Rankin and Grandson Todd Hrobowski.*

Those who still cherish her memories are her daughter and caregiver, *Marian Rankin White Hrobowski* of the home; *grandson, Kyle Hrobowski,* Atlanta, Ga.; *step-daughter, Lenora Heaggans Reid; brothers, William Rankin (Peggye),* Southfield, Michigan, *Rev. James Henry Rankin (Mary Emma)* Salisbury; *sisters-in-law*: *Thelma Rankin,* Detroit, Michigan, *Virginia Rankin,* Brooklyn, N.Y., *Carolyn Mack Lipscomb White,* Mooresville; *and a host of nieces, nephews, cousins, friends and other family members.*

My Family Tree

A Poem For Black Hearts

Please Have Pride in Yourself

My People Listen Closely To My Words

My People Stand Up As A Race

Please Be Strong

Be Blessed You Are Black

Say What Is On Your Mind

Do Not Be Afraid Of The Beast

The Beast Can Not Control You

Only GOD Can

Be Happy You Are God's People

Show The Beast We Can Stand

Walk and Talk Together As One

Talk Together Without Harmful Words

Do You Hear Your People Voices Are Crying Out

My People Stand Still

Listen To What The Voices Are Saying To You

Our Time Is Coming To Take Back What Is Ours

Please Do Not Close Your Eyes or Ears

Do Not Turn Away

Please Listen To The Voices That Are Crying Out For Your Help

Please Help Them

Your Race Needs Your Help To Fight The Battle Against The Beast

See What The Beast Is Doing To Your Race

Hear What They Are Saying About Us And You

We Have To Do Something About It Before We Lose Our Pride

And Become Slaves Into Their System With No Way Out

The Beast Has Kept Us As Slaves For More Than Four Hundred Years

Kept Us Away From Our Language

Our Way Of Life

My Family Tree

And Our God

Please Be Strong Black People

We Are Dying So Young

And Not Even Caring

Over Guns

Drugs

Alcohol

All Types Of Diseases

Gangs And Broken Homes

The Beast Is Sitting Back Watching Blacks Kill [Our] Own Race Off This Earth

The Beast Just Wants To Use Us To Bring Down Our Race

By Using Us Against Each Other

To Save Them The Headache

The Beast Do Not Want Us To Know About Our GOD or Our History As Black People

The Beast Tells Us What They Want Us To Know About Our GOD And Our History

The Beast Knows We Are Powerful People, But We Do Not Know We Are Powerful People

We Can Be Powerful People Again

Only If We Put Our Heads and Voices Together And Think As A People And Not against Our People

Maybe You Do Not Remember Our Ancestors Were Here Before Them

Your Ancestors Were Kings And Queens In Our Homeland

We Can Be Kings And Queens Again In Our Homeland And Anywhere Else

The Time For Waiting Is Over

We Have To Do It Now

By Stephanie M. Mason © 2024

⌘

My Family Tree

From our Family Albums

Left side (Big Grand Mommy) Hazel L. Mason, (Poppie) Napoleon J. Mason, (Mommy) Norma J. Mason, (Dad) Eugene N. Mason, (Little Grand Mommy) Levonia M. Cowan and Bishop, Gary M. Simpson

My Family Tree

Bishop, Gary M. Simpson

My Family Tree

Left side Aunt Litha R. Mason, Iris A. Nicholas, (Mommy) Norma J. Mason and Stephanie M. Mason

Mr. JJ Nicholas IV

My Family Tree

Grandma Ellen Jefferson Mason   Grandpa Samuel M. Mason

William Robert Workman, Grace Louise Workman Browning, Grandma Euphonia Bernice Orr Workman, and Hazel Lorraine Workman

My Family Tree

Ruth W. Hairston Hairston and (her husband) William Thomas Hairston

Aunt Jetta Malinda Faulkner Childs and her sister Grandma Levonia Margaret Carey Cowan

My Family Tree

Aunt Jetta Malinda Faulkner Child   Aunt Mattie Mason

George Beamon Faulkner (Jetta's Dad)

Grandma Helen Bass Carey

My Family Tree

Uncle Wilbur C. Carey I   Aunt Vereece Carolyn Carey

Sabreen L. Salahuddin   Abdul R. Salahuddin

My Family Tree

Tariq Lydick, Ameerah Salahuddin Lydick, Hamazah Lydick, Ridhwana Lydick, and Safadin Lydick

Uncle Tony on the left side, Aunt Euphonia in the middle, Dad on the right and Uncle Bobby in the front

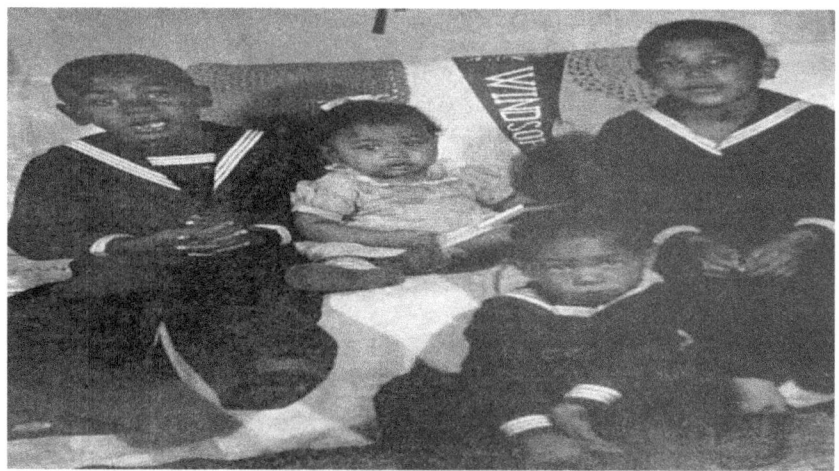

My Family Tree

Mildred E. Peppers, Blanche Y. Sawyer, Darren A. Sawyer, and Ronnie C. Peppers

Mildred E. and Ronnie C. Peppers   Francis V. Peppers

My Family Tree

Angela E. Bassett Vance and Courtney B. Vance

Carrington S. Pledger

Mildred E. Pepper, Xavier J. Sawyer, and Maria J. Strickland

My Family Tree

(Left to Right) Uncle Robert (Bobby), Uncle William (Tony), Napoleon (Poppie), Hazel (Grandma), Eugene (Gene – Dad) and Aunt Euphonia (Phonia)

The Mason Clan

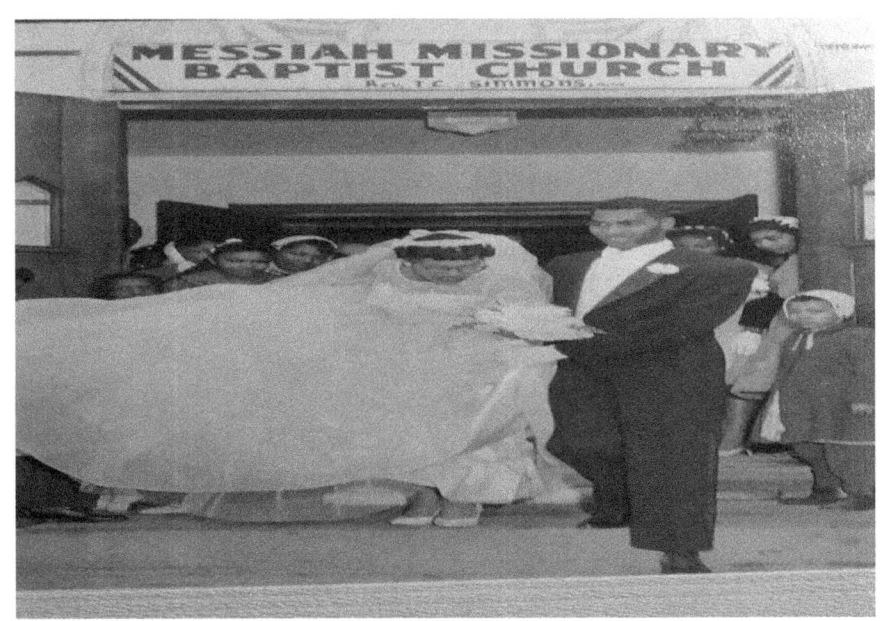

Aunt Litha Ruth Walker Mason and Uncle William Anthony Mason (Tony)

My Family Tree

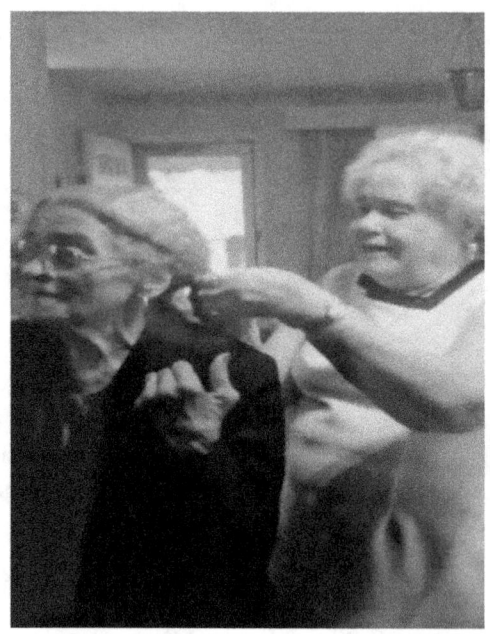

Gladys Childs and her sister Mary Childs

Louise Mason

My Family Tree

Euphonia Bernice Orr Workman & William Essix Workman Marriage License

My Family Tree

Household Record
1880 United States Census

Search results | Download   Previous Household   Next Household

Household:

Name	Relation	Marital Status	Gender	Race	Age	Birthplace	Occupation	Father's Birthplace	Mother's Birthplace
Rubin CUNNINGHAM	Self	M 1820	Male	B	60	VA	Farmer	VA	VA
Lucia CUNNINGHAM	Wife	M 1842	Female	B	38	NC	Keeps House	NC	NC
Kate CUNNINGHAM	Dau	S 1865	Female	B	15	NC	At Home	NC	NC
Sarah CUNNINGHAM	Dau	S 1867	Female	B	13	NC		NC	NC
Harriett CUNNINGHAM	Dau	S 1869	Female	B	11	NC		NC	NC
Martha CUNNINGHAM	Dau	S 1871	Female	B	9	NC		NC	NC
Edmon CUNNINGHAM	Son	S 1874	Male	B	6	NC		NC	NC

Source Information:

Census Place   Mount Carmel, Halifax, Virginia
Family History Library Film   1255369
NA Film Number   T9-1369
Page Number   270D

View original image — for a fee at Ancestry.com

My Family Tree

Joseph Bass

My Family Tree

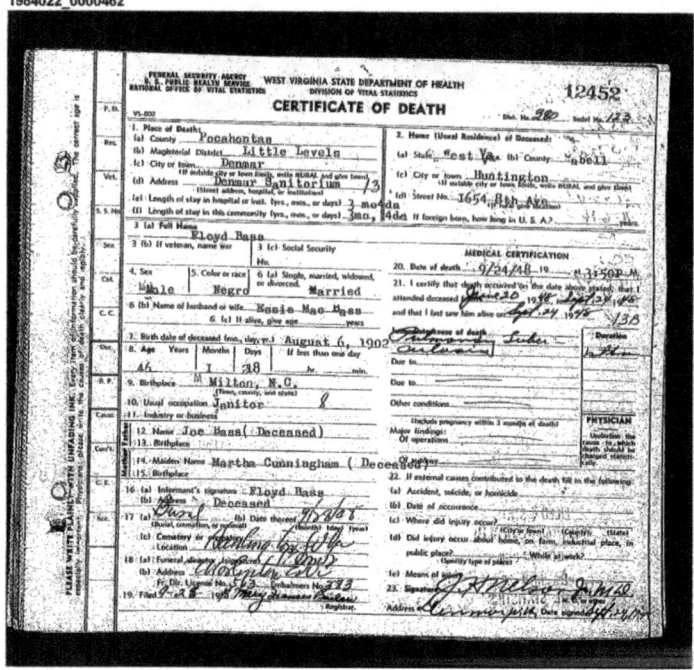

Floyd Cordest Bass

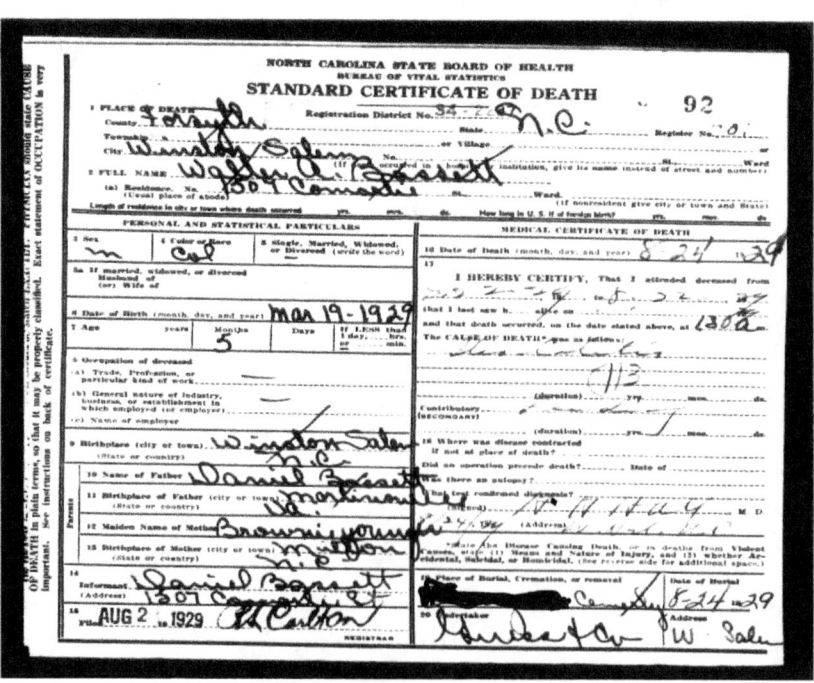

Walter A. Bassett – 5 months old

My Family Tree

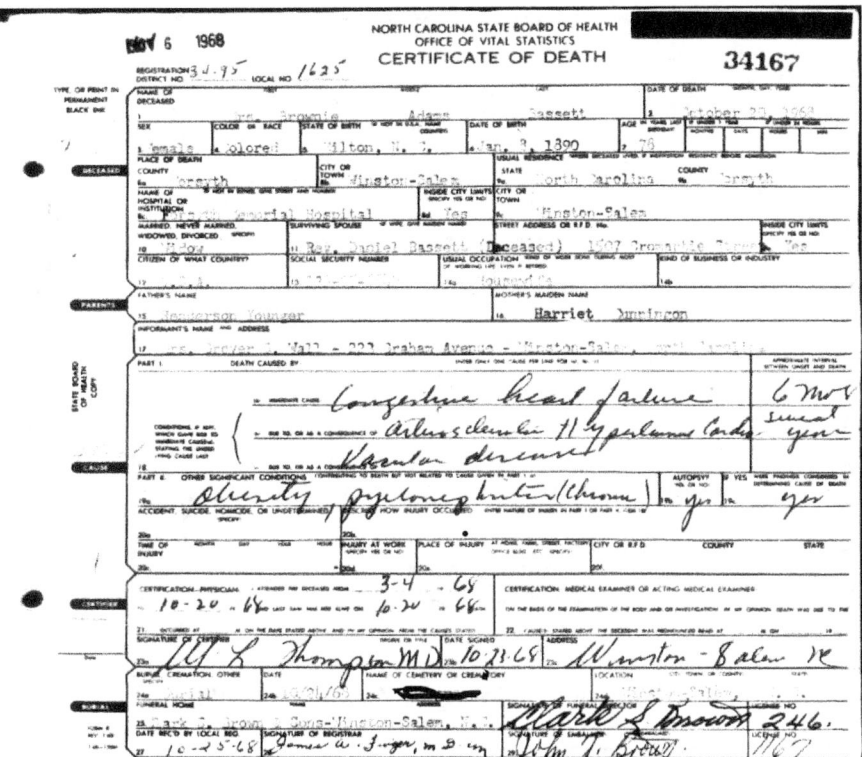

Brownie Younger Bassett

Jettie Ann Hairston Mason Brown

My Family Tree

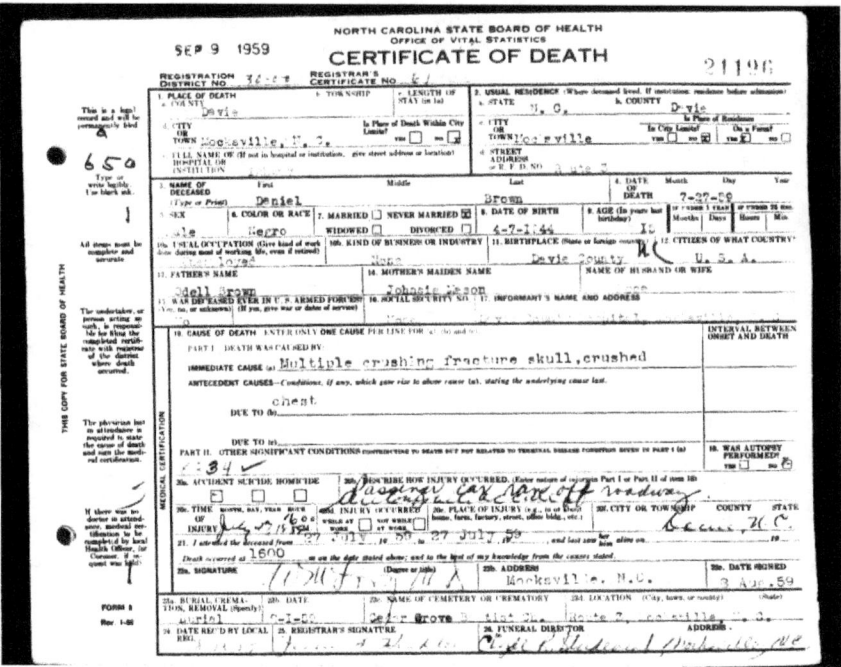

Daniel Brown – Johnsie Mason Brown's son

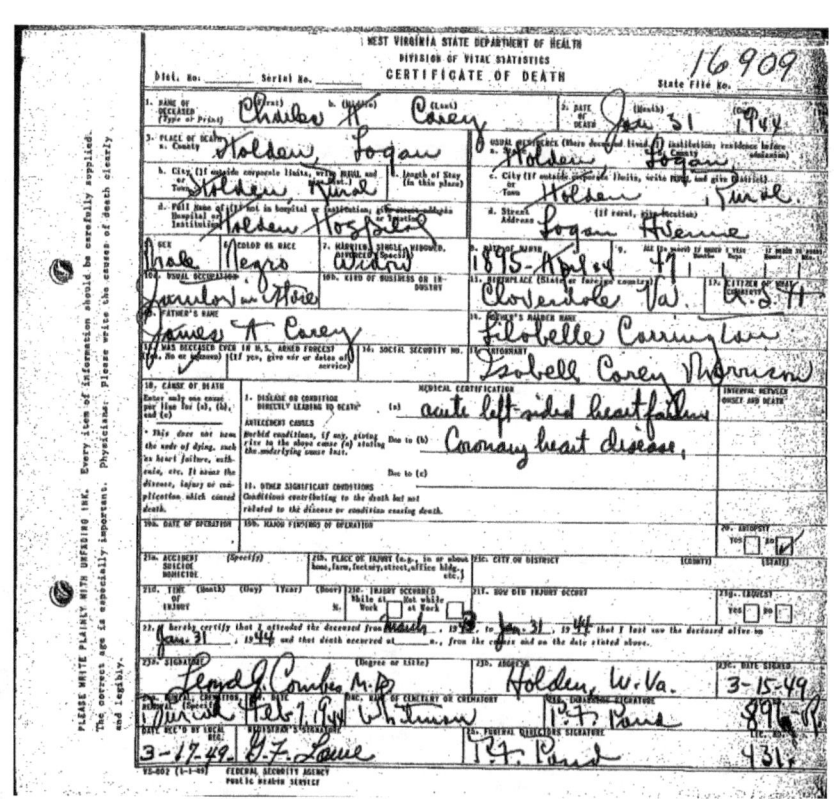

Charles A. Carey

My Family Tree

Johnsie J. Mason Brown

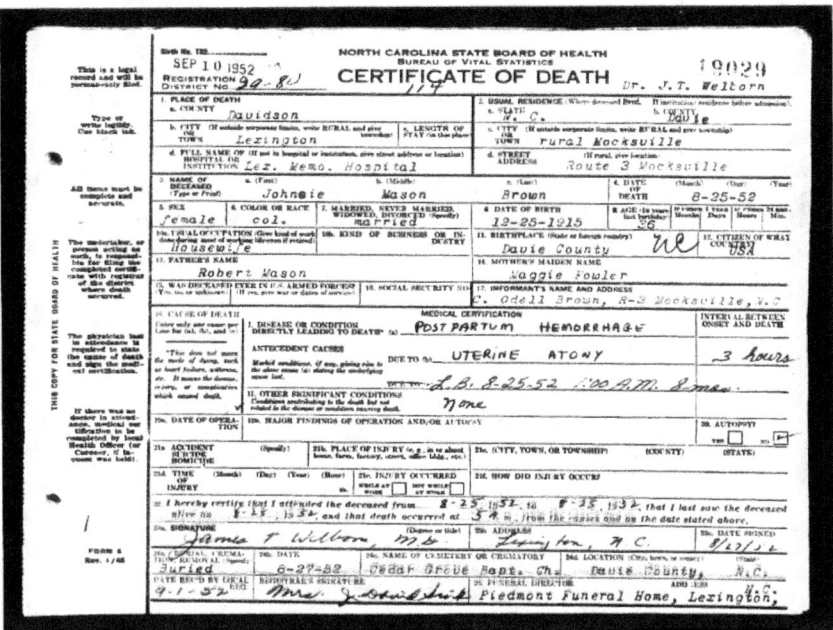

Lillie Belle Carrington Carey, the daughter of Suan Beverly Carrington and Abraham Carrington

My Family Tree

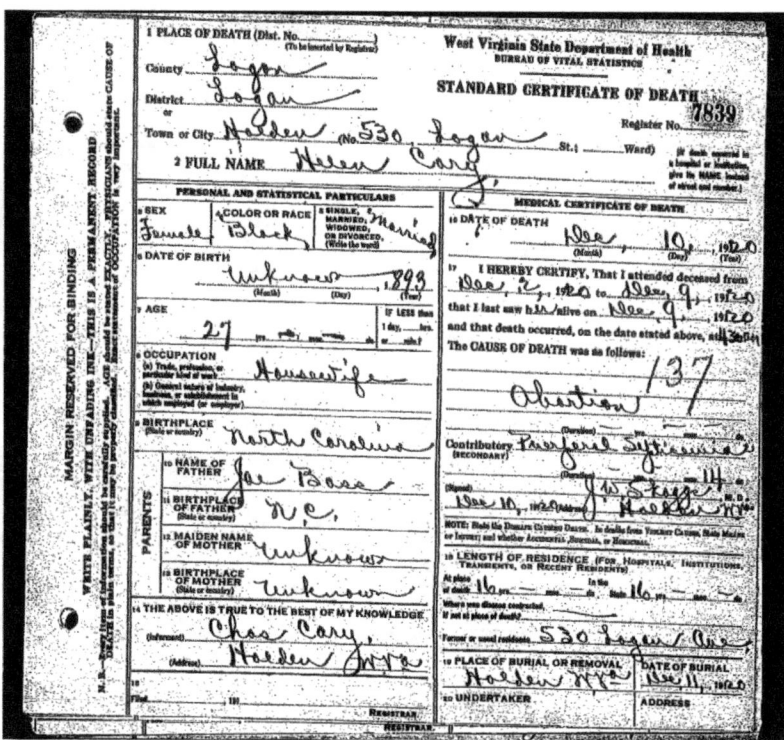

Helen Bass Carey

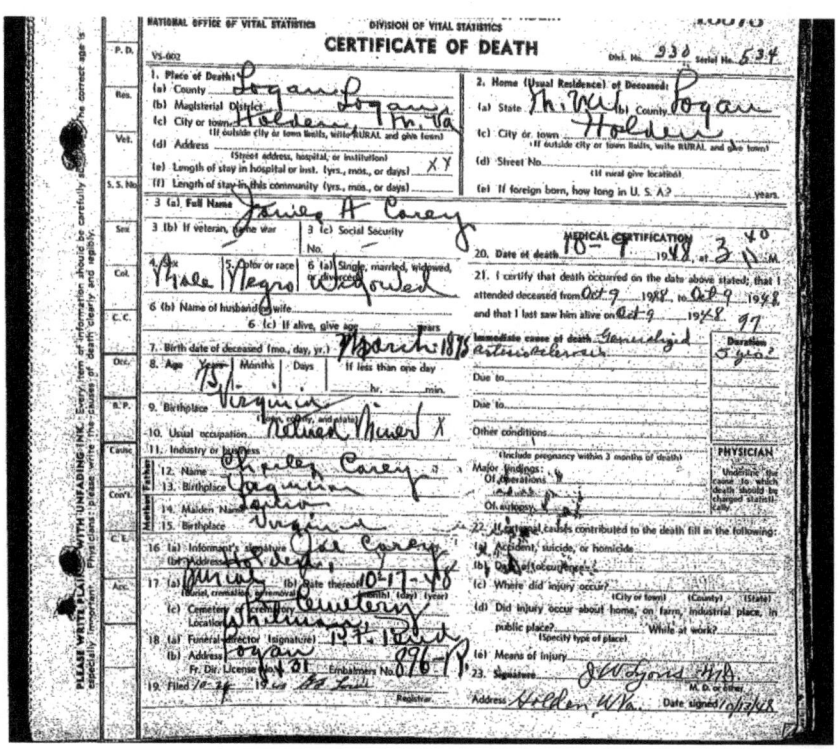

James A. Carey

My Family Tree

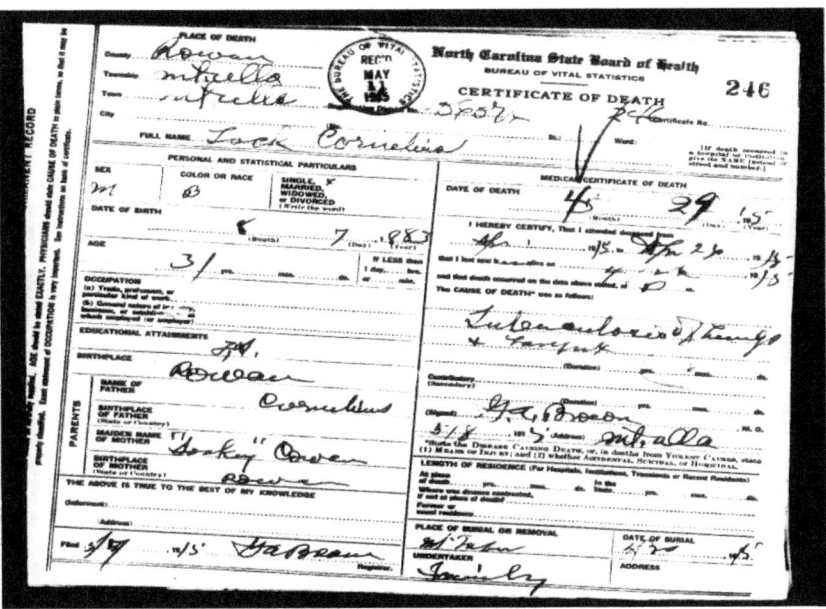

Locke A. Cornelius

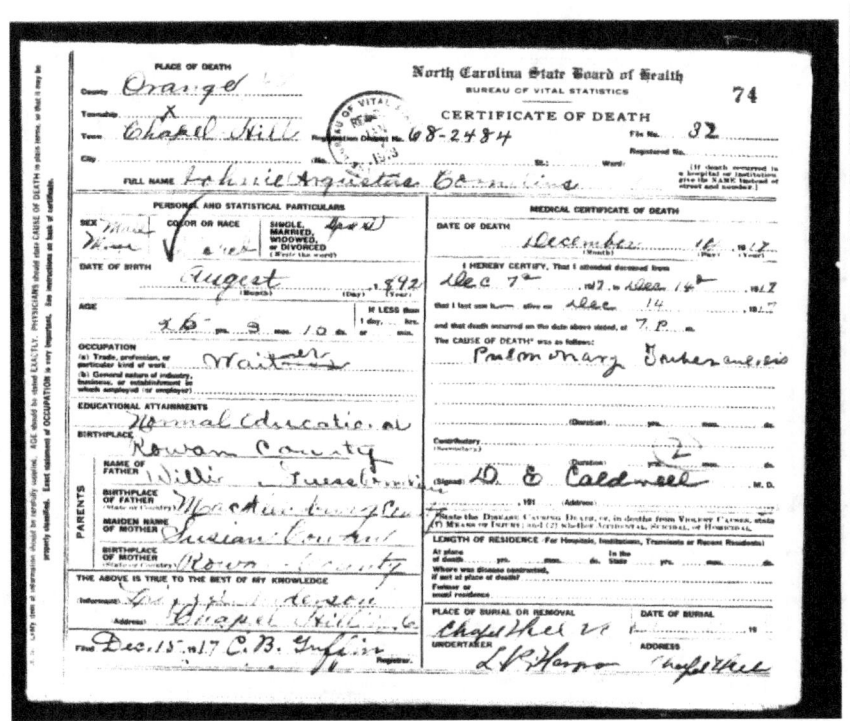

Johnnie Augustus Cornelius

My Family Tree

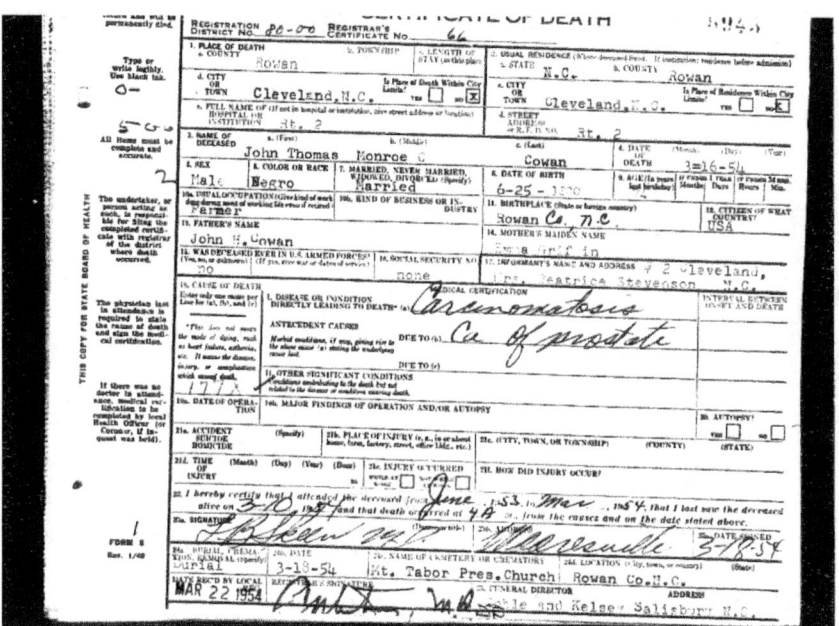

John Thomas Monroe Cowan

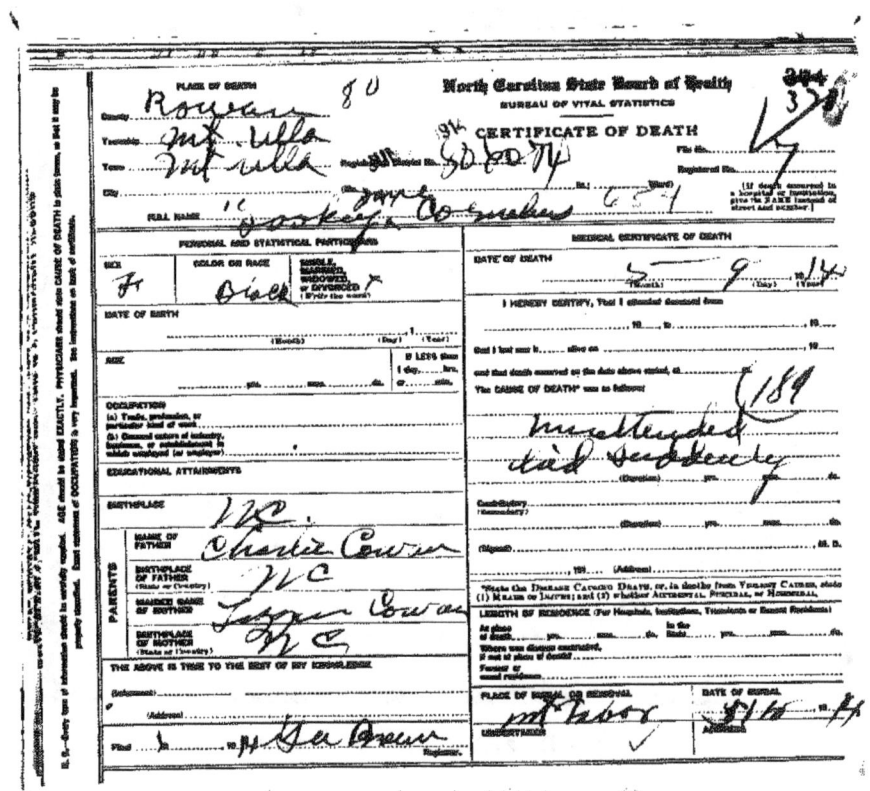

Susan Jane Cowan Cornelius (Sookey)

My Family Tree

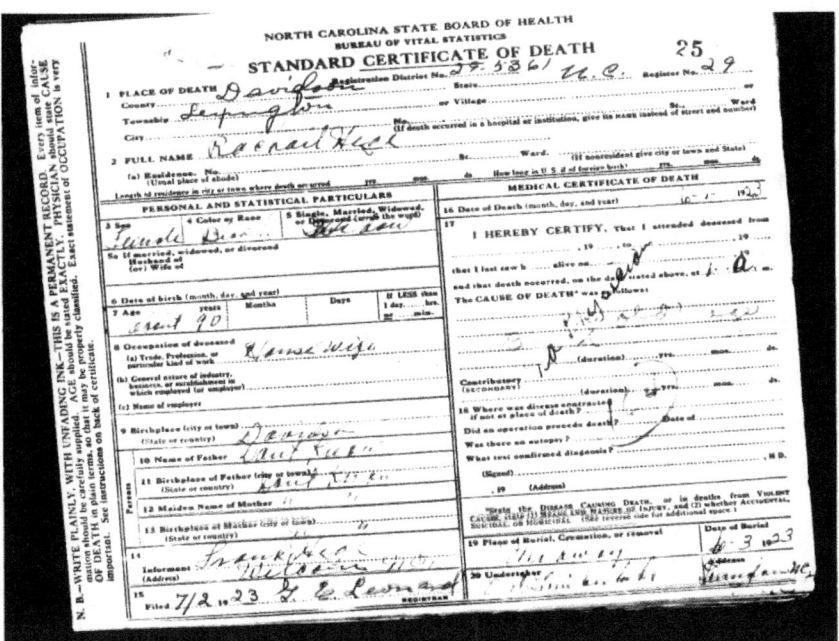

Rachael Hege Conrad

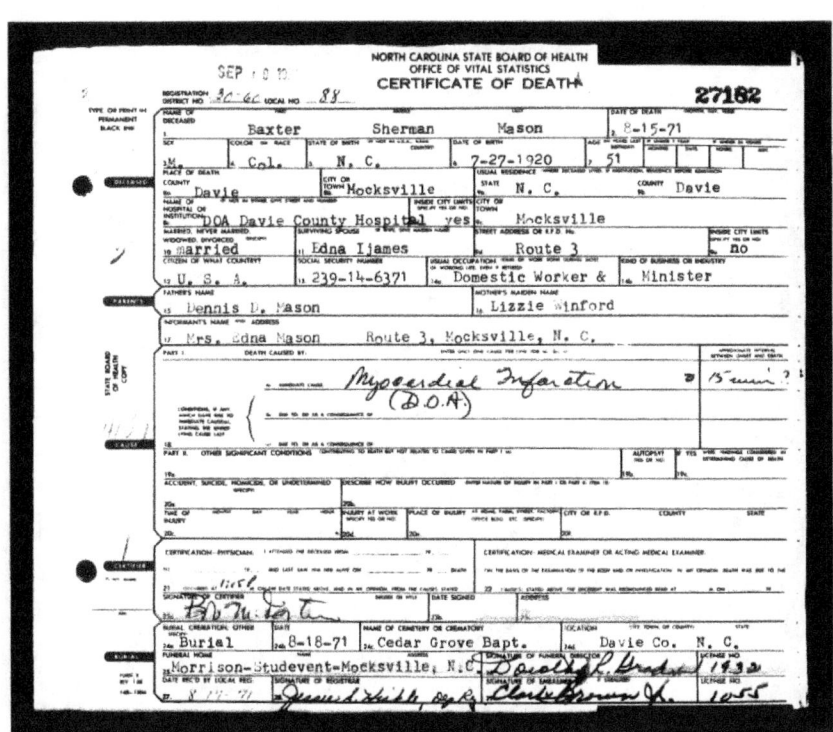

Baxter Sherman Mason

My Family Tree

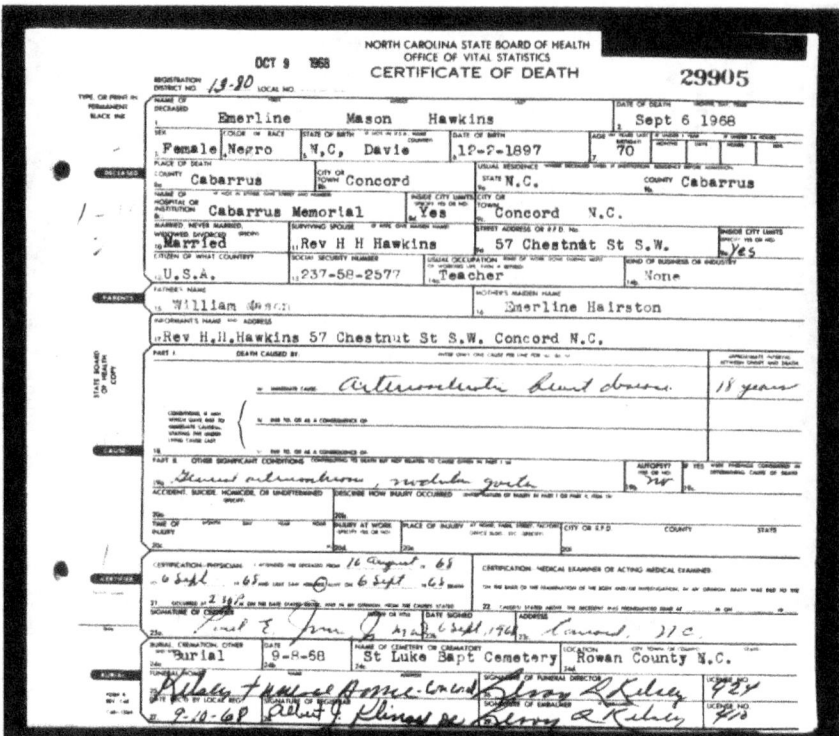

Emerline Wachovia Mason Hawkins

Lewis E. Hege II

My Family Tree

Washington A. Orr II (Wash)

John H. Cowan

My Family Tree

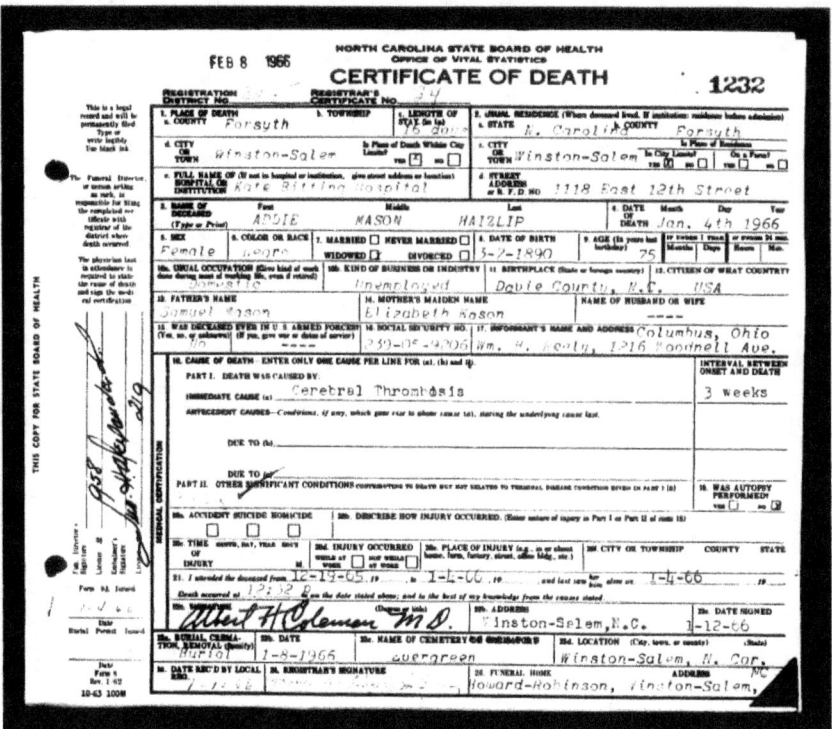

Addie Mason Haizlip

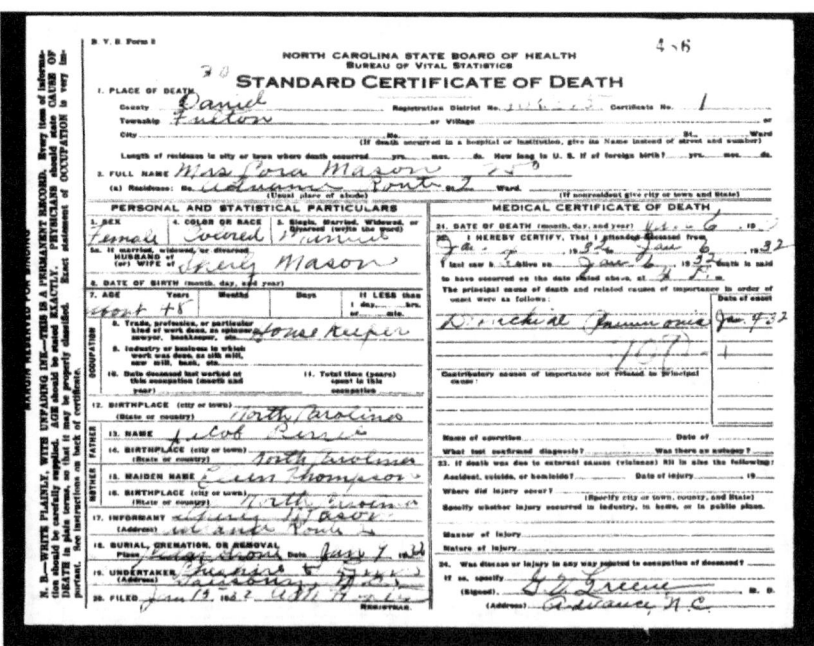

Cora Perrell Mason

My Family Tree

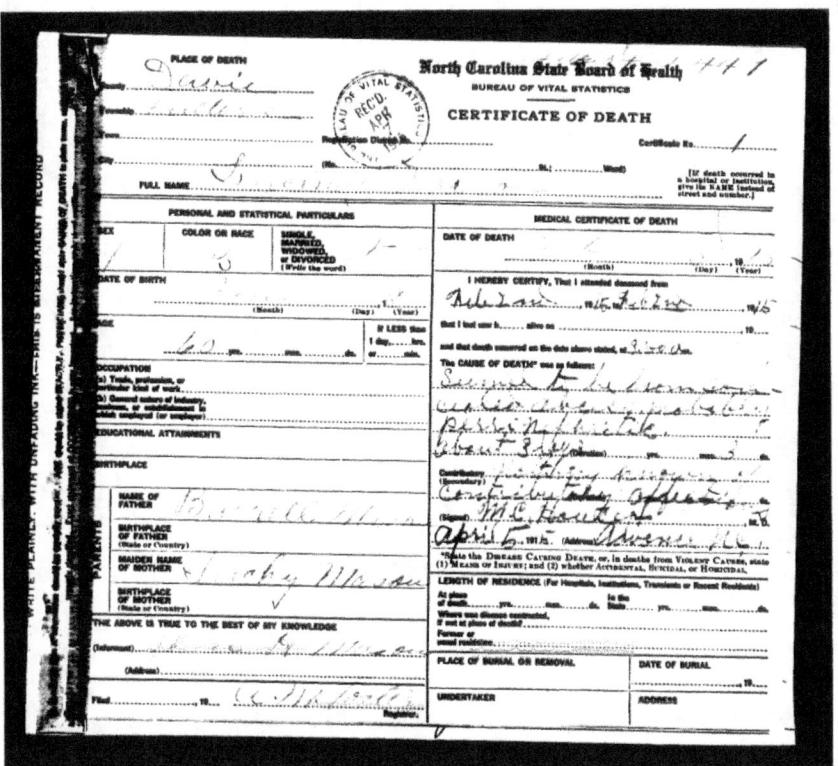

Lucinda Mason Mason

Ernest I. Mason

My Family Tree

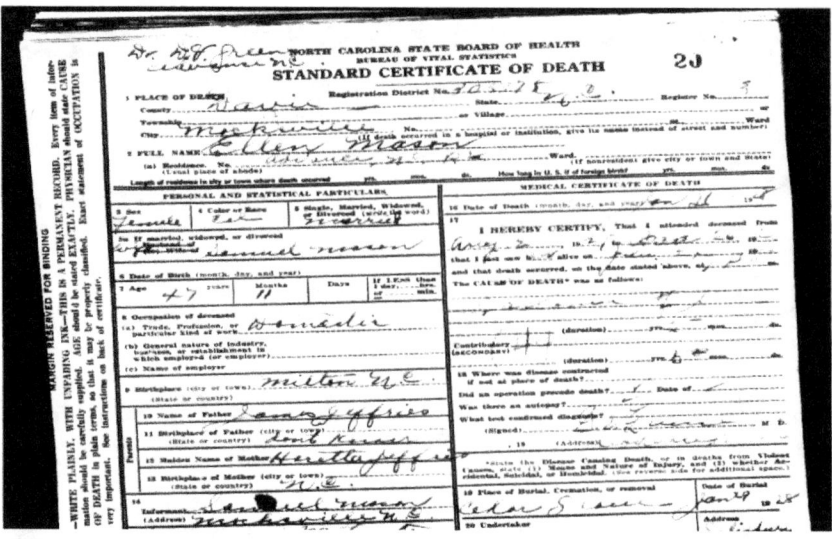

Ellen Jefferson Mason

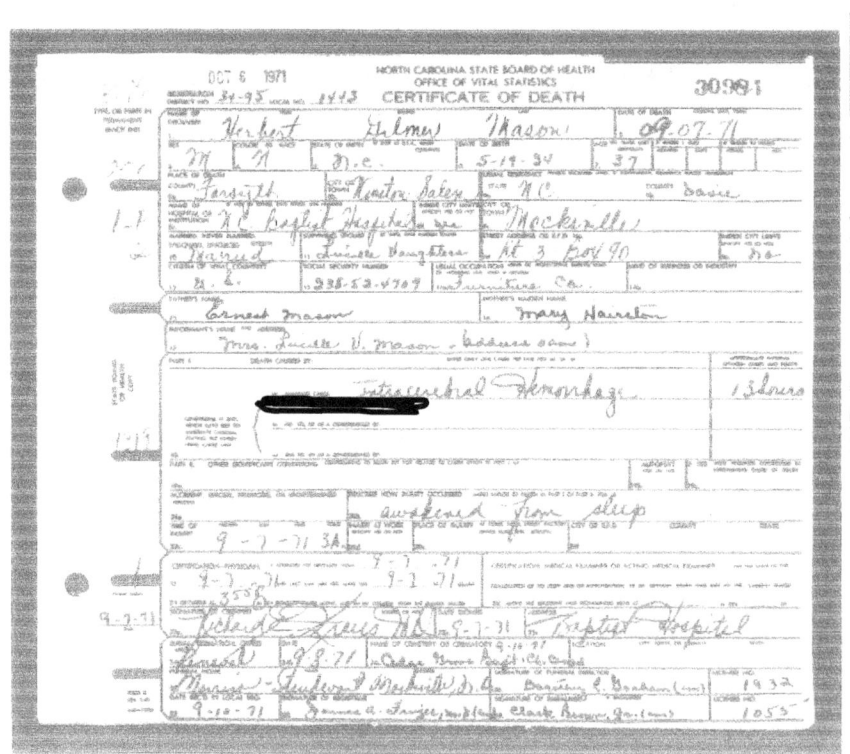

Herbert Gilmer Mason

My Family Tree

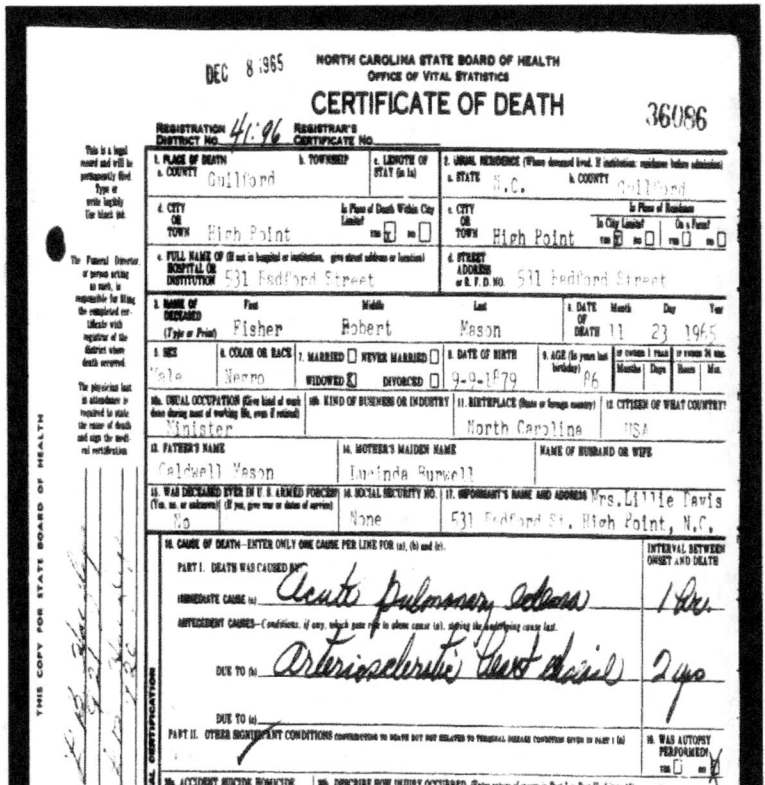

Fisher Robert Mason

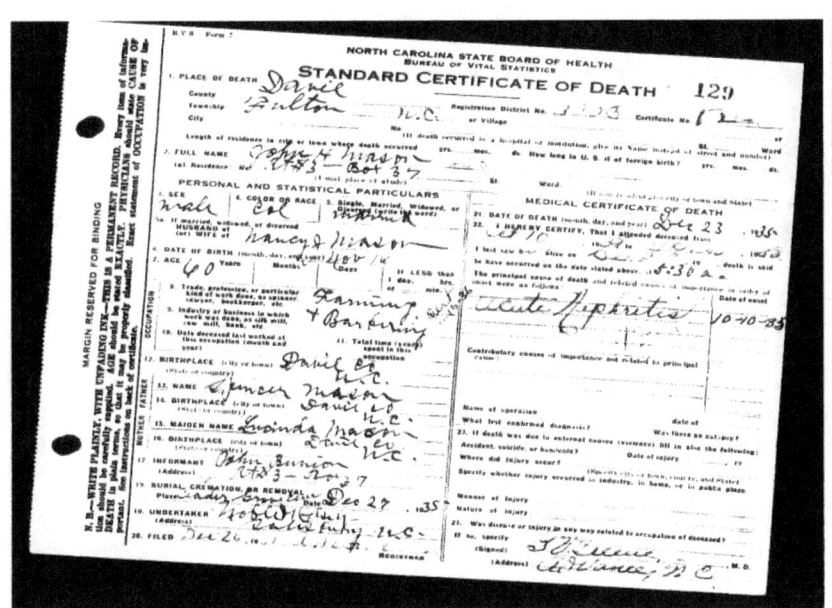

John Henry Mason, the son of Lucinda Mason Mason and Spencer Mason

My Family Tree

Ida Mason Carter

John Bunyon Mason II

My Family Tree

Sherlie H. Mason

William B. Mason II

My Family Tree

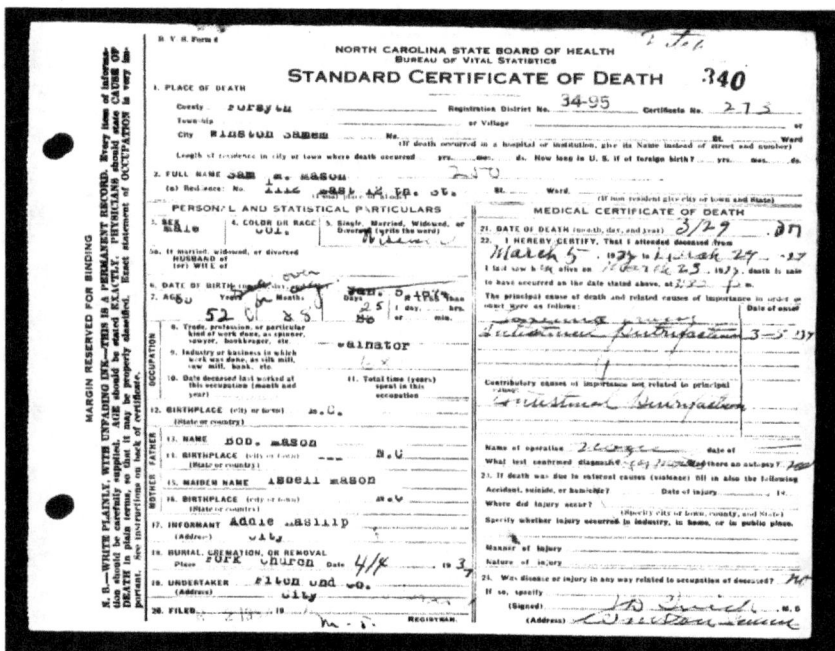

Samuel M. Mason

David L. Neely

My Family Tree

Annie Cornelius Hege Orr

My Family Tree

North Carolina Death Certificates, 1909-1975 - Ancestry.com

North Carolina Death Certificates, 1909-1975

Name:	**Daniel B Bassett**
Gender:	Male
Race:	Black
Age:	41
Birth Date:	28 Sep 1893
Birth Place:	Virginia, United States
Death Date:	14 Apr 1935
Death Location:	Greensboro, Guilford
Spouse's Name:	Brownie Bassett

My Family Tree

Ancestry.com - North Carolina Death Collection, 1908-1996

North Carolina Death Collection, 1908-1996
Record
about Brownie Bassett

Name:	**Brownie Bassett**
Death Date:	20 Oct 1968
Death City:	Winston-Salem
Death County:	Forsyth
Date Death Recorded:	1968
Death Age:	78
Burial Type:	
Birth Date:	abt. 1890
Residence City:	Winston-Salem
Residence County:	Forsyth
Gender:	Female
Race:	Black
Marital Status:	Widowed
Autopsy:	Yes
Institution:	General Hospital
Attendant:	Physician

My Family Tree

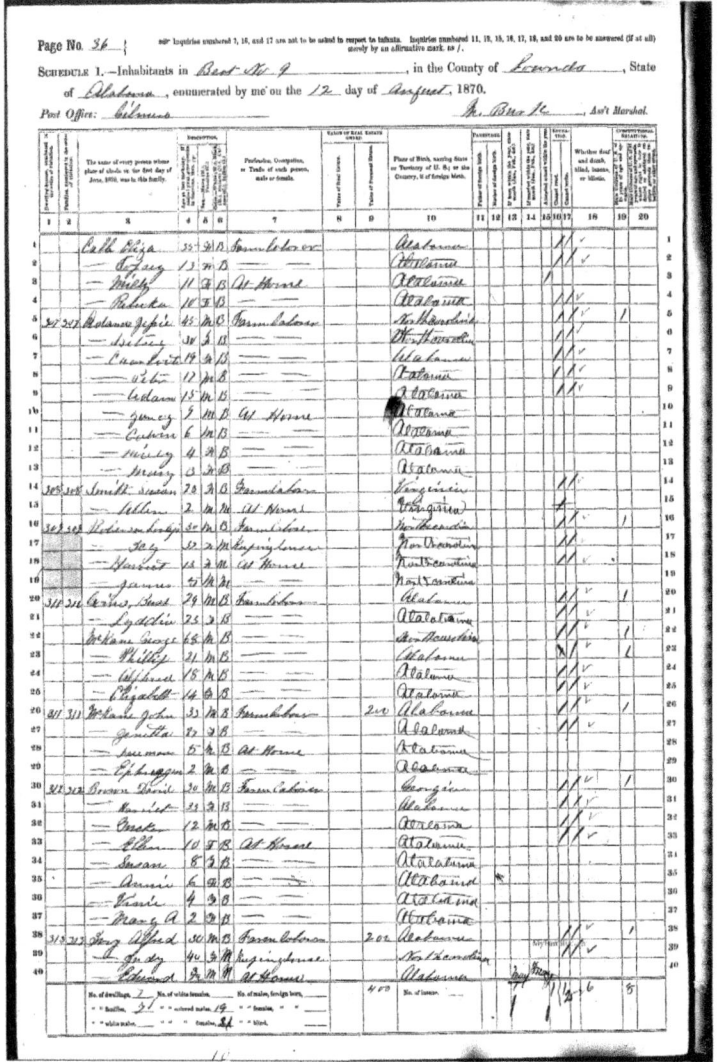

My Family Tree

1900 United States Federal Census - Ancestry.com

1900 United States Federal Census

Name:	**Ellen Younger**
Home in 1900:	Winston Ward 2, Forsyth, North Carolina
Age:	20
Estimated Birth Year:	abt 1880
Birthplace:	North Carolina
Relationship to head-of-house:	Daughter
Parent's Name:	Harriet
Race:	Black
Occupation:	
Neighbors:	

Household Members:

Name		Age
Harriet Younger	June 1860	40
Ellen Younger	Feb 1880	20
Icy Younger	July 1886	14
Eliza Younger	Dec 1887	12
Purcilla Younger	Sept 1889	10
Dora Younger	May 1897	3

http://search.ancestry.com/cgi-bin/sse.dll?indiv=1&db=1900usfedcen%2c&rank=0&gsfn=... 2/29/2008

My Family Tree

1920 United States Federal Census - Ancestry.com

1920 United States Federal Census

Name:	**Icy Roberson** [Illa Roberson]
Home in 1920:	Winston-Salem Ward 4, Forsyth, North Carolina
Age:	84 years
Estimated Birth Year:	abt 1836
Birthplace:	North Carolina
Relation to Head of House:	Grandmother, Grandma *(Grandmother)*
Father's Birth Place:	North Carolina
Mother's Birth Place:	North Carolina
Marital Status:	Widow
Race:	Black [Colored *(Black)*]
Sex:	Female
Able to read:	No
Able to Write:	No
Image:	514
Neighbors:	
Household Members:	

Name	Age
Brown A Adams	30
Harrie Snow	62
Icy Roberson	84
Graham Cathey	22

http://search.ancestry.com/cgi-bin/sse.dll?rank=1&gsfn=ICY&gsln=ROBERSON&=&aaf... 2/27/2008

My Family Tree

1880 United States Census Household Record

Household Record

1880 United States Census

Household:

Name	Relation	Marital Status	Gender	Race	Age	Birthplace	Occupation	Father's Birthplace	Mother's Birthplace
Isaac ORR	Self	M	Male	B	46	NC	Section Hand On R.R.	NC	NC
Caroline ORR	Wife	M	Female	B	47	NC	Housekeeping	NC	NC
Wash ORR	Son	S	Male	B	15	NC	At Home	NC	NC
Lee ORR	Son	S	Male	B	15	NC	At Home	NC	NC
Venus ORR	Dau	S	Female	B	13	NC	At Home	NC	NC
Elick ORR	Son	S	Male	B	11	NC	At School	NC	NC
Lou ORR	Dau	S	Female	B	11	NC	At School	NC	NC
William MAY	Other		Male	B	47	TN	Railroad Hand	TN	TN

Source Information:

- **Census Place:** Pineville, Mecklenburg, North Carolina
- **Family History Library Film:** 1254972
- **NA Film Number:** T9-0972
- **Page Number:** 540D

My Family Tree

1900 United States Federal Census - Ancestry.com

1900 United States Federal Census

Name:	Sam H Mason
Home in 1900:	Winston Ward 2, Forsyth, North Carolina
Age:	30
Estimated Birth Year:	abt 1870
Birthplace:	North Carolina
Relationship to head-of-house:	Head
Spouse's Name:	Mary
Race:	Black
Occupation:	View Image
Neighbors:	View others on page

Household Members:	Name	Age
	Sam H Mason	30
	Mary Mason Nov 1873	26
	Addie Mason Mar 1885	15
	Etta Mason June 1887	13
	Ella Mason July 1887(?)	12
	Green Mason Dec 1892	7
	Nebraska Mason Mar 1897	2
	Nevada Mason Feb 1900	1.12
	Mack Smith	30

http://search.ancestry.com/cgi-bin/sse.dll?indiv=1&rank=0&gsfn=SAM&gsln=MASON&... 4/13/2008

My Family Tree

North Carolina Death Certificates, 1909-1975 - Ancestry.com

Name:	**Mrs Brownie Adams Basset** [Mrs Brownie Adams Younger]
Gender:	Female
Race:	Black
Age:	78
Birth Date:	8 Jan 1890
Birth Place:	Milton, North Carolina, United States
Death Date:	20 Oct 1968
Death Location:	Winston-Salem, Forsyth
Spouse's name:	Rev Deceased Daniel Bassett
Father's Name:	Henderson Younger
Mother's Name:	Harriet Cunningon
RESIDENCE:	Winston-Salem, Forsyth, North Carolina

http://search.ancestry.com/cgi-bin/sse.dll?ti=0&indiv=try&db=ncdeathcerts&h=532895   5/29/2009

My Family Tree

1870 United States Federal Census - Ancestry.com   Page 1 of 1

1870 United States Federal Census

Name:	**Susan J Cowan** (Sookey) Cornelius
Estimated Birth Year:	abt 1858
Age in 1870:	12
Birthplace:	North Carolina
Home in 1870:	Salisbury, Rowan, North Carolina
Race:	Mulatto (Black)
Gender:	Female
Value of real estate:	View Image
Post Office:	Salisbury

1880
s m w a - 22

Household Members:	Name		Age	
	Charles Cowan	1825	45	
	John Cowan	1851 Jan 17 -	19	DC copied
	Rhody Cowan	1854	16	
	Lucinda Cowan	1856	14	
	Susan J Cowan	1858	12	DC
	Charles Cowan	1862	8	
	William Cowan	1864	6	
	Eliza Cowan	1868	2	
	Mary Cowan	1870	4/12	
	Elizabeth Cowan	1830	40	

Lilli Cowan 1869 Indian (age 1)
1885 - Living in Mt Ulla Rowan County

http://search.ancestry.com/cgi-bin/sse.dll?indiv=1&rank=0&gsfn=SUSAN&gsln=COWAN...   6/2/2008

My Family Tree

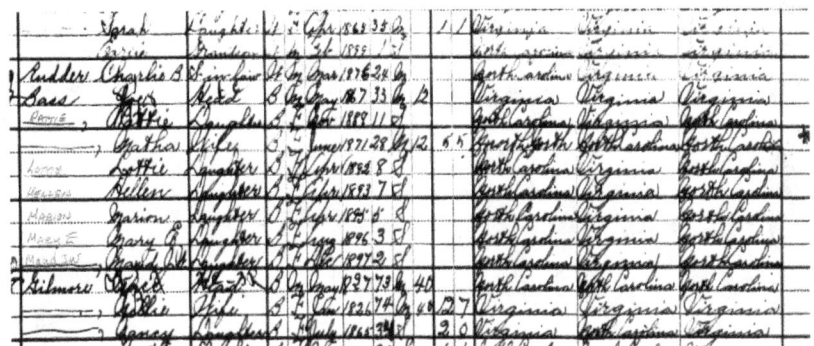

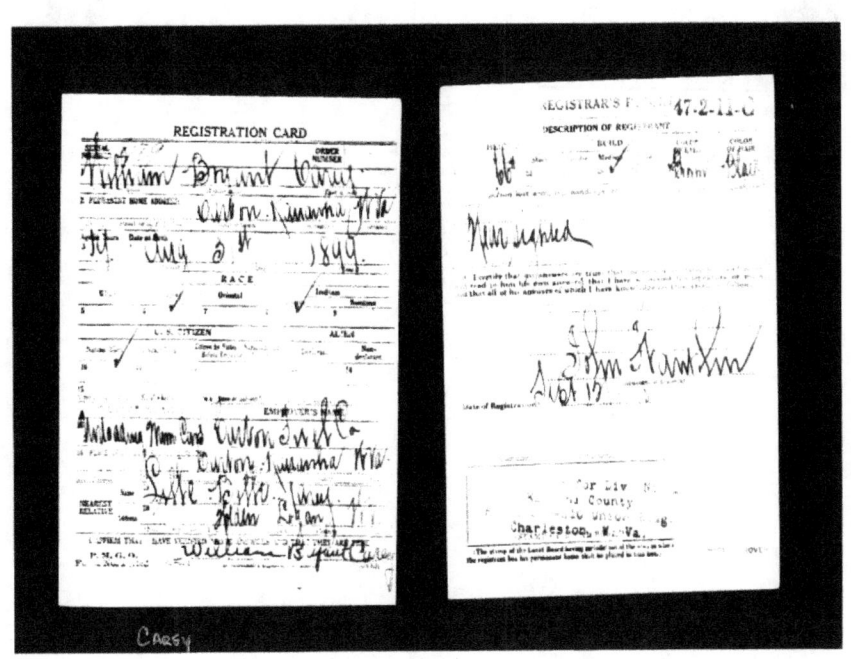

William Bryant Carey

My Family Tree

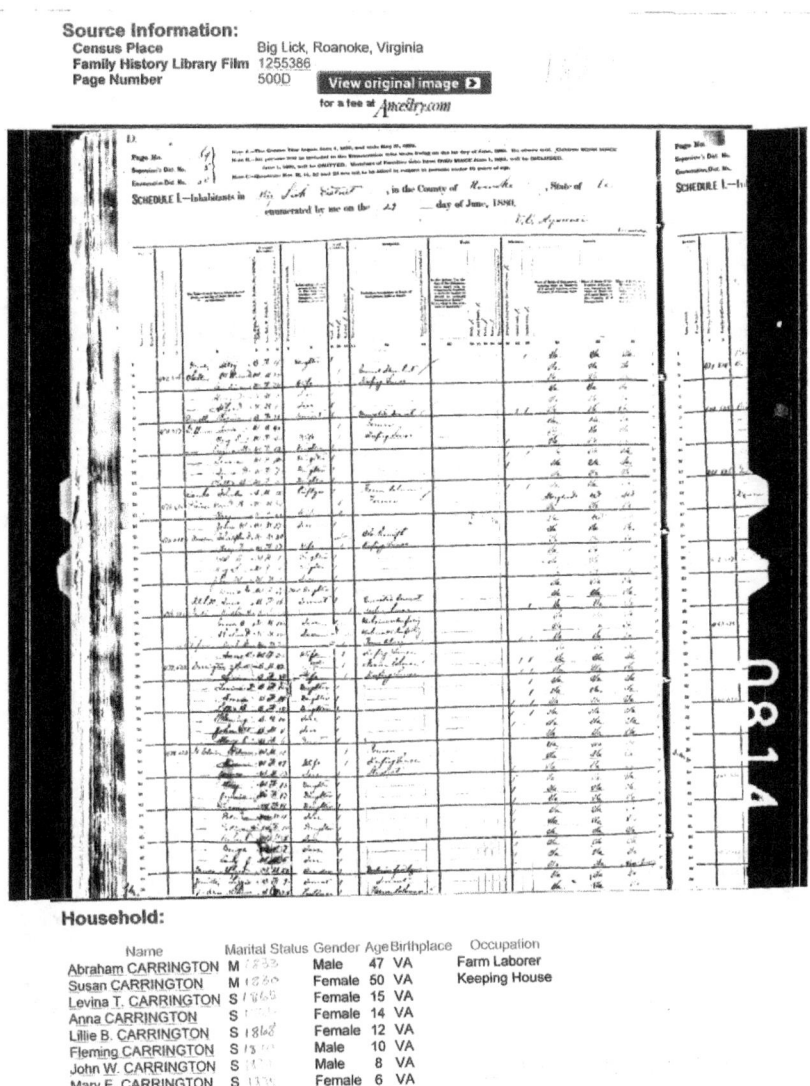

Source Information:
Census Place: Big Lick, Roanoke, Virginia
Family History Library Film: 1255386
Page Number: 500D

Household:

Name	Marital Status	Gender	Age	Birthplace	Occupation
Abraham CARRINGTON	M 1833	Male	47	VA	Farm Laborer
Susan CARRINGTON	M 1830	Female	50	VA	Keeping House
Levina T. CARRINGTON	S 1865	Female	15	VA	
Anna CARRINGTON	S	Female	14	VA	
Lillie B. CARRINGTON	S 1868	Female	12	VA	
Fleming CARRINGTON	S	Male	10	VA	
John W. CARRINGTON	S	Male	8	VA	
Mary E. CARRINGTON	S	Female	6	VA	

My Family Tree

1880 United States Federal Census - Ancestry.com

1880 United States Federal Census

Name:	**Lucinda Mason**
Home in 1880:	Fulton, Davie, North Carolina
Age:	28
Estimated Birth Year:	abt 1852
Birthplace:	North Carolina
Relation to Head of Household:	Self *(Head)*
Father's birthplace:	North Carolina
Mother's birthplace:	North Carolina
Neighbors:	View others on page
Occupation:	Laborer
Marital Status:	Single
Race:	Black
Gender:	Female
Cannot read/write:	
Blind:	
Deaf and dumb:	View Image
Otherwise disabled:	
Idiotic or insane:	

Household Members:	Name	Age
	Lucinda Mason	28
	Pinnix Mason	11
	John Mason	9
	Mary Mason	4
	Fisher Mason	3
	Alex Mason	21
	Julia Brooks	20
	James Brooks	2
	Lizzie Mason	15
	Dock Mason	10
	Julia Mason	9

Source Citation: Year: *1880*; Census Place: *Fulton, Davie, North Carolina*; Roll: *T9_961*; Family History Film: *1254961*; Page: *309.3000*; Enumeration District: *55*; Image: *0693.*

Source Information:
Ancestry.com and The Church of Jesus Christ of Latter-day Saints. *1880 United States Federal Census* [database on-line]. Provo, UT, USA: The Generations Network, Inc., 2005. 1880 U.S. Census Index provided by The Church of Jesus Christ of Latter-day Saints © Copyright 1999 Intellectual Reserve, Inc. All rights reserved. All use is subject to the limited use license and other terms and conditions applicable to this site. Original data: United States of America, Bureau of the Census. *Tenth Census of the United States, 1880.* Washington, D.C.: National Archives and Records Administration, 1880. T9, 1,454 rolls.

Description:
This database is an index to 50 million individuals enumerated in the 1880 United States Federal Census. Census takers recorded many details including each person's name, address, occupation, relationship to the head of household, race, sex, age at last birthday, marital status, place of birth, parents' place of birth. Additionally, the names of those listed on the population schedule are linked to actual images of the 1880 Federal Census. Learn more...

http://search.ancestry.com/cgi-bin/sse.dll?indiv=1&viewrecord=1&ti=0&r=an&db=1880usf... 6/4/2008

My Family Tree

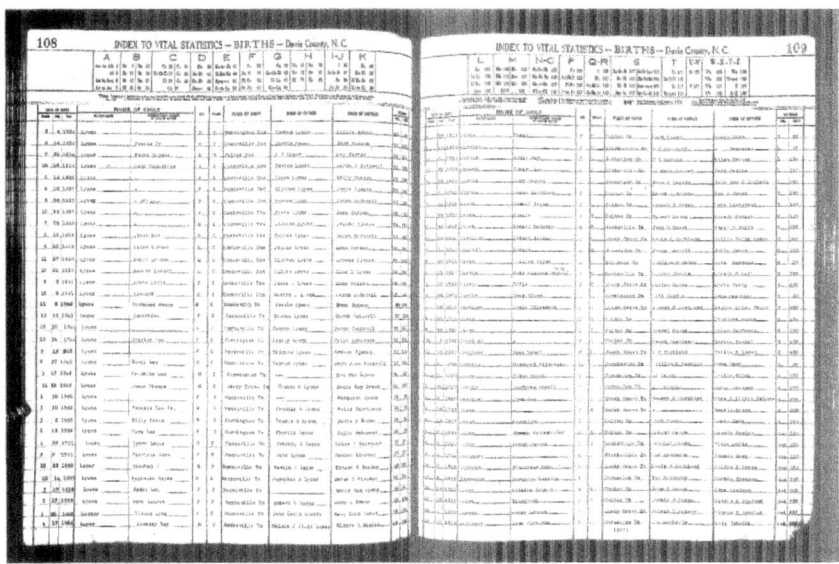

Dorothea Younger

My Family Tree

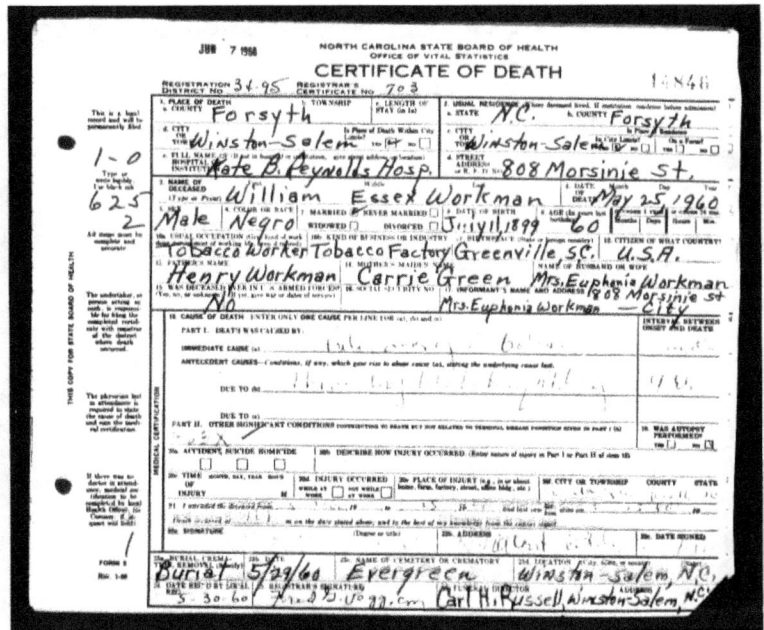

William Essix Workman

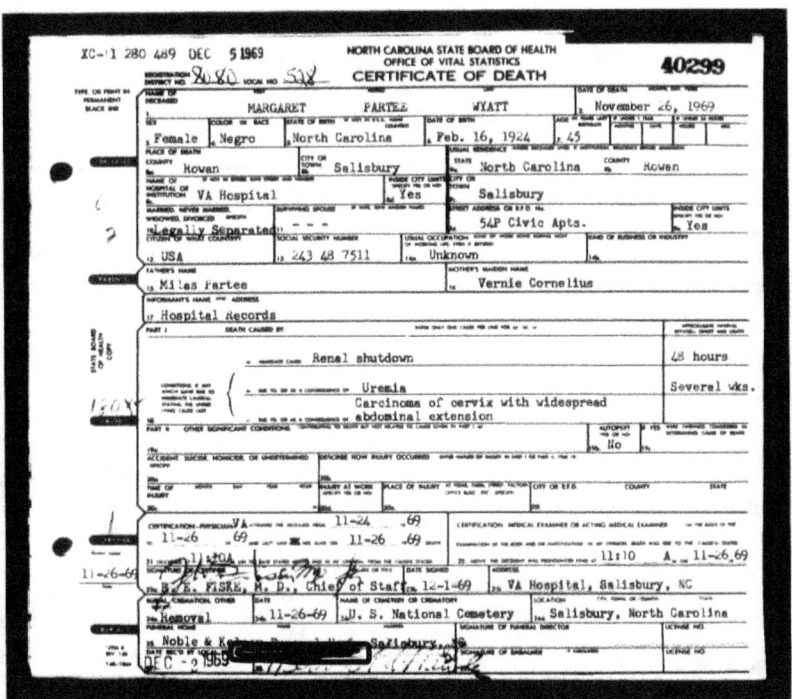

Margaret Ruth Partee Wyatt

My Family Tree

Eugene N. Workman

Jay Hugh White

My Family Tree

Isie Elliott Roberson

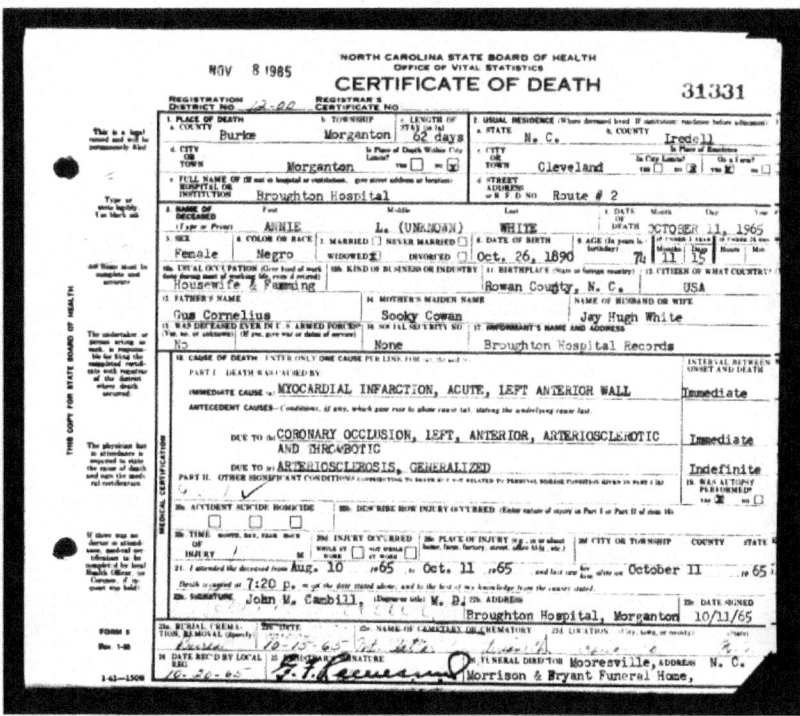

Annie Lee Cornelius White

My Family Tree

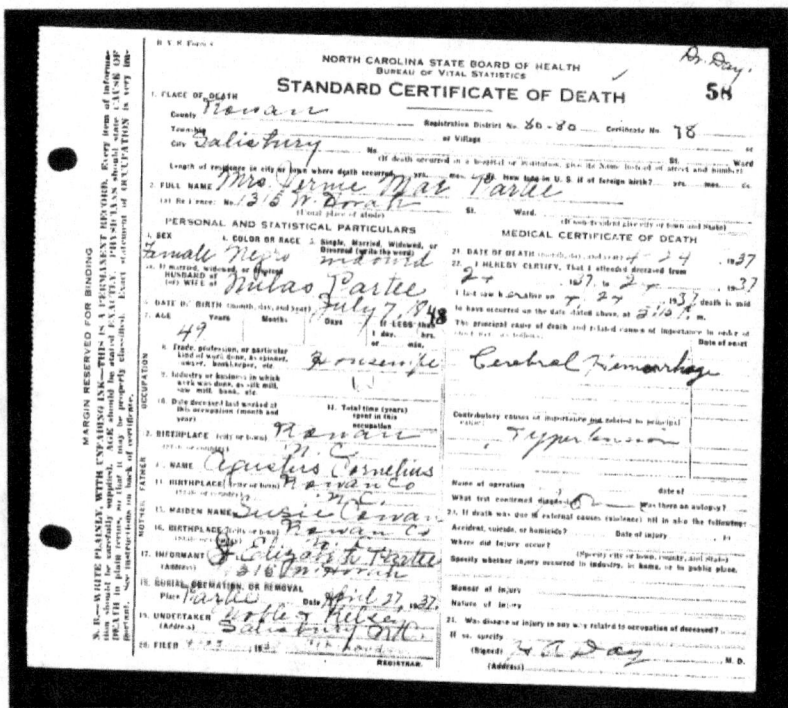

Vernie Mae Cornelius Partee

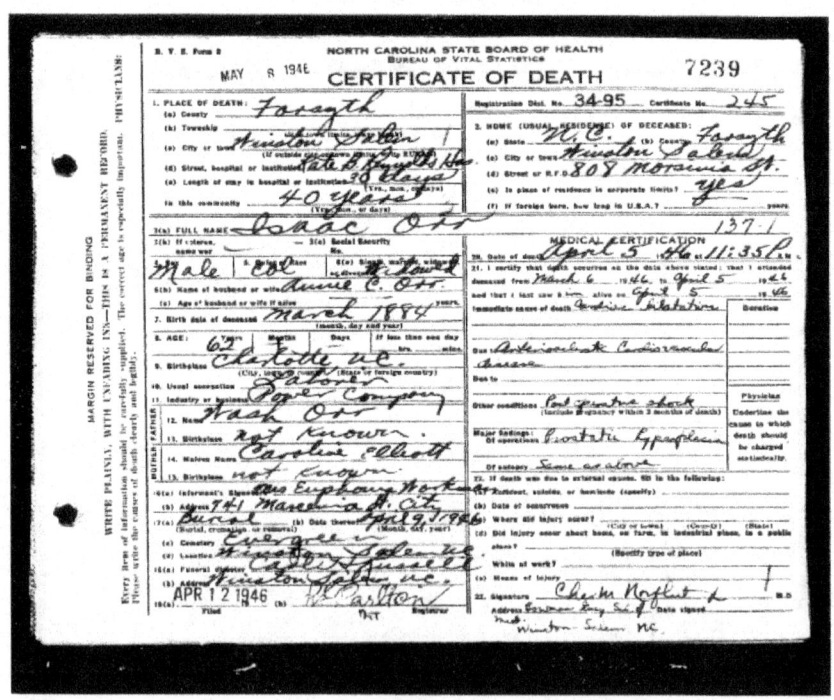

Isaac Orr

My Family Tree

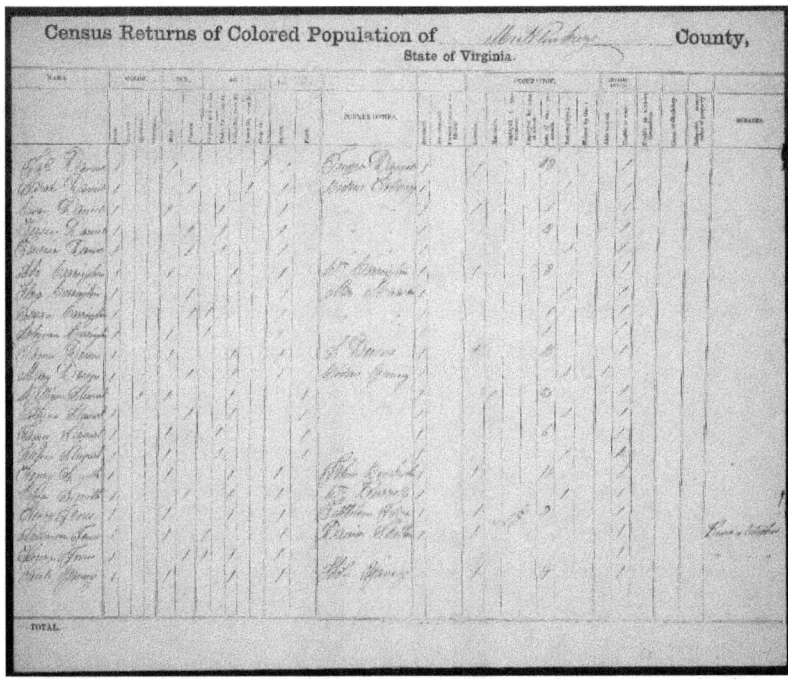

Susan Beverly Carrington, Abraham Carrington, Flora Carrington, and Abe Carrington's names were listed on Virginia Freedmen's Bureau Field Office Records, 1865-1872 Census Returns of Colored Population of Mecklenburg County, State of Virginia noted that Susan and Abraham identified their former slave masters: William Carrington (slave – Flora, Abe and Abraham,) and Mr. Mason (slave – Susan Beverly).

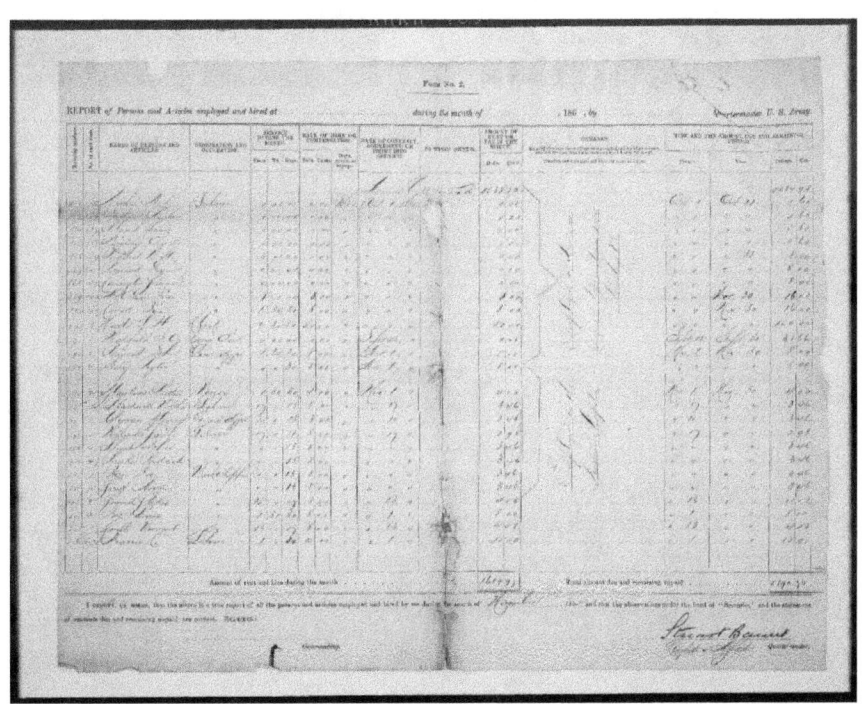

Samuel C. Carrington [I] as a Quartermaster in the United States Army Wednesday, August 9, 1865

My Family Tree

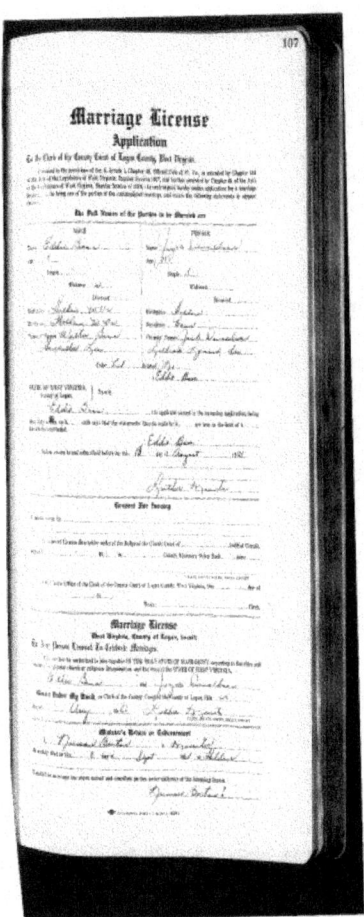 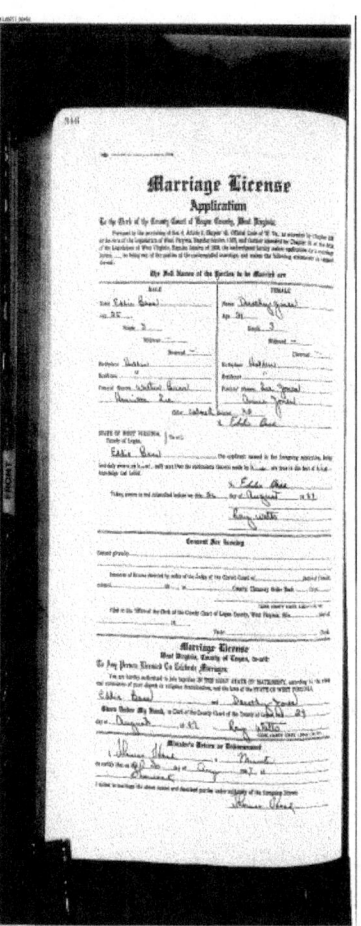

Eddie Bass I, Joyce Lavern Donaldson Bass, and Dorothy Jones Harris Bass marriage license

My Family Tree

Postscript

As I moved through the changes in my life – emotional and spiritual, a new focus developed from within. The importance of purpose began to take hold, not the least of which was my education. Obstacles, derision, and delays would no longer be tolerated. The task at hand was a goal to be achieved. Those who know me understand the depth of my obsession that motivates me to keep my word. Thus, has been the inspiration and driven force behind MY FAMILY TREE! In my spared time for over 20 years, I did a lot of research on how to establish and document my family bloodlines.

From the moment in 2000 when my mind latched on to the idea of recording my family line, I began looking for ways by which to retrieve information. I wanted a centralized document that could be easily accessed by members of the family – families. The project could not be accomplished unless comprehensive records from both sides of the family (mother and father) were available. I recognized early that social trend sources were not the answer. From where did they retrieve their information? If these commercial entities could gather information and make people believe that they were intense in their efforts, there was no reason I could not put forth the effort on behalf of those near and dear to my heart and mind.

With each step along the journey, new vistas opened themselves to me. The reporting of births, deaths, marriages, and off-spring was not enough. In order for this tome to have meaning to have depth, to have a means by which to touch the hearts and minds of future generations, there had to be something different. There had to be more than just statistics and records. The thoughts of family members, their memories of events, situations, conditions, words of advice and personal messages of love had to be part of the record. The effort of past generations reaching out to future generations would be a touchstone, a connection and a bond that would endure through the ages. These additions would create a link not possible in general history books.

Dad's family was generally centralized and rooted, with blended families in North Carolina, and I am ever grateful to *Cousin Frances* for her generous assistance. There was a reticence in tracing my mother's family, not in small part due to blended families or the fact that records had to be traced from a three-state area – North Carolina, Virginia, and West Virginia.

The support, encouragement and prodding from my parents, sister, grandparents and god-parents has been invaluable. The constant foundation of knowledge and spiritual strength provided by *Bishop Simpson* touches my heart in a manner that no words could ever competently express. As well there is a well-spring of appreciation for the on-going tutelage, mentorship, and friendship of *Mrs. Tess Haney and Mr. William C. Roberson,* who has walked with me in this effort.

Without the guidance of God, who gave us the name **"I AM,"** none of this would have ever been possible. So, it is to each of you who have been part of this journey that I render a heartfelt "Thank you!"

⌘

My Family Tree

DNA Results

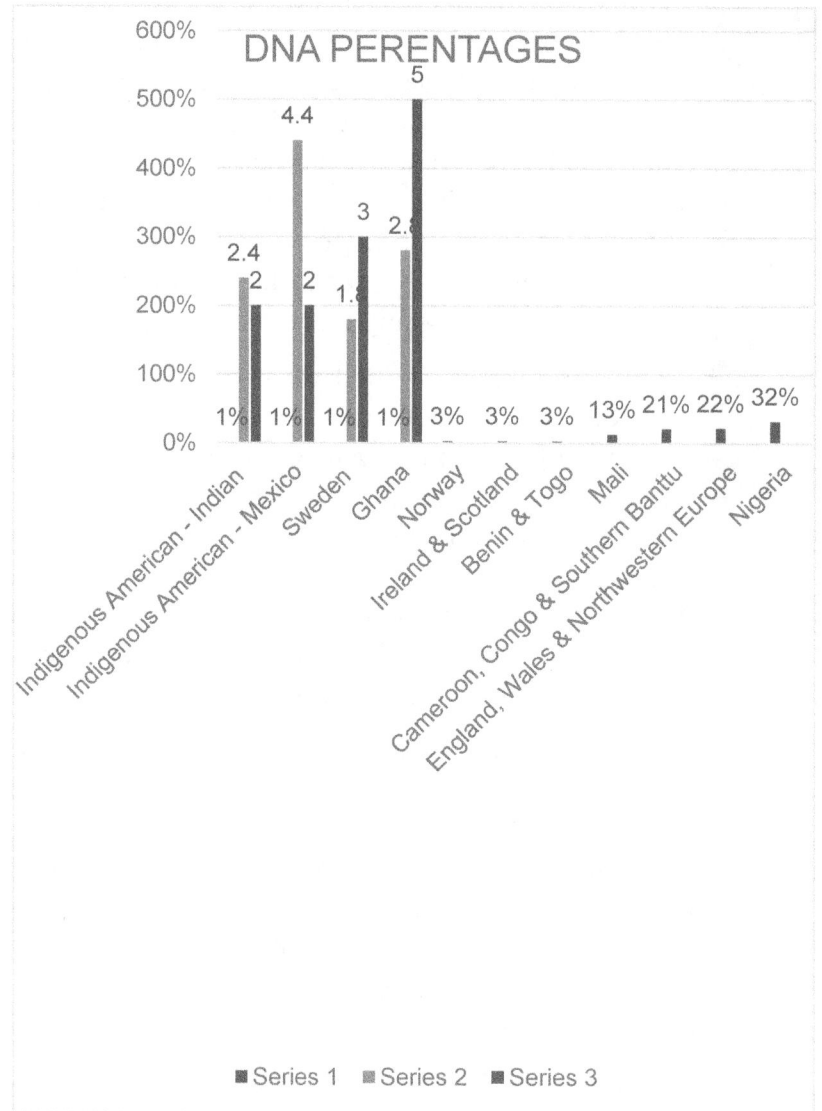

We have Native American ancestors on both sides of the family through my dad's mother's side, and my mother's mother's side, but Native American DNA only shows 1% in my DNA testing. Studies have shown that anyone who has Native-Americans in their family, no matter how far it goes back. DNA is passed down to the next generation in chunks, each parent passes half of their DNA to their child. But if something happened to the chromosomes, it could skip generations, there would be a good chance that you will not get DNA from your grandparents, great, great-great, and so on, it could be lost.

⌘

My Family Tree

Carey and Mason Bloodline – Index

Abraham...21, 214, 224, 264, 313, 316, 319, 360, 455, 456, 528, 588, 620
Ada R. Bradshaw...411, 436, 443, 448, 453, 517, 519, 520, 533
Addie...48, 58, 168, 224, 255, 380, 535, 537, 558, 560, 595
Addie Vaughters 224
Agnes 302, 345, 457
Albert Alexander 378
Alberta Mae 164
Alberta Mae Brown................................ 164
Alberta R 62, 136, 137
Alex..38, 111, 119, 129, 153, 247, 271, 343, 456
Alexander..24, 37, 38, 103, 107, 114, 120, 147, 158, 247, 252, 253, 254, 270, 271, 332, 335, 380, 385, 388, 395, 399, 426, 455, 456, 458, 496, 497, 507, 516, 546, 561, 564
Alfonzo 127
Alfred K 155
Alice..38, 61, 76, 107, 118, 172, 189, 210, 227, 232, 234, 236, 246, 247, 254, 282, 330, 422, 455, 456, 457, 458, 542, 559, 561
Alice Foster 246, 247, 282
Alice Gaither ... 172, 227, 232, 234, 236, 456
Alice M 107, 118, 330, 422, 455, 458
Alice Mack 118
Alice Patricia................................... 76, 457
Alice Roberson 61, 457
Alice Wallace 38, 254, 458
Allen..24, 87, 125, 133, 189, 196, 211, 213, 214, 310, 330, 355, 380, 397, 402, 422, 430, 455, 456, 457, 458, 463, 491, 495, 498, 504, 516, 528, 545, 552, 560, 564
Allie.. 255, 327, 456
Almeta Robinson 129, 458
Alphonso 543, 550
Alva Jean....................................... 104, 507
Alva Jean Davis 104, 507
Amanda 28, 37, 198, 455
Amanda Elizabeth.................................... 28
Amber Rose 81, 461, 494, 504

Ameerah...........385, 410, 411, 483, 522, 540
Amelia... 317, 456
Ana 22, 354, 385, 456, 537
Ana Barber 22, 354, 385, 456, 537
Anderson..21, 43, 105, 303, 309, 310, 332, 337, 381, 399, 400, 455, 457, 458, 492, 496, 561
Angela..144, 204, 206, 207, 208, 483, 484, 485, 543, 550, 579
Angela Evelyn................. 207, 208, 483, 485
Angeline... 189
Ann..21, 30, 57, 77, 179, 380, 386, 407, 408, 476, 478, 485, 487, 500, 548, 554, 567
Anna 65, 314, 315, 317, 455, 650
Anna Whitfield................................ 65, 455
Anne Lou 324, 372, 518
Annette................................ 77, 529, 535
Annie..22, 30, 38, 43, 55, 57, 114, 116, 135, 159, 160, 206, 207, 217, 232, 236, 255, 256, 257, 258, 271, 272, 281, 303, 304, 323, 324, 326, 333, 355, 370, 371, 372, 373, 374, 375, 376, 377, 385, 439, 441, 454, 456, 457, 458, 518, 521, 547, 548, 561, 567, 602, 618
Annie Cornelius...22, 30, 43, 55, 57, 521, 602
Annie Cornelius Hege..22, 30, 43, 55, 57, 521, 602
Annie E 114, 116, 567
Annie Ellis 567
Annie Geneva......................... 159, 160, 303
Annie Geneva Mason.............. 159, 160, 303
Annie Lee Cornelius...22, 323, 326, 333, 355, 370, 385, 518, 547, 548, 618
Annie Lucille 232, 236
Annie Mae...................... 303, 304, 441, 454
Annie Mae Miller.......................... 303, 304
Annie Ruth 281
Annie Ruth Neely 281
Anthony...8, 24, 68, 75, 76, 81, 82, 86, 87, 88, 89, 90, 96, 108, 132, 225, 406, 455, 457, 461, 468, 472, 478, 479, 491, 494, 495, 498, 499, 501, 504, 506, 520, 526,

529, 534, 535, 536, 543, 559, 563, 565, 566, 580
Anthony Jefferson 82, 461, 494, 504, 563
Anthony Troy 88, 89, 494, 563
Arabelle 41, 457
Arthur 109, 333, 423
Asberry 189
Ashley Sherrin 90, 494, 504
Askew, Alexandra 543, 550
Audradella 356, 396
Audrey F. Holloway..81, 88, 461, 494, 522, 529, 535
Aurelia Pearson 118
Austin Shane 89, 494, 504
Barbara...89, 140, 155, 165, 172, 400, 481, 502, 554
Barbara B 165, 172, 481
Barbara B. Brown 165, 172
Barbara Elenola 400
Barbara Jean Carson 155
Bashie 230, 457, 513
Beana Mae 149, 150
Beathric C 188
Beatrice 114, 116, 262, 263, 316, 360, 457
Beatrice Hairston 262, 263, 457
Bell 42, 51, 65
Benjamin....21, 27, 28, 32, 49, 50, 119, 202, 204, 205, 207, 209, 211, 239, 316, 457, 483, 497, 543
Benjamin Franklin 119
Bernice 68, 69, 262, 373, 457
Bernis 229, 296, 457
Bertha...345, 357, 358, 362, 374, 508, 559, 560
Bertha Martin 357, 358, 362, 559
Bessie...114, 115, 116, 121, 122, 129, 133, 227, 234, 235, 288, 289, 300, 333, 388, 417, 425, 456, 457, 527
Bessie C 227, 234, 235, 288, 289
Bessie C. Mason 227, 234, 235, 288
Bessie Hooper 300, 457
Bessie Lee Stockton 417, 527
Bessie Mae 114, 121, 122, 133
Bessie Mae Mason 114, 121, 122, 133
Bessie Mason 115, 129
Bessie Partee 333, 425

Bettie..54, 118, 161, 162, 197, 200, 313, 316, 348, 349, 364, 365, 457, 542, 544
Bettie Click 118, 457
Bettie Hairston 54, 161, 162, 197
Bettie Holmes 542
Bettie Louise 313, 348, 349, 364, 544
Bettie Louise Jones Carey 348, 349, 364
Betty...98, 99, 165, 167, 172, 204, 206, 207, 483, 484, 559, 567
Betty B 165, 172
Betty B. Brown 165, 172
Betty J. Burrs 98
Betty Jane 204, 206, 207, 483
Betty Jane Gilbert 204, 206, 207, 483
Beulah Irene 177, 280
Beulah Watt Shoaf 293, 457
Beverly 309, 310, 534, 545, 588, 620
Bill 43, 355, 371, 380, 450, 473, 537, 541
Blanche Lucille 146, 457
Blanche Lucille Vaughters 146, 457
Blanche Y...102, 103, 106, 496, 497, 507, 546, 558, 561, 578
Blanche Y. Peppers 102, 497, 507
Bobby....65, 68, 77, 93, 478, 494, 500, 501, 502, 504, 523, 524, 525, 529, 531, 532, 533, 534, 559, 577, 580
Brenda Ann 236
Brian 543
Bronwyn Golden 207, 484, 485
Brownie Mae 48, 69, 537
Brownie Younger44, 49, 50, 202, 207, 212, 543, 586
Bryan Walter 355
Bud 22, 53, 217, 263, 382, 455, 533, 535
Burrell T 179, 180, 199, 228, 457
Bush 199, 457
Buxton F 182, 215, 216
Calvin 76, 218, 456, 493, 562
Carey, Albert Martin 358
Carlton James 445, 446, 519
Carolina Austin 133
Caroline...21, 27, 28, 29, 35, 120, 217, 250, 252, 254, 315, 316, 362, 456, 457, 458
Caroline Elliott...21, 27, 28, 29, 217, 250, 252, 254

Carolyn...67, 96, 108, 373, 374, 395, 396, 508, 518, 548, 557, 567
Carolyn Collen...................................... 96, 108
Carolyn Mack Lipscombs....373, 508, 518, 548, 567
Carrie....22, 56, 57, 163, 210, 287, 379, 380, 457, 516, 538
Carrie Francis Bassett.............................. 210
Carrie Green................... 22, 56, 57, 287, 457
Carrie Hairston... 163
Carrie Mozella 379, 516, 538
Carrie Mozella Clement 379, 516, 538
Cary....227, 320, 341, 352, 354, 356, 357, 456
Cassandra 107, 110
Castle...................... 354, 465, 470, 480, 537
Catherine....114, 126, 127, 128, 150, 225, 227, 242, 243, 266, 383, 456, 493, 562
Catherine Bailey...................... 126, 242, 243
Catherine Mason 114, 127, 128, 266
Cavicka S 110
Celesta................................ 147, 275, 458
Celestia.. 187
Celia 228, 264, 456, 457
Celia Atkinson................................. 264, 456
Charles....21, 22, 34, 35, 70, 154, 221, 292, 293, 311, 312, 313, 316, 319, 325, 326, 327, 329, 331, 333, 341, 348, 350, 352, 353, 362, 365, 377, 379, 380, 385, 388, 395, 398, 411, 418, 425, 454, 455, 456, 457, 497, 516, 527, 538, 539, 547, 548, 587
Charles Alexander....22, 313, 341, 348, 352, 353, 362, 385, 388, 395
Charles E....327, 379, 380, 454, 456, 516, 538, 548
Charles J... 292
Charley........................ 33, 34, 222, 250, 458
Charlie....34, 63, 95, 114, 126, 127, 147, 242, 243, 277, 557
Charlie Lee 63, 95
Charlie Robert................................. 147, 277
Charline.. 154
Charline Mason..................................... 154
Charlotte Hodge 21, 45, 458
Chester 349, 417, 436, 457, 519
Childs, Doris Alorie 353

Christine.. 356, 402, 432, 456, 458, 545, 555
Christine Tucker............................... 402, 458
Christopher.............................. 171, 241, 553
Christy... 241, 553
Clara Clementine...412, 441, 442, 443, 448, 517, 519, 520, 541
Clara Clementine Rankin...412, 441, 442, 443, 448, 517, 519, 520, 541
Clarabelle 65
Clarabelle Berry....................................... 65
Clarence....59, 60, 98, 99, 123, 141, 152, 165, 174, 175, 262, 328, 332, 333, 399, 400, 413, 424, 456
Clarence C...................................... 328, 413
Clarence D 333, 424
Claude DeWitt...................................... 378
Claudine 282
Clayborn....................... 179, 187, 228, 457
Clemistine 560
Cleveland....37, 120, 122, 166, 219, 253, 254, 308, 325, 326, 327, 328, 330, 331, 332, 354, 355, 356, 371, 372, 373, 374, 375, 384, 417, 421, 433, 434, 435, 436, 437, 438, 439, 440, 441, 442, 450, 453, 454, 455, 456, 476, 478, 516, 517, 518, 519, 520, 528, 533, 537, 538, 540, 541, 542, 567
Clifton 67
Clinton..... 122, 133, 138, 279, 495, 503, 564
Clydie Mae Mason................... 158, 159, 192
Coleen 542
Columbia DeAnn 189, 196, 564, 565
Columbia Veatrice............................ 189, 564
Columbia Veatrice Sturdevant 189, 564
Columbus Sylvester 266
Colwell.... 179, 182, 185, 227, 238, 457, 515
Congera 431, 455
Connie...............113, 390, 406, 456, 458, 555
Connie Hairston 113, 456
Conroy Bernard..................................... 208
Cora....34, 63, 181, 182, 185, 215, 250, 290, 357, 363, 364, 446, 447, 457, 537, 595
Cora Patterson............................... 185, 457
Cora Pauline........................ 446, 447, 537
Cora Pauline Glaspy 446, 447, 537
Cora Perrell 181, 182, 215, 595

Cora Scales 290
Cora Young 63, 457
Cordeline 359, 458
Cornelia 238, 560
Cornelius....22, 37, 48, 64, 92, 253, 308, 309, 310, 324, 326, 331, 332, 333, 334, 370, 378, 379, 385, 396, 397, 423, 456, 494, 503, 537, 542, 590, 591
Cornelius Alexander 378, 542
Cornelius Vanderbilt 37, 253
Countess L. 210
Courtney Bernard 207, 484
Cozette 438, 544
Cozette Graham 438, 544
Creolla Ann 151, 152, 457
Creolla Ann Mason 151, 152, 457
Cuttie 282
Cynthia 171, 242, 534, 553
Daniel....49, 50, 123, 143, 191, 202, 204, 205, 207, 209, 211, 319, 339, 458, 483, 484, 531, 543, 587
Daniel W 209
David....85, 86, 178, 216, 315, 320, 333, 366, 374, 425, 434, 435, 442, 443, 450, 519, 537, 538, 539, 541, 567, 601
David L ... 178, 434, 442, 443, 519, 537, 601
David Lee 434, 442, 443, 519, 537
DeAndre 472
DeAnnette E 565
Debbie 534, 543, 567
Debbie C 543
Debby 337, 455
Deborah 41, 282, 390, 406, 429, 464, 555
Deborah Michelle 390, 406
Deidre Marie 408, 485, 487
Deidre Marie Trent 408, 486, 487
Delia 199, 222, 458
Della M. Howard 137
Dellwyn 559
Delmar 542
Delores 533
Dene R 191
Denise 555
Derrick 171, 241, 553
Dest 262
Dewey Arnold 224

DeWitt Shuford 324, 373, 508
Diana Malone 21, 30, 39, 43
Dinah 40, 315
Dixie 100, 456
Doc 35, 349, 455
Dock 349, 364, 366, 367
Donald....104, 371, 380, 441, 450, 451, 507, 519, 520, 538, 541, 542, 548
Donald R....104, 371, 441, 450, 451, 507, 519, 520, 541
Donald Ray 441, 450, 451, 519, 520, 541
Donna 355, 358, 363, 451, 518, 528, 560
Donna Jean 358, 363, 560
Dora 132, 438, 457, 543
Dora Wallace 132, 457
Doris Alorie Childs 368
Doris Amentia Siegel 451, 456
Doris Faya Quick 111
Dorotha 44, 52
Dorothy....37, 61, 109, 127, 253, 254, 347, 348, 354, 505, 534, 537, 549, 560, 621
Dorothy Jones Harris 347, 621
Dorothy L 37, 253, 254
Dorothy Mae Grier 127
Dorothy Speas 109
Dorsey 147, 272, 458
Dorthea M 62, 137, 138, 527
Dorthea M. Mason 62, 137, 138, 527
Douglas 211, 214, 310, 404, 455
Dunbar, Aaron DeVanta 557
Dwayne 533
Dwight 330, 421
Earl 110, 114, 125, 328, 415, 517, 518
Earlene 462, 470, 478, 479, 526
Early B 163
Earnest 94, 111, 121, 204, 458
Ebony Latifah 385, 409, 483
Ed 118, 344, 457, 463, 550
Eddie....135, 195, 200, 201, 345, 346, 347, 348, 386, 407, 408, 458, 485, 486, 487, 522, 537, 540, 551, 560, 566, 621
Eddie Andrew I 485
Eddie Andrew II 485
Eddie I 195, 201, 386, 407
Eddie II 201, 407
Edgar 287

Edith Elaine 201
Edith Elaine Ables 201
Edmon 338, 456
Edna Bell 147, 157, 159, 271
Edna Bell Winford 147, 157, 159, 271
Edna Dillard 211, 213, 214
Edna Dillard Bassett 211, 213, 214
Edna Elizabeth 149, 189, 196, 564
Edna Elizabeth Ijames 189, 196, 564
Edna Elizabeth Ijames Mason. 189, 196, 564
Edvern Dallas 353, 368
Edward....55, 72, 108, 183, 191, 239, 282, 328, 339, 340, 386, 412, 413, 437, 438, 450, 455, 469, 514, 516, 517, 521, 528, 529, 533, 538, 541, 542, 544, 548, 551
Edward Alvis 108
Edward Ray 55, 72, 517, 521, 528, 529
Edwin 21, 57, 114, 117, 457
Effie....161, 175, 176, 229, 233, 296, 350, 447, 455, 457
Effie Fisher 161, 455
Effie Gilbreath 350, 457
Effie Neely 175, 176, 233
Elaine 373, 472
Elbert James 358, 363, 560
Eldora Knox 440
Electra Jean 389, 391, 556, 557
Eli Barr 328
Elias 255
Elijah 345, 457, 528
Elijah Gadson 457
Elise....305, 353, 354, 367, 385, 386, 387, 407, 408, 485, 486, 487, 522, 537, 540, 543, 550, 551
Eliza....21, 39, 44, 51, 53, 57, 96, 114, 116, 133, 284, 285, 316, 317, 318, 329, 418, 455, 457, 458
Eliza Elizabeth 329, 418
Eliza Elizabeth Cowan 329, 418
Eliza Little 21, 57, 284, 285
Eliza Morton 316, 317
Eliza Palmer 318
Eliza Wilson 39, 457
Eliza Younger 44, 51
Elizabeth....21, 22, 28, 48, 54, 57, 58, 65, 71, 94, 101, 102, 105, 106, 124, 136, 147, 157, 158, 183, 187, 188, 196, 200, 206, 224, 254, 260, 272, 279, 296, 313, 325, 326, 331, 350, 377, 383, 398, 399, 411, 418, 444, 457, 458, 496, 497, 500, 501, 507, 513, 514, 519, 533, 535, 541, 557, 558, 560
Elizabeth Gay 65, 458
Elizabeth Mason....22, 48, 54, 57, 58, 65, 94, 224, 457, 535
Elizabeth O....28, 147, 157, 158, 187, 188, 196, 200, 224, 272
Elizabeth O. Winford....147, 157, 158, 187, 188, 196, 200, 224, 272
Elizabeth Patterson 444
Elizabeth Payne 260, 279
Elizabeth Roberts 254
Elizabeth Victoria 124, 136
Elizabeth Victoria Mason 124, 136
Elizabeth Witherspoon 21, 325, 326, 331, 377, 411, 418
Ella....32, 33, 48, 59, 60, 62, 98, 140, 147, 175, 217, 218, 220, 268, 269, 274, 346, 350, 354, 456, 457, 458, 536, 537, 554
Ella Audrey 32, 33, 217, 218
Ella M....33, 48, 59, 60, 62, 98, 140, 175, 220, 346, 457, 536, 537, 554
Ella M. Mason....48, 59, 60, 62, 98, 140, 175, 536, 537
Ella Mae 33, 220
Ella Mae Orr 33, 220
Ella T 268, 269
Ella T. Chaplin 268, 269
Ella Wilson 350, 354, 456, 537
Ella Wilson Crummie 354, 537
Ellen....22, 47, 48, 54, 57, 61, 74, 92, 94, 136, 175, 182, 270, 271, 272, 273, 274, 356, 429, 430, 458, 533, 535, 536, 555, 573, 597
Ellen Clement.. 270, 271, 272, 273, 274, 458
Ellen Jefferson....22, 47, 48, 54, 57, 74, 92, 94, 136, 175, 533, 535, 536, 573, 597
Ellen Moore 356, 429, 430, 555
Ellen Thompson 182
Elmer 295, 412, 436, 513, 517, 519
Elmer Howitt 295, 513
Eloise 374, 445, 518, 547, 567
Eloise R. Garner 445

Eloise Rankin 374, 518, 547, 567
Elouise Margaret Darr Henley 277
Elsie 60, 174, 277
Elsie Hawkins 60, 174, 277
Elva 413
Elvira Anderson 21, 337, 338
Emerline....99, 111, 129, 180, 199, 200, 456, 593
Emerline Butler 99, 456
Emerline Hairston 180, 199
Emerline Lord 111, 129, 456
Emerline Wachovia 180, 199, 200, 593
Emerline Wachovia Mason....180, 199, 200, 593
Emery J 333, 423
Emily 21, 33, 45, 206, 455
Emily Robinson 33, 455
Emma....33, 50, 114, 116, 129, 147, 180, 205, 206, 218, 219, 275, 285, 286, 304, 327, 377, 378, 380, 433, 456, 457, 458, 516, 538, 547
Emma Ferron 380, 456, 516
Emma H. Griffith 327, 377, 433
Emma Jean 205, 206
Emma Jean Stokes 205, 206
Emma L 380, 538, 547
Emma L. Lyons 380, 538, 547
Emma Orr 33, 218, 219
Emmett Jake 430
Ennis 54, 161, 162, 197
Ephraim Coleman 203
Equila Francena 96, 107, 110
Equila Francena Hege 96, 107, 110
Eric....50, 77, 85, 140, 191, 389, 392, 396, 463, 520, 522, 529, 535, 539, 554, 556, 557
Eric Creighton 85, 520
Eric James 389, 556, 557
Eric Todd 392, 557
Ernest...114, 120, 121, 145, 201, 259, 284, 401, 402, 415, 455, 458, 517, 560, 596
Ernest I 114, 120, 121, 145, 259, 596
Ernest Lee 284, 458
Ernestine Lavawn 449
Espy Lee 328, 414
Essex 56, 287, 294, 369
Essie Mae 374, 567

Essie Mae Ellis 374, 567
Essre Myricle 154, 456
Estell 247
Estella....76, 186, 187, 328, 358, 415, 416, 457, 493, 559, 562
Estella Ina 328, 415, 416
Estella Ina Rankin 328, 415, 416
Estella Lewis 76, 493, 562
Estella Novella 186, 187
Estella Novella Mason 186, 187
Estella Young 358, 457, 559
Esther....29, 114, 120, 244, 245, 256, 267, 282, 294, 332, 401, 457, 541, 549, 562
Esther Chaplin 244, 245, 267, 282, 562
Esther Lee 29, 256
Esther Mason 114, 120
Esther Naomi 332, 401, 541
Ethel Baker Burney 382
Ethel Leona 281
Ethel Mae....412, 440, 441, 453, 454, 517, 519, 533
Ethel Mae Rankin....412, 440, 441, 453, 454, 517, 519, 533
Ethel Perry 346, 455
Ethel Perry Martin 346, 455
Etta 48, 59, 61, 337, 343, 457, 535, 536, 537
Etta Bass 337, 343, 457
Eugene.... 22, 27, 29, 38, 39, 43, 53, 55, 56, 57, 68, 69, 71, 74, 75, 76, 78, 129, 159, 279, 385, 450, 457, 462, 467, 468, 469, 472, 478, 479, 480, 501, 504, 517, 518, 520, 521, 522, 528, 529, 531, 534, 536, 539, 541, 542, 559, 563, 565, 570, 580, 617
Eugene J 159
Eugene N,.... 22, 27, 29, 38, 39, 43, 53, 55, 56, 57, 68, 69, 71, 74, 75, 78, 279, 385, 462, 469, 478, 479, 517, 518, 520, 521, 522, 528, 529, 534, 536, 542, 559, 570, 617
Eugene Napoleon....22, 27, 29, 38, 39, 43, 53, 55, 56, 57, 68, 69, 74, 75, 78, 385, 462, 469, 478, 520, 521, 522, 529, 534, 536, 559
Eugenia B 326, 333, 456
Eugina 542
Eula Van Easton 247, 456
Eulia 292
Eunice 33, 221, 222

Eunice Orr 33, 221, 222
Euphonia Bernice....22, 30, 55, 56, 57, 68, 69, 74, 82, 287, 501, 517, 520, 523, 528, 542, 573, 582
Euphonia Bernice Orr....22, 30, 55, 56, 57, 68, 69, 74, 82, 287, 501, 517, 520, 523, 528, 542, 573, 582
Euphonia C....68, 77, 78, 84, 478, 519, 520, 529, 534, 536, 539, 559
Euphonia C. Mason....68, 77, 78, 84, 478, 519, 520, 529, 534, 539, 559
Euphonia Tracy 8, 84, 86, 520, 527, 539
Eureka Jean 389, 393, 394, 395, 556, 557
Eureka Jean Morrison...389, 393, 394, 395, 556, 557
Eva 64, 92, 163, 210, 347, 457, 558, 567
Eva Brown 163
Eva Day 347, 457
Eva Parker 64, 92
Eva Rankin 567
Eveline 153
Evelyn....73, 140, 458, 518, 521, 529, 535, 554
Evelyn T 73, 458, 518, 521, 529, 535
Everett....182, 183, 238, 415, 455, 470, 514, 517
Everett H 183, 238, 514
Fallie 147, 272
Fallie Winford 147, 272
Fannie....41, 113, 149, 180, 181, 182, 183, 232, 237, 238, 247, 287, 302, 412, 456, 457, 458, 514, 533, 559, 561
Fannie Elizabeth...... 232, 237, 238, 559, 561
Fannie Elizabeth Goolsby....232, 237, 238, 561
Fannie Hargraves 180, 181
Fannie Harris 247
Fannie L. Parks 412
Fannie M 182, 183, 238, 514, 533
Fannie M. Bryant 182, 183, 238, 514, 533
Fannie P 149, 457
Faye 533, 542
Febby 303, 458
Felix 517, 544
Ferrell 354, 537
Fisher S 184, 246, 247, 282
Fleming 209, 318, 457
Fletcher 415, 455, 517
Flora 21, 262, 313, 314, 456, 479, 620
Flora Hairston 262
Florence... 138, 200, 322, 332, 344, 456, 457
Florence Abney 138
Florence Ferguson 344, 457
Florence Gray 332, 456
Flossie 204
Floyd Cordest 337, 345, 346, 585
Forest....157, 169, 245, 254, 310, 322, 345, 347, 348, 429, 458, 490, 553, 557, 560
Frances.... 63, 96, 97, 100, 101, 102, 216, 272, 465, 490, 492, 493, 496, 500, 507, 523, 546, 557, 558, 561, 562, 622
Frances Martin 216
Frances Rebecca....63, 96, 97, 100, 490, 492, 496, 557, 558, 561
Frances Rebecca Hege....63, 96, 97, 100, 490, 492, 496, 557, 558, 561
Frances V 102, 496, 507, 546, 558, 561
Francis..31, 32, 411, 412, 441, 448, 541, 578
Francis James 31, 32
Francis Lee 441, 448, 541
Frank....123, 144, 166, 168, 169, 180, 183, 194, 209, 211, 214, 239, 247, 285, 321, 322, 333, 356, 412, 426, 429, 437, 438, 455, 457, 458, 514, 517, 533, 541, 544, 547, 554, 555, 558
Frankie 245, 246, 481, 528, 557, 562
Frankie Lee 528
Frankie Marie 245
Frankie Marie Hargraves 245
Franklin....21, 41, 46, 47, 55, 57, 59, 62, 65, 66, 69, 98, 99, 100, 137, 138, 139, 140, 149, 174, 209, 210, 243, 284, 285, 358, 363, 396, 450, 455, 458, 521, 527
Fred 284, 391, 543, 556, 557
Freddie 435, 538
Frederick 15, 184, 268, 307, 456, 550
Frederick Talmage 268
G. G 179, 452, 457, 515, 519, 520, 541
Gail 191, 542
Galva L 257, 458
Garfield Alexander 441, 453
Garland 431

Gary....75, 79, 304, 305, 386, 388, 462, 469, 471, 473, 478, 480, 481, 510, 522, 525, 528, 545, 570, 571, 649
Gaston....35, 97, 99, 125, 254, 284, 292, 370, 545
Gayberns Lamard 109
Gayle 140, 554
Gayle Mason 140, 554
Gelia Jean 393, 557
Gene Edward 386, 486, 537, 540, 551
Geneva 413
Genie Elizabeth 332, 398, 399, 540
Gennellia 158, 194
Gennellia Mason 158, 194
Genola 330, 419, 456
George....21, 22, 33, 39, 50, 53, 59, 65, 68, 94, 120, 154, 166, 174, 176, 177, 186, 187, 188, 208, 209, 211, 213, 223, 224, 234, 235, 236, 277, 281, 282, 283, 284, 294, 306, 313, 320, 321, 322, 333, 341, 351, 352, 353, 367, 370, 382, 390, 392, 393, 394, 395, 404, 455, 456, 457, 458, 488, 498, 502, 513, 524, 532, 575
George A ... 33, 223, 236, 313, 351, 456, 457
George Adam 236, 456
George Cornelius 284, 458
George Edward 353, 367
George Fountain 59
George Henry 166, 281
George I 208, 209, 457
George R.,....21, 176, 186, 187, 320, 321, 333, 370
George Rufus 186, 187
George Thomas 294, 513
George W,....21, 177, 188, 209, 211, 213, 224, 234, 235, 277, 282, 306, 321, 322, 382, 455, 456, 458, 498, 502, 524, 532
George Washington....177, 188, 209, 211, 213, 224, 234, 235, 277, 306, 455, 502, 524, 532
Geraldine 171, 239, 553
Geraldine Tatum 171, 239, 553
Gertrude 40, 41, 297, 414
Gertrude Carter 40
Gertrude Cowan 414
Gertrude Crump 297

Gilbert 24, 205, 206, 207, 380, 456, 516
Giovanni Alexavier 392, 557
Gladys 183, 239, 353, 369, 533, 581
Gladys Beatrice Haith 183, 239, 533
Glaspy, Ada G. 441
Glenn....24, 44, 47, 63, 108, 277, 282, 310, 456, 457, 486, 487, 560
Glenna 282
Gloria....372, 389, 390, 394, 458, 468, 481, 518, 556
Gordon 24, 206, 296, 457, 513
Grace....22, 55, 69, 70, 82, 104, 212, 269, 270, 323, 324, 370, 375, 376, 377, 391, 456, 458, 498, 499, 501, 504, 505, 517, 518, 521, 527, 528, 529, 531, 542, 548, 549, 550, 557, 573, 649
Grace Colwell Thornton...212, 504, 505, 548
Grace E 22, 323, 370, 375, 376, 458
Grace Louise....55, 69, 70, 82, 517, 521, 527, 528, 529, 542, 573
Grace Louise Workman....55, 69, 70, 82, 517, 527, 528, 529, 542, 573
Grace Virginia 269, 270, 456
Grace Virginia Hargraves 269, 270, 456
Grace Vivian 324, 376, 377, 518
Gregory....89, 429, 450, 502, 522, 529, 535, 541, 555, 559
Griffin 127, 377, 455
Grover....203, 284, 383, 435, 456, 528, 538, 543
Grover Cleveland 203
Gwendolyn 140, 167, 554, 559
H. W 257, 458
Hal 533
Hallie Bell Owens 353, 456
Hallie Jane 436, 456, 519
Hallie Jane Rankin 436, 456, 519
Hallie Rankin 438
Hamazah 411, 483, 540, 577
Hanna 162, 558
Hannah Elizabeth 166, 558
Hannah Elizabeth Brown 166, 558
Harold 109, 135, 402, 458, 545
Harriett 336
Harry 50, 348, 457, 560
Harry Edward 348, 560

My Family Tree

Harvey Boyd 173
Harvey Lee 546
Hattie Ivory 66, 458
Haywood 46, 457
Hazel....8, 22, 55, 67, 68, 69, 74, 78, 84, 85, 86, 87, 305, 344, 375, 457, 458, 461, 462, 465, 478, 500, 501, 517, 518, 519, 520, 521, 522, 527, 528, 529, 534, 536, 542, 559, 565, 570, 573, 580
Hazel Dell McElmore 375, 458, 518
Hazel Lorraine....22, 55, 67, 68, 69, 74, 78, 84, 87, 461, 501, 517, 519, 520, 521, 522, 527, 528, 529, 534, 542, 559, 565, 573
Hazel Lorraine Workman....22, 55, 67, 68, 69, 74, 78, 84, 87, 461, 501, 517, 519, 520, 521, 522, 527, 528, 529, 534, 542, 559, 565, 573
Heaven 393, 521, 557, 566
Helen....22, 49, 124, 135, 202, 259, 272, 337, 340, 341, 342, 348, 352, 353, 362, 367, 385, 388, 395, 457, 481, 539, 547, 567, 575, 589
Helen Bass....22, 337, 340, 341, 342, 348, 352, 362, 367, 385, 388, 395, 539, 547, 575, 589
Helen Faith....................................... 124, 135
Helen M 259, 272, 457
Helen Trent... 567
Helen W 49, 202
Henderson . 22, 28, 44, 45, 49, 200, 202, 458
Henrietta....22, 43, 44, 45, 46, 47, 48, 49, 53, 62, 202, 206, 344, 345, 346
Henrietta Lee 344, 346
Henry....22, 50, 56, 57, 60, 76, 108, 131, 174, 175, 176, 181, 203, 206, 208, 210, 211, 212, 213, 214, 215, 217, 232, 263, 271, 277, 287, 301, 316, 321, 324, 327, 330, 345, 358, 363, 381, 382, 398, 399, 417, 420, 455, 456, 457, 484, 486, 493, 520, 522, 527, 560, 562, 649
Henry Alvis 108
Henry Caldwell 327, 381, 382
Henry F 358, 363, 486, 520, 522, 560
Henry Luther 417, 527
Henry M 176, 181, 457
Henry P 232, 457

Herbert 121, 146, 432, 457, 597
Herbert Gilmer 121, 146, 597
Herman 242, 449, 458, 540, 553
Hester 235, 263, 273, 288, 457
Hester Doulin 263, 457
Hilda 412, 439, 541
Hilda Rankin 412, 439, 541
Hollan Reid 417
Holloway 24, 250
Hope Marie 560
Horace....77, 78, 84, 85, 210, 233, 456, 520, 522, 525, 529, 532, 535, 539
Horace Reginale 85, 520
Horace William 210
Houston 68, 316, 457
Howard....24, 283, 310, 330, 337, 338, 339, 412, 439, 457, 491, 517, 519, 520, 533, 558
Howard V 412, 439, 517, 519, 520, 533
Icy 44, 50, 51, 457
Icy A 44, 50, 51
Icy A. Snow 44, 50, 51
Ida....55, 167, 197, 198, 236, 316, 332, 355, 361, 366, 398, 456, 528, 558, 599
Ida Doreatha 167, 236
Ida Doreatha Brown 167, 236
Ida Mae 332, 398, 528
Ida Mae Partee 332, 398
Ida Mary 55, 197, 198
Ida Mary Mason 55, 197, 198
Ida N 316, 361, 456
Ida Octavia Hawkins 366
Ilar 127, 457
Inez 377, 555
Infant....34, 114, 121, 123, 126, 127, 145, 164, 251
Ione 34, 252, 458
Irdee 381
Iredle 359, 458
Irene 359, 389, 547, 555, 556
Irene Morrison 359, 389, 555, 556
Iris A....23, 75, 76, 79, 80, 305, 469, 473, 478, 494, 518, 522, 525, 529, 535, 559, 563, 572
Iris A. Mason....75, 76, 305, 494, 518, 522, 525, 529, 535, 559
Irma 565

My Family Tree

Isaac....22, 28, 30, 43, 55, 57, 113, 323, 341, 352, 375, 456, 458, 518, 521, 619
Isaac E 323, 375, 458, 518
Isabel 49, 455
Isabela 21, 27, 28, 29, 256, 456
Isabella 30, 411, 456, 457
Isabelle....22, 47, 48, 53, 197, 341, 358, 359, 388, 390, 406, 473, 475, 476, 482, 535, 539, 546, 547, 555, 556
Isabelle Carey....341, 358, 359, 388, 390, 406, 473, 539, 546, 555, 556
Isabelle Dubose 22, 47, 48, 53, 197, 535
Iseral H 229
Isiah 129, 458
Isie 21, 43, 44, 618
Isie Elliott 21, 43, 44, 618
Ivory 24, 234, 235, 288, 484, 543
Ivory Shack 234, 235, 288
Iza 312, 456
J. T 295, 458
J. T. Hairston 295
Jack 37, 49, 220, 348, 455, 456, 516, 561
Jackson....8, 24, 37, 68, 77, 78, 84, 85, 86, 97, 105, 302, 310, 345, 355, 455, 457, 478, 484, 505, 519, 520, 522, 526, 527, 528, 529, 535, 539, 549, 559
Jacob 182, 186, 296, 455, 457, 513, 516
Jacob Perrie 182
Jadon Carl 105, 496
James....12, 21, 22, 23, 24, 29, 30, 32, 33, 35, 43, 44, 46, 47, 48, 50, 51, 55, 58, 63, 73, 79, 80, 88, 95, 102, 114, 116, 123, 128, 129, 131, 132, 141, 144, 149, 158, 161, 162, 165, 169, 170, 171, 177, 185, 192, 193, 198, 200, 209, 223, 236, 239, 246, 256, 257, 269, 270, 273, 274, 278, 282, 286, 287, 304, 305, 312, 313, 315, 316, 319, 328, 337, 338, 341, 342, 348, 350, 352, 354, 358, 364, 365, 384, 385, 386, 387, 388, 389, 404, 405, 407, 411, 412, 429, 436, 439, 443, 448, 453, 456, 457, 458, 467, 468, 471, 472, 473, 479, 481, 482, 485, 489, 492, 499, 501, 503, 505, 517, 518, 519, 520, 521, 523, 528, 529, 533, 535, 537, 539, 540, 541, 542, 546, 547, 549, 553, 557, 558, 559, 560, 561, 562, 563, 565, 566, 567, 589
James A....22, 29, 35, 58, 102, 312, 313, 319, 341, 342, 348, 352, 354, 358, 364, 384, 385, 386, 387, 388, 404, 405, 407, 457, 458, 482, 485, 489, 492, 537, 539, 540, 546, 589
James Avery....22, 354, 384, 385, 386, 387, 388, 404, 405, 407, 482, 485, 489, 492, 537, 540
James B....21, 33, 123, 141, 144, 149, 161, 162, 165, 169, 170, 171, 198, 223, 236, 239, 337, 338, 553, 558
James Carr 315
James D 429, 456, 557
James Edison 304
James Edward 365
James Francis....328, 411, 412, 436, 443, 448, 453, 517, 519, 520, 533
James H....22, 44, 46, 47, 48, 50, 51, 63, 95, 185, 273, 274, 457, 567
James Henderson 22, 44, 46, 47, 48
James I 30, 50, 80, 209, 305, 456, 543
James II 80
James J 286
James K 177, 278
James L....55, 73, 269, 270, 316, 457, 518, 521, 528, 529, 535, 542
James Roosevelt 246, 562
James Thomas 269
James W 200, 282, 287, 389, 458
Jamie 560
Jamie Martin 560
Jane....21, 33, 123, 142, 143, 222, 247, 311, 321, 326, 372, 396, 457, 458, 518, 591
Jane E. Alison 21, 321, 458
Jane Frohop 247, 457
Jane White 21, 311, 372, 458
Janet 124, 135, 380, 457, 548
Janet Secreca Britton 124, 135, 457
Janie Taylor 214, 455
Jasper 185, 187, 294, 513
Jasper Mason 185, 187
Jasper Roland 294, 513
Jay Allen 441, 451, 519, 520, 541
Jay Lawrence 326, 332

Jay Roger 324, 372, 518
Jean....75, 366, 367, 385, 389, 390, 391, 392, 393, 394, 395, 473, 481, 482, 486, 506, 539, 543, 544, 550, 556, 567
Jean Freeman Barnes 366, 544
Jeff................................ 21, 37, 45, 348, 458, 560
Jefferson....13, 22, 24, 37, 43, 44, 46, 47, 48, 67, 68, 69, 221, 252, 253, 320, 375, 457, 529, 531, 534, 536, 542
Jefferson, Ellen 44
Jenean Evette 88, 494, 495, 563
Jenette 567
Jerell 435, 538
Jeri 241, 553
Jerryl Jairus 435, 538
Jesse....63, 94, 95, 100, 107, 123, 141, 149, 161, 162, 165, 169, 170, 171, 198, 229, 236, 239, 348, 355, 528, 553, 555, 557, 558, 560
Jesse Lanei 348
Jessica Darlene 171, 240
Jessica Marie 91, 498, 499, 506
Jessie....33, 63, 88, 114, 123, 124, 125, 141, 219, 220, 301, 369, 456, 457, 499, 534
Jessie B 33, 123, 141, 219, 220
Jessie B. Orr 33, 219, 220
Jessie Durham 369, 456
Jessie Mae 88, 114, 124, 125, 301, 499
Jessie Mae Collie 301
Jessie Mae Mason 114, 124, 125
Jethro Benjamin 49, 205
Jetta Malinda....341, 352, 353, 367, 539, 540, 547, 574, 575
Jetta Malinda Faulkner....341, 352, 353, 367, 539, 540, 547, 574, 575
Jettie Ann....55, 123, 141, 149, 161, 162, 169, 170, 198, 558, 586
Jettie Ann Hairston....55, 123, 141, 149, 161, 162, 169, 170, 198, 558, 586
Jettie Ann Hairston Mason....55, 123, 141, 149, 161, 162, 169, 170, 198, 558, 586
Jettie E. C 250
Jettie Elizabeth 165, 173
Jettie Elizabeth Brown 165, 173
Jim....10, 15, 21, 256, 293, 337, 358, 455, 457, 550, 559

Jimmie T 206, 207
Jimmy Ray 146
JoAnn McGuire 77
Joe....33, 34, 101, 252, 455, 458, 491, 545, 650
Joel S 558
John....22, 27, 36, 42, 50, 63, 95, 96, 97, 104, 107, 109, 110, 118, 122, 127, 130, 140, 147, 149, 155, 156, 157, 158, 159, 165, 167, 170, 171, 176, 180, 184, 188, 189, 193, 194, 209, 210, 216, 219, 226, 227, 229, 230, 232, 233, 236, 244, 245, 248, 250, 258, 267, 269, 272, 281, 282, 284, 288, 293, 294, 295, 302, 303, 304, 313, 316, 318, 319, 320, 321, 324, 325, 327, 330, 335, 341, 351, 354, 373, 374, 377, 378, 384, 385, 403, 418, 433, 441, 442, 443, 448, 455, 456, 457, 458, 472, 478, 485, 486, 487, 513, 518, 519, 520, 537, 541, 542, 547, 554, 557, 558, 561, 562, 564, 565, 567, 591, 594, 598, 599
John Alexander 189
John C. Charlie 248
John Gaither 330, 418
John H. 27, 327, 377, 378, 433, 594
John Hairston I 170
John Henry....147, 155, 156, 157, 176, 180, 188, 209, 226, 227, 232, 236, 267, 284, 288, 303, 598
John I 107, 542
John L....97, 149, 170, 316, 330, 418, 441, 442, 443, 448, 455, 457, 519, 520, 537, 541, 565
John Lester 565
John Louis 149, 170
John M.A 321, 324
John Thomas....63, 95, 96, 107, 109, 110, 140, 165, 171, 184, 193, 194, 229, 230, 244, 267, 282, 293, 294, 295, 327, 384, 513, 562, 591
John W....42, 188, 189, 258, 281, 303, 304, 318, 319, 335, 456, 458
John Wesley 188, 189
John Westly 281
Johnny 348, 378, 560
Johnsie J 114, 122, 123, 141, 165, 588

Johnsie J. Mason....114, 122, 123, 141, 165, 588
Jonathan 355, 407, 543, 545, 550
Jonathan Darrell 407
Joneice C....102, 104, 105, 496, 500, 501, 546, 558, 561
Jonnie 102, 332, 398, 404, 546
Jonnie E 332, 404
Jordan....24, 62, 91, 226, 296, 457, 483, 491, 498, 499, 513, 563, 566
Joseph....22, 120, 127, 177, 243, 278, 279, 313, 323, 337, 338, 340, 341, 346, 351, 352, 358, 359, 364, 366, 367, 370, 439, 444, 455, 456, 518, 519, 541, 542, 544, 545, 560, 584
Joseph Bailey 127, 243
Joseph C.. 358, 359, 364, 366, 544, 545, 560
Joseph David 313, 351, 456
Joseph Frank 177, 278, 279, 444, 519
Joseph Franklin 444, 519
Joseph Knox 439, 541
Joseph Lee 542
Joseph Linzie 370, 518
Josephine 381, 429, 456
Josephine Cowan 381
Joshua 21, 177, 277, 311, 458
Joshua S 177, 277
Josie Ann 284, 458
Joyce Lavern 347, 560, 621
Joyce Lavern Donaldson 347, 560, 621
Juanita Cuthrell 123, 559
Juanita L 438, 450, 517, 544
Juanita L. Graham 438, 450, 544
Judge 206, 552
Judy....67, 283, 305, 354, 387, 388, 404, 457, 488, 489, 522, 537, 540, 551, 561
Judy Carol....354, 387, 388, 404, 488, 489, 537, 540, 551
Judy Carol Cowan....354, 387, 388, 404, 488, 489, 540, 551
Judy Wilson 283, 457
Julia....43, 166, 227, 233, 234, 235, 311, 415, 418, 455, 457, 516, 558
Julia Ellen 227, 233, 234, 235
Julia Ellen Mason 227, 233, 234, 235
Julia Friday 166
Julia Higgins 415, 455, 516
Julia Lyerly 418
Julia White 43, 457
Julian 295, 458
Julius 134, 456
June L 358, 363, 560
Jura 330, 421
Justin Merrick 84, 527
Kaiyela 396
Karl Anthony 367, 544
Karma L 565
Kate 335
Kathryn L 80
Kathy 354, 537, 545, 560
Katie 175, 210, 441, 452, 519, 520, 541
Katie Geneva........... 441, 452, 519, 520, 541
Keith 144, 388, 406, 493, 533, 551
Keith Jerome 388, 406, 493, 551
Kelvin 367, 544
Kenneth....154, 165, 171, 348, 387, 489, 542, 551, 560
Kenneth Dwight 489, 551
Kenneth O 165, 171
Kenneth S 348
Kent 439, 541
Kevin 408, 487
Kim 348, 392, 560
Kouri 408, 487, 567
Lacy Belle Everlina 543
Lacy Belle Everlina Gray 543
Lacy Belle Everlina Gray Graham 543
LaKeisha Renee 225
LaKeisha Renee Thues 225
Larry 282
Lashonia 472
Laura....21, 46, 147, 181, 184, 273, 274, 293, 311, 319, 321, 455, 457, 458
Laura Florence Winfred 273
Laura J 46, 181, 457
Laura Law 184
Laura Palmer 21, 311, 319
Laura Witherspoon 293, 455
Lawrence....38, 171, 187, 204, 240, 254, 255, 481, 553
Lawrence O'Neal 187
Leah 95, 99, 457

Leah M 99
Leah M. Chubbs 99
Leander 153
LeAnn Haynes 234
LeAnn Jacob 389
LeAnn Jacobs 389
Leatha 111
Leatha Adams 111
Lee....24, 31, 32, 63, 94, 95, 100, 107, 152, 169, 195, 200, 201, 206, 207, 272, 310, 320, 345, 356, 371, 380, 385, 408, 412, 414, 429, 456, 457, 458, 462, 470, 478, 479, 481, 526, 541, 554, 557, 567
Lee Thomas 152, 169, 457, 541
Lemuel Arthur 49
Lena E 159
Lenora W 71, 542
Lenora W. Workman 71
Lenore 374
Leona 148, 168, 169, 558
Leona Brown 148, 168, 169, 558
Leonard Radney 76, 457
LeRoy 149, 205, 281, 396
LeRoy Thurmon 281
Leroy Wilson 378
Leslie 208, 380, 456, 484, 516
Leslie Antia Daniels 208
Lessee 140, 554
Lester LeRoy 116, 132, 133
Letitia 301, 302
Letitia Goolsby 301
Lettie F 165, 167, 170, 232, 236, 239, 561
Lettie F. Goolsby....165, 167, 170, 232, 236, 239, 561
Levenia Moore 174, 457
Levi Mitchell 247
Levina T 315, 456
Levonia Margaret....22, 75, 78, 353, 354, 384, 385, 404, 405, 407, 408, 428, 473, 482, 485, 489, 492, 537, 539, 547, 551, 574
Levonia Margaret Carey....22, 75, 78, 353, 354, 384, 385, 404, 405, 407, 408, 428, 473, 482, 485, 489, 492, 537, 539, 547, 551, 574
Levonz Wallace 131, 132
Lillian 33, 218, 248, 348, 456
Lillian Lynard 348, 456
Lillian Mae Dalton 248
Lillian Orr 33, 218
Lillie....22, 34, 58, 59, 127, 182, 183, 224, 225, 239, 251, 281, 312, 313, 316, 319, 327, 342, 348, 352, 360, 378, 379, 455, 456, 457, 458, 514, 542, 588
Lillie B....22, 127, 312, 316, 319, 342, 348, 352, 360, 455, 456, 588
Lillie Belle....22, 312, 319, 342, 348, 352, 588
Lillie Belle Carrington....22, 312, 319, 342, 348, 352, 588
Lillie C 379
Lillie D. 327, 378, 379, 542
Lillie D. Cowan 327, 378, 379, 542
Lillie Doulin 281
Lillie Mae....58, 59, 183, 224, 225, 239, 378, 457
Lillie Mae Haizlip 58, 224, 225
Lillie Mae Rankin 378
Lillie Mae Webster 59, 457
Lillie May Mason 514
Linda....77, 102, 167, 207, 241, 481, 484, 522, 529, 535, 543, 546, 550, 553, 559, 561
Linda D 543, 550
Linda Goolsby 167, 559
Linda Mason 77, 522, 529, 535, 559
Lino 330, 421
Lisa....207, 386, 407, 408, 435, 484, 485, 487, 489, 522, 533, 537, 538, 540, 543, 550, 567
Lissie 447
Lissie Ramsey 447
Litha Ruth....76, 81, 88, 89, 461, 478, 493, 495, 520, 522, 526, 535, 559, 562, 580
Litha Ruth Walker....76, 81, 88, 89, 461, 478, 493, 495, 520, 522, 526, 535, 562, 580
Lizzie....53, 114, 119, 158, 231, 325, 444, 457
Llie 161
Locke A. 326, 331, 590
Lois 62, 138, 280, 457, 554
Lois Mason 62, 138, 457, 554
Lois Rebecca Turner 280
Lolo 33, 222, 458

Loren 138
Loretta Jean Hill 254
Lori 191
Lori Mason 191
Lottie 218, 337, 339, 340, 456
Lottie Bass 337, 339, 340
Lottie Rush 218, 456
Lou 37, 123, 144, 380, 456
Lou Etta 123, 144
Louisa 37, 114, 199, 252, 253, 333, 428, 457, 458
Louisa Sadler 37, 252, 253
Louisa Sadler Orr 37, 252, 253
Louise 21, 41, 69, 70, 71, 77, 105, 118, 119, 258, 262, 312, 341, 352, 353, 456, 457, 581
Louise Constans 21, 312, 456
Louise Hairston 41, 258, 262, 457
Louise Harris 118, 119
Louise Johnson 105, 457
Louise Lockhart 77
Louise Mason 341, 352, 353, 456, 581
Louisiana 128, 212, 244, 263, 264, 306, 504, 542
Louisiana Hairston 128, 244, 263, 264
Loula 418
Loula Bradshaw 418
Loveless 21, 43, 46
Lovvenia 316, 361, 456
Lowell 356, 400, 432, 555
Lowell Goode 400
Lucia 21, 335, 338
Lucile 291, 301
Lucille 22, 96, 107, 110, 182, 191, 216, 217, 294, 355, 371, 402, 513, 518, 528
Lucille Boozer 96, 107, 110
Lucille Boozer Woody 96, 107, 110
Lucille Bruce-Wilson 22, 355, 371, 518, 528
Lucille Ingram 294, 513
Lucille Mason 182, 216, 217
Lucille V 191
Lucinda 147, 156, 176, 179, 199, 215, 227, 234, 235, 238, 244, 282, 286, 287, 329, 456, 458, 514, 515, 596, 598
Lucinda Jane 234, 235

Lucinda Mason 147, 156, 176, 179, 199, 215, 227, 238, 244, 282, 514, 515, 596, 598
Lucinda Williams 286, 458
Lucy 22, 157, 171, 184, 209, 210, 211, 242, 312, 341, 356, 385, 428, 456, 457, 458, 554
Lucy Hettie 209
Lucy Jane Staples 210
Lucy Michelle 171, 242, 554
Lucy Michelle Brown 171, 242
Lucy Nancy 22, 356, 385, 428, 458, 554
Lueco G 198
Lula 41, 97, 122, 158, 165, 167, 170, 188, 224, 227, 232, 233, 236, 247, 260, 279, 383, 434, 456, 457, 528, 559, 561
Lula Goolsby 167, 559
Lula Hege 41
Lula M 122, 165, 167, 170, 227, 232, 233, 236, 247, 260, 279, 456, 561
Lula M. Mason 122, 165, 167, 227, 232, 233, 236, 561
Lula Malone 247, 260, 279, 456
Lula Shields 97, 457
Lula Virginia 383, 434, 528
Luna 358, 456
Lunlu 174
Lura L 330, 420, 455
Luther 216, 542, 550
Luvie 243
Luvie Scott 243
Lydia 36
Lydick, Ameerah Salahuddin 577
M. Angeline Penry 424, 458
Mac 350, 456
Mack 24, 118, 228, 229, 287, 298, 374, 457, 508
Mack Charles 287
Maddie Mae 498
Madeline Allen 368, 456
Madison Rene 225, 491, 499
Mae Eva Cram 367, 456
Maggie 22, 35, 113, 114, 116, 122, 129, 133, 135, 145, 147, 242, 259, 263, 266, 276, 277, 281, 323, 370, 371, 384, 456, 457, 458
Maggie Doulin 263, 457

Maggie Fowler....113, 114, 116, 129, 133, 135, 145, 242, 259, 266
Maggie M. 122, 133, 456
Maggie M. Davis 122, 133, 456
Maggie McCall 22, 323, 370, 371, 458
Maggie Tate................................... 35, 458
Mahaley..560
Malik.. 392, 557
Malinda 29, 36
Malinda Orr... 29, 36
Malva J.. 358, 363, 560
Mamie 127, 187, 382, 444, 455, 456
Mamie Clarke................................. 444, 456
Mamie Minton 127
Mamie Suggs 187
Manuel....151, 152, 169, 249, 321, 340, 389, 392, 457, 542
Margaret....48, 66, 95, 113, 127, 139, 229, 258, 279, 298, 332, 333, 384, 385, 403, 404, 405, 407, 408, 420, 423, 432, 434, 442, 443, 449, 455, 456, 457, 458, 519, 537, 555, 563, 565, 616
Margaret A. McHenry............................. 384
Margaret Harris 420, 455
Margaret Lula 434, 442, 443, 519, 537
Margaret Lula Allison....434, 442, 443, 519, 537
Margaret Mason 48, 66, 139, 458, 537
Margaret S. L 449
Margaret Sturdevant....................... 279, 563
Margaret Summer 333, 423
Margie 127, 436, 519
Margie Ann 127
Margie Ann Chaplin............................... 127
Marguerite... 93, 457
Maria....83, 97, 101, 187, 387, 404, 465, 472, 486, 488, 489, 492, 496, 517, 522, 537, 540, 546, 557, 558, 561, 579
Maria Antoinette 387, 404, 488, 489
Maria Price... 187
Mariah 32, 457
Mariah Holmes.................................. 32, 457
Marian 274, 337, 343, 567
Marian Bass 337, 343
Marian Hairston 274
Marian Hairston Lewis 274
Marie....121, 146, 158, 185, 186, 191, 264, 397, 408, 436, 439, 446, 456, 457, 504, 516, 519, 533, 541
Marie Antoinette 185, 186, 516
Marie Antoinette Alston.......... 185, 186, 516
Marie Mason 121, 146, 158, 191, 457
Marie P 439, 541
Marie Waddell.. 446
Marion................. 139, 374, 547, 562
Marion White.. 374
Marjorie...293
Mark.. 396
Marshall Rankin.............................. 441, 453
Martha....22, 45, 50, 51, 108, 184, 207, 209, 213, 228, 229, 282, 283, 292, 293, 294, 295, 327, 330, 332, 337, 338, 346, 348, 352, 377, 383, 402, 433, 443, 446, 454, 455, 456, 457, 458, 484, 513, 528, 538, 541, 545, 550, 560
Martha Allen 337, 455
Martha Ann 348
Martha Bratcher 560
Martha Cunningham....22, 337, 338, 346, 352, 455
Martha Doulin 184, 282, 283
Martha Douthit.............................. 108, 455
Martha Elizabeth............. 327, 383, 433, 443
Martha Hairston 229, 292, 293
Martha Jane 50, 209, 213, 330
Martha Jane Cowan................................ 330
Martha Jane Price..................... 50, 209, 213
Martha Jean 207, 484
Martha Louise Rogers............................. 446
Martha Lucille.......... 332, 402, 454, 541, 545
Martha Lucille Partee...... 332, 402, 541, 545
Martha Y 45, 51, 294, 295, 458, 513
Martha Y. Jordan 294, 295, 513
Marva Lorraine 82, 517, 527, 543
Marva Lorraine Browning..82, 517, 527, 543
Marvin..................... 385, 408, 446, 482, 551
Marvinah Nyderah 385, 410, 483
Mary....21, 22, 31, 35, 37, 41, 47, 48, 54, 57, 59, 63, 65, 87, 90, 92, 98, 101, 112, 121, 122, 130, 134, 138, 139, 140, 145, 147, 152, 156, 157, 158, 164, 168, 169, 176, 177, 183, 184, 191, 209, 210, 220, 223,

227, 232, 233, 234, 245, 246, 247, 249, 250, 253, 259, 263, 267, 270, 271, 273, 275, 276, 277, 282, 283, 288, 289, 303, 304, 316, 319, 320, 321, 324, 326, 327, 328, 330, 331, 333, 334, 337, 340, 342, 353, 354, 360, 370, 371, 383, 386, 399, 400, 416, 417, 426, 429, 430, 435, 444, 447, 448, 455, 456, 457, 458, 491, 495, 498, 502, 518, 526, 535, 537, 538, 541, 543, 555, 558, 565, 567, 581

Mary A....59, 140, 177, 209, 220, 277, 328, 331, 416, 417, 457, 458, 518, 526, 543, 558

Mary A. Simms 140, 457
Mary Alexander 220, 458
Mary Alice 543
Mary Ann....59, 177, 277, 328, 331, 416, 417, 457, 518, 526, 558
Mary Ann Ijames............................. 177, 277
Mary Ann Lash 59, 457
Mary Ann Rankin.... 328, 416, 417, 518, 526
Mary Bell....47, 147, 158, 270, 271, 275, 276, 324, 371, 399, 455, 457, 518
Mary Belle....147, 158, 270, 271, 275, 276, 399, 455
Mary Belle Doulin....147, 158, 270, 271, 275, 276
Mary Belle Sharpe 399, 455
Mary C....21, 156, 164, 288, 289, 303, 321, 333, 353, 354, 370, 400, 456, 457, 537, 581
Mary C. Chambers 303
Mary C. Summers 21, 321, 333, 370
Mary Causer 400, 456
Mary Clodfelter............................... 164, 457
Mary Cornelia 288, 289, 457
Mary Cornelia Martin 288, 289, 457
Mary Dingess 429, 555
Mary Doulin.................................... 249, 250
Mary E....35, 37, 65, 92, 122, 134, 138, 152, 158, 168, 191, 253, 282, 319, 320, 326, 333, 334, 337, 342, 426, 455, 456, 458, 541, 567
Mary E.....35, 319, 326, 334, 337, 342, 455, 456, 458
Mary E. Whitworth 35, 458
Mary Elizabeth....37, 122, 134, 152, 158, 168, 191, 253, 282, 320, 541

Mary Elizabeth Holmes 152, 168, 541
Mary Ella 333, 426
Mary Ella Partee 333, 426
Mary Ellen 65, 92, 138
Mary Ellen Eason................................. 138
Mary Emma 567
Mary Frances Clinkscales... 87, 90, 498, 502
Mary Francis 340
Mary Francis Brown 340
Mary Glaspy................................... 447, 448
Mary Hairston . 121, 145, 259, 263, 283, 457
Mary Haynes................................. 435, 538
Mary Jane....176, 227, 232, 234, 288, 330, 456, 457
Mary Jane Brown....176, 227, 232, 234, 288, 457
Mary Jane Taylor 330, 456
Mary Jones 139
Mary Langhorne............................. 316, 360
Mary Leak 41, 456
Mary Mason....22, 48, 54, 57, 98, 183, 184, 245, 246, 247, 267, 282, 456, 535
Mary McClain...................................... 444
Mary N. 327, 383
Mary N. Cowan.............................. 327, 383
Mary P. 130, 209
Mary P. Smith..................................... 130
Mary Rose 448, 458
Mary Smith 122, 456
Mary Taylor................................... 157, 458
Mary Travis 210
Mary Wilbur.................................. 430, 456
Mary Wilma Dobson.............................. 63
Mary Winford................................ 147, 273
Matt 21, 38, 339, 456, 457
Matthew 210, 217, 565
Mattie....122, 134, 210, 224, 257, 282, 346, 353, 444, 575
Mattie Arwilda 224
Mattie Arwilda Steelman 224
Mattie Bass.. 346
Mattie Green 210
Mattie Green Price 210
Mattie Heath...................................... 257
Mattie Louise 282
Mattie Louise Neely 282

Mattie Odessa Leazer 444
Mattie Ruth 122, 134
Mattie Ruth Davis 122, 134
Maud J W 342
Maude 350, 456
Maude Martin 350, 456
Maynard 543
Mayo, Irene 149
McIver Holman 278
McKenzie 374, 508
McQueene 196, 455
Melba Elizabeth 71, 518, 521, 535
Melba Elizabeth Thompson 71, 518, 521, 535
Melba Louise Lindsay 71, 542
Melik 411
Melissa 348, 560
Mellon 380, 456
Melvin 62, 127, 140, 172, 438, 457, 543, 554
Melvina 542
Merissa Douglas 488
Merle Inay 376
Merle Inay Gamble Polk 376
Merriel 140
Michael 24, 162, 171, 239, 240, 393, 394, 395, 542, 543, 553, 556, 557, 558
Michaela 240, 553
Mildred 48, 63, 67, 73, 94, 95, 97, 100, 101, 102, 105, 106, 107, 210, 282, 291, 300, 380, 417, 432, 456, 458, 465, 466, 496, 497, 500, 507, 516, 518, 521, 523, 529, 531, 535, 536, 537, 542, 546, 549, 555, 557, 558, 560, 561, 578, 579
Mildred Ann 48, 63, 94, 95, 100, 107, 500, 537, 557
Mildred Ann Mason 48, 63, 94, 95, 100, 107, 500, 537, 557
Mildred B. Hairston 291, 300
Mildred Delores 73, 282, 518, 521, 529, 535
Mildred Delores Cherry 73, 518, 521, 529, 535
Mildred Holmes 542
Mildred Inez 417
Mildred Inez Stockton 417
Mildred Mason 432, 458, 555

Miles 21, 51, 312, 332, 333, 396, 397, 399, 423, 456, 458, 540, 545
Miles Allen 332, 397
Miles Harrison 332, 333, 396, 397, 423
Millie 33, 34, 250, 458, 549
Millie Barber 33, 250, 458
Milly 279, 457
Milton 43, 44, 45, 46, 47, 49, 220, 330, 333, 344, 419, 427, 455, 458, 536, 559
Milton McKinley 330, 419, 455
Milton Walker 220
Minnie 116, 127, 130, 131, 132, 205, 206, 207, 243
Minnie Lee 205, 206, 207, 243
Minnie Lee Jackson 205, 206, 207
Minnie Lee Johnson 243
Minnie M 116, 130, 131
Mitchell Lewis 381
Mollie 41, 209, 457
Mollie Ellis 41, 457
Molly A. Hairston 121, 258, 259
Mona Louise 83, 517
Mona Louise Browning 83, 517
Monica 450, 541
Monika 450, 541
Monique Anthony 406, 493, 505, 551
Monroe Walker 314
Morgan Elizabeth 542
Mosella Doulin Neely 184, 284
Murlee 381
Mustafa 411, 483, 540
Myron 94
Nancy 45, 147, 155, 156, 157, 180, 188, 217, 229, 237, 294, 295, 303, 310, 327, 382, 383, 385, 434, 456, 457, 513, 528, 538, 561
Nancy Alice 294, 295, 513
Nancy Alice Wright 294, 295, 513
Nancy Cinora 383, 434, 528, 538
Nancy Cinora Cowan 383, 434, 528, 538
Nancy E 327, 382
Nancy Goolsby 237, 457, 561
Nancy Jane 147, 155, 156, 157, 180, 188, 303
Nancy Jane Crump 147, 155, 156, 157, 180, 188, 303

Nancy Lois 229, 294
Nancy Lois Hairston 229, 294
Nanna 157, 458
Nannie 151, 190, 191, 458
Nannie B 151, 458
Nannie E. 190
Nannie E. Sullivan 190
Naomi 227, 401, 458, 545
Naomi Bailey 227, 458
Napoleon Jefferson 22, 48, 67, 68, 69, 74, 78, 84, 87, 461, 501, 518, 519, 520, 521, 522, 527, 529, 533, 534, 535, 537, 559, 565
Nash 41, 456
Nat 14, 40, 57, 72, 298, 456
Nathaniel 157, 291, 300, 323, 375, 439, 518, 541
Nathaniel A 157
Nathaniel H 291, 300
Nebraska 48, 60, 458, 536, 537
NeKeith 240, 553
Nellie 291, 299, 355, 377, 528
Nellie Hairston 291, 299
Nelly J 45, 458
Nelly J. Carey 45, 458
Nermaryha 392
Nettie Langton 333
Nevada 48, 61, 458, 536, 537
Newell Virgil 22, 356, 384, 385, 408, 428, 429, 482
Newton 21, 321, 458, 561
Noah 229, 298
Nona Bell 364, 544, 547
Nona Bell Hicklen 364, 544, 547
Norma J, ... 22, 74, 75, 76, 78, 311, 313, 320, 325, 331, 335, 338, 348, 352, 354, 355, 370, 385, 462, 469, 473, 495, 518, 520, 522, 529, 547, 551, 557, 559, 563, 566, 570, 572
Norman Eugene 177, 280
Nyema 201
Obadiah H 261
Oberian 94, 457
Odell 114, 118, 119, 123, 141, 151, 152, 165, 169, 324, 375, 456, 458, 518, 542, 558
Odell Buck 114, 118, 119
Odena 415, 516

Odena Allison 415, 516
Ola 125, 199, 432, 458
Ola Moody 432, 458
Ola Winford 199, 458
Oliver 359, 458, 543
Olivia Mills 186, 455, 516
Ollie 378
Olympia Nicole 538
Ona 51, 457
Onelle 123, 143
Ophelia 125, 152, 169, 291, 298, 457, 458, 541
Ophelia Gray 125, 458
Ophelia Tillman 152, 169, 457, 541
Ora Mae 281, 458
Ora Mae Holman 281, 458
Osborn 114, 457
Oscar 209, 344, 457, 484
Osee 247, 457
Ossie Holman 278
Ossie Holman Wilson 278
Otha David 443, 444, 537
Otho 371, 458, 518
Otis 59, 187, 259, 261, 295, 356, 365, 432, 458, 513, 555
Otis C 365
Otis D 259, 261
Otis L 187, 295, 458, 513
Otis Livingston 187, 458
Ouida 159
Ouida Jackson 159
Pamela 140, 554
Pamela Mason 140, 554
Pansy 119, 152, 456
Pansy Annette 152
Pansy Annette Mason 152
Pansy Harris 119, 456
Paris Ashley 542
Paschal 262, 263
Paten Richard 63
Patricia 282, 364, 454, 455, 522, 529, 535
Patricia Ann 454, 455
Patrick 283
Pattie 337, 338, 339, 457
Pattie Bass 337, 338, 339, 457
Paul 26, 51, 124, 127, 255, 457, 557

Pauline 262, 457
Pearl 108, 151, 455, 458, 560
Pearl Brandon 108, 455
Pearline 356, 430, 431, 555, 558
Pearline Moore 356, 430, 431, 555
Peggy....68, 77, 478, 500, 520, 522, 525, 534, 537, 565
Peggye 567
Penix M 184, 458
Pennix Marshall 187
Perley 229, 296, 457
Perry Lee 146
Peter 229, 302, 303, 545, 565, 566
Peter E 565, 566
Phil 346, 457
Philo 330, 419
Phyllis A....155, 179, 226, 290, 434, 456, 458, 513, 515, 528
Phyllis Ann....155, 179, 226, 290, 458, 513, 515
Phyllis Ann Brown 155, 179, 226, 290, 458, 513, 515
Phyllis L. Kittler 328
Pinkney C 328, 411, 436, 518, 526
Powell 434, 528, 567
Preneet 327, 456
Preston 41, 149, 210, 456
Prince....340, 347, 390, 392, 393, 394, 395, 404, 457, 488, 521, 534, 537
Princess Irene 290
Princess Irene Tatum 290
Priscilla 44, 50, 52, 114, 178, 456, 458
Priscilla E 50, 456
Priscilla E. Holton 50, 456
Priscilla Hargraves 114, 458
Priscilla Mason 178, 456
Queen 499, 562, 650
Quince 353, 369
Quinn 542
Rachel Bradley 380, 548
Ralph 67, 189, 455, 537, 564
Ramiyah Kimberly 91, 499, 507
Ramonia L 140
Ramonia L. Mason 140
Ramsey, Charmaine 438
Randy 355, 390, 478, 518, 528

Raphael Santi Pasamonte 392, 557
Rashad Amin 77
Raven 101, 491, 558
Ray....72, 140, 451, 462, 470, 478, 481, 526, 554
Raymond....48, 62, 66, 100, 136, 139, 140, 218, 368, 378, 456, 493, 527, 537, 554
Raymond Bundrant 368
Raymond D. I 136
Raymond Wilford 378
Rebecca....130, 158, 194, 195, 261, 270, 271, 272, 276, 277, 337, 382, 455, 456
Rebecca Clement 261
Rebecca Ellis-Young....270, 271, 272, 276, 277
Rebecca Solter 130
Rebektah 317, 455
Reginald 365, 542
Reginald Thomas 542
Renee 90, 390, 491, 498, 499, 506, 535
Rhody Isabella 328, 411, 436, 518, 526
Rhody Isabella Cowan....328, 411, 436, 518, 526
Rhonda 542
Richard....51, 55, 65, 73, 74, 92, 107, 110, 282, 291, 299, 378, 406, 416, 447, 501, 518, 521, 523, 528, 529, 535, 541, 542, 563
Richard Aubrey 291, 299
Richard Elihue 378
Richard L....55, 73, 74, 107, 110, 447, 518, 521, 528, 529, 535, 542
Richard LeRoy I 521
Richmond....175, 186, 223, 306, 319, 320, 367, 457, 516, 544, 554
Rickey E 542
Ridhwana 411, 483, 540, 577
Righteous 164, 457
Rilla 196, 455
Robert....22, 29, 47, 48, 53, 55, 65, 66, 68, 70, 71, 76, 93, 114, 115, 116, 123, 124, 127, 128, 129, 131, 132, 133, 135, 139, 142, 145, 179, 182, 183, 184, 194, 197, 229, 238, 242, 245, 246, 247, 259, 266, 267, 282, 283, 284, 293, 302, 320, 327, 332, 333, 349, 364, 365, 367, 369, 380, 382, 400, 401, 402, 412, 423, 424, 439,

440, 441, 451, 456, 457, 458, 478, 501, 514, 518, 519, 520, 521, 522, 528, 529, 531, 533, 534, 535, 536, 541, 542, 544, 545, 548, 559, 573, 580, 598

Robert Baxter 229, 293
Robert Bruce 131
Robert Flood 115, 116, 129
Robert I 93, 114, 135
Robert II 114, 135
Robert Junior 284
Robert L....184, 194, 302, 412, 439, 440, 441, 451, 457, 519, 520, 533, 541
Robert Lee 302
Robert Lewis....412, 439, 440, 441, 451, 519, 520, 533, 541
Robert M. I 116
Robert M. II 116
Robert Mason....47, 48, 53, 65, 93, 114, 123, 124, 135, 142, 179, 182, 183, 197, 238, 458, 514, 533, 535, 598
Robert V 542
Robert Willard 542
Robin 543, 550
Rodney....22, 75, 78, 274, 305, 450, 478, 518, 522, 525, 541
Rodney Allen 22, 78, 305, 478, 518, 522
Rodney Kenneth 274
Roosevelt 96, 266, 456, 458, 536
Rosa....132, 257, 302, 303, 436, 484, 519, 549
Rosa E. Williams 302, 303
Rosa Williams 436, 519
Rosanna 256, 257
Rosanna Witherspoon 257
Rosco Corklin 267, 268
Roscoe....41, 149, 150, 359, 388, 390, 406, 457, 473, 482, 547, 555, 556
Roscoe I 406
Roscoe II 406
Rosena Gist 110
Rowan....33, 36, 114, 124, 152, 166, 174, 180, 182, 183, 198, 199, 200, 238, 239, 240, 241, 242, 247, 259, 262, 263, 269, 279, 280, 281, 283, 308, 322, 323, 325, 326, 327, 328, 329, 330, 331, 332, 333, 334, 354, 355, 371, 372, 373, 374, 375, 378, 379, 380, 381, 382, 383, 384, 397, 398, 399, 400, 401, 402, 403, 411, 412, 413, 414, 415, 416, 417, 418, 419, 420, 421, 422, 423, 424, 425, 426, 427, 428, 433, 434, 435, 436, 437, 438, 439, 440, 441, 442, 443, 444, 446, 447, 448, 449, 451, 453, 454, 455, 458, 516, 517, 518, 519, 520, 527, 528, 533, 537, 538, 540, 541, 542, 547, 567
Roxanna S. Smith 62, 136, 527, 554
Roxie....46, 47, 354, 356, 385, 408, 428, 457, 476, 482, 540, 551
Roxie Lee 354, 356, 385, 408, 551
Roxie Lee Carey 354, 356, 385, 408, 551
Roxie Martin 46, 457
Roy....55, 73, 74, 164, 304, 354, 431, 455, 535, 537
Roy Charles 304
Roy Righteous 164
Royale 88, 499
Rubin 21, 335, 338, 456
Ruby 149
Ruby Brown 149
Rudolph 151, 458
Rufus 58, 247, 312, 456, 457
Rufus C 247, 456
Rugina 102, 546, 561
Russell Alberta....383, 433, 434, 443, 528, 537, 538
Ruth....160, 281, 302, 303, 332, 403, 412, 436, 449, 456, 457, 517, 519, 539, 574, 616
Ruth D 449
Ruth D. Sanders 449
Ruth W. Hairston 160, 303, 574
Ruthie 298, 456
Ruthie Bailey 298, 456
Sabe 199
Sabreen Lavonia 385, 409, 483
Sadie 47, 291, 298, 397
Sadie Long 291, 298
Sadie Marie 397
Sadie Marie Miller 397
Safadin 411, 483, 540, 577
Salem....12, 13, 30, 39, 40, 41, 43, 44, 45, 48, 49, 50, 51, 52, 55, 56, 58, 59, 61, 63, 68, 69, 70, 71, 72, 73, 74, 75, 77, 96, 97, 98,

My Family Tree

99, 100, 101, 102, 103, 104, 105, 106, 107, 108, 109, 110, 111, 113, 114, 115, 116, 118, 119, 120, 122, 123, 124, 125, 127, 128, 129, 130, 131, 132, 133, 134, 135, 144, 146, 149, 152, 166, 169, 173, 175, 176, 178, 181, 193, 202, 203, 204, 205, 209, 211, 214, 224, 225, 230, 235, 240, 255, 256, 262, 263, 267, 272, 274, 277, 289, 290, 291, 292, 293, 297, 298, 299, 300, 301, 302, 303, 330, 445, 457, 465, 466, 490, 491, 492, 496, 497, 500, 501, 502, 507, 508, 517, 518, 519, 521, 522, 524, 527, 528, 529, 531, 532, 534, 536, 541, 542, 543, 546, 553, 557, 559, 561, 563, 565

Sallie 63, 133, 176, 291, 458
Sallie Luanna 133
Sallie Luanna Martin.................. 133
Sallie May Farris 176, 458
Sallie Weaver 291
Sally 140, 209, 457, 458, 557
Sally Mae 140, 458
Sally Mae Jones 140, 458
Sam 21, 29, 45, 48, 97, 140, 316, 554
Samuel....22, 27, 28, 29, 47, 48, 54, 57, 58, 59, 61, 74, 92, 94, 97, 98, 100, 121, 136, 175, 200, 207, 224, 229, 256, 258, 265, 283, 303, 315, 316, 317, 332, 360, 362, 377, 399, 401, 402, 417, 455, 456, 465, 490, 492, 496, 533, 535, 536, 557, 561, 573, 601, 620
Samuel Allen.................. 402
Samuel H.................. 121, 229, 258, 283
Samuel I 97, 360
Samuel J 332, 377, 401
Samuel M.....22, 47, 48, 54, 57, 59, 61, 74, 92, 94, 98, 136, 175, 200, 224, 533, 535, 536, 573, 601
Samuel Maye 200
Samuel R.................. 399, 455
Sandar Lewin....89, 494, 522, 529, 535, 559, 563
Sandra Kay.................. 109
Sandra Kay Simpson.................. 109
Sara 359, 458, 543
Sarah . 37, 102, 210, 253, 274, 284, 336, 546
Sarah Cunningham.................. 336

Sarah Georganna.................. 284
Sarah Lee 102, 546
Sarah Maggie 274
Savannah.................. 259, 260, 281
Savannah Hairston 259, 260
Savannah Latner Myers 281
Sawyer, Alexander J.................. 558
Scott Reid.................. 441, 449, 519, 520, 541
Seaila.................. 261
Seaila Wilson 261
Sean.................. 406, 493, 537, 540, 545, 551
Sebastian 391, 556, 557
Sequita Renee.................. 533
Sharon 28, 223, 251, 449, 533
Shawn Manuel 389, 392
Sheila Moore 555
Shelia.................. 429
Sid 47, 457
Sidney 493
Silla Bruce 179, 458
Simon 114
Slater Josiah 207, 484, 485
Slater Samuel 205, 206, 207
Sophia Anna 302
Spencer....147, 156, 179, 181, 182, 227, 398, 425, 426, 427, 428, 458, 514, 519, 540, 545, 598
Stanley Eric.................. 372
Stella 34, 259, 260, 458, 480
Stella W.................. 259, 260
Stephanie M, 7, 9, 23, 75, 76, 79, 460, 462, 478, 494, 508, 509, 510, 512, 518, 522, 525, 529, 535, 539, 540, 545, 552, 559, 563, 566, 569, 572
Stephanie McCluney.................. 545
Stimson 156, 456
Sue Morrow 35, 455
Sue Pearl 132, 133
Sue Pearl Barksdale 132, 133
Sukie 179, 226, 227, 232, 458
Susan....21, 22, 46, 114, 117, 178, 229, 230, 255, 290, 298, 313, 314, 319, 324, 326, 331, 339, 360, 370, 396, 423, 456, 457, 513, 591, 620
Susan Ann 255, 456

My Family Tree

Susan Beverly....21, 313, 314, 319, 360, 456, 620
Susan Jane (Sookey)....22, 324, 331, 370, 396, 423
Susan Johnson.. 46
Susan Mason....114, 117, 229, 230, 290, 298, 513
Susan McIver 178
Susan McIver Brown 178
Susan Winston.................................... 339, 457
Susie 58, 149, 229, 277, 457, 513
Susie Shannon 277
Susie Shannon Glenn 277
Suzanne Maria 81, 461, 494
Suzette D....97, 100, 101, 490, 491, 557, 558, 561
Suzette D. Strickland 97
Sylvester....189, 197, 221, 222, 245, 246, 310, 353, 367, 368, 412, 438, 561, 562, 564
Sylvester R 412, 438
Sylvia 136, 192, 458
Sylvia Ijames 136, 458
Sylvia Mae 192
Sylvorn Eugene 447, 448
Tallie 147, 276, 458
Tame...114
Tameka 109
Tamika.. 545
Tanya 393, 394, 556, 557
Tariq 411, 483, 540, 577
Teresa Laverne 451
Terrence 77, 522, 559
Terry.. 390
Thelma....50, 97, 128, 129, 182, 217, 266, 292, 359, 378, 456, 457, 458, 542, 567
Thelma Miller 128, 129
Thelma W... 97
Theodore76, 81, 88, 209, 212, 461, 494, 502, 503, 505, 522, 529, 535, 559, 562, 563, 566, 567
Theodore Cornelius....81, 88, 461, 494, 502, 503, 563
Theodore Roosevelt 209, 212, 505
Theola W... 543
Theresa Jean 392, 557
Thessalonia 265, 456

Thomas....25, 34, 38, 42, 43, 83, 85, 86, 128, 150, 168, 169, 172, 222, 244, 253, 255, 262, 263, 264, 269, 282, 284, 294, 303, 328, 330, 350, 384, 413, 456, 457, 458, 464, 469, 472, 479, 539, 541, 542, 558
Thomas A 172, 222, 456, 458
Thomas Brice 542
Thomas C 262, 328, 413, 542
Thomas Christopher 542
Thomas Fisher.. 150
Thomas J 128, 244, 253, 263
Thomas Jonas..................... 128, 244, 263
Thomas Ray 350
Thouston Conrad..................................... 374
Thurman Roscoe 260, 261, 457
Tinsie Mae C 381
Tinsie Mae C. Baity 381
Titus 35, 458
Tobe... 133, 455
Todd 392, 567
Tolston... 254
Tom 55, 168, 264, 277, 456, 457
Tommy Lee 439, 541
Tommy P 456
Toni Sue 354, 388, 405, 492, 505, 537, 540, 551
Tony....68, 76, 144, 461, 465, 471, 473, 478, 485, 494, 495, 498, 499, 500, 501, 523, 524, 525, 526, 529, 531, 532, 534, 543, 559, 562, 563, 565, 566, 577, 580
Treva Mae ... 55, 72, 517, 521, 528, 529, 542
Trevon Deonte........................ 405, 493, 551
Trevor Anthony 520, 539
Trina 85, 86, 539
Tyrone 77, 522, 529, 535, 559
U Grant.. 58, 59, 224
Valeria Jean 389, 390, 556
Valeria Jean Harris-Johnson.... 389, 390, 556
Valerie 191, 481
Valerie Mason 191
Vallie Few 97
Vance Wiseman........ 229, 290, 291, 292, 298
Veada 48, 67, 500, 537
Veada Mason........................... 48, 67, 537
Velesha Edwards 542
Vendetta.. 96, 109

My Family Tree

Vendetta Hege 96, 109
Venus....29, 34, 35, 76, 87, 88, 90, 225, 455, 491, 494, 498, 499, 502, 506, 522, 529, 559, 563, 566
Venus Orr 29, 34, 35, 455
Venus Renee....87, 88, 90, 225, 491, 498, 499, 502, 506
Venus Renee Mason....87, 88, 90, 225, 491, 498, 499, 502, 506
Veola 246
Veola Parker 246
Vera Mae 205, 455
Vera Mae McDaniel 205, 455
Vereece Carolyn 356, 357, 395, 396, 576
Vereece Carolyn Carey....356, 357, 395, 396, 576
Vernell Mae Baxter 350, 456
Vernie Edith 332, 400
Vernie Edith Partee 332, 400
Vernie Grace.................................... 377
Vernie Mae....326, 332, 333, 396, 397, 423, 540, 545, 619
Vernie Mae Cornelius....326, 332, 333, 396, 397, 423, 540, 545, 619
Vernie Matilda........................ 324, 377, 518
Vernon Edward.. 92
Vesta... 476, 482
Victor...................... 406, 493, 505, 543, 550
Victor Richard 406, 505
Viola A 215
Viola A. Scales 215
Violet.. 35, 458
Virgil Eugene 368, 456
Virginia....10, 14, 45, 46, 50, 75, 80, 89, 90, 103, 106, 107, 111, 114, 131, 149, 154, 158, 174, 175, 179, 184, 186, 193, 194, 203, 209, 210, 211, 212, 213, 214, 215, 216, 223, 227, 229, 230, 264, 270, 290, 301, 306, 307, 308, 311, 312, 313, 314, 315, 316, 317, 318, 319, 320, 335, 336, 337, 339, 340, 341, 342, 343, 344, 345, 346, 347, 348, 349, 350, 351, 352, 353, 355, 356, 357, 358, 359, 360, 361, 362, 363, 364, 365, 366, 367, 368, 369, 370, 379, 380, 383, 385, 388, 389, 390, 391, 396, 398, 414, 429, 430, 431, 432, 433, 434, 441, 443, 452, 456, 458, 466, 467, 473, 476, 482, 494, 496, 497, 504, 507, 508, 514, 515, 516, 518, 519, 528, 537, 538, 539, 540, 541, 542, 544, 545, 547, 548, 550, 554, 555, 556, 559, 560, 563, 567, 620, 622, 650
Virginia Catherine....433, 434, 443, 519, 537, 538
Virginia Catherine Glaspy....433, 434, 443, 519, 537, 538
Virginia Mae 158, 193, 194
Virginia Mae Mason............... 158, 193, 194
Virginia Ruth......................... 441, 452, 541
Virginia Theodoric 433, 458, 538
Virginia Theodoric Cowan.............. 433, 538
Vivian...................... 383, 435, 528, 538, 567
Vivian Catherine 383, 435
Vivian Catherine Cowan 383, 435
Voncille 545
Vonnie 282
Vonnie Wilson................................... 282
Walker....25, 38, 76, 255, 310, 337, 339, 340, 400, 429, 456, 493, 529, 555, 562
Wallace Amzi 28
Wallace C 292
Walter....22, 34, 44, 46, 47, 49, 75, 78, 108, 129, 133, 175, 176, 202, 227, 233, 246, 249, 250, 251, 324, 337, 344, 345, 346, 348, 355, 371, 384, 385, 415, 418, 455, 456, 457, 458, 473, 478, 516, 518, 528, 537, 560, 585
Walter A 49, 202, 415, 455, 516, 585
Walter Earl 415, 517, 518
Walter Ellmore 418
Walter I... 47
Walter II 47
Walter Joe........................ 337, 344, 345, 346
Walter Wade 129
Wanne................................... 229, 298, 457
Wardell............................... 355, 456, 528
Warren....25, 58, 70, 176, 198, 224, 225, 294, 365, 513, 527
Warren G 294, 513
Warren L 198
Washington....21, 27, 28, 29, 32, 33, 41, 105, 151, 154, 217, 218, 222, 250, 252, 254,

404, 456, 458, 468, 469, 488, 508, 540, 550, 556, 594

Wayne....63, 67, 69, 70, 74, 75, 76, 77, 78, 79, 80, 81, 82, 83, 84, 85, 86, 87, 88, 89, 90, 91, 92, 95, 96, 123, 142, 177, 208, 267, 268, 269, 350, 354, 356, 368, 369, 374, 385, 386, 387, 388, 404, 405, 406, 407, 408, 430, 431, 461, 463, 464, 468, 470, 472, 476, 478, 479, 481, 484, 485, 486, 487, 488, 489, 491, 492, 493, 495, 498, 499, 517, 518, 519, 521, 527, 539, 551, 552, 566

Wendy 438, 544
Westley 257, 457
Whilhelmenia Jackson 500
Whilhelmenia Levonia 105
White, Andrew Wilson 324
Wilbur....310, 341, 356, 357, 358, 362, 363, 390, 396, 539, 547, 576
Wilbur C. I 362
Willard H 262, 457
William.... 17, 22, 28, 30, 44, 45, 50, 55, 56, 57, 59, 67, 68, 69, 70, 71, 72, 74, 75, 76, 81, 82, 87, 88, 89, 90, 91, 99, 100, 125, 128, 134, 137, 148, 149, 160, 161, 163, 168, 169, 170, 177, 180, 181, 183, 186, 188, 189, 194, 196, 197, 199, 203, 208, 209, 210, 213, 217, 225, 230, 231, 238, 260, 262, 263, 279, 281, 283, 287, 303, 313, 326, 327, 328, 330, 334, 345, 346, 350, 353, 378, 379, 380, 381, 398, 399, 417, 418, 426, 441, 445, 449, 455, 456, 457, 458, 461, 468, 478, 481, 491, 494, 495, 498, 499, 501, 504, 514, 516, 517, 518, 519, 520, 521, 522, 523, 526, 528, 529, 533, 534, 535, 536, 540, 541, 542, 548, 559, 562, 563, 564, 565, 566, 567, 573, 574, 580, 582, 600, 612, 616, 620, 622, 650
William A .... iv, 231, 330, 458, 522
William E....22, 30, 55, 56, 57, 68, 69, 74, 82, 161, 188, 189, 197, 210, 287, 455, 501, 517, 521, 523, 528, 529, 542, 582, 616
William E. 30, 161, 210, 455, 529
William Edward 188
William Ernest 189, 197
William Garlin 125, 128
William H....50, 59, 99, 100, 163, 183, 194, 208, 209, 213, 260, 262, 279, 283, 328, 398, 399, 417, 514, 540
William Henry....50, 208, 209, 213, 260, 279, 328, 398, 399, 417, 540
William Jacob 380
William Joe 345, 346
William John Bunyon 148, 168, 169
William Lee 327, 380, 381
William Lewis 149, 170
William McKinley 238
William N 161
William Odell 177, 281
William Olly 441, 449, 519, 520, 541
William Robert I 521
William Sherman 189, 196
William T....17, 160, 186, 303, 378, 458, 516, 574
William Theodore 378
William Thomas 160, 303, 574
Willie....80, 83, 88, 104, 105, 112, 116, 127, 129, 130, 149, 213, 214, 269, 288, 289, 290, 315, 380, 412, 438, 456, 457, 472, 496, 499, 500, 527, 545, 546, 560, 561
Willie Gladden 105, 457
Willie James 80, 83, 472
Willie Lee....104, 105, 412, 438, 456, 496, 500
Willie Mae 112, 456
Willie Martin 288, 289, 290
Willie Taylor 213, 214
Willie Wise 288, 289
Willimina 287
Wilson....25, 229, 246, 257, 258, 261, 271, 282, 303, 310, 333, 371, 378, 389, 425, 426, 435, 449, 456, 458, 485, 518, 533, 538, 546, 556, 557
Wilson Cooper 246, 458
Winnie Lee 278
Winnie Lee Thomas 278
Winston....12, 13, 30, 39, 40, 41, 42, 43, 44, 45, 47, 48, 49, 50, 51, 52, 55, 56, 58, 59, 60, 61, 63, 68, 69, 70, 71, 72, 73, 74, 75, 77, 96, 97, 98, 99, 100, 101, 102, 103, 104, 105, 106, 107, 108, 109, 110, 111, 113,

My Family Tree

114, 115, 116, 118, 119, 120, 122, 123, 124, 125, 127, 128, 129, 130, 131, 132, 133, 134, 135, 144, 146, 149, 152, 160, 166, 169, 173, 174, 175, 176, 178, 181, 182, 193, 199, 202, 203, 204, 205, 209, 211, 214, 224, 225, 230, 235, 240, 255, 256, 262, 263, 267, 272, 274, 277, 289, 290, 291, 292, 293, 297, 298, 299, 300, 301, 302, 303, 310, 330, 445, 457, 465, 466, 490, 491, 492, 496, 497, 500, 501, 502, 507, 508, 517, 518, 519, 521, 522, 524, 527, 528, 529, 531, 532, 534, 535, 536, 541, 542, 543, 546, 553, 557, 559, 561, 563, 565

Winston Ervin 160, 303
Wise 234, 288, 289, 369
Woodrow Wilburn 350, 456
Wurdy James 447
Wyatt 178, 310, 332, 403, 456, 616
Wyvonnia M 195, 196, 200
Wyvonnia M. Mason 195, 196, 200
Xavier J ... 103, 106, 496, 497, 507, 558, 579
Youorra 451
Zaddie 174
Zaiden 86
Zeffie Crawford 194
Zelma Thomas 279
Zepha 43, 458
Zsa Zsa Nicole Pasamonte 392, 557
Zula M 160, 161
Zula M. Mason 160, 161
Zulla 152, 456

My Family Tree

References

Ancestry. United States Federal Census Mortality Schedule, 1850-1885. (1997-2022). Retrieved from https://www.ancestry.com

Antioch Baptist Church Cemetery. Find A Grave. (2018). Retrieved from https://www.findagrave.com/cemetery/2410517/antioch-baptist-church-cemetery

Black Codes and Pigs Laws. Theme. Slavery by Another Name. PBS.org. Black Presence. (n.d.). Retrieved from National Archives- Exhibitions- Black Presence https://www.nationalarchives.gov.uk/pathways/blackhistory/rights/abolition.htm

Cedar Grove Baptist Church Cemetery. Find A Grave. (2018). Retrieved from https://www.findagrave.com/cemetery/2410517/cedar-grove-baptist-church-cemetery

Evergreen Cemetery. Find A Grave. (2018). Retrieved from
https://www.findagrave.com/cemetery/2410517/evergreen-cemetery

Falconbridge, A. (1792). The Manner in Which The Slaves Are Procured. In A. Falconbridge, An Account of the Slave Trade on the Coast of Africa. London: J Phillips.

Finding Your Roots. Henry Louis Gates, Jr. (October 26, 2014). (Bassett and Stokes) Retrieved from
https://www.PBS.org/weta/finding-your-roots

Gundaker, Gary. (July 2007). Hidden Education Among African Americans During Slavery. Teachers College Record. Vol 109, No7. Columbia, University. The Black Codes. (1996). Retrieved from https://www.en.m.wikipedia.org

Margolis, D. (February 17, 2006). Grace Bassett: foot soldier for justice Retrieved from People's Weekly World Continuing The Daily Worker https://peoplesworld.org

Mount Tabor Presbyterian Church Cemetery. Find A Grave. (2018). Retrieved from
https://www.findagrave.com/cemetery/2242720/mount-tabor-presbyterian-church-cemetery

Odd Fellow Cemetery. Find A Grave. (2018). Retrieved from
https://www.findagrave.com/cemetery/48289/odd-fellows-cemetery

Palmer, C. (1999). Defining And Studying the Modern African Diaspora. Retrieved from African Historical Association:
https://www.historians.org/publications-and-directories/perspectives-on-history/september-1998/defining-and   studying-the-modern-African-diaspora

Richardson, M. M. (2016). *Losing Citizenship: Racial Classification, Migration and Peoplehood.* Retrieved from Racial Choices: The Emergence of the Haliwa-Saponi Indian Tribe, 1835 -1971

https://search.proquest.com/openview/6677d1f665610be64243112d61eebf63/1.pdf?pq-origsite=gscholar&cbl=18750&diss=y

My Family Tree

Rogers, J. A. (1947). Anna Singha, Warrior Queen of Matamba. In J. A. Rogers, World's Great Men of Color (pp. 138-141). New York. Futuro Press Inc.

Setting The Record Straight About Native People: Southern Blackfoot. (n.d.). Retrieved from Native Languages: https://www.native-languages-org./inq18.html

The Schomburg Center for Research in the Black Culture. (n.d.) The Abolition of the Slave Trade. Retrieved from The Act of 1807: https://abolition.nypl.org/essays/us_constitution/5/

Trotter Jr., Joe William. "African American Heritage." e-WV: The West Virginia Encyclopedia (19 October 2010) (Web 07). Retrieved from https://www.wv.encyclopedia.org

Webb, L. Dean. (2006). The History of American Education. A Great American Experiment. Pearson Merrill Prentice Hall Columbus, Ohio. (2.Ibid, 3.Ibid and 5.Ibid).

Whiteman Cemetery. Find A Grave. (2018). Retrieved from https://www.findagrave.com/cemetery/80285/whitman-cemetery

NEW YORK WEEKLY

NEW YORK Weekly

Book Endorsement

Date: May 1st, 2025

To: Stephanie M. Mason

"My Family Tree: The Mason & Carey Bloodline" by Stephanie M. Mason is an evocative and meticulously researched memoir that intricately traces the intertwined histories of two African-American bloodlines. Drawing upon decades of oral history, archival records, and ancestral testimonies, Mason crafts a powerful tapestry that honors the resilience, sacrifices, and legacies of her forebears. From surviving slavery and enduring reconstruction to preserving dignity through generations of oppression and perseverance, her narrative offers both a deeply personal and broadly significant historical reflection.

Stephanie Mason's work is more than a genealogical exploration, it's a cultural reckoning. Her ability to breathe life into each generation's experiences is a testament to her commitment to truth-telling and historical preservation. This book serves as a timeless reminder of the strength found in family, faith, and heritage. Through "My Family Tree," Mason not only records history, she resurrects it with reverence and purpose.

A monumental tribute to ancestry and identity, Stephanie M. Mason's "My Family Tree" is a work of legacy-building that will inform, inspire, and empower readers for generations to come.

Willis Tucker

Senior Editor

© 2025 New York Weekly. All Rights Reserved.